Further praise for

FEAR ITSELF

"All of *Fear Itself* is suffused with the same sense of pure terror during the Roosevelt and Truman years as, say, Philip Roth's *The Plot Against America*. It's easy to forget not just how dangerous the situation was, at home and abroad, during the New Deal, but how palpable were outcomes far worse than what we got. . . . [Katznelson] has done something remarkable in *Fear Itself* in creating a large-scale, densely detailed tableau of the New Deal that feels fresh and unfamiliar." —Nicholas Lemann, *New York Review of Books*

"*Fear Itself* is a monumental history of the New Deal's greatest paradox, its connections with the Jim Crow South. Combining historical nuance with his clear eye for the big picture, Ira Katznelson contributes one of the most trenchant accounts yet of American liberalism at the height of its power in the 1930s and 1940s—a book of major importance in understanding our own political distempers and opportunities." —Sean Wilentz, author of *The Rise of American Democracy: Jefferson to Lincoln*

"An absorbing study that spans the period from Roosevelt's first term to the end of the Truman administration. . . . Readers of this insightful book may feel that the past, albeit in new ways, lives on." —*Economist*

"*Fear Itself* deeply reconceptualizes the New Deal and raises countless provocative questions." —David Kennedy, author of *Freedom from Fear: The American People in Depression and War, 1929–1945*

"With *Fear Itself*, Ira Katznelson accomplishes something almost impossible— making us think in entirely new ways about the New Deal and its complex and contradictory legacy for modern America, and about the long legacy of slavery in our politics and society." —Eric Foner, author of *The Fiery Trial: Abraham Lincoln and American Slavery*

"Ira Katznelson's *Fear Itself* is an extraordinary book that will change our understanding of the New Deal. He has shown the ways in which racism has shaped American life in the age of the Great Depression, and among other things he has brought the U.S. Congress to the front of the New Deal. It is a remarkable work of scholarship." —Alan Brinkley, author of *The End of Reform: New Deal Liberalism in Recession and War*

"In *Fear Itself*, Ira Katznelson has taken up an old subject and given it new life. In vivid prose, he reinterprets the causes and consequences of the New Deal and its aftermath, putting new emphasis on the role of Congress and southern legislators in the construction of domestic and foreign policy and the fighting of a world war and a cold war. His arguments are compelling, his documentation thorough. *Fear Itself* will, from this moment on, be the place to go for an understanding of the making of the New Deal and twentieth-century America." —David Nasaw, author of *Andrew Carnegie*

"How the Northern and Southern wings of the Democratic Party reconciled themselves to each other in this period was the central dynamic of American politics . . . and it provides the basis for Katznelson's enthralling new history of the New Deal. . . . The result was a 'Janus-faced' politics: outwardly assertive, interventionist, crusading, moralising, always looking to take the fight to the enemy; inwardly constrained, laissez-faire, decentralized, protective of private interests, reluctant to uphold the public good." —David Runciman, *London Review of Books*

"Engrossing. . . . It is an exhilarating pleasure to lose yourself in this old-fashioned example of original historical scholarship. *Fear Itself* is a sprawling, ambitious book that offers illuminating insights on nearly every page. Among

Katznelson's gifts is the one most valuable to readers and most in danger of extinction in the American academy: He writes clear, energetic prose without a whiff of academic jargon or pretension. . . . Entertaining and enlightening."

—Robert G. Kaiser, *Washington Post*

"Brilliant. . . . One of the many strengths of *Fear Itself* is that it brings Congress back to center stage in the New Deal era. American politics past tend to be retrospectively seen through the lens of the presidency, an impulse that is particularly understandable with respect to FDR, who almost certainly did more to shape the political landscape than any politician of the last century."

—Scott Lemieux, *American Prospect*

"In *Fear Itself*, Ira Katznelson . . . has produced an excellent work of synthesis about the political and economic terms of the New Deal. It forms a bittersweet homage to the period he has long thought of as the pivotal moment in the development of both American democracy and the US national security state, founded on foreign and domestic policy designed around the 'containment' of threats. . . . His powerful and well-paced account begins in 1933 at the start of FDR's extended presidency and ends with the inauguration of Dwight Eisenhower 20 years later. . . . Anyone wanting an intelligent guide to the ideas that still shape its place in our own fractious times should begin by reading this book."

—Duncan Kelly, *Financial Times*

"*Fear Itself* is a provocative look at how modern America—created three-quarters of a century ago by the very Southern barons who were so important a part of the New Deal—was shaped. We think of history as a settled thing, tucked safely in a faraway past. This book is a reminder of how very surprising it can be."

—David Shribman, *Boston Globe*

"By casting fear as the linchpin of politics and policymaking in the New Deal era, Katznelson tackles a big topic and makes it even bigger. . . . A work of sprawling ambition and nervy iconoclasm. . . . The book is an extraordinary achievement. Katznelson has permanently discredited selective, nostalgic, impressions of the New Deal era. By taking readers back to a time of

perpetual crises, doomed moral compromises, and ill-begotten political alliances, *Fear Itself* is an urgent reminder that, in Katznelson's words, 'not just whether but also how we find our way truly matters.' "   —Taeku Lee,
Foreign Affairs

"A wholly new approach to the New Deal takes history we thought we knew and makes it even richer and more complex. In this deeply erudite, beautifully written history, Katznelson . . . adopts an expansive view of the New Deal, extending it to the end of the Truman administration."
     —*Kirkus Reviews*

"Positing that the New Deal preserved liberal democracy, but at the expense of compromises with illiberal forces, Katznelson's hefty history weighs other historians' interpretations of the New Deal as it knowledgeably advances its own."
     —*Booklist*

"Katznelson moves deftly between striking anecdotes and incisive analysis, demonstrating along the way his command of both the domestic and international scenes. . . . [It] is truly a masterful work. If you wonder whether politics matter, read this book. More than just a defining history of the New Deal, it is a penetrating look at the origins of our time." —Heath W. Carter,
Christian Century

FEAR
ITSELF

ALSO BY IRA KATZNELSON

Black Men, White Cities: Race, Politics,
and Migration in the United States, 1900–1930,
and Britain, 1948–1968

City Trenches: Urban Politics and the Patterning
of Class in the United States

Schooling for All: Class, Race, and the Decline
of the Democratic Ideal (with Margaret Weir)

Marxism and the City

Liberalism's Crooked Circle: Letters
to Adam Michnik

FEAR ITSELF

The New Deal

AND THE

Origins of Our Time

IRA KATZNELSON

LIVERIGHT PUBLISHING CORPORATION

A Division of W. W. Norton & Company

New York • London

∎

For Deborah, and her
ever-expanding bounty

∎

For information about permission to reproduce selections from this book,
write to Permissions, Liveright Publishing Corporation,
a division of W. W. Norton & Company, Inc.,
500 Fifth Avenue, New York, NY 10110

For information about special discounts for bulk purchases, please contact
W. W. Norton Special Sales at specialsales@wwnorton.com or 800-233-4830

Manufacturing by LSC Harrisonburg
Book design by Abbate Design
Production manager: Anna Oler

Library of Congress Cataloging-in-Publication Data

Katznelson, Ira.
Fear itself : the New Deal and the origins of our time / Ira Katznelson. —
First Edition.
      pages cm
Includes bibliographical references and index.
ISBN 978-0-87140-450-3 (hardcover)
1. New Deal, 1933–1939. 2. United States—Politics and government—1933–1945.
3. World politics, 1933–1945. 4. Political culture—United States—History—
20th century. I. Title.
E806.K37 2013
973.917—dc23
                    2012041794

ISBN 978-0-87140-738-2 pbk.

Liveright Publishing Corporation
500 Fifth Avenue, New York, N.Y. 10110
www.wwnorton.com

W. W. Norton & Company Ltd.
15 Carlisle Street, London W1D 3BS

4 5 6 7 8 9 0

I live in an age of fear.

■

E. B. White, letter to the
New York Herald Tribune,
November 29, 1947

CONTENTS

FEAR
ITSELF

❧ Triumph and Sorrow

L ESS THAN A YEAR after Franklin Roosevelt assumed the presidency, Charles Beard, the nation's leading historian, reported how, "with astounding profusion, the presses are pouring out books, pamphlets, and articles on the New Deal."[1] Ever since Beard's observation, copious attention has been paid to how the Roosevelt and Truman administrations brought energy to despair.[2] Indeed, we possess hundreds of thematic histories, countless studies of public affairs, and abundant biographies of key persons during this time of great historical density. Scholars and journalists have exhaustively analyzed the epoch's increasingly powerful bureaucracy, the Supreme Court as it evolved, the thicket of policies concerning economic regulation and social welfare, and the country's growing military capacity and global leadership. Their resonant pages emphasize the character, the actions, and prose of its two presidents—one mesmerizing, larger than life, the other plain but not simple. They are crowded with other grand characters we have come to know well, including the grandiloquent union leader, John L. Lewis; the lanky congressman and senator from Texas, Lyndon Baines Johnson; the erudite African-American scholar and activist, W. E. B. Du Bois; and a colorful parade of spies and spy catchers, radio preachers and generals, atomic scientists and war-crimes lawyers.

With the protean twenty-year epoch of Democratic Party rule long understood as "a watershed . . . that separates politics past from politics present and future," why present another portrait of the New Deal? Is there anything new to be said about this "defining time—like the Revolution and the establishment of the new nation—that set . . . the terms of American politics and government for generations to come"?[3]

I.

DRAWN TO the mystery and beauty of Venice, Henry James set numerous sketches, stories, and novels in that city, "where the mere use of one's eyes . . . is happiness enough."[4] Writing in 1882 as "a brooding tourist," he cautioned that "an originality of attitude is completely impossible." After all, the "golden" city had been "painted and described many thousands of times," and there was "nothing new to be said." With "as little mystery about the Grand Canal as about our local thoroughfare, and the name of St. Mark . . . as familiar as the postman's ring," James conceded that there was "a certain impudence in pretending to add anything."[5]

James defended his depiction. "It is not forbidden . . . to speak of familiar things" or present "a fillip to . . . memory" when a writer "is himself in love with his theme."[6] One reason for writing is just such veneration. The New Deal—the designation I use for the full period of Democratic Party rule that begins with FDR's election in 1932 and closes with Dwight Eisenhower's two decades later—reconsidered and rebuilt the country's long-established political order. In so doing, it engaged in a contest with the dictatorships, of both the Right and the Left, about the validity of liberal democracy. Bleak uncertainty marked most of these years. By successfully defining and securing liberal democracy, the New Deal offers the past century's most striking example of how a democracy grappled with fear-generating crises.

A gloom of incomparable force was setting in when the New Deal began. In July 1932, Benito Mussolini celebrated, if prematurely, how "the liberal state is destined to perish." Reporting how "worn out" constitutional democracies had been "deserted by the peoples who feel [it will] lead the world to ruin," he boasted, in prose ghostwritten by the philosopher Giovanni Gentile, that "all the political experiments of our day are antiliberal."[7] The New Deal's rearrangement of values and institutions, and its support for the Western liberal political tradition, answered this challenge. Its battles were fought on many fronts, from the effort to revive capitalism to the struggle to incorporate the working class and contain the dangerous features of a mass society. Its international objectives were no less weighty, from the mission to defeat Nazi Germany, Fascist Italy, and militarist Japan to the desire to keep Soviet Communism in check, while maintaining internal solidarity and security in the process. These achievements are especially impressive when one realizes that they had to be accomplished virtually all at once, like a galloping Thoroughbred carrying not one rider but four.

From the early days of the New Deal, the democratic world watched with great curiosity. Many were convinced that there was a nearly perfect coincidence between the particular causes of the United States and the universal causes of humanity.[8] Five months to the day after FDR's inauguration, Jawaharlal Nehru saluted the president for coming to democracy's rescue from a New Delhi British prison cell.[9] In a December 1933 letter sent to Roosevelt, John Maynard Keynes affirmed, "You have made yourself the trustee for those in every country who seek to mend the evils of our condition by reasoned experiment within the framework of the existing social system."[10] "Our generation," the German novelist Stefan Zweig, who would later commit suicide in exile in Brazil, observed, "grew up in the ardent, inflexible faith in the mission of Europe. . . . Though Europe has now proved so shamefully false to its most sacred mission, has destroyed itself in wanton self-laceration, though individual countries have made of moral irresponsibility a doctrine and of brutality a creed, we shall not be false to our faith. We shall place our trust in the youth of younger countries—America above all; it is for them to save the freedom of the mind, the humanity of the heart, for the world."[11]

This trust was not misplaced. The New Deal ultimately proved Mussolini wrong. The Gods of liberalism did not die. The dictatorships' vortex of violence and brutality was not only met but also trumped by a model of constitutionalism and law. Of the New Deal's many achievements, none was more important than the demonstration that liberal democracy, a political system with a legislature at its heart, could govern effectively in the face of great danger.[12] In a decisive break with the old, the New Deal intentionally crafted not just a new set of policies but also new forms of institutional meaning, language, and possibility for a model that had been invented 150 years before.[13] By buttressing the country's constitutional order despite the many frustrations inherent in its separation of powers and federal organization, the New Deal demonstrated that not all attempts at nonrevolutionary reform need fail.[14]

These achievements were widely recognized, almost immediately so. The editors of *The New Republic* reviewed the New Deal's panoply of policies in May 1940. They persuasively judged the first two Roosevelt administrations "to have done far more for the general welfare of the country and its citizens than any administration in the previous history of the nation."[15] That year, a twenty-nine-year-old graduate student by the name of Hubert Humphrey, completing a master's degree in political science at Louisiana State University, noted how much had been accomplished by "refusing to be bound by time-worn ideas as to the function of the state."[16] Likewise, the historian E. H. Carr observed the same year that the New Deal's program of reform had created a "vital democracy" as a global model.[17] A decade later, the best-selling author John Gunther praised the New Deal for accomplishing "one of the few gradualist revolutions in history," with "profound emotional results in lifting up the mental climate of most of the nation, stirring citizens to new hope and faith."[18] Looking backward, Oxford's Isaiah Berlin remarked in 1955 how "Mr. Roosevelt's example strengthened democracy everywhere—that is to say, the view that the promotion of social justice and individual liberty does not necessarily mean the end of all efficient government."[19]

By transcending the limits of traditional liberalism, conservatism, and orthodox socialism to take effective decisions on democracy's behalf, the

New Deal designed a template of options and possibilities with wide appeal beyond the United States. Marked by the "brilliant invocation of democratic resources against the perils of depression and war,"[20] the federal government reinvigorated constitutional democracy by countering economic and political cruelty. Prosperous and effectively armed by the end of this epoch, the country became democracy's global leader. It is inconceivable that liberal democracy today would enjoy legitimacy and prestige without the actions taken by the "long Roosevelt Administration"[21] that effectively responded to the era's naysayers, who claimed that liberal democracies were too pusillanimous to challenge the treacherous dictatorships, too effete to mobilize their citizens, and too enthralled with free markets to manage a modern economy successfully.

The New Deal's sustained defense of liberal democracy surely deserves at least as much admiration as Henry James expressed for golden Venice. Yet with so many facts familiar, archives exhausted, and competing interpretations long established, high regard cannot justify this book, certainly not a book of this length. The question lingers. Why paint, yet again, the most painted political landscape of twentieth-century America?

II.

A WISE COMMENTATOR once wrote of *King Lear* that "the sheer greatness of this work grossly magnifies its defects . . . that stand between certain scenes and their possible perfection."[22] Esteem for the New Deal paradoxically should draw attention to its most profound imperfections; it should motivate efforts to discern the causes of its defects. Seeking to understand not only the New Deal's manifest successes but also its ironies and limitations, I explore the complicated and sometimes unprincipled relationships between democracy and dictatorship, and between democracy and racism. Eschewing the traditional division separating foreign from domestic affairs, the book examines the fringes of liberal civilization and the ways in which illiberal political orders, both within and outside the United States, influenced key New Deal decisions.

The New Deal inhabited a space filled with tension. It unfolded at a moment of profound crisis. In their texts, the Greeks used the term in law, theology, and medicine to designate how a crisis imposes "choices between stark alternatives—right or wrong, salvation or damnation, life or death."[23] As the great economic historian Alexander Gerschenkron explained during World War II, "should Germany win, there will be no reconstruction in which the peoples of the world can take an active part; there will be nothing but the construction of pyramids for the new pharaohs."[24] But, in the 1930s and 1940s, the capacity for unblemished choices had disappeared. The Manichean world of right and wrong, where alternatives are nonnegotiable—a philosophy that derived from the ancient world—could no longer be sustained. Untainted partners no longer existed. No decisions could be made that were not influenced by practical and moral compromise.

At the time, it was not at all clear that America's constitutional state possessed the means to meet the era's challenges or make these judgments effectively. Writing in 1940, even before the conflagration spread beyond the borders of Europe, a leading political scientist, Pendleton Herring of Harvard, put the challenge this way:

> We face a world where discipline, organization, and the concentration of authority are placed before freedom for the individual and restraints on government. Internal economic problems likewise call for a greater degree of continuity and consistency in public policy. Yet our government was originally designed for no such complex necessities. What can we do with what we have? Can our government meet the challenge of totalitarianism and remain democratic? Is the separation of powers between the legislative and executive branches compatible with the need for authority? In seeking firm leadership do we open ourselves to the danger of dictatorship?[25]

This is a book about democracy and fear. Faced with emergency, the New Deal urgently had to navigate dangerous borderlands where freedom and the lack of freedom overlapped. By exploring how the New Deal dealt with these challenges, *Fear Itself* probes not just the achievements but the cost of doing what was necessary to preserve liberal democracy and protect its values.

To depict the effects of fear on the character and resilience of liberal democracy, I have found it necessary to rearrange the geography of New

PK's foci

Deal history, making it both wider and more narrowly focused.[26] Placing American developments within a broader global context, I ascribe to the New Deal an import almost on a par with that of the French Revolution. It becomes here not merely an important event in the history of the United States but the most important twentieth-century testing ground for representative democracy in an age of mass politics. Recasting more familiar narratives that have traditionally been centered on presidents and the executive branch, I primarily emphasize congressional lawmaking and the content of policy decisions.

Neither traditional history nor customary political science, this book aims to bring vital aspects of the New Deal into view more sharply, and thus to illuminate features that otherwise might remain indistinct or might even disappear.[27] By elevating the New Deal to a global drama, the book refuses to treat domestic and international affairs as disconnected subjects. By elongating the temporal contours of the New Deal to include the Truman years, it analyzes a time period more expansive than almost all New Deal histories.[28] In refusing to contract the time frame of the New Deal to the period before World War II, or to the Roosevelt years alone, the book, in effect, alters what we can see because it expands the years in which catastrophic events challenged American democracy and altered the national state. By shifting attention to Congress and the ways its votes remade the country's policies and institutions, it highlights the central importance of legislative bodies to vibrant liberal democracies.[29] By honing in on the role played by southern members of the House and Senate, it emphasizes how America's deepest regional divide altered the country's history, and shows how the South's commitments to a hierarchical racial order affected the full range of New Deal policies and accomplishments.

Fear Itself examines issues frequently avoided in the past, such as necessary evil and "dirty hands," an expression that connotes taking wrong action in a right cause.[30] As a liberal democracy without the luxury of sticking to a policy of high moral probity, the United States engaged dubious allies, abroad and at home. Although the United States provided the globe's only major example of a liberal democracy successfully experimenting and resisting radical tyranny, it did not—indeed, could not—remain unaffected by its associations with totalitarian governments or domestic racism. Concentrating on the New Deal era's new democratic beginnings under grave and chal-

lenging conditions, the book assesses the results fashioned by these necessary
but often costly illiberal alliances.

Reminding us that "all historians are prisoners of their own experience
and servitors to their own prepossessions," one of the most eminent historians
of the New Deal, Arthur Schlesinger Jr., thoughtfully recalled shortly before
his death how his own writings, especially the dramatic three volumes of
The Age of Roosevelt,[31] had been "conditioned by the passions of my era." He
wrote:

> Conceptions of the past are far from stable. They are perennially
> revised by the urgencies of the present. When new urgencies arise
> in our own times and lives, the historian's spotlight shifts, probing
> now into the shadows, throwing into sharp relief things that were
> always there but that earlier historians had carelessly excised from
> collective memory. New voices ring out of the historical darkness
> and demand attention.[32]

Schlesinger's history presented a New Deal narrative focused on Franklin Roosevelt, arguably the most dominant American figure of the twentieth century. It showed how this president mobilized a coalition of diverse
voters—native and immigrant, white and black, northern and southern. It
let readers see how the New Deal grappled with popular disaffection with
the business class, and with feelings of exclusion by workers, farmers, and
ethnic minorities. It chronicled how public policies led the transition to modern capitalism. It also demonstrated the ways pragmatic experimentation
helped conquer fear by expanding the ability of the national state to confront
unprecedented economic failure. Schlesinger's powerful and moving story
about the growth of government, the curtailment of unregulated business,
and the renewal of America as a land of opportunity remains persuasive even
today. But it is no longer sufficient.

Read in light of recent capitalist volatility, religious zealotry, and military insecurity, *The Age of Roosevelt,* and indeed much of the scholarship
on the New Deal, seems too insular and too limited. Our current age has
produced anxieties perhaps not of the same magnitude as those of the 1930s
and 1940s, but I believe we are being tested in similar ways. These dilemmas, then and now, are not unlike those that Alexis de Tocqueville, usually

known in the United States only for his 1835 and 1840 volumes on American democracy, sought to probe when he worried about French liberty and despotism in the 1850s. Referring to the "immense transformation of everything" that had taken place in 1789, and alarmed by the wayward political course that France had taken during the decades that followed, he was convinced that "today we are situated at just the right place to best see and judge this great thing." With time, the Revolution looked different, he argued. New acts could be witnessed; new questions could be asked; old certainties could be revisited.[33]

In composing this work, I returned repeatedly to Tocqueville's remarkable text, for today we are situated at approximately the same distance form the New Deal as he stood from his subject. Written in the mid-nineteenth century, *The Old Regime and the French Revolution* declared that France was "far enough from the Revolution to feel only fleetingly the passions that troubled the view of those who made it," but "we are . . . still close enough to be able to enter into and comprehend the spirit that brought it about." With a sense of exigency, and possessed with an understanding that a certain distance can produce a revealing perspective, Tocqueville set about composing "not a history of the French Revolution, whose story has been too brilliantly told for me to imagine retelling it," but, rather, "a study of the Revolution" that "never entirely lost sight of our modern society." Combining warm empathy and cold detachment, he blended close observation with historical sensibilities in order to probe his core subject, the fragile relationship between democracy and freedom. "I have written the present work without prejudice, but I do not pretend to have written it without passion," he explained. "My purpose has been to paint a picture both accurate and instructive."[34]

Like the French Revolution, the New Deal was a moment when the most fundamental contours of politics, including political institutions, language, and values, were deeply unsettled.[35] Inspired by Tocqueville's lesson that objects alter in changing conditions of time, I have tried to paint a picture that is accurate but not dispassionate, just "far enough above the details," as the historian Bernard Bailyn summed up his ambition, "to see the outlines of the overall architecture, and . . . to sketch a line—a principle—of reconstruction."[36] I hope to adjust the landscape of our historical perception and illuminate a seminal era in American history that explains much about our own times.[37]

III.

"Fear," one informant told Studs Terkel when the latter conducted an oral history of the 1930s, "unsettled the securities, apparently false securities that people had. People haven't felt unfearful since." Another reported how "everyone was emotionally affected. We developed a fear of the future that was very difficult to overcome . . . there was this constant dread. . . . It does distort your outlook and your feeling. Lost time and lost faith."[38] Hope proved elusive. The rumble of deep uncertainty, a sense of proceeding without a map, remained relentless and enveloping. A climate of universal fear deeply affected political understandings and concerns. Nothing was sure.

Over the course of the Roosevelt and Truman administrations, the country confronted three acute sources of fear.[39] First was the deep worry that the globe's leading liberal democracies could not compete successfully with the dictatorships. This period witnessed the disintegration and decay of democratic politics and liberal hopes.[40] Parliamentary democracies were widely thought to be weak and incapable when compared to the assertive energies of Fascist Italy, Nazi Germany, imperial Japan, and the Communist USSR. At the heart of this concern was a widespread belief that legislative politics, a politics polarized by competing political parties and ideological positions, made it impossible for liberal democracies to achieve sufficient dexterity and proficiency to solve the big problems of the day.

This problem seemed especially acute in the United States, whose government reflected the most radical separation of powers between the executive and legislative branches of government in the world. "If this country ever needed a Mussolini, it needs one now," Pennsylvania's Republican senator David Reed declared in 1932. "Leave it to Congress," he explained, "we will fiddle around here all summer trying to satisfy every lobbyist, and we will get nowhere. The country does not want that. The country wants stern action, and action taken quickly."[41] We will see that a similar call issued by the business weekly *Barron's* on the eve of Franklin Roosevelt's presidency for "a mild species of dictatorship [that] will help us over the roughest spots in the road ahead," and the claim by the American Legion that the crisis Roosevelt faced could not be "promptly and efficiently met by existing political methods" were neither isolated nor idiosyncratic.[42]

While competition with the dictatorships created the first fear, exponential growth in sophisticated weaponry proved the second, reflected in an accelerating arms race both before and after World War II, the radical intensification of warfare during that epochal conflagration, and the capacity to kill on a once-unimagined scale. With the global face-off between the two great powers after the war, a confrontation exacerbated by the Soviet Union's acquisition of nuclear weapons and the standoff in the Korean War, it became impossible for the United States to return to isolation or to disarm, as it previously had done after prior large-scale military mobilizations. By the early 1950s, America's military was *ten times* the size it had been in 1939, creating a new political reality "that could not be solved by a return to the happy days of 1939 or 1919 or 1914."[43]

Fear about warfare and global violence became a permanent condition. It became an inextricable part of American consciousness, helping to produce an obsession with national security, one that risked political repression. The new nuclear calculus, more than anything else, altered the geopolitics of the world as we knew it. Before, even the most flagrant examples of human suffering could be overcome. Slavery could be abolished. Decolonization could triumph over imperialism. But with radically enlarged prospects of vast and irrational killing fields, domestic and international politics came to be informed by a new and permanent amplification of danger and fear at a moment, ironically, when history's course held out possibilities of profound human improvement. Everyday politics became the stuff of unprecedented and awful apprehension. "Quite ordinary civilian rulers," Denis Brogan, a leading British historian of the United States, remarked in a 1956 lecture devoted to the implications for democracy in an atomic world, "are in the position of Milton's God."[44]

"The limitations imposed by the scale, the necessary secrecy, the necessary authoritarian character of the military establishment," he further observed, made the role of Congress especially problematic. Reporting on a wartime conversation he had had with a leading New Deal Democratic senator who had complained that the White House was bypassing his chamber in making key decisions about military matters, Brogan wrote:

> I was able to silence or, at any rate baffle him, by asking a question. How could the Senate be expected to be taken seriously when it kept at the heads of the Military and Naval Affairs Committees Senators

[Robert] Reynolds [of North Carolina] and [David] Walsh [of Massachusetts], not because anybody in the Senate or out of it thought them fit, but simply because they had a "right," by seniority, to these positions of power?[45]

By contrast, Harry Truman "ran up against a blank wall" when his committee investigating the national defense program "stumbled on the vast, secret enterprise 'Manhattan Project' that developed the country's atomic bomb." That moment, Brogan acutely commented, "when Senator Truman's investigators were turned away from the Manhattan Project was the constitutional turning point of no return, not when President Truman decided that 'it' was to be dropped on Hiroshima."[46]

 The racial structure of the South generated the era's third pervasive fear, a source of worry for both its defenders and its adversaries. Writing for the New Deal's Federal Writers' Project, Mississippi-born Richard Wright, later to write *Native Son,* described "the ethics of living Jim Crow." Reporting lessons he had learned in "how to live as a Negro," he told how his "Jim Crow education" had communicated messages confirming unquestioned white control.

Wright recalled one incident that occurred when he had worked as a teenager in a clothing store:

> The boss and his twenty-year old son got out of their car and half-dragged and half-kicked a Negro woman into the store. A policeman standing at the corner looked on, twirling his nightstick. . . . After a few minutes, I heard shrill screams coming from the rear of the store. Later the woman stumbled out, bleeding, crying, and holding her stomach. When she reached the end of the block, the policeman grabbed her and accused her of being drunk. Silently I watched him throw her into a patrol wagon. . . . No doubt I must have appeared pretty shocked, for the boss slapped me reassuringly on the back. "Boy, that's what we do to niggers when they don't want to pay their bills," he said laughing. His son looked at me and grinned. "Here, hava cigarette," he said.[47]

Southern politics was an integral part of such performative racism. Even the section's white racial moderates, such as the historian and Chattanooga newspaper publisher George Fort Milton, thought that the South's political order, including its restricted franchise and racial segregation, was "the fruit of the grim necessity of Reconstruction," the "means for redemption of a prostrate people."[48] In all, organized politics below the Mason-Dixon Line before the civil rights revolution not only functioned within a white-dominated society but served as the means to ensure it.

The role this system played in national politics is the most overlooked theme in almost all previous histories of the New Deal. Of course, a system of racial hierarchy was not limited to the South; race was embedded as a mark of division in every region. "The Negro problem is not the sole property of the South," W. E. B. Du Bois convincingly noted.[49] Much of the country outside the South marginalized and isolated African-Americans, practiced de facto segregation in housing, schooling, and employment, and looked the other way when antiblack violence proceeded.[50] The non-South, in the main, also was unconcerned about Jim Crow, unresponsive to black demands, and ignorant about the major works of social analysis by African-Americans and a few white scholars, including Du Bois, Charles Johnson, St. Clair Drake, Horace Cayton, Allison Davis, and Gunnar Myrdal, who chronicled America's racist matrix.[51]

Make no mistake, though. The South was singular. There, a racial hierarchy and the exclusion of African-Americans from the civic body were hardwired in law, protected by patterns of policing and accepted private violence, which created an entrenched system of racial humiliation that became everyday practice. No more than 4 percent of African-Americans could vote as late as 1938.[52] Buttressed by this limited franchise and protected by a one-party political system, rigid, fiercely policed segregation below the Mason-Dixon Line seemed like an unalterable fact of nature. "The further South one went," a shrewd historian of the era observed, "the smaller the impact of the New Deal in reshaping the political order."[53]

Reciprocally, the farther South one went in the United States, the greater the influence in shaping the content of the New Deal. We will discover the central role played by the once-slave South in Congress, where representatives from the seventeen states mandating racial segregation were pivotal members of the House and Senate. Democrats nearly to a person, they were the most important "veto players" in American politics.[54] Both the content and the moral tenor of the New Deal were profoundly affected. Setting terms not just for their constituencies but for the country as a whole, these members of Congress reduced the full repertoire of possibilities for policy to a narrower set of feasible options that met with their approval, or at least their forbearance. No noteworthy lawmaking the New Deal accomplished could have passed without their consent. Reciprocally, almost every initiative of significance conformed to their wishes.

Crucially, the South permitted American liberal democracy the space within which to proceed, but it restricted American policymaking to what I call a "southern cage," from which there was no escape. We will see how during the midpoint of the New Deal era, especially during World War II, southern politicians became increasingly obsessed with what they rightly perceived to be growing dangers for their racial order. This fear resulted in important changes to their political behavior in Congress. This historic shift within the Democratic Party, in which southern representatives were increasingly willing to team up with Republicans to create what later came to be called the "conservative coalition," was yet another fateful contribution the South made to the character of modern American politics.

The New Deal navigated each of these three indefinite sources of fear. A central goal of this book is to establish how these distinct fears became entwined. Manifestly present from the start, the contrast between democracy and dictatorship became an ever-more-visible theme of American politics and rhetoric. Questions about might and the conduct of war were different. Sometimes, those issues generated passionate debate; increasingly common, though, was a growing zone of secrecy and insulation from the normal give-and-take of political life. Southern racism in the early years was mostly taken as a given, but during World War II the combination of acceptance and invisibility became untenable.

The need to contend with the dictatorships to protect liberal democracy required alliances and arrangements that paradoxically violated widely accepted moral norms, a precedent that continues today. A striking example of such Faustian bargains is the "Darlan deal" of 1942, in which American officials, hardly excluding Gen. Dwight Eisenhower, recognized the authority of Vichy's Adm. Jean-François Darlan in French North Africa, despite his paramount role in rounding up Jews for deportation, in exchange for his cooperation with the impending Allied invasion.[55] Such transactions could no longer be avoided as the United States entered the globe's center ring.

It was Machiavelli who famously first argued that political leaders cannot simply follow traditional ethical prescriptions, because they cannot assume that their enemies, or their allies, will do the same. The path of virtue is the path of defeat. To promote the common good, Machiavelli claimed, it is necessary to perform ethically dubious acts. The New Deal could not but face this dilemma. The vaunted "Citty on a Hill," the phrase John Winthrop borrowed from the Sermon on the Mount's Parable of Salt and Light in 1630, could no longer luxuriate in its self-imposed isolation. Faced with such challenges, key issues were posed. When, and with whom, should Washington engage? How would the balance between the benefits and drawbacks, the good secured and the cost paid, be assessed? How, and to whom, should these actions be made accountable?

The United States recurrently compromised its liberal principles to make common cause with its ideological adversaries in Fascist Italy during the 1930s. It did so as well with unmistakably brutal Soviet Russia during World War II, and with postwar Germany, when a veritable army of Nazi veterans—political, administrative, and scientific servants of Hitler's regime—was enlisted in the Cold War.[56] These problematic partnerships were provisional. Treating Fascist Italy as a respectable government, despite its harsh treatment of many citizens at home and its horrific incursions in Ethiopia, was motivated in part by a wish to learn economic and administrative lessons about how to find a way out of the economic collapse and modernize the federal government. Making the Soviet Union a well-armed ally, despite Stalin's murder of millions, was far more than a desirable strategic consideration. That country's stalwart resistance, battlefield victories, and immense casualties were indispensable. Without them, the fight against Nazi Germany could not have been won.[57]

Far more enduring was the New Deal's intimate partnership with those in the South who preached white supremacy. For this whole period—the last in American history when public racism was legitimate in speech and action—southern representatives acted not on the fringes but as an indispensable part of the governing political party. New Deal lawmaking would have failed without the active consent and legislative creativity of these southern members of Congress. Here lay an acute incongruity. The New Deal permitted, or at least turned a blind eye toward, an organized system of racial cruelty. This alliance was a crucial part of its supportive structure. The

New Deal thus collaborated with the South's racial hegemony as it advanced liberal democracy at home and campaigned to promote liberal democracy abroad. In pursuing these purposes, the New Deal did not just tolerate discrimination and social exclusion; its most notable, and noble, achievements stood on the shoulders of this southern bulwark, all the while ultimately creating conditions for their amelioration.

In rejecting idealized versions that trivialize or conceal the era's morally ambiguous and sometimes heinous features, I aim not, as critics from the Left and the Right sometimes have wished, to diminish or make less legitimate what was accomplished during the New Deal. Rather, my lasting affinity for the New Deal is tempered by a kind of realism best expressed by the theologian Reinhold Niebuhr, who noted, in 1932, how "politics will, to the end of history, be an area where conscience and power meet, where the ethical and coercive factors of human life will interpenetrate and work out their tentative and uneasy compromises."[58] Even though the New Deal shimmied up, tantalizingly so, to the dictatorships, it did in the end keep faith with liberal democracy. Even though the New Deal patently ignored the South's violations of black rights and worked closely with many who were prepared to go to any length to protect the system of racial domination, it kept the South inside the Democratic Party, and thus inside the ambit of democratic politics. In contrast to the 1860s, a united republic ultimately held fast to its constitutional order. But this course was less assured, less definite, less pat, and, in some pivotal aspects, more damaging than historical portraits typically depict.

IV.

PROVIDING FUNDAMENTAL adjustments to the character of government and governance, the New Deal made many historic contributions, but its most enduring one was a novel national state. Quite securely in place by the close of the Truman administration, this new state boasted an unusual construction.[59] Much like the Roman God Janus, it possessed two distinctive faces. The first was that of procedural government. On this side, the national state collapsed into interests.[60] The federal government was defined less by objectives than by rules, less by purpose than by process, less by assertiveness than by access. This form of liberal democracy "legitimizes decisions on the basis of formal, procedural, legal correctness," rather than on the basis of content, substantive justice, or ultimate values.[61] It also rests on the commitment that "the role of government is one of ensuring access particularly to the most effectively organized, and of ratifying the agreements and adjustments worked out among the competing leaders and their claims." This is government, the political scientist Theodore Lowi observed, "in which there is no formal specification of means and ends . . . there is therefore no substance. Neither is there procedure. There is only process."[62] Such procedural government constitutes "the Adam Smith 'hidden hand' model applied to groups."[63] As numerous critics, including C. Wright Mills, Michael Sandel, and Lowi have argued,[64] this permeable state lacked instruments of collective civic purpose. The differences between political parties became less a matter of intrinsic ideology than a product of the interest groups with whom they identified and to whom they offered special access in exchange for electoral and financial support.[65]

The national state's second face was that of a crusader.[66] It provided marked contrasts with the first. Unlike its procedural partner, this countenance avowed a strong sense of the public interest. Charged with ideological purpose, it actively organized the defense and advancement of freedom.[67] Cordell Hull, who had represented Tennessee in the U.S. Senate before becoming Franklin Roosevelt's secretary of state in 1933, summarized this aim shortly after his abrupt retirement in 1944 as a quest "with hope and with deep faith for a period of great democratic accomplishment," a pursuit shaped by a concern that "the free peoples of this world, through any absence of action on our part, sink into weakness and despair."[68] This side of the state was nearly unbounded. Deploying power in an unprecedented way, its reach exceeded that of any prior national state or empire. It acted without inherent constraints or tied hands. Respecting few limits, it actively battled illiberal enemies. Linking great power ambitions with the high ground of idealism and moral legitimacy, it put planning, science, and technology at the service of couriers of violence. Symbolized by the immense Pentagon, at one point only temporary headquarters for a military at war,[69] it deployed itself in a myriad of ways, including extensive military outposts, clandestine subversion, and cultural education, often neglecting to disclose the source of its sponsorship. As Dwight Eisenhower succeeded Harry Truman, the country was spending 14 percent of its gross domestic product on the military, almost three times the rate of 1941 and almost as high as in 1942, the year following Pearl Harbor.[70]

The twin-pronged new state provided the New Deal with its most profound and enduring response to the challenge of navigating emergencies and managing the conflicts that are inherent in efforts to guard liberal democracy, while safeguarding its own institutions and advancing its values. This dual form of governance has lasted. It also has been prone to pathology. Ever since its creation, the dual state's discomfiting features—its nearly unconstrained public capacity contrasting with its nearly unconstrained private power, especially business power—have recurrently made an appearance.

V.

MUCH OF this volume is devoted to examining how this national state got fashioned. This task leads to Congress, the fulcrum of the book. One cannot understand the New Deal without appreciating the activist lawmaking that resulted from many bouts of arguing, bargaining, and voting in the U.S. Senate and House of Representatives. These policy achievements demonstrably challenged the period's common claim that national legislatures had become incapable and obsolete.

In the United States, the legislature remained an effective center of political life. As evidenced by the welter of lawmaking this book examines, Congress maintained a pride of place in a system of coequal branches. Its constitutional role was not supplanted. The Senate and House of Representatives continued, when they wished, to say no even to presidents at the peak of their popularity. Working through Congress, the New Deal falsified the idea that legislative politics must ensure democratic failure. To the contrary, Congress crafted policies that changed how capitalism worked, in part by promoting unions that gave the working class a voice both at the workplace and in national politics. It also organized responses to the challenges of global violence and national security. It was, in short, the central operative role of Congress that most distinguished the United States from the forces of brutality and the absence of political competition that characterized the dictatorships.[71]

Yet inside Congress, we hear an obbligato—the deep and mournful sound of southern political power determined to hold on to a distinctive way of life that also was indispensable to the era's legislative majorities. The region's representatives were located at the very center of the era's winning coalitions when the country faced a cascade of grave crises, and when its character as a liberal polity was being fundamentally reshaped.

Students of Congress know that, in addition to personal preferences, members of Congress are most influenced by party and constituency pressures. At a time of widespread racial bias and segregated arrangements hardly confined to the South, the men who represented the Jim Crow South constituted the pivotal bloc in the national legislature. With their local constituencies artificially limited through restrictive voting arrangements, and with such institutional rules as the Senate filibuster at their command, the southern bloc gained a key role within Congress, often playing captain to a diverse crew of other officers. Significantly, their votes tended to count for more than one. Buttressed by virtually all-white electorates in one-party constituencies, and possessing the powers of seniority, they dominated the committee system and the leadership of the House and Senate, thus serving as the legislature's main gatekeepers.

In all, the enhanced representation of the South in the powerful national legislature with an internal decision-making structure that experienced southern legislators skillfully negotiated and deployed made questions of region and race matter more than we often have appreciated in shaping what the New Deal could, and did, accomplish. Commanding the institution's lawmaking switchboard, southern members were in a position to determine the shape and content of key legislation. Although they—and the institution in Washington they knew most intimately—did not make the key difference at every turn, the South's capacity to veto what the region did not want and its ability to promote, as a pivotal actor, the policies it did favor mattered regularly and insistently over the course of the Roosevelt and Truman years. As a result, we live in a different country, different from what might have been without the exercise of power by southern members within America's uniquely capable national legislature.

To be sure, the southern region did not exist in isolation.[72] The ability of the House and Senate to refashion American liberal democracy depended on harnessing the Jim Crow South to the majority coalition of the Democratic Party. Without the South, there could have been no New Deal. When southern support was withheld, the outcome was different. With southern support, the New Deal could proceed, but there always was a cost, either tacit or explicit.

Much as the Constitution could never have been adopted without cross-sectional backing, and much as Lincoln understood that he could not win the Civil War without the support of Delaware, Kentucky, Maryland, and Missouri, the slave states that stayed loyal to the Union, so Presidents Roosevelt and Truman recognized their own limitations and how much they needed votes cast by their party's representatives from across the swath of the South to govern effectively. They understood that without the South, the country could not discover policies commanding majorities to steer precariously between the failed or inadequate status quo and nostrums pursued by the world's dictatorships.

Despite its centrality, southern power has always hovered at the fringe of most New Deal portraits.[73] When present at all, the South is usually slotted into a list of elements in the New Deal coalition—"a unique alliance of big-city bosses, the white South, farmers and workers, Jews and Irish Catholics, ethnic minorities, and African Americans"[74]—as if these were equivalent units of political power. The failure to place the special, often determining role of the Jim Crow South front and center, I believe, has had much the same effect as the "willful critical blindness" about race that Toni Morrison has identified so tellingly. "It is possible," she mournfully noted, ". . . to read Henry James scholarship exhaustively and never arrive at a nodding mention, much less a satisfactory treatment of the black woman who lubricates the turn of the plot and becomes the agency of moral choice and meaning in *What Maisie Knew*."[75] During the New Deal, it was the white South that acted as the key agent in Congress of just such moral choice and meaning. To record the history of the 1930s, 1940s, and early 1950s as if this were not the case would be as much a distortion as writing American history without its African-American sorrow songs.[76]

The South, then, was America's "wild card." Scholarship about the social roots of Fascism in interwar Europe has shown how the fate of democracy frequently hinged on choices made by the leaders and voters from that continent's least prosperous and most "backward" areas, those who were most afflicted by economic volatility, ethnic conflict, demagogic politics, and a sense of isolation from modern life's main currents.[77] This was also the case in Latin America, where agrarian districts, characterized by repressive labor practices, often rejected democratic governance, preferring various forms of authoritarian government.[78]

Both liberal and illiberal, progressive and racist, the large bloc of southern states played more than one role in national life, including that of advancing a radically anti-liberal white populism, with a family resemblance to European Fascism that combined "demagogic appeals to lower-income white farmers, bitter denunciations of large corporations and Wall Street, and vitriolic personal abuse of their opponents."[79] This most active form of political racism was perhaps best typified on the national scene by South Carolina governor Strom Thurmond, who ran for president in 1948 and carried four Deep South states, and by Alabama governor George Wallace, who carried five such states in 1968. But such third-party efforts were not the norm. Opting in the main to stay within the Democratic Party, the region empowered most New Deal initiatives in Congress, all the while holding fast to the ideology and institutions of official racism. The result was a Democratic Party—then the party of governance—that internalized the deepest contradictions in American life.

The region's representatives, who manifested strong preferences and effective strategic means to pursue them, imposed their wishes on each facet of New Deal policymaking. They determined which policies were feasible and which were not. The period's remarkable burst of invention reconstituted modern liberalism by reorganizing the country's political rules and public policies, but only within the limits imposed by the most illiberal part of the political order. In yet another ironic turn, these southern politicians helped save liberal democracy so successfully that they ultimately undermined the presuppositions of white supremacy.[80]

Often placing their supremacist values first, these representatives fought fiercely, if ultimately unsuccessfully, to preserve their region's racial tyranny. Their main national instrument, the Democratic Party, confederated two radically disparate political systems. One, northern and western, was primarily rooted in cities that featured urban machines, Catholic and Jewish immigrant populations, labor unions, and the working class. The other, southern, was essentially rural, native, Protestant, antilabor, and exclusively white. Writing about "American liberalism today" shortly after the conclusion of the extended New Deal, Denis Brogan sharply observed in 1957 the dynamics of this cross-sectional coalition:

The Liberal conscience is most deeply touched and his political behaviour seems (to the unfriendly outsider) most schizophrenic. The representative Liberal is a Democrat, or an ally of the Democrats, but in the ranks of "the Democracy" are most of the most violent enemies of the integration of the Negro into the American community. This is no doubt accidental; it arises from the localization of the most acute form of the colour problem in the region where the Democratic Party is traditionally strongest. The necessity of holding the national party together makes for strange bedfellows and strange deals.[81]

To properly understand the New Deal, it is just these bedfellows—their deals, successes, and failures—whom we need to place front and center.

But if there is a lesson, it is not one of retrospective judgment, as if the possibility then existed to rescue liberal democracy and pursue racial justice simultaneously. It later turned out that the first would prove to be a condition of the second. But there is no reason not to brood about the confining cage of explicit and willful racism in the Roosevelt and Truman years, or not to weigh its implications.

In a prior book, *When Affirmative Action Was White*,[82] I examined how southern power in Congress damaged the prospects of African-Americans. Shaped by the South, national policies in the 1930s and 1940s regarding Social Security, labor law, military race relations, and the treatment of veterans, I argued, reinforced inequality and deepened the racial divide. Missing from that book, however, was a discussion of how housing segregation was encouraged by the Federal Housing Authority, and the failure of the federal government to contravene segregation in its own facilities, whether in Washington, D.C., or even at the atomic bomb research center in Oak Ridge, Tennessee. I might even have mentioned how "African American journalists were excluded from both the president's and Mrs. Roosevelt's press conferences," or how the Civilian Conservation Corps (CCC) camps were segregated.[83]

Though I return to such themes and their implications in terms of racial justice in discussing soldier voting, antilynching measures, and other, mostly abortive, civil rights initiatives, in *Fear Itself* I examine primarily how the South exercised its critical position to affect decisions concerning global power, national security, civil liberty, unions, and the character of capitalism. The southern wing of the Democratic Party, I show, composed the most persistently effective political force that determined the content and boundaries of this momentous "constitutional moment."[84]

If history plays tricks, southern congressional power in the last era of Jim Crow was a big one. The ability of the New Deal to confront the era's most heinous dictatorships by reshaping liberal democracy required accommodating the most violent and illiberal part of the political system, keeping the South inside the game of democracy. While it would be folly to argue that members of the southern wing of the Democratic Party alone determined the choices the New Deal made, their relative cohesion and their assessment of policy choices through the filter of an anxious protection of white supremacy often proved decisive.

The triumph, in short, cannot be severed from the sorrow. Liberal democracy prospered as a result of an accommodation with racial humiliation and its system of lawful exclusion and principled terror. Each constituted the other like "the united double nature of both soul and body" in Goethe's *Faust*. This combination confers a larger message—a lesson that concerns the persistence of emergency, the inescapability of moral ambiguity, and perhaps the inevitability of a politics of discomfiting allies, abroad as well as at home. It also reminds us that not just whether but also how we find our way truly matters.

PART I

FIGHT AGAINST FEAR

1 ⟫ A Journey without Maps

EAR, MICHEL DE MONTAIGNE maintained in the sixteenth century, "exceeds all other disorders in intensity."[1] Likewise, Francis Bacon thought that "nothing is terrible except fear itself"; the statesman and political theorist Edmund Burke observed that "no passion so effectually robs the mind of all its powers of acting and reasoning as fear"; and Henry David Thoreau believed that "nothing is so much to be feared as fear."[2]

Why might this be the case? What distinguishes deep anxieties that generate fear from more ordinary uncertainties and risks? Taking such admonitions and claims seriously during the Roosevelt and Truman years requires identifying the era's objects of fear. The politics and policymaking of the period were not conducted in ordinary circumstances. Spreading like fire from rooftop to rooftop, fear provided a context and served as a motivation for thought and action both for America's leaders and ordinary citizens.

Without grappling adequately with this political and cultural climate, the historical landscape tends to be seen like a series of disconnected but well-mapped roads, each with specific factors said to have caused this or that key outcome. We consider, as examples, how legacies from the past helped cause one landmark law of 1933, the National Industrial Recovery Act, to fail, but another, the Agricultural Adjustment Act, to succeed; we ask whether the 1935 Wagner Act, which established a framework for union development, was the result of labor pressure or business interests; we evaluate the reasons for, and the consequences of, the lapse into deep recession in 1937–1938; and we investigate whether the global preferences of internationally oriented capitalists propelled the foreign and domestic policies of the United States.[3]

The background assumption in such studies is that the politics and policymaking of the period were conducted in customary circumstances of risk. But they were not. Overall, the New Deal had to travel uncharted territory, often without maps in hand.[4] To comprehend its achievements and their price, we must incorporate uncertainty's state of doubt, and identify the objects of fear and the effects of being frightened.[5]

I.

DELIVERING AN address to a Charter Day audience at Berkeley on March 23, 1933, the very day the Reichstag passed its powers to Adolf Hitler and Germany's first concentration camp opened at Dachau,[6] the journalist and political commentator Walter Lippmann sought to understand the time's deep uncertainty. He noted how "the certain landmarks are gone," and how "the fixed points by which our fathers steered the ship of state have vanished." He further identified the rupture between past and present—in the democracies as well as the dictatorships—with two revolutionary developments in modern politics he believed to be "wholly without precedent in history." First was the active and self-conscious participation in government by "the masses of men," making of "modern government in our Western World, even under the dictatorships," something of "a daily plebiscite." The legitimacy of any government thus had come to depend on its ability to solve problems and formulate policies to which the governed would offer consent, both active and passive. Second was the vastly enlarged scope of governmental action. "Never before has government been on so vast a scale, touching such numbers of men in the vital concerns of their lives. The interests which modern governments are called upon to manage are as novel as they are complicated," and they now included issues that no nineteenth-century government had faced. These new questions included "relationships between producers and their markets," "forms of economic organization," including a place for labor, profound challenges of war and peace in an age of warfare fought by conscript armies and revolutionary violence, and problems of "external and internal political control."[7] To this list concerning capitalism, workers, military might, and security, he might have added the issue of citizenship, for if politics had become a politics of masses, then defining the qualifications for membership had become ever more pressing. In all, "there is a widespread feeling today among the people" that older codes, conventions, rules, policies, and institutions "lack the power to guide action."[8]

In accepting the Nobel Prize in Literature a quarter of a century later, Albert Camus summed up the shocking sequence of overlapping developments that his generation had endured during "more than twenty years of an insane history."

> These men who were born at the beginning of the First World War, who were twenty when Hitler came to power and the first revolutionary trials were beginning, who were then confronted as a completion of their education with the Spanish Civil War, the Second World War, the world of concentration camps, a Europe of torture and prisons—these men must today rear their sons and create their works in a world threatened by nuclear destruction.[9]

Not only to Camus but to so many others, as well, this was an age of broken certainties. "When the World War, in which aircraft was employed for the first time on an intensive scale as an instrument of combat broke out, there were few conventional rules and naturally little or no customary law in existence," a learned commentator wrote in 1924.[10] Across a wide swath of domestic and international issues, policymakers and the public alike had to proceed in similar circumstances. With Western civilization robbed of much of its ethical and political authority, the New Deal confronted novel challenges. The key political question was whether democracies, with their fractious parties, parliaments, and polarization, could invent solutions and find their way while holding on to their core convictions and practices.

Many inside the democracies had serious doubts. Their misgivings grew when economic recovery proved sporadic. Over the course of the 1930s, the globe's circumstances grew more forbidding. Violence became more common, more intense, more threatening. Security seemed elusive. Commenting in 1936, the English novelist Graham Greene wrote how "our world seems particularly susceptible to brutality."[11] The constitutional scholar Karl Loewenstein noted in 1937 how dictatorial, antidemocratic regimes possessing seductive emotional power are "no longer an isolated incident in the individual history of a few countries." Rather, they have "developed into a universal movement which in its seemingly irresistible surge is comparable to the rising of European liberalism against absolutism after the French Revolution."[12] No one, the U.S. ambassador to Germany, William Dodd, wrote in 1938, "can fail to see increasing evidence that democracy is in grave danger." Stationed in Berlin from 1933 to 1938, Dodd witnessed the dramatic crumbling of a once-democratic republic. The United States, he warned, "facing the same dangers ahead," is not exempt.[13] That year, before Nazi armies crossed into Poland to begin the European phase of World War II, the distinguished émigré sociologist Pitirim Sorokin announced that the twentieth century had become "the bloodiest century in the whole history of the Western World."[14] That year as well, George Kennan, then the head of the Russian desk at the Department of State and soon to be the most important architect of the strategy of anti-Soviet containment during the Cold War, started drafting a book recommending that the United States travel "along the road which leads through constitutional change to the authoritarian state," a state he believed would have to be led by a specialized elite who "would have to subject themselves to discipline as they would if they entered a religious order."[15]

What these observers and commentators shared was an understanding that theirs was a time when uncommon uncertainty at a depth that generates fear had overtaken the degree of common risk that cannot be avoided. Any circumstance of contingency is marked by risk of the usual kind. Choices are made based on past experience. Because the properties of most things remain fairly constant, and because the relationship between cause and effect is mostly predictable, it is possible to assess probabilities intelligently. When firms invest, when parents decide which school to select for their children, when individuals buy a house, or when political leaders bargain, vote, and make laws, most of the time the distribution of likely results from particular actions can be calculated, either intuitively or on the basis of statistical analysis. This is the basis for most strategic calculations and rational estimates based on a reasonable degree of confidence.

But when deep uncertainty looms, the ability to choose is transformed. The University of Chicago economist Frank Knight identified such circumstances of "unmeasurable uncertainty" as those that are uncommonly unsure because any valid basis for classifying instances is absent. Effects and outcomes of action cannot be calculated because such situations are unlike any other. In commonplace risk he wrote, "the distribution in a group of instances is known . . . while in the case of uncertainty this is not true, the reason being in general that it is impossible to form a group of instances, because the situation dealt with is in a high degree unique." The novelty and depth of this kind of uncertainty is radical. It is the kind of risk that cannot be ensured against, for the very premises underlying prediction are undermined. Looking ahead, estimates of possibilities and effects grow increasingly opaque. Modeling the future becomes ever more elusive.[16]

Measurable risk generates worry. Unmeasurable risk about the duration and magnitude of uncertainty spawns fear. A large and growing literature in social psychology has examined the question of how persons deal with such realities in thought, feeling, and behavior by attempting to reorganize situations in order to restore consistency and predictability. Under conditions of fear, these various theories and studies about the management of uncertainty reveal that people develop a heightened mindfulness and self-awareness about the constraints on free action, and take, as a central goal, the desire to restore a higher degree of coherence and certainty; that is, they try to reduce deep uncertainty to ordinary risk.[17]

This is how I have come to understand the New Deal. Over the course of its two decades, the reality of deep uncertainty progressively extended the sense that the United States confronted unparalleled dangers. Faced with economic collapse, total war, genocide, atomic weapons, and postwar struggles with Communism, political leaders sought to find means to restore a sense of normal risk. Because they possessed no fixed or sure policy approaches or remedies for the domestic and global crises of the day, they could consider a very wide repertoire of policies. The collective result of the various choices and selections they made to reduce uncertainty to risk, particularly in Congress, where southern members played a disproportionate role, became, in effect, a new national state, a state with a procedural and a crusading face.

II.

CURIOUSLY, THOUGH, a time when the presence of fear was pervasive is not how the New Deal era is ordinarily portrayed. A fit of amnesia distorts the era, thus risking an excessively sentimental and simple set of understandings. This tendency appeared from the beginning. Within a week of Franklin Roosevelt's inauguration, Walter Lippmann, who only weeks earlier had spoken of the uncertainty of the times, celebrated how "the manner in which the Administration has conducted itself fully justifies the public approval which is manifest everywhere. It has proceeded rapidly, surely, and boldly, dealing directly with the essentials, accepting responsibility without hesitation, relying confidently upon the willingness of the people to face realities." Heralding a redemptive theme that later organized the narrative of most New Deal histories, Lippmann rejoiced in how "the nation, which had lost confidence in everything and everybody, has regained confidence in the government and in itself."[18] It was as if he had worried too much at Berkeley; yet he had not.

The president's own inaugural rhetoric, announcing that fear itself was unjustified, had the virtue of avoiding fearmongering, of not promoting hysteria, and thus not worsening the quality of democratic thought and deliberation. Unlike some appeals to fear, it was not a free-floating invocation of insecurity, without content, the all-too-familiar kind that can open the door to demagoguery, manipulation, and control.[19] Insisting that "we are stricken by no plague of locusts," but by a crisis caused by speculative greed and misguided policy decisions, Roosevelt called for "an end to a conduct in banking and in business which too often has given to a sacred trust the likeness of callous and selfish wrongdoing," and he identified "safeguards against a return of the evils of the old order; there must be a strict supervision of all banking and credits and investments; there must be an end to speculation with other people's money, and there must be provision for an adequate but sound currency."

By presenting a sober and realistic account of danger without crossing the line into apprehension so acute as to be paralyzing, FDR offered reassurance. His political narrative featured how public policy could overcome fear. This was how his formulation about fear itself was intended, and this, as it turned out, was how he later would represent his administration's achievements. Accepting his party's nomination for a second term in June 1936, Roosevelt laid claim to having vanquished fear itself. "In those days, we feared fear. That was why we fought fear. And today, my friends, we have won against the most dangerous of our foes—we have conquered fear," he stated, patently ignoring the developing maelstrom that was laying siege to the European and Asian continents.[20]

Moving from deep trouble to a positive resolution, this appealing rendering soon became the norm for historians, journalists, and social scientists. It successfully organized many strands into a coherent story. But this came at a high price, bypassing, as the literary critic Alfred Kazin remarked, "the permanent crisis that is the truth of our times," thus letting pass "the truth that cannot be fitted in, the jagged edges that would detract from the straight frame and the smooth design."[21]

Among historians, this theme of rescue and salvation was first projected by Arthur Meier Schlesinger in *The New Deal in Action, 1933–1937,* the earliest serious assessment by a member of his profession and one that set the main contours for later scholarship.[22] In just thirty-six printed pages, he represented the New Deal as a successful response to economic catastrophe and political crisis. This text famously distinguished the First New Deal's measures of relief and recovery to prevent starvation, ameliorate suffering, and jolt the capitalist economy from the Second New Deal's long-term measures of economic regulation and social policy, including the 1934 Securities Exchange Act and the 1935 Social Security Act. By radically transforming the range and scale of the national state, by curbing and controlling market excesses, and by adding social rights to citizenship, the New Deal, he argued, had restored trust and loyalty, hopefulness and popular support.

Like Schlesinger, the great majority of historians have underscored these achievements, stressing how they redrew the country's lines of civil society and the geometry of political pressure, and how, in just over half a decade, President Roosevelt's program transformed not only the range and scale of government but also the character of the country's economy and the scope of American citizenship. It is impossible to write about this subject without attending to these matters. This book is no exception. From the inauguration of Franklin Roosevelt to the 1939 outbreak of World War II in Europe, the New Deal substantially increased the domestic scope of government. A federal civil service that had 572,000 employees grew to one of 920,000 in just those six years, and spending nearly doubled, going from $4.6 billion to $8.8 billion, as a host of alphabet agencies and programs—AAA, CWA, PWA, REA, TVA, WPA, NRA, SEC, NLRB, FLSA, FHA, FSA, and more—undertook unprecedented responsibility for public employment and public works, relief payments, labor policy, and the regulation of capitalism.[23] "More than anything else," Hubert Humphrey recalled in 1970, "the New Deal was a change in the scope of public responsibility."[24]

After World War I, the liberal intellectual Harold Stearns had reflected on the lessons conveyed by that war's massive bloodletting, enhanced state power, reduction to the scope of freedom, and jingoistic hysteria. He perceptively predicted an uncertain future for the liberal democratic political tradition in the West. He thought such governments could not survive as effective actors unless they could devise social revolutions without violence to carve out a space for reason in the face of the intensifying conflict between labor and capital, and the virulent nationalism characterizing relations among countries.[25] The familiar story of the New Deal as a movement from fear to expectation, brought about by retrofitting capitalism and shaping a welfare state, appropriately focuses on how the New Deal achieved what Stearns meant by a social revolution without violence. It captures, as the historian Richard Hofstadter put it, how the remarkable combination of Roosevelt's "opportunistic virtuosity" and his administration's policy improvisations, "in their totality, carried the politics and administration of the United States farther from the conditions of 1914 than those had been from the conditions of 1880."[26] But it misses both the perception and the reality of persistent fear.[27]

To be sure, despondency and insecurity at the New Deal's founding has long been a familiar theme. The stock market crash and capitalism's global crisis starkly posed the question whether prosperity and liberty could be renewed simultaneously under democratic auspices. "The Politics of Hard Times" and "Winter of Despair" open William Leuchtenburg's classic *Franklin Roosevelt and the New Deal.*[28] Following in his father's footsteps, the no less venerable Arthur Schlesinger Jr. defined the subject of his evocative trilogy, *The Age of Roosevelt,* as "The Crisis of the Old Order."[29] He recalled how, from 1929 to 1932, farm income had dropped by 70 percent, automobile production by 65 percent, and the value of the stock market by over 80 percent. Industrial production dropped precipitously. Thirteen million Americans had lost their jobs. Before the crash in October and November 1929, some 3 percent of Americans had been out of work. The proportion of unemployed thereafter had reached a calamitous 24 percent, and those lucky enough to keep their jobs often had their pay cut.[30] Farmers who could not keep up with their mortgage payments lost their land; many homeowners, a minority at the time, lost their homes; and tenants who could not pay their rent lost their dwellings. More broadly, the system of credit and banking had broken down, posing a major threat to the continuation of market capitalism. With factories "ghostly and silent, like extinct volcanoes," families sleeping "in tarpaper shacks and tin-lined caves," and "thousands of vagabond children . . . roaming the land," Schlesinger wrote, the country faced a "mood of helplessness." A "contagion of fear" and "a fog of despair hung over the land."[31]

But in these, and in a great many other, estimable histories, fear and uncertainty drop out too soon.[32] Stirred perhaps by President Roosevelt's "firm belief that the only thing we have to fear is fear itself," the New Deal is presented as a story of how assertive economic policies overcame doubt and restored confidence during President Roosevelt's first term.[33] Measuring where things stood late in 1936, Schlesinger applauded how "the fog began to lift." The president, he wrote, "was apparently succeeding; and people could start to believe again in the free state and its capacity to solve problems of economic instability and social injustice. Free society, in consequence, might not yet be finished; it had a future; it might have the strength and steadfastness to surmount the totalitarian challenge."[34] With successful legislative and policy achievements, Franklin Roosevelt's initial term had transformed the politics of upheaval into a politics of hope.[35]

III.

I N FACT, the entire New Deal period, lasting until the inauguration of Dwight Eisenhower in 1953, reflects an unremitting sense of fragility. From the Great Depression to the blood-filled battlefields in Korea, persistent, nearly unremitting anxiety conditioned the era's "normal politics" of voting, public opinion, pressure groups, federalism, and the separation of powers among the executive, legislative, and judicial branches of government. Faced with desolation, the New Deal proceeded in an anguish-filled environment. In such a world, the most constant features of American political life continually threatened to become unstable, if not unhinged. The ability of leaders to cope with menacing economic, ideological, and military threats never could seem quite sure.

It must be underscored that fear was not banished after just four years of the New Deal. To the contrary, it only deepened. Schlesinger's temporal limits, substantive foci, and vivid theatrical structure in *The Age of Roosevelt* understate the sheer range of tests American democracy faced as it lacked assured policies to rescue capitalism, confront the dictatorships, and deal with global power and conflict. The presentation of the era's challenges to liberal democracy as primarily those of American economic suffering had also been too limited. The Depression deepened and spread virally across the globe, sparing virtually no place and no economic sector. Collapsing production and consumption, shrinking markets, diminishing trade, the loss of credit and liquidity, and especially a sweeping increase in unemployment were not countered by effective remedies anywhere for something like half a decade. First responses, including high tariffs and stringent austerity policies, only made things worse. Among all social classes and groups, confidence about capitalism plummeted, and the prestige of private business fell off radically. The World Economic Conference of 1933 failed. Even when economic recovery began, it proved fitful, remaining well below late 1920s levels for most of the 1930s.

The global crisis to which the New Deal had to respond, moreover, transcended economic duress. During the period covered by *The Age of Roosevelt*, international and multilateral institutions to keep the peace and prevent a return to the carnage of World War I, most notably the League of Nations and the Kellogg-Briand Pact, began to collapse in the face of imperial Japan's conquest of Manchuria and its attack on Shanghai.[36] The range of political repression also broadened. The Soviet Gulag as a branch of State Security was officially born in 1930 to manage camp complexes, most in Siberia, that ultimately housed millions. Many were mobilized for immense projects of rapid industrialization, including the White Sea Canal. A growing network of German concentration camps imprisoned people for who they were and what they believed rather than for how they had acted, thus housing "a particular type of noncriminal, civilian prisoner, the members of an 'enemy' group, or at any rate a category of people who, for reasons of their race or presumed politics, are judged to be dangerous or extraneous to society."[37] Though the majority of Americans were not yet alert to the severity and consequences of these distant developments, the country's leaders were keenly aware that threats to liberal democracy were proliferating in a way that was without precedent.

The pressures on liberal democracy did not stop in the second half of FDR's first term. At home, the economic recovery left many millions in dire circumstances. An environmental crisis ravaged agriculture.[38] Racial violence erupted. Anti-Semitism reared its head. Labor unrest grew. Demagogues talked louder.[39] Of course it would be an exaggeration to state that the United States was on the verge of joining the democratic collapse that was spreading like a domino effect during the 1930s. But there were plenty of dangers at home and a continuing atrophy for liberal democracy abroad.

The United States possessed many of the same features that Hannah Arendt was soon to associate with the rise of totalitarianism. These included racism as a robust ideology, imperial expansion, and the control of subject populations. Proud of their diaspora nationalism, there was much ethnic admiration, even loyalty, to German and Italian Fascism, ideological attachment to the USSR to the point of spying, and there was a good deal of anti–civil liberties counterpunching by Congress, the courts, and the executive branch. American democracy may not have risked the same apocalyptic fate as the Weimar Republic. Nevertheless, there was a real set of pitfalls. At issue were prospects of executive usurpation and excessive congressional delegation, the projection of antidemocratic (and racist) mass populism and instances of private violence against targeted groups, an increase in surveillance and pressures on civil liberties, suspensions of due process, and, most broadly, a loss of democratic legitimacy.

The period's various forms of political tyranny—including Fascism, Nazism, Stalinist Bolshevism, Peronist populism, and Japanese militarism—grew in number and became more confident and overbearing. Over the course of the decade, these various regimes that sought to move "forward from liberalism"[40] claimed to make constitutional democracy obsolete, a mere stage of history. Emerging like an irresistible tide and professing to be riding the wave of the future, these various governments legitimated torture, police terror, and show trials. They also concentrated power, extinguishing all but the ruling party. They geared "the whole of society and the private life of the citizen to the system of political domination."[41] By late 1938, "only Britain, France, the Low Countries, and Scandinavia" had experienced success "in any sense preserving those 'liberal' freedoms which had spread across Europe since 1789."[42] "The outstanding feature of our time is insecurity," England's leading political analyst, Harold Laski, declared in 1939. "The liberal society of the epoch before 1914 is unthinkable in our age."[43]

The scope of sources generating fear continued to grow. In the two years before the outbreak of World War II in Europe, Nazi Germany "had regained a dominance in Europe at least comparable to that of Bismarck; and like that of Bismarck, it was exercised with the willing consent of the British government and the glum acquiescence of the French."[44] With American neutrality, the relative absence of opposition to Hitler's hegemony, near silence about Nazism's fierce discrimination and humiliation of German Jews, and widespread democratic exhaustion and indifference, the surviving democracies seemed limp and incapable. Even more seemed lost in the demoralizing dislocations at the start of the 1940s. Poland, France, and a host of other countries were seized by the Nazis. Collaboration, whether official, as with France's Vichy government, or quotidian, was far more common than resistance. The stream of refugees became a torrent on a biblical scale.[45] The sudden fall of France in June 1940 was especially shocking. Late that month, the president of the Swiss Confederation, Marcel Pilet-Golaz, addressed the country by radio. He counseled that "this is not the time to look with melancholy toward the past," explaining why the country's legislative procedures would be suspended. "The government has to act. Conscious of its responsibilities, the executive branch will fully assume them. Outside and above party lines, the Federal Council will serve all Swiss. . . . Confederates, you will have to follow the Federal Council as a devoted and steady guide. We will not always have the opportunity to explain, comment, and justify our decisions. Events are happening fast; we have to adapt to their pace."[46] The morale of the other democracies was also shaken.

Wartime violence placed civilians at a risk higher than they had faced during World War I. Then, as with prior wars, if on a much more intense scale of killing, "the armies destroyed everything in their path, but the path was narrow, and towns a little way out of the path were hardly affected."[47] The road of devastation was not nearly as narrow the second time around. Rotterdam was entirely razed from the air in May 1940. German bombers conducted raids across the Channel, hitting Sheffield, Birmingham, Hull, Plymouth, Glasgow, Coventry (smashing its cathedral and putting one-third of its homes in ruin), and London, damaging the Tower and Westminster Abbey, demolishing the northern wing of Parliament, and devastating much of the East End—at a cost of 30,000 lives and 100,000 homes. "Entire chunks of the city centre, including the busy shopping and office area between St Mary-le-Bow and St Paul's Cathedral, returned to the primal state of the old London, a wilderness of mud, rubble, and tall grass, a plain where only a few footpaths bore the names of former streets," anticipating by three decades the apocalyptic scenery imagined by J. G. Ballard.[48] Despite its ill-fated August 1939 Non-Aggression Pact with Germany, the Soviet Union was being pummeled even more spectacularly. Hitler's exterminationist empire was confidently on the march.[49] In what Timothy Snyder has called the "forgotten Holocaust,"[50] SS Einsatzgruppen murdered tens of thousands each day in Belarus and Ukraine; in July 1941, orders were given to shoot all the Jews of Minsk; in just two days, September 29 and 30, 33,771 Jews who had been rounded up at Kiev were executed, naked and their faces to the ground, in an immense ravine at Babi Yar. More Jews were put to death behind the front that year than Soviet troops killed by German soldiers in battle.[51] Japanese militarism controlled much of the Pacific and the Asian mainland, having conquered the Philippines, Burma, Hong Kong, Malaya, Singapore, and the Dutch East Indies. Australia was threatened by invasion.[52] China seemed quite likely to yield to Japanese force. America faced an uncertain two-front war that was exacting high casualties. "Nationalism, capitalism, liberalism are in the crucible; it may take years," the lawyer and sociologist David Riesman declared in 1942, "before a new amalgam of social forces emerges which can give promise of some stability and peace."[53]

Even before the Cold War rent the alliance between the Soviet Union and the Allied powers, scorning postwar hopes for a United Nations that would mean more than a new global institution, World War II had proved to be "a tainted triumph."[54] The United States fought with a segregated army. Xenophobia and racism helped frame the campaign against Japan; "Admiral Ernest King, Chief of Naval Operations, wrote to President Roosevelt in March 1942 that the USA could not permit the 'white man's countries' of Australia and New Zealand to be conquered by Japan 'because of the repercussions among the non-white races of the world.'"[55] Terrible destruction had been wrought by incendiary carpet bombing, then by atomic weapons.[56] City after city, by war's end, not just in Europe but also in Asia, lay in ruins.[57] And even before the inevitable diffusion of the relevant knowledge and capacity, the very existence of the first nuclear bombs utterly transformed the human condition. The rain of actual and potential destruction had grown more intense, more widespread, far more promiscuous. And there was no turning back.

Above all, the victory of 1945 was tarnished by the discovery of the Holocaust, an orgy of organized slaughter that exceeded earlier twentieth-century instances, including the attempt, between 1904 and 1907, to exterminate the Herero and Namaqua peoples of German Southwest Africa by driving them into the Omaheke desert and poisoning their wells after their insurgency against colonial rule, or the Ottoman Empire's mass killing and starvation of Armenians during World War I. This shocking enlargement of genocide had been accompanied mainly by passivity or complicity.[58] After the war, a swollen mass of forced emigrants and displaced persons again filled the roads. "It was estimated that by May 1945 there were perhaps 40.5 million uprooted people in Europe, excluding non-German forced labourers and Germans who fled before the advancing Soviet armies."[59] Writing about the death camps, the Holocaust survivor Paul Celan described it as a time of "black milk" in his poem "Todesfuge."[60]

Even after the fighting stopped, there was no escape from its unprecedented compound of violence, willful mass murder, ideological fervor, and radical versions of state and party. The war, moreover, left the United States deeply unsure about how to deal with Stalin's Soviet Union. "At best optimistic and at worst naïve," the historian John Morton Blum judged, American policymakers had "projected their own understanding of American politics beyond the borders of its relevance," and thus found themselves, both in East Europe and in Asia, caught between an unwillingness to impose liberal democracy by brute force, especially in a confrontation with the Soviet Union at war's end, and an acceptance of a division of the world by realist, great power, principles, and thus the acceptance of the actuality of Communist global power.[61]

"The war changed everything," Tony Judt observed, making key features of the past "unrecoverable."[62] Moreover, fear did not dissipate once the fighting stopped. It became pervasive, persistently constitutive, both deeply particular and broadly abstract. With unlimited power having joined unlimited violence, and with killing, married to passionate causes, having gone beyond any reasonable assessment of instrumental utility, even what had remained of conventional standards after World War I eroded. Only with the depredations of World War II was it absolutely clear, as Leszek Kolakowski has put the point, that "evil is not contingent. It is not the absence of deformation, or subversion of virtue . . . but a stubborn and unredeemable fact."[63] Only then did all humankind, even its most advantaged, fall within the ambit of a permanent fear.

IV.

EVEN IN the mid-1930s, when the New Deal's domestic achievements seemed most apparent, many contemporaries were not convinced that fear had been conquered. Howard Odum, for example, a sober southern moderate who was a leading student of the demography, culture, and economy of his region, strongly supported President Roosevelt's initiatives. Odum warned in 1935 (the year the Wagner Act, chartering unions, and the Social Security Act passed into law) that American democracy was at risk from the country's "multiplied inequalities of opportunity for the majority of the people." He noted the "increasing injustice throughout the Nation," "a well-nigh universal lack of security," and "widespread confusion, unrest, distrust, and despair." Describing "a mixed picture," he took note of American "movements toward violent revolution," "the movement toward fascism and dictatorship," and various messianic currents and regional discontents. Despite the apparent solidity of the two-party system and constitutional arrangements, a strong possibility existed, he believed, for "anything but orderly transitional democracy," especially in the South. Calling for unprecedented national planning, he concluded "in simple language . . . that there will be no democracy or formal alternative to democracy in the United States for the next period, say twelve years." Rather, he predicted that the nation would experience a deeply uncertain "struggle to evolve an orderly democracy . . . in competition with the other alternatives of chaos, revolution, super-corporate control and centralization, socialism, communism, and fascism."[64]

Of course, no single essay can accurately reflect the ethos of an era. But even if judged to be an overstatement of actual danger for American democracy, Odum's words of warning in fact were characteristic. They were echoed many times over. Explaining in *I'm for Roosevelt* why he supported the president, Joseph P. Kennedy, then the first chairman of the Securities and Exchange Commission (and the father of the nineteen-year-old John Fitzgerald, the eleven-year-old Robert Francis, and the four-year-old Edward Moore), commented in 1936 that "democracy will not be safe for this country unless we constructively deal with causes of dictatorships. . . . If our democracy is to survive the attacks of dictatorship, whether open or veiled, we must solve the problem of security."[65] In an election-eve radio address in November 1938, even President Roosevelt mused aloud about the safety of the American political system when "in other lands across the water the flares of militarism and conquest, terrorism and intolerance" had grown. "Comparisons in this world are unavoidable," he noted, arguing that "in these tense and dangerous situations in the world, democracy will save itself with the average man and woman by proving itself worth saving." He then ventured "the challenging statement that if American democracy ceases to move forward as a living force, seeking day and night by peaceful means to better the lot of our citizens, then Fascism and Communism . . . will grow in strength in our land."[66]

By the late 1930s, Walter Lippmann had become a sharp critic of the New Deal. Referring to Woodrow Wilson's unredeemed promise of global peace, the Republican party's ill-fated guarantee of permanent prosperity in the 1920s, and what he thought to be the New Deal's still-unrealized pledge to end the economic devastation of the Great Depression, Lippmann wrote of how mass disaffection after the deep recession of 1937–1938 had caused popular hopes that the economy was recovering to recede. He attributed America's vulnerability to the power and lure of the globe's dictatorships in 1939 to "the accumulated disappointments of the post-War era," reminding his readers that "three times in these twenty years the American people have had great hope and three times they have been greatly disappointed."[67] The idea of hope restored rang hollow.

The next year, Lewis Mumford, one of the country's most prominent intellectuals, was troubled by "the disintegration of liberalism." Notwithstanding the enactment of all the major New Deal legislative achievements, he cautioned:

> . . . the philosophy of liberalism has been dissolving before our eyes during the last decade: too noble to surrender, too sick to fight. The liberal has begun to lack confidence in himself and in the validity of his ideals. . . . Unable to take measure of our present catastrophe, and unable because of their inner doubts and contradictions and subtleties to make effective decisions, liberals have lost most of their essential convictions: for ideals remain real only when one continues to realize them. . . . If we are to save the human core of liberalism—and it is one of the most precious parts of the entire human heritage—we must slough off the morbid growths that now surround it.[68]

The scope of the era's fearful concern for democracy soon widened. In 1941, the University of Chicago political scientist Harold Lasswell identified the "garrison state" as a new form of rule, presided over by specialists in violence, that cut across the distinction between democracies and dictatorships. The maturation of total war as a concept after World War I, he feared, had utterly transformed not just the technology of warfare and the mobilization of production and propaganda. It had also altered the very character of modern states, including the United States. "With the socialization of danger as a permanent characteristic of modern violence the nation becomes one unified technical enterprise." In such circumstances, he asked in anguish, "what democratic values can be preserved, and how?"[69]

Lasswell's University of Chicago colleague, the prominent sociologist

David Riesman, took up this theme a year later. Considering "civil liberties in a period of transition," he showed how the traditional distinction between normal and special times had become obsolete. "It is unrealistic," he cautioned, "to rely on sharp distinctions between war and peace to test the limits of civil liberty," for "today, it is 'peace' which is anomalous, not war." He predicted "that after this war (which may last for many years), it is most unlikely that we can, or even if we can we will want to, return to 'normalcy.'" Liberal democracy, he argued, must be rethought in this context of permanent uncertainty and civic mobilization in order to discover how, by way of "affirmative governmental action . . . an aggressive public policy might substitute new liberties for the vanishing liberty of atomistic individuals." Haunted by the collapse of Germany's Weimar Republic, he concluded with a charged warning about Fascism in America: "Like a flood, it begins in general erosions of traditional beliefs, in the ideological dust storms of long ago, in little rivulets of lies, not caught by authorized channels."[70]

Much as Riesman projected, deep uncertainty about the character and prospects of liberal democracy lingered after World War II had been won. The eminent philosopher Morris Raphael Cohen closed his 1946 collection of essays expressing "the faith of a liberal" by underscoring the doctrine's vulnerability in an inhospitable world: "We are now entering into the world arena, and the question is no longer that of the special type of liberal civilization which once existed in the United States, but whether any type of liberal civilization can exist in America."[71]

John F. Kennedy responded to a Harvard University class questionnaire that year by noting, "I am pessimistic about the future of the country." Half of the fifteen thousand business executives polled by *Fortune* projected an "extended major depression with large-scale unemployment in the next ten years."[72] Reflecting on the West's cultural and political crisis, the economic sociologist Paul Meadows cautioned that "the close of the recent war can hardly change the fact that the ideological revolutions in Europe during the 'twenties and 'thirties bludgeoned liberals into a reeling retreat," and that unless the liberal political tradition learned to live in a world of power, it would continue to surrender to this retreat.[73] This moment of despondency soon was followed by the Maoist victory in China, the fright of nuclear proliferation, intensified conflicts about race and civil liberty, and a bloody war in Korea, claiming some three million lives, overwhelmingly civilian, that was marked by gross miscalculations of Chinese intentions and fighting ability, a disastrous retreat, a counterattack restoring the thirty-eight parallel as the dividing line between the North and South, and a showdown between Gen. Douglas MacArthur and President Truman, in which the president repulsed a stark challenge to the civilian control of the military.[74]

During the era's last phase—marked by the Cold War, Stalinist and anti-Communist fanaticism, atomic fear, and a new hot war in Asia—many learned observers worried whether liberal democracy could maintain its balance and élan. With Roosevelt gone, Richard Hofstadter was quite unsure. He concluded a 1948 assessment by writing:

> [FDR] is bound to be the dominant figure in the mythology of any resurgent American liberalism. There are ample texts in his writing for men of good will to feed upon; but it would be fatal to rest content with his belief in personal benevolence, personal arrangements, the self-sufficiency of good intentions, and month-to-month improvisation, without trying to achieve a more inclusive and systematic conception of what is happening in the world.[75]

Permanent violence and permanent insecurity loomed. "Our own outlook, as well as the world's outlook," Columbia University's Asia specialist Nathaniel Peffer asserted in 1948, "is darker than before 1914 or even 1939. . . . We have not even the assurance of a transient peace, to say nothing of a long truce, as after Waterloo and the Congress of Vienna. On all the evidence before us, we are now in the state of prelude to war." At a moment marked by ever "sharper fears," the "pendant issue" is that of "absolutism versus democracy, or, better put, representative government," with "democracy losing by default," judging that its "lease on life is precarious again, perhaps more so than before the war. Again it appears to be in danger of being ground between Right and Left."[76] Looking inward in this situation, the poet Archibald MacLeish cautioned a Pomona College graduating class in 1950 that the country found itself in a "trap of fear and hate."[77]

Surrounded by wild and intense insecurity, American political institutions and processes could not look to fixed points or a guiding status quo. As the novelist Robert Musil once described turn-of-the-century Austria, no one "could quite distinguish what was above and what was below, between what was moving forward and backward."[78] Decision making had to proceed under conditions that made it uncommonly difficult to assign probabilities to what might lie ahead based on past experience.

Intense uncertainty, the kind that makes the usual sense of the term *status quo* virtually irrelevant, became a source of fear. No one quite knew whether the era's constellation of crises indicated "a state of greater or lesser permanence, as in a longer or shorter transition towards something better or worse or towards something altogether different."[79] The federal government proceeded in circumstances of recurring and escalating emergency without the benefit of an established starting point and without a fixed repertoire of public policies that were effective and legitimate. As Presidents Roosevelt and Truman sought to reduce such deep uncertainty to a more tolerable level of risk, they lacked fixed or sure preferences about public policy. As a result, the field of policy invention was uncommonly open but also largely uncharted. Unusually unconstrained by existing public policy, the New Deal possessed a wider array of policy possibilities than any prior set of government initiatives in American history. It could learn from a store of initiatives tested both by liberal democracies and by illiberal dictatorships in Europe. It could emulate experiments the various states had initiated, and adapt policies developed under different conditions by progressives in both major parties, by democratic socialists, by the labor movement, and even by mainstream Republicans in the Hoover administration. It could draw on a wide array of options developed by policy intellectuals who worked in university social science departments, law schools, and recently established think tanks, and who sought to invent alternatives in the space that lay between an insufficient status quo and the designs offered by the era's dictatorships. But could it succeed despite the self-seeking partisanship of politicians and the polarization inherent in the legislative process?

V.

NOT SURPRISINGLY, America's émigré intellectuals who had come close to the abyss acutely comprehended the stakes. Imbued with concerns about "the evil of politics and the ethics of evil,"[80] they were particularly attuned to liberal democracy's difficult, intransigent, and unresolved dilemmas.[81] They possessed a discriminating sense of the insufficiency of older models of liberal democracy, combined with a keen alertness about the present. Like Henry James in Venice, they often thought of themselves as brooding tourists, brooding because they understood that the time was marked by many unimaginably bad choices.

During the academic year 1935–1936, the small but remarkable group of refugee scholars who constituted the Graduate Faculty of the New School for Social Research in New York assembled in regular sessions of what they called their "General Seminar" to assess the prospects for political economic democracy on the understanding, as the institution's president, Alvin Johnson, put the point, that "democracy is the central problem of all present day serious political thinking."[82] This was a regular gathering of members of the primarily German and Jewish cohort of social scientists who had escaped Fascism. Their lives had ruptured. Their commitment to democracy was marked less by an ameliorative instinct—though they did have strong views about how to make liberal democracy and modern capitalism work better—than by resistance to all forms of dictatorship. From the perspective of these newcomers, the faith of American liberals—the very idea that fear had been supplanted by hope—seemed too simple, rather credulous, even provincial.

The issues they took up in their General Seminar concerned the roots of Fascism, the vulnerability and excesses of democracy, the era's sources of mass irrationality, and deformations in public opinion. In doing so, they compelled attention to what, arguably, were the most vital challenges of their time, defending liberal democracy in an open, rich, and cosmopolitan way. Reports of their meetings record how they grappled with the strengths and weaknesses of parliamentary representation, the role of political parties, and the rule of law in circumstances where "everyone today pictures democracy and parliamentary institutions on the defensive or already definitely in retreat. . . . Thus it is a crucial question for the future," Hans Simons wrote, "whether democracy and parliamentarism can gain in strength and influence not only in comparison with dictatorship, but in their intrinsic value and in their capacity for expansion."[83] Also striking is how these intellectuals linked those broad and fundamental concerns about democracy to specific policy discussions about economic planning, trade unions and the regulation of labor conflicts, taxation and the distribution of wealth, and foreign policy, on the understanding that whether liberal democracy could thrive depended considerably on what kind of liberal democracy might be fashioned in hard times.[84] All this was occurring at the very moment when fear was said to have been vanquished.

Two years after these intellectuals met, Thomas Mann crossed the United States from February to May 1938 to lecture to audiences totaling some sixty thousand in order to help marshal "the coming victory of democracy." Mann spoke of a "lust for human degradation which it would be too much honour to call devilish." Worried that "democracy as a whole is still far from acquiring a clear conception of this fascist concentration, of the fanaticism and absolutism of the totalitarian state," he stressed that "democracy and fascism live, so to speak, on different planets." He reminded his listeners that, as a degenerated regime, a travesty of democracy, "it is in physical and mental oppression that fascism believes. . . . Oppression is not only the ultimate goal, but the first principle of fascism." Such dictatorships, "hostile to freedom," mobilize nationalism as "a thoroughly aggressive impulse, directed against the outer world; its concern is not with conscience, but with power; not with human achievement, but with war." With the Final Solution still some years off, he also brought to light "the treatment of the Jews in Germany, the concentration camps and the things which took place and are still taking place in them," including the "ignominious distinctions such as the cutting of the hair and the yellow spot."[85]

These brooding immigrants, together with other newcomers, whose numbers included Hannah Arendt, Theodor Adorno, Leo Strauss, Franz Neumann, and Hans Morgenthau, had no illusions about the era's depths of despair, the constitutive features of fear, or the fragility of liberal democracy.[86] "Exiled in paradise," they composed a particularly attentive group that watched and evaluated how the New Deal took up custody for liberal democracy. Perhaps more attentively than other Americans, they painfully observed how, in pursuing liberal guardianship, Washington risked—indeed, had to risk—informal cooperation and formal alliances with illiberal partners, and they acutely noticed when the federal government pushed constitutional processes right to the limit of rights and liberties, sometimes beyond.[87] More than most, they also comprehended that the global contest with the dictatorships of the Right and the Left was a struggle about the persistence and competence of representative parliamentary government in a situation of deep uncertainty. With more reason than most to be unsure of the ultimate outcome, they never underestimated either the achievement or its costs. "Something new, a new world began," Stefan Zweig wrote about transformations to democratic culture and politics in the United States shortly before his suicide in Brazil, in February 1942. "But how many hells, how many purgatories had to be crossed before it could be reached!"[88]

VI.

THE CREDIBILITY of the claims made both by the dictatorships and by the democracies depended on the degree to which they could innovate to solve the major problems of the day and thus reduce uncertainty to risk.[89] These were matters both of reality and of its perception. With the development of film and radio, dictators and democratic leaders alike could address their nations directly in regular talks and addresses. To be persuasive, they had to be seen to be inventing genuine answers to pressing questions. The period's contest between the dictatorships and the democracies was a competition to find responses to central dilemmas, and to discover whether parliamentary democracies could do as well as the illiberal regimes in this struggle for supremacy.[90]

The dictatorships projected many alluring answers. With market capitalism performing so poorly, the Italians put forward a corporatist model that coordinated matters of labor and capital under the auspices of the state. The Germans advanced a highly managed capitalism. The Soviets, who had eliminated private property and markets altogether, pushed ahead with an ever-more-ambitious planned economy.[91] These economic nostrums had big implications for the character of social class and the role of labor. Italy folded unions into its authoritarian corporatism, making them compliant. Germany eviscerated their independence. The Soviet Union created the form of union representation but without the content, having integrated it into the Communist Party apparatus. Each claimed in its own way to have surmounted class conflict, the bane of market capitalism, while creating a united people, based on solidarities of a singular nation, race, or class, and a commitment to the common welfare of its members. In all, these initiatives seemed to herald the future at a time when the advanced economies of the world seemed to be moving, in one form or another, from competitive to planned economies.[92]

While the United States was struggling with how it might engage with global affairs, the dictatorships projected a sense of assurance and apparent know-how to enhance their might and maintain national security. They promoted a pervasive militarism. For the Italians, the armed forces, especially Italo Balbo's air force, were key symbols of national revival and Fascist modernity. For the Soviets, a decision was taken in 1931 and 1932 to accelerate large-scale military investment, moving from 1.8 billion rubles in 1931 to 4 billion the next year, and fully 14.8 billion by 1936, then accelerating to 40.88 billion in 1939, or approximately 4 billion U.S. dollars. Similarly, Nazi Germany's spending on arms and soldiers spiraled from under 1 billion reichsmarks in 1933 to 10.2 billion in 1936, and 38 billion by 1939, a level approximating 9 billion U.S. dollars.[93] By contrast, the United States, in the grip of isolationist sentiment, spent just $0.6 billion on military defense in 1933, 0.9 in 1936, and 1.3 in 1939.[94] The high level of spending by the dictatorships was accompanied by a widespread militarization of political and popular life, and the armed forces, following purges in the second half of the 1930s in Germany and the Soviet Union, were tied ever more closely to the ruling parties and to decisions taken directly by Stalin and Hitler. Their regimes, and the Italian, routinely utilized vocabularies charged with violent metaphors that symbolically created united countries ready for war.

The dictatorships introduced advanced models of internal security reflecting strictly defined strong criteria for membership, based on ideology, nation, and race. Their programs of control were not compromised by attention to the liberties of citizens. The Soviet Union, which described itself as a union of peoples, imposed class criteria for full citizenship, downplaying nationalism, while in Germany a racially defined conception of nation—the nation as *Volk*—set limits for how Nazism sanctioned citizenship (German Jews could not qualify as ethnic Germans), presenting a model that was copied, if more moderately, by the Italian government in 1938. Each of these countries induced order from the willing and imposed it on those who were not. Each used police powers with hardly any constraints. Each justified its repressive apparatus with Manichean language, sharply distinguishing foes from friends, the certainty of these divisions intrinsically appealing in such dark times. Germany and the USSR established immensely complex and far-flung camp systems (with the Soviet, before World War II, being considerably larger, housing nearly 1.7 million people in 1939, compared with 60,000 in Germany) that isolated, punished, restricted, and reformed dissenters in immense numbers, well before Germany first built death camps in 1941. Tolerance was equated with weakness, and enemies were defined as those whose support was suspect. The cost of dissent was more than physical insecurity, but the loss of individual identity and the capacity to communicate.

The dictatorships professed to solve these various problems better than the democracies. They also claimed to be better democracies. As antiliberal democracies, they offered mass mobilization and participation through approved political parties, buttressed by strong images of popular support and national unity.[95] Their governments, they insisted, were modern, secular, and largely popular, sustained by consent alongside repression. By advancing a social agenda, producing economic results, and mobilizing the population, they "caught the parliamentary powers off guard" by advancing policy answers without going through the route of democratic lawmaking.[96] "The Fascist State," Giovanni Gentile wrote, "is a people's state, and, as such, the democratic State *par excellence.*" Through the party, it uses and reflects "the thought and will of the masses." For this reason, the regime undertakes what he described as "the enormous task" of "trying to bring the whole mass of the people . . . inside the fold of the Party."[97] Similarly, Stalin declared in 1936, "We understand democracy as the raising of the activeness and consciousness of the party mass, as the systematic involving of the party mass not only in the discussion of questions but also in the leadership to work."[98] According to these readings, the key to democracy was just the reverse of its liberal understanding, which insisted on the separation of state and society. Here, by contrast, the ethical and political unity of the people and their state was a central principle, thus bypassing entirely the need for representative legislative institutions.

The countries on both sides of the divide were aware of what the others were doing. They knew and studied one another's policy prescriptions, observed their political and technical counterparts, and borrowed where they thought appropriate. "The Soviet-watching Nazis suppressed existing trade unions, and sought to organize their own new ones; the Japanese, watching the Nazis, would do the same."[99] And the United States watched as well, absorbing and learning where possible, as the Roosevelt administration did when it sent Louis Brownlow, Charles Merriam, and Luther Gulick—each a leading student of public administration who, together, composed the president's Committee on Administrative Management, which Brownlow chaired—to Rome to study how Benito Mussolini's government had organized Fascism's administration, and then used what they found to make extensive recommendations for the reorganization of America's national government. It called for the abolition of regulatory agencies in order to strengthen the executive branch, advocating placing them under the authority of the president's cabinet departments, a suggestion Congress refused to enact.[100]

Facing many common challenges, each regime measured the accomplishments of its arts of ruling by where it stood in this competitive game.[101] "Notwithstanding the distinctiveness of their ideology and many of their practices," the historian of the Soviet Union Stephen Kotkin has observed, these regimes "were part of an international conjuncture, and compared themselves to others."[102] They sometimes produced similar policy prescriptions, such as the use of public labor camps to put redundant labor to work.[103]

In the 1930s and early 1940s, the competition pit the constitutional democracies in Europe and North America against a wide array of authoritarian alternatives. Most, including Japanese militarism, Italian Fascism, and German Nazism, were defeated during World War II. But the rivalry between dictatorship and democracy did not come to an end after the war; rather, it took a new form, with Soviet Communism facing off against late–New Deal America, and with each crusading, literally armed to the teeth.

Although American majorities were never drawn to the models crafted by the dictatorships, their seeming success did attract tens of thousands, including visible and articulate intellectuals and organizational leaders. In the United States, other forms of economy and politics beckoned. Some looked to the Soviet Union, envious of its capacity to deploy multiyear plans to rapidly modernize and surmount the speculative boom and crisis patterns of capitalism, and for its propertyless class structure. Over the course of the 1930s, Communist Party rallies often filled the twenty thousand seats in New York's Madison Square Garden. By 1938, some 75,000 Americans had joined the Communist Party, and many others participated in post–1935 popular-front organizations, many of which were sponsored by the Party.[104]

Excitement about the Soviet experiment formed a component of left-of-center ideology during the 1930s and 1940s. Famously, Walter Duranty, a *New York Times* journalist with a strong pro-Soviet tilt, explained why he had decided not to file deliberately "lost stories" that described the human cost of the first Five-Year Plan, stating that "what matters to me is the facts, that is to say whether the Soviet drive to Socialism is or is not successful irrespective of the cost. . . . In the course of the last seven years, this country has made an unprecedented capital investment in socialized industry and has simultaneously converted agriculture from narrow and obsolete individualism to modern Socialist methods. What is more both of these operations have been carried out with success. Their cost in blood and other terms of human suffering has been prodigious, but I am not prepared to say that it is unjustified," he stated, concluding that "any plan, however rigid, is better than no plan at all and that any altruistic end, however remote, may justify any means, however cruel."[105]

In June 1936, in assessing Stalin's new constitution as a welcome "loosening of the bonds of dictatorship," the editors of *The New Republic* drew on the adulatory report of Beatrice and Sidney Webb and an account by the journalist Louis Fischer (who had declared, despite March 1933 reports about the massive famine, especially in Ukraine, that "there is no starvation in Russia," a statement he later recanted in *The God That Failed*[106]) that "the Soviet system has always contained more genuine democracy than outsiders have realized. . . . The essential power in the Soviet Union has never rested entirely with the government," citing the Webbs, who had concluded that the Soviet Union "has been the very opposite of dictatorship."[107]

The appeal of the Soviet Union extended into unexpected places, including the American Civil Liberties Union. "If American workers, with no real liberties but to change masters, or, rarely, to escape from the working class, could understand their class interests," its director, Roger Baldwin, wrote in 1934, "Soviet 'workers democracy' would be their goal." Baldwin had been a champion of freedom at home. He had led the ACLU's challenge of the ban on *Ulysses,* and had involved his organization in the Scopes trial and the murder trial of Ferdinando Sacco and Bartolomeo Vanzetti. Yet he endorsed the abandonment of liberal democracy in the Soviet Union. Freedom in the USSR, he wrote, is "fixed on the only ground on which liberty really matters—economic. No class to exploit the workers and peasants; wide sharing of control in the economic organizations; and the wealth produced is common property," and he declared that "the Soviet Union has already created liberties far greater than exist elsewhere in the world."[108] Baldwin was hardly alone; he was joined in his sentiments by, for example, Edmund Wilson, who extolled the Soviet Union in *Travels in Two Democracies.*[109]

Others flirted with Fascism, and still more, including leaders of the country's most important universities, refused to take principled stands against such regimes.[110] Some were attracted to strong-leader right-wing models. Richard Washburn Child, reflecting on his experiences in Rome as ambassador when the fascists had seized power, celebrated the young regime in 1924 in *The Saturday Evening Post,* the country's largest weekly magazine, with a circulation of nearly four million: "When a spirited people cannot stand it any longer, they act." The institutions of liberal democracy, he mused, "are luxuries enjoyed by these people who do not face intolerable situations. . . . When a people face an intolerable situation the real ravenous hunger is not for a program, but for a man."[111] Four years later, he gushed in a foreword to the Duce's *Autobiography* that "it may be forecast that no man will exhibit dimensions of permanent greatness equal to that of Mussolini," a "man who had made a state. . . . He takes responsibility for everything—for discipline, for censorship, for measures which, were less rigor required, would appear repressive and cruel. . . . Time has shown he is wise and humane."[112] Even in the mid-1930s, not on the fringe but in the *Annals of the American Academy of Political and Social Science,* the most moderate and respectable of learned journals, a pro-Fascist opponent of the New Deal (tried for sedition in 1944) explained why he did not agree with those, such as former president Herbert Hoover and Socialist Norman Thomas, who attacked the New Deal as similar to Fascism. They were assuming, Lawrence Dennis wrote, that "fascism is per se something to be feared or fought." Rather, he argued, "it appears to me that prevailing social forces the world over make a fascist trend the inevitable alternative to chaos or communism."[113]

Many Americans drawn to Fascism were attracted by its trope of ethnic solidarity. The Italian-American linguist Mario Pei celebrated in 1935 how "the Italian people today are enjoying a new and different type of liberty. They are enjoying themselves as members, part and parcel, of a powerful, organic state, which rules for the welfare of everybody and not in the interests of a chosen few, a state which has social justice within and international prestige without its borders."[114] Led by the self-styled American Führer, Fritz Kuhn, the pro-Nazi Amerikadeutscher Bund (German American Bund) attracted approximately 100,000 members. Some twenty thousand, many dressed in Nazi garb and chanting "Heil Hitler," descended on Madison Square Garden, which was decorated with swastikas and American flags for this "Mass Demonstration for True Americanism" on February 20, 1939, where they listened as speakers asserted the rights of Gentiles, denounced the New Deal as a "Jew Deal," and referred to President Roosevelt as "Frank D. Rosenfeld." By this time, the Bund was closely cooperating with Father Charles Coughlin, whose appeals had grown stridently anti-Semitic.

VII.

WITH THE boundaries and capacities of liberal democracy in question, and with incremental fine tuning to the status quo absent as a real option, fear defined the context within which political action in the United States proceeded. It also served as a motivation to act. Such circumstances required making decisions that were more fundamental than picking alternatives or choosing possibilities. Fateful and transformative, New Deal decisions were more fundamental, more likely to be irrevocable. What was unclear was whether America's political institutions could tame fear and produce tolerable risk at least as well as the dictatorships.[115]

This was what Franklin Roosevelt pledged to do on that blustery March day in 1933 when he had identified how "fear itself ... paralyzes needed efforts to convert retreat into advance." As he, his successor, and their colleagues sought to counter the dictatorships in an increasingly desperate world, they risked informal cooperation and formal alliances with partners of necessity. As anxiety, disillusion, and doubt afflicted the American polity, neither the dilemma of dirty hands nor questions about democracy's abilities could be evaded.

2 ▶ Pilot, Judge, Senator

DRESSED IN HIS pilot's garb and seated in an open cockpit, Gen. Italo Balbo, Benito Mussolini's dashing minister of aviation,[1] commanded the cover of *Time* on June 26, 1933. Celebrating ten years of Fascist rule, his squadron of seaplane pilots were preparing for the "Cruise of the Decade" at the navigation school of the Italian Air Force at Orbetello, north of Rome, on the Tuscan coast. Led by Balbo, the crew of this Crociera del Decennale would soon travel 6,100 miles in forty-eight hours, journeying from Rome—via Amsterdam, Londonderry, Reykjavik, the Labrador coast, New Brunswick, and Montreal—to the "Century of Progress" world's fair in Chicago.[2]

The International Military Tribunal met briefly in Berlin

in October 1945, then in Nuremberg for eleven months, to try the surviving senior leadership of the defeated Nazi regime. The Soviet judge, Iola Nikitchenko, had been born in 1895 in Dom Voisko Province, the center of Cossack culture. He had gone to work in the Donbass coal mines at thirteen, before joining the Red Army, then fought in the Russian Civil War. After studying law at Moscow University, he ascended to be vice president and divisional military jurist on the panel of the Military Collegium of the Supreme Court of the USSR and a lecturer in criminal law at Moscow's Academy of Military Jurisprudence.[3]

On May 17, 1948, memorial services were conducted in a joint meeting of U.S. Senate and House of Representatives to commemorate the lives and achievements of seven members who had died during the prior session. Their number included Democrat Theodore Bilbo, who, following terms in the state senate, as lieutenant governor, and twice as governor, had served as a senator from Mississippi from January 1935 until his death in August 1947.[4] The main tribute, delivered by his successor, John Stennis, identified Bilbo with "progressive forces" and "service to the common people," and as "a faithful friend" to FDR who had delighted in the "inspiration and hope" provided by the New Deal.[5]

As individuals, the energetic, dapper Balbo, the pale, thin-faced Nikitchenko, and the paunchy, florid Bilbo could not have been more different. But in one crucial respect, they were very much alike. The role played by these servants of an authoritarian regime illuminates how the Roosevelt and Truman administrations were obliged to pursue their often dangerous efforts to secure liberal democratic alternatives under deeply uncertain conditions. By attending to these largely forgotten major figures in public life, we can begin to observe the character and consequences of the New Deal's partnerships with discomfiting confederates.

I.

*T*IME's ACCOUNT of Italo Balbo's impending flight was lighthearted and sympathetic, a tone that was not surprising given the sympathies of its publisher, Henry Luce.[6] Intent on making these Fascist pilots more palatable to an American readership, the article eschewed the nativist cant that had been widely used only six years before in describing the two "swarthy"

Italians, the anarchists Sacco and Vanzetti, before their execution. "With discipline relaxed," so the article proclaimed, these valiant pilots "amused themselves like college footballers on the eve of a Big Game." For months, "the men had been confined in monastic seclusion lest any of them get off mental or emotional balance." In high spirits "having been joined on the eve of their departure by females young & old, beauteous & unlovely . . . permitted to roam the air station arm-in-arm with the flyers," they "awaited the signal to start the biggest show ever staged by Italian aviation."[7]

The article drew no link between Italy's fearless Fascist fliers and the Nazis who had just ransacked a Jewish-owned department store in Vienna, and it did not comment on how the same issue's foreign news section was highlighting how, five months after Hitler's dramatic rise to power, pre-Anschluss Austria was erupting in Nazi-inspired violence, which included attempts to assassinate senior officials and bomb the city's main Jewish quarter.[8]

That week's lead centered instead on developments at home, focusing on early New Deal achievements. It recorded how "the 20 hours between the adjournment of Congress and his departure for a New England vacation last week" had been "some of the busiest President Roosevelt had put in since taking office." Celebrating effective collaboration between the executive and legislative branches, the story took note of "the finest fruit of that cooperation . . . the vast Industrial Recovery Act," which sought to reorganize a deeply distressed economy, a bill "the president signed with a vim." The piece also reported on a new Banking Act, named for Senator Carter Glass of Virginia and Congressman Henry Bascom Steagall of Alabama, a historic piece of legislation that provided for the separation of banking and brokerage companies, which would not be repealed until 1999.[9] The article closed with an account of how a "happy" Franklin Roosevelt "turned out the light and went to sleep conscious that he had been blessed as few presidents are: he had 1) got Congress to pass most of the laws he wanted, and 2) got rid of Congress . . . before Congress got completely out of control."[10]

Time also noted the death, at seventy-five, of Clara Zetkin, the "grandmother of German Communism," who, "in the face of Nazi fury," valiantly insisted only months before her passing on "her rights as oldest deputy to open the Reichstag," despite having to be "carried in on a stretcher" into Germany's legislative chamber. The magazine also announced the prema-

ture death of the fifty-one-year-old Ukrainian-born immigrant Josef (Yos-
sele) Rosenblatt, "world famed synagog cantor and concert singer; of a heart
attack after completing a film for the American-Palestine Fox Film Co. in
Jerusalem. An orthodox Jew whose voice drew comparisons to Caruso, had
refused to remove his vast beard even when offered $3,000 a night to sing
La Juive for the Chicago Opera Company."[11] And commenting on an event
halfway around the world, the magazine also took note of a "revolutionary
marriage" between Mahatma Gandhi's son Devadas, a Vaishya (the caste of
shopkeepers) to a Congress Party leader's Brahmin daughter.

The issue's fullest and splashiest report, however, was devoted to Balbo's
undertaking. It extravagantly described the rigorous training, flight plans,
advanced technology, and aesthetics of how "the Italians fly in a cavalcade of
seven compact triads and one quartet" led by "Balbo's plane, identified by a
large black star on the fuselage." It richly portrayed the send-off ceremony
at Orbetello, as the fliers and visitors gathered to face "the 25 big seaplanes
bobbing at moorings," each painted either in Fascist black or the white and
green colors of the Italian flag, each carrying the Fascist emblem that had
been inscribed on air force planes on Balbo's orders since 1928:

> The stage was set. Upon it stepped the imposing figure of General
> Italo Balbo, Minister of Aviation, supreme commander of the Atlan-
> tic flight. . . . "I greet you all as a commander and a companion. We
> are ready with tranquil spirit. I am not unmindful of the dangers.
> . . . But these are not inferior to our destiny." Right arms extended,
> commander & crew recited in unison the Fascist oath: "We will
> make ourselves worthy soldiers of the King and worthy soldiers of
> the Italy created by our leader [*nostro Duce*]." A priest came forward,
> prayed over the men, sprinkled holy water toward the seaplanes,
> and invoked the blessing of the Virgin of Loreto.[12]

This mission was hardly the first. From the start of his terms as undersecretary in 1926 and minister in 1929, Balbo had undertaken to promote
thoroughly choreographed mass flights. In an age fascinated by such mod-
ernist spectacles, entranced by the daring of audacious pilots like Wiley Post,
Roscoe Turner, James Mollison, and Charles Lindbergh, Balbo wished to
demonstrate the technological capacities, military prowess, discipline, and

personal heroism of Italy, and, more specifically, Italian Fascism.[13] Immediately on assuming power eleven years earlier, in 1922, Mussolini had moved to establish an independent air force, less as an instrument of war than a means to build a Fascist "civilization" based on the values of dynamism and innovation. His *Autobiography,* eagerly published in English by the venerable firm of Scribner's, which also published the work of Hemingway and Fitzgerald, recalls how he had turned "immediately" to build a "new type of armed force," boasting in 1928 how "I dedicated myself to a reorganization of aviation, which had been abandoned to utter decay by the former administrations." Even at this early stage, he noted how "the flights in squadrons . . . have demonstrated that Italian aviation has recently acquired great expertness and prestige, not only in Italy, but wherever there is air to fly in."[14]

The historical link between aviation and Fascism had been already established a decade earlier. The connection had been reinforced by images and words, and by spectacular feats.[15] Introducing his book *Mussolini aviatore* in 1935, the journalist Guido Mattioli explained that "every aviator is a born fascist." Mussolini himself had trained to fly in 1920, at age thirty-seven, to pursue what Mattioli called the "necessary and intimate spiritual connection" linking Fascism to aviation.[16]

Like millions of others around the world, Balbo had been mesmerized when Lindbergh had piloted the *Spirit of St. Louis* from Long Island to Paris in 1927, and he would visit the United States for a month the following year, where he reported pleasure at seeing the first Mickey Mouse cartoon, *Plane Crazy,* in which Mickey takes Minnie for a near-disastrous ride in an airplane converted from a car. The Lindbergh frenzy crossed geographic and ideological lines. Even the left-wing playwright Bertolt Brecht got in on the action, writing *Der Lindberghflug,* a radio play celebrating the achievement for the 1928 Baden-Baden music festival, with music by Kurt Weill and Paul Hindemith. Yet Italian reverence for Lindbergh was particularly intense. Millions of Italians sang "The Eagle of the USA" and learned to dance the Lindy.[17] From May 26 to June 2, 1928, Balbo, dressed in the uniform of a Fascist militia general, led his first mass flight, a voyage of sixty-one seaplanes, including light bombers, that took off from Orbetello and traveled to six Spanish and French ports in the western Mediterranean. A longer mission followed, in 1929, when Balbo directed a fleet of thirty-six bombers to the eastern Mediterranean, stopping in Athens, Istanbul, Varna, and finally

Odessa, in part to explore whether Italy and the Soviet Union had common ground in their lack of sympathy for constitutional democracies, which Balbo announced to be "rotten to the bone, lying and false."[18] On his first Atlantic crossing, in 1931, Balbo led twelve seaplanes from Rome to Rio de Janeiro, making stops in West Africa and northern Brazil.[19] Each flier, his memoir reports, was "given Fascist Party membership cards before leaving Orbetello and the crews don black shirts for the Atlantic crossing, as a symbol of their 'Fascist will' to conquer the ocean."[20]

Known for his megalomania, for his radicalism within the Fascist Party, and for his violent and fanatical tendencies as "an intransigent squadrista, founder of the blackshirts and first head of the Fascist militia,"[21] Balbo had made his mark as a brutal *ras* (chief) of the Blackshirt militia of Ferrara and Emilia after service in the Alpine Corps in World War I, earning a bronze medal and two silver medals for bravery.[22] Notably, he had been one of the four paramilitary leaders of the October 1922 March on Rome, which swept away the liberal state he disparaged as "a nest of owls."[23] "When I returned from the War," his diary recorded in 1922, "I hated politics and politicians," and decided to "deny everything" about liberal Italy, especially its parliamentary politics.[24]

Balbo's fanatical militarism was hardly atypical, and his actions reflected a right-wing paramilitary response not only to the devastation of World War I but also to the rise in socialist and Communist activity following the war. He explained in 1922 that the Blackshirt battle cry, "I don't give a damn," had been rightly interpreted by the socialist newspaper *Avanti!* as expressing "contempt for every norm of established government." The country's liberal parliamentary regime, he wrote in a March 2, 1922 diary entry, was "our battle objective. We want to destroy it with all of its venerated institutions. The greater the scandal generated by our actions the happier we are."[25] Most important, as if anticipating the views of Germany's Nazis, he observed that it was impossible to reconcile the Fascist theory of violence with liberal principles: "Above all, how can one practice violence and preach respect for all opinions? The truth is one. Who believes that he possesses it must defend it with his life. And whoever does not believe that he possesses the truth in himself, absolute and unique, cannot be a Fascist. . . . It appears to me absurd that others do not think like me."[26]

Balbo, though glowingly portrayed by *Time* in 1933, was widely thought to have been the most extreme of Fascism's leaders when he first served as inspector of the regime's militia in the mid-1920s. As a strong advocate of Fascist-Nazi collaboration, he visited Hermann Göring, in Berlin in December 1932, only one month before Hitler's historic selection as chancellor, when Göring chaired the Reichstag as the representative of the largest parliamentary party, which had been elected six months earlier. Göring, who became minister of civil aviation after Hitler assumed power on January 30, 1933, soon commanded the Luftwaffe. He developed a close friendship with Balbo, who initiated covert training for German pilots, a step prohibited by the Treaty of Versailles.[27]

The apprehension and dread that later marked responses to Nazi aggression were hardly apparent when Balbo began his tour of various democratic countries in July 1933. Even though the Italian fliers represented militarized Fascism, Balbo and his crew were greeted and hailed as heroes in each of these democracies.[28] As leader of "the greatest transoceanic flight in the history of aviation,"[29] Balbo achieved—in Lindbergh fashion—mass adulation, a sentiment widely echoed in the press and in laudatory receptions by local and national political leaders. In Northern Ireland, the top officers of the Royal Air Force, the mayor of Belfast, and other leading provincial and national politicians were on hand when the Italians landed. Thousands cheered as "flowers and rose petals were thrown in General Balbo's path by pretty girls inside the square." A call was placed to Mussolini to report on the flight's progress.[30]

When the Italians approached Montreal, a laudatory message to Balbo arrived from Berlin: "Congratulations on your thrilling achievement. Admiringly, Adolf Hitler."[31] As with Mussolini, the nexus between aviation and politics had not been lost on Hitler. During his election campaign in 1932, Hitler had been inspired by Balbo's prior Fascist flights, and he had crisscrossed Germany by air in a dramatic demonstration of *"Hitler über Deutschland"* that identified Nazism with a modern and bright German future.[32]

The Balbo spectacle finally reached heartland America in mid-July of 1933. The *New York Times* reporter on the scene at Chicago's downtown lakefront captured the excitement generated by the Italian armada:

It was soon after 1 o'clock when the first group of six planes, led by General Balbo, came into sight over the horizon. They were flying at about 1,500 feet, and as they headed into the sun, the light flashed from their propellers and other gleaming metal parts. . . . The thousands gathered on the shore and those who had access to the jetty greeted them with a cheer. An Italian Fascist band played "La Giovanezza" and the lines of the black-shirted Fascists on the jetty raised their arms in salute.[33]

Accompanied by U.S. Army planes in formation spelling *Italia,* Balbo's air fleet reached Chicago eleven days after Independence Day, sweeping past the Century of Progress Exposition as they landed in eight groups of three in Lake Michigan. The Commerce Department cabled a salute for "the triumphant flight of your aircraft," which it called "an epochal achievement."[34] Pope Pius XI, who had been personally following the path of the flight by placing Italian and papal flags on a large map Balbo had presented before departing, instructed Cardinal Mundelein to confer his blessing.[35] The Mass he led at Holy Name Cathedral the next day was followed by the reading of "a telegram of congratulations and blessing from the Vatican, written by the future Pope, Pius XII, Cardinal Eugenio Pacelli."[36] Anne and Charles Lindbergh telegrammed "our congratulations on your splendid flight," with Balbo responding that "the greeting of America's outstanding transoceanic flier, who performed a legendary enterprise, flatters and honors the crew of the Italian air fleet."[37] As the news filtered into Italy, "people paraded the streets, singing Fascist hymns and cheering Il Duce and General Balbo," as if the invasion of Sherwood Anderson's mythical American heartland represented a return to Roman glory.[38] When the planes finally descended, some 100,000 Chicago observers gathered near the Navy Pier. Their numbers included a rear admiral, the governor, who read warm messages of greeting from the new national administration's secretary of war and secretary of the navy, and the mayor, who compared Balbo to the fifteenth-century discoverer Columbus, proclaimed "Italo Balbo Day," and renamed Seventh Street as Balbo Avenue, a name it still has.

At the lakefront, a monument to Christopher Columbus was inaugurated with the inscription "This monument has seen the glory of the wings of Italy led by Italo Balbo, July 15, 1933." Small indignant demonstrations by the Italian Socialist Federation and the Italian League for the Rights of Man were dwarfed by the far more dominant mood of the day. That evening, a dinner for some five thousand of the city's political, economic, and religious leaders was held at the recently opened Stevens Hotel (now the Chicago Hilton), which occupied the full city block on Michigan Avenue between Seventh and Eighth streets.[39] Many rose to offer a Fascist salute when Balbo and his squadron entered the ballroom. At dinner, "girls and women fought for the chance to dance with the dashing flier."[40] The event was chaired by a former American ambassador to Fascist Italy and the room was decorated by a huge black silhouette of Mussolini. The gathering heard an invocation by the bishop of Chicago, addresses by Mayor Edward Kelly and the president of Loyola University, who proffered an out-of-season honorary degree, and, as a highlight, a message of salutation sent by the president of the United States. The next day, America's new Fascist hero was made an honorary Sioux at the world's fair and was dubbed "the Flying Eagle." Perhaps reluctant to be tainted by an association with a group he thought inferior and defeated, and afraid it might sully his image as a representatives of Il Duce, Balbo accepted this honor from Chief Black Horn only reluctantly.[41]

Following a night at a local casino, Balbo and his crew left Chicago, serenaded by a parade attended by no fewer than one million onlookers along the full length of Michigan Avenue. It was as if the Cubs had brought a World Series victory back to Chicago, only it was July 18. The Italian airmen next traveled to New York, invited by Mayor John Patrick O'Brien and Governor Herbert Lehman, who had reminded Balbo that "the great Empire City of New York ... includes among its population the largest group of Italians in any city in the world outside Rome."[42] In New York, the festivities were no less intense. The fliers landed at Floyd Bennett Field in Brooklyn, to a nineteen-gun salute from the navy, which was followed by a flight down the Hudson, skirting Manhattan's shore. The event was witnessed by euphoric crowds estimated by the *New York Times* as "millions," and reported by a broadcaster perched at the top of the Empire State Building.[43]

This stay in New York was brief, and the airmen traveled to Washington the next day. Here, Balbo was greeted along the Potomac by a nineteen-gun salute before laying a wreath at Arlington Cemetery's Tomb of the Unknown Solider and stopping at the Lincoln Memorial. Secretary of the Navy Claude Swanson (a Virginian who previously had served seven terms in the House of Representatives, four years as governor, and four terms in the U.S. Senate) saluted him for his "enviable reputation" and "remarkable capacity for organization and leadership."[44] The trip climaxed at the White House on July 20, where President and Mrs. Roosevelt hosted a luncheon in Balbo's honor, a day before receiving Prince Ras Desta Demtu, the son-in-law of Haile Selassie, emperor of Ethiopia, whose country Italy would ravage just three years later.[45] Swept up by the national frenzy, the president tried to persuade Balbo to prolong his visit for some months to undertake a countrywide tour. The *New York Times* glowingly described how, "to the youthful and bearded leader of Italian aviation," the president's "words conveyed genuine feeling," and that the "Air Minister left the White House with his face wreathed in smiles."[46] Balbo then returned to New York, where this wreath of smiles must have been perpetuated, for he was sent off by some two million New Yorkers in a massive downtown ticker-tape parade. The festivities terminated at a gathering of 65,000, most Italian-American, at the Madison Square Garden Bowl. Balbo, the newspaper reported, "had deliberately given a speech there of political propaganda character, accentuating its Fascist tone, 'to show those who still do not believe that the miserable remains of international anti-Fascism is forced to resort to a bluff destitute of any seriousness and consistency'." Wiring a report to Mussolini before returning to Europe, Balbo observed "that the existence of anti-Fascist sentiment abroad was a myth which was exploded by the enthusiastic welcome his air squadron has received in America."[47]

Echoes of the thunderous reception resounded across the ocean. The following day, the U.S. ambassador to Italy, Breckenridge Long, a Princeton classmate of Woodrow Wilson who bred horses,[48] visited Mussolini to communicate "President Roosevelt's admiration for the flight of General Italo Balbo and his men to America," and to report how "the American people had acclaimed them with enthusiasm and admiration."[49]

Back in Italy, Balbo and his crew, resplendent in white dress uniforms, were greeted by a triumphal procession, bedecked with Fascist banners, to Rome's Domitian's Stadium on August 13. Balbo was promoted to air marshal and praised by Mussolini, dressed in the uniform of a commander of the Blackshirt militia, for having "consecrated Fascist revolution in the skies of two continents." In turn, Balbo presented Mussolini with an air marshal's hat, announced that Il Duce had guided the enterprise with his daily telegrams, and fawned about how "the whole credit for the Italian armada's successful flight was due to Premier Mussolini."[50] As the ceremony ended, "the fliers saluted in the Roman fashion and gave the Fascist cry, 'A Noi'. . . while cannon boomed and thousands of Fascist women threw flowers and laurel leaves in their path."[51]

American expressions of appreciation hardly ceased that summer, a dire one, with the Depression economy showing no sign of recovery. In April 1934, Columbia University, whose president, Nicholas Murray Butler, though hardly known for his support of ethnic diversity, compared Mussolini to Cromwell,[52] announced an Italo Balbo Crociera Atlantica Fellowship for graduate students at the university's Casa Italiana, a copy of a fifteenth-century Roman palazzo that had been opened on Amsterdam Avenue in 1927 at a ceremony whose keynote speaker, representing Mussolini, was Guglielmo Marconi, the Nobel laureate pioneer of telegraphy, and a committed Fascist.[53] The creation of this fellowship for study in Italy was followed four months later by a ceremony in Rome in which Mussolini awarded high decorations to ninety-nine Americans, recognizing the assistance they had given to Balbo's armada. The highest honor—the Grand Cordon of the order of the Crown of Italy—went to three men: Secretary of the Navy Claude Swanson; Chief of Naval Operations Adm. William Standley; and Gen. Douglas MacArthur, the army's chief of staff.[54] In May 1935, only six months before Mussolini sent 500,000 troops to conquer Ethiopia, Ambassador Long responded in kind by visiting Tripoli to confer the United States Distinguished Flying Cross on Balbo, an award that had been approved by Congress and confirmed in April by President Roosevelt.[55]

At the time of his decoration, Balbo had become governor-general of the Italian colony of Libya, a post he had assumed at the start of 1934, all the while continuing to run *Corriere Padano,* the leading Fascist newspaper in Ferrara. Only months later, Long sang a more ominous tune, reporting to Secretary of State Cordell Hull that Italy was preparing for war against Ethiopia. Factories in Milan were suddenly turning out tanks, trucks, and artillery at a breakneck pace. Fascist troops were being shifted surreptitiously, shipping out from Naples, camouflaged as part of the merchant marine, and moving through Balbo's Libya and Italian Somaliland.[56]

Dropping bombs and grenades laden with mustard gas, targeting not only soldiers but also civilians and Red Cross camps, Balbo's beloved Aeronautica became the first air force to be deployed against a sovereign enemy since World War I. Instrumental in subduing Ethiopia, the fliers, heralded only two years earlier by America's leaders, citizens, and press, helped initiate a reign of terror that included mass executions, chemical weapons, and forced labor camps, having been ordered by Mussolini to conduct a murderous campaign of systematic terror against any resistance. "Aircraft," Balbo prophetically had explained in 1933, "must be used in masses like infantry in the next war."[57] Now they were.[58]

The United States took no action. Echoing isolationist sentiment that prevailed in the United States, and still apparently convinced of Italy's inherent attractiveness, Ambassador Long counseled against an oil embargo as a rejoinder to Italian imperialism shortly before his resignation in 1936. By accepting this advice, the *Chicago Tribune* observed, the country had decided "to work out America's relations with the new Italian empire without a loss of face."[59] A willingness to countenance horrendous human rights violations in the name of realism, which would become even more apparent in 1938 with Kristallnacht, thus already was evident in the aftermath of this aggressive Italian war.

That February, a botched attempt to kill Rodolfo Graziani, the Italian viceroy in Ethiopia, served as the pretext for a campaign of counterterror by Italian forces that killed some thirty thousand civilians. The colonial government further responded by introducing residential segregation based on race, an action to which the United States could not have been expected to object.[60] More broadly, the Italians understood how to play American opinion during this period between the initiation of this repression and Mussolini's Libyan tour. At just this moment, Charles Lindbergh and his wife, the pilot Anne Morrow Lindbergh, were welcomed by Balbo in Tripoli, where he greeted the couple.[61] The reunion of Lindbergh and Balbo brought together the two figures who had been most responsible for placing aviation in the firmament of Western imagination.

A leading isolationist, Lindbergh chose not to disentangle himself from the Fascist web in Europe. In fact, he had made five trips to Nazi Germany in the 1930s, including a celebrated appearance at the opening ceremony of the 1936 Berlin Olympic Games. Even after the Nuremberg Laws of 1935 extruded Germany's Jews from civil, economic, and political society, the anti-Semitic Lindbergh characterized Hitler as "undoubtedly a great man . . . having far more character and vision than . . . painted in so many different ways by accounts in America and England."[62] By comparison, the flogging of two Jews in Tripoli in December 1936 because they had "rebelled against Governor Italo Balbo's ordinance" that they "keep their shops open Saturdays" seemed like a small, even petty violation.[63] Aware of his predilections, Air Marshal Hermann Göring, Hitler's designated successor and Germany's own pilot hero, presented Lindbergh, in 1938, "in the name of the Führer," with a medallion ornamented with four swastikas, the Service Cross of the Order of the German Eagle, the second-highest German decoration, for service by foreigners to the Third Reich.[64]

Addressing a rally at Chicago's Soldier Field in August 1940, eleven months after the start of war in Europe and in the midst of the Battle of Britain, Lindbergh called for cooperation with Germany should it win the war, "adding that an agreement could maintain peace and civilization throughout the world."[65] In July 1941, after the Soviet Union had been invaded, he told a San Francisco mass meeting of the America First Committee, the country's leading isolationist pressure group, that he would prefer an alliance "with Germany with all her faults" than with "Soviet Russia."[66] Two months later, as Hitler threatened Britain after the conquests and occupation of Poland, Belgium, the Netherlands, Norway, Denmark, and France, and with the Final Solution under way, Lindbergh singled out "the Jewish race," at an America First Committee rally he addressed in Des Moines, as "one of the most important groups who have been pressing this country toward war."[67]

A full year before Lindbergh's campaign on behalf of isolation, Balbo had died mysteriously, with eight other Italian officers, when his plane crashed in flames at Tobruk, in northeastern Libya, near the Egyptian border, on June 28, 1940. Like their Nazi allies, who rarely missed an opportunity to falsify facts or accept responsibility, the Italian government blamed the event on the Royal Air Force, which, it alleged, had brought down Balbo's plane after it had engaged the British in battle.[68] In fact, Balbo was piloting a nine-seat passenger craft, and no such airplane had been encountered during the RAF's bombing raid.[69]

Major Balbo's death was accorded the pomp of a national hero. There were many scenes of public mourning as his body was transported from Tobruk to Bengasi. Balbo was immediately succeeded as commander of all the armed forces of North Africa by Rodolfo Graziani.[70] A requiem Mass was held at the Church of St. Francis in Tripoli. Mussolini paid tribute by ordering that the Seventy-fifth Legion of Fascist Militia of Ferrara be named the Italo Balbo Legion.[71] Germany's message of condolence was sent by Hermann Göring: "The personality of the first Air Marshal of fascism was for all of us, in these times, a guarantee of victory. In this hour, which is so tragic for Italy, I send you, Il Duce, my deepest sympathy, and that of my air force."[72]

II.

B RECKENRIDGE LONG's and Charles Lindbergh's vision of American policy could not hold unless the United States under Franklin Roosevelt would abandon its commitments to democracy to become a bedfellow of Europe's fascist dictatorships. This, of course, did not happen. With the war over, and with Mussolini and Hitler dead and defeated, the events of the fall of 1945 provided a stark contrast to the fanfare that had greeted Balbo in Chicago and New York just twelve years earlier.

The Grand Conference Room of Berlin's Supreme Court Building, the seat of the Allied Control Council, provided the site for the opening session, on October 18, 1945, of the International Military Tribunal,[73] marking the first time the leaders of a defeated power were tried in an international court.[74] With Lord Justice Geoffrey Lawrence of Britain, Henri Donnedieu de Vabres of France, Francis Biddle of the United States, and Iola Nikitchenko of the Soviet Union on the bench, the tribunal began the process in which it would receive evidence, including captured film documenting atrocities, that had been generated by a massive staff working with the prosecutors of each of the Allies, and would hear riveting testimony, including substantiation by deathcamp survivors.

In part to counteract the idea that the tribunal was nothing more than an American court dressed up as a cross-national enterprise, Britain's Lawrence had been selected as president, or chief judge, while Nikitchenko, who had objected to this choice, was asked to preside over the opening session in Berlin.[75] Though he had little sympathy for Western-style jurisprudence, Nikitchenko utilized his manifestly keen intelligence to master its basic features once he had been tapped to join the tribunal in Nuremberg. A British Foreign Office observer at the trial thought him to be "of the highest calibre and genuinely interested in Anglo-Saxon legal principles and in preserving the dignity of the court."[76]

Dressed in a sharply creased chocolate-colored Red Army uniform with gold epaulets and green trim, which strongly contrasted with the gowns of the Western judges, Nikitchenko called the autumn proceedings to order at 10:30 A.M.[77] Most of the first day was devoted to reading lengthy capital indictments. The twenty-two accused were Germans from the highest rungs of the Nazi regime, including Governor-General of Poland Hans Frank; Minister of Internal Affairs Wilhelm Frick; Gestapo head and the Third Reich's second-in-command, Hermann Göring; Deputy Führer Rudolf Hess; Field Marshal Wilhelm Keitel; Foreign Minister Joachim von Ribbentrop; Minister for the Occupied Eastern Territories Alfred Rosenberg; architect and armaments minister Albert Speer; and the editor of the virulently anti-Semitic weekly *Der Stürmer,* Julius Streicher. They faced four sets of charges. First was the allegation of having conspired "to commit, or which involved commission of, Crimes Against Peace, War Crimes, and Crimes Against Humanity." Second was the contention that they had, in practice, committed such crimes by planning, preparing, initiating, and waging aggressive warfare. Third was the charge of executing war crimes, which the indictment identified with the mistreatment of civilians, the use of slave labor, and the wanton destruction of villages, towns, and cities, thus violating the customs and laws of war, including the Hague and Geneva Conventions. Fourth, and most novel, was the accusation of having performed crimes against humanity on political, racial, and religious grounds, including persecution and mass extermination.[78] There was no specific count for the murder of the Jews, but what later came to be called the Holocaust was the most important element in this charge.[79]

The tribunal gathered in a shell of what had been Germany's most vibrant city. Berlin had been the target of more than 350 British and, later, American bombing raids since August 1940. A concerted British campaign between November 1943 and March 1944 had killed some 4,000 civilians and rendered 450,000 homeless. Carried out by the American Eighth Air Force on February 3 and February 26, 1945, the last major attacks killed approximately 3,100 people, and some 190,000 lost their homes.[80] An official American history of the air war offers a sense of the intensity of this assault, a relatively moderate use of force for World War II:

The next day the Eighth sent all three of its air divisions over the capital of the Reich (Berlin), where 1,089 effective sorties employed

H2X to drop 2,778 tons of bombs, 44 percent of them incendiaries, through 10/10 clouds. Each division attempted to hit a separate rail station. The Schlesischer, Alexanderplatz, and Berlin-North stations were all located within two miles of the center of Berlin. The bombing started large fires and killed many civilians. RAF Mosquito nightintruder bombers attacking 12 hours later reported fires still burning. After the 26 February mission, with its 500,000 fire bomblets, the typical Berliner, with reason, would have been hard put to distinguish between RAF area bombing and AAF precision bombing.[81]

The tribunal soon moved to room 600 in Nuremberg's bomb-damaged but largely intact Palace of Justice, a building that had been restored by a workforce of 875, using "5,200 gallons of paint, 250,000 bricks, 100,000 board feet of lumber, a million feet of wire and cable," a harbinger of the larger postwar reconstruction to come.[82] The Bavarian city, famous as a leading manufacturing center for toys, had been reduced to rubble in a devastating bombing raid, lasting less than an hour, on January 2, 1945, when "the castle, three churches full of art treasures and at least 2,000 medieval houses went up in flames."[83] Writing as the trial opened, an American correspondent observed how the old town, flattened to ash and rubble, resembled "a medieval walled town razed by a giant catastrophe, a great fire or an earthquake."[84]

The court sat in Nuremberg from November 20, 1945 until the announcement of verdicts on September 30 and October 1, 1946. It had been Nikitchenko who had first suggested a city closely associated with the birth of Hitler's party.[85] There, starting in 1923, the Nazis had conducted mass demonstrations in conjunction with their annual party conference. During the first six years of the Third Reich, from 1933 to 1938, massive rallies, spectacularly choreographed by Albert Speer with dramatic lighting, a flotilla of fluttering flags, and theatrical torches, were held at the vast rally area he had designed. This immense site included a marching field, a "great road" more than a mile long that served as a parade ground and a field for military maneuvers, a congress hall, and two large stadiums. One of the stadiums, the Luitpold Arena, alone could hold some 150,000. It was here that Leni Riefenstahl's first Nuremberg documentary, *Der Sieg des Glaubens* (*The Victory of Faith*), recorded the Fifth Nazi Party Rally of 1933, while her second, *Triumph des Willens* (*Triumph of the Will*), famously captured the Sixth, in 1934.

A year later, in September of 1935, the Law for the Protection of German Blood and German Honor, the Reich Flag Law, and the Reich Citizenship Law were all passed at a special session of the Reichstag that was convened at the close of the "the Rally of Freedom," as the Seventh Party Congress was called. This legislation, dreaded by the nearly 500,000 Jews living in Germany, imposed an official shape on what had been previously an unsystematic and haphazard, though virulent, form of racial persecution.[86] These Nuremberg Laws, as they came to be known, forbade Jews to marry or have sex with "citizens of German or kindred blood." Jews, they announced, could no longer employ Gentile women domestics or display the national flag and colors. Most important, Jews no longer qualified for citizenship. Henceforth, "a Reich citizen" was to be defined as "a subject of the State who is of German or related blood, who proves by his conduct that he is willing and fit faithfully to serve the German people and Reich." In announcing these decrees at the rally's closing speech, Hitler portentously warned that if "international Jewish agitation should continue" to remonstrate against the way Jews are treated in Germany, their circumstances would be "handed over to the National Socialist Party for final resolution."[87] A decade later, the ultimate results of this more radical phase of persecution would be judged in Nuremberg.

The opening statement for the United States was delivered on November 21 by Robert Jackson, the U.S. Supreme Court justice who served as the country's chief counsel, although he had never attended college or earned a law degree. He underscored how Nuremberg had been selected as an object lesson. He observed that "it is not necessary among the ruins of this ancient and beautiful city, with untold numbers of its civilian inhabitants still buried in its rubble, to argue the proposition that to start or wage a war of aggression has the moral qualities of the worst of crimes."[88] As the tribunal met, no fewer than thirty thousand bodies were decaying under the city's reeking remains.[89] Though the level of destruction and casualties did not equal those caused by the carpet bombing and firestorms in Cologne, Hamburg, or Dresden, the city already had suffered grievous damage to its population and infrastructure even before the last raids only eight months earlier, on March 16 and 17, which killed 500 and rendered 35,000 homeless, and burned down the Steinbuhl, the only district that had still been standing.[90] During the course of that month, the fiercest in the Allied air war, a greater tonnage of bombs was dropped on Germany—67,000 tons—than had been deployed during the war's first three years combined (though no firepower had been directed at concentration camps in Germany or death camps in Poland). So extensive were the raids that at month's end, on March 28, Prime Minister Winston Churchill wrote to his army chief of staff to ask whether, in the wake of such ferocity, "the moment has come when the question of bombing German cities simply for the sake of increasing the terror, though under other pretexts, should be reviewed."[91]

Such bombing arguably violated prewar treaties and international ethical benchmarks, though the Allies would assert that it destroyed the war-making capacity of the enemy, saved the lives of soldiers, and shortened the duration and thus the destructiveness of the war. But this degree of inflicted desolation undermined the effort at Nuremberg to restore and reinforce international law and moral standards.[92]

The decision to create a means to punish Axis war crimes had been announced on October 30, 1943, at the conclusion of a twelve-day meeting in Moscow attended by Secretary of State Cordell Hull and Foreign Ministers Anthony Eden and Vyacheslav Molotov at a time when cooperation between the two democracies and the USSR was at a peak, and the Red Army was bearing the brunt of the war. The Moscow Declaration, signed by Roosevelt, Churchill, and Stalin, stipulated that hostilities would continue until the Axis powers surrendered unconditionally, and it announced the intention to create a new international organization to secure global security and keep the peace. The last section, a "Statement on Atrocities," proved more germane to the events unfolding in Nuremberg in 1945. It declared:

> Let those who have hitherto not imbrued their hands with innocent blood beware lest they join the ranks of the guilty, for most assuredly the three Allied Powers will pursue them to the uttermost ends of earth and will deliver them to their accusers in order that justice may be done. The above declaration is without prejudice to the case of the major criminals, whose offenses have no particular geographical localization and who will be punished by the joint decision of the Government of the Allies.[93]

By mid-1945, as the concentration camps were being liberated and the civilized world began to confront the unimaginable horrors perpetuated by the Third Reich, the time had come. Yet a precise policy remained to be formulated. Since the Moscow Declaration, the three Allies had not discussed the question of war-crimes trials. On June 26, Robert Jackson of the United States, Robert Falco of liberated France, David Maxwell Fyfe of Great Britain, and Iola Nikitchenko of the Soviet Union opened six weeks of strenuous negotiation in London to determine the protocols that would govern future proceedings.[94] One important determination concerned the scope and particularity of the charges against the Nazi defendants. The Soviets at first demanded that the crime of aggressive war be limited to actions by the European Axis powers, arguing against a general condemnation and urging that a war-crimes trial stick to "aggressions started by Nazis in this war." The other delegations thought the Soviets either had their November 1939 invasion of Finland in mind or were trying to insulate themselves against condemnation for their own future activities by distinguishing justified "peoples wars" from unjustified imperialist ones. The resolution of this dispute split the difference. A general, abstract definition was adopted, but its application was limited to crimes "carried out by the European Axis."[95]

Even more significant was the key decision, arduously achieved, to create an international court, rather than proceed either by convening military tribunals or having each country deal with crimes against its own citizens. Its procedures, the August 8 London Charter stipulated, would be directed by established liberal legal procedures, not by summary justice. Jackson summarized this achievement in his final report on the proceedings to President Truman, on October 7, 1946, noting how the London Charter had "devised a workable procedure for the trial of crimes which reconciled the basic conflicts in Anglo-American, French, and Soviet procedures. . . . The Charter set up a few simple rules which assured all the elements of a full and fair hearing, including counsel for the defense."[96]

Situated in time between war and peace, the trial thus sought to reimpose legality, notwithstanding problems of post hoc justice by the victors, on what had been an especially barbaric war marked by unprecedented genocide, and a 3:1 ratio of civilian to military deaths. "The nature of these crimes," Justice Jackson argued in his opening statement, "is such that both prosecution and judgment must be by victor nations over vanquished foes." Especially in that light, he insisted, what was critical was that the proceedings not cross the line that divides "just and measured retribution" from "the unthinking cry for vengeance which arises from the anguish of war."[97] At stake was the character of post–Nazi Germany, and the creation of multilateral institutions that could articulate broadly liberal values and pragmatically shift probabilities toward peace and decent human values.[98] The approach was one of "measured judicial retribution—not silent amnesty or indiscriminate vengeance."[99]

As a negotiator in London, the rather stiff Nikitchenko, quite different from the genial, witty Robert Jackson, initially insisted on features of Soviet-style justice, recommending a quick determination of guilt followed by swift execution. "We are dealing here with the chief war criminals who have already been convicted and whose conviction has already been announced by both the Moscow and Crimea declarations by the heads of government," he argued as the pretrial procedural negotiations were taking place. "The fact that the Nazi leaders are criminals has already been established. The task of the Tribunal is only to determine the measure of guilt of each particular person and mete out the necessary punishment, the sentences." He further cautioned that "if such procedures is adopted that the judge is supposed to be impartial, it would only lead to unnecessary delays."[100] During the trial, moreover, Nikitchenko was visibly uneasy when Göring argued, in mitigation, that the Führer principle was indeed practiced in the USSR. He might have been thinking of how the poet Osip Mandelstam, who had critiqued Stalin in earlier poetry, felt pressured during the period of the purge trials to compose an "Ode to Stalin" in late 1936 and early 1937, though this act would not prevent his exile to the northern Urals or his death in the Gulag.

Nikitchenko faced an almost Shakespearean dilemma in representing the USSR as a victor and moral nation, having to sweep aside its purges and terror, which had resulted in the death of millions. He often voted to refuse witnesses the defense wanted to hear, and opposed allowing the defendants the right to testify under oath when they sat in the same witness box that had been used by prosecution witnesses, arguing there should be no equivalence between the prosecution and the defense.[101] Perhaps reacting to the brevity of his own nation's show trials, he complained that the Nuremberg trial was taking far too long. At its end, he argued that two of four votes should be sufficient to convict, objected to votes by the other judges that produced acquittals or sentences short of death, dismissed the discussion of the verdicts as "ridiculous trifles," and insisted that hanging be the tribunal's form of capital punishment. As deliberations proceeded, he urged his colleagues to remember that the tribunal was meant to be "practical, not a discussion club."[102]

In London, however, Nikitchenko's conception of due process did not prevail. Led by Justice Jackson, America's negotiators successfully argued that the Moscow and Yalta summit declarations had not been convictions, but accusations. Their truth would be determined in court. The United States, Jackson insisted, would not agree to set up "a mere formal judicial body to ratify a political decision to convict," and would resist "political executions." He maintained that "if we are going to have a trial, then it must be an actual trial."[103] Later, in October, after initial resistance by Nikitchenko, the tribunal agreed to allow the defendants to have lawyers of their choice, even if they had been visible and active Nazis, and permit them free rein in mounting a defense.[104]

Judge Nikitchenko's opening speech betrayed no disagreement. In harmony with Jackson's views and the London Charter, he stressed the right to counsel, and he underscored the importance of the soon to be issued "Rules of Procedure," which would govern how witnesses would be produced and which documents could be placed in the record. Using language that might have been written by the American Civil Liberties Union, he resolutely asserted that the tribunal would guarantee the defendants nothing less than an impartial trial, marked by evenhanded regulations and a thorough opportunity to present their defense.[105]

Nikitchenko previously had presided over many cases at the Military Collegium of the Supreme Court of the USSR. That panel was best known for superintending key trials during the high point of Stalinism's search for internal enemies and conspiracies, a process the party boss of Moscow, Nikita Khrushchev, characterized in August 1937 as a particular form of courage: "Our hand must not tremble . . . we must march across the corpses of the enemy."[106] After the second show trial, in January 1937, Khrushchev addressed a demonstration of 200,000 in Red Square, supporting what its banners called "the People's Verdict." Insisting that "Stalin is hope . . . Stalin is our banner, Stalin is our will, Stalin is our victory," he declared that those who had been convicted had "raised their hand against all the best that humanity has."[107] Apocalyptic language dominated the public sphere. Stalin's speeches to the Central Committee Plenum, which met from the fall of 1936 to June 1937, were published under the chilling title *Measures to Liquidate the Trotskyists and Other Double-Dealers*.[108]

Between January 1935 and June 1941, when Germany, in violation of the Nazi-Soviet Non-Aggression Pact signed two years earlier, launched Operation Barbarossa, the regime initiated a period of purge and terror that combined public repression by tribunals with secret extralegal repression by political police. The era's agonizingly protracted spasm of violence, directed both at elites and at the broader society, was controlled from the top. It was marked by a profound sense of insecurity about "spies and enemies," a deep concern for conspiracy, a quest for uniform social solidarity, and by what the historian Stephen Kotkin has called a pseudo class war that identified four groups of targets—senior Party and military figures, Party and economic cadres, ordinary Russians, and targeted non-Russian groups—who were thought to be insufficiently stalwart and loyal.[109] Neighbors and loved ones disappeared in the night. "Some returned, most did not," noted Kotkin.[110] In the volatile years of 1937 and 1938, some eight million Soviet citizens were arrested, and "the quota, authorized by Stalin, for 'enemies of the people' to be executed was set at 356,105, though the actual number who lost their lives was more than twice that."[111] With some 636,000 new prisoners in those two years alone, the Gulag was transformed "from indifferently managed prisons in which people died by accident, into genuinely deadly camps where prisoners were deliberately worked to death, or actually murdered, in far larger numbers than they had been in the past."[112]

The Great Terror, preceding the creation of the Nazi abattoirs by several years, was marked by rituals that already had been refined. "One by one party members were called in front of an ad hoc commission formed by representatives of local party leaderships" in the iron and steel region of Magnitogorsk, a symbol of Soviet urbanism based on heavy industry, in 1933:

> Approaching the front of the room, Communists placed their party cards on a red-draped table and, with portraits of the party's leaders in the background, recited their political biographies and prepared to answer questions.... In the buildup to the purge, special receptacles had been installed inside all institutions for the collection of signed or more often anonymous testimony about the Communists in that organization. No party member could be certain of what the commission had managed to find out or might ask.[113]

A new wave of investigations, expulsions, and executions was inaugurated by the murder, perhaps on Stalin's order, of Leningrad's Communist Party leader, Sergei Kirov, outside his Smolny Institute office in December 1934. Kirov, in whose memory the Mariinsky Ballet was renamed, had administered the construction of the great showpiece of the First Five-Year Plan, the 141-mile-long Baltic White Sea Canal built by 100,000 Gulag convicts, 20,000 of whom died during the twenty months between 1931 and 1933.[114] Stalin utilized the killing to open a drive to eradicate opposition, real and imagined, to purify the Communist Party, much as the Nazis sought to "purify" their own country, and as the occasion to promulgate the "Law of December 1," with agreement by the Politburo, which sanctioned rapid trials without legal representation and authorized prompt executions.[115] Lev Kamenev and Grigori Zinoviev, who had been members of Lenin's original eight-member Politburo in 1917 and had ruled the Soviet Union in a triumvirate with Stalin when Lenin took ill in 1923, and who had lined up with Stalin against Trotsky at the pivotal Thirteenth Party Congress in May–June 1924, were put on trial. Convicted of "moral complicity" in the murder that had been carried out by Leonid Nikolayev (who, with thirteen others, was tried secretly and immediately shot), they were sentenced to prison terms of five and ten years, respectively.[116]

Soon they were retried by a military court, over which Nikitchenko presided, nine years before his appearance at Nuremberg. They were the star defendants, alongside fourteen other leading Communists, in one of the court's most notable trials, conducted from August 19 to 24, 1936.[117] Each faced accusations of counterrevolutionary conspiracy as members of "the Trotskyite-Zinovievite *bloc* . . . a group of unprincipled, political adventurers and assassins striving at only one thing, namely, to make their way to power even through terrorism."[118] The court case unfolded in the October Hall of Moscow's Trade Union building, the pre-Revolutionary Noble's Club, decorated with pale blue walls and white Corinthian columns and adorned with a stucco frieze of dancing girls. The indictment once again alleged participation in plots to assassinate Sergei Kirov, and to kill other leading Party figures, including Stalin. The audience consisted of some 30 foreign journalists and diplomats, and 150 junior members of the NKVD, the Soviet Secret police, who had been ordered to begin a disturbance should any of the accused depart from the agreed script of contrition. Relatives of the accused, even officials of the Central Committee, were not admitted.[119]

The charges, running to some thirty closely printed pages, were submitted by State Prosecutor Andrei Vyshinsky, the key theorist of Soviet law, whose 1932 book, *Revolutionary Legality in the Contemporary Period,* provided the basis for the political jurisprudence that governed such cases, making the case for class law rather than what he dismissed as bourgeois legal formalism. Under Communism, he insisted, law is neither autonomous nor a protector of individual rights, but an integral part of the state's revolutionary purposes: "Law and state cannot be regarded as separate from each other," as "the law obtains its power and content from the state."[120] Later foreign minister, then Soviet ambassador at the United Nations, he referred to the show trial defendants as "hybrids of foxes and pigs," "reptiles" and "filthy dogs . . . from whose mouth a bloody venom drips . . . mad dogs of capitalism, who want to tear to pieces the flower of our new Soviet nation! Let's push the bestial hatred they bear our leaders back down their own throats!"[121]

This, the first of the three sensational stage-managed trials, the others following in January 1937 and March 1938,[122] produced surreal scenes. "Stalin orchestrated the proceedings from behind an opaque screen, occasionally signifying his presence with puffs of smoke from his Dunhill pipe" as the trial unfolded beneath a large slogan reading "Workers of Moscow! To the mad dogs—a dog's death."[123] No documentation was offered by the prosecution. No defense was produced by the accused. Each person, having "refused" a lawyer, responded to his examination by confession. In a last plea, Mrachkovsky declared, "I took a despicable path, the path of deception of the party. . . . I want to depart from life without carrying any filth with me." Evdokimov averred that "the difference between us and the fascists is very much in our disfavour. Fascism openly and frankly inscribed on its banners, 'Death to Communism.' On our lips we had all the time, 'Long Live Communism,' whereas by our deeds we were fighting socialism victorious in the U.S.S.R." Bakayev announced, "I am heavily oppressed by the thought that I became an obedient tool in the hands of Zinoviev and Kamenev, became an agent of the counter-revolution, that I raised my hand against Stalin." In turn, each defendant, including Kamenev and Zinoviev, acknowledged culpability. "And the proletarian state will deal with me as I deserve," Berman-Yurin declared. "It is too late for contrition." Kamenev averred, "No matter what my sentence will be, I in advance consider it just," and advised his sons, "Go forward . . . Follow Stalin."[124] Zinoviev confessed to how "my defective Bolshevism became transformed into anti-Bolshevism, and through Trotskyism

I arrived at Fascism. Trotskyism is a variety of Fascism and Zinovievism is a variety of Trostskyism."[125] Just before Nikitchenko, only seven years before his appearance at Nuremberg, led his colleagues to the Council Chamber to consider their verdicts, Ter-Vaganyan added, "I am crushed by the weight of all that was revealed here. . . . I bow my head before the Court and say: whatever your decision may be, however stern your verdict, I accept it as deserved."[126]

Vyshinsky closed his summary speech with "the demand that these dogs gone mad should be shot—every one of them."[127] Years later, Khrushchev reported that Stalin had prepared their death sentences before the proceedings had begun.[128] Each of the sixteen was shot in the basement of the Lubyanka prison hours after the trial terminated, in contravention to promises that had been offered six of the political prisoners, including Kamenev and Zinoviev, that, with contrition, their lives would be spared.[129] Nikolai Bukharin, the Marxist theorist and member of the Central Committee who was to lose his own life in March 1938 after being convicted for conspiring to overthrow the state at the third show trial, told Vyshinsky, "I am terribly glad the dogs have been shot."[130]

The 1939 *History of the Communist Party of the Soviet Union*, later numbered among Stalin's *Collected Works*, offered the official version of these proceedings. The illiberal flavor of the prose is remarkable. It included a litany of "villainies over a period of twenty years" that had been committed "to destroy the Party and the Soviet state, to undermine the defensive power of the country, to assist foreign military intervention, to prepare the way for the defeat of the Red Army, to bring about the dismemberment of the U.S.S.R., to hand over the Soviet Maritime Region to the Japanese, Soviet Byelorussia to the Poles, and Soviet Ukraine to the Germans, to destroy the gains of the workers and collective farmers, and to restore capitalist slavery in the U.S.S.R." Stalin reported how, after the execution of these "dregs of humanity," "whiteguard pigmies" and "whiteguard insects," the USSR "passed on to next business."[131]

For their loyal work, Nikitchenko and Vyshinsky were awarded the Order of Lenin.[132] Like Nikitchenko, Vyshinsky would prominently surface after the war. During the Nuremberg proceedings, despite having no official role, he acted as Stalin's proxy by advising, indeed supervising, Nikitchenko and the Soviet delegation. At a party for the judges and the prosecutors on November 27, the day he first arrived, unheralded, for a monthlong stay as a member of the Soviet prosecution team, Vyshinsky proposed a toast in Russian: "Death as soon as possible to the defendants," he declared, thereby betraying a rather off-center sensibility.[133] His recurring visits sought to ensure that various embarrassments would not enter into the proceedings, like the secret protocols of the August 23, 1939, Non-Aggression Pact with Nazi Germany, and the March 5, 1940, mass execution of 22,000 Poles in the Katyn Forest, including 8,000 officers who had been taken prisoner during the fall of 1939 in the Soviet conquest of eastern Poland.[134] Not only did Vyshinsky seek to bury this Soviet crime but he also pressed an audacious counterstrategy, insisting that the Germans should be charged with this atrocity.[135]

Nikitchenko died in 1967. We know little about how or why. Attempts by American and British lawyers to stay in touch after his return to Moscow had been blocked. Letters and presents were never acknowledged. No reply ever came. Of his life after the trial, nothing is "known beyond a Soviet report of his death."[136] His April 1967 *New York Times* obituary observed that "when he was named to serve . . . at the Nuremberg war crimes trial before this trial, Major General Nikitchenko already had wide experience in the judiciary."[137]

III.

AFTER A rose had been placed in a vase to mark the absence of the late senator Theodore Bilbo, Republican congressman Everett Dirksen of Illinois observed at the May 1948 congressional memorial service that Bilbo had been "a man of deep and abiding conviction."[138] He had been just that. "The course of Bilbo's career," the Mississippi historian Chester Morgan has commented, singled him out as one of the New Deal's "most effective evangelists," a supporter whose commitment to "New Deal liberalism . . . never wavered," but with a caveat—"so long as the rights of the people of his state were not infringed."[139] In that regard, Bilbo had been the Senate's most furious racist, a proud member of the Ku Klux Klan.

This severe racism was curious. His political base had not been in the state's plantation-dominated black belt or the urbanized and relatively cosmopolitan Gulf Coast, but in the hill country of central and northern Mississippi, where the farms were small, the soil poor, and the land without great value, as well as in the primarily white, fundamentalist, impoverished piney woods region of the state's south, the location of Bilbo's own Pearl River County, where most of the once-fecund forests had been stripped by the timber industry and where growing cotton on small parcels with relatively primitive methods produced deep poverty. There, literacy rates were low, schools were pitiful, and housing consisted mainly of wooden shacks lacking electricity and running water. Because the legislature apportioned seats by population, the minority of whites in the heavily populated, predominantly black Delta counties enjoyed a structural advantage. Nearly sixty years earlier, in 1890, the planter-dominated Democratic Party had convened a constitutional convention that established a literacy test and a four-dollar poll tax payable during the course of the two years before an election. These measures not only eliminated black voting but radically reduced the white electorate, as well.

Bilbo could not have risen as a political force had the state's Democratic Party continued to select nominees for governor by a nominating convention dominated by Delta politicians.[140] In 1902, despite the opposition of those counties, white legislators from the other sections, no longer concerned about black voters or multiracial populism, substituted a primary system, thus giving birth to a new type of flamboyant popular politics based primarily on appeals to mostly poor rural whites. The first governor to be elected this way, the fiercely racist James K. Vardaman, pioneered in combining exuberant campaigning at mass rallies, antiblack rhetoric, including support for lynching, and class-based appeals against the "money power."[141] Serving as mentor, Vardaman nourished Bilbo's early political career, successfully boosting his election as lieutenant governor in 1911. With Vardaman's move to the U.S. Senate, Bilbo was elected to his first term as governor in 1916. As a populist Democrat in the nation's poorest state, he championed a politics of class resentment despite the reduced white electorate, a politics whose rhetoric railed against the planters of the Delta and against Yankee capitalism. In office, he became "the undisputed leader of the reform wing of the state Democratic party," by initiating a vibrant program of progressive legislation, including the equalization of land assessments, banking and prison reform, hospital construction, conservation, road building and the redistribution of public school funds to poorer districts to equalize education across the state.[142]

Despite his very unaristocratic origins in the Deep South, Bilbo ardently supported Governor Roosevelt of New York for president in 1932. Shortly after FDR's inauguration, Bilbo found himself rewarded by a patronage appointment at the new Agricultural Adjustment Administration, having been recommended by Pat Harrison, his state's senior senator.[143] Bilbo then ran successfully for the Senate against the two-term incumbent Hubert Stephens in 1934, as an enthusiastic New Dealer "pledging himself to support the efforts of the Roosevelt administration to bring the Nation out of the depression, to aid the farmer and the laboring man." After winning the Democratic primary, assuring his election in November, he promised to make "noise for the common people," and "raise the same kind of hell as President Roosevelt." He recalled his loyalty to the national party, even when, in 1928, it had nominated a Catholic for president: "I stumped the state for Al Smith in 1928—me a Baptist a dry and a Ku Klux Klansman—and I saved the state for the Democrats."[144]

Mississippi's members in the House of Representatives also stressed Bilbo's New Deal liberalism in their chamber's memorial event. As a "representative of the toiling masses," noted that state's John Rankin, arguably the chamber's most vocal racist, Bilbo's "heart went out to the toiling people of his state, and whenever their interest was at stake they knew exactly where he stood." William Whittington recalled how Bilbo, as "the champion" of "progressive and liberal policies . . . advocated measures in the interest of the average man. With him, the welfare of the common man was paramount." Jamie Whitten rightly observed how "contrary to the reputation built up in the national press during recent years, Senator Bilbo was identified with liberal measures."[145] Joseph Keenan, the secretary of the Chicago Federation of Labor, who had just moved to serve on President Roosevelt's National Defense Advisory Commission (the agency that oversaw the mobilization of the defense industries in the face of Hitler's successes on the ground in Europe), had had good reason to write to Bilbo in 1940 to express the administration's appreciation for his recent primary win: "I was delighted to learn of your splendid victory . . . assuring six more years of a real friend of liberal government.[146] Running for reelection that year, Bilbo pronounced himself, and his state, to be "100 percent for Roosevelt . . . and the New Deal."[147]

When a leading historian of the South in twentieth-century American politics reflected on how "President Roosevelt's leadership inspired and directed a hardy band of southern liberals in Congress," his list included

Maury Maverick and Lyndon Johnson in the House, and Alben Barkley, Hugo Black, Claude Pepper, and Bilbo in the Senate.[148] He had been a "liberal fire-eater," a political scientist observed shortly after Bilbo's death, "despite his ranting on the race issue."[149] He also had been, as Georgia governor Eugene Talmadge admiringly assessed, "a bulldog for protecting traditions of the South."[150] John Stennis's eulogy in the Senate did not shy away from Bilbo's fierce avowal of racial segregation. Stennis saluted his late colleague for having fought "back with all the vigor of the rough-and-tumble political fights that had enlivened his public career . . . when measures were brought before the Congress affecting the established customs and traditions of Mississippi and the Southern States." Congressman Rankin likewise commented that "Senator Bilbo stood for those traditions which have characterized the people of the South from the earliest settlements and for those policies of segregation by which alone the two races can live together in peace and harmony in that great section of the country."[151]

Compared with the facts of Bilbo's utterances, these speeches offered measured recollections, for no one in public life, certainly no other New Dealer, articulated racist commitments more openly and emphatically. During his first term as governor, the *New York World* had wired Bilbo to ask what he was doing to prevent lynching. He replied how "it is practically impossible, without great loss of life, especially at the present time, to prevent lynching of Negro rapists when the crime is committed against the white women of the South," adding that the United States is "strictly a white man's country, with a white man's civilization, and any dream on the part of the Negro Race to share social and political equality will be shattered in the end."[152]

From the 1938 consideration of the Wagner–Van Nuys bill to make lynching a federal crime to debates in the 1940s about the poll tax, absentee voting by soldiers, and the Fair Employment Practices Commission, Bilbo emerged as the Senate's leading unashamed crusader for racism. Pleading against "mongrelization" in the antilynching debate of 1938, a process he claimed had destroyed white civilization over much of the globe, Bilbo took a page from Hitler's *Mein Kampf* to assert that merely "one drop of Negro blood placed in the veins of the purest Caucasian destroys the inventive genius of his mind and strikes palsied his creative faculty."[153] During the filibuster to derail the bill, he sought to instruct his colleagues about "the difference in the intellect, in the brain, in the mind" between blacks and whites, making "the white man throughout all time . . . the superior race, the ruling race, the race of creating power, the race of art, the race of literature, the race of music that moves the soul."[154]

Bilbo's fulminations were hardly limited to African-Americans. The next year, he wrote to attack the "New York Jew kikes that are fraternizing and socializing with Negroes for selfish and political reasons" after the National Committee to Combat Anti-Semitism protested his views about race.[155] In July 1945, he responded to a letter by Benjamin Fischler, a New York accountant who had objected to Bilbo's efforts to prevent the Senate from voting to create a permanent Fair Employment Practices Commission, recalling that Jews had "denied and crucified Christ," and, moreover, did not practice a "code of square dealing, especially in your business relationships."[156] Referring to the FEPC bill on the Senate floor as "a damnable, Communist, poisonous piece of legislation," Bilbo fulminated about having learned that "some Catholics are linked with some rabbis trying to bring about racial equality for niggers. . . . The niggers and Jews of New York are working hand in hand."[157] He also observed during the course of that filibuster that "it has just occurred to me that the editor of the *Washington Post* is a Jew and that his wife is a Jewess . . . are the ones who have been back of this vicious legislation. Therefore, we find the editor of the *Washington Post,* a Jew, fighting against me, accusing me, and denouncing me and any other man who dares to disagree with him with regard to this proposed legislation, and calling us bankrupt men. I resent it."[158] Four months later, Miriam Golombeck, a student at New York's Hunter College, informed Bilbo in writing that "a meeting attended by 600 Hunter girls had adopted a resolution calling upon members of Congress to institute impeachment proceedings against him" and had condemned his views as Fascist. Calling these students "'Communists,' 'Negro gals,' 'mongrel,' and 'uneducated,'" he replied that "the mere fact that I believe in racial purity which every decent and self-respecting Negro ought to believe in does not make me a fascist."[159]

Bilbo's extreme rhetoric as well as his style of dress, which favored loud check suits and brash ties,[160] were something of an embarrassment to more reserved political leaders, including many fellow southerners in Congress, though his racial and religious bigotry, while particularly excessive, was not radically different from common prejudices of the time, the difference being that others chose to express in polite or nonverbal ways what Bilbo so vocally conveyed in demagogic fashion. In any event, his extreme rhetoric did not prevent the legislature's rules of seniority from doing their work when it was Bilbo's turn, in 1944, to be designated chair of the Senate Committee on the District of Columbia, effectively making him the city's mayor. He governed that segregated city, where nearly one in three residents was black, as he had ruled as governor of Mississippi. Immediately after his selection, Bilbo declared his intention to make Washington "a model city," pledging to "press for the best police force in the nation, the best water system, elimination of slums, reduction of juvenile delinquency, and renovation of the city's hospitals."[161] It was as if his crude nativist and racist sentiments had become both sanctioned and legitimized as his responsibilities grew. As committee chair, he did, in fact, secure a new hospital center for the city, improve transportation over the Potomac, enhance housing conditions, and build new parks, much as Mussolini had done in his Fascist petri dish. All the while, Bilbo worked assiduously to deepen the city's Jim Crow arrangements, discharging his responsibilities much as the president of the local branch of the NAACP, Arthur Gray, had feared: "On the basis of Bilbo's record and statements, Negroes cannot expect any kind of fair treatment under his administration of District affairs."[162]

Shortly before Bilbo's selection, students at Howard University, whose federal grants Bilbo worked unsuccessfully to block, pioneered the sit-in to protest segregation in the nation's capital, a decade and a half before the sit-in at the Woolworth lunch counter in Greensboro, North Carolina, in February 1960, set off a wave of such nonviolent protests. In the face of these demonstrations, Bilbo sought to enforce segregation in the city's federal parks, convened discussions in his committee concerning "how to maintain racial discrimination at the National Airport" in Virginia (concerned that "Negroes can fraternize by eating in the white person's dining room"), actively opposed home rule, and enforced barriers to black voting. Calling multiracial children "a motley melee of misceginated mongrels," he strongly advocated a law to ban racial intermarriage in Washington, arguing that "the purity of the blood of the Anglo-Saxon, the Celt, and the Teuton in this America of ours is now being threatened."[163]

Campaigning in Mississippi for reelection in 1946, Bilbo reported to his audience in Greenville about a meeting he had held with a delegation of black labor leaders in the District of Columbia in February 1944. The group, headed by the lawyer B. V. Lawson, included Dorothy Strange, administrative secretary of the Washington Council of the National Negro Congress, and representatives from the Fraternal Council of Negro Churches, the CIO, the Brotherhood of Sleeping Car Porters, the United Cafeteria and Restaurant Workers, and the Industrial Union Council. Having been reminded by the group that black soldiers "are fighting and dying to preserve and extend American democracy to all, regardless of race, creed, and color," Bilbo rejoined by announcing an intention to "renew his 'Back to Africa' campaign for the Negro people," stating, according to the delegation's spokesman, that "Negroes can only hope for a continued practice of discrimination and oppression after the war. Liberia is the place where they must settle to obtain security and equal opportunity—not America."[164] In espousing such return-to-Africa views, Bilbo was resorting to a crude and unrealistic perspective that had waxed and waned, particularly during the nineteenth century, since the republic's beginnings, a view that had at times been favored by such "enlightened" slave owners as Thomas Jefferson, and even by the Emancipator, Abraham Lincoln. Yet coming in the 1940s, the idea of a reverse movement to Africa was at best anachronistic, presenting a view that no longer had a national constituency, or even much support among other segregationists in the South.

Bilbo's own recollection of the encounter was pungent:

> You know, folks, I run Washington. I'm Mayor there. . . . Some niggers came to see me one time in Washington to try to get the right to vote there. The leader was a smart nigger. Of course he was half white. I told him that the nigger would never vote in Washington. Hell, if we give 'em the right to vote up there, half the niggers in the South will move into Washington and we'll have a black Government. No Southerner would sit in Congress under those conditions.[165]

Bilbo's public racism peaked during the 1946 Mississippi primary, just as the state's white and black war veterans were returning home. He campaigned almost exclusively as the defender of the southern way of life, a bulwark against racial change that might be imposed from without. When *Life* ranked Bilbo the Senate's worst member, he characteristically retorted that its publisher's wife, Clare Boothe Luce, was "the greatest nigger-lover in the

North." When Eleanor Roosevelt spoke up for black rights, as she had in sponsoring Marian Anderson's concert at the Lincoln Memorial in 1939 and in supporting antilynching legislation in Congress, Bilbo insisted that she would like to compel "Southern girls to use the stools and toilets of damn syphilitic nigger women." Characterized by such vitriolic rhetoric, this election, which followed the Supreme Court's 1944 *Smith v. Allwright* ruling that such all-white primaries were unconstitutional, was particularly tense.[166]

The combination of this judgment and the return to Mississippi of tens of thousands of black veterans, who, like white soldiers, were exempted from the poll tax because of their service in the armed forces, opened the possibility for substantial black voting. So severe were the repercussions in Mississippi that one might have thought that the era of Reconstruction was being exhumed. On June 22, Bilbo spoke from Jackson in a broadcast carried throughout the state just "hours after a Negro Army veteran charged that he had been beaten and flogged by four white men when he sought to register." The former soldier, who had served for twenty-three months in the South Pacific, had asked to register at Brandon. "After he left," the *New York Times* reported, "four men seized him, carried him to some woods, stripped him and flogged him with a heavy wire cable, and threatened him with death if he made another attempt to register." Bilbo's radio speech cautioned that "the white people of Mississippi were sitting on a volcano." If blacks were to vote even in small numbers in the July 2 primary, more would the following year, "and from there on it will grow into a mighty surge." During the campaign, he had observed "northern niggers teaching them how to register and how to vote."[167] He now implored every "red-blooded Anglo-Saxon man in Mississippi to resort to any means to keep hundreds of Negroes from the polls." He asserted that "white people will be justified in going to any extreme to keep the nigger from voting. You and I know what's the best way to keep the nigger from voting. You do it the night before the election. I don't have to tell you any more than that. Red-blooded men know what I mean."[168]

Bilbo published *Take Your Choice: Separation or Mongrelization*, a racist screed published by a local Mississippi press, shortly before his death in 1947, a death commemorated by the striking Andrew Tibbs blues song "Bilbo Is Dead." Warning that "the great majority of white Americans have failed to realize the intensity of [the] campaign for racial equality and the abolition of racial segregation in this Nation," the ill senator, suffering from oral cancer, cautioned that "the race problem lives on and on and sometimes rages with all the fury of a jungle beast. It gnaws at the very vitals of our existence, in time it will sap our strength and destroy the greatness of our American way of life unless solved properly and permanently . . . only by the physical separation of the races."[169]

Bilbo's rhetorical extremism, even in a Senate that regularly countenanced much racist talk, eventually put his membership at risk. Article 1, Section 5, of the Constitution of the United States states, "Each house shall be the judge of the elections, returns, and qualifications of its own members." In September 1946, a predominantly black group of fifty Mississippi residents contended that the July 2 primary should be declared invalid because Senator Bilbo had fostered the intimidation and acts of violence that had kept Negroes from the polls. Starting on December 2, a Special Committee to Investigate Campaign Expenditures convened four days of hearings in Mississippi. The two Republican senators, Styles Bridges of New Hampshire and Bourke Hickenlooper of Iowa, found in favor of the complainants, but they were outvoted by the three Democrats, each from a Jim Crow state— Burnet Maybank of South Carolina, Elmer Thomas of Oklahoma, and the chairman, Allen Ellender of Louisiana. Having heard thirty-four white witnesses and sixty-eight black witnesses, the committee's majority found that Bilbo was nonetheless entitled to his Senate seat even though his oratory had been "crude and in poor taste." The majority wrote:

> We are of the opinion that the record demonstrates conclusively that any difficulties experienced by the Negro in his attempts to register and vote in the July 2 primary resulted from the traditional feeling between white and Negroes and their ideas of the laws in that state as regards participation by Negroes in Democratic primaries and it would have been the same irrespective of who the candidates might have been. And we further feel that nothing that Senator Bilbo actually said was responsible in any way for any illegality shown in the evidence presented to the committee to have taken place in the Mississippi registration or voting.

Twisting the facts, and keen to protect a fellow southerner, the committee's Democrats further found Bilbo's campaign remarks to have been justified because of what they called "unwarranted interference with the internal affairs of the state of Mississippi by outside agitators, seeking not to benefit Negroes but merely to further their own selfish political ends."[170]

Later that month, as the Republican Eightieth Congress convened, the Special Committee to Investigate the National Defense Program heard testimony regarding "transactions between Senator Bilbo and various war contractors." It found that Bilbo had, in fact, profited from such dealings by extracting thirty thousand dollars from three contractors to use in his 1946 campaign. Senator Ellender judged this accusation to be a partisan effort "to capture the nigger vote."[171] In early February, the Senate put off a decision on Bilbo's credentials until the Senate physician certified he was physically fit after an operation to remove cancer from his jaw.[172] Never well enough to return to Washington, Bilbo died on August 21, 1947. At the burial in Poplarville, the Pearl River County seat in southern Mississippi where Bilbo had been born, some five thousand mourners gathered at the Juniper Grove Cemetery. They were led by Governor Fielding Wright, who would run for vice president on the Dixiecrat ticket the next year, and by Senator James Eastland, like Bilbo a stalwart opponent of black rights. The first of many eulogies was offered by his local pastor, the Reverend D. W. Nix. The senator, proclaimed the minister, had "died a martyr . . . to the real, true principles of American Democracy."[173]

IV.

THE NEW Deal's partnerships with Italo Balbo, Iola Nikitchenko, and Theodore Bilbo underscore how policymaking during the Roosevelt and Truman administrations proceeded in an atmosphere of unremitting uncertainty about liberal democracy's capacity and fate. For an emerging power like the United States, there was no place to hide, no means to keep liberal democracy unsullied in often desperate conditions of economic collapse, total war, genocide, atomic weaponry, and Cold War.

During the period from the rallying call by the new president to confront fear itself on March 4, 1933, to the Nazi invasion of Poland six years later, the New Deal was concerned, above all, with questions of political economy. Could capitalism be rescued? On what terms? With what degree of public support? The core policymakers in this initial phase of the New Deal never thought the USSR or Nazi Germany could provide workable models. But they were drawn to Mussolini's Italy, which self-identified as a country that had saved capitalism.[174] No wonder Balbo, with all his military insignia, appeared so appealing. It was not just antiegalitarian figures like the philosopher George Santayana or the poet Ezra Pound who famously celebrated Italy's Fascist regime. It was not just the breathless masses that thronged the streets at Chicago and New York to welcome the flamboyant Balbo and his fliers. Italy's administrative reforms and corporatist organization of relationships between the state and economy caught the imagination of such pragmatists and policy scholars in the 1920s as Horace Kallen, the student of ethnicity and pluralism at the New School for Social Research, and Charles Merriam, a leading early behavioral political scientist and a specialist in public administration at the University of Chicago, who found appealing "its experimental nature, antidogmatic temper, and moral *élan*."[175] Mussolini also was keenly admired by none other than Hugh Johnson, the former army officer who led the National Recovery Administration in the early New Deal, who distributed copies of Raffaello Viglione's Fascist pamphlet, *The Corporate State,* to members of the cabinet and hung a portrait of Mussolini in his office.[176]

Desperate for tools and itself in an experimental mood, the Roosevelt administration in the 1930s did not so much adopt a pro-Mussolini stance as seek to associate with Italian Fascism, of course on American terms for America's own purposes, seeking to find policy models that could be put to use under democratic conditions. Throughout the 1930s, the United States, which continued to have robust cultural ties with Italy (participating avidly in the new 1932 Venice Film Festival, and enthusiastically receiving Italy's most imposing pavilion at Chicago's Century of Progress Exposition), also broadly admired that country's combination of optimism and commitment to technology. The United States engaged eagerly with Italy on trade, though it later introduced a copper embargo, as it sought to encourage Mussolini's comparatively moderate Fascism as a counterweight to National Socialism.[177] Thus, in the summer of 1936, one year after the Italian conquest of Ethiopia, both Merriam and Louis Brownlow, who had been a city manager in Knoxville, Tennessee, and, with Merriam, one of the founders of the Public Administration Center clearinghouse at the University of Chicago, journeyed to Italy to study modern administrative methods for the President's Committee on Administrative Management, which FDR had created to recommend a reorganization of the federal government to increase the capacity and effectiveness of the executive branch.[178] "There is," its report observed, "but one grand purpose, namely, to make democracy work today in our National Government; that is, to make our Government an up-to-date, efficient, and effective instrument for carrying out the will of the Nation."[179] The report failed, of course, to mention the Italian campaign of 1935–1936 that had produced Ethiopian killing fields.

Affectionate as the feelings had been between the Fascist regime and progressive American policymakers, the infatuation did not last, dashing the hopes of ardent American sympathizers like Ambassador Long. With the outbreak of war in Europe and the Pacific, Italy unavoidably moved to the enemy camp. When Hitler reneged on his Non-Aggression Pact with the Soviet Union two years later, Stalin's regime became America's most valuable military ally. Ideological principles and liberal commitments became subordinate as a Metternichean sense of Realpolitik came to dominate American overseas policy, a new way of advancing the United States in the world. The United States, accordingly, made common cause with Stalinism at its most ruthless and repressive moment. Joined under the anti-Fascist banner Moscow first proclaimed with popular-front policies in the mid-1930s, the country once distinguished as the deepest enemy of liberal and democratic values was welcomed into an association of nations fighting against Hitler, and defending Enlightenment virtues and liberties.[180] Anti-Fascism, the erstwhile Communist French historian François Furet recognized,

> purged Soviet Communism of much of the antibourgeois aggressiveness with which Lenin had imbued it in order to separate Bolshevism from Social Democracy. . . . To isolate Hitler, the Soviet Union drew closer to the democracies. Being still distinct from them, it was a lap ahead on the path to freedom, which is how the Soviets explained Hitler's particular hostility to the USSR. . . . By inscribing the Soviet Union at the top of the list of democratic nations engaged in the battle against the Fascist powers, Stalin gained an enormous advantage—a fierce enemy, deprived of the amenities of freedom, identifiable yet ubiquitous.[181]

With this advantage, the Soviet Union managed simultaneously to join the defense of democracy from Nazism and its allies while justifying domestic repression as anti-Fascist. After all, a central theme at the show trials of 1936–1938 was the accusation that such leading Party figures as Zinoviev and Kamenev were guilty of collaborating with the Gestapo.[182]

Thus the placement of the Soviet Union inside the global coalition against Nazism, while drawing a sharp line between Hitlerism and the Enlightenment's values of liberty and equality, came to be justified not only by sober military realism or, later, by the enormity of the crimes revealed to have been committed by Germany but also by what appeared to be common values. Based during the war on a willful disregard of the means of Soviet rule and on taking no notice of fundamental geopolitical and ideological differences, this alliance did not endure after the collapse of Fascism in its various forms as a viable social order. Seen from this perspective, Nikitchenko's role at Nuremberg brought to a close the period in which the United States deliberately chose to look the other way in the face of extreme human rights violations. Absent a common enemy, the liberal West again confronted a totalitarian power, this time across an Iron Curtain. The term *Cold War,* when viewed from a remove of sixty years, underestimates the depth of anxiety and violence during the last phase of the Roosevelt-Truman era. As this period was coming to an end, the United States had lost the nuclear monopoly it had maintained only less than a handful of years. Fighting an enervating and brutal war in Korea, the United States, especially through its foreign policy and covert actions, was beginning to build what has proved to be a massive and permanent national security state.

The nation's fondness for Italian Fascism, once symbolized by Balbo's tumultuous reception, and its toleration of Soviet hypocrisy under the banner of anti-Fascism, signified by Nikitchenko's seat on Nuremberg's bench, would prove ephemeral. Both were based more on instrumental realism than on deep or enduring affiliation.

Bilbo and his fellow southern Democrats, by contrast, made up an essential and permanent part of the New Deal, for they commanded votes required for any of the domestic and international programs advanced by Presidents Roosevelt and Truman to become law. The Jim Crow South was the one collaborator America's democracy could not do without. If we are to understand the world in which we currently live, we must examine the very real lingering effects of that New Deal alliance with those politicians whose views Bilbo expressed, albeit in extreme form.

3 ▷ "Strong Medicine"

THE START OF 1933 witnessed an upsurge in lynching in the American South. In mid-March, the *Chicago Defender,* one of the country's leading black newspapers, chronicled these gruesome events:

> Harry Ross was shot and killed January 3 by three white men, outside of Memphis, Tennessee. They reported they were taking him into the city to lay charges of "having made improper proposals to a white woman" against him, when he "tried to escape" from their moving car.

Fell Jenkins, 20 years old, was beaten to death by three white farmers, at Aycock, Louisiana, January 11. They said he had been trespassing on the property of one of them.

Three members of a family of fishermen were hacked to death on Tavernier Island, one of the Florida Keys, January 19, by an invading gang of white men. Their names were not reported in the press and authorities have not responded to queries for more details.

Robert Richardson was shot to death in Baton Rouge, Louisiana, February 9, while "attempting to escape" from a gang of 25, headed by a deputy sheriff, which raided his house on a report, given out later, that he "had annoyed a white woman."

Nelson Nash, 21 years old, was hanged from a tree by a gang of men at Ringgold, Louisiana, February 19.

George Cheater died February 19, at Aiken, South Carolina, from a beating administered by three white men who later said he had "stolen their whiskey."

Levon Carlock, 19 years old, [was] beaten, tortured and shot to death by six policemen in Memphis, Tennessee.[1]

In early March, Edith Frank posed with her daughters Margot, just seven, and Anne, three months shy of her fourth birthday, at Frankfurt's Tietz department store and the nearby Café Hauptwache. Geert Mak reports:

Three days later, the SA raised the swastika banner above the balcony of the town hall, and three weeks later a boycott was pronounced against most Jewish shops and businesses. After the Easter holidays, Margot's non-Aryan teacher seems to have disappeared into thin air. During those same weeks, Otto Frank began making plans to emigrate. Within a year the whole family was living on Merwedeplein in Amsterdam. The rest of the story we know.[2]

With barbarism advancing at home and abroad, Franklin Delano Roosevelt was inaugurated as the thirty-second president of the United States on March 4, 1933.

I.

THE LATE-WINTER day was cool, gray, and windy, mostly cloudy, with a trace of sun. The freezing rain and sleet that fell four years later on the president's 1937 inaugural, when he returned to the White House in an open car with a half inch of rain splashing on its floor, might have been more appropriate for the start of an era tinged with fear. Franklin Roosevelt took office just over a year after the Seventeenth Congress of the Communist Party of the USSR had confidently initiated its Second Five-Year Plan; ten months after Japan's prime minister, Inukai Tsuyoshi, had been assassinated in his official residence by a group of right-wing naval officers and army cadets, exposing the tenuous circumstances of the country's democratic politics;[3] five weeks after Adolf Hitler launched the SA, the SS, and the Prussian police, led by Hermann Göring, to rule the streets; just days after President Hindenburg and Chancellor Hitler had invoked Article 48 of the Weimar Constitution to suspend civil liberties at a time of national emergency; and nineteen days before the Reichstag, by a vote of 494–94, overwhelmingly passed the Enabling Act, which legally created the Nazi dictatorship by giving the chancellor and the cabinet the right to draft legislation, enact laws, and rule by executive decree.[4] Confronted by seemingly more successful dictatorships on the Right and the Left, the president of the United States was about to lead a democracy that was unsure of its practical abilities and moral authority.

"Fear itself": evocative and shocking, it is a visceral phrase. It was just this "nameless, unreasoning, unjustified terror which paralyzes needed efforts to convert retreat into advance" that Roosevelt pledged to dispel in his first minutes as president. It is, he famously said, "the only thing we have to fear."[5] Nameless and unreasoning, perhaps, but not unjustified, and not the only thing Americans had to fear. When he spoke, capitalism had collapsed, spreading misery everywhere. Liberal parliamentary regimes were toppling. Dictatorships led by iron men and motivated by unforgiving ideological zeal seemed to have seized the future. Rearmament had begun against the backdrop of the experience and lessons of total war. Of course, FDR could not have foreseen the vast expansion of powers by predatory states, the imminent intensification of violence, or the radical evil of mass killing that lay just ahead. But we can see how even at the time, FDR's summons "to wage a war against the emergency" understated the perils and prospects of evil, all of which soon enhanced reasons for dread, apprehension, and alarm.

As the president spoke, there already was more than enough cause to evoke "fear itself." This was no speech born of hyperbole. "Several of the forces propelling Hitler into power," the journalist John Gunther recalled, "were much the same as those that put Mr. Roosevelt into office—mass despair in the midst of unprecedented economic crisis, impassioned hatred of the *status quo,* and a burning desire by a great majority of people to find a savior who might bring luck"[6] unless adjustments to the traditional constitutional balance were carried out.

Front and center was the global economic failure. On Inauguration Day, a quarter of the wage force was out of work, and a massive banking crisis was robbing the middle class of its savings. The Great Depression had taken "a more violent form" in the United States, its place of origin, than anywhere else. The nation's collapsing national income accounted for more than half the world's decline in industrial production. The New Deal historian William Leuchtenburg has judged that "when economic disaster struck, no major country in the world was so ill-prepared as the United States to cope with it," for its national state lacked "both instruments of control and a tradition of state responsibility."[7]

The profound economic crisis was but one of the shocks that marked the two decades between 1913, when FDR began his seven years of service as assistant secretary of the U.S. Navy in the Wilson administration, and his presidential inaugural. Hope that bellicosity and significant investments in arms could be offset by an international order that could guard the peace and control warfare seemed irreparably dashed. In 1897, the English barrister John Shuckburgh Risley, later a legal assistant in the Colonial Office, had published *The Law of War,* a massive compendium for lawyers and the general public. Looking at the bright side of efforts then under way to contain warfare, Risley observed:

The Rules of War are pervaded by one grand animating principle—
to obtain justice as speedily as possible at the least possible cost of suf-

fering and loss to the enemy, or to neutrals, as the result of belligerent operations. On this principle, for example, the wanton devastation of territory, the slaughter of unarmed prisoners, or the poisoning of an enemy's wells are recognized forms of illegal violence. . . . That the policy of nations has not been to increase or diminish the horrors of warfare is sufficiently proved by the Convention of Geneva, 1864, and the Declaration of St. Petersburg, 1868.[8]

The twelfth volume of *The Cambridge Modern History,* devoted to "the latest age," was published in 1910.[9] Armed peace, it suggested, was a leading achievement of modern times. This assessment recognized the ongoing arms race, noting how the five great Continental powers—France and Russia joined in a Dual Alliance; Austria, Germany, and Italy in the Triple Alliance—had placed more than two million men under arms, and could mobilize some twenty million. It acknowledged that the arms race begun in the late 1880s was accelerating, that the production of armaments was ever more integrated into the larger economy, and that annual military spending, for just these five countries, had jumped to 158 million pounds.[10] Yet a sense of optimism prevailed. "The existence of this tremendous military equipment," the opening essay confidently declared, "makes for peace. The consequences of war would be felt in every household; and statesmen, as well as nations, shrink from the thought of a conflict between forces so immense." National passions, it further observed, had "lost their operative power."[11]

The Great War's vast support and remarkable bloodletting mocked these outlooks. Little did they anticipate the wave of enthusiasm by mass populations, politicians, generals, and intellectuals for the brutal intensity of mobilization and combat, or for the manner in which warfare could unite a nation across the lines of class, region, and religion. A passion for war infected some of the greatest intellectuals of the day, including the novelist Thomas Mann, who saluted the war for its promise of "purification, liberation, and an immense hope," and the sociologist Max Weber, who assessed how "*this war is great and wonderful . . . however* it turns out."[12]

The carnage that soon followed dashed any expectation that the new war would replicate the relatively moderate level of killing that had characterized the last major European conflict, the brief but brutally decisive Franco-Prussian War of 1870–1871, and the killing fields that marked the colonial territorial race that had taken place between 1880 and 1910 that had been out of sight for most Europeans. On the western front, in the first two months of the Great War, the number of Germans killed, wounded, ill, or missing by the count of the army medical service reached 373,369. Fully five of every eight members of the Belgian army's force of 200,000 died, and the initial British Expeditionary Force of some 117,000 was almost entirely wiped out. By Christmas, 747,000 German and 854,000 French soldiers had been killed or wounded in just the first six months of war since the archduke had been assassinated in Sarajevo.[13]

These astonishing early losses were inflicted by immense armies and fierce firepower before defensive positions could be constructed. Once deep trenches were built, the contending armies settled in for four more years of extraordinary bloodshed. At Verdun, for example, between February and December 1916, some 800,000 soldiers were killed, wounded, or went missing; at the Somme, between June and November 1916, casualties reached 1.1 million.[14] Mired in the ice and slush of the Dolomites and the Alps, half of all Italian forces died or were missing by the fall of 1917, having fought to move just twelve miles beyond Austrian lines from the border of 1915.[15] In all, of the 65 million soldiers mobilized to fight, 8 million were killed, 7 million were enduringly disabled, and 15 million were wounded.[16]

As fear and terror directed at civilians became instruments of warfare, there also was collateral damage, killing five million noncombatants, often in assaults that were incidental to military advantage. "There is good reason to believe," a postwar observer acutely noted, "that one of the motives, possibly the leading motive, which animated those who were responsible for those attacks was the psychological effect which it was believed that terrorization of the civilian inhabitants would cause and which might lead them to demand peace."[17] Further, as the historian Alan Kramer has noted, "the enemy was not merely the enemy army, but the enemy nation and the culture through which it defined itself."[18]

This transformation to the nature of war was first signified by the destruction of the Belgian university town of Louvain and its great university library, the shelling of the cathedral, and the deliberate murder of hundreds of civilians in Rheims, followed later in 1914 by mass executions conducted by German troops in Dinant and the Ardennes. Violence took especially stark form from the air, the source of disembodied killing. When a leading student of foreign affairs proposed rules to regulate such warfare in 1924, he underscored how "an aviator who flies over a city at great height during the night, when all lights are extinguished, as was the general practice during this World War," could not possibly "identify the persons and things to be bombarded."[19]

Not all killing, though, was anonymous or indifferent as to its victims. The Armenian massacre between 1915 and 1917, which cost at least 800,000 lives, perhaps as many as 1.5 million,[20] introduced genocide, the type of mass murder identified by Raphael Lemkin three decades after 1914, and defined in 1948 by a United Nations Convention adopted by the General Assembly, as the deliberate and systematic destruction, in whole or in part, of an ethnic, racial, religious or national group.[21] Not constrained by utilitarian motivations or simple self-interest, this radical evil crossed a line distinguishing real from putatively objective enemies.[22]

Notwithstanding the catastrophic scale of destruction wreaked by the Great War, many believed it would be possible finally to realize Risley's disappointed hope for international institutions. A number of global instruments indeed were fashioned to keep the peace. These included not just the League of Nations but also the Washington Naval Conference of 1921–1922, which produced a series of treaties limiting the construction and scale of battleship fleets, and the Kellogg-Briand Pact of 1928, providing "for the renunciation of war as an instrument of national policy." Good sense seemed to triumph. As late as September 10, 1931, Britain's Robert Cecil, 1st Viscount Cecil of Chelwood (who would win the Nobel Peace Prize in 1937), announced to the League's Assembly, "I am sure that no one in this vast assemblage will rise to contradict me when I say that war was never more remote, nor peace more secure."[23]

Nine days later, imperial Japan invaded Manchuria (a huge area, one-fourth the size of China), and completed its conquest by February 1932. Japan also attacked Shanghai from January to March 1932, leaving hundreds of Chinese dead. The League proved helpless and ineffective.[24] The international security system soon disintegrated. In October 1933, Adolf Hitler withdrew Germany from the League and from the World Disarmament Conference the League had summoned in 1931. Interwar efforts to limit military spending began to fail. In 1933, both Germany and the Soviet Union started down the path to become the world's first military superpowers. With the acceleration of civil upheaval in China and anticolonial challenges to the Great Powers, most conspicuously in India, global anarchy became more prominent. "The 'hinge years' of 1929–33," Zara Steiner's monumental study of international history concluded, "witnessed the threat to the hopes and institutions nurtured during the previous decade and the collapse of many of them." With the mood visibly darkening, she observed, national interests clearly trumped international attempts to replace the pre–World War I European system with a peaceful global order. Germany's radical turn and Japan's military assertion of regional dominance made clear that future events and attempts to keep the peace "would take place outside the Washington treaties, the Kellogg-Briand Pact, and the League of Nations."[25] It was during this darkening international atmosphere that Franklin Roosevelt would assume the presidency.

Amid the shift from expectation to disappointment that preceded his election, the United States stood aloof. Not a participant in the League of Nations, the country repeated a familiar pattern of military demobilization, secure, it was thought, behind two great oceans.[26] At the close of the Civil War, the United States, despite grievous losses on both sides, had possessed the world's most powerful army and its second-greatest naval force. Protected by geography, the nation disarmed after the emergency passed. Following the Armistice of November 1918, another "great army was disbanded; all attempts to maintain a serious military force failed."[27] A long-term peace did seem at hand. The Washington Naval Treaty of 1922, which set limits on construction in order to prevent a new arms race, proved the Harding administration's most popular achievement. Despite the far-reaching military potential of the United States, its armed forces numbered only some 230,000 army and navy personnel at the start of the 1930s, less than half of Italy's services, even though the United States had more than three times the population of Italy. U.S. spending on arms and manpower, moreover, totaled just a quarter of that of the Soviet Union.[28]

For a time, it seemed that this American absence would not much matter. In the war's glowing aftermath, as "the world seemed dedicated to reconstruction," recalled the novelist Stefan Zweig, "it seemed as if a normal life was again in store for our much-tried generation."[29] The projection made by *The Cambridge Modern History* before the war of a global victory for liberal democracy did not seem far-fetched. Its prediction that an arc of membership in a global "European brotherhood, ruled under the same forms of government, practicing the same arts, pursuing the same commerce and industry by the same financial methods, in short as States created and living after the European pattern" based on "the steady advance" of liberal democracy looked prescient.[30] In 1918, the American historian James Harvey Robinson observed how "the opening years of the twentieth century have witnessed a steady increase in people's control of their governments," noting that "the House of Lords in England has been forced to admit that the final word in lawmaking rests with the House of Commons; the monarchy has been overthrown in Portugal; Turkey has tried to establish a constitution and a parliament; China, having overturned the imperial administration, has founded a republic; and Russia has dethroned the Tsar."[31]

Common to all such existing and potential democracies, both Robinson and *The Cambridge Modern History* stressed, was a place of privilege for their national legislatures. "In every country where the Constitution is democratic, representative institutions afford a means, however imperfect, for the expression of popular sentiments; they act as a real check on the executive authorities and exercise a modifying influence upon older national institutions and customs." Through this process of political representation, the essay confidently announced, "the interests of the masses" become central to political life without engendering "warfare of class against class."[32]

The war's settlement ushered in what the English Liberal constitutional scholar James Bryce portrayed as liberal democracy's "universal acceptance . . . as the normal and natural form of government."[33] With a European "belt of democracies—stretching from the Baltic Sea down through Germany and Poland to the Balkans,"[34] and with the establishment of parliamentary democracies on other continents, President Woodrow Wilson's assured 1918 declaration that "democracy seems about universally to prevail," and his confident analysis of how "the spread of democratic institutions . . . promise[s] to reduce politics to a single form . . . by reducing all forms of government to Democracy" seemed confirmed.[35]

These expectations were cruelly deflated even before the spectacular fall of the Weimar Republic, the leading example of the general failure of European democracy.[36] Lost illusions put the liberal democracies on trial.[37] "The public press," as a Harvard political scientist noted in 1926, "not only of this country but of England and of Continental Europe as well, is full of current prophecies that the age of democratic liberalism is dead and done for."[38] Such foretelling was prescient. Caught between mass parties of the Left, some inspired by the Bolshevik experiment, and nationalist, Catholic, conservative, and frankly Fascist parties on the Right, enthusiasm for liberal democracy hollowed out. Mass support frequently was lacking. Political and technical elites often grew impatient with the give-and-take of parliamentary government. "Liberalism's triumph proved short-lived," an overview of the period has noted. "By the 1930's, parliaments seemed to be going the way of kings."[39]

Especially significant was the tragedy of German democracy. From the start, it was placed under exceptional political and intellectual stress. Aping the themes and apocalyptic language that marked the fledgling Nazi movement, a 1923 best-seller, Arthur Moeller van den Bruck's *Das Dritte Reich* (*The Third Reich*), announced that "liberalism is the death of nations." It identified liberal democracy as "a dangerous mental infection" and "a disintegrating atmosphere . . . which spreads moral disease amongst nations, and ruins the nation whom it dominates."[40] This tome epitomized a broad and growing current of thought that advanced what the historian Carl Schorske identified as "post-rational politics" that sought to "organize masses neglected or rejected by liberalism in ascendancy."[41] Each of the era's dictatorships, however different, advanced van den Bruck's claims about liberal democracy. Led by iron men and motivated by unforgiving ideological zeal, these tyrannies seemed to have seized the future.

On the eve of his presidency, Franklin Roosevelt faced a world rather different from the one Woodrow Wilson had envisioned. By 1933, the European map of democracies no longer included Russia, Germany, Italy, Portugal, Austria, Poland, Yugoslavia, Bulgaria, Romania, Hungary, Latvia, or Estonia.[42] With the exception of Britain, Scandinavia, and (still) France, all of interwar Europe turned authoritarian, dictatorial, or Fascist.[43] Concurrently, Stalin extended and intensified Lenin's revolutionary heritage by leading an effort to strengthen Party control over all spheres of Soviet life, to purify the thoughts and composition of Communist cadres, to remake agriculture in a collectivist image, notwithstanding the risk of famine on a mass scale, and to make a massive leap forward in industrialization, whatever the human price.

Writing shortly before going to Yale from the University of Munich, a leading émigré lawyer, Karl Loewenstein, correctly observed in 1935 how "by far the greater part of European territory and of European population is under dictatorial rule of one kind or another," and concluded that "fear persists today more than ever that the contagious spread of dictatorships cannot be checked."[44] He might also have taken notice of antidemocratic transformations in Japan, and various types of limitation on democracy across Latin America. Writing again in 1937, he worried that the antidemocratic tide had "developed into a universal movement which in its seemingly irresistible surge is comparable to the rising of European liberalism against absolutism after the French Revolution."[45] Loewenstein concluded that "perhaps the time has come when it is no longer wise to close one's eyes to the fact that liberal democracy . . . is beginning to lose the day to the awakened masses."[46] Thin and defensive, the democracies seemed no match for the vigor and dynamism of the radical one-party dictatorships.

Half a decade earlier, as Roosevelt prepared his presidency, none of the era's emerging dictatorships had achieved full and complete legitimacy or control. Some looked back, nostalgically, but the newest kinds of dictatorship, the ones that came to be designated as totalitarian, were revolutionary responses to modern democracy that boldly pointed to the future. Frequently rejecting tradition, and seizing instruments of mass politics, they had a variety of ideological goals and utopian projects—leveling the class order, achieving racial purity, rebuilding traditional religious cultures, expanding or defending territory, among others. Across the Left-Right divide, they identified others as implacable enemies.[47] German Nazism and Italian Fascism declared an overwhelming opposition to Russian Bolshevism that was heartily reciprocated. But individually and collectively, their contrast with liberal democracy was profound. Even Europe's pre-1914 authoritarian states had more than one party and respected parliamentary forms, however weak their legislature or limited their electorate. By contrast, the era's revolutionary dictatorships introduced the one-party state as a righteous innovation. They made the ideological party, not the national state, the regime's driving force. This novelty was their answer to what Ortega y Gasset, the influential Spanish philosopher, identified in 1930 as "the coming of the masses," the "one fact which, whether for good or ill, is of utmost importance in the public life of Europe at the present moment."[48]

These dictatorships claimed to be vanguards that could discern directions to history. Their parties—Fascist, Nazi Communist—took ultimate responsibility for what their states did, and for shaping how members of society should think and behave. As vigilant guardians that fought subversion by combining persuasion and rewards with intimidation and coercive violence, their power was unconstrained by liberal rules and rights. As Carl Schmitt, the Berlin law professor, put the point after joining the Nazi Party in May 1933, the party can administer "the highest justice" and it is "the *Führer* [who] protects the Law" as "the highest judge of the nation and the highest lawgiver."[49]

Proudly opposed to parliamentary democracy, the dictatorships produced an antiliberal moral universe that rejected any government based on rights, political representation, and the rule of law as flaccid and incapable. Their political parties did not compete for power, appeal to distinct constituencies, or represent constellations of interests, each of which they thought to be pathologies in the democratic world. Rather, by supervising, persuading, coercing, and integrating their societies, the parties in each of the revolutionary dictatorships "supplied the practical means to bind population to their citizens."[50] Though the dictatorships maintained constitutional structures, these were routinely overridden by an extraconstitutional state under the rubric, as Hitler put things in July 1933, of the "Unity of Party and State."

These, in the main, were dictatorships by consent.[51] Backed by a demonstrated propensity for violence, claiming to advance the wishes, beliefs, and interests of the whole community, and acting as the key hinge between the population and the state, these parties secured active participation and the committed backing of most of their citizens. Of course, it is hard to gauge the degree to which the broad support offered by the public reflected genuine enthusiasm or a pragmatic set of adaptations to make it possible to get on with family life and continuing employment. Writing about Fascism, Hans Morgenthau, the noted émigré student of international affairs, stressed how "it derived its rule from the source that America had thought to be peculiarly its own: the consent of the governed. Fascism laid claim to the democratic title as did America, and even claimed an exclusive title as America once had done; for, pointing to the crisis of the American purpose, it proclaimed the superiority of its own democracy over the sham democracies of the West."[52]

Yet underneath this "consent" lay unprecedented repression justified by a strident language of cleansing and enforced by ruthless persecution. These dictatorships brought into line teachers, university professors, and independent labor leaders, lawyers and civil servants, journalists and writers, and musicians and artists (preferring the didactic and heroic to the expressive and abstract). Placing their rule on a single philosophical base, they did not hesitate to eliminate potential sources of opposition aggressively. Aiming to bolster and toughen the collective body of citizens based on solidarities of race, nation, or class, they respected no zone of privacy and personal identity, and rejected the idea of an independent civil society. Economy and society were conceptualized and organized in service to the party state. Toleration for diversity and pluralism of any kind was coded as weakness. They routinely deployed military metaphors to justify their other policies and behavior.

In constructing governance along these lines, the rituals and practices of the dictatorships worked to undo the sordid mess they believed liberal and democratic government had produced.[53] They claimed to be correcting the politics of division—whether between classes, factions, parties, or divided national loyalties—in the public interest. "In each case," the historian Richard Overy has observed, the dictatorships defined superior, nonliberal democracy "as the absence of political division and the true representation of popular interests, the creation of a united mass public into a singular people capable of acting to solve society's most pressing problems."[54]

II.

HAVING ESCAPED to the United States in 1940, the historian Konrad Heiden wrote a study of Hitler's rise to power, stressing how German democracy had failed to protect itself from willful subversion and hooligan violence. He noted how, "from the afternoon of March 23, 1933, Hitler was dictator, created by democracy and appointed by parliament."[55] But this had hardly been a free vote. Needing a two-thirds majority, Hitler appealed to the Reichstag for the passage of the Enabling Act in person at the Kroll Opera House, less than three weeks after Franklin Roosevelt had begun his presidency. The chamber was dominated by a large swastika. Dressed in the brown shirt signifying his role as Nazi Party leader, and surrounded by "a mass of swastika flags and banners," with the parliamentary "corridors and aisles . . . lined with brown-shirted SA men," he spoke for two and a half hours, outlining the substantive program to combat unemployment, protect the peasantry, place the armed forces on a parity with other countries, and promote a program of moral renewal that his government would pursue once the act was passed. All the exits were guarded and the building surrounded by uniformed Nazi loyalists. Threatening the Reichstag's parties with war if it refused his request, and appealing "in this hour to the German Reichstag to grant us that which we could have taken anyway," he justified the need for executive power by arguing that "it would be against the meaning of the national uprising and would hamper its intended purposes if the government were to negotiate with and petition for the Reichstag's approval of its measures from case to case."[56] "The mob unleashed by the government ruled the capital and the vote was taken in an indescribable atmosphere of terrorization and coercion."[57] Commenting the next day in his diary, Joseph Goebbels recorded, "Now we are also constitutionally the masters of the Reich."[58]

Although the Reichstag lingered on for a period, and though Hitler used it from time to time to legitimate the government's decisions, as he did by having parliament pass the anti-Semitic Nuremberg Laws in 1935, parliamentary government effectively ended. The institution survived as an empty shell, merely a platform for Hitler's speech making.

This transfer of power and authority was not unprecedented. Such a shift to lawmaking authority had also characterized the first year of Italian Fascist rule in 1922. The historian Charles Maier has recalled how parliament had been "generally compliant before Mussolini and quickly endorsed a grant of 'full powers.'"[59] This supersession of parliamentary democracy was the deepest-possible negation of a central liberal political principle. In 1690, in the *Second Treatise of Government,* John Locke had anticipated, and rejected, the possibility that an elected assembly might pass along its ability to make laws to other persons and institutions. "The power of the *legislative*," he wrote, being derived from the people by a positive voluntary grant and institution, can be no other than what that positive grant conveyed, which being only to make *laws,* and not to make *legislators,* the *legislative* can have no power to transfer their authority of making laws, and place it in other hands."[60] In a democracy, moreover, it is the task of the legislature and the representatives who people it to manage a robust relationship with citizens, balancing the good of all with the specific good of constituents, judging merits both as individuals and as members of political groups open to external influence, and seeking a balance between responsiveness and craven behavior.[61]

Looking back in 1936, Karl Loewenstein recalled how "dictation according to the leadership principle was substituted for deliberation and majority vote in parliamentary bodies." The separation of powers, moreover, which ever since Montesquieu's *Spirit of the Laws* (1748) had been considered a guarantee of political liberty, "was superseded by a unity of command and the concentration of authority in the hands of the 'Führer' and his associates."[62]

Democracy's frictions were made to disappear. So, too, were civil liberties and the independent rule of law, notwithstanding the Weimar Constitution, which formally protected liberal rights, though they were never formally abolished. But such "fundamental rights which create free spheres for individuals untouchable by the state," the Nazi judge Roland Freisler announced, "are irreconcilable with the totalitarian principle of the new state." So much so, that judges were given the capacity to punish behavior deemed a crime even if no law had been passed defining it as illegal. As secretary of state in the Reich Ministry of Justice, Freisler urged judges to avoid what he called "exaggerated caution" in applying due process to criminals, especially in instances where the correct punishment was sterilization or castration.[63] In these ways, Nazi Germany and the other dictatorships turned the resurgence of executive power that had been deployed into an emergency device during World War I into a permanent principle.[64]

The last open election in Germany took place the day following FDR's ascent to the presidency. Gaining 44 percent of the vote, the Nazi Party emerged as the dominant player in the Reichstag, far outstripping the Social Democratic Party, with 18 percent, and the Communists, with 12. The democracy that had been hatched at Weimar seemed like a distant mirage. Forming a government of the National Union with the German National People's Party, which secured 8 percent of the vote, assured Hitler's control of the legislative process. Following the Enabling Act, there was a torrent of lawmaking, but not ordinarily by parliament, which established the basic contours of the Nazi dictatorship.[65] These statutes were not subject to judicial review. Under these rules, a federal state was transformed into a unitary and centralized national government, and a one-party executive state replaced a multiparty parliamentary regime. These decrees often included stipulations of delegation, leaving it up to individual ministers or to the cabinet as a whole how a given law would be carried out. Arbitrariness obtained the sanction of law. When elections to the Reichstag were conducted, as they were on

November 12, 1933, and March 29, 1936, only one party ticket was on offer, the others having been outlawed in July 1933. Jews, including those with mixed parentage, were barred from participating in the second election. The emancipation that had come to Germany's Jews some six decades earlier was harshly abrogated as citizenship came to be defined by blood.

Haunting the new Roosevelt presidency, the March 1933 Nazi domination of the Reichstag and the liquidation of parliament were accompanied by new realities on the ground. "The day after the March election, stormtroopers rampaged along the Kurfürstendamm, a fashionable shopping street in Berlin, hunting down Jews and beating them up." Episodes of mass beatings and intimidation of Jews also took place in Hamburg, Frankfurt, Braunschweig, Wiesbaden, and Kassel. There and elsewhere, "synagogues were trashed, while all over Germany gangs of brownshirts burst into courthouses and dragged off Jewish judges and lawyers, beating them with rubber truncheons and telling them not to return."[66] The historian Peter Fritzsche notes that "everything changed for Germany's Jews in two months, March and April 1933. After the 5 March elections, a wave of violence descended upon Jews. As thousands of new converts joined the paramilitary units of the SA, whose numbers shot up ninefold from 500,000 in January 1933 to 4.5 million one year later, the scale of antisemitic actions expanded dramatically. Becoming a Nazi meant trying to become an antisemite as well." In that period, "nearly one in every four active adult men in Germany had turned himself into an *SA-Mann*; many other Germans stood in the ranks of Hitler Youth or the Nazi Party itself."[67] By May, Jews were being fired from large and small firms and asked to leave corporate boards, their shops were passed by, and books were being burned in Berlin's Bebelplatz and in eighteen other university towns and cities, declaring a cultural war against modernism and the role of Jews (speaking as the Berlin bonfire proceeded, Goebbels declared that "Jewish intellectualism is dead").[68] By July, more than 100,000 Germans had been arrested, and 26,000 were behind barbed wire.[69]

"Fascism is action," declared Mussolini, gloating, his words suggesting a stark contrast to the deliberative institutions of the liberal democracies. Unlike such governments that place legislative lawmaking at their center, making it possible for citizens to shape public policy, "the Fascist conception of the State is all-embracing; outside of it no human or spiritual values can exist, much less have value. Thus understood," he observed, "Fascism is totalitarian, and the Fascist State—a synthesis and a unit inclusive of all values—interprets, develops, and potentates the whole life of the people. No individuals or groups (political parties, cultural associations, economic unions, social classes) exist outside the state."[70]

Mussolini's political theory of unchecked executive power, an ideology of destiny, and a cult of heroism was based on the claim that liberal democracies simply were unable to confront central problems in the modern era of mass politics, capitalist economics, and total warfare. He had good reason to suspect that governments based on the central liberal values of consent, pluralism, toleration, rights, and legislative representation could not face up to these complex challenges or govern effectively.[71] He had experienced the lack of confidence Italy's liberals had had in their own parliamentary institutions, and their willingness to share power with Fascism at the start of his rule.[72] He would have observed how many foreign commentators, including those with no particular sympathy for Fascism, attributed his regime's rise to Italy's loss of confidence in the ability of parliamentary institutions and liberal political ideas to deal with the country's ailing economy, incessant labor struggles, and mass emigration.[73]

His claim on the eve of Franklin Roosevelt's inauguration that "the Gods of liberalism" were dying seemed vindicated. Liberal Italy before the March on Rome had experienced a stunted parliamentarianism, "an affair of narrow elites" characterized by shallow social roots, great fragmentation, endemic violence, political and policy paralysis, and mass parliamentary parties that were driven by strong extraparliamentary movements. Parliament simply could not absorb and manage the deep divisions between Liberals, Socialists, and Catholics, let alone the emergent Fascist forces. At least a year before Mussolini took command in revolt against the liberal state, "whatever authority liberal parliamentarianism had once enjoyed in Italy had vanished."[74] In Germany, antisystem parties vied on roughly equal terms with Weimar's defenders from the very start of the postwar republic. They sought to bear out the wartime view of Otto Hintze, arguably German's leading early-twentieth-century international relations analyst, who had argued that "in the face of a world of enemies," it is necessary to decisively rebuff "a transformation" of political life "that would place the government in the hands of changing majorities and subject the army to corrupt parliamentary influences."[75] Like many others writing in this period, he feared that party divisions, personal dishonesty, and ideological disunity that he associated with parliamentary government would cripple the capacity to govern and make difficult but necessary decisions. All through the later years of the Weimar Republic, before Hitler ascended to power, the German Reichstag, Europe's most visible and significant democratic emblem, had begun a sharp descent into irrelevance. Article 48 of the Weimar Constitution stated, "If public security and order are seriously disturbed or endangered within the Reich, the President of the Reich may take measures necessary for their restoration," and this resulted in more than 250 suspensions of constitutional rights, mostly concerning matters of economic emergency.[76] Starting in 1930, the Reichstag met less and less often when it became impossible to find parliamentary majorities that could sustain any of the period's governments or support their lawmaking initiatives. As a result, Germany came to be ruled more and more by emergency decrees by the president that were authorized by the republic's constitution.[77]

Mussolini's view that "liberalism is preparing to close the doors of its temples," having piled "up innumerable Gordian Knots," and having failed "to cut them with the sword of the world war," also was confidently asserted in Moscow and Berlin.[78] Josef Stalin similarly identified the problem of liberal democracy as one of representing parts of a divided society in fractious and fragmented parliamentary politics. Bolshevism differed, he argued, because it united the whole country to build a radiant future. The Soviet Union, he claimed, had overcome divisions between "capitalists and workers, landlords and peasants" by instituting one-party government unconstrained by liberal rules, democratic procedures, and legislative institutions that brought social divisions to the center of the state.[79] As early as April 1920, Adolf Hitler had recorded a comparable opinion. Parliamentarianism would destroy Germany unless "one day a [man with an] iron skull shall come, with muddy boots, perhaps, but with a clear conscience and a steel fist, who will end the blathering of these [Reichstag] drawing room heroes. . . . We need a dictator who is a genius, if we wish to rise again."[80] Speaking thirteen years later as chancellor to representatives of German agriculture in early April 1933, some nine weeks after assuming power and just two weeks after the Reichstag had been stripped of its power to legislate, Hitler boasted that "the German people has been freed and released for the first time from the party views and considerations of our former representative assembly."[81]

Such beliefs and opinions were not limited to dictators and dictatorships. As Roosevelt prepared to speak, skepticism was prevalent about whether representative parliamentary democracies could cope within their liberal constitutional bounds with capitalism's utter collapse, the manifest military ambitions by the dictatorships, or international politics characterized by ultranationalist territorial demands. Hesitation, alarm, and democratic exhaustion were widespread. By the 1920s, political analysts as divergent as Germany's Carl Schmitt, then an advocate for a democracy more militant than that on offer in the Weimar Republic but also a deep skeptic about parliamentary capabilities,[82] and England's James Bryce, the strong Liberal who was dubious about the effects of mass democracy, were calling into question the qualities and the desirability of democratic legislatures to grapple with challenges of governance and legitimacy.[83] Their doubts echoed the postwar ruminations of Max Weber, who, in 1918, had projected what he thought to be the inevitable decay of national legislatures.[84]

Despite its long and relatively secure constitutional heritage, the United States could not stand apart. The panoply of anxiety was too extensive, the sense of disappointment too profound, the criticisms of liberal democracy too relentless, the defenders of democracy too plagued by doubt, and the problems of depth, difficulty, and urgency too insistent. Americans had reason to worry that their frail and undersized federal government lacked effective means to exercise global power, revive capitalism, or calm the widespread disquiet of the American people. The rise of the dictatorships along with the means they had adopted to address economic problems and rebalance international might and power revealed that familiar policies would no longer suffice.

At the start of the Roosevelt administration, Reinhold Niebuhr, America's most prominent Protestant thinker, worried that "our western society is obviously in the process of disintegration." He designated an end to the "philosophy of unqualified optimism [that] has attended the entire brief reign of modern capitalism," and he offered "the basic conviction . . . that the liberal culture of modernity is quite unable to give guidance and direction to a confused generation which faces the disintegration of a social system and the task of building a new one." Looking across the sea at Fascist ascendance and Communist assertiveness, Niebuhr agonized about the very fate of democracy, warning that "a dying social order hastens its death in the frantic effort to avoid or postpone it." He further expressed concern about how "a dying capitalism is under the necessity of abolishing or circumscribing democracy, not only to rob its foes of a weapon, but to save itself from its own anarchy."[85] The next year, William Ernest Hocking, the distinguished Harvard philosopher, declared that the time for political liberalism "has already passed," for it is "incapable of achieving social unity." Liberal democracy, he predicted, "has no future. . . . Its once negligible weaknesses have developed into menacing evils." Commenting on how, for growing numbers of people across the globe, liberal political alternatives had come to seem unfeasible or beside the point, he wrote that "present reactions against Liberalism, crude, bedeviled, and alloyed as they are, move under the necessity of an historical dialectic, so far as they tend to reassert the reality of the total interest of society." Despite rejecting how "contemporary dictatorships have taken the easy path" in seeking to gain "social unity at the cost of the individual," he nonetheless argued that such a "total interest" would have to be more fully recognized in the United States by moving toward "a more unified society, capable of using its voice and its muscles, with a sterner internal discipline and a new emotional basis."[86]

Niebuhr and his colleagues were hardly alone in voicing these concerns. It is an understatement to say that positive outcomes were not assured. The crisis of capitalism, they discerned, was a good deal more than an economic predicament, for it had produced a crisis of democratic confidence.[87] As Hans Morgenthau recalled, "the impact of economic crisis upon American consciousness was not limited to denying the ability of America to achieve its purpose; it put into question the purpose itself." Democracy, for many, seemed hollow and incapable. "Freedom there still was, but it was now experienced as a freedom to sell apples on the street. Power there still was, but it was now experienced as the meaningless gesture of casting a ballot." With democracy caught "in a drama of disillusionment and frustration," capitalism's failures remade "America in the image of Europe," and "seemed to have made a mockery of the American purpose and put an end to the American experiment itself."[88] In the period leading up to Franklin Roosevelt's inaugural, Nicholas Murray Butler, Columbia University's president, who was no stranger to ethnic quotas, which he rigidly enforced, instructed the freshman class that the dictatorships were putting forward "men of far greater intelligence, far stronger character and far more courage than the system of elections."[89] Even the relatively optimistic Lindsay Rogers, the Columbia

University political scientist, believed, in 1934, that representative institutions "must reconcile themselves to laying down general principles within the limits of which they will give executives free hands." Such "considerable revamping of the machinery of representative government [that] will come quickly is greatly to be desired." It might not, he worried, because such "crisis government in the United States is considerably more difficult than it is in European countries."[90]

During the early 1930s, these anxieties found even more widespread expression in democratic Europe, especially in the mainstay democracies of Great Britain and France. Arnold Toynbee, who wrote about the rise and fall of civilizations, cautioned that "men and women all over the world [are] seriously contemplating and frankly discussing the possibility that the Western system of society might break down and cease to work."[91] A prominent historian of ideas, F. J. C. Hearnshaw, noted that "it would seem as though autocracy were sweeping the Western world," and he "freely admitted," despite his own strong democratic orientation, "that Italy under Mussolini's rule has enjoyed a distinctly more efficient régime than that of the corrupt and incompetent democracy which it superseded."[92]

Out of phase with the historical moment, the capacities of the era's democratic governments thus seemed vastly inferior to the instruments of mass mobilization and problem solving that the dictatorships had fashioned. Claiming the ability to liberate humankind from profound crises and deep traps by comprehending the tides of history, those antiliberal governments fashioned support and created complicity, drew an absolute distinction between friends and foes, and did not shrink from redemptive violence and targeted hatred. They, not the West's democracies, it seemed, had seized a future, one that was starkly symbolized by Balbo's squadron of planes that crossed the world.

The pressures on all the democracies, including that of the United States, were intense. Writing in 1932 about "the breakdown of the old order," "the immediate economic and social needs of labor," and "the exploitation of the farmers," the economist and future U.S. senator Paul Douglas exhorted fellow advocates of peaceful and democratic change that all had not yet been lost. "If enough men and women become filled with this spirit, then the future will not belong to the Mussolinis, the Lenins, or to the plutocracy." But he thought he was pushing against the odds. "And if ultimate failure is, nevertheless, the result, there will still be the joy of going down under a worthy flag. Happily," he concluded, "I do not believe that such need be the fate of our democracy. If men will but organize and act intelligently, we can still obtain social change without catastrophe. But we do not have much time to lose."[93]

The crisis of liberal democracy in Europe, Latin America, and East Asia, in short, generated widespread apprehension about democratic incapacity as Franklin Roosevelt was about to assume the presidency. As he and the country faced a night sky illuminated by barbarism in early 1933, they confronted confounding and pressing uncertainties. Could the political system meet its most urgent tests without suspending its rules? Might it be necessary to fashion a crisis government and transcend the limitations of ordinary procedures in order to confront the economic crisis, respond to the dictators, and rescue the system? Unless these questions could find persuasive answers, there might indeed be a great deal more to fear than fear itself.

III.

A s THE presidential limousine transported Herbert Hoover and Franklin Roosevelt from the White House to the Capitol on March 4, 1933, they must have wondered whether the economic desolation, social malaise, and political disappointment caused by the Great Depression might undermine America's democracy unless the country's traditional constitutional balance could be adjusted.

During the interregnum between the presidential election in November and this March Inauguration Day, a jarring, even incendiary, debate had been waged about the need for emergency government to overcome democracy's greatest source of weakness, legislative power. From abroad, German, Italian, and Soviet leaders were claiming to have found effective means to direct economic growth, eliminate class conflict, build global might, and preserve national security. Worried that Congress would be unable to cope with these challenges, some of the country's leading intellectuals and journalists advocated a new presidency, with a decidedly more elastic Constitution. Unlike the dictatorships that had abolished meaningful legislative institutions, the government of the United States, they thought, was hampered by the requirement that policies could pass into law only through open, and often divisive, legislative politics. At issue was not whether the United States would permanently lose its democracy but whether, faced with grave dangers, it would have to undergo a period of emergency rule, a constitutional dictatorship in which uncommon powers would be delegated from Congress to the president and the executive branch.[94]

Writing a series of widely noted articles for *The New Republic* under the rubric of "A New Deal for America," the economist Stuart Chase offered "a survey for a third road" between violent Fascist or Communist revolution, whose "road . . . is blocked," and a "business dictatorship" whose "road . . . has mud holes and soft shoulders." He called for a "third and last road," a path that "may entail a temporary dictatorship," though one that "will not tear up customs, traditions and behavior patterns to any such extent as promised by either the Red or the Black dictatorship."[95]

Walter Lippmann was no less vocal. At the start of 1933, the popular historian James Truslow Adams identified Lippmann, then in his mid-forties, as "one of the most potent political forces in the nation," the one truly national voice that had emerged since the war.[96] Lippmann's widely respected syndicated column in the *New York Herald Tribune* offered a combination of learning, incisiveness, and detachment.[97] With President Hoover's term ending, the Great Depression exacting an expanding toll, and fears of endless economic catastrophe becoming widespread, Lippmann worried that Congress could not govern effectively or quickly in the emergency.

The "situation," he wrote, "requires strong medicine." In advocating a grant of "extraordinary powers" to the incoming president, he insisted that "the danger we have to fear is not that Congress will give Franklin D. Roosevelt too much power, but that it will deny him the power he needs. The danger is not that we shall lose our liberties, but that we shall not be able to act with the necessary speed and comprehensiveness." Extraordinary authority, he proposed, should give the president, "for a period say of a year, the widest and fullest powers under the most liberal interpretation of the Constitution." Concurrently, Congress should "suspend temporarily the rule of both houses, to limit drastically the right of amendment and debate, to put the majority in both houses under the decisions of a caucus." This supersession of normal politics, he concluded, "is the necessary thing to do. If the American nation desires action and results, this is the way to get them."[98] Lippmann directed the same advice to his good friend, the president-elect.

During a February 1 visit to Warm Springs, Georgia, he counseled how "the situation is critical, Franklin. You may have no alternative but to assume dictatorial powers."[99]

Lippmann did not have Rome or Berlin, let alone Moscow, in mind. Rather, he was arguing that the need for democratic protection required a temporary violation of normal constitutional procedures, much as James Madison had written in The *Federalist Papers* about how "constitutional barriers" are not relevant when faced with the "spirit of self-preservation."[100] The imperatives of the day, Lippmann asserted, required the president and his executive to have the ability to act swiftly with prompt discretion in the present emergency without being constrained by the usual checks and balances. He thus wanted the Constitution's ambiguous language about presidential power—including its vesting in the president "the executive power of the United States," giving him responsibility for taking care "that the laws be faithfully executed," and declaring him "Commander-in Chief"—to be interpreted expansively, treating the economic emergency as a wartime situation. Congress, Lippmann hoped, would authorize and thus legitimate a soft dictatorship in which the new president, on the model of Abraham Lincoln, could be what Lord Bryce had designated as "almost a dictator."[101] The president would not seize power, but have it conferred on him, based on an uncommonly expansive reading of the Constitution of the United States.

There were competing voices. "Do We Need a Dictator?" *The Nation*'s lead editorial inquired during inauguration week. The magazine's answer, though quite different from Lippmann's, signaled deep apprehension about the future balance of executive and legislative capacity. "Emphatically not! Nothing in the existing situation, grave, critical, and menacing as it is, warrants the overthrow of our system of government." However "stupid and frightened" Congress might be, the editors cautioned, "if we muzzle Congress, muzzles for the rest of us will come as a matter of course, particularly if the emergency becomes more critical."[102] Such palpable anxiety was not confined to the left-of-center niche occupied by *The Nation*. At the close of the 1932 campaign, on October 31, President Herbert Hoover warned a mass rally in New York's Madison Square Garden that a Roosevelt-led New Deal threatened to concentrate power in the presidency and thus "break down the dikes of American freedom" based on "the Trojan Horse of emergency."[103]

IV.

O NE OF only a small number of Jewish students at Harvard, Lippmann had entered the university just months after his most important teacher, William James, the great pragmatist philosopher and psychologist, and older brother of the novelist Henry James, had returned from a visiting professorship at Stanford. James's stay had been cut short by the great earthquake of April 18, 1906, which leveled much of nearby San Francisco and destroyed a good deal of the Palo Alto campus. In February, James had addressed a well-attended Stanford assembly on the topic "The Moral Equivalent of War."[104] The globe, he worried, even in 1906, might soon be galvanized by a "fear regime." Warfare, he presciently projected, would shortly be revered as "a sort of sacrament" in which "whole nations are the armies." The world, he thus argued, was in desperate need to discover a peaceful alternative based on civic honor and collective discipline. As it turned out, these were the very ideas Franklin Roosevelt would invoke immediately upon taking the oath of office.

Unlike Lippmann, whom he preceded at Harvard by six years, and unlike his cousin Theodore, FDR never studied with William James. But like most undergraduates at Harvard, and especially as editor of the *Harvard Crimson,* he must have been aware of James's views and high standing as one of the country's most luminous scholars, and might well have heard discussion about the 1901–1902 Gifford Lectures, *The Varieties of Religious Experience,* when James first called for a moral equivalent of war.[105]

The ideas and language of William James resonated in President Roosevelt's inaugural address. Suffused with Jamesian language, it reverberated with military similes. Preaching "the clear consciousness of seeking old and precious moral values," President Roosevelt identified "the clean satisfaction that comes from the stern performance of duty by old and young alike," and exhorted Americans on behalf of "the warm courage of national unity."[106] Assuming "unhesitantly the leadership of this great army of our people dedicated to a disciplined attack upon our common problems," the country's new leader called on his fellow citizens to "move as a trained and loyal army willing to sacrifice for the good of a common discipline, because without such discipline no progress is made, no leadership becomes effective." Concerned with the current crisis, Roosevelt affirmed a Jamesian quest for warfare's equivalent. "We are, I know, ready and willing to submit our lives and property to such discipline, because it makes possible a leadership which aims at a larger good. This I propose to offer, pledging that the larger purposes will bind upon us all as a sacred obligation with a unity of duty hitherto evoked only in time of armed strife."

The new president and his audience knew the stakes. Could constitutional democracy endure "when confronted with an emergency that has the potential to undermine the democracy itself"?[107] He went on to voice confidence that it would be possible to find a way within the Constitution of the United States to respond effectively.[108] "Our Constitution is so simple and practical," he reassured with a high degree of ambiguity, "that it is possible always to meet extraordinary needs by changes in emphasis and arrangement without loss of essential form."

But with what "changes in emphasis and arrangement"? In grim and testing conditions, how much adjustment, and of what kind, might be necessary? To what extent must a belief in the values of democracy respond to "the demands of the hour ... even at the risk and cost of violating fundamental principles"?[109] To what extent would emergency powers and procedures be required for the essentially conservative purpose of protecting the legitimacy and effectiveness of democratic government?[110] Having drawn a parallel between economic and military emergencies, and having identified his own position as that of commander, the president identified his constitutionally authorized powers as broadly as possible while staying inside the document's formal stipulated scope.[111] Would he seek to find a space to act lawfully beyond that authorized by congressional lawmaking? If so, how broad and how durable would this zone be?

Flirting with Walter Lippmann's extraconstitutional proposals, the president voiced misgivings about the ability of Congress to cope within traditional bounds. Speaking in terms both portentous and measured, Roosevelt ominously cautioned how "it may be that an unprecedented demand and need for undelayed action may call for temporary departure from that normal balance of public procedure." Should Congress not act promptly and decisively, he warned, "I shall not evade the clear course of duty that will then confront me. I shall ask the Congress for the one remaining instrument to meet the crisis—broad Executive power to wage a war against the emergency, as great as the power that would be given to me if we were in fact invaded by a foreign foe." He also spoke of how, at the last election, the American people had conferred "a mandate that they want direct, vigorous action. They have asked for discipline and direction under leadership. They have made me the instrument of their wishes. In the spirit of the gift, I take it."

The phrase "as great as the power that would be given to me if we were in fact invaded by a foreign foe" was no mere abstraction. When the new president indicated he would ask Congress for such powers, he evoked the near-term history of World War I. Franklin Roosevelt had been at hand, of course, in Washington during the war as assistant secretary of the navy, with regular access to the cabinet, the armed forces, and the president. With the war not a remote historical event but present in popular and elite historical memory, FDR would have recalled the 1917 Espionage Act, which mandated sentences up to twenty years for individuals who encouraged "disloyalty" in wartime, as well as the 1918 Alien Act, which authorized Washington to deport members of anarchist organizations. The same year, a Sedition Act made it illegal to use "disloyal, profane, scurrilous, or abusive language" about the flag, the armed forces, and the country during the war. He also would have remembered that era's unprecedented congressional delegations of economic power, constituting what the political scientist Lindsay Rogers identified at war's end as a history of "presidential dictatorship."[112]

With Franklin Roosevelt invoking the prospect of wartime powers, the *New York Times* ran a banner headline that prophesied what Roosevelt would do: WILL ASK WAR-TIME POWERS IF NEEDED. The paper's chief political correspondent, James A. Hagerty,[113] reported that "there seemed to be a general opinion that Congress would grant him this power if it should become necessary," and observed that this proposal had been greeted favorably by members and leaders of Congress of both parties.[114]

To be sure, as the historian Frank Freidel has commented, the inaugural's "strong words . . . bespoke no intent on the part of Roosevelt to assume the role of a Mussolini or Hitler,"[115] but his claim to embody a singular popular will, coupled to his suggestion that the legislative branch might be surpassed or displaced, did seem to announce a willingness to convene an emergency and extraconstitutional government that would dodge the federal government's traditional separation of powers. At this opening moment of the New Deal, even the president was intimating that American liberal democracy, with Congress at its center, might falter, or at least require a substantial, if only provisional, modification to the distinction between legislative and executive power.[116]

As the New Deal's early months unfolded, many, including Roosevelt supporters, thought that Lippmann's arguments had won the day. Writing for the *New York Times* at the start of May, the superb, rare woman journalist Anne O'Hare McCormick described "the atmosphere" in Washington as "strangely reminiscent of Rome in the first weeks after the march of the Blackshirts, or Moscow at the beginning of the Five Year Plan." The American people, she observed, "trust the discretion of the President more than they trust Congress." Rather than a seizure of power of the kind that had brought the Bolsheviks or the Italian Fascists to power, the New Deal, she reported, rested on mass popular consent that "vests the president with the authority of a dictator. The authority is a free gift, a sort of unanimous power of attorney. . . . all the other powers—industry, commerce, finance, labor, farmer and householder, State and city—virtually abdicate in his favor. America today literally asks for orders. . . . Nobody is much disturbed by the idea of dictatorship."[117]

Looking back on those months from the vantage of Harry Truman's presidency, the political scientist Clinton Rossiter recalled how Roosevelt had launched "an unvarnished crisis government" that shifted many powers from Congress to the White House. The run on the banks the very day of his address put the private banking structure of the country at risk, threatening an even greater economic catastrophe. Two days later, referring to the national emergency, the president proclaimed a bank holiday, stopped transactions in foreign exchange, and forbade the exporting of silver and gold, all without explicit congressional authorization, basing his authority on the dubious claim that it was sanctioned by the Trading with the Enemy Act of 1917, which had long been considered defunct in peacetime. Only three days later, with the Emergency Banking Act, did the House and Senate ratify what he had done.[118]

In all, the emergency legislation that Congress enacted in the administration's Hundred Days was marked by three unprecedented features. First, it was almost entirely drafted, in detail, by the executive branch. The Emergency Banking Act, the Economy Act, and the Unemployment Relief Act of March; the Agricultural Adjustment Act, the Emergency Farm Mortgage Act, and the Federal Emergency Relief Act of May; and the Home Owners

Loan Act, the Farm Credit Act, the Emergency Railroad Transportation Act, and the National Industrial Recovery Act of June were passed virtually unchanged from the texts the president had sent to the Hill. In this sense, the president seemed more like a prime minister than a traditional American president.[119]

Second, while the form of lawmaking was preserved, and no formal institutional rules were violated, the legislative process was pushed forward in a highly abbreviated way. Debate was cut short, limited for the eleven most significant statutes to under four hours. Amendments from the floor were barred unless they had been approved by a congressional committee.[120]

Third, these measures were characterized by immense powers delegated from the legislature to the executive branch that dramatically expanded the powers of federal agencies, many of which were new. To be sure, this assignment of authority stopped well short of the German Enabling Act. The president and his cabinet did not issue or make laws, but the presidency, as we will see when we consider this era's radical moment, did gain extraordinary discretion under very broad and often not very well-specified emergency legislation.[121]

Notwithstanding these features of the early months of the New Deal, it would be a mistake to conclude that Walter Lippmann won the argument. This initial phase proved ephemeral, and the manner in which lawmaking proceeded soon largely returned to preemergency conditions. To be sure, delegation by Congress to the president and the executive branch and a greatly extended public administration became enduring features of the federal government.[122] These changes, which rapidly advanced in the opening months of the New Deal, did have long-term implications for the content and form of the country's democracy. But crucially, Congress not only reasserted its lawmaking prerogatives; it also developed enhanced means to control the growing administrative system of the federal government, at least in domestic affairs.

In fact, the process Lippmann had advocated came closest to fruition only at the very beginning of the Hundred Days, when the Banking Act conferred blanket powers, resembling those of wartime circumstances. But as an overall portrayal, the idea that Congress acted as if an Enabling Act had been passed is a vast exaggeration. Ironically, the most extensive legislative grant of executive power gave Roosevelt the power to cut the size of the federal government as he saw fit, not enlarge it. More broadly, FDR did not compel Congress to legislate. Rather, he persuaded members to pass his emergency program, and often he had to compromise, as he did to secure the Farm Act and in accepting a vast program of public works that he did not want.[123] Speaking by radio in his second fireside chat on May 7, 1933, President Roosevelt explicitly sought to reassure the public in just these terms by stressing how, in passing the laws he had recommended, there had been "no actual surrender of power. Congress," he underscored, "still retained its constitutional authority and no one has the slightest desire to change the balance of these powers."[124]

Still, in placing the recovery program almost entirely in the president's hands, Congress did flirt with what might be thought of as a functional Enabling Act. But flirt though it did, the institution also did not cross the line. Congress kept, and increasingly asserted, its legislative prerogatives. Even during the Hundred Days, the legislature dealt with the economic emergency through ordinary legislation, however novel and far-reaching, rather than by yielding lawmaking to the executive branch or declaring a state of exception. After the Hundred Days, congressional forms of dispute, debate, and decision survived and thrived. Intense differences of view about the proper role for government and the character of good public policy were located inside the institution, which the full range of perspectives and political actors respected as the legitimate place for decisions to be made. Congress thus was not a casualty of the country's crises, but an instrument that sought to overcome them. Even the nineteenth-century ideal of a deliberate legislature where lawmakers sought to persuade one another by rational argument did not entirely disappear.[125] Nor was there a lapse into dictatorship. Even when the New Deal governed at the beginning almost as an emergency government, this was not a dictatorship anything like the real thing. Rights were not suppressed, and the legislature did not abdicate.[126] In all, the central place of Congress was maintained. Even more, the crucial lawmaking role that it undertook offered a practical answer to critics who thought the days of legislative institutions had passed.

America's separation of powers and democratic lawmaking as core features of the rule of law persisted. This was a notable, even extraordinary, attainment. The New Deal managed, as a leading political scientist put the point in 1940 in Homeric terms, to "sail a precarious passage between the

Scylla of sufficient power to solve a temporary but severe crisis and the Charybdis of this power becoming unrestrained and permanent."[127] It did so not by extreme constitutional measures, but by pioneering "a new model of emergency powers—the legislative model . . . [that] handles emergencies by enacting ordinary statutes that delegate special and temporary powers to the executive."[128]

From this perspective, the New Deal can be understood as a period of democratic learning and adjustment. Though similar in some ways to paths traveled elsewhere, the New Deal's course was different. While there were family resemblances to features of governance pursued by the period's dictatorships, there was not an identity. Constitutional democracy was sustained, if bruised, in the world's most long-lived liberal regime, with the legislative authority of Congress intact. Executive and legislative powers remained separate and divided. During the 1930s, as it responded to economic predicaments and offered many institutional inventions, the national government did not create an emergency regime side by side with the normal separation of powers system, even though it seemed, certainly at the start, that this departure from constitutional procedures might be necessary.

During the Roosevelt and Truman years, Washington successfully wrestled with the problem of how to find a durable and democratic role for Congress in the face of crises characterized by fear and an urgent need for action. The breakdown of so many democracies between the two world wars was marked by the failure to find productive answers to this challenge. Indeed, the very triumphant assertiveness of the dictatorships was rooted in their rejection of the need to find an answer, since they totally discarded the eighteenth- and nineteenth-century liberal idea of a separation of powers and promoted the utter collapse of a parliamentary system. The United States, by contrast, stood for the ways in which American democracy secured the capacities of Congress to make laws and oversee their consequences. Congress did not become obsolete or irrelevant. It was not an anachronism. To the contrary, it kept and utilized the authority that liberal principles and democratic practices required that it not cede to others.

During the administrations of Roosevelt and Truman, Congress firmly established itself as a forum where detailed answers could be crafted to the main substantive challenges of a historically dense and difficult era. The institution's historical legislative functions were guarded zealously and in some respects expanded, often to the frustration of the epoch's two presidents. Here, then, a course many thought not possible was pursued. It was the attempt to reconcile political representation, the cornerstone principle of liberal democracy, with the requirements of government in complex and frightful times. In that painful and uneven process, the legislature was recast and reinvigorated as a site of decision and governance. This achievement should not be underestimated.

V.

N OR, HOWEVER, should the vital role played by powers and preferences of the South's congressional members. These were representatives with a difference.

No member of Congress at any time during the full New Deal era would have thought that the South did not comprise a discrete and coherent entity. Like that of other Democrats, the patronage, influence, and seniority of southern members depended on these members securing their party's majority status. But as guardians of their region's racial order, they assessed New Deal policies for compatibility with organized white supremacy.

Of course, southern members shared other interests. Mainly representing agriculture, they favored programs that would help specific crops: cotton, rice, and tobacco. They promoted free trade so that they could sell these crops and import low-cost machines and finished goods. With destitution more acute in the South than anywhere else in the country, they also sought to relieve agrarian and urban poverty. They largely approved robust federal spending and expansive fiscal policies. During the late nineteenth and early twentieth centuries, what the historian C. Vann Woodward called a "paradoxical combination of white supremacy and progressivism" characterized the dominant strain of southern politics. This view identified the railroads, the banks, the utilities, and other northern-controlled capitalist firms as targets for regulation and reform.[129] Operating in a mainly rural environment characterized by dispersed and isolated communities, southern representatives promoted administrative modernization, infrastructural development, and social policies to deal with the region's hardships.[130]

But these and other policy stances were all filtered by one common concern, "the real basis for southern unity, the Negro," as V. O. Key Jr.'s landmark *Southern Politics in State and Nation* put the point in 1949. Distinguished by a fervent commitment to make racial arrangements safe, "the one-party system of the South," Key observed, "is an institution with an odd dual personality. In state politics the Democratic party is no party at all but a multiplicity of factions struggling for office. In national politics, on the contrary, the party is the Solid South; it is, or at least has been, the instrument for the conduct of the 'foreign relations' of the South with the rest of the nation."[131] This was the basis on which the white South fought so vehemently to preserve the region's system of white hegemony and fight against what they considered to be federal intrusion ever since the end of Reconstruction.

To be sure, the politicians advanced by the single-party South covered quite a range. Personal styles ran the full gamut from the cautious and cerebral (figures like Alabama senator Lister Hill, Georgia senator Richard Russell, and Arkansas senator William Fulbright) to the impulsive and flamboyant (characters like Louisiana's senator Huey Long as well as Mississippi's Theodore Bilbo). They also did not share identical views about the full range of public policies, including those that concerned budgets and the desirable degree of federal economic regulation. In Congress, though, such differences did not so much disappear as enfold within a shared dedication to protect southern autonomy. Refusing to acknowledge any incompatibility between the system of segregation and wider American values and visions, they sought to legislate without having to choose among their valued objectives.

Washington's responses to the era's challenges were shaped in fundamental ways by how the representatives selected from within this region chose to legislate. Without their leadership, legislative experience, and votes, the New Deal's efforts to secure American democracy and resist the globe's dictatorships would not have happened. With southern support, liberal democracy could be redeemed, but only along a pathway constituted in critical respects by organized racism.

Like other members of Congress, southern representatives understood the pressing need to confront the central challenges of the time. They, too, grappled with how to remake capitalism and deal with issues of global power. Over the course of the New Deal, we will observe, these representatives frequently were the pivotal members of winning coalitions in the House and Senate, thus in a position to choose which solutions should form the basis for public policy.

Without southern votes, successful lawmaking that falsified claims about the incapacity of liberal democracy could not have happened, and American constitutional democracy would have stuttered. With the South's active legislative participation, the New Deal produced results that otherwise would have been different. With their votes, a new American state was created.

KEEP POOLESV.
WHITE
INTEGRATION
IS
UNCHRISTIAN
STOP
INTEGRATIO
KEEP POOL
WHIT
INTEGRATION
IS
LEGAL"
PUT ME "DOWN
AS "NO"
"NIGGER-LOVER"
INTEGRATION
IS
"COMMUNISM"

PART II

SOUTHERN CAGE

4 ⬖ American with a Difference

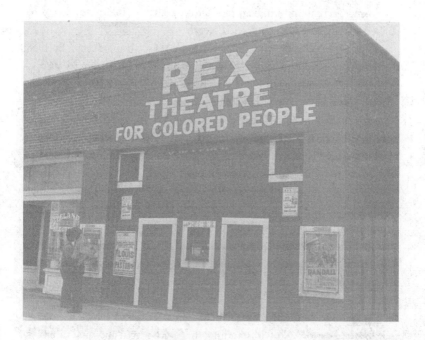

S IX EXTRAORDINARY PARAGRAPHS sit in the midst of an uncommonly turgid address delivered by William Howard Taft as he took the oath of office on March 4, 1909, a dozen years after the Supreme Court, in *Plessy v. Ferguson,* had sanctioned the South's laws requiring racial segregation in public facilities, and twenty-four years to the day before Franklin Roosevelt would become president. The contents are striking. Taft proclaimed that the Republican Party—the party of Lincoln, of Emancipation, of the Thirteenth, Fourteenth, and Fifteenth Amendments, and of Reconstruction—would no longer champion the cause of black rights. "It is not the disposition or within the province of the Federal Government," Taft declared, "to interfere with the regulation by Southern States of their domestic affairs."

As he was assuming the presidency, the South was crafting a distinctive racial order suffused with beliefs and practices signifying white dominance and black inferiority in all spheres of life. Shielded by law and underpinned by violence, actual and implicit, Jim Crow applied an inferior and circumscribed status to every person coded Negro.

Politics served as an instrument to secure these arrangements. By 1908, the South had perfected a political system to guard white supremacy successfully even in counties with black majorities. A host of mechanisms ensured virtually no chance to vote for African-Americans, and a low-turnout franchise for white citizens.[1] These devices included white primaries, declarations that political parties were restricted private clubs, poll taxes, property tests, literacy tests, and understanding clauses that tested for arcane knowledge of the provisions in state constitutions.[2]

To be sure, race suffused the expectations and possibilities of whites and blacks across the country. The majority of whites outside the South, it is important to note, betrayed no particular passion for the cause of racial equality. Most opposed living with black neighbors, working with them as colleagues, or sending their children to integrated schools. Summarizing an early-twentieth-century tour of the South, the journalist Ray Stannard Baker accurately reported for *The American Magazine* that "the attitude of the North," like the South, "did not believe in a democracy which had a place in it for the Negro."[3] Notwithstanding, the South's rigid and total racial system did set the region apart. There, the tension that marked the relationship between racial inequality and the country's rights-based political system based on free citizenship—an association that had vexed the American republic from its first days—was more insistent and most acute.

In the conclusion of *Yankee Leviathan,* his magisterial treatment of how a modern American nation-state emerged from the carnage of the Civil War, the political scientist Richard Bensel reminded us that "the United States in the late nineteenth century was really two nations joined together by force of arms."[4] It was this division that President Taft declared to have finally come to an end. "There was a time," Taft noted, "when Northerners who sympathized with the negro in his necessary struggle for better conditions sought to give him the suffrage as a protection to enforce its exercise against the prevailing sentiment of the South." No longer. That "movement proved to be a failure." Consistent with the Fifteenth Amendment's "attempt to secure the negro against any deprivation of the privilege to vote because he was a negro," he argued, the South had succeeded in finding means to protect itself against "the domination of an ignorant, irresponsible element" by enacting "laws which shall exclude from voting both negroes and whites not having education or other qualifications thought necessary. The danger of the control of an ignorant electorate has therefore passed." Leaving the South to its own devices, moreover, would reconcile whites to the Union and increase "feeling on the part of all the people in the South that this Government is their Government, and that its officers in their states are their officers."

"The negroes," Taft continued, "are now Americans." With citizenship, "this is their only country, and their only flag." Yet there was an unmistakable division between the "we" who were political actors and the "they" who were not. "We are charged with the sacred duty of making their path as smooth and easy as we can." Carrying out this trust, he counseled, required caution, as "race feeling is so widespread and acute." The government must practice restraint in appointing blacks to federal offices lest "the recurrence and increase of race feeling which such an appointment is likely to engender" outweigh the "encouragement to the race." More broadly, Taft advised against any move that would diminish the prospects for the further development of "the already good feeling between the South and the other sections of the country."[5]

This declaration of federal inaction initiated a period, lasting well into the New Deal, when the federal government took a hands-off stance with respect to southern race relations. Other than their ability, sporadic at best, to move northward, southern blacks found themselves without power, trapped in a system of organized fear and humiliation, and faced no realistic prospect that Washington would act to underwrite or enforce their status as citizens of the United States.[6]

I.

WHEN FRANKLIN ROOSEVELT spoke in March 1933 of the need to overcome fear itself, the South was still highly distinctive, having been protected by a quarter century of willful federal inaction. A combination of tradition, demography, and anxiety continued to place the race question at that region's social, economic, and political center in a manner not present anywhere else, especially as the great majority of African-Americans who still lived in the region were compelled by custom and law to experience a rigid and circumscribed status.

As the New Deal drama began, the Mason-Dixon Line presented a real boundary. This frontier resembled the border that Alexis de Tocqueville had distinguished when he had visited the United States a century earlier. On January 4, 1832, he had set out, with Gustave de Beaumont, on a stage-coach route through the Deep South, which he called the "Midi," echoing the common term for southern France. Covering a thousand miles in twelve days, he discovered an America deeply divided by the geography of slavery.[7] Tocqueville wrote:

> On both banks of the Ohio stretched undulating ground with soil continually offering the cultivator inexhaustible treasures; on both banks the air is equally healthy and the climate temperate; they both form the frontier of a vast state: that which follows the innumerable windings of the Ohio on the left bank is called Kentucky; the other takes its name from the river itself. There is only one difference between the two states: Kentucky allows slaves, but Ohio refuses to have them.[8]

When the southern historian Ulrich Phillips searched, in the late 1920s, for "the central theme of southern history," he was drawn, like Tocqueville, to the banks of the Ohio River. "The northern shore," Phillips wrote, "is American without question; the southern is American with a difference."[9] It was that difference, we will see, that powerfully shaped not just whether but also how the New Deal grappled with fear itself.

A century after Tocqueville published *Democracy in America,* a still-distinct geography, marked not by slavery but by Jim Crow, took hold in Alabama, Arkansas, Delaware, Florida, Georgia, Kentucky, Louisiana, Maryland, Mississippi, Missouri, North Carolina, Oklahoma, South Carolina, Tennessee, Texas, Virginia, and West Virginia.[10] Fifteen of these states had practiced chattel slavery on the eve of the Civil War. These, plus West Virginia, which then was part of Virginia, and Oklahoma, which achieved statehood only in 1907, all required racial segregation, until it was outlawed

outlawed in

in public schools by the 1954 *Brown* decision. Furthermore, these states prohibited interracial marriage as late as 1967, the year the Court ruled such bans to be unconstitutional in *Loving v. Virginia*.[11]

In the 1830s, Tocqueville had already emphasized the baneful effects of slavery on economic and social life. He had told how "the traveler who lets the current carry him down the Ohio till it joins the Mississippi sails, so to say, between freedom and slavery; and he has only to glance around to see instantly which is best for mankind." That person would see that in Kentucky, "on the left of the river the population is sparse; from time to time one sees a troop of slaves loitering through half-deserted fields; the primeval forest is constantly reappearing; one might say that society had gone to sleep; it is nature that seems active and alive, whereas man is idle." But in Ohio, "on the right bank a confused hum proclaims from afar that men are busily at work; fine crops cover the fields; elegant dwellings testify to the taste and industry of the workers; on all sides there is evidence of comfort; man appears rich and contented; he works."[12]

Professor Phillips famously devoted his career to proving Tocqueville wrong. The slave South, he argued, had not been a land of industrial slackness. As efficient, profit-seeking economic units, plantations had resembled other American firms and enterprises.[13] The South also was not "a political entity with boundaries clearly marked by treaty, constitution, or law."[14] If not its economy or its formal political frontiers, what, Phillips asked, made the South stand apart? How, then, was it American, but with a difference?

The answer, he argued, was the South's commitment to white supremacy, the region's single nonnegotiable value, the reason it was "a land of unity."[15] Decades after Reconstruction, the South made no particular sense as a coherent unit without this connecting tissue.[16] From Delaware to Florida, from South Carolina to Oklahoma, "white folk [are] a people with a common resolve indomitably maintained—that it shall be and remain a white man's country." This, Phillips approvingly concluded, was both "the cardinal test of a Southerner" and "the central theme of Southern history," whether "expressed with the frenzy of a demagogue or maintained with a patrician's quietude."[17]

During the years Presidents Roosevelt and Truman governed, it would have been hard to find a contrary view. Phillips was hardly a racial moderate, and more fixed in his views than many leading intellectuals. But his outlook expressed the era's common sense across the ideological and racial spectrum. This, for example, is how Ralph Bunche, the most important African-American member of the team that produced Gunnar Myrdal's influential study, *An American Dilemma*,[18] defined southern distinctiveness at the start of the 1940s. Writing an extended report about the political status of the period's blacks, Bunche took note of the region's great heterogeneity, "except in its traditional adherence to the doctrine of white supremacy ... and to the political derivative of that doctrine—a blind allegiance to the one party system."[19]

When the New Deal was getting under way, the director of the University of North Carolina Press, W. T. Couch, who took care to publish some African-American writers and offered a home to the South's liberal regional studies movement centered in his university, similarly summarized white southern racial views:

> There is no question as to what the dominant opinion is. It holds that the Negro is inferior to the white man, and shades all the way from the prevailing opinion of two centuries as given in the Dred Scott Decision to the less extreme opinion that the Negro, while inferior, nevertheless has some rights and should be encouraged to develop a culture parallel to and dependent on that of whites.[20]

A decade later, his press published *What the Negro Wants?*—a collection of essays edited by the African-American historian Rayford Logan and written by leading black intellectuals and activists, including W. E. B. Du Bois, Langston Hughes, A. Philip Randolph, and Roy Wilkins. Couch, who had commissioned the book, felt compelled to write a defensive publisher's introduction to answer the demands Logan and his colleagues had put for an end to segregation and "an equal share not only in the performance of responsibilities and obligations, but also in enjoyment of rights and opportunities" in voting, legal standing, employment, schooling, housing, and social security.[21] Broadly, they endorsed the position that had been articulated by the polymath African-American author James Weldon Johnson, in 1935, when he had charted a course for blacks to become "an integral part of the nation." Johnson had counseled blacks to gain strength and experience from "the system of imposed segregation," but to "use that experience and strength steadily and as rapidly as possible to destroy the system."[22] Effectively speaking not only for himself but for his press and university, Couch strongly demurred. After awkwardly thanking the book's contributors, he announced, "I disagree with the editor and most of the contributors on basic problems."[23]

Like many southern moderates, Couch rejected biological reasoning about black inferiority. Equally, he repudiated the idea that recently had been articulated by Myrdal's study, whose central theme Couch summarized as "the view that the Negro is not inferior to the white man, that he only appears to be so, that his condition is wholly and completely a product of race prejudice, and the consequent disabilities inflicted on the Negro by the white man." Rather, citing Abraham Lincoln's Peoria speech of October 16, 1854, which assailed slavery but rejected black equality ("What next? Free them, and make them politically and socially our equals? My own feelings will not admit of this"), Couch endorsed a third position, "the theory that the Negro's condition is produced by inferiority, but that this inferiority can be overcome, and the prejudice resulting from it can be cured." He cautioned, however, that efforts at Negro development "must not be done in such manner as to weaken the barrier between the races."[24]

Later in the decade, an influential book urged southerners to bolt from the Democratic Party because it had become an uncontrollable instrument for something worse. The Alabama lawyer and archsegregationist Charles Wallace Collins, like Phillips, proudly underscored in 1947 how the South was not like any other part of the country. There, "the doctrine of white supremacy is akin to a religious belief. . . . It is rooted in the very fiber of the southern soul." Collins was not a fringe crank. Until 1927, he had served in major posts in Washington, including librarian of the Supreme Court, law librarian for Congress, and general counsel for both the Bureau of the Budget and Office of the Comptroller of the Currency. He went on to become a leading figure in the Bank of America, and served as special counsel for the American Bankers Association. One purpose of *Whither Solid South?* was to analyze the capacity of what he identified as the South's "three bars across the path of those Negroes whose aspirations embrace the entry into every phase of American society." These he named the bar of blood, the bar of suffrage, and the bar of segregation.[25]

The first, the barrier of blood,[26] was widely shared across the United States. As an indicator, Collins noted how the Red Cross distinguished white

Bar of Blood

from black blood everywhere, on the understanding that white Americans, irrespective of region, would object to being given black blood, despite the absence of any chemical difference. Although such racism was national, the bar of blood, he stressed, was not as universal or as absolute as it was inside the South. By contrast, "its full pattern . . . which flows from the doctrine of white supremacy . . . is set only in the South where the mass of Negroes reside and where the white population is predominantly of British descent with hardly a trace of foreign born." There, he was pleased to indicate, "white supremacy . . . is taken for granted and is not open to debate." In the South, "white supremacy is a political doctrine. It is not a question of scientific proof."[27]

Bar of Suffrage

If ideas and practices related to the meaning of race were not confined to the South, the other two barriers blacks confronted were, Collins wrote, unique to that region. The bar of suffrage followed from an absolute commitment to white supremacy, for "inherent in that doctrine" is "the principle that the Negro shall have no part in governing the white people." The restricted franchise was the region's most important political defense, for black voting promised a return to the dreaded conditions of Reconstruction. "If the Negro in the South were admitted to the polls simply on the qualifications of citizenship, age, residence, and sound mind, as many now advocate, he would gain political control over the richest agricultural regions of the Deep South—the lands of the old Cotton Kingdom . . . In States like Alabama, South Carolina, Mississippi, Georgia, and Louisiana, many counties would be controlled by Negroes. The county offices would fall into their hands," and, as a result, "the fate of the white people would be at the mercy of the Negroes."[28]

Bar of Segregation

The third barrier, the bar of legally required segregation, did not mean that blacks and whites lived entirely separate lives. After all, they were in daily contact, especially in urban and rural workplaces. What formalized segregation intended, rather, Collins acutely observed, was to make it certain "that the Negro could not aspire to social equality in intercourse with the whites." Segregation was imposed everywhere that racial contact might be thought to entail social equality; hence blacks and white were kept apart when they ate, played or watched sports, attended movies or theatrical events, rode buses and trains, even when they had to use a public toilet.[29]

Collins might have added a fourth barrier, one he chose not to mention—the region's pervasive climate of public and private violence, including vigilante lynching, what a historian of the Ku Klux Klan calls racist "thought in action."[30] Between 1900 and 1930, 1,886 such killings occurred in the United States. Though only nine states had none, the greatest number took place in the South—not just in Georgia (302), Mississippi (285), Texas (201), or Alabama (132) but also in Tennessee (76), Kentucky (68), and Missouri (41).[31] This form of violence was ebbing by the early 1930s, but it hardly had disappeared. The United States witnessed 28 lynchings in 1933, the first year of the New Deal. In November, one year after FDR's election, Lloyd Warner was burned alive before a cheering crowd of ten thousand in Princess Anne, Maryland, after the attempt to hang him had failed. David Gregory was lynched in Kountze, Texas, his body burned and his heart and genitals carved from his corpse. Cord Cheek of Columbia, Tennessee, was found hanging from a tree limb after a grand jury had refused to indict him for molesting an eleven-year-old white girl. Freddy Moore was killed in Assumption Parish, Louisiana, for the murder of a white girl (another man, who was white, later admitted to the killing).[32]

Moderates like W. T. Couch abhorred lynching. But this type of justice was a significant feature of the South's racial order during the early New Deal, much as it had been since the close of Reconstruction. Lynching signified both an ultimate commitment to white domination and the region's fixation on black sexuality. Even the erudite Collins, whose prose was very different from the brutal racist talk of the Klan or political figures like Theodore Bilbo, underscored the central role played in the white southern imagination by fears of racial mixing.

II.

I F LYNCHING was the least civilized means the white South used to protect its racial hegemony, electoral politics and congressional representation were perhaps the most. In the language of political science, "the critical intervening variable between agenda change and policy change is the congressional process."[33] It was just this space in the legislative process that the South commanded by virtue of its electoral system and its implications for congressional experience and seniority.

"For seventy years, the South has voted in the Negro question," Anne

O'Hare McCormick summarized in a remarkable 1930 series of articles on the South. "The Negro is its perpetual inhibition. The revenge of the slave is to place his masters in such subjection that they can make no decision, political, social, economical, or ethical, without reference to him. . . . Voteless, he dominates politics." A dozen years later, Marian Irish's study of the one-party system in the South underscored the inescapability of "the elementary determinant in the southern pattern," which she described as "an intense negro phobia which has scarcely abated since Reconstruction. . . . No issue seems more important than the exclusion of negroes from public affairs. The Solid South is white; the one-party system has been devised primarily to perpetuate the political supremacy of whites."[34]

This authoritarian and racist political system repressed groups and a diversity of views. Speaking of the last quarter of the nineteenth century, the historian Morgan Kousser noted:

> A third to a half of Southern voters had been unreconstructed oppositionists. Despite ingenious gerrymandering, a few white Republicans, Independents, Populists, and even Negroes sat in every session of every state legislature. Some non-Democrats filled congressional, gubernatorial, and senatorial seats. How much more rationalized was the South after 1900! Virtually every elected officeholder was a white Democrat.[35]

The polity they controlled was formally democratic. Even its domination by a single party did not make it a dictatorship, for the Democratic Party within the South was chaotic and anarchic, not centrally controlled or ideologically rigid. But it had powerful authoritarian tendencies and a strong exclusionary tilt. Rules designed to repress black political participation also kept white voting rates down. Poll taxes, as an example, arguably kept more poor whites from the polls than African-americans, often making "a travesty of many [southern] elections," as "political machines and individual candidates commonly buy votes by paying the poll taxes of those who will 'vote right.'" Across the country as a whole, nearly 60 percent of eligible persons voted in the 1940 presidential election. In the South, no state reached a 50 percent level. In Alabama, Georgia, Mississippi, and South Carolina turnout rates were at or below 20 percent.[36]

Midterm congressional elections attracted even fewer voters. In 1938, Mississippi had a population of 2,183,796, of whom 49 percent were African-American, yet all of its seven Democrats in the House—Ross Collins, William Colmer, Wall Doxey, Aaron Ford, Dan McGehee, John Rankin, and William Whittington—ran unopposed that year. Collins was elected with 11,540 votes, a good deal higher than Colmer's 4,873, McGehee's 4,834, Rankin's 4,384, Doxey's 4,134, Ford's 3,502, or Whittington's 2,172. In all, voters in Mississippi cast 35,439 votes. In neighboring Alabama, where four seats were contested (with the non-Democrats receiving 28, 12, 7, and less than 1 percent of the vote), the winning candidates in its nine districts secured between 10,266 and 17,903 ballots. Even the border states had relatively low turnouts. Successful candidates in Kentucky, for example, each running in a contested race (one of whom was a Republican), earned an average of 38,000 votes. In California, by contrast, no member of the House from any of its twenty districts, each contested, received fewer than 52,516 votes. Most winning candidates took many more, reaching a peak of 119,236. In the Twelfth District, Jerry Voorhis, later famously defeated by Richard Nixon, was supported by 75,003 voters, or 61 percent of the 123,363 votes cast in a three-way race.[37] For each voter in Mississippi's First District, which elected John Rankin, there were twenty-five who cast a ballot for Voorhis or his opponents in California's Twelfth.[38]

Once the region's elected representatives entered Congress, they acted as a distinctive unit on the national stage. Charles Wallace Collins was right to observe that "it is a well known fact that no person could be elected to any public office in the South who failed to subscribe to . . . the doctrine of white supremacy" in the form taken by segregation's barriers to social equality. Even "the warmest southern friends of the Negro race," he correctly noted about the era's white moderates and liberals who favored gradual racial change, the elimination of poll taxes, and a growing black franchise, "do not favor the breakdown of the pattern of segregation in the South."[39]

Collins was indubitably correct. The red lines that southern liberals would not cross had been crisply articulated in a *Virginia Quarterly* article just one month after FDR took office. Its author, R. Charlton Wright, was the recently retired editor of the Columbia, South Carolina, *Record* and had crusaded against "the tragic cost of thousands of lynchings, numerous race riots, and many acts of glaring injustice and inhumanity to the Negro." His "Southern Man and the Negro," a document on which he had been working since 1929, expressed "hostility to any and all approaches to the intermixes of the races," chastised black leaders for "advanced radical" demands that "are not compatible with any attitudes the South will entertain, or tolerate in practice within its confines, while it can prevent them," and underscored how "the white race cannot acquiesce safely in any compromises that would vitiate its age-long hereditary attitudes and convictions."[40]

Collins recalled how Mark Ethridge, the liberal editor of Louisville's *Courier-Journal*, pointedly sought to reassure a skeptical audience in Birmingham in 1942, soon after he had been appointed by President Roosevelt as the first chair of the new wartime Committee on Fair Employment Practices. "There is no power in the world," Ethridge state, "not even in all the mechanized armies of the earth, Allied or Axis, which could now force the Southern white people to abandonment of the principle of social segregation. It is a cruel disillusionment," he insisted, "bearing the germs of strife and perhaps tragedy, for any of their [Negroes'] leaders to tell them that they can expect it, or that they can exact it as the price of their participation in the war."[41] He might also have cited how the most racially liberal southerner in the House, Florida's Claude Pepper, had explained his opposition to federal antilynching legislation in August 1937 by announcing that "whatever may be written into the Constitution, whatever may be placed upon the statute books of this Nation, however many soldiers may be stationed about the ballot boxes of the Southland, the colored race will not vote, because in so doing . . . they endanger the supremacy of a race to which God has committed the destiny of a continent, perhaps of the world."[42]

Refusing to acknowledge any incompatibility between the system of segregation and wider American values and visions, southern politicians sought to legislate without having to choose among their valued objectives. Most had brought an activist agenda to Washington well before the New Deal. The southern bloc strongly pressed the federal regulation of railroads by advocating repairs to strengthen the Interstate Commerce Act of 1887. It fought to reduce tariff rates, campaigned for stronger controls over credit and banking, and played a crucial role in creating the Federal Reserve System. It strongly championed antimonopoly policies to bring big corporations under control. It supported federal aid to agricultural education. Though often ambivalent about organized labor, southern congressmen also were prepared to promote union interests in the hopes of forging a farmer-labor alliance within the Democratic Party.[43] In all, many of the South's congressional initiatives were progressive.

This turn-of-the-century program culminated in the election of Virginia-born Woodrow Wilson to the presidency in 1912, followed by his promotion of these policies under the label of "the New Freedom." Coming on the heels of the South's institutionalization of racial segregation and black disenfranchisement, both with the sanction of the Supreme Court, Wilson's presidency offered white southerners confirmation of their successful return to the union. "Long ago I had despaired of ever seeing a man of Southern birth President," Benjamin F. Long, a superior court judge in North Carolina, wrote in March 1913 to Walter Hines Page, the distinguished North Carolina–born journalist and publisher newly appointed as ambassador to Great Britain. That development, he observed, marked "an era in our national life. With it we have the ascendancy of men of Southern birth and residence to the seats of power and responsibility such as has never been seen in our day."[44] As a Virginian and the first southern-born president since the Civil War, Wilson combined progressivism with aggressive racism by segregating federal departments in workstations, lunchrooms, and bathrooms, removing most blacks from supervisory positions in the federal civil service, celebrating the Ku Klux Klan by screening *The Birth of a Nation* in the White House before his assembled cabinet, and successfully resisting a condemnation of racial inequality in the Treaty of Versailles.[45]

During the Wilson years, the composite of racism and progressive liberalism came to dominate the Democratic Party, and, with it, the content and boundaries of social reform.[46] Wilson had been elected in a three-party race, winning a majority of the vote only in southern states and one non-southern state, Arizona. As he took office, more than half the Democratic majority in the Senate was southern, and just over 40 percent in the House. Champ Clark of Missouri was Speaker of the House, with Oscar Underwood of Alabama serving as majority leader. Southern senators chaired twelve of fourteen committees, and southern representatives presided over eleven of thirteen.

Southern representatives pushed the Wilson administration in interventionist directions, driving it to move beyond an original and more moderate emphasis on lowering tariffs and opening markets. Southern members, Arthur Link has stressed, led a crusade advocating "government's duty to intervene directly in economic affairs in order to benefit submerged or politically impotent economic interests." In so doing, "they helped make Wilson an advanced progressive and helped to commit his administration to a broad program of welfare legislation." Though historians have debated whether southerners in Congress were the lone prime movers, southern preferences and votes clearly played a central role in crafting and passing President Wilson's legislative program.[47] In all, "the imprint of the triumphant South on the domestic agenda of Wilson's New Freedom," the historian Michael Perman has rightly noted, was "indisputable." Key legislation concerned with tariffs, economic monopolies, the currency, banking, farm relief, railroad regulation, and child labor "was brought forward and steered to passage by southern congressmen, while receiving overwhelming support from the southern delegations."[48]

With the era's Republicans more concerned with winning white votes in the South than with promoting the rights of their black supporters, and with the Democratic Party so tightly bound to the region's segregated order, southern members were free in the main to vote their substantive preferences without much concern for the security of white supremacy.[49] Understanding, however, that a growing federal role might well invite national oversight and supervision, they deployed their structural power in the legislature to block even the most limited of such efforts.

A revealing example concerns legislation that aimed to bring modern techniques to farmers through scientific education, the first federal government program to offer grants-in-aid.[50] Sponsored in the Senate by Hoke Smith of Georgia and in the House by Asbury Lever of South Carolina, the bill expanded earlier programs based on federal farm stations managed by state agricultural colleges. Moneys were to be allocated in proportion to each state's farm population, a stipulation designed by the sponsors to send the bulk of federal dollars to the South.[51]

Having been passed by the House in January 1914, the bill came to the Senate with a provision inserted by Congressman Lever that would effectively permit southern states to direct federal funds exclusively to white institutions. The language provided that "in any State in which two or more such colleges have been or hereafter may be established, the appropriation hereinafter made to such State shall be administered by such college or colleges as the legislature of such State may direct." This designation, critics rightly observed, was designed to exclude black land-grant colleges and black farmers. During the Senate debate, Senator Hoke Smith explicitly argued that the administration of funds should be left in white hands, as they would "do more for the negro than the negro could do for himself," and by James Vardaman of Mississippi, who insisted that agricultural extension work could be performed properly only by "the Anglo-Saxon, the man of proven judgment, initiative, wisdom, and experience."[52] An amendment advocated by the NAACP and sponsored by Senator Wesley Jones of Washington to guarantee Negro colleges a fair share was rejected by a 32–23 margin. Only two Democrats[53] supported the effort to open the program to black schools. A weaker alternative, which shifted responsibility from state legislatures to governors and their secretaries of agriculture "without discrimination as to race," but without any enforcement mechanisms, was endorsed without a roll-call vote.[54] This provision did not survive the conference between the House and the Senate. There, the bill's sponsors, Smith and Lever, blocked even this limited constraint on southern autonomy. When the act became law in May 1914, responsibility for allocating extension funds was assigned exclusively to each state's legislature, and the antidiscrimination language had been removed.

During the 1920s, Alabama's Oscar Underwood and Joseph Robinson of Arkansas led the Democratic Party in the House; Senate Democrats were led by Claude Kitchin of North Carolina until 1923, then by Finis Garrett of Tennessee. With no realistic threat to segregation on the horizon, southern members often allied successfully with western Republican progressives led by Robert LaFollette of Wisconsin and George Norris of Nebraska. This coalition propelled reform legislation that included the Water Power Act of 1920 and the Merchant Marine Act of the same year, as well as tax laws that maintained the progressive income, inheritance, and excess profits provisions that had been brought in during World War I.[55] It also passed the Maternity and Infancy Welfare Act of 1921, jointly sponsored in the House by the Texas Democrat Morris Sheppard and Iowa Republican Horace Towner, whose pattern of local administration sharply discriminated against black families in the South.[56] The South's Democrats also supported collective bargaining for unions in the railroad industry, and large-scale power projects, including the epic construction of Boulder Dam, a project that would not be undertaken until 1931. Their tax policies, in the main, grew more moderate after the 1924 Republican landslide, which weakened that party's progressive wing, but even the more conservative southern Democrats, like Underwood, "sustained much more 'progressive' voting records than their Republican colleagues from New England and the mid-American states" throughout the 1920s.

III.

THE YEARS immediately preceding the New Deal represented a high point for white southern security about the still-fresh arrangements of Jim Crow. Forty years had elapsed since the last major legislative effort to guarantee African-Americans political rights. In 1890 and 1891, Representative Henry Cabot Lodge, the Massachusetts Republican,[57] proposed a federal-elections bill, which would have placed elections to the House of Representatives under national supervision, placing responsibilities for the conduct of fair elections in the hands of federal circuit courts rather than state election boards. After complicated legislative maneuvering, including a filibuster lasting thirty-three days, the "force bill" went down to defeat in the Senate. Debate ended after "the bill lost majority support primarily due to the machinations of a handful of silver Republicans who cared far less about civil rights than adopting currency legislation, which required close cooperation with Democrats."[58] Such was political life at the end of the nineteenth century.

In 1894, with the Democratic Party in control, the House and Senate repealed the remaining Enforcement Acts of Reconstruction, dating from 1870 and 1871, which had provided federal supervision for state elections. Strengthened by these confirmations that racial questions would take a backseat to other policies in Washington, the South pushed ahead with the systematic disenfranchisement and segregation of its black citizens, all the while pressing to achieve an assertive national policy agenda. North of the Mason-Dixon Line, Republicans took black votes for granted, offering little but the fact of not being Democrats, the party associated with slavery and white supremacy. Within the South, Republican acquiescence placed segregation and voting restrictions beyond question. As President Taft had predicted in 1909, this new stance, abandoning the cause of racial justice, made it possible for several members of the party to find favor with the electorate in some border states.[59]

Over the arc of an entire half century before the New Deal, every effort in Congress to protect black rights failed. A turn-of-the-century endeavor to reduce southern representation as African-Americans were purged from voting rolls and an attempt to pass federal antilynching legislation in 1922, a year marked by fifty-seven such killings, were particularly notable. With that bill "displaced by the indifference of its friends and the strategy of its enemies," who successfully mounted a Senate filibuster, race disappeared from the agenda of national politics.[60] Congress would mount no other efforts to deal with the deepening of Jim Crow and the persistence of lynching before the New Deal began.

By March 1933, the issue, at least on the political surface, no longer seemed to exist. As the southern region returned to more traditional voting patterns, southern racial confidence seemed safe. FDR—also a New York governor, but a Protestant opposed to Prohibition—won large majorities in every segregated state but Delaware. With Congress also swinging dramatically in a Democratic direction, the 1932 election was an all-too-often-overlooked watershed that thrust the South into a pivotal lawmaking position.

In Congress, southern members held three trump cards: uncommon longevity, disproportionate numbers, and a commitment to racial hierarchy more passionate than that of their opponents. Many key figures—including Senators Ellison "Cotton Ed" Smith of South Carolina, Walter George of Georgia, and Kenneth McKellar of Tennessee, and House members Martin Dies of Texas, Robert Ramspeck of Georgia, and Howard Smith of Virginia—had already become congressional fixtures who were destined to serve over many decades. Often unopposed, southern Senators and members of the House amassed uncommon seniority, the key factor that produced access to the most influential committees and positions. When President Roosevelt was elected, congressional committees had grown more significant and entrenched than they had been during the Wilson years. Southerners chaired twenty-nine of the forty-seven committees in the House, including Appropriations, Banking and Currency, Judiciary, Foreign Affairs, Agriculture, Military Affairs, and Ways and Means, which handled all tax matters.

13 out of
33 Committees

In the Senate as well, southerners held sway; they headed thirteen of thirty-three committees, counting the most significant, including Agriculture, Appropriations, Banking and Currency, Commerce, Finance, and Military Affairs.[61]

With seniority also came experience; with experience, legislative skill based on the command of issues and rules. "With such knowledge and experience in national affairs," moreover, "they become the logical leaders of the Party in Congress," as Marian Irish noted in 1942, when Sam Rayburn of Texas was Speaker of the House and Alben Barkley of Kentucky was majority leader. In all, she concluded, "there is no doubt but that the one-party system enables the South to exert more influence in Congress than it could by any other political means."[62]

Notwithstanding the relatively modest proportion of actual voters in the South, the representation of these districts and states in Washington remained unaffected. Each state automatically secured two U.S. Senate seats, a feature of the Constitution. In turn, seats in the House of Representatives were apportioned by population—the total population, irrespective of who was kept from voting and how many eligible persons actually appeared at the polls on Election Day. As a result, the South achieved numbers and influence in each chamber far in excess of its actual voters. Further, the southern presence in the House and Senate was sanitized. Once a member was sworn in, each chamber repressed any knowledge of racial exclusion, franchise-reducing rules, limited voting, or unopposed elections, let alone the pervasive atmosphere of violence that accompanied many, especially rural, southern elections. In Congress, each elected member was treated like every other. Each possessed the same prerogatives. Each was free to play by the same institutional rules.

After the economic and political upheavals of the late nineteenth century, the Democratic Party in Congress came to consist mainly of representatives from the South. From the Democratic Party debacle of 1896 to the election of Franklin Roosevelt in 1932, Democratic congressional candidates outside the South were able to secure only some 40 percent of the popular vote, but the party's vote totals within the South never fell below 86 percent.[63] As a result, during the first three decades of the twentieth century, two out of every three Democrats in Congress were elected from southern constituencies.

With Warren Harding, Calvin Coolidge, and Herbert Hoover in the

White House in the 1920s and early 1930s, Republican majorities in the Senate and the House were constant, and often large. As a result, southern members dominated the Democratic Party in both houses of Congress. During this period, 67 percent of all Democrats in the Senate and fully 72 percent in the House hailed from the South.[64] During the last Congress to serve before the Democratic Party's landslide in the 1932 elections, 30 of the 47 Democratic members of the Senate and 136 of the 216 in the House represented southern constituencies.

The partisan transformation of 1932 altered the region's place in the legislature. Across the country, Democratic Party candidates secured a remarkable 72.4 percent of the vote for the House of Representatives and won fully 63 percent of the ballots cast for the Senate. A House that had been divided between 218 Republicans and 216 Democrats (and one independent) after the midterm election of 1930 was replaced by a chamber with 311 Democrats and just 117 Republicans, so severe was the impact of the Depression and the Roosevelt landslide.[65] In the Senate, the Democrats gained twelve seats, giving them a decisive majority of 59–36.[66] When the Seventy-third Congress assembled in March 1933, the South no longer commanded a majority of Democratic seats; 46 percent of Democrats in the House and 49 percent in the Senate represented southern districts and states. These shares fell further when the party's majorities grew in 1934 and 1936.

Still, southern power persisted. Nonsouthern Democrats could not pass legislation without southern support. At no time during the New Deal did the southern cohort drop below 44 percent of Democrats in the Senate and 41 percent in the House. These numbers were sufficient to block any initiatives they did not approve. During the heyday of the Roosevelt administration's great legislative productivity, every law had to pass southern scrutiny. Even when the presence of Republicans in the House was reduced to a paltry 88 seats after the election of 1936, the 192 nonsouthern Democrats could not muster majorities on their own. Although only 16 Republicans served in the Senate that convened after that Democratic rout, the 43 nonsouthern Democrats likewise constituted only a minority of that chamber. Without southern acquiescence, the party's national program could not pass.

Republicans began a steep comeback in 1938. That midterm election followed President Roosevelt's failed effort to enlarge the Supreme Court, and took place in the context of labor unrest, a severe economic dip (unemployment nearly doubled in the nine months following August 1937, and farm prices fell by some 30 percent), and a foreign policy that many judged to lack a strategy to confront the dictatorships.[67] Despite the Republican Party's gain of eighty seats in the House, the Democrats maintained a comfortable majority, but its composition changed. Southern members once again commanded a majority of their party, 54 percent. Never again during the Roosevelt and Truman administrations did their share fall below half of all House Democrats. Party turnover in the Senate was slower, as the Republicans gained eight seats. A southern majority of Democrats did not emerge until the next election, in 1940. By the end of the Truman administration, fully 63 percent of Democrats in the Senate hailed from the South.

IV.

THE ASSUMPTIONS, institutions, and practices within which southern congressional voting took place in the 1920s soon expired. The reform impulses of southern members had taken aim at northern capital in circumstances marked by national economic prosperity, a postwar disengagement from world affairs, and a federal system that relegated issues of property rights and the organization of the economy to the forty-eight states.[68] When these circumstances altered during the New Deal, the South was confronted with difficult choices about policies and preferences, choices that grew more difficult as the period unfolded.

During the course of the New Deal, the character and content of policy majorities depended on these southern decisions. On its own, the region did not command a majority of the House or the Senate. Statistically, representatives from the South were no more central to getting legislation passed than other Democrats or Republicans. In a technical sense, each of these three sets of representatives was pivotal, as each group was in a position to provide the votes that were needed by at least one other to gain a winning margin. Overall, though, the South was the bloc most vital to lawmaking. Unlike other members of the House and Senate, whose substantive preferences and propensity to vote were located predictably on a left-to-right spectrum, southern members were more pliable and less predictable with respect to their views and votes. Unlike the others, they made policy decisions on the basis of two dimensions, not just one, those of partisanship and regional concerns.

And when the latter was in play, it almost always took priority over commitments to the national Democratic Party and its policy preferences. The level of intensity felt for each was not symmetrical.[69]

Each time they prepared to cast a vote on the floor of the House or Senate, southern congressmen had to decide with whom to align. These decisions produced four types of roll calls, as shown in Figure 1. When they joined their Democratic Party colleagues with a high degree of likeness,[70] but not with Republicans, their vote was "partisan." When the three blocs behaved similarly, the result was "cross-partisan." When southern actions differed both from those of nonsouthern Democrats and Republicans, the choice was "sectional." And when Southern members sided with Republicans and against fellow Democrats, they became "disloyal."

During the course of the Roosevelt and Truman administrations, the House of Representatives cast 1,898 roll calls about public policy and the Senate 2,533.[71] When these votes are sorted as partisan, cross-partisan, sectional, or disloyal, we discover a dramatic shift from the first decade of the New Deal era to the second. During the initial period, southern representatives overwhelmingly made partisan and cross-partisan choices. The picture

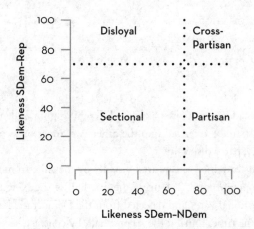

FIGURE I. *Types of Roll Call Votes Cast by Southern Members of Congress, 1933–1952*

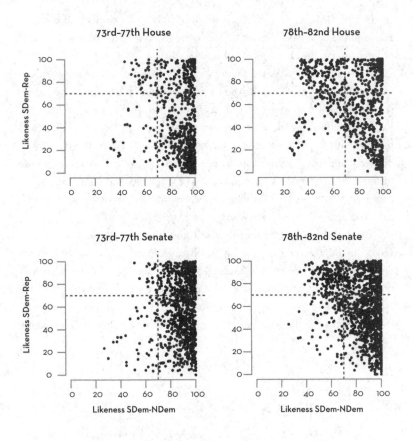

FIGURE 2. *Southern Votes in Congress, 1933–1952*

the second decade presents is strikingly different. Figure 2 identifies how a much larger share of votes fell into the other two zones of sectional voting and, especially, party disloyalty.

This transformation is captured visually by the shift from a vertical to a diagonal slope in Figure 2. During the first half of the New Deal, southerners cast sectional votes and defected from the Democratic Party position 5 percent of the time. During the second half, by contrast, sectional voting doubled, to 10 percent of the total, and the decision to defect was taken fully 19 percent of the time. This dramatic transformation raises questions of three kinds. Why did southern congressional behavior change so dramatically? On which issues did the South move from partisan and cross-partisan to sectional and defection voting? What was the impact of these decisions on the character and content of lawmaking, and thus on the contours and prospects of American democracy? Parsing these questions in the remaining chapters, we will discover not just whether but how the South made the New Deal.

5 ⨠ Jim Crow Congress

Named for the Roman consul and dictator, Lucius Quintus Cincinnatus Lamar was a nineteenth-century planter, lawyer, soldier, diplomat, and scholar. He resigned from the House of Representatives in 1860 to draft Mississippi's Ordinance of Secession. During the Civil War, he fought at Bull Run, served as army judge advocate, and traveled to England and France as a Confederate envoy. He returned to the House with Reconstruction nearing its end, then was elected to the Senate after the Compromise of 1877, which restored home rule and withdrew federal troops from the South. Chosen by President Grover Cleveland to be his secretary of the interior in 1885, Lamar joined the Supreme Court three years later, the first southern justice since 1853.[1]

For his "effort to reconcile the North and South in the face of enormous calumny in the aftermath of the Civil War," Lamar was selected by John F. Kennedy as one of eight U.S. senators to enter the pantheon of "profiles in courage."[2] As a strong supporter of white supremacy, and as a tireless campaigner for the restoration of white Democratic Party rule after Reconstruction, Lamar was also a hero to many New Deal–era southerners. These included the Southern Agrarians, the circle of literary intellectuals centered in Nashville, whose 1930 volume, *I'll Take My Stand,*[3] resisted an industrializing "New South" and promoted a traditional and unified region. The Agrarians celebrated Lamar as "one of the truly great men in American history."[4] He inspired modernizing southern liberals as well, people who looked forward to a less provincial South. A leader of that group, Virginius Dabney of the *Richmond Times-Dispatch,* recalled in 1932 how Lamar had backed strong federal measures to bolster the region's economy, including supporting federal subsidies to lower shipping costs to the South by rail, and how, with the close of Reconstruction, he had predicted that "the Southern people would now forget about the Negro as an issue and turn their attention to more important matters."[5]

Across this range of views, leading southern thinkers and politicians in the early 1930s, including members of the House and Senate, were confident the time to realize Lamar's forecast had arrived. Convinced that race no longer was an issue in national politics, they propelled policies that could realize a long-standing regional desire for economic rectification. In 1874, one of Lamar's Senate colleagues, North Carolina's Augustus Merrimon, had asked "Congress to inaugurate a policy" to redistribute "the industrial and capital interests of the country" from the "vast accumulation of capital and population in the Eastern States" to the South.[6] Merrimon understood what the distinguished economist William Parker would observe a century later when stating that an alternative to the South's disadvantaged status after Reconstruction "could hardly have occurred except . . . as part of a national economic and social policy which would have redistributed labor and capital within the nation."[7] For even as industrialization was proceeding elsewhere, the South remained overwhelmingly rural and poor, with depleted land, a quasi-feudal tenure system based on debt and fear,

Reasons
for
South
backward
ness

and many bankruptcies and foreclosures.[8] The New Deal thus was a boon for a hardscrabble region that faced many barriers to economic development. These included a poorly educated and low-skilled white and black population, inferior roads, the outmigration of ambitious workers, a shortage of local investment capital, fewer native mineral resources than other regions, and a paucity of industrial research facilities. The South also experienced high freight rates, high tariffs, low commodity prices, and patterns of ownership that placed the control of financial, mining, manufacturing, transportation, and communications corporations mainly in the hands of northeastern capitalists, a pattern many southern commentators thought to be colonial in nature.[9]

Most of the region's political leaders almost giddily propelled the New Deal's radical economic policies, a program that offered the South the chance to escape its colonized status while keeping its racial order safe. They were reassured by its strong resemblances to Wilson's New Freedom, in policy, personnel, and, it seemed, questions of race. Drawing on that history of reform and regulation, the region's representatives saw a golden opportunity to advance progressive priorities in both the region's and nation's interest. Economic concerns, at last, could displace race in what Congressman Maury Maverick, a liberal Texan, celebrated in 1936 as "another southern rebellion." This time, by contrast, it would be a rebellion "in which northerners—damned Yankees—lend assistance to the grandsons of the ragged troopers who starved and fought and died with Jackson and Lee. Both have found that they have a common enemy—and that enemy is not to be seen in terms of sectional cleavage but in terms of economic power."[10] Looking back with nostalgia from his professorial perch at the University of North Carolina a decade later, Howard Odum recalled how the region had assumed "a new sort of normal and logical participation in the total national effort" after 1933, without regional or racial issues coming to the fore.[11] Somewhere, Senators Lamar and Merrimon were smiling.

They would also have been pleased to know that in the generation before the New Deal, a "powerful sentiment" had developed within the South "to dampen the rekindled fires of racial feeling and to discourage any further public discussion of race." They almost certainly would have been impressed by how, in turn, the main concerns of the Democratic Party's burgeoning nonsouthern wing found no place for racial rectification.[12]

At the start of the New Deal, racial segregation seemed immovable, almost natural. The country's political class had come to terms with a system of differentiated citizenship based on race, a system in which some Americans, thought to be incorrigibly inferior, were accorded only limited rights. The conciliatory culture that celebrated the reunion of the sections after the Civil War remained vibrant across party lines. A white consensus that existing racial patterns should not be disturbed seemed durable, notwithstanding the ways the southern system contradicted the most basic commitments of the country's liberal ideals and democratic political culture.

As the New Deal began, southern civil society appeared safe. The South's daring policy positions were premised on this security. Southern members of Congress had little reason to fear the large number of their new nonsouthern colleagues in the House and Senate. Almost to a person, these newcomers had no particular focus on racial segregation, and no interest in confronting the legislature's southern leaders. Not one Democrat in Congress was African-American.[13] Few of the constituents of nonsouthern Democrats, or Republicans, were black. Effective lawmaking, they understood, demanded an alliance with their more experienced southern colleagues. And that, in turn, could not happen unless they overlooked Jim Crow.

Southern members of the House and Senate also had no cause to worry that the new president, who had been nominated with robust southern support, spent long periods in Warm Springs, Georgia, and had selected a segregationist Texan, John Nance Garner, as his vice president, would do anything but make the Great Depression a priority.[14] His election brought comfort to elected southern officials who understood that his success would depend on overcoming the divisions that had split the southern and nonsouthern wings of the Democratic Party during the 1928 presidential election. During his long term of office, Franklin Roosevelt never pushed civil rights legislation.[15] His staff had a southern slant. James "Jimmy" Byrnes, then a new Democratic senator from South Carolina and a key speechwriter and strategist for the 1932 campaign, "believed unquestioningly in the total supremacy of the Caucasian race."[16] The administration's press secretary, the Virginian Stephen Early, "was always on the alert for any piece of legislation, White House appointment, or firm pronouncement that risked an impression of special concern for racial discrimination."[17] The Justice Department at the start of the New Deal studiously ignored all African-American pleas for help. Emblematic New Deal institutions, including the Civilian Conservation Corps and the Tennessee Valley Authority, were directed by explicit racists who limited black participation. Walter White, the secretary of the NAACP, famously reported how FDR explained why he would remain silent during the Senate filibuster of the antilynching bill first introduced in January 1934 by two of his party's senators, Colorado's Edward Costigan and New York's Robert Wagner. "I've got to get legislation passed by Congress to save America. . . . If I come out for the anti-lynching bill, [the southerners] will block every bill I ask Congress to pass to keep America from collapsing. I just can't take that risk."[18]

In all, southern lawmakers had no grounds to believe that anything threatening would be done to challenge segregation and white political domination beyond the occasional symbolic gesture. With no pressure about civil rights from their colleagues or from the president in the early New Deal, they "not only insisted on strict adherence to the imperatives of white supremacy in administering New Deal programs in their own section, but also imposed their prejudices on Capitol Hill."[19] Fusing white supremacy with American nationalism, most white southerners, including most politicians, saw little conflict between systematic racism and liberal democratic government. This combination controlled how the region stayed within the ambit of national politics through the instrument of the Democratic Party. "No wonder they thought they could pretty much shape a New Deal to suit themselves."[20]

This equilibrium did not prove stable. Looking back, Odum ruefully remembered its collapse. "Then," he wrote, "a strange thing happened, a sudden revivification of the old sectional conflict," and a recovery "of the terms North and South." By reopening "the old race conflict," sectional divisions in national politics and especially within the Democratic Party had brought "the South to its gravest crisis and the nation again to one of its chief domestic problems since the Civil War."[21]

The developments to which he referred did, in fact, change the course of the New Deal. Pressured in many unexpected ways, the white South became uncertain and unsure, perplexed about how simultaneously to maintain its commitments to racism and to a changing Democratic Party, its long-standing political home. As southern power grew more guarded and fearful, the New Deal moved from a first phase of radical reform to a second, in which its social democratic wings were clipped. A third and decisive phase followed. In the 1940s, southerners in Congress became an increasingly independent force, one whose decisions forged a double-sided procedural and crusading national state. With pivotal powers, these southern choices defined the country's institutional realities and moral geography.

I.

T HE EMBARGO on racial issues after the decisive Democratic Party victory in 1932 opened up the attractive prospect that economic policies crafted in Washington might transform the region's desperate plight without endangering Jim Crow. Of course, not every southern member was on board. On the Left, Louisiana's senator Huey Long thought the program did not go far enough to constrain business and redistribute income and wealth. His Share Our Wealth movement, calling for confiscatory taxation on fortunes worth more than one million dollars and a guaranteed family income of more than two thousand dollars, generated a national, not just a southern, movement with mass support.[22] Long, however, never mobilized serious congressional backing. Nor did a small group of adversaries at the other end of the region's ideological spectrum, including Senators Carter Glass and Harry F. Byrd of Virginia, Thomas Gore of Oklahoma, Millard Tydings of Maryland, and Josiah Bailey of North Carolina, who were deeply anxious about the growth of federal power. Just after the Hundred Days, Glass wrote to Walter Lippmann to decry the New Deal "as an utterly dangerous effort of the federal government to transplant Hitlerism to every corner of the nation."[23]

Neither Long nor the opposition on the Right spoke for the greater part of the South. With race at bay, they failed to come close to commanding southern majorities in the House and Senate, which eagerly supported the New Deal's ambitious legislative agenda and "moved White House proposals through Congress . . . to a remarkable degree."[24] The South's congressional leaders, whose legislative skills and powers he surely understood, were cultivated and flattered by FDR. Offered both patronage and recognition, they enjoyed the prerogatives that came with being in the majority. In all, pressure by the southern rank and file in Congress made the first years of the New Deal more forceful and less circumscribed than they otherwise might have been.

With racial southern autonomy not in question, the region's representatives were free to pursue their other substantive preferences to great effect. During the early New Deal, they collaborated closely with the White House to achieve their own long-standing desire to regulate and control the market economy. Applying ideas about planning and corporatism, they shaped and endorsed remedies to heal a sick economy that promoted an unprecedented degree of national state intervention. At least as enthusiastically as other Democrats, often more passionately, congressional southerners constrained how business and the stock exchanges could operate. They also joined other Democrats to find a place for labor unions, support massive jobs programs, get behind large-scale public infrastructure projects, restructure American agriculture, open conduits for global trade, and develop a modern welfare state. The milestone laws they helped craft and adopt included the National Industrial Relations Act of 1933, which promoted an economic recovery by moving well beyond laissez-faire; the Banking Act of 1933, which rescued the financial system; the Securities Exchange Act of 1934, which regulated Wall Street and other stock exchanges; the Reciprocal Trade Act of 1934, which began to help fashion a more open global economy; the National Industrial Recovery Act of 1935, which gave unions a fighting chance to organize; the Public Utility Holding Company Act of 1935, "an astonishing piece of reform legislation" that President Roosevelt called "his greatest legislative victory,"[25] which sharply constrained the gas and electric industries; the Revenue Act of 1935, which raised the surtax rate on incomes over $50,000 from 59 to 75 percent; and the Social Security Act of 1935, which not only provided for old-age pensions but created a larger framework to ensure against unemployment and provide assistance to impoverished mothers with children.

Richard Hofstadter's judgment during the first Eisenhower administration about the far-reaching quality of these legislative accomplishments still rings true. "In the years 1933–8 the New Deal sponsored a series of legislative changes that made the enactments of the Progressive era seem timid by comparison."[26] With the brief exception of World War I, such policies had previously stood outside the scope of imagined possibilities. In embracing features of planning that had been identified mainly with the radical program of the Bolsheviks, in supporting features of corporatism that principally had been associated with Fascist Italy, and in backing the delegation of great power to administrative agencies that regulated the private economy in a manner that had a family resemblance to the active economic project of Nazi Germany, the South helped show that each of these policies could be turned in a democratic, not totalitarian, direction.[27] In so doing, the South helped the United States respond to the gibes of the dictatorships that liberal democracies could not restore an effective capitalism or manage class conflict.

Concurrently, southern members of the House and Senate did more than defend the racial status quo by blocking all efforts to advance black rights. As economic legislation advanced, they fortified Jim Crow by making certain that southern employers could continue to draw without hindrance on the still-enormous supply of inexpensive and vulnerable black labor. They did so by ensuring that key New Deal bills on subjects sensitive for the South, such as labor relations, would be adapted to meet the test of not disturbing the region's racial structure. The main techniques by which this goal was accomplished were a decentralization of responsibility that placed administrative discretion in the hands of state and local officials whenever possible, a recognition in law of regional differentials in wage levels, and the exclusion of maids and farmworkers—fully two-thirds of southern black employees— from key New Deal programs.[28]

Southern legislators understood that their region's agrarian interests and racial arrangements were inextricably entwined. Farm labor dominated the economy of the South as in no other region of the country. Of all people engaged in agricultural labor nationwide, 53 percent worked in the South in 1930, and 50 percent in 1940. Of the massive southern agricultural labor force, 40 percent of those classified by the census as "laborers" were black in 1940, and 55 percent of the region's sharecroppers.[29] Only a small proportion of black farmers, about one in ten, owned their own land. Others were sharecroppers, the vast majority, or tenants. By excluding these persons from New Deal legislation, it remained possible to maintain racial inequality in southern labor markets by dictating the terms and conditions for African-American labor.[30] What southern members might have done if these provisions had not been adopted is impossible to know. But with these adjustments, southern whites rallied to the New Deal in Congress and beyond. As one commentator put the point in referring to Senate Majority Leader Joseph Robinson of Arkansas, "So long as they [New Dealers] fought the money power and the big industries—so long as they were pro-farmer and did not stir up the niggers—he was with them."[31]

The uncommonly wide repertoire of ideas and techniques that were considered and adopted during this era's "chaos of experimentation"[32] simply would have been impossible without the willing audacity of the segregated South. None of the early New Deal could have happened had the South not been convinced that the Democratic Party would continue to protect its racial order. Once the provisions advanced by the South were made integral parts of New Deal legislation, southern representatives were free to treat their congressional votes primarily as choices about party faithfulness and ideological conviction. Facing no threat in Washington to Jim Crow, southern party loyalty was high, with virtually no gap between the voting behavior of the party's members who hailed from different parts of the country. As Figure 1 indicates, between 1933 and 1936, fully 96 percent of roll calls fell into the partisan and cross-partisan quadrants in the House of Representatives, and 95 percent in the Senate. In this period, sectional votes were concerned with civil rights in circumstances where it was widely understood that such initiatives stood no chance of passage through the gauntlet of the Senate, and the tiny number of defection votes primarily were related to efforts to protect the region's distinctive labor market. Otherwise, southern Democrats stood shoulder-to-shoulder with fellow Democrats in a remarkable display of party solidarity.

These decisions to back the New Deal and President Roosevelt were ratified at the polls. FDR, "who frequently thought of himself as a Georgian,"[33] had developed credibility in the region as a southerner who had led a great political project in a manner that was consistent with its central preferences. In October 1936, Broadus Mitchell, the Johns Hopkins economist who later ran as the Socialist candidate for governor of Maryland, reflected on this happy experience. "Since Franklin Roosevelt came into office," he wrote, "the South has been a chief beneficiary of national projects and expenditure. . . . But with all of this cordial, even avid, acceptance of outside money and enterprise," he hastened to add, "we have continued to insist that our Southern problems are peculiar, that they must not be proved by strangers, that all critical inquiries and negotiations must have the certificate of Southern personnel." This the New Deal had done.[34]

Running against Kansas governor Alf Landon in 1936, FDR won a landslide 61 percent of the national popular vote, an achievement that was inflated by his average southern state vote of 75 percent. Even more remarkable was the degree of support he secured across the Deep South. Roosevelt's reelec-

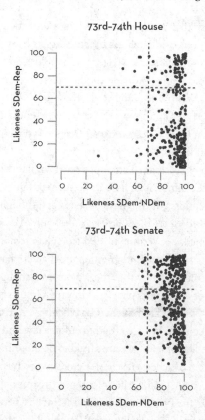

FIGURE 1. *Southern Votes in Congress, 1933–1936*

tion was endorsed by 87 percent of voters in Alabama, Georgia, and Texas, 89 percent in Louisiana, and an astonishing 97 percent in Mississippi and 99 percent in South Carolina, where some counties reported not one Republican vote. The lopsidedness of the numbers seemed like something Stalin might have fabricated in the Soviet Union, yet this indeed was an election carried out on American soil. By contrast, when Woodrow Wilson ran successfully for a second term in 1916, he averaged 61 percent in the South, and lost by thin margins to Charles Evans Hughes in Delaware and West Virginia.

This level of approval was an expression of gratitude for more than the New Deal's economic policies. As the campaign unfolded, the high degree

"Racial autonomy" of racial autonomy that southerners had long demanded remained intact, notwithstanding a renewed attention to lynching, its least defensible feature. Later, this issue would serve as a wedge that, hand in hand with other unsettling debates, would begin to divide the Democratic Party along sectional lines. But not yet. With winks and nods, those in both wings of the party understood the gestures and moves the other was required to make, all the while knowing that there was no prospect that antilynching legislation could actually be enacted into law.

Card

When the last congressional attempt to curb vigilante killings had failed in 1922, the South claimed it could handle such extrajudicial murder without federal intervention.[35] In the next dozen years, though, 277 instances of lynching were recorded. Of the southern states, only Alabama strengthened its own antilynching laws. Writing in 1931 to explain to nonsouthern Americans why "southern violence and emotional debauch" had not produced a successful countermovement within the region, even though "our conscience is the conscience of a religious people," Howard Odum explained that "the great body of people who are horrified by lynching . . . are afraid to protest. We are afraid to legislate. We are afraid to enforce law and liberty. . . . Rationalizing amid the fear of fears, we are afraid to do anything. There are practically no exceptions. Teacher, preacher, doctor, lawyer, business man, farmer, laborer, artist and craftsman, writer of poems, dreamer of dreams—we are all afraid. Among the Negroes," he added, "fear . . . becomes stark terror. The Negroes are afraid to do anything. Why shouldn't they be afraid?"[36]

The year 1933 was particularly appalling. The South recorded twenty-six lynchings, the second-highest annual total in a decade.[37] By year's end, "lynching dominated the headlines as at no other time in American history,"[38] its prevalence a reflection of how dark economic fears can be expressed through racial malignancy. At the start of 1934, Senators Wagner and Costigan introduced legislation that made it a federal crime for state officials to neglect or collude with lynching. State governments were to be given thirty days to respond; if they did not, the Department of Justice would step in. Any state official allowing a prisoner to be taken by a mob would face five years imprisonment and a five-thousand-dollar fine; any state officer colluding with lynchers could be punished by a sentence of up to twenty-five years; and any county in which the lynching occurred would face a fine of up to ten thousand dollars, with the funds paid to the victim's family as restitution.

"Wagner" "Costigan"

The bill went nowhere, despite the continued resurgence of lynching and the particularly ghastly October 1934 murder of Claude Neal, who had been accused of rape and murder. With a crowd of some four thousand, including many children, bearing witness, Neal was stabbed, burned, and castrated. He was forced to eat his own genitals before being dragged by an automobile to his death; then his body, mutilated and nude, was suspended from a tree in the courthouse square of Marianna, Florida. Photographs were sold for fifty cents. Neal's toes and fingers were put on display.[39]

With the Justice Department refusing to intervene during the next half year, despite the fact that Neal had been seized from a jail in Alabama and thus had been transported across state lines,[40] Wagner and Costigan moved to have the Senate take up the bill in April 1935. The president remained silent. In March, Eleanor Roosevelt explained to Walter White, "The President feels that that lynching is a question of education in the states, rallying good citizens, and creating public opinion so that the localities themselves will wipe it out. However, if it were done by a Northerner, it will have an antagonistic effect."[41] Southern senators successfully killed the proposed law by preventing the legislation from coming to a vote. They did not, in the main, defend vigilante justice. Rather, they argued that Congress lacked authority to pass such a law; in assaulting states' rights, it violated the Constitution.[42] They also again claimed that their region could control lynching on its own, citing efforts where governors had intervened to stop such violence, and insisted that southern race relations, marked by bonds of affection, were superior to those of the North. James Byrnes contrasted southern paternalism to New York's gang murders. Hugo Black, another future Supreme Court justice, feared a return to Reconstruction conditions.[43]

To stymie the bill, the South launched a filibuster, threatening to "speak night and day if necessary," thus "delaying other important legislation."[44] The debate "was a godsend" to southern progressives, who could demonstrate to their constituents that notwithstanding their strong and often leading position regarding New Deal legislation, they would not be moved when it came to federal interference in matters of race.[45]

During the Senate's consideration, it was widely understood that the debate would not lead to a roll call. Reporting how the "antilynching measure meets dogged hostility," the *New York Times* commented that its "well-intentioned" sponsors were mistaken if they thought the proposal ever

would come to a vote.[46] Plainly exasperated by the members of his party
who had insisted on bringing the bill to the floor, President Roosevelt pushed
"for greater speed on his legislative program,"[47] including a veterans bonus
compromise bill sponsored by Mississippi's senator Pat Harrison. Majority
Leader Robinson initiated a series of procedural moves to kill the legislation
by voting on adjournment. A vote on April 26 failed, but its narrow 33–34
defeat signaled that supporters of the legislation lacked the two-thirds that
would have been necessary to stop the southern filibuster.

What is striking about this vote is not the overwhelming support by
southern Democrats or the comparable degree of opposition by Republicans.
It is, rather, the critical support for adjournment provided by nonsouthern
Democrats, almost half of whom voted to support the South's procedural
move. With this demonstration, a decisive effort to adjourn easily passed by
48–32, with the majority composed of 44 Democrats and just 4 Republicans.[48]
"The effort to displace the Costigan-Wagner bill could not have succeeded
without the support of northern Democrats."[49] As their southern colleagues
knew all along, they were playing for audiences of constituents rather than
making a serious effort to actually put an antilynching law on the books. The
plea by South Carolina's Cotton Ed Smith that the Democratic Party should
rally to protect the South as "'our pillar of a cloud' by day and our 'pillar of
fire' by night" was heeded.[50]

II.

THE ROOSEVELT administration pursued a strategy of pragmatic forgetful-
ness with regard to racial matters as long as it could. Relying on southern intellectuals like Howard Odum and other students of economic and
social regionalism, this policy consisted of two key rhetorical and intellectual
elements. First was an equilibrium of silence. By excising the sharpness of
Jim Crow's racial dimension, the South was transformed analytically into a
more ordinary, if poor, region that could be melded within a larger American sectional mosaic. The South itself, this perspective stressed, was no less
internally complex than other regions. Delaware and Maryland were as different, say, from Louisiana and Georgia as Connecticut was from Colorado.
Looking at such considerations, many New Deal contemporaries argued that
the day of southern exceptionalism had passed. Odum, for one, took notice of

how "'North' and 'South' in the early New Deal were no longer valid realities in the new America that was developing, except as they reflected a tragic past which the nation wanted to forget."[51] Regions still mattered, but not in a way that would make the South any more singular or remarkable than the Midwest, the Northwest, or any other area of the country. Moreover, as a historian of the Civil War, Ella Lonn, stressed in her presidential address to the Southern Historical Association, American similarities after the Civil War and Reconstruction had become vastly more important than North-South differences. "Fundamentally," she explained, "we were one people. There were no barriers of language such as exist when two different nations engage in combat. Further, both sections were dominated by the same Anglo-Saxon traditions, both had the same English background and developed through the same pioneer experience." In addition, "both sections were devoted to the same system of government."[52]

2| A second feature of the strategy dealt with the conduct of policy research. Using the tools of modern social science, enlightened empirical scholarship conducted in settings like the Institute for Research in Social Science, which Odum led in Chapel Hill, amassed data that could be classified by many other categories than race. Drawing on southern regional studies, this approach chronicled the South's distinct character and circumstances this way.[53] Like Odum, a good number of leading white southern intellectuals who were racial moderates understood that any attempt to confront race head-on was doomed to fail.[54] In these circumstances, they sought to find a vantage from which to explore southern realities while bypassing the region's racial conundrums. They thought this course to be ethically advantageous. Such an equilibrium of silence, they believed, might shift the dominant language from an explicit and often embarrassing justification of white supremacy to a concern for the South irrespective of race. Segregation would stay, but there would be no need to talk about it.

This position offered New Dealers a way to discuss and assess the South without mounting a frontal assault on its racial system. On June 22, 1938, Franklin Roosevelt wrote to Lowell Mellett, the executive director of the National Emergency Council, to commission a report on the economic conditions of the South that would pursue this approach. The council had been created in 1935 to coordinate the recovery agencies of the early New Deal. Mellett was a political ally; a former editor at the *Washington Daily News,* he

had angered his bosses at the Scripps-Howard newspaper chain by supporting FDR's 1937 plan to enlarge the Supreme Court. Getting ready to purge
recalcitrant southern members of Congress in party primaries for the 1938
midterm election, Roosevelt came to think that a report "on the problems
and needs of the South" might prove politically useful. His formal request
took an elevated tone, noting how "discussions in Congress and elsewhere
in connection with legislation affecting the economic welfare of the Nation
have served to point out the differences in the problems and needs of the different sections of the country." As the report was being prepared, the president underscored "his intimate interest in all that concerns the South." This
consisted, he said, of a good deal "more than a sentimental attachment born
of considerable residence in your section and of close personal friendship for
so many of your people." Addressing a July 4 gathering in Washington of
the Conference on Economic Conditions in the South, a group of southern
liberals who focused on the dire economic status of the region while staying
largely silent about racial questions, Roosevelt recorded his "conviction that
the South presents right now the Nation's No. 1 economic problem—the
Nation's problem, not merely the South's."[55]

The report underpinned the claim made by southern regional studies
that only a reinvigorated New Deal could end the quasi-colonial status of
the region. "If it is true that the South is 'the Nation's No. 1 economic problem,'" the historian B. B. Kendrick argued before the Southern Historical
Association in Atlanta in November 1941, "the fundamental historical explanation of that condition is to be found in the fact that for more than three
centuries this region has occupied the status of a colony."[56] The largely agrarian South in the last third of the nineteenth century and the first third of
the twentieth was relatively impoverished, and found itself integrated into
the larger American economy on dependent terms dictated principally by
northern capitalists. In such circumstances, white southerners, and especially
plantation elites, fashioned a politics that was concerned simultaneously with
advancing regional interests against this nationally dominant class and with
protecting their distinctive racial civilization.

Issued on July 25, 1938, the fifty-nine-page *Report on Economic Conditions of the South* underscored the meaning of the region's colonial status
without addressing its racial complexion. It stressed the region's poverty, and
its underutilized human and physical resources. It sketched great depriva-

tion. "Ever since the War between the States the South has been the poorest section of the Nation. The richest State in the South ranks lower in per capita income than the poorest State outside the region." The average income in 1937 for all Americans was $604; in the South, it was nearly half that, at $314. The average southern farmer had a gross income of just $186 per year, compared to $528 elsewhere. More than half had no land of their own, but were sharecroppers or tenants. These had lower incomes still. On cotton plantations, "the average tenant family received an income of only $73 per person for a year's work. Earnings of share croppers ranged from $38 to $87 per person, and an income of $38 annually means only a little more than 10 cents a day." That very year, Congress had passed the Fair Labor Standards Act, establishing a minimum wage at twenty-five cents per hour, soon to rise to forty cents. Farm workers and maids, at southern insistence, had been deliberately left out.[57] Southern poverty, the report concluded, was fully "comparable to that of the poorest peasants in Europe."[58]

Public services, especially the schools, were terrible, well below the level "necessary in any civilized community." Tax collections were meager, averaging, in the states, just $28.88 per person, compared to $51.54 in the country as a whole. With 28 percent of the population, the South contributed just 12 percent of income tax receipts. And the tax burden mainly fell, through sales taxes, on those least able to pay. As southern communities desperately sought to attract capital investment, they promised, and delivered, low-wage workers and low-tax environments. Education was pitiful. The section had one-third of the country's children but just one-sixth of its revenues for schooling. Teachers in Arkansas were paid 80 percent less than teachers in New York. The latter state spent $141.43 per child in 1936; $27.47 was the amount spent in Mississippi, where "there were actually 1,500 school centers . . . without school buildings, requiring children to attend school in lodge halls, abandoned tenant houses, country churches, and, in some instances, even cotton pens." Not surprisingly, southern illiteracy was high, at nearly one in ten persons.[59]

Health was deplorable, especially for those at the bottom—"a belt of sickness, misery, and unnecessary death." The South lacked doctors, hospitals, and clinics. "Many counties have no facilities at all." Pellegra, a disease of malnutrition, was rampant; so, too, were tuberculosis and pneumonia. Despite the region's abundant water supply, water pollution was widespread. Flooding was common, often accompanied by malaria—which annually was infecting more than two million persons, especially in areas without adequate drainage. "More people in the southern area than elsewhere die without medical aid."[60] One cause of such poor health was the state of the region's housing. Half of all the homes in the South were mere hovels, well below a minimum standard. Most lacked running water, and many water supplies were impure. Of all the farmhouses in the South, only 5.7 percent had water piped to the house, and only 3.4 percent to the bathroom. The great majority lacked not only indoor toilets but any system of sanitation.[61]

This document was compelling but deeply misleading. Without exception, all its data lumped blacks and whites together. The report made no mention whatsoever of segregation. Its powerful catalog of regional economic ailments reads as if the race issue did not exist. Yet the South's racial order was an integral part of the region's slow industrialization and backward agriculture, its low wages and poor public services, its keen opposition to unions and stunted strategies of economic development. Organized white supremacy was the foundation for virtually every aspect of southern economics, politics, and society.

The report's silence was motivated by a devout but ultimately forlorn hope not just by the regional scholars whose views the document reflected but also by the national leaders of the Democratic Party that the New Deal might continue to set the race question aside. By the time the document appeared, however, this course already was proving impossible to sustain. By drawing attention to southern deprivation, the New Deal's most focused effort on the South undermined its own presuppositions. It sparked a defensive response by southern politicians and promoted a closer examination of how racial disparities helped constitute the forces it described. By 1938, the willful amnesia and quiet accommodation of racism on the part of New Deal leaders were becoming untenable.

III.

As HAS been noted, southern racial security did not last, and anxiety, if not outright paranoia, became more palpable as the decade was coming to an end. The most important reason was the growth of a far more ambitious and often more militant labor movement than had been anticipated when Congress passed the National Industrial Labor Relations Act in 1935.

A roiling working-class insurgency raised the stakes. At the heart of the corporate economy—in the automobile, rubber, textile, and steel industries—factory workers were seizing factories to demand recognition for the unions affiliated with the newly established Congress of Industrial Organizations (CIO). Rubber workers took over the Goodyear plant in Akron, Ohio, in November 1935, in January 1936, and, again, in February. Organizing huge picket lines and arming themselves with clubs and sawed-off billiard cues to resist efforts by police to end the disturbance, those involved in this "epic struggle" won a settlement for the new United Rubber Workers (URW) union on March 21.[62] At year's end, starting on December 30, workers seeking recognition for the fledgling United Automobile Workers (UAW) occupied the General Motors plants in Flint, Michigan. Sitting down and locking themselves in, the workers at Fisher Body Plant No. 1 and Chevrolet Plant No. 4 fended off tear-gas assaults by the police, and ignored court injunctions to leave until their union was recognized, as it was on February 11. By the close of 1937, the UAW had recruited half a million members.[63] That year also witnessed a mass sit-down strike at Republic Steel and Youngstown Sheet and Tube that was broken up by state troopers. In all, during the period between September 1936 and May 1937, "sit down strikes directly involved 484,711 workers and closed plants employing 600,000 others."[64] According to official government statistics, 1937 alone witnessed 2,200 strikes for union recognition, with the participation of 941,802 workers, which led to success for 711,060. An additional 262,000 workers won union recognition that year through the electoral process sanctioned by the National Labor Relations Act of 1935.[65]

On the eve of the 1935 Wagner Act, which provided a supportive legal framework for labor organizing, 12 percent of nonagricultural workers had belonged to trade unions. By 1939, the proportion more than doubled, reaching 29 percent, thus making it increasingly likely that labor might come to play a central role in national politics in a manner similar to that it had come to perform in Scandinavia, France, and Great Britain. Most telling, because most militant, was the remarkable growth of the CIO. As an excited account of "labor on the march" by a union activist recorded at the time, "by the end of 1937 the affiliated international unions of the CIO had grown from the founding ten to thirty-two; its membership from less than a million in December 1935 to 1,296,500 in July 1936; to 1,460,000 in December;

to 1,804,000 in March, 1937; and by September of 1937 to 3,718,000." The American Federation of Labor (AFL) also expanded, if in a more measured way, growing from 3,218,000 members in 1935 to 3,878,000 by 1939.[66] Both labor federations swiftly made clear that their policy concerns transcended workplace agreements. In November 1939, the AFL announced a comprehensive program for "Next Steps in Social Insurance"; five months later, the CIO issued its far-reaching plans to achieve "Security for the People."[67]

In Congress, the southern wing of the party observed how the interests of "labor" appeared to supplant those of the "farmer" in the Democratic Party's "farmer-labor" coalition. The new unions that "added to the base of social reformism," and "gave the later New Deal a social democratic tinge that had never before been present in American reform movements,"[68] began to organize black as well as white southern workers in the late 1930s. Some unions also worked closely with advocates of racial change within the South. Already in 1934, some two in three mostly white southern textile workers had joined a strike called by AFL's United Textile Workers of America; it was repressed by authorities, who called out the National Guard, used physical force, and set up internment facilities for strikers. Seen as an exception that was handled effectively, this labor conflict did not raise the alarm bells rung by the activities of the CIO's industrial unions in the region.[69] Between 1936 and 1938, there was a successful sit-down strike in Atlanta by the United Automobile Workers at the Fisher Body and Chevrolet plants of General Motors; violent clashes with United Rubber Workers organizers in Gadsden, Alabama; a Tennessee Coal and Iron contract with the United Steelworkers of America; success by the Amalgamated Clothing Workers and the United Garment workers in scattered clothing plants; gains by the United Textile Workers; and triumphant organizing by the Oil Workers International Union in Oklahoma and Texas. By one careful estimate, there were 627,000 union members across the South by 1939, with some 60 percent in building trade, railroad, printing, tobacco, and other AFL unions, about 15 percent in the independent United Mine Workers, and the remaining 25 percent in the new industrial CIO unions.[70]

Relationships between unions and African-Americans were often fraught. A survey in the early 1940s noted how fully thirteen AFL affiliates excluded black members by provisions in their constitutions or by the tacit consent of their members, and how seven more gave black members only

segregated auxiliary status. "In most instances the exclusionist and discriminatory practices have been in effect for many years, and there is no doubt but
that they have the support of the majority of the membership of the unions."
Despite the persistence of such racial discrimination in many unions, and
despite the practice of segregation by numerous southern locals, labor groups
pioneered racial integration in American life. This role included some AFL
unions, such as those of the bricklayers, masons, plasterers, and cement fin-
ishers, as well as the hod carriers' union, the longshoremen's union, and various garment workers' unions that offered equal treatment across the racial
divide; some even fined members who discriminated on the basis of race.[71]

Most striking, though, was how the new CIO unions cultivated African-
American membership and played a key role in forging links "between
urban liberals and the black struggle." They quickly became the most
racially integrated institutions in American life. In all, these unions were the
most important force in making it difficult for across-the-board southern
support for the New Deal to persist. The developing labor movement added
backing for legislation to punish lynching and eliminate the poll tax, thus
helping to emplace civil rights on the agenda of Congress in a serious way
for the first time in nearly five decades.[72]

Southerners had additional reasons to become anxious about the vulnerability of their racial order. The color line was coming under increasing
pressure. Black voices were growing louder and more assertive. The mounting ideological contrast between democracy and totalitarianism drew attention to parallels between the patterns of exclusion that characterized the
lives of African-Americans and German Jews. Further, white southerners
could observe the first signs of change in national white opinion, notice the
president's Court-packing plan, and watch the 1939 creation of a Civil Liberties Unit in the Department of Justice, whose remit included race-related
litigation.[73] President Roosevelt himself seemed less reliable, especially after
he had attempted an unsuccessful purge in 1938 of southern members of
Congress who had begun to resist his legislative agenda.[74] To be sure, he
"seemed ready enough to leave well enough alone in questions that involved
white supremacy," yet he also did not want to forgo northern support, black
as well as white, especially after African-Americans had begun to vote
for the Democratic Party. In 1932, two in three African-Americans voted
for Hoover. The midterm elections two years later witnessed a dramatic

shift, as many blacks soberly recognized that no other available arrangements were better than those offered by the New Deal. By 1936, the slope of
electoral change had grown steeper. Days after the president opened a new
chemistry building at Howard University, the nation's leading black institution, declaring that "among American citizens there shall be no forgotten
men and no forgotten races," support by black voters topped his national
share of 60 percent.[75] The *Baltimore Sun*'s columnist Frank Kent announced
that "nothing of more far-reaching significance has happened in politics for
a good many years."[76]

This electoral swing underscores the dire circumstances black Americans faced at the time. They were attracted to the New Deal by its economic
program, which, however discriminatory, offered real material benefits to
a desperate population. Blacks who had been entirely shut out before 1933
could draw on some public programs, especially federal relief, public works,
and housing assistance.[77] "They say Roosevelt saved them from starvation,
gave them aid when they were in distress," a South Carolina voter regis-
trar reported.[78] The Civilian Conservation Corps (CCC) segregated whites
and blacks, but it put to work some 200,000 young African-Americans.[79]
Blacks also drew comfort from the government's limited and halting racial
appeals, and appreciated unprecedented access to the White House and
federal agencies and the creation of a "black cabinet." They were thankful
for how some federal orders slowed racial discrimination, such as the 1935
directive by the president to the Works Progress Administration, in which
he stated that qualified persons should not be "discriminated against on any
grounds whatsoever."[80] They noticed Eleanor Roosevelt's outspoken support
for greater racial equity, how she promoted education for black Americans
as the ultimate civil right, and how she spoke out against the crime of lynching and advocated federal legislation to curb it.[81] They also took note of how
Harold Ickes, a key Roosevelt confidant who served as secretary of the interior from 1933 to 1946, had been president of the Chicago chapter of the
NAACP; that some administration figures, such as Aubrey Williams, the
National Youth Administration's leader, spent about one-third of his budget on black students; how the New Deal brought tens of talented African-
Americans to Washington, including Ralph Bunche, Rayford Logan, and
William Hastie; and even how a black minister was selected to open a session
of the Democratic Party's 1936 national convention.[82]

Southern Democrats noticed, as well. They understood that no president had been elected in recent decades without carrying Illinois, New York, Ohio, and Pennsylvania, states with 135 electoral votes, a quarter of the national total. Commanding between 4 and 5 percent of the electorate in these states with closely divided white participants, black voters had become potentially pivotal.[83] More broadly, southerners understood that they faced an increasingly unappealing electoral dilemma. From the end of Reconstruction to the New Deal, Democrats lost national elections most of the time because their only sure base was in the South, and Republicans had consolidated a voting advantage in the rest of the country. Only by becoming competitive outside the South, while holding on to their base in the region, had the Democratic Party put together the winning coalition that propelled southern members of Congress into prominent, indeed central, legislative positions.

The South also observed growing black aspirations and outmigration, demands for better education, the heightened activism of an assortment of liberals, union organizers, Communists, and socialists, and a general unsettling of race relations.[84] They took in how some national unions in major industries like steel, rubber, automobile, oil, and mining included a growing multiracial membership, and how northern politicians had begun to cultivate black votes.[85] They worried that efforts to create a national minimum wage would undermine the racial order. "There is a racial question here," Martin Dies, the Texas Democrat, told the House in 1937. "And you cannot prescribe the same wage for the black man as for the white man."[86] At issue was not whether segregation would collapse, at least not in the near term, but whether these developments portended more fundamental change in the future.[87]

Such worries helped revive talk of states' rights, and exacerbated tensions within the Democratic Party's caucuses in the House and Senate. Long-dormant questions were transformed into accusatory challenges. These concerns made even those southern members most inclined toward the New Deal become wary about the strong national powers they had done so much to fashion. James Byrnes, soon to be a Supreme Court justice, then the country's secretary of state, and long "the President's favorite senator," ripped into the New Deal in 1938 for how its decisions about unions and wages undermined southern racial patterns. The Democratic Party, he argued, had fallen under the sway of "the Negroes of the North." He lamented how the South, by contrast, "has been deserted by the Democrats."[88] Many other southern political leaders and journalists also began to realize that New Deal initiatives, ranging from agriculture to industry, threatened to destabilize Jim Crow. It was the first intimation of the possibility that later would cause many southern Democrats to abandon their party entirely.

With the increasing importance of labor union members and northern urban voters, including African-Americans, to the party's electoral base, some even put into question the long-standing affiliation between the South and the Democratic Party.[89] "Southern states," Mississippi's *Fayette Chronicle* editorialized in September 1937, "which for so long have given absolute loyalty to the Democratic party . . . have been actuated by one consideration—the preservation of white supremacy in the south," which it believed had been called into question by the party's cultivation of black constituents. Thus, it counseled that the New Deal had "absolved southerners from any further obligation to a party that has betrayed its most loyal adherents."[90] In January 1940, Mississippi's John Rankin rose in the House to caution his nonsouthern party colleagues not to test the South's sufferance by supporting civil rights initiatives. "Remember," he warned, "southern Democrats now have the balance of power in both Houses of Congress. By your conduct you may make it impossible for us to support many of you for important committee assignments, and other positions to which you aspire." In attacking the southern system, he asserted, "you Democrats . . . are destroying your usefulness here."[91]

The increasingly tenuous coalition of strange bedfellows that composed the Democratic Party had already become manifest when Congress took up two contentious proposals in the first part of 1937. In February, Roosevelt proposed a judiciary organization bill, which would have allowed the president to appoint a new Supreme Court justice, and, more broadly, a new federal judge each time a sitting member over the age of seventy, with ten years of service, did not retire. The goal was to overcome the decisions against key New Deal legislation that had begun in May 1935 when the Supreme Court had ruled the NIRA to be unconstitutional, later followed by judgments that invalidated the tax provisions of the AAA, and the price-setting provisions of the Bituminous Coal Conservation Act of 1935. Some southerners, especially the minority who long had opposed the New Deal, sought to mobilize their fellow regional representatives by arguing that a transformation of race relations was part of the agenda of enlargement. Referring to the plan, Josiah Bailey claimed that Roosevelt "is determined to get the Negro vote, and I do not have to tell you what *this* means." Carter Glass maintained that the bill offered evidence that FDR was courting and helping African-Americans more "than any President except Lincoln." To them, the ill-fated court proposal "was the first step toward the destruction of white supremacy." This appeal persuaded key Senate figures like Champ Clark of Missouri and Tom Connally of Texas, who had backed administration legislation in the past, to break with Roosevelt.[92]

A second jarring proposal was the resurrection of the Costigan-Wagner bill about lynching in the spring 1937 by New York's Joseph Gavagan, a white House Democrat whose district included largely black Harlem (whose first African-American representative, Adam Clayton Powell Jr., was not elected until 1944). With the bill bottled up in the Judiciary Committee, led by Hatton Sumners of Texas, Gavagan pried it loose with a discharge petition that carried 218 signatures, a majority of the chamber. Such a procedural move had not been attempted in the House during the earlier New Deal antilynching effort.[93] Three days later, on April 15, 1937, the House passed the bill by an overwhelming margin, 277–120, with nearly unanimous nonsouthern Democratic support. This was the first civil rights bill sponsored by Democrats ever to pass the House. But it did not survive a six-week filibuster that opened in November 1937 in a Senate with a huge Democratic majority. With solid southern opposition, two cloture votes to end debate failed on January 27 and February 16, 1938. All but one, then three, of the chamber's sixteen Republicans also opposed cloture. Unlike the southerners, they expressed support for the bill. But they announced an unwillingness to give up what their leader, Charles McNarry of Oregon, called "the last barrier to tyranny," the protection filibusters could offer to intense minorities.[94] The black press speculated that Republicans wanted to prevent Democrats from passing legislation they had failed to advance when they had a majority, and that they were exacting retribution for the shift of the black electorate to Roosevelt and congressional Democrats. The *Washington Post*'s analysis claimed that the Republicans had calculated an advantage to demonstrating Democratic divisions by keeping the antilynching question alive, and thought they could appeal to black votes by stating strong substantive agreement with the bill while allowing it to go down, with a Democratic majority taking the blame.[95]

A hallmark of growing southern anxiety was the intensification of rhetoric in the House and Senate compared with the prior debate.[96] As before, southern members argued that the proposed law was unconstitutional, unnecessary, and unfair because it singled out a specific region and only one type of violent behavior. But there was more to be said. Declaring that "the color line in the South is a permanent institution," Georgia's Edward Cox identified the bill as "but one of a series that is intended to be put upon the country in an effort to break the spirit of the white South and, in time, bring about social equality."[97] Georgia senator Richard Russell likewise argued that the bill heralded a wider assault on "the rights of the Southern states," which would culminate in "social equality between the races which includes wiping out all segregation of the races in schools and colleges and churches and hospitals and in homes and in every public place." Byrnes of South Carolina agreed, arguing that to "vote for this bill . . . will require acquiescence to . . . [such] subsequent demands."[98] Explicitly racist speech grew more frequent. Louisiana's Allen Ellender and Mississippi's Theodore Bilbo remonstrated about "mongrelization." Ellender offered an account of the fall of civilizations as a result of racial crossbreeding. Bilbo told the bill's supporters that "upon your garments and the garments of those who are responsible for this measure will be the blood of the raped and outraged daughters of Dixie, as well as the blood of the perpetrators of these crimes that the red-blooded Anglo-Saxon white southern men will not tolerate."[99] Mississippi's John Rankin opined that "decent white people are not going to sit supinely by and let these brutes outrage defenseless women in this manner, law or no." These habitually racist speakers were not alone. They were joined in this line of talk by a range of usually more contained figures, including Representative Sumners and Senator Byrnes.[100]

In 1935, southern members had still been able to count on fellow Democrats not to pass such legislation. This was no longer true. Georgia's Malcolm Tarver asked, "When an overwhelmingly Democratic House supports by a sectional vote such a legislative monstrosity as this Gavagan bill, it is time for the people of the South to ask themselves, 'What protection have we from the unconstitutional interference with our handling of our race problems?'"[101] With Georgia's Paul Brown identifying the legislation as "little more than an emotional appeal to large groups of Negro voters in the North," and Rankin calling it "a bill to make Harlem safe for Tammany," many southern mem-

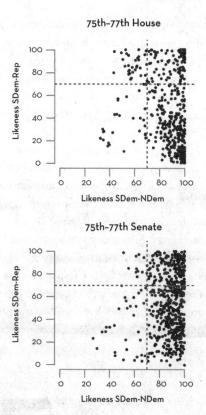

FIGURE 2. *Southern Votes in Congress, 1937–1942*

bers denounced their colleagues for betraying their southern partners.[102] "For more than 100 years," Cox declared, "the people of the South have kept life in the Democratic Party. At times they have been its only friends, and now when the party has grown strong and powerful, it turns upon them and proposes to deal to them this wicked and cowardly blow."[103] Even the most progressive southern member of the Senate, Florida's newly arrived Claude Pepper, spoke out for states' rights, and complained, if in more measured and empirically accurate prose, that "this tragic proposition is out of harmony with the spirit of that philosophy which has prevailed in the national life of this country since the 4th of March 1933, known under the terminology of the New Deal."[104]

Southern voting patterns in Congress increasingly began to shift. Party loyalty grew less sure. Compared with the nearly straight-line party voting during President Roosevelt's first term, the six years that preceded World War II witnessed a still modest but unmistakable change.[105] In the House, partisan and cross-partisan voting declined by 10 percent; 14 percent of roll calls now elicited southern defection to the Republicans or sectional voting. In the Senate, the level of such voting reached 9 percent, twice the level of the earlier period. In the main, partisanship still ruled the day. But as we will see in chapter 10, this turn away from party voting on a growing number of roll calls by southern representatives, especially on proposals dealing with labor markets and trade unions as well as some aspects of social welfare, brought into question those features of the early New Deal that most resembled European social democracy. Simultaneously, as discussed in chapter 11, the South rejected German appeals of racial solidarity and stood in the front line of those in Congress who supported active responses to the growing military might of the German, Italian, Japanese, and Soviet dictatorships. These were the first glimmerings of the essential role southern representatives would soon play in fashioning a new national state with two distinct facets.

IV.

THE WAR years witnessed the growth of an ever-more-obsessive anxiety about race by vigilant southern legislators. The Democratic Party's grip on the region came loose as the South began to lose its capacity to control the racial agenda. The implicit compact that underlay southern enthusiasm for the early New Deal was no longer sufficient, for it became increasingly difficult to secure the section's accustomed freedom of action. Much as the region's leaders before the Civil War "seriously exaggerated the strength of Northern abolitionism and curiously underestimated their own political strength in the nation,"[106] southern congressional delegations in the late 1930s and early 1940s arguably had amplified their vulnerabilities. But when World War II jolted the South's economy, accelerated black population movements and economic mobility, emboldened civil rights activists, and produced major union gains, Jim Crow, in fact, was placed under great ideological and practical pressure.

Both the North and the South were dramatically transformed. The war brought about the recruitment of black labor for work in northern factories, most of which were unionized. In 1940, some 77 percent of black Americans lived in the South, only a 2 percent decrease in share from 1930; by 1950, one in three of the country's fifteen million African-Americans lived outside the region.[107] As voters, they were allied with the liberal wing of the Democratic Party. Although many northern whites were ambivalent, at best, about civil rights, there was an increasing alignment at the mass level of a configuration that included Democratic Party identification, support for New Deal economic policies, and a growing degree of racial liberalism.[108] Further, by the mid-1940s, nonsouthern Democratic party activists and officials composed the political force most in favor of civil rights initiatives.[109] Party competition could proceed no longer without regard for black rights.

The South also changed during the war.[110] One in four farmworkers left the land.[111] Very tight labor markets emboldened union forcefulness. When Congress passed the National Industrial Relations Act in 1935 with southern support, the presence of unions in the region had been slight. During the prewar period, the unionization movement had primarily been concentrated in large urban areas in the Northeast and Midwest, where mass-production industries were situated. With the exception of gains on the docks in New Orleans and in the packinghouses and steel mills of Birmingham, the South was largely left out of the union surge of the 1930s. Labor organizing in the South faced high hurdles. The region was less industrialized than the rest of the country, and its factories were widely dispersed in small and middle-size towns where resistance often was relentless. The huge supply of desperately poor persons depressed wages and made union organizing very difficult. The region's racial order also partitioned workers by race, making divide-and-conquer strategies by employers a ready tool with which to defeat union drives. Many efforts to build southern unions, including a large organizing drive conducted by the AFL in the teeth of the Depression, had come to naught.[112] Thus despite some gains, "the union movement of the South in 1939 ... lagged markedly behind the Northeast, Midwest, and West coast in reacting to the stimulus of the New Deal."[113]

During the war, however, both the AFL and the CIO secured dramatic gains. The labor market induced by wartime industrial expansion and fueled by large federal investments facilitated aggressive union efforts. In just two years, from Pearl Harbor to late 1943, industrial employment in the

South grew from 1.6 million to 2.3 million workers. Southern trends were brought more in line with national developments. Between 1938 and 1948, the two data points in the leading study of labor trends, the region's union membership more than doubled, from just under half a million to more than one million.[114] Indeed, as World War II drew to a close, H. F. Douty, the chief labor economist at the Department of Labor, observed that "with respect to the South, the existing situation is different from any existing in the past." Cotton mill unionism had begun to function, and important collective bargaining agreements had been reached with the major tobacco companies (covering some 90 percent of all workers in the industry) and in the cigar industry (covering about 50 percent). Steel unionism became strongly established, and there were important successes in oil, rubber, clothing, and a wide array of war-related industries. Because "the Negro constitutes a relatively large and permanent part of the southern industrial labor force in such industries as tobacco, lumber, and iron and steel," Douty noted, ". . . successful unionization of such industries require[s] the organization of colored workers." He added that, based on wartime experiences, including experiments with multiracial union locals, there "is evidence to the effect that workers among both races are beginning to realize that economic cooperation is not only possible, but desirable."[115] Assessing future prospects, he concluded, in 1946, that "union organization in the South is substantial in character and is no longer restricted in its traditional spheres in railroading, printing, and a few other industries."[116] These dramatic achievements obviously threatened the traditional South and prodded the development of an antilabor obsession that connected unions to racial change and unrest.

Wartime's labor experiences were only part of a larger pattern of profound change.[117] The mechanization of southern farming accelerated. Literally millions of nonsouthern Americans were trained in southern military camps, more than a million in Texas alone. Attempts to lure industry to the region finally began to succeed.[118] The region's occupational structure and technological capacity underwent pressured change. A huge investment, one exceeding ten billion dollars, in Department of War facilities and war industries accelerated road construction, helping to overcome the poverty of isolation and the isolation of poverty. War plants manufactured planes, ships, and ordnance, fashioned industrial momentum, and formed a more permanent industrial base. More than a million new civilian jobs were created. Military

service emptied many towns and villages at just the moment the new economy fostered urban development. Racial unrest surrounded army camps as
black soldiers in the still-segregated army became emboldened to resist Jim
Crow restrictions when they left their bases.

For the first time in many decades, the Supreme Court began to rule in
favor of more equal rights. In 1938, it found that Missouri had deprived a
black citizen of constitutionally mandated equal protection by excluding him
from law school, even though the state was willing to fund his legal education elsewhere. In 1941, it held that Arkansas likewise had violated the Constitution by denying an African-American access to a white Pullman railcar
when it had not provided a comparable facility for blacks. Most important,
the Court tackled the question of whether party primaries fell within the
purview of federal constitutionalism, an issue that was especially important
in the one-party South, where party primaries in effect constituted the only
democratic elections. In 1935, in *Grovey v. Townsend,* a Texas case, the Court
had ruled that the white primary, excluding blacks from electoral participation, did not fall within the purview of the Fourteenth Amendment's guarantee of equal protection, or the Fifteenth Amendment's insurance of the
franchise, because it was a private activity by the Democratic Party that proceeded without regulation or authorization by the state. In 1944, the Court
ruled differently in *Smith v. Allwright.* It outlawed such primaries on the
grounds that state law made such party elections an inherent part of the electoral process.[119] The decision had an immediate effect on black political participation. Within three years, the proportion of southern blacks registered to
vote more than doubled, reaching some 12 percent.[120]

In the South, as well as outside it, African-Americans were mobilized by
an active black press and civil rights organizations, including a rapidly growing NAACP, to support a "Double V" campaign for democracy at home
as well as overseas. Within the region, white dissent also grew. Tentative
and often limited to criticism of the most outrageous features of the racial
order, southern liberals advocated a heretical platform for racial reform that
linked educational improvement, better access to doctors and hospitals, support for the modernization of state government that would administer programs without regard to race, assaults on egregious inequality and the lack
of economic opportunity, and campaigns against restrictions on voting—all
of which they linked to the wartime struggle against Fascism.[121]

The war also witnessed the first focused effort by the federal government to restrict racial discrimination. Concerned with the potential for mass disorder if A. Philip Randolph, the president of the Brotherhood of Sleeping Car Porters, a black union, were to mount his projected march on Washington to rally against segregation in the armed forces and call for an end to hiring bias in defense industries, President Roosevelt issued his Executive Order 8802 on June 25, 1941. Establishing a five-person Fair Employment Practice Committee (FEPC) to "receive and investigate complaints of discrimination" and "take appropriate steps to redress valid grievances," the order banned "discriminatory employment practices because of race, color, creed, or national origin in government service, defense industries, and by trade unions."[122] From the perspective of the white South, this nightmare of conjunction of union power, labor market issues, and race relations was mitigated by the persistence of racial segregation in the military and by the limited capacity of a body that operated with little money, without real teeth, and without the sanction of a congressional statute. Yet in conjuring the prospect of a labor-based civil rights movement, and its potential for an assault on the economic foundations of Jim Crow, the FEPC crystallized growing southern fears.[123]

Writing in 1949, Richard Hofstadter compared the 1940s to the pre–Civil War crisis, when "a cleavage between North and South became acute during a time of general social ferment in the North, and also of widespread criticism of the slave system." He went on say, "In the recent past, great social changes have again been telescoped within a relatively brief period. Simultaneously, the Negro has gained friends and allies outside the South, numerous enough to give him powerful leverage in changing his racial position. Again the South has reacted militantly."[124]

From the perspective of blacks and the minority of whites who found the South's racial order to be embarrassing, excessive, offensive, or simply wrong, World War II was "a liberating war."[125] But for the South's large white majority, the war, as Odum wrote in 1943, was a "story of the crisis of the South." He counted the ways. These, he observed, included "a general pressure movement to force the hand of the South to eliminate segregation," the rise of black militancy among the group's leaders, and a growing hatred of racial segregation on the part the black masses. In all, Odum argued, the war had increased the "unmeasurable and unbridgeable distance between the white South and the reasonable expectation of the Negro." As a result, the South had come face-to-face with "a supreme test" whose outcome was not clear. Chronicling "the rising tide of tension," he presciently projected that "the outcome of this crisis of race" would have a direct bearing on national politics in postwar America, especially "the problem of labor groups," and the role of government in economic life. "In each of these, both in philosophy and in action," he predicted, "race would be heavily involved," and the South "might be a balance of power."[126]

Odum wrote as a concerned moderate, hoping that a way could be found to navigate this uncertain future. Others responded with violence and with strategies of resistance. "An epidemic of random murder and mayhem was sweeping like a fever through the region, fueled by white fears that black veterans might become a revolutionary force, and that blacks in general would no longer stay in their place." For the first time in many years, the Ku Klux Klan rallied at Stone Mountain, Georgia, burning a cross that could be seen sixty miles away, a signal that southern mores would be enforced by any means necessary. The South experienced six lynchings within three months of the August 15, 1945, end of the war with Japan, followed by seven more in 1946. At least five black veterans were killed by the Birmingham, Alabama, police force, led by Eugene "Bull" Connor, whose brutal treatment of civil rights demonstrators would galvanize the nation two decades later.[127]

The leading southern theorist of resistance, the Alabama lawyer Charles Wallace Collins, sought to counter what he perceived as black control over the national Democratic Party in tandem with organized labor that "strongly advocates and fights for the whole Negro program of equality." Southern anxiety, he wrote, appropriately had reached fever pitch because a new situation had arisen "within the Democratic Party." He went on to say, "The northern wing insists that the Party should strive to give equality to the Negro, including the ballot and the abolition of segregation in the South." This he declared to be "a burning issue for which no compromise solution is possible." The southern political dilemma, he added, was unprecedented. "And for the first time in the history of the country, the South finds itself without political allies north of the Mason-Dixon Line."[128] Fearing that the filibuster would not be a sufficient guardian, Collins identified two options that could utilize the political capacity of the South: an independent southern political party that "would hold the balance of power in the Congress as do the southern Democrats now," or a new two-party alignment, in which the South would vote increasingly in tandem with conservative Republicans in "a logical though unorganized alliance."[129]

The fretful concerns of the South's leaders peaked when a broad-based movement with congressional support mounted an effort to create a permanent FEPC. The World War II FEPC, which was closed when its funding was cut off at war's end, had, in fact, made a significant difference to black employment prospects in war industries, but largely in the North.[130] In the South, it had failed to break out of the confines of segregated employment patterns because the institution on which it relied, the U.S. Employment Service (USES), continued operating as it had traditionally. It maintained segregated offices, routinely placed blacks only in menial and heavy labor, and failed to direct blacks to skilled blue-collar or white-collar jobs. In key war-industry factories, welders and other skilled black laborers were offered only unskilled work as porters or busboys. The FEPC did investigate southern defense industries, received numerous complaints about bias in the USES, and publicized findings of job discrimination discovered in hearings held in May 1942. Yet a combination of little money, determined opposition from southern officials, and the don't-rock-the-boat attitude of the Wartime Manpower Commission, under whose authority the FEPC was located, made it impossible for the committee to make significant headway in the South.[131]

As the war ended, white southern anxiety continued to grow as the region witnessed the return of hundreds of thousands of black veterans who were impatient for change. As they prepared to reenter the workforce, fair-employment legislation covering all employers of six or more persons reached the floor of the Senate in January 1946. This bill promised an aggressive federal effort to secure racial equality that would be significantly more far-reaching than the wartime FEPC, which had included only the federal government and companies engaged in contracting with it.[132] The proposal for a permanent FEPC would have prohibited discrimination based upon race, creed, color, national origin, or ancestry not only by the federal or state governments but also by private employers, with no exemptions for agricultural labor, and by unions. Richard Russell was quick to recognize the radical character of the bill, rightly noting that "there is no more comparison between the powers which were sought to be vested in the FEPC created by Executive order and the agency which is sought to be created by the pending legislation than there is between a rat and an elephant, the existing committee being the rat, and the body proposed to be set up being the elephant which would trample down the last private rights of business in the country."[133]

Far more threatening to segregation than antilynching initiatives, this legislation, a bill, in Russell's words, that "would create class and racial consciousness," evoked a range of negative arguments by southern senators that combined reasoned objections to federal power in the private economy with exaggerated, even panic-stricken and hysterical prose. The bill, which crystallized the main sources of southern anxiety at the junction of race and class, Russell insisted, would "nationalize all employment in industry, business, agriculture, and all other lines of work," taking "away from the employer the fundamental right to say whom he shall hire, whom he shall promote, whom he shall discharge." Alabama's Lister Hill likewise raised the specter in this "first step toward the nationalization of American business and American enterprise" of "a little bureaucrat, clothed with all the power and majesty of the Federal Government, [who] would come out of Washington and would walk into a man's castle—his business—and there would assume to tell him and to dictate to him whom he could employ and whom he could not employ." Byrd of Virginia described such bureaucrats as "snoopers and busybodies, smellers and agitators, alleged do gooders."[134]

This combination of authority and intervention was, it was argued, a harbinger of totalitarianism. Many speakers from the South deployed innuendos and resorted to scapegoating. For Walter George of Georgia, the FEPC bill represented the "philosophy of totalitarian government, pure and simple, in its most extreme form and expression. . . . The latest example is Nazi Germany." For John Bankhead of Alabama, the bill's supporters were "the Bolshevik crowd, the Communist crowd." For Wilbert O'Daniel of Texas, "the philosophy of this FECP bill is purely communistic, and I should not be surprised to learn that it originally came from Moscow."[135]

These were relatively measured comments. James Eastland of Mississippi cast his argument that "the bill would rape Magna Carta itself" in anti-Catholic and anti-Jewish terms. He blamed the "school of thought [that] has grown up in this country which expresses the ideals of these people of southern and eastern Europe. For 50 years that school of thought has grown as immigrants have come to this country, and from it there has been a concerted attempt to destroy our Anglo-Saxon system of jurisprudence, of justice, and of liberty, a school of thought which reaches the high point in this bill, which is part of a campaign to destroy the America which we have loved, and which thousands of men have laid down their lives to create and preserve."

Not to be outdone, Olin Johnston, South Carolina's former governor and now a first-term senator, railed against this assault on the natural order of things. Racial separation, he explained, "is due to an inborn instinct . . . that cannot be changed by legislation." The flagrant Mississippi racist Bilbo likewise described how "segregation is perfectly natural in nature. It is natural in the animal world. We do not see horses out in the meadow land lining up with the cows. . . . That general law also applies to the human race." Underscoring his greatest fear, he regretted "that there are many white people in this country who have no regard for the integrity of their white blood, who are encouraging and aiding and abetting the attempt, the fight, the campaign, the movement which is on to bring about the mongrelization of their own white blood. I say that FEPC is one of the instruments they want to use to bring about that social equality which leads to miscegenation, mongrelization, intermixing."[136]

Much of the inflated rhetoric was directed at unions, especially the CIO, whose members were said to be outside agitators, both corrupt and Communist, "would be uplifters," as South Carolina's Burnet Maybank put it, "people from other sections of the country who do not know or understand the colored man, would use their efforts to stir up strife and prejudice among our people, which in the end would result only in unemployment, and not fair employment." A colloquy between Senators Eastland and Maybank likened the CIO to Reconstruction-era carpetbaggers, and noted, as Maybank put the point, that "the leaders of the CIO mainly are against the things for which the southern people stand."[137]

The ways race and labor had conjoined, these representatives understood, did, in fact, threaten to undermine segregation's establishment. The legislation, Maybank insisted, "is a pure and simple segregation bill . . . to do away with segregation." In terms ranging from moderate to intemperate, they joined as a solid South to denounce such interference by defending their customs and the region's time-honored autonomy. Johnston explained how "long ago the people of the South settled the race question in the only sensible way in which it could be settled, namely, by segregation," and how "segregation is not discrimination but, instead, it operates for the benefit of both the black and white races." With this happy record, Maybank cautioned, "the South will not accept any measure which has the undoubted intent of destroying segregation and at the same time permit social equality between the races. We believe that the colored people have their colleges, their elementary schools, and their churches. If they desire communities, they may have them also. Let them remain in them. Let the rest of us leave them alone."[138]

With the profound transformations of the war years, "leaving alone" was no longer an option. Tensions between the South's commitments to an assertive New Deal and to white supremacy progressively sharpened. The fact that the South was able to prevent a vote on the bill by mustering thirty-six votes to sustain cloture (with forty-eight voting to close debate) was not sufficiently reassuring.[139] In this unsettled and heated context, even milder and more indirect challenges than the FEPC proposal came to be viewed as acts of war, and every potential law, including the vast bulk of legislative proposals not overtly concerned with race, was assessed for how it might affect the region's autonomy. It was as if war clouds were looming once again, this time in the South, where an entire way of life seemed threatened.

Southern congressional evaluations of this situation profoundly shaped the content of the era's achievements as the old formula in which a southern presence within the Democratic Party "would have a check upon extreme violations of its interests" by having the "southern bloc exercise its influence upon the northern wing of its group" no longer was sufficient. As a result, southern power during the 1940s became more pronounced and assertive, so much so that Hofstadter ended his assessment this way, following the successful filibuster of February and March 1949:

> It became clear that the southerners still possessed, and were determined to exercise, the balance of power, which they were free to do at any time by bolting and voting with conservative Republicans; and that no legislation could be passed, on either economic affairs or race relations, which they would not accept. . . . The Democratic party thus finds itself in the anomalous position of being a party of "liberalism," whose achievements are subject to veto by a reactionary faction.[140]

Emerging as the median voter in Congress, the southern bloc became an increasingly independent third force between nonsouthern Democrats and Republicans. Still mostly left of center in ideology, its members preferred to vote with their party when they considered the racial order not to be at stake, and so they still did most of the time. Their fearful apprehension, however, often shading into apocalyptic judgments should the white South lose ground, produced a willingness to join with Republicans or go their own way when they believed that a given substantive issue would jeopardize Jim Crow. Such defections grew increasingly frequent, and the South became the self-conscious arbiter of what could, and what could not, become law.

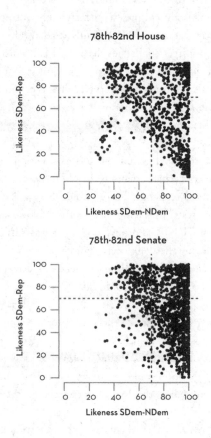

FIGURE 3. *Southern Votes in Congress, 1943–1952*

Before the Civil War, when the strategy of emplacing a southern presence in each major party seemed insufficient to protect the region's vital interest in the slave system, John C. Calhoun, fearing that the South might be defeated by sectional interests, formulated the constitutional idea of a concurrent majority that would give a state, or combinations of states, the ability to veto federal legislation that violated its core interests. In the 1940s, as the South lost confidence that it could stand "firm under a combination of the master-race theory and the one-party state" because race relations and the doctrine of white supremacy had become unsteady and vulnerable, it turned to a reprise of Calhoun's strategy—not, to be sure, as a matter of constitutional federalism, but as a design for southern solidarity and veto rights in Congress, based on shifting alliances depending on the substantive content of a given piece of legislation.[141]

During the FEPC debate, Senator Byrd, whose political machine dominated Virginia politics, underscored how "the South is the backbone of the Democratic Party. No one can deny that. Without the support of the South the Democratic Party could not survive as a national party," and he added that he was "unable to see why our Democratic colleagues from the West and from the North persist time and time again in proposing measures which are without justice and without reason but which are irritating to the South." Overton of Louisiana wondered "how long will the National Democratic Party continue to bite the hand that feeds it?" There would be consequences, a good many argued. O'Daniel beckoned Republicans to join southern Democrats in a new coalition to restrict the use of federal power. "Then we will let the northern Democrats who believe in this philosophy of government, and who can not be elected without getting the Negro votes, go over to the other side and occupy the empty chairs there." Bilbo joined in. Pointing to the division between Republican and Democratic desks on the Senate floor, he warned that "if the northern Democrats keep on monkeying with us southern Democrats we are going to draw the line of separation over on this side."[142]

And so, selectively, they did. In adopting an increasingly independent role, the South, we will discover, did more than make a last stand against fundamental racial change. With the rest of the country divided between liberals and conservatives, Democrats and Republicans, a united Democratic South could defend its interests by determining legislative outcomes.

Its strategic voting behavior, and its search for various winning coalitions for different types of public policy, strongly affected the nation's much wider repertoire of policies. What once had seemed like a domestic policy horizon of far-reaching openness, which included planning and corporatist-interest representation backed by the growing strength of organized labor, gave way to a more restricted vision and less assertive policy instruments, tools that ultimately shaped the procedural face of America's national state. Concurrently, it was also the South's representatives in Washington, we will see, who organized the means for the country's crusading enterprise of might and national security, the state's second face.

As this history unfolded, the calculated substantive orientation adopted by southern Democrats also had a strong impact on the calculations of the two other voting blocs in Congress. We have already seen how in the second phase of the New Deal, starting in the later 1930s, a new repertoire of considered moves, one that was less simple and less predictable than a stark partisan division, selectively began to appear. It occurred when some southern Democrats, on several matters of particular concern, joined with Republicans to endorse positions at odds with the New Deal. Then, during the war, a different pattern emerged, one that carried into the postwar period. Republicans were confronted with a new, if charged, opportunity to forge voting alliances with the majority of members on the other side of the aisle who were increasingly ready, as a united group, to defect from established Democratic Party positions. Nonsouthern Democrats, in turn, who badly needed southern votes to achieve their aims, had to gauge ever more precisely the outer limits of southern tolerance. Where possible, they tried to adjust the contours of legislation to suit those preferences.

We can see these judgments and processes of this third phase of the New Deal as they emerged during the debates about soldier voting that convulsed Congress in 1942 and again in 1944, the subject to which we now turn.

6 ▶ Ballots for Soldiers

R ECOVERING FROM what he described as the flu, perhaps
still exhausted from grueling travel that had taken
him to Cairo in late November to meet with Winston
Churchill and Chiang Kai-shek, then to Teheran for a summit with Churchill and Stalin, Franklin Roosevelt delivered his
January 11, 1944, State of the Union message as a fireside chat.[1]
The Teheran Conference, called to plan the invasion of France,
consider the future of Germany, and begin to fashion the postwar division of Eastern and central Europe, had concluded on
December 1 with a Declaration of the Three Powers affirm-
ing "plans for the destruction of the German forces." With the
Red Army advancing into Poland, having crossed the border on
January 6, with a second European front yet to be established,

and with costly island-to-island battles under way in the Pacific, the president sought to galvanize support for his wartime policies.

In contrast to his March 1933 "Fear Itself" speech, which called on Americans to discover a moral equivalent to war, FDR was now urgently exhorting the country not to tire of the burdens of the raging global war. He urged a quickening of war production, promoted a plan for compulsory national labor service, and summoned Americans to "subordinate individual or group selfishness for the national good." Facing labor unrest and growing impatience with the rationing of sugar, coffee, and tires, rising prices, pervasive shortages, overcrowded housing, and long work hours, he appealed for national unity by attacking advantages being taken by "pests who swarm through the lobbies of the Congress and the cocktail bars of Washington ... to make profits for themselves at the expense of their neighbors," and, most notably, by pledging a postwar "Second Bill of Rights" to guarantee work and economic security, supply health care, provide decent housing, and enhance public education. He also asked Congress to enact "legislation which would preserve for our soldiers and sailors and marines the fundamental prerogative of citizenship—in other words, the right to vote," observing how "surely the signers of the Constitution did not intend a document which, even in wartime, would be construed to take away the franchise of any of those who are fighting to preserve the Constitution itself."[2]

By attending to the history and fate of soldier voting during World War II, we can learn much about how the South was decisively shaping public affairs and policy choices at a time when fundamental postwar domestic and international plans were being conceived. Though it was quite impossible for any member of Congress to oppose, in principle, the idea that citizens who were risking their lives in battle should have the chance to cast a ballot, southern representatives were keenly concerned that an effective federal role of the kind the president was proposing threatened to undermine the restrictions on voting that their states had crafted over many decades. As a result of their legislative craftsmanship, the soldier-voting bills that were adopted satisfied southern preferences.

In proposing a strong federal role, Roosevelt must have recalled how, at the end of June 1918, when he was serving as assistant secretary of the navy, the Department of War had issued a statement observing that almost none of the states provided "a practicable method of taking soldiers' votes under prevailing conditions in Europe," and thus had failed to live up to Secretary

Newton Baker's announced criteria for voting by the one million men serving overseas in the American Expeditionary Force, requiring that plans for voting not impede military efficiency.[3] The president's impetus to promote an effective soldier-voting bill surely also took into consideration the feeble results that had been produced by the unwieldy Servicemen's Voting Act of 1942. That year, final passage did not occur until September 16, only a month and a half before Election Day. That complex statute had ordered each secretary of state to send ballots to soldiers qualified by state law who had declared a wish to vote by returning a postcard provided by the military. Marked ballots were mailed to the secretary's office in each state capitol, accompanied by an oath of eligibility sworn in front of a commissioned officer. Once received, these ballots were transmitted to election officials in the appropriate constituency. "Time was short; shipping was a problem," *Newsweek* recalled as Congress began to consider what to do in 1944. "And in the South, Democratic primaries tantamount to election had long since been decided."[4] In all, 78,589 applications were received;[5] in a total electorate of 29,448,320, a mere 28,051 war ballots had been cast and counted.[6]

The issue was more pressing in 1944. Not since the Civil War had such a large proportion of young American men been exposed to the probability of death or injury. The country had entered a raging global war in December 1941 with an army of just under 1.7 million, and a navy, marine corps, and coast guard with a combined force of 486,000. Two years later, as Congress geared up to decide how soldiers might vote, the army had grown to some 7,582,000, and the navy, marine corps, and coast guard to 2,958,000.[7] On Christmas Eve of 1943, reporting on Cairo and Teheran and announcing the appointment of Gen. Dwight Eisenhower as the commander who would lead "a gigantic attack on Germany," Roosevelt had broadcast the warning that "the war is now reaching the stage when we shall all have to look forward to large casualty lists."[8] By the time he was reelected to a fourth term, nearly 140,000 Americans had been killed, and more than 70,000 others, missing in action, were presumed to have died.[9]

Without a federal soldier-voting framework, President Roosevelt argued in his January State of the Union message, "the men and women in our armed forces" would experience "unjustifiable discrimination" because "the overwhelming majority of them will be deprived of the opportunity to vote if the voting machinery is left exclusively to the States under existing State laws."[10] Reporting how the army and navy indicated "that it will be impossible effectively to administer forty-eight different soldier-voting laws" (but implicitly noting that the administration of the franchise was ordinarily a prerogative of the states[11]), he argued it was essential to preserve this fundamental right of citizenship for those fighting in the service of the nation.[12]

Within weeks, Roosevelt failed to deliver on this goal. Considering it impossible to veto, lest the only system in place be the ineffective arrangements that had been used so feebly in 1942, he let what he himself admitted was a "wholly inadequate" and "defective" bill pass into law at the end of March without his presidential signature.[13] "Out of conference between the House and the Senate," the historian Frank Freidel correctly summarized, "came a bill that bore little more than the semblance of a soldiers' vote bill,"[14] if not quite, as Philadelphia Democrat Michael Bradley told the House, "a bill to make it difficult for soldiers to vote."[15] Despite powerful practical and ethical impulses favoring direct, simple procedures for soldier voting, the outcome hovered between democracy and its betrayal.

Immediately after Congress heard a message from the president on March 31, in which he explained his very reluctant passive endorsement and requested amendments that would ensure delivery "to men and women in the service . . . a short, uniform Federal ballot,"[16] Mississippi's John Rankin, who had led the legislative effort to craft an alternative to the administration bill in the House, "rose to say that he had no intention 'to quarrel with the President,' but asserted that 'we have provided the very best law we could under the circumstances.'"[17]

What were these countervailing circumstances? Why was an assertive president, who was invoking military sacrifice on behalf of a basic right of democratic citizenship, placed in the discomfiting position of waiting until twelve hours before the deadline for a presidential decision to accept, veto, or decline to sign before passively permitting what the *New York Times* called "the 'States rights' soldier vote bill" to take effect, not only in contravention to his own wishes but in the face of a national elite and mass consensus that favored expedited soldier voting?

I.

WITHOUT EXCEPTION, members of the House and Senate who discussed the issue in committee or on the floor backed soldier voting. Further, as the *Congressional Digest* observed, "even assuming that a Senator or Representative might feel that the absentee soldiers might not vote for him, sheer political sense would prevent his opposing the soldier vote, actively or passively. It would be political suicide for him to do so."[18] "Every one concedes that the men who are fighting to preserve our American form of government should participate in the elections of that government while they are in service," the once-isolationist *Chicago Tribune* editorialized.[19] Who could, or would, disagree? In January 1944, the National Opinion Research Center asked respondents whether "you think that men and women over 21 in the armed forces who are stationed outside of this country should be able to vote in the Presidential election next November, or don't you think they should?" Positive replies were offered by 92 percent.[20]

Soldier-voting legislation first passed the House in 1942 by an overwhelming 134–19 margin; final passage in the Senate was achieved on an emphatic 47–5 roll call.[21] After the war, in 1946, soldier voting was affirmed unanimously by voice vote in both congressional chambers. No case ever was advanced in Congress, or indeed by any political leader or commentator, to oppose voting rights for soldiers, sailors, and marines. "We all agree that the war has taken the soldier away from the ballot box back in his own State," Texas Democrat Eugene Worley, who chaired the Committee on Elections, told the House, noting that "no true American can disagree with [the] premise . . . that it is the solemn duty of Congress and the States to do everything within their legal and constitutional power they can do to take the ballot box to the soldier, wherever he may be."[22] Largely for this reason, the military-voting initiatives of World War II usually are remembered as efforts to protect and extend voting rights.[23]

This legislation is particularly celebrated for lifting the poll tax, a suspension first enacted in 1942 for soldiers who lived in one of eight former Confederate states (Alabama, Arkansas, Georgia, Mississippi, South Carolina, Tennessee, Texas, and Virginia[24]) that still required this payment of between one and two dollars, sometimes cumulatively, in order to vote. Although this was a partial and temporary deferral—only for soldiers, only for the duration of the war, and only for federal posts in the general election[25]—the heat of opposition in the Deep South revealed its significance. There and more widely, it was recognized as a noteworthy advance to black rights in a nation at arms at the site where racism collided with the language and values of republican citizenship. This "limited retreat from the poll tax system"[26] constituted the first enacted congressional civil rights initiative since the wave of procedures that had been introduced to disenfranchise black citizens at the end of the nineteenth century and the start of the twentieth. A November 29, 1943, political summary, one of a series regularly sent by Oxford's Isaiah Berlin to the Foreign Office from the Special Survey Section of the British embassy in Washington, reported that the "bill to enable soldiers abroad to vote in presidential election (though it seems not in primaries) has stirred up powerful opposition among Southern Democrats." They were especially exercised by the "danger to [the] poll tax system since Southern colored soldiers cannot well be prevented from voting with their white comrades, which would establish a powerful new precedent."[27] Nearly half a century after the fact, the person most responsible for drafting the administration's preferred bill for 1944, the legal scholar Herbert Wechsler, similarly recalled how "the Southern point of view" was marked by "the fear that this was an opening wedge for congressional intrusion in the electoral process, with its ultimate implications for breaking down the disenfranchisement of blacks. And the Southerners were absolutely right about that."[28] For African-Americans, long denied meaningful political participation, rescinding the poll tax seemed remarkable, a kind of miracle. Edgar Brown, the president of the Negro Federal Workers Employees Union, who had served as adviser on Negro Affairs for the Civilian Conservation Corps, thus celebrated this "first implementation of the Thirteenth, Fourteenth, and Fifteenth Amendments to the Constitution . . . the greatest contribution to democracy since the signing of the Emancipation Proclamation by President Lincoln."[29]

In assessing the effects of war on liberal democracy, Ronald Krebs has underscored how the pressures of total war in the 1940s enhanced political participation.[30] David Mayhew's examination of warfare's impact on American political history identifies soldier-voting rights, including the poll tax exemption, as one of nine key policy advances of World War II.[31] Even more expansively, the historian Reeve Huston has written that "during the war, Congress passed Soldier Voting Acts, which enabled all soldiers to vote without racial exclusions."[32] Mayhew's and Huston's source is Alexander Keyssar's grand history of the evolution of suffrage in the United States, which stressed how, over the course of American history, it was warfare and its sacrifice for democratic values that emboldened the disenfranchised and placed opponents on the defensive. Keyssar characterized the World War II measures as "standardizing and federalizing" the right to vote for members of the armed forces. Appraising this development as "not surprising" at a time of patriotic fervor and national cohesion, he positively judged soldier voting to have been a critical step toward nationalizing and advancing voting rights for all American adults.[33]

In light of these assessments, it seems curious to read a dry scholarly monograph that dramatically takes note of the legislation's "enormous controversy"; to discover a leading student of soldier voting summarizing how the issue was "seething with controversy"; to come across *Newsweek*'s report of how "the soldier-vote promised to be one of the most explosive of this 78th Congress [and] could turn the 1944 election into one of the most controversial in history"; to notice that the journalist (later novelist) Allen Drury recorded in his contemporaneous Senate journal that "the soldier-vote bill" is "rather less of a patriotic contest than the public has been led to believe"; to see Samuel Rosenman, a key Roosevelt adviser and White House counsel between 1943 and 1946, recalling how "the bitter fights with Congress . . . on soldier voting" revealed that the president "had lost control . . . of his own party in Congress"; to become aware of the *Chicago Tribune*'s report of how, in "one of the wildest sessions in years," lasting "nearly four tumultuous hours, the Mississippian [John Rankin] fought to prevent his colleagues from considering legislation to permit members of the armed forces serving in the continental limits of the United States and Alaska to cast absentee ballots in the forthcoming November election"; and to read *The Nation*'s description of the soldier-vote issue "as one of the most partisan fights in American history."[34]

It is even more unexpected to learn that fully fifty-three members of the House of Representatives voted against the soldier-voting bill in September 1942; and to discover that, in July 1944, the Senate approved soldier voting by a 47–38 margin, hardly an indicator of a sweeping consensus about liberal rights, democratic imperatives, and republican citizenship at a time of national peril.

The disputes that split Congress and ultimately led to President Roosevelt's humiliation lay precisely with the "standardizing and federalizing" attributes that Keyssar's account appreciatively, but wrongly, portrays as the legislation's primary features. These questions strained the spirit of national unity that Roosevelt had started to invoke even before Pearl Harbor. In his "Four Freedoms" State of the Union message of January 1941, the president had underscored, wishfully, how circumstances in Europe and Asia called on all Americans to build a shield for democracy beyond special interest or partisan divisions. Calling for "an all-inclusive national defense," expressing a determination to keep "war away from our Hemisphere" by "resisting aggression," and refusing "to acquiesce in a peace dictated by aggressors and sponsored by appeasers," the speech utilized the phrase "by an impressive expression of the public will and without regard to partisanship" to begin the three consecutive paragraphs expressing, in this way, "our determination that the democratic cause shall prevail."[35] Echoing this language, Massachusetts Republican Joseph Martin, the House minority leader and chairman of the Republican National Committee, who later led his party's support for soldier-voting legislation, underscored that "partisan politics have no place in the consideration of war activities."[36]

Yet by moving questions about federalism and eligibility to the fore, soldier voting pit such calls for national unity against other strongly held beliefs and values, most notably inclinations to favor a modest federal role and protect Jim Crow. These preferences sometimes coalesced. In an atmosphere of heightened anxiety on the part of some southern members in the House and Senate about the war's impact on the persistence of white supremacy, debate in both chambers disclosed tensions within the usually solid South on matters that concerned race. Further, in 1942, and again in 1944, the House proved more willing to acquiesce to southern anti–poll tax sentiment, just the reverse of the voting pattern that prevailed when the poll tax was considered in a freestanding manner, thus exposing tensions between symbolic and sincere behavior with regard to civil rights.

Contrary to Keyssar's canonical assessment, the most notable features characterizing both the burdensome process that was authorized in 1942 and the simpler and more timely 1944 statute were, in fact, decisions not to standardize the ballot and not to give significant powers of oversight, implementation, and sanction to the federal government despite the imperatives of total war.

Technically a set of amendments to the existing act, the 1944 law did gesture toward a standard federal role by establishing a three-person Federal Ballot Commission (the secretaries of war and navy, and the administrator of the War Shipping Administration) to prepare, deliver, and receive ballots for federal offices. This procedure was intended to facilitate voting when a state did not provide for absentee voting, or when a soldier would swear an oath after October 1 that a state ballot properly applied for had not been received. Votes cast by soldiers utilizing this federal ballot would be counted in the tally for national offices in the local jurisdictions to which they would be delivered. Further, the amended act did not repeal—at least not explicitly—the poll tax waiver for soldiers.

Nevertheless, what stands out is not the "not surprising" impulse to extend voting possibilities to members of the armed services but the "emasculation of a stronger Soldier Vote Act"[37] by a congressional coalition that successfully resisted the vigorous effort Roosevelt and his administration mounted to offer all soldiers a standard federal ballot.

In all, the 1944 statute contained numerous features that made it a pantomime of federally secured voting rights. Its provisions incorporated features the president had denounced as "fraud on the soldiers, sailors, and marines now fighting for us, and a fraud upon the American people" in late January, when they first had appeared as the defining elements of a bill for soldier voting sponsored in the House by John Rankin and in the Senate by James Eastland, also from Mississippi.[38] "The bill reduced the United States War Ballot Commission to largely printing, compiling, and record keeping, it had 'no general supervisory authority' to judge the qualifications of potential military voters."[39] The statute's provisions included the requirement of an oath of qualification, and a stipulation that "under this act the states are free to determine for themselves whether or not the voters under the act are qualified to vote under the laws of the state." The law simply recommended, but did not mandate, that states waive their registration requirements for voters in the armed forces. It only suggested that they make available absentee ballots for state and local as well as federal positions in both primary and general elections.[40] The federal ballot applied exclusively to members of the armed services serving *outside* the country, unless the person's state made no provision for absentee voting whatsoever (at the time, only Kentucky and New Mexico met this test). Most important, Title III stipulated that the federal balloting provisions of the law would be subject to state-by-state legislative approval. Each governor would have to confirm that "the use of ballots provided for by this title is authorized by the laws of such State," thus ensuring that the standard federal ballot would be counted only in states that officially and publicly certified their use by July 15. Any conflict between federal provisions and state law, moreover, would privilege the latter.

Just twenty of the forty-eight states approved the federal ballot. Fewer than 85,000 soldier voters utilized it. Of the 9,225,000 persons of voting age in the military in 1944, 2,961,160 voted, the vast majority by utilizing ordinary state procedures for absentee voting. This turnout clearly was a huge advance over that of 1942, but it fell well short of widespread expectations, including the estimate of 6,000,000 soldier voters that had been offered by statisticians at the American Institute of Public Opinion months earlier.[41] In a March 1952 message to Congress about soldier voting in the midst of the Korean War, President Truman judged this record, without elaboration or an explanation of the cause, to have been "not good,"[42] observing how "during World War II, an effort was made through State action and congressional action to facilitate voting by men and women in the armed services, but it was never really as successful as it should have been."[43] In 1944, the South had lagged far behind. The poorest military-turnout performers were Alabama, South Carolina, Delaware, Texas, Arkansas, Mississippi, and Louisiana. With the exceptions of Georgia and Virginia, where state governments actively courted white soldier voters, the turnout record in the other southern states was only marginally better.[44] Of the weakest southern performers, only one, Texas, sanctioned the federal ballot.

Not just the federal ballot but also the poll tax dispensation first enacted in 1942 hinged on the certification by governors that the federal ballot would be an acceptable form of soldier voting. Asked by Iowa Republican Karl LeCompte if the poll tax provisions of the earlier law had been repealed, Eugene Worley replied, "I say they are not expressly repealed, but they are effectively nullified. We have tied them down to such an extent that they are dead unless the Governors make the necessary certification. . . . Until he makes such certification, [the 1942 stipulations] are stone dead."[45] In all, with these provisions and stipulations, the symbols but not the substance of voting rights were extended to American soldiers.

II.

FROM START to finish, the South's qualms hung over soldier voting. Any account must show how, under the leadership of Senator Eastland and Congressman Rankin, southern members sought to mobilize sectional solidarity, command congressional rules, and invoke cherished values associated with the federal principle of limited central government. Crafting a states' rights alternative to Wechsler's Department of Justice bill, which came to be sponsored by Democratic senators Theodore Green of Rhode Island and Scott Lucas of Illinois,[46] they sought to ensure that any enacted legislation would not upend the region's rules for, or control over, its low-franchise, exclusionary voting system.

John Rankin had represented Mississippi's First District for twenty-four years. He had been a leader in the House in crafting legislation that created the Tennessee Valley Authority in 1933, and was a consistent supporter of the expansion of public-power facilities. As chairman of the Committee on World War Veterans Legislation, he had championed general pensions for World War I widows and orphans, and played a key role in 1944 in writing the GI Bill during the period soldier voting was being debated.[47] He also was a fervent and unashamed racist, famous for having labeled antilynching legislation a proposal to encourage rape, for threatening "that thousands of blacks would be killed" if the poll tax were to be repealed by the federal government, for supporting Japanese internment on racial grounds ("The white man's civilization has come into conflict with Japanese barbarism. . . . Once a Jap always a Jap"), and for rabid public anti-Semitism.[48] In 1942, his speech had been dependably unconstrained, calling the bill "an insult to the uniform" that had been "pushed by the Communist Party, through the C.I.O. for the purpose of giving those radical elements power over our electoral machinery."[49] By contrast, during the soldier-ballot debates of 1943 and 1944, Rankin spoke fairly loftily about constitutional law, remonstrating that a federal ballot would "destroy the States' control of elections, wipe out the independence of our elections, and destroy the States' election machinery," characterizing the administration's initiative as "one of the most dangerous measures so far as the welfare and safety of our American institutions are concerned that has ever been proposed to the Congress of the United States."[50] Explaining how the House conferees had managed to accede to the formalities of a federal prohibition of the poll tax while ensuring that it could be nullified, he more laconically observed, "We were trying to bring this law within the scope of the Constitution of the United States."[51]

James Eastland's soldier-vote rhetoric was rather less restrained. Starting the first of five terms—a career that culminated in a long chairmanship of the Judiciary Committee and service as permanent Senate president when the vice presidency was twice vacant in the 1970s, he rose to "speak the sentiments of the hundreds of thousands of young men from Mississippi and the South who wear the uniform of their country. When they return to take over," he declared, "they desire more than anything else to see the integrity of the social institutions of the South unimpaired. They desire to see white supremacy maintained." Affirming "that we shall maintain control of our own elections, and our election machinery, and that we will protect and preserve white supremacy throughout eternity," Eastland, who controlled his family's six-thousand-acre plantation in the Delta's overwhelmingly black Sunflower County, insisted that he was doing no more than representing his soldier constituents, "the men in the armed forces of Mississippi and from other states in the South." Hundreds, he reported, had written to convey that "above all things they do not desire to see the election laws of the South or the powers of the States in defining the qualifications of electors tampered with. Those boys are fighting to maintain the rights of the States. Those boys are fighting to maintain white supremacy."[52]

Such unconcealed sentiments are scattered throughout these debates. "We of the South are proud, indeed, of the purity of blood which flows through our veins," Peterson "Pete" Bryant Jarman of Alabama informed the House when soldier voting was first considered, in 1942. Arguing that such a federal measure constitutes "an attack on our southern way of life and on white supremacy in which we have every reason to take much pride," he concluded that this "entering wedge looking toward the destruction of our State-supervised election systems, our way of life, and possibly white supremacy . . . is really an arrow aimed directly at the heart of the South, which has always been, is now, and ever must be, white supremacy."[53] Ellison DuRant Smith, who had been a leading figure in the Southern Cotton Association (hence his nickname, "Cotton Ed") before his election to the Senate from South Carolina in 1908, who had led the charge for immigration restriction in 1924 ("I think we have a sufficient population in our country for us to shut the door and to breed up a pure, unadulterated American citizenship"[54]), and who famously had walked out of the Democratic National Convention in 1936 when a black minister was about to offer the invocation, took the floor in 1943 to characterize national ballots for soldiers as "but a camouflage to enrage a race that does not understand it."[55]

The southern role in the legislative history of soldier voting, however, was both more variegated and more complex than this racist rhetoric might indicate. Three features stand out. First, the year 1942 was notable for how southern congressional moderates, led by Tennessee's Estes Kefauver in the House and Florida's Claude Pepper in the Senate, sought to develop an independent voice on behalf of steady, if measured, racial progress, a view they shared with moderate journalists, intellectuals, activists, and politicians who advocated the growth of industry and the acceleration of urbanization as forces that could shape a more modern South.[56]

Second, soldier voting proved a harbinger of massive resistance and the larger failure of the moderates.[57] Because the issue so deeply resonated with fundamental American values—what Gunnar Myrdal at just this moment was labeling "the American Creed"[58]—and with the rhetoric of rights announced by the Atlantic Charter and President Roosevelt's talk of Four Freedoms, the possibility that the federal government might assume an assertive voting-rights role raised hard-core southern anxiety to a pitched level. Eastland's rhetoric reflected this acute panic for the extreme South. Under these circumstances, the alliance that had brought together such strange bedfellows in the Democratic Party was placed under great stress as southern Democrats and Republicans gingerly discovered how they might join together in alliances of convenience.

Third, alongside wartime lawmaking about organized labor,[59] soldier voting provides the most observable setting in which to watch this crucial process of coalition shifting that significantly widened the spectrum of possibilities within national politics. In 1942, nonsouthern Democrats found common cause with moderate southerners to pass a soldier-voting law that protected states' rights and shielded segregation without overtly endorsing restrictive racial practices. Over the course of the next two years, an alliance of southern Democrats and Republicans came to devise effective means to resist President Roosevelt's plan for a federal ballot. Southern votes supplied pivotal support for both winning coalitions.

III.

THE RULES Committee of South Carolina's Democratic State Convention gathered in Columbia on May 21, 1942. By a vote of 40–1, its members resolved to keep the party's upcoming September primary all-white, despite a petition by a small group of white liberals that called attention to the war and its values, and raised questions about soldier voting. Referring to the exigencies of the time, the decision to maintain the status quo was folded into a motion to suspend action on "all controversial matters."[60] The next month, the two leading candidates for governor—Wyndham Manning, who later, in 1947, was appointed superintendent of South Carolina's prison system by Governor Strom Thurmond, and the fervent New Dealer Olin Johnston, who had held the gubernatorial office from 1935 to 1939 and went on to defeat Manning in the party primary—debated problems of war and peace at a June 9 mass meeting in Lexington, which had been called to consider the impact of World War II on the state. Near the evening's conclusion, "A. B. Hogan," described as a "liberal white," made reference to the convention's decision regarding black primary voting, by civilians and soldiers, and asked for the candidates' views, according to the *Pittsburgh Courier,* the country's leading black paper. "I'll be glad to answer that," said Johnston. "I believe in white voters staying in the Democratic party. If the colored people want a party, let them organize one." Manning replied, "I'm surprised that such a question should be asked. The Democratic party is a white man's party and must be so maintained."[61]

In a situation marked by an imminent congressional election, and with more than 200,000 African-Americans already serving in the country's armed forces, the question of black voting did in fact get asked over the course of the next two summer months on Capitol Hill as the House and Senate fashioned the Servicemen's Ballot Act for the 1942 election. Strikingly, the poll tax issue was placed on the agenda not by Republicans or nonsouthern Democrats but by southern moderates.

Nonsouthern members had taken pains to reassure the South that they had no intention of disturbing existing practices. Raymond Springer, an Indiana Republican, confirmed in the House, "[T]his proposed legislation refers only to those who are "otherwise qualified to vote under the law of the State of his residence. . . . It does not seek to modify or change the qualifications of the voters of any State."[62] After the Rules Committee sent the bill he had sponsored to the floor, the Democratic representative for West Virginia, Robert Ramsay, offered similar guarantees. The law, he declared, would not affect state requirements for voting, "such as payment of a poll tax."[63] Ramsay's fellow Democrat, Rhode Island's Theodore Green, the floor manager for the legislation in the Senate, explained that "in view of the need for speedy passage, it was more urgent now to give the service men from the other . . . States their chance to vote than to risk delay by making a stand for the men from the . . . poll tax states."[64] He justified this position, one he had taken alongside other pro–civil rights Democrats, by arguing that the poll tax was controversial and the committee had decided it would omit all such controversial questions.[65]

By contrast, it was Senator Pepper, a fiery New Dealer, Harvard Law School graduate, and a racial moderate, who insisted that "it is inconsistent with the spirit of American institutions to make a soldier pay a poll tax. . . . That is not democracy," and Representative Kefauver, a Yale Law School graduate who took to wearing a coonskin cap after he had been likened to a cunning raccoon by his conservative opponents in Tennessee, who resolutely argued that "no poll tax should be required of men in the armed services who wish to exercise their right to vote while they are away from home," as "one of the principal rights every citizen should have is that of franchise, and this should be without the imposition of financial conditions."[66] In introducing his amendment to suspend the poll tax, Kefauver articulated the tension-charged position of the region's moderates, noting, "I realize that my position on this bill and to some similar matters is not in conformity with many of my colleagues from the South," but insisting "that if we feel that these boys are capable of serving on the battlefield to protect us and our country, we ought to feel they are capable of voting in an election without registration and without the payment of a poll tax."[67]

When soldier voting was first approved in the House, on July 23, this issue did not elicit much passion. A quite empty and seemingly indifferent House rejected Kefauver's poll tax amendment by a vote of 33–65.[68] With this question out of the way, the bill passed by a 139–19 margin,[69] but only after committed opponents, led vocally by John Rankin and Pete Jarman, offered "persistent but futile objections," forced four roll calls to confirm the existence of a quorum, and challenged the legality of the Rules Committee's report ("obtained by fraud," claimed Rankin, "clandestinely held or held without notifying the other members"). Though there is no official record of the individual distribution of votes, as this was a standing vote, the press reported that the nineteen all were southern—the hardest of the hard core from the Deep South, for these were representatives who shared Rankin's view that the bill was "merely an attempt to get the camel's nose under the tent and destroy the election laws in every State in the Union," despite the failure of his colleagues, to that point, to put the poll tax on hold, despite the bill's affirmation of the right of the states to set qualifications for voting, despite the applicability of this version of the bill exclusively to soldiers stationed inside the United States, and even though the only modification it proposed to state elections laws was that of overriding any requirements that voters must appear in person to register or cast their vote.[70] What Rankin and his supporters feared was federal action of any kind in the area of voting rights.[71]

The difficulty was that once the southern moderates had taken the lead on the poll tax question in the Senate, Green and most other Democrats no longer could refrain from endorsing the suspension. Republicans, in turn, saw an opportunity to divide the Democrats, make them uncomfortable, and appeal to northern black voters.[72] They seized the issue as their own. Charles Wayland Brooks of Illinois, who was running for reelection in a tight race, managed to get his Republican anti–poll tax amendment, rather than that of Democrat Pepper, recognized as being in order in the Senate.[73] The black press widely praised Brooks; a convention of 3,500 ministers "gave a rising vote of thanks to Sen. Wayland Brooks [R., Ill.] for his successful sponsorship of the anti-poll tax amendment to the soldiers' vote bill" at the Memphis National Baptist Convention in September 1942; Dr. D. V. Jamison, the president of the National Baptist Convention, citing Brooks, "called upon Negroes to vote for republican candidates for congress as the only way for colored people to secure justice and freedom"; and the African-American vote did exhibit a swing back to Republican voting in the 1942 congressional elections. Walter White, the executive secretary of the NAACP, was quick to claim credit for Republican gains, noting in a press statement that "the shift in a number of Congressional districts of Negro voters from Democratic to the Republican side is in large measure due to resentment against the domination of national policy on the Negro by the reactionary South," a group he described as "Negro hating Southern Democrats." The sociologist Horace R. Cayton Jr. ascribed the black Republican turn in Chicago that boosted Brooks to "his courage and alertness that eliminated the necessity for payment of poll tax by soldiers and sailors from eight southern states."[74]

Approved by a 33–20 margin, the Brooks amendment was one of three liberalizing changes made by the Senate to the House bill. The other liberalizing changes in the Senate authorized soldier voting to include primary elections, the ones that really counted in the South, by an even closer, 28–25 vote; and, by voice vote, extended absentee voting to soldiers and sailors stationed overseas. This broadening of scope to include troops abroad was considered a technical matter, not an issue of principle and, for this election at least, not much more than a gesture; "if it should prove impossible to get the votes back in time," said Robert Ramsay, summarizing the meaning of the Senate's action for the House, "it would at least give the boys a chance to vote and enable Congress to say we are going to take the ballot to every man who is a citizen."[75]

In light of the bill's time frame, the issue of whether soldiers should be permitted to vote in primaries likewise was rather abstract, since all the South's primaries took place before the bill could become law. Nevertheless, the manner in which votes were cast on this amendment, which was proposed by Republican John Danaher of Connecticut, is quite revealing. With fifteen of the twenty-eight positive votes, the core of the winning coalition supporting a more liberal bill was Republican. Not surprisingly, the core of the negative vote was southern. Perhaps less expected was how the fourteen southern nay votes were joined by eleven, a majority, of nonsouthern Democrats, including Green of Rhode Island, who were struggling at just this time with how to maintain cross-regional party unity in the face of an increasingly assertive Republican Party.[76]

Of the three changes to the House bill introduced by the Senate, the poll tax issue was the most contentious. The "simple issue" of soldier voting, the *Washington Post* observed, "has been virtually lost to sight in the quarrel over Southern poll taxes and the one-party system in the South."[77] The opponents were not just the hard-core rejectionists from the Deep South, such as Mississippi's Theodore Bilbo or South Carolina's Cotton Ed Smith; they included Kentucky's Alben Barkley, the Senate's majority leader, and Missouri's Harry Truman. Breaking with the southern consensus were five senators from the region's periphery, who joined Pepper to support the amendment. Coming from West Virginia, North Carolina, Tennessee, and Delaware, they represented states without a poll tax.[78]

Whereas the chamber's Republicans voted with perfect cohesion to support the Brooks amendment, the nonsouthern Democrats divided 12–7. Coming from Arizona, Idaho, Indiana, Iowa, Pennsylvania, and Rhode Island, none of the negative voters either supported or represented states with a poll tax. What motivated them was a concern that approval of this amendment might ultimately doom the legislation and split the party. The degree of likeness between southern and nonsouthern Democrats[79] was considerably higher than Republican and nonsouthern Democratic likeness,[80] and surprisingly closer to the more expected low likeness of southern Democrats and Republicans.[81] In short, this was a vote that pitted a unanimous Republican Party against Democrats from all regions who found themselves torn between principle, both for and against, and instrumental calculation.

For more than half a century, civil rights voting in the House had provided a form of theater. Those casting votes about lynching or the poll tax understood that southerners in the Senate would filibuster to block the legislation. For the first time in decades, the subject of soldier voting detached this veto instrument. Like their House compatriots, southern senators in the main understood that they could not afford to be seen to block soldier voting. Moreover, most southern representatives found explicit talk promoting white supremacy to be discomfiting and instrumentally counterproductive. They appreciated that such language, as distinct from constitutional argument, risked appearing unpatriotic, insufficiently committed to the war against the dictatorships. Expressing this ambivalence, Nat Patton, a former judge and a member of the House from East Texas, remarked in late August, "I don't want to disturb the poll tax, but I don't want to deprive the boys of their chance to vote."[82] Cross-pressured this way, and also aware that "their objections were dealing a death blow to their party's campaign in the North," where "the Negro vote in northern cities which swung away from Republicans in 1933 was going back to the party of Abraham Lincoln as a result of the poll tax discussion,"[83] the representatives from the eight poll tax states agreed not to block the House's consideration of soldier voting by procedural objection, and thus permitted the chamber to send the bill to a congressional conference by unanimous consent.[84] Nonsouthern Democrats were keenly aware that the era's Great Migration was bringing new black voters to their constituencies who might decide close elections.[85] The poll tax issue was especially attractive to these Democrats because it offered a chance to endorse and secure black sentiments without challenging or offending their white constituents. Most southern representatives, in turn, knew the poll tax was the least important of the barriers to black voting, and the one most difficult to defend at a time of war.[86] So they principally looked to other, less emblematic but more essential, means to preserve the region's electoral exclusions.

Furthermore, southern members in the main understood that if they went too far and were too insistent in opposing soldier voting because of its poll tax feature, they might endanger the period's mostly tacit but sometimes explicit agreement to leave well enough alone south of the Mason-Dixon Line. Especially during the war, there was little interest on the part of Congress to press the South to transform its exclusionary franchise, for much the same reason the armed forces had justified the decision to maintain military segregation. John J. McCloy, then assistant secretary of war, who headed the Advisory Committee on Negro Troop Policies, wrote in July 1942 that this was no time to confront racial prejudice and discriminatory acts "irrespective of whether the White or the Colored man is responsible for starting them," adding, with respect to segregation, "I doubt that you can convince the people of the United States that the basic issues of freedom are involved in such a question." This position restated the policy of racial separation that President Roosevelt had endorsed in 1940, which argued that "changes now would produce situations destructive to morale and detrimental to the preparation for national defense. . . . It is the opinion of the War Department that no experiments should be tried with the organizational set-up of these units at this critical time."[87]

Writing in the *Atlanta World*, the South's principal black newspaper, the African-American columnist Charles Howard Sr. wondered at the start of the soldier-vote debate in May 1942 whether "the law makers in Congress are going to disfranchise a couple of million white boys to keep a couple of thousand Negroes from exercising the prerogative of American citizenship." Observing that "it is going to be pretty hard to grant the ballot to one group and deny it to the other," he quite presciently predicted that "the anti-Negro group in Congress is pretty ingenious."[88] So it proved to be. Faced with these various conflicting currents of language and value, southern members crafted strategies, made choices, and offered justifications that could somehow reconcile, or appear to reconcile, democratic norms with the desire shared by committed racists and moderates alike to maintain segregation and determine the character and pace of change without external intervention.

Even with the poll tax suspension, the 1942 act met this test. With the compliant assistance of fellow party members from other parts of the country, the Democratic majority crafted a bill that through its timing, burdensome procedures, and states' rights protections that minimized the federal role offered only the appearance of remedies for the severe logistical problems posed by soldier voting.

This had been an issue the Democrats had initially preferred to avoid. The first bill to clarify how that might actually happen had been introduced in April 1942 by Joseph Martin, the Republican minority leader and chairman of the Republican National Committee, who declared that the three million individuals scheduled to be serving by November "ought not to be deprived" of the chance to vote.[89] President Roosevelt, by contrast, "not at all certain that much can be done about it," thought the task of soldier voting to be so imposing that, in May, he simply advised the Department of War and the Department of the Navy to "remind the boys by posting notices . . . summarizing laws in each state." He also considered issuing an executive order commanding the armed services to work with existing state regulations to facilitate voting by absent soldiers.[90]

As Martin had insisted, soldier voting was an issue Congress was mandated to consider. Even before U.S. entry into the war, the Selective Service Act of 1940 had stipulated that conscripts be permitted to vote in all elections under the laws of their state, either in person, without being required to take a leave of absence of more than one day to do so, or by absentee ballot (in turn, they were not eligible to vote in other states in which they were stationed). The diversity and patchiness of existing state laws in 1942 made necessary at least some degree of federal inducement and oversight along the lines Martin proposed to advance cooperation between state authorities and the military if soldiers were to have any realistic chance to vote. Moreover, a high premium was placed on the successful functioning of American democracy in the dire circumstances of that spring, marked by the surrender of American forces to the Japanese on the Bataan Peninsula and on Corregidor, the drive led by Germany's Field Marshal Erwin Rommel from Libya toward Alexandria, the visible ban in France of Jews from public facilities, including restaurants, libraries, and public gardens, and the less visible start to mass killings at Auschwitz.[91] With only Rankin objecting ("It seems to me that we have enough on our hands to whip Germany, Italy, and Japan without pandering to those vicious elements who are constantly waging war on private enterprise and on the white people of the South"[92]), the House conferees accepted the Senate version, including the poll tax suspension and the inclusion of primary elections. The bill also suspended the requirement that prospective voters had to register in person. Passed in mid-September by overwhelming votes (47–5 in the Senate; 248–53 in the House) that were characterized by uncommonly unified voting by Republicans and nonsouthern Democrats, the statute, as we have seen, rendered these features moot in practice because only 1 percent of the armed forces succeeded in utilizing its procedures. It also did not disturb in any way the capacity of each state to establish qualifications for voting and judge whether a citizen had met them. To Maryland's Millard Tydings, who had asked, "Is it the Senator's contention that any proper limitation upon the qualification of a voter is not wiped out by the measure now proposed?" Senator Green replied, "That is correct . . . the bill has nothing to do with the qualification of electors. They all remain as they were, whether they are right or wrong, constitutional or unconstitutional."[93]

IV.

WHEN CONGRESS again debated soldier voting in 1944, voting patterns had changed dramatically. The two crucial House votes—the 328–69 passage of the Rankin states-rights version, and a narrower 273–111 vote to agree to the conference report, which tilted ever so slightly in the direction preferred by President Roosevelt—were passed by a coalition of Republicans and southern Democrats. Only nonsouthern Democrats supported the type of federal ballot that he had proposed.

As discussion unfolded, the southern and nonsouthern wings of the Democratic Party first tried to find common ground to maintain party unity. That effort did not succeed. The maximum the South was willing to countenance and the minimum that pro-administration nonsouthern Democrats were ready to tolerate did not mesh. The Republicans, in turn, faced with the chance to build a winning coalition, performed a volte-face from their assertive rhetoric and vote pattern of 1942, shifting to a states' rights position that meshed with that of the southern Democrats. As a result, soldier voting played a key role during the early stages of the development of ties between southern Democrats who feared for their social order and Republicans who especially disliked the New Deal's alteration of the balance between capital and labor, who found the administration's centralization of policy and administration objectionable, and who yearned for another chance to govern. "More than any other episode during the war, the controversy over the soldier vote cemented a Southern Democratic-Republican alliance," a detailed study of wartime public policy concluded.[94] "I am actually getting to the point," remarked Cotton Ed Smith, "where I turn to the Republicans when I want the real fundamental constitutional laws of this country adhered to."[95]

The collision of regional and party interests with the imperatives of national unity had been minimized and managed in 1942, albeit at the cost of adopting an ineffective statute. By 1944, striking political changes had altered the stakes of soldier voting for each of the three partisan groups in Congress. The Republicans were enjoying a remarkable resurgence, one that had been advanced, many observers believed, because millions of soldiers had not been able to vote in 1942, when the party had elected 209 members of the House, picking up 47 seats, close in number to the 220 secured by the Democrats.[96] The Republican Party also gained 10 senators, up to 38, a number sufficient to control efforts at cloture. For the first time in a decade, moreover, Democrats secured less than half the party vote. Republican control of both chambers now was within hailing distance. Even more enticing was the prospect of the 1944 election. With Roosevelt's candidacy uncertain, the Republicans could anticipate a campaign against either a new candidate or an aging candidate running for an unprecedented fourth term. In turn, the Democratic Party became more proportionately southern than it had been at any time since 1932, as most of its losses were sustained in nonsouthern competitive races.

With wartime planning for production and the allocation of labor, price controls and rationing, corruption and war profiteering, recriminations and qualms about loyalty, and the inevitable clumsiness of wartime management and resentment at how executive and emergency powers were being deployed, suspicion of the federal government had grown sufficiently to bring the Republican Party's smaller domestic government ethos in tune with popular disillusionments and resentments. Finding allies among southern Democrats, Republicans had begun to close a raft of New Deal agencies, including the National Resources Planning Board, the National Youth

Administration, the Civilian Conservation Corps, and the Works Progress Administration, and sought to return Congress to its pre–New Deal role of "negotiating the local and regional adjustments to the national policies the president was advocating."[97]

How ballots for soldiers would be organized, it was widely understood, might matter quite a lot in 1944. The federal government clearly could not decline to facilitate political participation by the country's far-flung military. But how to do so was a subject of intense and distinct interest to each party's legislators. Eleven months before the election that would produce a new term for Franklin Roosevelt and place Harry Truman in the vice presidency with 25,613,916 votes to 22,017,929 for the Republican ticket of Thomas Dewey and John Bricker, George Gallup appraised the two parties as "running neck in neck in terms of voting strength among the civilian population." He thus projected that "if the presidential election were being held at this time, the outcome would therefore be determined by the soldier vote."[98] With many Americans exhausted by the war and skeptical about a president running for a fourth term, a June 1944 Gallup poll put the distance between Roosevelt and Dewey at only two points. That summer, two students of that election found that the age group of those twenty-one to twenty-nine was "11 points more Democratic than is the entire voting population," and thus concluded that "the Democrats will be losers to the extent to which service men do not vote."[99] Another, earlier analysis by Gallup had calculated the party gap in the military to be significantly higher, 61 percent Democratic to 39 percent Republican.[100] An August analysis also saw a near dead heat in electoral votes, assessing 248 for Roosevelt and 229 for Dewey.[101] Even with two million of the ten million persons under arms disqualified by their age, the military electorate promised to be pivotal.

Southern Democrats had good reason for concern about the war's effects on the foundations of white supremacy. Eleven months before Pearl Harbor, President Roosevelt cast World War II as an "armed defense of democratic existence," and "a great emergency" that challenged "every realist" who "knows that the democratic way of life is at this moment being directly assailed in every part of the world," and he spoke of "a decent respect for the rights and the dignity of all our fellow men within our gates" as the foundation for the country's unity and the credibility of its foreign policy "based on a decent respect for the rights and dignity of all nations."[102] With the United

States at war a year later, the president spoke even more vigorously about the need to "be particularly vigilant against racial discrimination in any of its ugly forms," cautioning that Hitler would seek to "breed mistrust and suspicion between . . . one race and another."[103] Taking such talk seriously, a growing number of African-Americans began to mobilize in an unprecedented way for, in the words of a nationwide "Double V" campaign, "victory over our enemies at home and victory over our enemies on the battlefields abroad."[104] Racial violence increased, some at and adjacent to segregated military bases in the South in the spring and summer of 1943. By early summer, "serious disorders occurred at Camp Van Dorn, Mississippi; Camp Stewart, Georgia; Lake Charles, Louisiana; March Field and Camp San Luis Obispo, California; Camp Bliss, Texas; Camp Phillips, Kansas; Camp Breckenridge, Kentucky; and Camp Shenango, Pennsylvania."[105] One report chronicled 242 incidents in forty-seven cities, the most visible and costly to lives and property being the riots in Detroit and New York during the summer of 1943.[106] The threat of a march on Washington had induced President Roosevelt to issue Executive Order 8802 in June 1941, creating the Fair Employment Practices Committee, which made federal investigation and remediation of discrimination in the workplace a reality for the first time. Lawyers oriented to civil rights staffed the Civil Liberties section of the Department of Justice. Unions, some on a multiracial basis, were making unprecedented advances in the South under tight labor-market conditions. Legislation to curb poll taxes was debated in Congress. Gunnar Myrdal was finishing his massive and unsentimental *An American Dilemma,* which was organized to reveal the full range of contradictions that his subtitle characterized as *The Negro Problem and Modern Democracy.*[107] The Supreme Court, which had begun to consider the status of the white primary, was about to pronounce it unconstitutional in *Smith v. Allwright.*

Soldier voting placed southerners who wished to protect regional racial patterns, or at least ensure that change would come from within rather than be imposed from without, in a difficult position. They did not wish to be portrayed, once again, as opponents of soldier voting, placing racial hierarchy above national obligation. As Isaiah Berlin discerned when the debate over the issue of soldier voting in the 1944 election opened, the opposition to a federal ballot "is in an embarrassing position since it cannot very well afford to be accused of wishing to deprive 'soldier boys' of an opportunity to vote in face of all efforts of the President and Administration to give them that right."[108] But southerners feared that a standardized national approach to military balloting would establish a powerful precedent they would be unable to resist when more fundamental challenges regarding voting rights arose.

Shifts to Republican fortunes and prospects presented the welcome possibility of a new set of solutions, simultaneously favoring soldier voting while defending states' rights. Republican members of the House and Senate who had argued passionately for a strong bill in 1942 now were assessing soldier voting anew, anxiously, lest its terms foreclose opportunity. Concerned their chance to win back the presidency and the House of Representatives might slip away if soldiers were to vote by federal ballot, with the process overseen by the commander in chief and the Departments of War and Navy, they came to advocate a weak federal role, and proposed to limit the flow of information to soldiers serving abroad. To realize these preferences, they required southern votes. The language spoken by the two groups often became interchangeable. Warnings like those of Ohio's Republican senator Robert Taft to the effect that a federal role would place the country "on very dangerous ground indeed," and his insistence that the war did not justify superseding what he took to be the "express language of the Constitution," were not easy to distinguish from Democratic senator Eastland's admonition that "the proposed legislation is the first step toward Federal control, toward bureaucratic control of the entire election machinery of this country," and thus a violation of constitutional provisions for state supervision of elections.[109]

Observing this alliance develop were two representatives who expressed more than a little puzzlement and unease regarding the shift in Republican preferences, Estes Kefauver and John Sparkman. Both men would later become senators, and each ran as vice president with Adlai Stevenson, Sparkman in 1952 and Kefauver in 1956. Kefauver, who favored the federal ballot, wryly observed how "no great cry of States' rights was raised by many who are going to vote against this measure when we eliminated the requirement for registration and poll tax as a prerequisite of voting for servicemen in September 1942. It is strange that many of those who voted for that measure have become so suddenly converted to the doctrine of States' rights."[110] Alabama Democrat John Sparkman responded sardonically to Republican talk about constitutional federalism, most recently articulated on the House floor by

New York Republican Hamilton Fish ("For years we have seen States rights vanish, one after the other under the New Deal"[111]), by noting how members from that party who were lecturing their colleagues about states' rights had not done so during debates about lynching or the poll tax.[112] In turn, Senator James Tunnell, a Delaware Democrat who backed the federal ballot, also took note of the strange bedfellows alliance that had emerged. "The Senator from Mississippi," he observed, "was perfectly frank when he introduced the bill. His position cannot be criticized. He has his own problem. He said the bill is one to maintain white supremacy." But how ironic it was, he insisted, that "Senators from the southern part of the country, who are interested in white supremacy," were now joined at the hip with members from what once had been "the party of Thad Stevens," the powerful Pennsylvania Republican who, when serving in the House from 1859 to 1868, had sought to use federal power to promote the equality of freedmen.[113]

However uncomfortable, the alliance of southern Democrats and Republicans found common ground in utilizing a language of democracy to oppose the federal ballot as insufficient, because it would apply only to national offices and general elections. Administratively and politically, liberal Democrats, including the president, understood that they had no chance to create a federal long ballot, since they lacked the means to manage the votes of soldiers for the full range of offices at the local and state level. Listing all candidates from sheriff on up would lead to impossible logistical and shipping problems. This opened the possibility for the opponents of any federal role to contend that what they labeled "the bobtailed ballot" discriminated against military personnel. In the southern version of the argument, the federal ballot was labeled discriminatory because it did not include state-level primaries.[114] In the Republican version, it was the failure to offer soldiers means to vote for local and state offices that mattered.[115]

The first point of inflection changing long-familiar voting coalitions came in the Senate when the Green-Lucas administration bill for a federal ballot and a strong oversight commission with enforcement capacity reached the floor in late November 1943. Into the first days of December, a united Democratic Party had weakened the powers of the elections commission and had included the Merchant Marine, Red Cross, Society of Friends, USO employees, the Women's Airforce Service Pilots, and the Women's Auxiliary Ferrying Squadron within the compass of the bill. This marked an effort by its sponsors to find a sufficient number of votes to over-come Republican resistance. Those roll calls, together with votes regulating the distribution of partisan propaganda and political literature to troops, and another that rejected proxy voting by parents or designated relatives, moved along party lines.

The radical shift took place on December 3, when the Eastland substi-tute, "Requiring That the Method for Absentee Voting Must Be Provided and Regulated by the States Rather Than the Federal Government," passed on a 42–37 vote, a "startling defeat" for soldier voting by a federal ballot under national jurisdiction.[116] The replacement bill eliminated the Fed-eral War Ballot Commission, and simply recommended to the states that they provide means for eligible absentees to vote. The bill also included an amendment offered by Senator Taft to regulate and limit the written mate-rials soldiers could receive.[117] Southern members who had supported the weakening amendments to the standardizing federal ballot bill shifted to vote instead for this alternative. Of the forty-two ayes, twenty-four were cast by southern Democrats and eighteen by Republicans; they were opposed by twenty-five Democrats, some from border states, and twelve Republicans. Of the three possible coalitions among Republicans, southern Democrats, and nonsouthern Democrats, the most robust was that of southern Democrats and Republicans.[118]

In the House, the Rankin version of the Eastland bill passed by the wide margin of 328–69. A nearly unanimous southern bloc[119] was joined by an even more united Republican Party,[120] together with roughly half the non-southern Democrats (who were torn between rejecting this bill or having at least some mechanism for soldier voting),[121] to form the majority.[122] "Freedom Wins," the *Chicago Tribune* exulted, having long forgotten its many 1942 edi-torials excoriating the South for putting states' rights in the way of effective soldier voting.[123]

One last effort was made to preserve some federal role in the Sen-ate. Watching the president's State of the Union appeal for soldier voting get emasculated, an embarrassed Roosevelt administration backed what amounted to a new version of the Green-Lucas bill, one that combined East-land's provisions with a weaker version of the federal ballot. "The new mea-sure," the disappointed *Pittsburgh Courier* commented, "answers the demand for a soldier vote law while guaranteeing that the Negro vote be 'taken care of' by election in precincts, counties, and other state units, and therefore is satisfactory to all except Negroes. . . . Our legislators have not yet learned the truth that you cannot have democracy and white supremacy at one and the same time."[124]

After much legislative maneuvering, a diluted federal ballot, weakened further by requiring voters to write in the name of their preferred candidates, rather than simply vote by party designation or names already present, was added to the Eastland states' rights bill.[125] This modified legislation, passed by a 47–38 margin, was the version of soldier voting that ultimately became law. The federal ballot that it authorized was utilized by only 3 percent of the members of the armed forces who voted.

Two years later, the fight was over. The Democratic soldier-voting bill introduced in early 1946 in the House by Herbert Bonner of North Carolina and in the Senate by Theodore Green of Rhode Island eliminated the federal ballot altogether. It passed both houses in April by unanimous voice votes.[126]

PART III

EMERGENCY

7 ▶ Radical Moment

S IX MONTHS AFTER Franklin Roosevelt's inauguration,
and only two months after Chicago and New York had
feted Italo Balbo with euphoric pageants, nearly two
million persons, standing seven to fourteen deep, watched
more than a quarter of a million New Yorkers parade up Fifth
Avenue, from Washington Square to Seventy-second Street.
They gathered to salute not a hero or a sports team, but a law,

the National Industrial Recovery Act (NIRA). Enthusiasm had been grow-ing for days. Participation had to be limited by quota. President Roosevelt wired the organizers to affirm that "such evidence of support is highly grat-ifying and supplies real inspiration to those of us in Washington who are working to establish the NRA and bring this country back to better times."[1]

As ticker tape fell steadily from the sky on September 13, 1933, just a few days after Labor Day, Eleanor Roosevelt was joined on the grandstand in front of the grand marble façade of the New York Public Library, just south of Forty-second Street, by Gen. Hugh Johnson, the administrator of the National Recovery Administration; New York's governor, Herbert Lehman; the state's former governor Alfred E. Smith; Secretary of Labor Frances Perkins; New York senator Robert Wagner; and secretary to the president Louis Howe, who had lost thirty-two pounds while campaigning tirelessly for Roosevelt during the presidential election, and who effectively served as the president's chief of staff. Starting in the early afternoon, the parade they witnessed lasted many hours longer than planned, nearly to midnight. Led by Elise and Doris Ford of Brooklyn, models for the artist Howard Chan-dler Christy,[2] dressed as "Miss Liberty" and "Miss NRA," the event was organized into seventy-seven trade and industry divisions—including law firms, taxi garages, florists, furriers, barbers, banks, and laundries—many of whose members dressed in costume ("the restaurant section with fifty Chi-nese girls in native costumes, the warehouse men and coal men in the garb of miners"). Flags, banners, and celebratory bunting draped almost every Fifth Avenue building. An immense ninety-by-seventy-five-foot Blue Eagle, the NRA's ubiquitous symbol, hung from the B. Altman department store, later converted into the building of the City University of New York Gradu-ate Center, just north of Thirty-fourth Street. Two hundred bands, imported from near and far, gleefully serenaded the marchers. Trumping Balbo, forty-three army and navy planes and thirty civilian ones flew overhead in a series of dramatic tactical maneuvers, "a demonstration from the air ... without equal in the city." FERVOR SWEEPS THRONGS, the *New York Times* headlined, THE GREAT OUTPOURING TO SHOW FAITH IN NRA RECALLS ARMISTICE. NIGHT SCENE IS BRILLIANT. NOTABLES AND HUMBLE FROM ALL OCCUPA-TIONS MARCH UNDER AVENUE'S GOLDEN LIGHTS.[3] A cooler *Wall Street Journal* described "the celebration" as "one of the greatest in the nation's history."[4]

Convened by the White House, this colorful event seemed to confirm widespread popular support for what FDR had called "the most important and far-reaching legislation ever enacted by the American Congress."[5] It was the most visible culmination of a self-conscious campaign to mobilize the public. Broadcasting to the country on July 24, Roosevelt had once again likened the effort to confront economic misery to the challenges of large-scale warfare.[6] "In war, in the gloom of night attack," he had told the American people, "soldiers wear a bright badge on their shoulders to be sure that comrades do not fire on comrades. On that principle, those who cooperate in this program must know each other at a glance."[7] With the slogan "We Do Our Part," the Blue Eagle served as that badge of recognition.

By the time of the parade, there had been a "national surge around the Blue Eagle."[8] The new law, with its wide scope and a sharp bite, the president reported, represented "a connected and logical whole" program for American capitalism based on "a rounded leadership" for the economy "by the federal government."[9] Though initially skeptical, he had become increasingly enthusiastic about the planning aspects of this program.[10] A key member of his "Brains Trust," Rexford Tugwell, explained how this unparalleled initiative authorized "the national government to assume the leadership of private enterprise."[11] Facing deep insecurity and the loss of profit, many business leaders welcomed what Nelson Gaskill, president of the Lead Pencil Association, called "an economic sovereignty the like of which the world has never seen," a system that replaces "old theories of fierce competition" with "regulated competition or a systematized democracy." Likewise, Henry Harriman, president of the U.S. Chamber of Commerce, welcomed the "philosophy of planned national economy."[12] These measures, the *New York Times* rightly argued, were undertaken to create a scale of economic regulation and oversight "entirely new in the United States."[13]

Stating that "a national emergency productive of widespread unemployment and disorganization of industry . . . is hereby declared to exist," the statute sought to curb chaotic market competition by releasing firms from antitrust requirements, and it looked for means to jump-start the economy by raising wages to put more money in the hands of consumers. The centerpiece of these efforts was a massive voluntary endeavor, underpinned by public authority, that harnessed the capacities not of individual companies but of the country's trade associations, such as the Drug Institute of America, the National Coal Association, the American Textile Machinery Association, and the National Automobile Chamber. Working in tandem with labor unions, these organizations were instructed to create "codes of fair practices" that would establish production targets and set wages and prices. These negotiated agreements were to be reviewed, sector by sector, by an Industrial Advisory Board, a Labor Advisory Board, and a Consumers' Advisory Board before being sent by NRA staff to the president for confirmation.[14] He was granted the authority to impose standards and rules should such agreements not be reached voluntarily.[15] The statute singled out the collapsing oil industry for particularly robust public oversight at a time of rampant overproduction, cutthroat competition, and poor working conditions. Oil prices had plummeted, with a barrel of East Texas crude costing just four cents, "less than a bottle of the newly legal 3.2 percent beer." Reflecting concerns that oil companies would be unable to find ways to cooperate with one another, the law regulated oil pipelines, established prices for the transportation of petroleum products, and authorized the president to seize pipeline companies should they not comply with these directives.[16]

Further, this ambitious law guaranteed workers the right to form and join unions. Section 7(a) stated that "employees shall have the right to organize and bargain collectively through representatives of their own choosing," and thus banned "yellow-dog" contracts that forbade union membership. John L. Lewis, the president of the United Mine Workers, assessed these labor provisions as the most striking American advancement for human rights since the Emancipation Proclamation, and, in characteristically more tempered prose by William Green, the president of the American Federation of Labor (AFL), as having "brought [a] complete and almost instantaneous change in the union situation,"[17] including the chance to shape how industry would be governed by offering "representatives of wage-earners . . . a voice in every stage of code-making."[18]

Further, in a concession to the insistence of key members of Congress that vied with the president's fiscal conservatism, the act launched a $3.3 billion public works program to build roads and bridges, make river and harbor improvements, control floodwaters, and construct other infrastructure projects. To make these ventures happen, income tax rates were increased, corporate dividends were no longer exempt from such taxation, and a limit was placed on the deduction of capital losses. Congress also approved the use of eminent domain. With such compulsory purchase orders, the federal government could appropriate the land, buildings, and materials the law's economic-stimulus projects required without obtaining the consent of their owners. Additionally, the bill authorized the federal government to sell or lease any property built or acquired by the NRA.

An unamended version passed the House on May 26. The Senate approved an amended bill on June 9. A conference report reconciling these versions was endorsed by the House the very next day, and approved by the Senate just two days later. On June 16, the president affixed his signature, thus initiating a potentially renewable two-year period in which he was enjoined to carry out the purposes of the law.

No one could gainsay that the NRA was off to a quick start. Just five weeks after FDR had signed the act into law, his July fireside speech celebrated the Cotton Textile Code for its swift elimination of child labor—"an old evil" that "no employer acting alone was able to wipe out"—and reported on how he had sent a model "blanket code" to every employer in the country, calling for an immediate minimum wage of thirty cents an hour, a factory workweek of thirty-five hours, and the full abolition of child labor. By the beginning of September, fully 690 draft codes had been submitted to the NRA, including rules for the steel, automobile, and lumber industries where their drafting had proved contentious.[19]

Nothing like this comprehensive restructuring of market capitalism by a national state ever had been tried before in a constitutional democracy, even in countries governed by social democratic parties. Nor did the NRA simply reproduce what the dictatorships were doing. Above all, it combined tools of planning and corporatism borrowed from those regimes with American Progressive ideas about the regulation of business and the rights of labor. In preserving many features of the independence of these organizations, this vast scheme sought to create a more vibrant and less unequal capitalism in a manner that would be consistent with democratic values. While the new Nazi government, for example, had begun to renew German industrial power by stepping up orders by the state for goods, notably including weapons, in order to reactivate unused productive capacity, at the same time dissolving trade unions and mandating that wages and prices not rise above depression levels, the NRA sought to refloat capitalism and sustain a balanced private economy by finding a steering role for the national state that maintained democratic sensibilities, private powers, and constitutional procedures.[20]

Indeed, this Recovery Act initiated the most radical economic policy moment in American history. It did not stand alone. Marking the New Deal's first year, the *New York Times* named as many as forty "Alphabet New Deal Agencies," ranging from the AAA (Agricultural Adjustment Administration) to the USES (United States Employment Service), that Congress had created.[21] And that initial year was followed by a further torrent of lawmaking.

In all, by passing new rules for banking and investing, by convening new large-scale programs to build infrastructure and advance conservation, by providing public employment, and by comprehensively enlarging labor rights and creating America's first fully modern program of social insurance, the administrators of the New Deal forcefully rejected what the new president, at his inaugural, had called "an outworn tradition" of political economy that thought markets to be self-correcting. The economic collapse had vastly reduced the appeal, even the legitimacy, of these older ideas and had marginalized, at least for the moment, those scholars and policy advocates who resisted a robust economic role for the nation's government. In one of many tens of such articles to appear in popular and academic outlets, Rexford Tugwell argued that new types of federal intervention had become necessary because the very idea of an independent and free market was no longer compelling. "The jig is up. The cat is out of the bag. There is no invisible hand. There never was. If the depression has not taught us that, we are incapable of education." Washington, he announced, was "recapturing the vision of a government equipped to fight and overcome the forces of economic disintegration. A strong government with an executive amply empowered by legislative delegation," he thus concluded, "is the one way out of our dilemma, and forward to the realization of our vast social and economic possibilities."[22]

Seeking to reduce paralyzing national fear to more manageable risk, this array of programs shaped by this activist sensibility guided industrial decisions, regulated the economy's commanding heights, organized countervailing powers for working people, and provided security for persons who fell outside labor markets for reasons of age, infirmity, or unemployment. Donald Richberg, the general counsel of the National Recovery Administration, and later Hugh Johnson's successor, declared that the central goal of these initiatives was "to promote a more stable and more evenly distributed prosperity, and to prevent the inevitable breakdown of an undisciplined, uncoordinated control of the business enterprises upon which our security and freedom depend."[23] By so doing, these programs did more than repudiate unfettered market capitalism. They showed that economic purposes in the public interest could be galvanized within a constitutional democracy under great stress, thus rejecting the claim by the dictatorships that democratic legislatures could not confront the toughest problems of the day.[24] "The great adventure of the Recovery Act," Richberg testified, "lies in this effort to find a democratic and a truly American solution of the problem that has produced dictatorships in at least three great nations since the World War."[25]

It is important to comprehend how these sweeping ambitions were distinguished from totalitarian programs and policies, how they could have happened in a country where markets, individualism, property, and a modest national state had been watchwords, and why, in turn, such extensive efforts to guide the economy did not last. The New Deal's policy intellectuals and political leaders were keenly aware that the ideas they were importing possessed features less benign than earlier policy borrowings from Europe.[26] They also understood that, however justified, the policy initiatives they supported would have to garner congressional majorities that, despite big Democratic Party margins in the House and Senate, were not always certain. Given the novelty of these programs, moreover, it was understood that their legitimacy would depend on gaining considerable support in the House and Senate.

During the New Deal's first phase, most southern members of Congress rallied to distinguish democratic from dictatorial planning and corporatism. Even as some of the region's representatives believed that the administration's legislative program was not radical enough and others, fewer in number, thought it went too far, all the New Deal's early flagship efforts to reorganize capitalism and reshape the economic role of government were propelled by the region's politicians.

The moment did not last. Though there was more than one cause, the ultimate failure of these New Deal initiatives resulted from the diminution of southern support for its economic affairs programs, which accelerated as the decade played out. Facing an emerging set of challenges to their racial order, southern Democrats became increasingly reluctant to empower efforts like the NRA that enhanced national economic power and reduced regional autonomy. Once southern politicians grew more anxious, such projects were foreclosed, and a new reality collided with the New Deal's loftier aspirations.

That shift marked the moment when domestic policies began to turn away from efforts to articulate a substantive public interest in favor of a less ambitious and more procedural orientation to the role of government.

I.

S PEAKING AT his 1933 inaugural, Roosevelt broke through the carpace of a political culture aptly described by Richard Hofstadter as "fiercely individualistic and capitalistic."[27] No other American leader had comparably chastised "the rulers of the exchange of mankind's goods" for "having failed through their own stubbornness, and their own incompetence." None had talked of the "unscrupulous money changers [who] stand indicted in the court of public opinion, rejected by the hearts and minds of men," or had identified the "generation of self-seekers" who pursued "the mad chase of evanescent profits." No other had called for "unifying relief activities" that "can be helped by national planning" and for a federal role so assertive that the country's national government would be called on to supervise "all forms of transportation and of communications and other utilities which have a definitely public character."

It was not just the collapse of capitalism that precipitated this search for new means to grapple with the economy but also the failure of what had been mainstream policy on the eve of the Great Depression. That repertoire had been three-pronged—a commitment to free markets that limited the role of government to the protection and enforcement of contracts; antitrust laws that sought to maintain efficient market competition; and guidelines for what President Hoover had called "associationalism," a policy that used the federal government to collect and disseminate information to firms and economic leaders in order to confront the worry that insufficient information could lead to market failure.[28]

Facing crumpled market policies, New Deal leaders searched elsewhere for economic designs. They had no wish to build a socialism in which the national state would supplant private firms to become the central economic actor, and they certainly did not want to discard private property in accordance with the Soviet model. During this initial phase, expansive fiscal policies also were ruled out. Three years before the 1936 publication of John Maynard Keynes's *General Theory of Employment, Interest, and Money,* the

New Deal remained committed to fiscal conservatism, the one orthodox economic idea still standing.[29] Most university and think-tank economists who advised the Roosevelt administration worried that large federal deficits would undercut the dollar's value, reduce national savings, and raise consumer prices unduly. Together, the president of the Chamber of Commerce, Henry Harriman, and the AFL's William Green implored the incoming president in late February 1933 to reduce federal spending sharply.[30] Within weeks, Roosevelt was urging Congress to pass the Economy Act to cut federal expenditures by $500 million, and permit him to reduce federal salaries and cut payments to veterans, stating that "too often in recent history liberal governments have been wrecked on the rocks of loose fiscal policy. We must avoid this danger."[31]

The government's economic policy repertoire thus came to focus on two principal options. First was economic planning, a capacious orientation to economic affairs in which the government, as an economic actor, sets terms for the movement of capital and labor, and intervenes directly in various sectors of the economy. Second was corporatism, an arrangement in which government participates in discussions, negotiations, and decisions with business and labor in order to reduce class conflict and produce a policy consensus. American versions of these two features of public intervention, Tugwell explained, aimed "to repair disaster, imminent, pressing," by providing "coordinated administration and negotiation" that could create "a control to conserve and maintain our economic existence" by acting "to eliminate the anarchy of the competitive system."[32]

Planning, of course, was closely identified with the Soviet Union and its encompassing Five-Year Plans, and corporatism with Italian Fascism. This certainly was how Herbert Hoover interpreted New Deal policies shortly after the NIRA's first anniversary. In "The Challenge to Liberty," his article in *The Saturday Evening Post,* the former president bemoaned how the United States had joined a process in which "peoples and governments are blindly wounding, even destroying, those fundamental human liberties which have been the foundation and the inspiration of Progress since the Middle Ages." Lamenting the "vast centralization of power in the executive," he cited the New Deal for its "economic regimentation" and what he viewed as its coercive "code restrictions on business." All told, he concluded, New Deal activism, characterized as "the daily dictation by Government, in every town and village every day in the week, of how men are to conduct their daily lives," represented "the most stupendous invasion of the whole spirit of liberty that the nation has witnessed since the days of Colonial America."[33]

To its congressional opponents, the 1933 creation of the NRA also seemed uncomfortably close to the antiliberal policies of the dictatorships. "The power that is conferred upon the President in this bill . . . makes the distinguished dictator, Mussolini, look like an Egyptian mummy," Frank Crowther, a New York Republican, told the House.[34] The bill "Russianizes the business of America," Pennsylvania Republican Harry Ransley pronounced."[35] It is "imitating Moscow," fellow Pennsylvania Republican James Beck declared.[36] It makes "a powerful appeal to Herr Hitler and Comrade Stalin," New York Republican John Taber asserted.[37] In all, Henry Watson, the Pennsylvania Republican, insisted, in Washington as in Europe, "dictators seem to be the political fashion of the hour."[38]

President Roosevelt, however, took care to distinguish his program from corresponding policies in Berlin, Moscow, and Rome. During his second fireside chat, on May 7, 1933, just as he was about to send the NRA code scheme to Congress, he underscored the law's voluntary character and how it preserved the vitality of civil society. "It is wholly wrong," he insisted, "to call the measures that we have taken Government control of farming, industry, and transportation. It is rather a partnership between Government and farming and industry and transportation, not a partnership in profits, for the profits still go to the citizens, but rather a partnership in planning, and a partnership to see that the plans are carried out."[39]

In all, as North Carolina Democrat Robert Lee Doughton put the point during the debate in the House, the New Deal was "walking a tightrope."[40] The Soviet, Italian, and German models were well known to the administration's policy planners, including Tugwell and other key Brains Trust members, especially Adolph Berle and Raymond Moley, and served as sources of ideas and possibilities. But "none of them gave the slightest indication of an affinity of anti-democratic solutions," as Alonzo Hamby has observed.[41] Set alongside "national planning in the communist Soviet Union, fascist Italy, Nazi Germany, or a militarized Japan," New Deal planning, Patrick Reagan similarly writes, "was not based on the traditional model of command and control planning led by the state to formulate blueprints intended to create a new kind of economy, society, and polity."[42]

Throughout the brief life span of the NRA, its leaders could be seen walking that line. During his very first week in office, Hugh Johnson urged manufacturers, especially the leading industries, to move swiftly to implement the law. He offered a double-sided message to business leaders. He told them that they were the key actors who would restore prosperity, while calling attention to the penalties that awaited should they not cooperate with the new law.[43] In early July of 1933, Donald Richberg reassured the Merchants Association that the NRA is "not trying to establish public management of private business," but, like his boss, he also warned that if industry failed to play its part, "the advance of political control over private industry is inevitable."[44]

The administration's community of policy experts was well aware that support by elites and the public at large required convincing accounts of why New Deal planning and corporatism were different, and truly American. Richberg often stressed how, in "seeking to bring about a purposeful, planned organization of trades and industries, so integrated and coordinated that the continuous production and exchange of necessary goods and services may be assured," the NRA was being administered "not in the exertion of a political control over business, but by encouraging and sanctioning measures of self-discipline that will provide a genuine self-government of industry." As such, he declared, New Deal planning is "essentially democratic and individualistic." Its voluntarism sets it apart both from Italian corporatism and from the "regimentation [that is] the product of the socialist doctrines of Karl Marx."[45]

Far from "a presidential dictatorship over industry," the country's relationship among business, labor, and government depended on "genuine cooperation between property men and labor men in developing a common program for their common benefit." This form of economic governance, Richberg asserted, was located in "a half-way house—a house of democratic cooperation and self-discipline—which lies between the anarchy of irresponsible individualism and the tyranny of state socialism."[46] Much was at stake. "If the half-way house cannot be established," he cautioned, "we may find soon that we have reached the end of democratic government."[47] Likewise, the Brookings Institution economist Lewis Lorwin warned that democratic planning policies are "the only alternative to dictatorial government."[48]

In defining national economic planning as "a collective procedure that treats all individual and separate plants, enterprises, and industries of a country as coordinated units of one single system for the purpose of achieving the maximum satisfaction of the needs of the people within a given interval of time," Lorwin conceded that "there is as yet very little of it outside Soviet Russia," and, to a lesser degree, in Italy and Germany. But planning, he insisted, was not of one type. While it might include "absolute socialist planning" on the Soviet model, or Fascist planning, in which the state stood above society and forced a resolution of class conflict into national cooperation, U.S. "social progressive planning" was proceeding within the framework of the country's democratic state.

The NRA's congressional supporters took up the argument that the survival of democracy under conditions of economic emergency required just such action. "Under normal times this measure would be unthinkable; but these are not normal conditions or times," Democratic senator David Walsh of Massachusetts proclaimed, for this is a moment of "economic war . . . that threatens the very destruction of our political institutions."[49] Even if it were plausible to label the NRA a "benign dictatorship," North Carolina's Edward Pou, the Democrat who chaired the House Rules Committee, argued, fears of dictatorship were misplaced because the bill, "dedicated to the welfare of the American people," would protect the very existence and legitimacy of democratic life.[50] Planning, in short, had been turned from a tool of the dictators into an instrument for democracy.

II.

As the Recovery Act quickly snaked its way through Congress, no one underestimated what was at stake for American democracy; New Jersey Republican congressman Charles Eaton designated it as the New Deal's effort "to remake the entire structure" of American capitalism.[51] "We all know that an emergency exists, that the economic structure has fallen," the Kentucky Democrat Fred Vinson told the House. Later secretary of the treasury from July 1945 to June 1946, then chief justice of the Supreme Court from 1946 to 1953, Vinson strongly defended the legislation's combination of planning, corporatism, and public works for its promise to "build anew upon the ruins."[52] All agreed, as Robert Doughton, its House sponsor, declared, that the proposed law was "something unusual, something extraordinary."[53]

This massive statute moved through Congress in less than a month with the support of the vast majority of Pou's, Vinson's, and Doughton's southern colleagues. It was Pou, a traditional segregationist serving in his thirty-fourth year in the House and one of the New Deal's most stalwart supporters before his death, in April 1934, who led his Rules Committee to pass a closed rule prohibiting amendments, despite the objections of House Republicans and some Democrats. Each of the key committees that had jurisdiction over this legislation was led by an enthusiastic southern backer: Doughton, who chaired the Committee on Ways and Means, and Mississippi's Pat Harrison, who chaired the Finance Committee in the Senate.

In all, southern legislators argued for and strongly advanced the bill in much the same terms as nonsouthern Democrats. Like their party colleagues, they underscored how the NIRA was moving through the lawmaking process with great popular support and widespread consent by business and labor. While ushering the law through the amendment process in the Senate, Harrison reported that "the representatives of labor who appeared before the committee know what is in the bill, and they have approved the bill. Representatives of the great industries of the country, and of the trade organizations, came before the committee and they approved the bill."[54] Doughton also noted how the bill "is favored or supported by industry, by agriculture, and by labor," and thus how "those three powerful organizations in this country are all behind this legislation." In attending to the bill's technical features, especially its tax provisions and funding allocations, he underlined their benefits, especially how they met "the prime need of millions of our citizens today, a job." This bill, he declared, "undertakes to make that a certainty."[55]

The Senate voted on fifteen amendments. Of these, fourteen were defeated or passed by starkly partisan votes that were marked by nearly identical patterns of support by southern and nonsouthern Democrats. One amendment, introduced by Missouri's Democratic senator Joel Bennett Clark, objected to the code-making process and the suspension of antitrust regulations for being insufficiently tough on business. This criticism from the Left deployed anticolonial and anti–big business rhetoric and analysis. Clark persuaded eight of the twenty-nine southern Democrats in the Senate at the time to join him to repeal Title I, the heart of the bill, because it would facilitate the concentration of industry.[56] This was the one moment when a cohort of more conservative southern senators, who included Harry Byrd of Virginia and Robert Reynolds of North Carolina, worried about the growth of federal power, joined the future Supreme Court justice Hugo Black of Alabama and Tom Connally of Texas, who were concerned that the bill was too generous to business, to defect from the New Deal Democratic consensus.

The bill passed the House by an overwhelming 323–76 margin on May 26. In all, there had been just five roll calls in this chamber. Two were procedural, one concerned the allocation formula for highway funds, another was a motion to recommit, and, most important, there was a vote on final passage (approval of the conference report came by voice vote). With the exception of a sectional vote on how to allocate money to various regions for roads, the bill elicited strong partisan votes, marked by a remarkable degree of of Democratic Party unity.[57] When the Senate passed the bill on June 9 by a 58–24 margin, with all but four Democrats voting in favor, there was a nearly comparable degree of high agreement between the southern and nonsouthern wings of the party.[58] Like other Democrats, most southern members in the House and Senate agreed with Doughton that the New Deal had successfully charted "a middle course between the ruinous or complete monopoly in vogue prior to the enactment of the Sherman antitrust law and the era of unfair competition that now has a strangle hold upon business. It sets up flexible machinery which the President may use to prevent monopoly on the one hand and ruinous competition on the other."[59]

Despite the similarities in talk and voting across the Democratic Party, distinctly southern voices could be heard expressing a concern for maintaining antitrust measures and the wish to control business. These positions were articulated most strongly by the tenacious and progressive Senator Black. Having closely studied the issue of unemployment, including the potential effects of a shorter workweek, he had proposed a thirty-hour cap in the interest of spreading existing jobs across a larger sector of the populace. His bill passed the Senate on April 6, 1933, but it did not advance in the House, in part because Roosevelt ordered his policy planners to design a recovery act with a more flexible provision for maximum hours. Rebuffed, Black did not support the new bill, despite the administration's offer that he should become its principal Senate sponsor.[60] In contrast to FDR, he had come from hard-scrabble roots in an impoverished family from the Appalachian foothills. He was especially concerned that the law would enhance rather than control business power, and that less economically developed southern states, like his own Alabama, which possessed weak industrial structures and a welter of endemic poverty, would find themselves at the mercy of code makers from richer states.[61] He was keen to place more robust controls on industry profits in order to place more money in the hands of workers and consumers, and he was especially exercised that the bill suspended antitrust legislation. During final passage, though, he cast an affirmative vote despite reservations caused by the removal of an amendment added by the Senate. This amendment, sponsored by William Borah, the progressive Idaho Republican, banned price fixing by NRA codes. When this stipulation was stripped from the bill in conference, Black, as well as eleven other senators, including four other southern members,[62] switched their votes, thus narrowing passage to a 46–39 margin.[63]

On these matters, Black found himself in a minority in his region. He and his colleagues were united and successful, however, in their insistence that the NRA must not undermine the South's racial system. The heart of that matter was the status of agricultural and domestic labor.

During the floor debate in both chambers, southern legislators voiced apprehension that the provisions of the act might extend to agricultural labor. Senators Huey Long of Louisiana and Joel Clark of Missouri complained that the law failed to define "industry," the category of activity it regulated, and thus expressed concern that the term might apply to agriculture.[64] Long stated that the bill as written applied to "every laboring man."[65] Concerned about southern votes, the law's principal congressional author, Robert Wagner of New York, responded by confirming that "in the act itself agriculture is specifically excluded."[66] Though the legislation contained no language declaring this exclusion, this claim did prove accurate. As it turned out, the NRA itself interpreted "industry" to exclude farming, and it explicitly announced that "Congress did not intend that codes of fair competition . . . be set up for farmers or persons engaged in agricultural production." No NRA codes were ever established for domestics or farmworkers, thus excluding the vast majority of southern blacks from their minimum wage and maximum hours benefits. Further, the definition of agriculture was extended to include industries related to it, such as canning, many of which were low-paid and had many black employees. The law explicitly delegated to the president the ability to pass his authority, in turn, to the secretary of agriculture, who could decide whether the scope of coverage took in these industries.

In a series of executive orders, Roosevelt took this course. As a result, such industries as citrus packing and cotton ginning remained outside the range of the NRA's industrial codes, leaving their workers unprotected. Within industries that were covered under the law, the NRA permitted codes to recognize regional wage differentials, with lower minimum wages authorized for southern workers. "It is not the purpose of the Administration," the president explained in April 1934 in a statement about the coal industry, "by sudden or explosive change, to impair southern industry by refusing to recognized traditional differentials." What gained an industry a classification as southern, moreover, was an employment pattern in which the majority of workers in a given state simply were African-American. This practice distinguished protected jobs performed by whites, who earned higher wages and worked fewer hours, from unprotected jobs performed by blacks. As an example, fertilizer production in Delaware, where nine out of ten workers were black, was assigned a southern code, while workplaces in that state were coded as northern when their workers were overwhelmingly white.[67] Although the NRA never recognized any racial basis for differentiating among workers, these occupational decisions effectively reinforced southern practices and reassured the region's politicians.

III.

THE IMMENSE turnout and the passion of the participants and spectators at the September NRA march, Governor Lehman argued, offered "proof that the NRA is going over." Maj. Gen. Dennis Nolan, the parade's organizer, remarked how "the entire spirit of the people has changed."[68] At a mass rally held the night before the parade at Madison Square Garden, General Johnson proclaimed that "the four years as grievous as ever plagued a people had begun to come to a close."[69]

During the next four months, a distinguished group of political leaders and policy intellectuals positively appraised the recovery program at a series of lectures held at Swarthmore College. John Dickinson, an assistant secretary of commerce, spoke of how "all groups and classes have been stirred to a recognition of the common national interest." Rexford Tugwell discussed how the NRA would lead to encouraging "long-term national policies." A. Heath Onthank, a senior official in the NRA, pointed with pride to how "every single person connected with the National Recovery Administration realizes he is in a fight for the future of America." Herbert Tily, the president of the National Retail Council and the man who led Strawbridge and Clothier, an East Coast department store chain, lauded the NRA's "attempt to give business and industry a mandate to control itself." And Leo Wolman, who chaired the NRA's Labor Advisory Board, talked glowingly of how the law had "effected unprecedented improvements in both prevailing rates of wages and in the length of the work week."[70]

Looking back, most historians and social scientists have judged differently. The NRA failed, nearly all agree, well before the Supreme Court ruled unanimously in a May 1935 landmark decision, *A. L. A. Schechter Poultry Corp. v. United States,* that the law's delegation of power to the president and the executive branch violated the Constitution.[71] A 1937 study by Charles Roos, an economist who had been one of the research directors for the NRA, set the tone by arguing that inadequate personnel, insufficient statistics, and clumsy economic interventions had limited its effectiveness. "Despite laudable reform efforts to abolish child labor, to eliminate intolerable unfair trade practices, to make competition function more smoothly through open prices, and, most important, to promote discussion of economic issues," he concluded, "the NRA must, as a whole, be regarded as a sincere but ineffective effort to alleviate depression."[72]

This judgment has stuck. Ellis Hawley's influential study recorded "administrative mistakes, the attempt to do too much all at once, the failure to get the public works program going when it was most needed ... mistaken assumptions about the altruism of businessmen" and "other errors of commission and omission."[73] The Blue Eagle, David Kennedy assessed, was less a "badge of honor" than a signal of "the poverty of the New Deal's imagination and the meagerness of the methods it could bring to bear at this time against the Depression." It was, he further concluded, "dead on arrival as recovery measure."[74] In all, Jonathan Alter's study of the Hundred Days concluded that "in retrospect, the NRA was a big, splashy, bad idea."[75]

Looking back, we can see how the NRA's implementation of its goals was checkered. Its complex organization often reached beyond its actual managerial abilities to superintend, manage, and enforce hundreds of codes or integrate the economy into large and inclusive pyramids. Franklin Roosevelt himself remarked in his State of the Union address in January 1937 how "we know now that its difficulties arose from the fact that it tried to do too much." The supposition that the NRA, as distinct from other forces, fell short in its goal to be the primary factor driving an economic recovery has been backed by reasonable analyses, even though the country did witness growth rates of 9, 10, and 14 percent in the three years following the passage of the Recovery Act, and a decline of the national unemployment rate from 25 percent in 1933 to 17 percent in 1936.[76] Clearer still is that the attempt to find a balance of power between business and labor failed to level the playing field. Even as the law did represent a "dramatic legal victory for organized labor" that facilitated the growth of independent and often militant unions,[77] uneven class power made planning for a cooperative capitalism difficult. As the first extended history of the New Deal observed in 1944, trade associations dominated by the largest corporations "not only formulated the codes but had also dominated the procedure of hearings, amendment, and adoption, while the influence of small businessmen, laborers, and consumers had been very slight."[78] In all, Louis Galambos and Joseph Pratt concluded, the National Industrial Recovery Act was "one of the most publicized and least significant of the programs" of the New Deal.[79]

However, this was not how the NRA was understood at the time. With support coming from most sectors of the country's economy, including many parts of business, the great majority of observers, some in favor and some against, were confident that the NRA would dramatically renovate American capitalism. A week after the passage of the new statute, the ordinarily market-oriented *Wall Street Journal* celebrated as "a matter for national rejoicing" how the NRA promised to end "murderous competition and the starvation wages which it compels or speciously condones. . . . If 'government interference' or 'regimentation of industry' is the only way to check these depression evils we must perforce accept even those distasteful emergency measures."[80] In September 1933, Henry Luce's business magazine, *Fortune*, applauded the NRA's "purpose to transplant the practice of democracy from the political field . . . to the industrial field," and it proclaimed how "the result may be not only the salvation of American industry but the rejuvenation of the now decayed and outmoded ideal of democracy itself."[81] Four months later, Gerard Swope, the president of General Electric, who helped design the NRA and who chaired the Executive Committee of the Business Advisory Council of the Department of Commerce while also serving on the NRA's Business Advisory Board, graded the law a success in how it was developing a form of planning and economic organization that was "enabling cooperative work on the part of competing units in commerce and industry," a gain he described as the "first but very important step" in what he hoped would be "the creation of a National Economic Council for long-range planning."[82]

Considered conclusions about achievements, we might acknowledge, are not the same as verdicts about the program's robustness. A focus on short-comings and disappointments can overlook the fundamental objectives and the changes in assumptions and possibilities that the law initiated. The negative verdicts that dominate historical memory and scholarly appraisal usually miss two quite fundamental aspects of the short-lived NRA. First is the law's sheer audacity. Invented under conditions of fear, the program's grand purposes, inventive arrangements, and elaborate means should not be underestimated. Second is the way this pioneering experiment was connected to other ambitious New Deal initiatives.

We know that the recovery legislation the administration sent to Capitol Hill was drafted quickly and somewhat haphazardly by at least three sets of policy groups. But what united them was quite remarkable. In undertaking the most assertive and thoroughgoing American attempt to restructure the economy under democratic auspices, they made use of instruments that had largely been invented and sponsored by antidemocratic regimes. In daring acts of transformation and inversion, these means were thoroughly modified. The NRA was designed to respect nongovernmental preferences and powers, and it inclined optimistically in the direction of showing how a constitutional government with a legislature at its heart could act effectively on behalf of the public interests even in the most difficult of conditions. There was, its supporters insisted, important space to be found and colonized between a failed market capitalism and the illiberal policies of the dictatorships, a democratic pathway to restore the shattered economy, by placing American capitalism under public supervision, a point made by John Dickinson in October 1933 from his position at the Department of Commerce.[83]

By combining purposive planning with voluntary code making, the NRA possessed capacities that were cut short by the agency's own limitations and, more decisively, by the Supreme Court. As a 1936 report recording how the NRA's program operated in the oil industry observed, "had it not been for the presence of legal obstacles, the Code might have become the instrument by which the government would eventually have controlled the whole of the oil industry."[84] When the NRA began, this largely anarchic industry faced massive problems of overproduction, falling prices, and dangerous conditions. It was weakly regulated, if at all, at the state level. Major producers, including Gulf, Shell, and Standard Oil, vied with independent companies in a clamor for control, pricing, and organization. Drilling scrambles led to cutthroat competition, which, in turn, led to a near-total neglect of environmental considerations. Clearly, the stakes were high—for the industry, survival and profit; for the country, economic success and national security—when the "NRA Code of Fair Competition for the Petroleum Industry" combined public authority with a collaborative and cooperative program that did effectively place oil production on a new and more secure basis.[85]

In all, Kenneth Finegold and Theda Skocpol are right to recall how, despite its flaws and uneven record, the NRA did add up to "an extraordinary new departure for the U.S. national government which abandoned its previous stance of minimal interference in the domestic market economy in favor of comprehensive attempts at administrative intervention."[86] Donald Brand's meticulous study also correctly judges this program to have been "radical" for the way the national state subordinated private power and transformed both business and labor into servants of the public interest.[87] If a key defect, as Alan Brinkley has noted, was how the act "did not so much resolve the tension" between economic planning and the model of creating industrial self-government through sponsored trade associations "as incorporate it into the new institution it was creating,"[88] this combination, paradoxically, also was the program's greatest strength, for it showed that it was within the scope of democratic public policy to use private consumer, worker, and business groups for public purposes.

Since this experiment was ended by judicial decision in 1935, we cannot know how it might have developed had it been renewed. Late in its life, Tugwell recalled, "the National Recovery Administration had fallen into awful chaos," beset by erratic leadership. "After a spectacular flight," he concluded, "the blue eagle's plumage was torn and ragged."[89] But spectacular the flight had been. Though manifestly beset by problems when it closed down, the NRA never had the chance to learn and adjust, build institutional capacity, or mobilize public powers to fully create a more balanced economic system by transforming its inherent tensions into a creative, rather than debilitating, site of friction and pressure. Though the NRA was quickly gone, its ideas, which the Supreme Court could not eradicate, did remain robust. Strikingly, when America's economy confronted a deep dip in 1937 and 1938, there was, as Brinkley notes, a "notable interest still in reviving something like the NRA" that could renew "efforts to limit competition and 'harmonize' the economy" by "making the federal government itself a powerful planning mechanism, capable of orchestrating corporate policies on prices, wages, and investments."[90] Later, the New Deal's short-lived configuration of democratic planning and corporatism was adopted as a model in much of postwar Western Europe, where administrative tools were developed with much success to achieve collaborative and egalitarian economic goals.[91] Despite its manifest and well-chronicled shortcomings, the NRA, in short, did lead the country's most far-reaching attempt in economic and social policymaking, before or since.

The second sizable cost exacted by a focus on the malfunctions and letdowns of the NRA concerns the organization of political time. In an important study of congressional behavior during the New Deal, James Patterson observed that "historians have not agreed whether the 'first' or 'second' New Deal was more radical," adding that "they have, however, usually agreed that about the time of the 'second' there was at least a shift in emphasis."[92] Indeed, one of the most familiar features of New Deal historiography is the construction of a boundary separating the First New Deal, whose main achievements were the creation, in 1933, of the National Recovery Administration and the Agricultural Adjustment Administration, from the Second New Deal, whose central legislative accomplishments in 1935 included the formation of a National Labor Relations Board and the establishment of Social Security. The influential 1937 essay by Arthur Schlesinger Sr. was the first to distinguish an initial moment that promoted economic reorganization to prevent starvation and ameliorate suffering from the next period, which created a modern American welfare state, and, by assisting organized labor, redrew the country's lines of power and influence.[93] Nearly a quarter of a century later, Arthur Schlesinger Jr. similarly identified how "1935 marked a watershed."[94]

Historians have come down on both sides of the timing of radicalism question. Setting the tone for one side of the debate, Basil Rauch's pioneering full-blown 1944 history of the New Deal characterized the start as cautious and friendly to business, and the second as expansive and oriented to the working class. Many others have also projected the position that the New Deal took flight as a progressive force only after it was liberated by the *Schechter* decision, which ended the NRA. Pressured by growing working-class militancy, it turned leftward to protect labor rights and build a program of social insurance.[95] However, there is an opposite view, first proposed by Arthur Schlesinger Jr. Rejecting the trajectory of a growing radicalism, he discerned just the reverse in how the Second New Deal drew back from the radical impulse of the First. A willingness to break through traditional limits to curb an unfettered marketplace and limit uncontrolled business power, he argued, had given way to "a certain lowering of ideals, waning of hopes, narrowing of possibilities." This second moment he believed to be "essentially more conservative," and only "ostensibly more radical."[96]

This debate forces a factitious choice. Though not entirely consistent, Schlesinger was rather more on the mark when he underscored how the New Deal's "objectives remained the same" during both times. Any change, he wrote, had been one of emphasis and style regarding "the manner in which these objectives were pursued."[97] Stressing continuities rather than differences, he took note of a letter he received in 1958 from Leon Keyserling, Senator Wagner's legislative assistant during FDR's first term, which underlined the unity of the 1933–1936 interval.[98]

This third orientation, the one I embrace, demonstrates that the division between the First and the Second New Deal signifies not a major break but a lesser inflection. This is the powerful message Alan Brinkley conveys in his study of how New Deal reformers defined their goals and articulated their ambitions. Moving from what Carl Degler called "the third American revolution," which had produced "a revolutionary response to a revolutionary situation,"[99] American liberalism's domestic policies became less expansive and more contained, Brinkley shows convincingly, during the period spanning 1937–1938 to World War II.[100] As both he and Schlesinger have revealed, it makes sense to focus a good deal less on differences within Roosevelt's first term and consider instead how those four years composed a tightly connected moment whose unprecedented actions were based on the persistent understanding that an unfettered and unbalanced capitalism could no longer be made to work.

Governor Roosevelt's presidential candidacy, we might recall, had been premised on this line of analysis. In a hallmark address to San Francisco's Commonwealth Club on September 23, 1932, he lamented how "equality of opportunity as we have known it no longer exists," and he sought to explain why "we are now providing a drab living for our own people." That speech offered a structural analysis. It identified a closed frontier, a built-up industrial structure, and "a steady course toward economic oligarchy" as the Depression's culprits. Needed in such circumstances were "new terms of the old social contract" . . . a new "economic constitutional order" in which "our government" would "restrict the operations of the speculator, the manipulator, even the financier." To check competitive markets and the reach of business power, FDR announced, would require plans in the public interest.

This signal speech explicitly rejected separating industrial policies from social welfare legislation, just the partition that commonly is said to distinguish the two phases of the New Deal's initial period. Economic guidelines devised to prevent a "state of anarchy," the candidate insisted, must not stand alone, but must move ahead in tandem with the kinds of welfare state programs Congress legislated three years later. "By no other means can men carry the burdens of those parts of life which, in the nature of things afford no chance of labor; childhood, sickness, old age. In all thought of property," the talk's stirring language announced, "this right is paramount; all other property rights must yield to it."[101]

Two years later, at just the moment many have identified with a shift from the First to the Second New Deal, President Roosevelt took to the radio to review the achievements of the second session of the Seventy-third Congress. Speaking to the country on June 28, 1934, he celebrated the legislature's long list of enactments in language that resonated with the forceful terms he had been using ever since his Commonwealth Club address to promote the assertive program that had been remaking the relationship between government and the economy. Noting that New Deal initiatives continued to face resistance, he identified its enemies with a "selfish minority." These opponents had been mounting arguments about the loss of liberty, "giving strange names to what we are doing. Sometimes they will call it 'Fascism,' sometimes 'Communism,' sometimes 'regimentation,' sometimes 'socialism.'" To counter such "prophets of calamity" who claim "a loss of individual liberty" and draw attention to parallels between the New Deal and "other nations [that] may sacrifice democracy for the transitory stimulation of old and discredited autocracies," the president asked his listeners to "answer this question. . . . Have you lost any of your rights or liberty or constitutional freedom or action and choice? . . . Read each provision of the Bill of Rights," he counseled, "and ask yourself whether you personally have suffered the impairment of a single jot of those real assurances."[102] Just over a year before he would sign both the National Labor Relations Act and the Social Security Act into law, this talk projected "the establishment of means to provide sound and adequate protection against the vicissitudes of modern life—in other words, social insurance" in terms that were identical to those he had offered in San Francisco.

Such rhetoric and analysis remained features of the radical moment from start to finish. Speaking to the assembled delegates in Philadelphia on June 27, 1936, Roosevelt accepted the Democratic Party nomination for a second term by boasting how the New Deal's comprehensive program to reshape American capitalism had countered the "economic royalists" who, "thirsting for power," had "created a new despotism," an "economic tyranny" in which "private enterprise, indeed, became too private." The New Deal had fought back against "the privileged princes of these new economic dynasties" by having refused to operate by older rules that distinguish "political freedom," which is "the business of the government," from "economic slavery," which is nobody's business."[103] Echoing the language and logic he had articulated both in San Francisco and in his inaugural address, the president's retrospective appraisals in early 1937 explained how, in making "the exercise of all power more democratic," the New Deal had created "the largest progressive democracy in the modern world." He did not back away from "the broad objectives of the National Recovery Act," which he called "sound," and he recalled how Washington had "begun to bring private autocratic powers into their proper subordination to the public's government" and how, by fashioning a welfare state and endorsing labor rights, it had constructed "new materials for social justice."[104]

The president also contrasted how this successful effort "to maintain a democracy"[105] had been carried out in a collaborative exercise between Congress and the executive branch, thus distinguishing America's response to the economic crisis from the ways the dictatorships had been addressing the same problems. In underscoring "mutual respect for each other's proper sphere of functioning in a democracy" and in stressing America's refusal "to permit unnecessary disagreement to arise between two of our branches of Government,"[106] he explicitly situated the early New Deal as engaged in a front-line struggle to disprove claims that liberal democracies could not function effectively. Explaining "why we have fought fear" as a display of "faith—in the soundness of democracy in the midst of dictatorships,"[107] the president insisted that the New Deal had been demonstrating "that democracies are best able to cope with the changing problems of modern civilization. . . ." Speaking before an assembled Congress on January 6, 1937, he proclaimed, "Ours was the task to prove that democracy could be made to function in the world of today," adding that "because all of us believe that our democratic form of government can cope adequately with modern problems as they arise," it had been vital to send "forth a message on behalf of all the democracies of the world to those Nations which live otherwise. Because such other Governments are perhaps more spectacular, it was high time for democracy to assert itself."[108]

At a time when so many observers thought that parliaments crippled liberal democracies, the president stressed how precisely the opposite had been occurring in the United States. America was confronting the problems of the Depression and economic insecurity, he reported, by passing "new laws consistent with an historic constitutionalist framework." He further underscored the central task of "the Legislative branch of our government" as it grapples with "the curbing of abuses, the extension of help to those who need help, or the better balancing of our interdependent economies."[109] In part a prelude to the impending and ill-fated proposal to enlarge the Supreme Court that had invalidated the NRA and other New Deal laws, this emphasis on congressional power underscored how problem solving in America required legislative action.

It was, in fact, a surge of statutes, not executive commands, that recast American capitalism. Every groundbreaking effort to place the federal government at the center of economic affairs and rebalance power in civil society proceeded through congressional lawmaking. The record is considerable. In addition to the NRA, which made industry its focus, the Hundred Days ushered in the Agricultural Adjustment Act, which profoundly reorganized American agriculture by tackling the problems of overproduction and low commodity prices through a program of subsidies to farmers in return for limiting their crops and the number of livestock. Repairing a system in desperate straits, the Banking Act of 1933 separated investment from depository banks. It also required institutions that were part of the Federal Reserve to possess sufficient capital reserves, allowed the Federal Reserve to regulate savings bank interest rates, and guaranteed the safety of deposits through a Federal Deposit Insurance Corporation.

The fusillade of laws continued. Following a nearly 90 percent decline in the value of the stock market between 1929 and 1933, the government also undertook to cleanse markets in securities. The Securities Act of 1933 mandated that stocks be registered, and demanded a great deal of disclosure before they could be sold. The Securities Exchange Act of 1934 further extended the scope of federal law to include all securities that were publicly traded, and put a new body, the Security and Exchange Commission (SEC), in charge of these regulations, with a mandate to prevent "manipulation and sudden and unreasonable fluctuations of security prices."[110] Congress passed the Tennessee Valley Authority Act in 1933, a sweeping project based on an existing dam and infrastructure facilities that had been constructed at Muscle Shoals, Alabama, during World War I. As an instrument of resource planning on a massive scale with powers of eminent domain, the TVA was fashioned as a public power company whose sole stockholder was the United States and whose three directors were to be appointed by the president with the consent of the Senate. In 1934, the House and Senate also fundamentally altered the rules for participation in foreign trade. The Reciprocal Trade Agreements Act promoted freer trade on the basis of tariff agreements that the president was authorized to negotiate. The next year witnessed passage of two additional landmarks: the National Labor Relations Act, which established a coherent and supportive framework for unions to recruit members and negotiate with business on a more level playing field, and the Social Security Act, which targeted assistance to needy families, created a federal framework for unemployment insurance, and guaranteed income to Americans upon their retirement.

IV.

T HE REMARKABLE legislative productivity of this radical moment—a moment when government embraced a strong sense of a domestic public purpose—was propelled as much by the South's elected representatives as by any other group in the House and Senate. Each of the era's milestone laws required their support; each would have been blocked without it. As it turned out, each not only achieved a threshold level of positive votes by southern members but also garnered extensive and usually eager backing. With their leadership positions and control of committees, moreover, southerners were often in the lead, even when a particular law did not have special sectional importance.

The TVA, of course, did have a regional focus. Passed into law on May 18, 1933, weeks after Congress established the Civilian Conservation Corps (CCC) to put 250,000 unemployed men to work, and just days after approving the AAA and the Federal Emergency Relief Act, which sent money to the states to put cash in the pockets of desperate citizens, the TVA Act offered resource development and economic planning on an immense scale. It authorized the construction of huge power and navigation dams on the Tennessee River to control flooding, advance reforestation of stripped land, and, especially, bring electricity at low cost to a backward region, and it sanctioned building plants the TVA would run to supply area farmers with affordable fertilizer. Not surprisingly, the South's representatives keenly backed the law, and welcomed Roosevelt's reversal of the rejection by Presidents Coolidge and Hoover of proposals to develop the Tennessee Valley extensively. Making good on a pledge he had made at a campaign appearance at Muscle Shoals, Roosevelt's proposal animated southern supporters for the arc of development it promised for a great swath of the South. The program for the river and its valley of some 40,660 square miles—the size of England—which originated in Missouri and moved through parts of Tennessee, Alabama, Georgia, North Carolina, Kentucky, and Virginia, had the potential, it was said, if with a degree of exaggeration, to generate some one million jobs for a population of six million.[111] It would produce, Mississippi's John Rankin informed the House, "hydroelectric power that will exceed in amount the amount of physical strength of all the slaves freed by the Civil War."[112]

Saluting the president's call in April 1933 for "national planning for a complete river watershed involving many States and the future lives and welfare of millions,"[113] southern representatives, particularly in the House, backed the legislation by articulating populist themes. "Let it be used to manufacture for the farmers of the United States cheaper and better fertilizer, and second, let it be used to protect the people against the Power Trusts of America," Tennessee's John Ridley Mitchell proclaimed. "Let it produce throughout the years the yardstick by which the people of the Nation may know the fair, legitimate, and actual cost of electricity," he stated, adding that "no one opposes this national project unless it is because of a selfish motive."[114] Samuel McReynolds, also of Tennessee, noted how desirable projects of this type were well beyond the scope of private capitalism. "No private interest could or would make this great development, and these great natural resources should always be held and controlled by the Government of this country for the best interest of its people."[115] Reporting how the legislation "has been bitterly fought by the manufactures of fertilizer, for the reason that they know when this plant is developed they cannot continue to get the price they are now getting," David Glover of Arkansas spoke for "the farmer at home [who] is not here, but we are here as his representatives to speak for him, and to hear his voice rather than to hear that of the lobbyist for these great concerns."[116] Robert Thomason of Texas claimed the TVA would put an end to the exploitation by "private interests" that have "taken charge of the streams that God put in this old world for the benefit of everybody," and he extolled the fact that electricity, which "has become as common and necessary as water, gas, and fuel," would be brought "within the reach of every man in America to use it upon terms that he can afford."[117]

What the *Washington Post* grudgingly came to call the country's "greatest experiment in social reform," and what the chairman of the TVA, Arthur E. Morgan, labeled a "laboratory for the nation," was brought into being by strong partisan votes.[118] Saluting how the federal government was successfully taking on the vigorous opposition of electric operating and holding companies and the area's large fertilizer firms, and encouraged by plans to work closely with local governments to improve health services, roads, and other facilities development would require,[119] all southern members but three (George Terrell of Texas in the House, and Thomas Gore of Oklahoma[120] and Millard Tydings of Maryland in the Senate) backed the TVA.

These supporters assumed that the law's administration would do nothing to disturb the racial order. They were correct. Like the Smith-Lever Act of the Wilson years, the TVA found no place in the fertilizer program for black colleges.[121] A classic 1949 assessment of the first decade and a half found that "the typical position of the TVA agriculturalist is one of white supremacy," marked by references "to 'good and bad niggers,'" and animated by the assumption that white landlords were taking proper care of their black tenants, "who are generally deemed to be satisfied with their lot." When blacks applied for jobs, a later analysis found, "they were relegated to the most menial positions. The authority barred them from vocational schools and from training sessions for higher-skilled jobs." Additionally, TVA communities were rigidly segregated, with no blacks at all inside Norris, Tennessee, its planned model community on the outskirts of Knoxville's metropolitan area.[122]

Southern politicians' support for the TVA, a federal program with such obvious benefits for their region, may not be surprising, but their central participation in other early initiatives also was critical. Two long-serving congressional southerners—each a strong supporter of racial segregation—led the rescue of the banking system. Senator Carter Glass of Virginia and Representative Henry Steagall of Alabama ushered the Banking Act through their committees and guided debate in each chamber. By restoring trust in the banks, this law provided the basis for all the economic policies that followed; without a solvent system, capitalism could not have functioned. Unlike most highly partisan votes on key bills in this era, this legislation garnered strong cross-party support, including that of southern members, who ranged from loyal New Dealers like Steagall[123] to conservatives like Glass, who wrote shortly, in August 1933, to Walter Lippmann to complain that the New Deal was "an utterly dangerous effort of the federal government to transplant Hitlerism to every corner of the nation."[124] Speaking to calm southern progressives who were concerned about legislation that would prop up banks and bankers, John Rankin argued that restoring confidence by insuring deposits was necessary to address the "terrible nightmare" caused by "the greatest economic catastrophe in history."[125] The Steagall bill passed the House by an overwhelming 262–19 vote (without a roll call), the Glass bill in the Senate by a voice vote. With differences ironed out, the Senate again approved the legislation by voice, and the House by a 191–6 margin (without a roll call).

A distinctive regional twang could be heard. In the House, Mississippi's William Colmer and Texas's William McFarlane and Wright Patman took up an old populist cause. Bemoaning how bankers were overpaid, they unsuccessfully offered amendments to restrict Federal Reserve salaries to no more than fifteen thousand dollars.[126] Southern members were particularly vehement in voicing concern about the durability of banks chartered by the states, rather than by the federal government. They also worried about the future of the Postal Savings System, which served primarily small depositors.

Patman was concerned that the bill would "use the Government's money to protect deposits in national banks aggregating $16,000,000,000, but you will exclude from protection of any kind whatsoever deposits in State banks amounting to $25,541,000,000."[127] Arkansas's Glover likewise expressed concern for state banks that would not fall under the protection of the Federal Reserve, but he was promised they would now come under its protective umbrella. With these apprehensions addressed, the southern wing of the Democratic party joined the overwhelming consensus.[128] In a characteristic statement, Senator Tom Connally of Texas told the Senate that he was not voting to support the banks, "but the people the banks serve," because the law will "furnish a reservoir of credit and money with which the people of this country can transact their normal business."[129] Perhaps most interesting is how even the region's most archsegregationists, people such as Rankin, betrayed no concern about the growth of federal regulatory power. With race clearly off the agenda, what they wanted was a guarantee that their region's state-level banks, which operated entirely on segregated principles, would emerge with enhanced security.

Well past the Hundred Days, as the New Deal filled the agenda of its radical moment, southern support rolled on, premised on this exchange of assurances about racial continuity. The Securities Exchange Act of 1934 was brought to the floor of the House by the Interstate and Foreign Commerce Committee, chaired by Sam Rayburn of Texas, and to the Senate by the Senate Banking and Currency Committee, led by Duncan Fletcher of Florida. Every southern senator but Thomas Gore and every southern representative but Missouri's James Claiborne, who wanted a more business-friendly bill, supported passage of this law that aimed to provide an honest market in securities and prevent a recurrence of the crash of 1929. The bill passed Congress with partisan divisions of 281–84 in the House and 62–13 in the Senate,[130] then by voice votes in each chamber to adopt the conference report. The final product was written by a conference in which two of the three House participants (Rayburn and George Huddleston of Alabama) and each of the Senate conferees (Alben Barkley of Kentucky, James Byrnes of South Carolina, Duncan Fletcher of Florida, and Phillips Goldsborough of Maryland) were southern.

There was disagreement within the region's voting bloc about whether regulatory responsibilities should be assigned to the existing Federal Trade

Commission (FTC) or placed, as they were, in the hands of a new Securities and Exchange Commission (SEC). There remained, though, broad southern agreement on the thrust of the bill, which, from the region's perspective, would harness Yankee finance capital that had helped impoverish their region ever since the Civil War. At issue, Rayburn explained, was how to oppose the "people who operate the exchanges" by lodging "authority, power, and directions" in the federal government "in the public interest."[131] Here, again, the dominant tone of southern contributions tilted toward populist strains like those spoken during the debate in the House by Virgil Chapman of Kentucky, who announced that "Wall Street and its minions are here full panoplied for battle."[132] It was to be hoped, Georgia's Edward Cox (later, a key southern reactionary) added, that the measure will "prevent the concentration of money in the great centers where the exchanges operate," and, as Oklahoma's Charles Truax colorfully expressed in terms that evoked anti-Jewish imagery, that it would control "the Wall Street bandits" by providing a "new declaration of independence from the strangling clutch of those long, bony talons of Morgan, Kuhn & Loeb, and the rest of the Wall Street racketeers, who have literally robbed this country of billions and billions of dollars."[133] Though Morgan was not Jewish, the reference to Kuhn and Loeb made the inference all too clear.

Domestic policy to reshape capitalism during the New Deal's radical period took further giant steps. Just six weeks after the Supreme Court struck down the NRA as unconstitutional, the National Labor Relations Act (NLRA), or Wagner Act, which empowered efforts to organize unions, was signed into law on July 5, 1935. Union insurgency, which had begun to develop under the umbrella of the NRA, found itself without a permissive legal framework until the passage of this legislation.[134] Reaffirming rights to organize and bargain collectively, the law specified detailed election procedures to ensure that employees could freely select their union representatives under the principle of majority rule. Crucially, this bill aimed, as it stated, "to promote equality of bargaining between employers and employees" and disallowed as "unfair labor practices" a variety of tactics commonly deployed by employers to subvert unionization. These included interference with striking and picketing; employer surveillance of union activities; discrimination against employees for union membership or activism; and offers by employers of benefits to employees who agreed to cease union activities.[135]

The NLRA also barred employers from providing financial assistance to, or attempting to control, labor organizations,[136] thus striking at the heart of company-dominated unions. Administratively, the act created the National Labor Relations Board (NLRB), a quasi-judicial expert board, appointed by the president, to investigate and adjudicate most labor disputes arising under the act. Independent from the Department of Labor, the NLRB was empowered to issue cease and desist orders, and its findings of fact were to be regarded as conclusive by federal courts.[137]

With this law, the federal government offered organized labor a broad legal umbrella under which to shelter.[138] Almost immediately, unions began to expand at a rapid rate. Both the AFL and the breakaway CIO quickly thrived. In 1929, labor unions had possessed fewer than four million members. A decade later, despite continuing mass unemployment (more than nine million Americans still were out of work in 1939), the new CIO alone matched that level of membership, while the AFL grew to more than four million members, and more than a million workers joined independent unions. Even before the wave of union expansion spurred by tight labor markets during World War II, this spectacular growth was altering the balance of power between labor and management.[139] Between 1930 and 1940, the proportion of manufacturing workers in unions rose from 9 percent to 34 percent and that of mining workers from 21 percent to 72 percent.[140]

On August 14, 1935, the president signed the historic Social Security Act. By establishing federally managed old-age pensions and unemployment insurance, it considerably altered the contours of America's labor markets by making it possible for the elderly to leave the workforce and by promising to cushion future economic downturns by keeping at least some purchasing power in the hands of those who lost their jobs with the provision of half pay, up to fifteen dollars each week, usually for sixteen weeks.[141] Most notably, at a time when just about half of all Americans over sixty-five were receiving relief payments,[142] the law created a system of social insurance that offered workers meaningful pensions when they retired. It also addressed issues of poverty by fashioning a program of social welfare that included cash assistance to the indigent elderly and the blind, including those who did not qualify for a pension, because they lacked a life history of employment, and aid to impoverished and dependent children, a program of welfare transfers whose costs were to be shared between the states and the federal government, with levels established by each state. Like the NLRA, this was an enactment that profoundly altered lives and, along with this, the character of American society.

On the face of things, neither the Wagner Act nor the Social Security Act, like the Banking Act, required southern votes. After all, the labor bill swept into law on a 63–12 margin in the Senate and a voice vote in the House; and Social Security was approved nearly without opposition by crushing bipartisan votes of 77–6 in the Senate and 372–33 in the House. That conclusion, however, would be premature. As these laws wended their way through the legislative process, southern support at critical junctures sustained their basic character in the face of serious challenges. In the case of the Wagner Act, it was only the high solidarity of the South's Democrats in the Senate with other Democrats[143] that made it impossible for a bloc to emerge sufficient in strength either to pass a crippling amendment offered by Maryland's Tydings or to mount a filibuster to block the bill without it.[144] Tydings's amendment would have added the language "free from coercion or intimidation from any source" at the end of the key paragraph offering employees the right to join unions and bargain collectively. He explained that without the additional wording, coercion would shift from business to labor.

Had this clause been adopted, union power would have been curbed, for it would have made opposition to a company union in an election to determine representation the equivalent of an employer's threat to fire a worker who wished to unionize. It also would have opened labor activity to the scrutiny of courts at a time when, as Senator Wagner observed, "the courts have said that a threat to strike is coercion."[145] Furthermore, the amendment had the potential to call into question the very core of the law, the closed shop that made it mandatory for workers to join a union after it had been recognized as the choice by the majority. By a vote of 21–50, the amendment failed. In addition to Tydings and his Maryland colleague George Radcliffe, it won the support of just five other southern Democrats. Had they been joined by the seventeen who voted no, the amendment would have carried by a 38–33 margin (another eight did not vote in this division).

Neither should the South's role in moving Social Security into law be underestimated. A crucial vote to recommit the bill to the House Committee on Ways and Means attracted all but one Republican. The amendment failed, 149–253, because southern Democrats stuck with the party position, voting at a high level with fellow Democrats.[146] Had the 141 Democrats in the chamber from the seventeen southern states resisted the legislation, it well might not have passed.

This is not a far-fetched alternative. It is likely that the southern wing of the party would have bolted if the legislation had taken the form initially proposed by the White House. On the basis of recommendations by the President's Committee on Economic Security, Social Security would have included farmworkers and maids. The committee explicitly opposed leaving these workers out, having noted their high degree of need: "In these groups are many who are at the very bottom of the economic scale."[147] Still, they were left out, extruded during the deliberations of the Senate Finance Committee and House Ways and Means Committee, each with strong southern representation (nine of fifteen Democrats in the Senate, including the chair, Harrison of Mississippi, and eight of eighteen in the House, including the chair, Doughton of North Carolina). The legislation also left it to the states to set levels of support both for unemployment insurance and for the welfare program of Aid to Dependent Children, programs that involved federal government matching funds for what the states decided to offer. As a consequence, southerners could vote for the bill that brought much needed funding to their poverty-stricken region while protecting the character of its racial arrangements.

Southern legislators similarly imposed occupational bars on the Wagner Act. The original bill that Senator Wagner introduced contained no language excluding any category of worker. But the version reported by the Senate Finance Committee explicitly stated that "the term employee ... shall not include any individual employed as an agricultural laborer." Addressing what it called "propaganda over the country in relation to this bill," the committee report affirmed that the bill it drafted "does not relate to employment as a domestic servant or as an agricultural laborer."[148] No effort was made on the floor of the Senate or the House to remove this condition. So assured, southern support became almost indistinguishable from that of other Democrats.[149] The Oregon Republican James Mott took notice. Remarking on Democratic solidarity during the debate on Social Security, he lamented how a party "machine so well oiled" had defeated every one of the forty-four amendments the House considered, "every one of them shouted down regardless of their merit by practically solid Democratic votes."[150]

V.

T HE DRAMATIC reorganization of American capitalism was not limited to domestic policy. In 1934, Congress passed the Reciprocal Trade Agreements Act (RTAA), a law that had been insistently advanced by the country's new secretary of state, Tennessee's Cordell Hull. A Wilsonian progressive and an active supporter of the South's racial system, he had championed lower tariffs during his service in the House, from 1907 to 1930, and in the Senate since 1931. Like most southern members with progressive commitments, he had long thought that high trade barriers "shifted the burden of financing government from the rich to the poor; concentrated wealth in the hands of industrialists influential enough to win favorable treatment for their products; and worked not as an effective source of revenue," but, "by reducing trade, actually lowered revenue."[151] Moreover, as he told Congress in 1934, he was convinced that the dramatic decline of some 70 percent in American exports and imports from 1929 to 1933 had caused massive reductions in consumption and in the country's standard of living. During this period, America's share of world trade also had fallen, from some 12 percent to 9 percent of global imports, and from 14 percent to 11 percent of exports.[152]

Prior to the passage of RTAA, tariffs had been set item by item in Congress. This process was dominated by special-interest lobbying and was prone to trades among legislators who sought to protect industries in their districts.[153] As a result, the institutional process tended to favor ever higher excise rates, especially when Republicans were in power. During the post-Reconstruction era, as the country underwent rapid industrialization, Republicans sought to protect domestic business from foreign competition, while Democrats, more oriented to the concerns of farmers and consumers, tried to keep them down and find alternative sources of revenue. Republican sectional and economic interest tended to gain, and Democratic sectional and economic interests to lose, when tariffs went up.[154] When Republicans controlled the legislative process rather more than Democrats in the late nineteenth and early twentieth centuries, foreign economic policy became increasingly protectionist. The McKinley Tariff of 1890 and the Dingley Tariff of 1897 had significantly raised rates at a time when such levies were still the country's main source of revenue.

With the ratification in 1913 of the sixteenth Amendment to the Constitution, authorizing the federal government to levy an income tax, questions about how to regulate imports and exports primarily became matters that placed contending economic interests and party coalitions in a policy competition to set desired levels. Revisions of tariffs when Republicans controlled the White House and Congress in 1922 raised rates on 88 percent of imported goods, reversing the policy of a Democratic government that had lowered rates on 91 percent in 1913.[155] The 1930 tariff act, named for Reed Smoot, a Utah Republican senator, and Willis Hawley, a Republican representative from Oregon, covered more than twenty thousand items and produced the highest tariff rates in American history.[156] Smoot-Hawley "was enacted at or near the peak of a great era of Republican supremacy, by a Congress in which this party had substantial majorities in both houses, following a presidential election in which Mr. Hoover defeated his Democratic opponent by more than 6,000,000 votes."[157] During the 1928 election, when the country turned its back on the Catholic candidate for president, New York governor Al Smith, the Republicans gained thirty seats in the House and seven in the Senate. With huge Republican majorities of 267–167 and 56–39, and with the Democratic Party largely reduced to its southern, anti-tariff, representation, Congress passed the new tariff schedule by overwhelmingly partisan votes (it garnered only seventeen Democratic votes in the House and five in the Senate).[158] The last of the "American System" Congress-centered protective tariff acts that sheltered America's huge domestic market from overseas competition, the Smoot-Hawley statute became infamous for having triggered a tariff-raising tit-for-tat process that raised barriers to world trade at just the moment when the global collapse of capitalism begged for the reverse.[159]

When Smoot-Hawley was considered, most of the debate was taken up with detailed discussion of the economic conditions in particular industries, including sugar, glass, metals, lumber, chemicals, leather, and textiles. These issues, and broader questions about protectionism, generated heated debate as well as intensely partisan votes. The most negative voices were southern and Democratic. They objected to the way tariffs raised prices and represented partial, not national, interests. Oklahoma's Jed Johnson remonstrated how lumber, wool, and the "gigantic steel and metal industry," with "little or no competition," and thus with monopoly pricing power, had made the case for protection. "The American public is going to demand to know just what constitutes a 'case' in the minds of these New England gentlemen who proudly boast of the authorship of this infamous tariff bill that is conceived for the purpose of adding additional millions to the coffers of the greedy industries of the East."[160] Missouri's Ralph Lozier echoed this populist position by seeking to reveal how "this act has enriched the manufacturing classes beyond the dreams of avarice."[161] Within the torrent of such southern objections, the most sustained and analytical argument for freer trade came from Cordell Hull. Five months before the Wall Street crash, he presciently projected that the law's "extreme protection system" would build agricultural and petroleum surpluses that could not find foreign markets. "Kept at home," he warned, "there would be depression and panic unrivaled in human history."[162]

Four years later, with Hull at the State Department crusading for lower rates, and with Democrats commanding a unified government, the New Deal undertook to change the institutional game significantly by removing Congress from the details of tariff setting. Sending a request to Congress for a new set of arrangements to jump-start American trade and revive depressed export industries, President Roosevelt took up Hull's idea that the capacity to set rates should shift to the president, who would be granted advance authority to negotiate trade agreements with other countries. Rather than set rates unilaterally, the legislation envisaged a mutual process of tariff reduction based on negotiated bilateral trade agreements. That would make it harder for subsequent Congresses to undo free trade deals, since tariffs no longer would simply be a domestic political matter but would be based on international bargains that would be costly to unravel. Hull's message to Congress underscored how the world's democracies and dictatorships had placed just such authority with their executives, and how, without such an arrangement, the United States faced the world without being "able to protect its trade against discriminations and against bargains injurious to its interests."[163] Such a process, he maintained, offered "the only feasible and practicable step" to revive American trade, a step required to get capitalism moving again.[164]

Technically an amendment to Smoot-Hawley, this statute heightened the chances that freer trade would prevail by shifting the political logic. Protectionist logrolling became more difficult, and the costs of high tariffs became more transparent, as they were no longer dispersed across hundreds of different constituency districts.[165] Since lower rates for imports were tied to more access to overseas markets, the change was palatable across the Democratic Party, even for recently elected members of Congress who came from previously Republican industrial districts with large working-class populations.[166]

Not surprisingly, southern Democrats dominated the positive side of the debate on the Hill. They condemned past practices that, as Lozier argued, had converted "the halls of Congress . . . into a marketplace" in which "so many votes for a tariff on this product were exchanged for so many votes for a tariff on another product."[167] They talked about the need for foreign markets, and the problems generated by trade wars; complained how farmers, and southern agriculture in particular, had suffered under Republican trade policies that raised the price for imported farm machinery while making it harder to sell cotton, tobacco, and rice overseas; and echoed Hull, as Representative Claude Fuller of Arkansas put the point, in arguing that international commerce "on a fair, mutual, and profitable basis" is both a privileged means "in the restoration of prosperity" and can "serve as a great civilizer and peacemaker."[168] They also fervently endorsed the new procedures, which Doughton argued were necessary to counter how "practically every other country in continental Europe, as well as England and her major dominions, and several of the countries of South America have vested authority in the executive branch of their respective governments to negotiate reciprocal trade agreements."[169]

The winning Democratic trade coalition was led by southerners. In his classic work, *Southern Politics in State and Nation*, V. O. Key Jr. noted how during the full 1933–1945 period he studied, "southern Democrats, on the average, voted 94.8 per cent for trade agreements, while on the average only 84.1 per cent of nonsouthern Democrats supported the program. On the other hand, on the average, 86.6 per cent of the Republicans opposed."[170] When the RTAA first passed in 1934, by a 57–33 margin in the Senate and a 271–111 margin in the House, Democratic Party solidarity was high across the board. Voting together, in the face of nearly unanimous Republican opposition, southern and nonsouthern Democrats stood tall together to support the global face of the radical moment.[171]

VI.

COMMENTING ON the New Deal's remarkable legislative productivity during the Seventy-fourth Congress, Lester Dickinson, an Iowa Republican senator, complained in February 1936 that "more legislation of far-reaching social and economic consequence was enacted last year than in any previous session." For liberal constitutional governments, he lamented, this was "a performance never equaled in the history of legislatures since those rump Parliaments which, under the Stuarts, so seriously jeopardized English liberty in the seventeenth century." Looking ahead, he anticipated Democratic Party gains in the November election, and worried that the New Deal seemed poised to advance ever more decisively.[172]

The landslide reelection in 1936 of Franklin Roosevelt, who carried forty-six of forty-eight states, helped generate remarkable majorities for the Democratic Party in Congress. The results reduced Republican representation to a mere eighty-nine seats in the House and sixteen in the Senate. With the one-party South intact and with the Democratic Party's gain of five seats in the Senate and twelve in the House, where it now controlled fully three-quarters of the chamber, the largest majority for any party since Reconstruction, Dickinson's worst-case scenario seemed confirmed. As the Seventy-fifth Congress was about to convene, the *New York Times'* congressional reporter, Turner Catledge, commented, "So large is the Democratic majority in the new Congress that, at least at the start, President Roosevelt's word will be law."[173] Furthermore, just as Roosevelt was proposing to enlarge the Supreme Court in order to unblock the barriers it had placed in the path of assertive federal action, the Supreme Court validated a state of Washington minimum-wage law in March; it decided to confirm the constitutionality of the Wagner Act in April, and, in May, it upheld the Social Security Act. That spring, there was little reason to think the trend of assertive New Deal lawmaking would weaken.

The success proved illusory, ephemeral at best. Even though no barrier, legislative or judicial, seemed to stand in the way, the trend of legislative achievement began to falter. Democratic unity proved unsteady. The South began selectively to withdraw its support. Despite the continued growth of the nonsouthern wing of the Democratic Party,[174] it did not control majorities. These required either Republican or southern Democratic votes, the latter, of course, being the more likely. Over the years that spanned the beginning of Franklin Roosevelt's second term in March 1937 to the start of the country's participation in World War II in December 1941, such southern support became more patchy and less assured. Danger signs appeared in the very first session of Congress after the massive electoral victory of 1936, when the level of opposition to New Deal proposals within the Democratic Party doubled, a trend led by a growing sectional divide.[175]

As it turned out, 1936 was a particularly good year for southern Democrats, who continued to dominate the region. Alabama senator John Bankhead was returned with 87 percent of the vote; Joseph Robinson, in Arkansas, with 82; Carter Glass, in Virginia, with 92. In Delaware, a twelve-point victory placed what had been a Republican seat in the hands of Democrat James Hughes. Claude Pepper won reelection unopposed in Florida. So did Richard Russell in Georgia, Pat Harrison in Mississippi, and Allen Ellender in Louisiana. Across the South, only a single Republican, John Townsend Jr. of Delaware, remained in the Senate.[176] On the other side of the Capitol, exactly the same distribution of seats was obtained by southern Democrats in this election as in the prior two. Across the region's seventeen states, 141 Democrats continued to overwhelm 4 Republicans (one each from Kentucky and Missouri, and two from the hill country constituencies in Tennessee).

After the new Congress assembled, more than one issue stressed the Democratic Party's sectional alliance. Taxes sometimes proved divisive. So, too, did the distribution of relief, utilities regulation, housing issues, payments to veterans, and, especially, Roosevelt's proposal to change the composition of the Supreme Court and the larger federal judiciary, lest it continue to negate New Deal statutes. Some southern members, especially those, like Carter Glass and Josiah Bailey, who had never been New Deal supporters, were persuaded that the president's successful courtship of northern black voters during the 1936 campaign portended a recast judiciary, one that would enhance the prospects for successful civil rights litigation. Joining Republicans in strategy meetings to plan the proposal's defeat, they induced other southern colleagues, including New Deal loyalists, to break with the president at a moment that coincided with the return of antilynching legislation to the congressional agenda.[177]

Above all, it was a cluster of issues concerning labor markets and labor unions that began to divide the Democratic Party more decisively. The South relied on its advantage in labor costs to recruit investors to a poverty-stricken and job-starved region. Only by following a low-wage development strategy, its business and political leaders argued, could it begin to overcome the economic dominion of northern industry and finance.[178] Its cotton, tobacco, and rice farming depended on subaltern labor, especially black labor, which was controlled by a mix of economic and political power, as well as by a pervasive threat of violence. The widespread system of sharecropping and tenancy was an intrinsic part of the racial order southern members were committed to defend.[179] During the House debate that ultimately produced the Fair Labor Standards Act (FLSA), setting minimum wages and establishing maximum hours, Representative James Mark Wilcox, a Florida Democrat, spoke about how "there has always been a difference in the wage scale of white and colored labor." Observing that "the Federal Government knows no color line and of necessity it cannot make any distinction between the races," he worried "that when we turn over to a federal bureau or board the power to fix wages, it will prescribe the same wage for the Negro that it prescribes for the white man," and he remonstrated that such equality "just will not work in the South. You cannot put the Negro and the white man on the same basis and get away with it. . . . This bill, like the antilynching bill, is another political goldbrick for the Negro."[180]

The White House proposed a labor standards bill after the NRA was ruled unconstitutional, thus eliminating federal supervision of labor market wages and hours. The Democratic Party's 1936 platform promised a legislative response. Announcing "the time has arrived for us to take further action to extend the frontiers of social progress" on May 24, 1937, when one in three American workers was earning less than thirty-three cents an hour,[181] President Roosevelt called on Congress to provide "A Fair Day's Pay for a Fair Day's Work." His message to a special session of Congress announced the hope that "legislation can . . . be passed at this session of the Congress further to help those who toil in factory and on farm."[182]

The bill followed a rocky path. Ultimately, thirteen months after this request, there was a bill to sign, but not before "one of the most desperately fought battles ever waged on the floor of congress."[183] Even as the New Deal ultimately won the ability to regulate labor markets, this struggle made clear that the radical moment was coming to a close. The new law appeared like a mere wraith of its predecessor, the NIRA, a substitute for its now-defunct labor standards.[184] Though vastly less ambitious than that law, which had passed quickly with southern leadership and much enthusiasm, the FLSA elicited great controversy and episodes of southern defection.

The full extent of the proposed law's troubles was not yet apparent when the Senate approved the measure, 56–28, on July 31, 1937, with southern and nonsouthern Democrats still voting much alike,[185] but not quite with as much solidarity as prior New Deal domestic proposals had secured.

Southern support depended on the introduction, once again, of agricultural exclusions that were equivalent to those that had characterized all prior relevant New Deal statutes, even though the president had advocated placing these workers under the law's protection. Though not mentioned explicitly, domestic workers also were effectively excluded by virtue of the bill's narrow embrace only of workers "engaged in commerce or in the production of goods for commerce."[186] Further, southern votes were forthcoming only after Alabama's Hugo Black successfully moved to table an antilynching provision that had been proposed by New York Democrat Royal Samuel Copeland. With Republicans unanimously voting to keep the Copeland proposal alive, and with southern Democrats predictably voting to table, the provision, which was defeated by a 46–39 vote, could have passed had it garnered just four more nonsouthern Democratic votes. These members of the party sharply split. Those voting with their southern colleagues understood that if the antilynching amendment were to be included, the larger bill surely would go down to defeat as a result of southern defections.

Early in the Senate hearings, Gardner Jackson, chairman of the National Committee on Rural and Social Planning, a labor-oriented advocacy organization, forcefully told the Senate Committee on Education and Labor "that agricultural laborers have been explicitly excluded from participation in any of the benefits of New Deal legislation, from the late (but not greatly lamented) N.R.A., down through the A.A.A., the Wagner-Connery Labor Relations Act and the Social Security Act, for the simple and effective reason that it has been deemed politically certain that their inclusion would have spelled death of the legislation in Congress." Continuing, he observed how, "in this proposed Black-Connery wages and hours bill, agricultural laborers are again explicitly excluded."[187]

Still, many southern senators hesitated. They wanted farmers to be excluded not only from the minimum-wage parts of the bill but also from the limitation on hours of work, and they were concerned that the definition of agriculture was rather narrow. They also worried about the amount of discretion to set wages and hours the law would grant to a board of five. But were reassured by modifications to the law. The final bill added exemptions on hours. It included the passage of an amendment, opposed by most nonsouthern Democrats,[188] that enlarged the exclusion of farmworkers to encompass the predominantly black employees who engaged in packing or processing agricultural goods during the harvesting season. Furthermore, with southerners not wishing to cross FDR yet again after having defeated his Court-packing plan, and with the rejection of antilynching provisions, sufficient numbers voted for passage. But along the way, a vote to kill the bill by recommitting it, a motion introduced by the once more liberal Tom Connally of Texas, had been supported by half the southern delegation and had failed by a close 36–48 vote, a harbinger of more opposition to come on labor questions.[189]

There was indeed trouble ahead. A combination of southern skittishness and Republican opposition made it difficult for the bill to move ahead in the House. The Committee on Education and Labor reported the Senate bill on August 6, but its way to the floor was blocked by the Rules Committee. That committee was composed of ten Democrats and four Republicans. Half the Democrats were southern.[190] With the Democrats split 5–5, the fate of the bill was placed in Republican hands. They joined the southerners in refusing to let the House consider the legislation. This was the first time the Rules Committee had successfully blocked a New Deal bill.

Nor would this be the last word. Addressing the country by radio on October 12, Roosevelt explained that he was calling Congress into special session. Still using the radical moment's assertive language of "financial oligarchies," he lamented how American workers had been "checked in their efforts to secure reasonable minimum wages and maximum hours," and called for swift action.[191] Despite the overwhelming majority his party commanded in the House, this effort failed. With the administration threatening to hold up a much-wanted farm bill, sufficient signatures for a chamber majority of 218 were obtained on a discharge petition on December 2 to circumvent the Rules Committee and get the bill to the floor. There, it ran into determined southern opposition.

A motion to recommit by New Jersey Republican Fred Hartley produced a debate dominated by southern voices. Among others, John McClellan of Arkansas remonstrated at the "raw deal" the bill offered agriculture as a result of its insufficient exclusions. William Whittington of Mississippi agreed. "If agriculture is to be exempt, surely industries engaged in producing, processing, distributing, and handling ... agricultural commodities should be exempt," he argued, adding that "the South cannot afford to pay unskilled labor the price it pays skilled labor." Joe Starnes of Alabama bemoaned the "dictatorship" the prospective law would create. "I would rather raise my right arm to strike down another bureaucracy in its inception than to water with blood and tears the flowers which will blossom upon the grave of our democracy." Wade Kitchens, of Arkansas, found the proposal to be "unworkable, un-American, impractical, and dangerous to our institutions," clearly referring to southern institutions. The bill, he explained, "will destroy state sovereignty, state rights, [and] local self-government." In turn, Hartley taunted the Democrats, noting how "the poorest paid labor of all, the farm labor," had been excluded as a matter of "political expediency" because coverage of agricultural labor, as everyone knew, surely would doom the bill's prospects.[192] When he called the question, his motion to send the bill back to committee succeeded.

KILL ROOSEVELT'S WAGE BILL, the *Chicago Tribune*'s banner headline exulted. HOUSE REJECTS DICTATOR RULE OF NATION'S LABOR.[193] This 216–198 decision constituted the most emphatic rejection of a major New Deal economic proposal since March 1933. It was a remarkable vote. The cross-sectional New Deal coalition came apart. A majority of the votes to recommit, 133 of the 216, had been cast by Democrats. These members were overwhelmingly southern; some eight in ten from below the Mason-Dixon Line voted to recommit (most others were rural Democrats from the West).[194] "The vote," reported the *Los Angeles Times*, "evoked a triumphant roar of applause from the southern bloc."[195]

The Fair Labor Standards Act did, in fact, become law in the spring of 1938. It established a minimum wage of twenty-five cents per hour for the first year following passage, thirty cents for the second year, and forty cents within a period of six years.[196] It provided for maximum working hours of forty-four hours per week in the first year following passage, forty-two in the second year, and forty hours per week thereafter.[197] The law also prohibited child labor in industries engaged in producing goods in interstate commerce.[198] The process by which defeat was turned to victory is instructive. In producing an act "far removed from the President's original request," it starkly demonstrated the dangers the New Deal faced when it dared to stray beyond the tolerance of the white South, especially when challenges to the racial system, generating white racial anxieties, were beginning to increase.[199]

Arm-twisting coupled with the manifest success of primary candidates in the South who supported the bill, including Claude Pepper in Florida just days before the House voted in late May, clearly helped produce the comfortable margin of 314–97. More fundamental were the substantive reasons. Along the way, the legislation underwent significant change to win southern, especially border-state, support. The scope of the agricultural exemption widened greatly. In the original bill, the extent of the agricultural exemption had been vague, left to the interpretation of the proposed administrative board in Washington, but "as the bill progressed the discretion became more and more narrow and the specific exemptions became larger and larger."[200] Now including "farming in all its branches," this classification incorporated every kind of work "in conjunction with farming operations, including preparation for market, delivery to storage or to market or to carriers for transportation to market."[201] Not only was the definition of agriculture broadened; so, too, was the understanding of who could count as a "person employed in agriculture," a category that expansively included any individual involved in the ginning or baling of cotton when the services of that person were seasonal, a definition clearly tailored to affect southern black labor.[202]

Other key changes helped tilt the balance. The concern that Washington bureaucrats could impose conditions that might be unsupportable for the South was addressed by setting fixed wages and hours by law. Even more important, a process was fashioned to create differentiated minimum-wage rates through the appointment of industry wage boards that were empowered to take into account "competitive conditions as affected by transportation, living, and production costs."[203] Though not based explicitly on region alone, this provision made it possible to reassure the South that it could maintain a low-wage, competitive advantage.

Sectional differentials proved the final hurdle. When a conference was convened to fashion a common bill from the one approved by the House and the version that long ago had been passed in the Senate, the Senate's majority leader, Kentucky's Alben Barkley, later Harry Truman's vice president, rallied southern support by promising that the final product would include regional guidelines, and he appointed both northern and southern conferees who supported them. When word initially came from the conference that these preferences had only partially advanced, eighteen of the South's members in the Senate threatened a filibuster. "Faced with a filibuster, the conferees reopened consideration of differentials" and agreed on the industry board solution by a 10–4 vote (opposed by three Republicans and only one Democrat, Walsh of Massachusetts).[204]

The Fair Labor Standards Act constituted the last lawmaking victory of the New Deal's radical moment. The tortuous legislative course of the wage and hour bill revealed a growing schism in the party, one that would become even more apparent in the 1940s. In many ways, it was a swan song to a time in the 1930s when the Democratic Party was transforming the ambitions and role of the government to tame capitalism and enhance economic security, and the prelude to ever-greater instances of southern defection from Democratic Party positions—a prelude, not yet the first act, because the labyrinthine history of the FLSA in 1937 and 1938 showed that so long as arrangements were made to tailor legislation to suit the region's concerns, southern representatives in sufficient numbers still would go along, in spite of their reservations. After all, they had much to gain from maintaining a coherent and broadly unified Democratic Party majority. But it also signaled that when such arrangements would be deemed insufficient, especially as the racial challenge mounted, the South would be prepared to defect.[205]

Even when the Fair Labor Standards Act finally was passed by the House on May 24, 1938, a year to the day of FDR's call to action, a majority of the negative votes, 56 of the 97, were cast by Democrats; and of these, fully 52 were by southern representatives. Three weeks later, the House approved the conference report, 291–89.[206] Notably, southern representatives divided their votes along geographic lines. Members elected from the seven Deep South states, those that first had seceded in 1860 and at present had the largest concentrations of African-Americans, nearly unanimously voted no, unlike their colleagues from the other ten states.[207] Within two years, this division had been erased. In 1940, Graham Barden of North Carolina sponsored an effort to undermine the FLSA by drastically contracting its coverage. His bill suffered a 206–175 defeat when the House voted to recommit. Across the South, Barden was joined by a virtually unanimous southern bloc,[208] thus splitting the Democratic Party in two.[209]

VII.

T HERE WAS yet one additional, even more powerful signal that not just the radical moment but also the party coalition on which it depended were being placed under enormous pressure. The passage of the National

Labor Relations Act in 1935—with southern support once farmworkers and domestics had been excluded—had ushered in a period of unprecedented labor militancy and organization, what David Greenstone called "the proletarian period in class politics."[210] A wave of sit-down strikes after workers seized industrial plants produced a recognition for CIO unions by General Motors, the United States Steel Corporation, and many other firms that had previously resisted organized labor. In turn, the AFL dramatically increased its recruiting efforts by investing in a threefold increase in its organizing budget from 1937 to 1939.[211]

After the 1938 passage of the FLSA, southerners paid ever more attention to the impact labor organizing might have in the region, while the schism in the party became more visible as southerners began to mount a furious campaign to undermine the legal framework of the Wagner Act. Most notable in this drive to contain labor was the creation in 1939 of a House Special Committee to Investigate the National Labor Relations Board, led by Virginia's Howard Smith.

Once constituted, the NLRB had acted forcefully to enforce the Wagner Act and facilitate union activity under the law. As it acted to check the antiunion behavior of many leading firms, including the Associated Press, Goodyear, Western Union, Standard Oil, Shell Oil, Inland and Republic Steel, Montgomery Ward, the Aluminum Company of America, Chevrolet, Ford, and United Fruit, the board seemed to be doing more than creating a level playing field for unions. By its administrative actions, it was returning to the impulses of the NRA, in which the federal government could act authoritatively to shape, limit, and direct key features of American capitalism. In dealing with the balance of power between labor and capital, the NLRB had worked to check "the widespread use of professional spies, armed guards, provocateurs, and strikebreakers." It also sought to stem antiunion business practices, which included bribing union leaders to dampen the militancy of their members, inciting violence against labor organizers who refused to play along, and firing workers for their union activities.[212]

Lasting into 1940, the Smith committee probe bypassed the House Labor Committee, which was dominated by union supporters, in order "to build opposition to the labor board and to frame legislation to scale back recent union gains."[213] Working closely with an up-and-coming Republican from Indiana, Charles Halleck, Howard Smith convened sessions that deployed tropes that almost immediately came to dominate the southern orientation to labor in Congress and beyond. Their themes, which became common during and just after World War II, included accusations of a government bias favoring the CIO and its anti–Jim Crow racial agenda, subversion by Communists, and a growing class bias against business and for labor. In advocating the passage of amendments to the NLRA to sharply limit the board's autonomy and capacity, Smith explained that the board "is definitely partial to the radical C.I.O. labor movement," and "is honeycombed with employees who do not even believe in our system of private ownership of property, upon which our whole industry is based."[214]

This truly was an opening act, not merely a prelude. House votes on Smith's various proposals also were harbingers of how an increasingly beleaguered white South would be torn between its commitment to its traditional political party and its commitment to white supremacy. When, on June 7, 1940, the chamber voted 246–137 to replace the existing board with a new three-member panel that would operate under more constrained rules, southern representatives split with their fellow Democrats[215] to join the move's wholehearted Republican supporters.[216] Appearing for the first time, this antiunion coalition would reappear again and again over the course of the decade.

Four weeks earlier, on May 10, having already conquered Poland and divided the spoils with the Soviet Union, Germany invaded the Low Countries and France. German victories were sudden and shocking, "so unbelievable," as the earl of Halifax, then British foreign secretary, remembered, "as to be almost surely unreal, and if not unreal then quite immeasurably catastrophic."[217] By June 14, Nazi troops had swept into Paris. On the seventeenth, Marshal Pétain, a hero of the French western front during World War I, called for an armistice, which was signed five days later. Before long, the country was divided between a German-occupied zone and Vichy France, whose government Pétain led.

Six days after the invasion, President Roosevelt addressed a joint session of Congress. "These are ominous days," he began, "days of swift and shocking developments." Taking note of how "the brutal force of modern offensive war has been loosed in all its horror," with "new powers of destruction, incredibly swift and deadly," he spoke of how the United States had become vulnerable, asked Congress to confront the new danger, and appealed for an unprecedented emergency appropriation of $896 million to equip and modernize the army and navy, deepen training, quadruple the country's capacity to build military planes, raising the number to fifty thousand a year, and "speed up to a twenty-four hour basis" all existing and future contracts for weapons.[218]

Here was a great new problem American democracy would have to solve despite skepticism about whether the dictatorships could be confronted successfully in a world of might. "There are some who say," Roosevelt reported, "that democracy cannot cope with the new techniques of Government developed in recent years by some countries—by a few countries which deny the freedoms that we maintain are essential to our democratic way of life."

Dramatically declaring, "That I reject," FDR closed by proclaiming a relationship and a rapport that soon would be sorely tested: "The Congress and the Chief Executive," he insisted, must "constitute a team where the defense of the land is concerned." At precisely the moment when Democratic Party solidarity was collapsing over questions of labor and race, the president was summoning Congress to a crusade "to give our service and even our lives for the maintenance of our American liberties." The partnership this campaign would require, we will soon see, could not have blossomed without the insistent support of the South.

8 ▷ The First Crusade

Putting their October issue to bed on Thursday, August 31, 1939, the editors of *Fortune* were startled to learn that Hitler's forces were moving into Poland. "All night long the teletype rattled out the unbelievable news," they reported. "Little groups of writers and researchers stood in the editorial offices reading the long streamers of tape, stumbling for the first time over the strange Polish names." Finishing their shift, the staff "walked out among the gray, deserted buildings of the city with the feeling that they had closed, not an issue of a magazine, but an era in human affairs."[1]

A decision was soon made to add a folded supplement called "The War of 1939." This insert was much more than a report about European events; it was an intervention in public affairs. Given the gravity of the impending war, *Fortune* would have to be more than a magazine about business. Its publisher,

Henry Luce, resolved to have *Fortune* "straighten out U.S. Businessmen (and 'Liberals') on the great matter of appeasement." He even toyed with changing the magazine from a publication about business to a "Magazine of America as a World Power."[2]

Identifying ideological stakes, "more striking than any since the medieval crusades," the October supplement confronted readers with a startling map: "Europe 1939." This image underscored the geopolitical advantages now attending an engorged Germany, which was colored in red, having already swallowed Austria in 1938 and Czechoslovakia in 1939. With the exception of Britain, France, and Poland, the Third Reich's only active adversaries, which were tinted in blue, the remaining countries were highlighted by a bright shade of yellow. Noting how "the outstanding feature of the present map is neutrality," the magazine's commentary observed that "what future historians will have to say about this war will depend almost entirely upon what the neutrals do in the fairly immediate future." Diplomats representing each of the combatants, it reported, were "shuttling back and forth" to elicit support from the neutral governments of Ireland, Spain, Portugal, the Netherlands, Sweden, Norway, Finland, Denmark, Hungary, Romania, Estonia, Latvia, Lithuania, Italy, Switzerland, Yugoslavia, Bulgaria, Greece, Turkey, and the USSR.

One country, however, was glaringly absent. Nowhere to be found was the United States, the globe's most important neutral country, whose capital lay some 4,200 miles west of Berlin. But that, *Fortune* insisted, was something of an illusion. The contours of Europe's map and the course of Europe's war, the editors argued, would depend on policy decisions soon to be taken in Washington. "As this supplement goes to press, the American Congress is about to convene for a momentous choice between two courses in world affairs." Noting that a robust battle for public support was under way, the insert included a snapshot survey of mass opinion about neutrality, military preparedness, and the use of force. Making the assumption that constituency views would affect how members of Congress would act, the report remarked that the battle for public opinion was "of the first importance to the whole world. For as the U.S. thinks, so will it probably do in the end. And what the U.S. does can turn the tides of history."

Fortune's portrait revealed dissonant popular views. The great majority of the public, 83 percent, sided with France, Great Britain, and Poland, and just 1 percent with Germany (16 percent said "neither side" or replied "don't know"). By contrast, the dominant policy position was "a definite though uneasy affirmation of 'neutrality.'"[3]

The survey asked about four options. First was immediate involvement in the war ("enter the war at once on the side of England, France, and Poland"). Second was a provisional endorsement of American military participation should the Allies face defeat, coupled in the meantime with shipments of food and war materials. Third was neutrality that would favor the Allies, stopping well short of active warfare ("supply England, France, and Poland with materials and food, and refuse to ship anything to Germany"). Fourth was strict neutrality based either on equal trade or an across-the-board economic boycott of all the belligerents. In all, only 3 percent of Americans favored abrupt and direct engagement. Another 14 percent supported American participation if the Allies were to face defeat. A larger cohort, 20 percent, backed uneven neutrality. A clear majority, 54 percent, endorsed existing strict neutrality, while another 9 percent were unsure.

These preferences varied markedly by region. Southern respondents were especially hawkish and anti-Nazi. A full 92 percent of those who responded in the South supported the British, French, and Polish Allies. Three in ten were ready to fight immediately or endorse American military efforts to prevent a German victory.[4] Another 18 percent backed active aid to the British-French-Polish alliance. No other region came close to this policy profile.[5]

When German forces crossed into Poland from the West in tandem with Soviet forces from the East, the democratic powers, notably including the United States, were in a far weaker condition than the dictatorships. Recalling that moment's shocking asymmetry of force, George Kennan observed in 1951 how "the overwhelming portion of the world's armed strength in land forces and air forces had accumulated in the hands of three political entities—Nazi Germany, Soviet Russia, and Imperial Japan," and how the Western democracies "had become militarily outclassed."[6] In 1938, President Roosevelt sent Bernard Baruch on a European mission to get a sense of the state of military preparedness in Germany and in Britain. In addition to confirming that Germany had made huge advances in producing synthetic oil and rubber, he found, and the Military Intelligence Division of the General Staff soon confirmed, a grim contrast:

The General Staff report credited Germany with having 3,353 medium and heavy bombers. . . . The second power in the air was Russia, whose bomber fleet was estimated at 1,300 to 1,900 planes. . . . France stood third, with 956 bombers; and Germany's ally, Italy, was right behind it with 916. Britain had only 715 bombers, but Japan had 660. And America, with less than half of Japan's strength, was the weakest of all the air powers.[7]

The United States also possessed too little ammunition for antiaircraft batteries, and all too few antitank guns.[8]

After the German invasion of the Low Countries and France in May 1940, the War Department informed President Roosevelt that Nazi forces in the West alone numbered more than two million, organized in some 160 divisions; in all, it had eight million under arms. The United States, by contrast, mustered fewer than 250,000 men, and could field only five divisions (each one-quarter under full complement) of its total of nine, with 80,000 soldiers, about the size of the Belgian force that Germany had quickly overwhelmed. By contrast, Germany possessed ninety field divisions, Japan fifty, and Italy forty-five. Ranked eighteenth in the world, America's armed forces possessed fewer than 350 usable tanks.[9] The country did have a large and capable navy, but it was geared almost exclusively to hemispheric defense.[10] A Council on Foreign Affairs report detailed how "today in Europe all the belligerents, both totalitarian and democratic, have subjected their economies to comprehensive government control" in order to pursue the necessities of total war.[11] The United States remained a conspicuous exception.

With the world balance of power so "decisively turned," three conditions would be required to repair American weakness: active rearmament, close alliance with Britain, and, ultimately, collaboration with the USSR.[12] It was a military buildup and an end to the isolationist version of neutrality that President Roosevelt sought in the run-up to American participation, neither of which could have been accomplished without legislative approval. But confronted with such divergent national views, *Fortune* expressed misgivings about whether Congress would reject isolationist positions, which were being "described by their advocates as the ways to safeguard the nation's peace." Noting how "the U.S. desire to remain at peace does not, however, seem to be accompanied by a firm conviction that we shall properly be able to keep out of war," the magazine combined its wish for engagement with apprehension that legislators would resist swift action to help block further Nazi advances.[13] This was not an abstract consideration. Fateful determinations about neutrality, preparedness, and conscription required congressional decision, despite inherent executive power to conduct foreign policy, command the armed forces, and exchange communications with other countries.[14] Absent congressional authorization and appropriations, Washington could not confront the Axis powers.

Fortune's anxiety about whether such votes could be mustered was well placed, for the outcome of the era's vibrant foreign and military policy disputes was in doubt. The magazine's editors understood that the shape of American foreign policy would be determined at least as much by Congress as by the executive branch.[15] When the October 1939 issue appeared, the Senate was about to consider a new Neutrality Act that would end the arms embargo on belligerents, a bill that had failed to reach the Senate floor after a more modest change had barely been passed by the House in June. As it turned out, military preparedness was widely supported by internationalists and isolationists alike (the former were worried about the fate of democratic Europe, especially Britain; the latter were concerned about securing an effective defensive perimeter to protect, in the spirit of the Monroe Doctrine, the Western Hemisphere), but almost all the other international decisions that the House and Senate acted on from 1939 through 1941 reflected the views of a polarized country, and were sanctioned only by close votes, some razor-thin, after tumultuous argument.

In a rough-and-tumble congressional process, the leery giant successfully began to confront problems it long had sought to set aside. The intense contests that accompanied this outcome should remind us that even when war and foreign policy were most at issue, Congress never abandoned its ability, one might say responsibility, to shape national policy. In considering these issues, its members worked almost nonstop. During the third session of the Seventy-sixth Congress alone, the longest in American history, which sat nearly every day between January 3, 1940, and January 3, 1941, issues concerning the war were front and center. The Compulsory Military Training Bill alone consumed 302 pages of debate in the *Congressional Record* in the House, and 665 in the Senate.[16]

The South made all the difference. Ever since World War I, a curiously

provincial internationalism—motivated by local concerns but looking assertively outward—had emerged in the region. When global questions grew
pressing, they were considered by the section's representatives within an
"unquestionably southern . . . frame of analysis," within which "each of the
issues that arose was evaluated in a peculiarly regional way and each found
its resolution in Southern terms."[17]

With mass opinion and elite decisions broadly in harmony, southern
Democrats led the coalition that overcame both a Republican Party that
overwhelmingly wanted to avoid overseas entanglements and the lesser but
still potent isolationist preferences of many nonsouthern Democrats who represented ethnic German, Italian, and Irish urban constituencies.[18] At just
the moment when many southern members were having second thoughts
about the domestic New Deal and its impact on the racial order, the very
same representatives, many of whom were courted by President Roosevelt to
support his increasingly assertive foreign policy, provided the pivotal votes.[19]
Combined with southern control of the key foreign relations and military
affairs committees, their nearly unanimous support for activist overseas policies made it possible for the House and Senate to endorse a massive buildup
of warships and planes, make thousands available to America's allies, and
sponsor the swift conscription of some 900,000 Americans during the initial
phase of the country's first peacetime draft.[20] Without the South, strict neutrality would have persisted, aid would not have followed so readily to U.S.
allies, and no person would have been subject to conscription for longer than
one year. Britain would have found it more difficult to resist a Nazi invasion, and the United States would have been far more vulnerable when Japan
attacked and Germany declared war early in December 1941.[21]

I.

DURING THE run-up to American participation in World War II, the
era's most influential mass pressure group, the America First Committee (AFC), argued that only by keeping out of the European war could
the United States secure its democracy. The AFC's policies curiously drew
support from across the political spectrum, notably from Norman Thomas
and Sinclair Lewis on the Left, and Herbert Hoover and Charles Lindbergh
on the Right.[22] Though rooted primarily in the Midwest, the organization

sought to mobilize all the country's regions, including the South, where it chartered chapters and clubs in Birmingham and Norfolk, Atlanta and Houston, Jackson and New Orleans.

Southern organizing proved the AFC's most conspicuous failure. Its members were almost exclusively drawn from the fringes of southern politics, mainly northern newcomers, some Republicans, and "a sprinkling of anti-Semites [and] German-Americans." In all, "in no section of the nation did the America First Committee encounter such uninterrupted, vehement, and effective opposition as it met in the South. . . . [T]he Committee had lost the foreign-policy debate in that section long before Pearl Harbor."[23] Commenting on the fact that southern sentiment was not only "overwhelmingly in favor of the fullest and most rapid rearmament program possible," Virginius Dabney, the editor of the *Richmond Times-Dispatch*, observed late in 1940 that "it also is in favor of committing mayhem upon anyone who desires Uncle Sam to offer appeasement to Hitler and Mussolini."[24]

The South's rejection of isolation must have seemed inexplicable to the leaders of the Third Reich, who were fascinated by America's South and who highlighted how much the new Germany shared with the Jim Crow system.[25] It certainly represented a failure of Nazi diplomatic policy. During the regime's first seven years, Berlin had actively sought friends and supporters below the Mason-Dixon Line. Offering expressions of racial solidarity to the most racially pure part of white America, and noting the obvious affinities between Germany's "progressive" racial laws and those in the United States, Nazi officials, newspapers, and journals persistently celebrated southern racism. From time to time, they urged the United States to repeal the Fourteenth and Fifteenth Amendments to the Constitution, which promised equal protection of the laws and the right to vote for all Americans, and urged Americans to push blacks out of the country.

Hitler denigrated blacks, admired American racism, and regretted the South's defeat in 1865, especially how "the beginnings of a great new social order based on the principle of slavery and inequality were destroyed by the war."[26] He complained when the French stationed African troops in the Rhineland, warned about racial mixing, and denounced "negrified music." His main direct sources of information about the South were a series of odd and skewed reports that were provided by a German resident of Florida who wrote about putative Jewish plans to mobilize American blacks to destroy the white race. Like other Nazi leaders, Hitler was fascinated in 1937 by *Vom Winde verweht,* the German edition of *Gone with the Wind.*[27] This melodramatic epic of the Civil War and Reconstruction was a best-seller. The film, not surprisingly, proved a big hit.[28] Nervous as he awaited the dawn invasion of the USSR, a move that would start Operation Barbarossa, Joseph Goebbels spent the hours after midnight on June 22, 1941, watching a prerelease German version with a group of invited friends, perhaps not aware that one of the film's stars, Leslie Howard, was a British Jew.[29]

When Americans complained about Nazi anti-Semitism, party officials rejoined by citing southern racial practices, claiming a kinship. The *Völkischer Beobachter,* the oldest Nazi Party newspaper, routinely disparaged Africans and African-Americans. Like much of the German press, it frequently printed antiblack cartoons, reminded its readers that southern public accommodations were segregated, and delighted in reporting how blacks, like German Jews, could not sleep in Pullman cars and could not exercise the right to vote. Lynching was a favorite subject. *Neues Volk* celebrated southern lynching for protecting white women from unrestrained black desire. The *Völkischer Beobachter* published many graphic stories that were intended to support lynching as a tool to shield white sexual purity. "The SS journal *Schwarze Korps* exclaimed that if lynching occurred in Germany as it did in the American South, the whole world would complain loudly."

German racial practices, of course, were primarily directed at Jews, but they also targeted blacks. When the Nazi Party began mobilizing mass support in the mid-1920s, *Der Weltkampf,* its ideological journal, reprinted speeches by the Imperial Wizard of the Ku Klux Klan about mongrelization. Alfred Rosenberg, the editor, announced that a new Reich would forbid any admission to Germany by "niggers." Three years before securing national power, Wilhelm Frick, the Nazi minister of the interior in Thuringia, prohibited jazz performances as part of a larger ban on Negro culture. With national power, the new regime limited the participation of blacks in German life, applied the 1935 Nuremberg Laws to them, and, in 1937, sterilized mixed-race children in the Rhineland who had African soldier fathers.

Late in the winter of 1941, Hans Habe, a prisoner of war, reported on the differential treatment that African troops, both Arab and black, had been experiencing after falling into German hands. Of the two million captured French, black Africans accounted for some 400,000. "The Negroes were mistreated even during their removal—on foot, of course—to their places of internment. . . . The heat was unbearable, and we would have collapsed with fatigue without water. The German guards had apparently received instructions to bar the Negroes from this solace. Though we were allowed to drink in every village we passed, the Negroes were prodded on with bared bayonets." In the camps, these soldiers were isolated, with their barracks cut off, surrounded, as they were, by barbed wire. These quarters were especially overcrowded, food rations were lower, and medical care was not provided to those who fell ill.[30]

As his camp's interpreter, Habe attended a series of training "courses that were organized to acquaint German soldiers and non-commissioned officers with the 'tasks of Germany as a colonial empire.' The whole curriculum was based on racial theories; Negroes from our camp were often taken to the lecture hall and exhibited as 'specimens.'" Organized by the General Staff in German-held territory, these classes taught that a leading factor in France's defeat had been its mixed-race fighting force. They also identified the core principles that Germany planned to uphold as a colonial power. These included white supremacy ("the colored people are an inferior race whose place must be fixed by the white 'master race'"), occupational restrictions, spatial segregation, a prohibition of sexual contact and intermarriage across racial lines, the absence of any electoral rights other than for whites, no access for blacks to white "railways, streetcars, restaurants, motion pictures, and all public establishments"; and bans on black membership in the National Socialist Party, any of its associated organizations, or in the army, with the exception of special labor battalions.[31]

During Hitler's and Roosevelt's early periods in office, Germans who were informed about the South expected the region to welcome the Führer's policies on race.[32] In correspondence with Rudolf Hess, Hitler's deputy, Count Felix von Luckner, who had served in Germany's navy and had traveled often to the United States, anticipated that the South "would be most receptive to Nazi racial propaganda." He believed that "Nazi racial views would be most appreciated by the '100 percent Americans' in the South and West where the black and Asian questions had already generated great anxiety among whites." Southerners, he thought, also would be responsive to Nazi anti-Semitic propaganda, since "they resented Jewish legal assistance to blacks in cases where white women had fallen prey to the 'lust of Negroes.'"

In 1934, the *Atlanta Constitution*'s European correspondent, Pierre van Paassen, reported that he had been told by German shipmates on an Atlantic crossing that "Hitler's ideas were 'very much respected' in the American South."[33]

Despite the affinities between the two systems of racial domination, southerners in the main did not reciprocate Nazi admiration. To be sure, a smattering of political figures, most notably Senator Robert "Bob" Reynolds of North Carolina, expressed sympathetic points of view. Combining racism with anti-Semitism, Reynolds founded the American Vindicators in January 1939, a society dedicated to fight immigration, prevent contamination of the country's white and Protestant stock, and keep the United States out of a European war against Germany. Closed to blacks and Jews, the Vindicators collaborated with leading members of the right-wing fringe, including the anti-Semitic Gerald L. K. Smith, who led the Christian Nationalist Crusade, and the poet George Viereck, America's leading pro-Nazi publicist, who had ties to the German Foreign Office and who later, in 1942, was jailed for a five-year term as a German agent.[34]

For sure, Reynolds was not alone. From time to time, a smattering of southern newspapers offered positive assessments of the Nazi regime. Pro-Nazi statements in southern newspapers ranged from the relatively mild, like those expressed by a 1934 editorial in the Starkville, Mississippi, *News,* which offered sympathy "with the viewpoint of the German radio commission which has banned Negro Jazz . . . [for] it belongs in Museums of ethnology" to the rabid, as in the dramatic 1935 offer by the Eupora, Mississippi, *Webster Progress* of a "Heil Hitler" for having "placed that downtrodden nation back into the ranks where it belongs! Heil Hitler, Crusher of Communism and Anarchy!" That year, the Memphis *Commercial Appeal* called for understanding Nazi Germany's wish to "live on terms that are tolerable" after the humiliations of World War I and the humbling conditions enforced at Versailles. Hitler's verbal assaults on these arrangements, it observed, were "similar to what the South said after the Civil War."[35] "We Southerners are as hostile to democracy as Hitler is," the *Charleston News and Courier* plainly declared in February 1938, "because we are unwilling for the negro masses to vote and have a part in governing us."[36]

Such positions, though, were uncommon and exceptional. Van Paassen's report "I did not notice anything in this respect myself a few weeks ago when

I visited several southern cities" captured the essential truth. "Despite their similarities," and despite sporadic interest in the Nazi program by small numbers of southerners, "the American South did not embrace Nazi Germany."[37] On the whole, editorial opinion in the region shared the anti-Nazi views most of the country's newspapers expressed. Southern newspapers, in the main, strongly disapproved of Germany's anti-Jewish policies and remonstrated against Germany's resurgent militarism and expansionist foreign policy. Some likened Nazism to the Ku Klux Klan. The *Birmingham News* identified the Klan, in 1933, as the "nearest approach that any American organization has to the Nazi party in Germany." Five years later, the *Clarke County Democrat* in Alabama noted the resemblance between German and Klan racism and cautioned that they "are similar enough to cause self-respecting Americans to hang [their] heads in shame." Over and again, the region's press rejected comparisons between violence against Jews in Germany and blacks in the South. Lynching, after all, was illegal, while the "crimes against humanity . . . thousands of miles away," as the *Raleigh News and Observer* noted, were sponsored and sanctioned by the state.[38] Senator Reynolds was increasingly cut off from the southern political mainstream; so much so that he dared not run for reelection in 1944, and the Vindicators withered.[39]

A systematic review of the era's southern press took note of how the region's newspapers "wrote editorials attacking racism abroad," but "defended it at home, either with openly racist arguments or by maintaining that racial pride required it for both whites and blacks."[40] As the South's press excoriated Nazi racism, it persistently argued that their own region's views and practices were fundamentally different. Though "hardly a champion of black causes," the *Washington Post* "condemned the Nazi's treatment of African-American athletes in the 1936 Olympics," and the *Atlanta Constitution* advocated a boycott of the games. Southern newspapers repeatedly criticized Nazi anti-Semitism, while ignoring their own parlor version of anti-Jewish sentiment. In July 1933, the *Montgomery Advertiser* took note of the regime's assaults on Jews, counseling that "Hitler will only gain respect in the U.S. if he stops persecuting the minority."[41] This contradiction was noted by the German ambassador to Washington in 1936. He reported bitterly that southerners, indeed most white Americans, rejected the idea that Jim Crow and Nazi anti-Semitism were comparable. Though "outraged by Nazi prejudice," even southern liberals "continued to support segregation in order to save the white race."[42]

In all, the South saw no contradiction between its racist and its pro-British commitments. "In the absence of any effective attack on southern racial practices," the circumstance that prevailed during the early years of Nazi rule in Germany, the historian George Tindall noted, "a powerful sentiment developed" in the region "to dampen the rekindled fires of racial feeling and to discourage any further public discussion of race."[43] Nazi appeals to the South that challenged this modus vivendi induced the great majority of the region's politicians and opinion leaders to underscore that southerners were patriotic Americans. They also elicited a defense of the southern system that differentiated it from the antidemocratic features of the German regime. As John Hope Franklin, the distinguished African-American historian, put the point, white southern thought and speech revealed "a section that has been continuously both southern and American and a people who rushed upon tragedy by making virtues of their vices."[44]

II.

I F THE South disappointed Germany, it also did not develop a particular voice on global affairs prior to late 1938 or early 1939. Before President Roosevelt began to lead the country toward global engagement, the South's positions broadly resembled those of other sections. During the first six years of the New Deal, there had been no southern push to move beyond strong neutrality, a modest military, and a defense strategy that protected trade lanes at sea. What demands explanation is not any constant southern internationalism, nor a particular wish to confront dictatorial Germany. Instead, it is how southern politicians came to lead an interventionist coalition at the end of the 1930s, after European efforts to assuage Hitler's territorial ambitions had collapsed.[45]

Early in World War II, John Temple Graves, a *Birmingham Age-Herald* columnist, posed just this question. To better understand the sources of "the greater belligerency of the South in the days before Pearl Harbor," he surveyed other white southern journalists and leading authors and intellectuals.[46] Their reasons clustered in three categories: cultural affinities, political calculations, and economic incentives.

Southerners, some noted, celebrated their martial traditions, and, as predominantly evangelical Protestants, resented Nazism's anti-Christian impulses. Others described the region's pro-British stance as ethnic solidarity. More than 90 percent of southern whites traced their roots back to England, Scotland, Wales, or Protestant Ireland, reflecting the negligible impact of mass Catholic and Jewish migration from southern and eastern Europe after 1880. Many identified with British values of liberty, recalled British sympathies for the Confederacy, and related to the pain afflicted by military occupation.

Several emphasized partisan calculations. Isolationism united the Republican Party. Democrats, led by President Roosevelt, tilted the other way. This gulf reproduced the division that had separated the parties when Congress debated whether to join the League of Nations after World War I. Then, as fellow Democrats, southerners had sided with Woodrow Wilson. Now, they backed FDR. "The one-party system in the South," Graves explained, "has been the agency of a total state as in Germany, Italy, and Russia, where the party is continually controlling and the control comes down from above." "In the South," he insisted, "the Democratic Party has had within itself divisions as sharp as any that have distinguished Democrats and Republicans elsewhere." To be sure, "each election time Southerners have had to recognize the party as a thing more important than all their contests within the party." One result was an "effect like a whole nation's recognition of itself when war comes," he argued, adding, "Perhaps that is another reason it was easier for the South to picture the country joined in a war against Hitler."[47]

More important still were economic considerations. Cotton and tobacco relied on overseas markets; so, too, did the oil industry in Oklahoma and Texas, the phosphate and sulfur mines of Florida, the steel producers in Alabama. The ports of Jacksonville, Tampa, New Orleans, Savannah, Mobile, Charleston, and Norfolk owed their economic life to these crops and goods. These cities also served as entry points for coffee, cocoa, bananas, manganese, and rubber, and for finished goods and machinery. Not surprisingly, the South had long supported low tariffs and open global trade.

Hitler's policies and conquests posed a direct threat to southern prosperity. Of the annual twelve billion bales of cotton the South was producing in the late 1930s, five billion were being cultivated for export. But given prewar tension and shipping hazards rising at sea, the South's warehouses buckled under surpluses. Nazi-dominated markets shut down. Czechoslovakia, as an example, had been an important importer of southern cotton before the

Munich pact of September 1938 assigned the Sudetenland, where two-thirds of Czech cotton mills were located, to Germany. Once these southwestern and western parts of the country were incorporated within the Third Reich, cotton imports from the South effectively stopped. The outbreak of war a year later also upset the South's tobacco commerce. "When Hitler's army began its march across the plains of Poland," Marian Irish noted, "the auctions on the 1939 flue cured tobacco were in progress in the southern warehouses when the British buyers were ordered by their government to cease purchasing." In November, the South's tobacco markets closed, if temporarily, because there were no Continental European or British customers.[48] By contrast, southern military camps and war production after 1939 produced a huge influx of federal government investment, which included a dramatic increase in the generation of hydroelectric power by the TVA, contracts to build ships and planes in or near the main port cities, increases in iron and steel production, and textile mill contracts for uniforms. Clearly, the South had an economic stake in activist policies.

Like policy imperatives in other areas, these reasons operated as causes only to the degree that the anti-isolationist course of action they helped conduce was consistent with the South's commitment to white supremacy. During World War I, the South had learned that this combination could be crafted, and, with it, the region could benefit from being active in a national patriotic project without compromising its racial system. What that experience had also shown was that economic imperatives, partisan loyalties, and ethnic solidarities would not operate to generate an internationalist orientation without these critical assurances.

With the eruption of war in 1914, it was anti-British sentiment, not anti-German, that first swept the South when the United Kingdom established an embargo to prevent the export of cotton to Austria-Hungary and Germany. Southern economic conditions rapidly declined. Since President Wilson was identified as pro-British, he was denounced widely in the South as a regional traitor, and warned that the Democratic Party's southern political supremacy might come into question.[49] The crisis passed only when Britain agreed to buy the cotton that otherwise would have gone to its enemies. But a second confrontation between Wilson and most southern representatives ensued when the president called for military preparedness after the Germans sank the British liner *Lusitania* in May 1915, with 120 Americans on board. Southern members of Congress worried that much of the bill would be paid by their section's farmers, and that weapons profits would go to hated northern capitalists. They also feared that expanded federal powers would come to haunt the region and threaten its racial system, especially if Republicans were to return to power. When the House voted to enlarge the army in 1916, fully 123 of the 216 negative votes were cast by southern representatives; they also opposed conscription more than any other part of the country.[50]

Wilson, in turn, understood that his policies badly needed southern support. He appealed to the region's patriotism and implied that support for the war would end imputations of southern disloyalty to the union. Writing in August 1918 for the *Jackson Daily News,* John Temple Graves identified World War I as having completed "the triple crown of Southern loyalty that we welded first at Manila Bay and then at Santiago, and now ready for the last service and sacrifice upon the plains of France. Henceforth, the South is at one with the republic."[51] The president also directed massive investment in wartime facilities to the South. Six of fifteen immense army camps, and fully thirteen of the sixteen National Guard camps, were placed in the region. So, too, were navy facilities and war-production factories. Additionally, and critically, southerners were reassured that their support for the war could proceed in a manner that actually reinforced the region's still-young system of Jim Crow. As Congress conducted hearings on a Selective Service Act in 1917, Secretary of War Newton Baker pledged to strictly enforce racial segregation in the military's training facilities and fighting units. All the while, the president was demonstrating that it was possible to fight "for democracy and ethnic self-determination abroad without threatening the system of segregation at home. . . . Southerners could embrace his work for democracy abroad without worrying that it would lead to democracy for blacks at home."[52] Later, southern politicians lined up, if unsuccessfully, to secure American membership in the League of Nations and the World Court. We cannot know with confidence how southern representatives would have acted had they not been reassured by a president with Wilson's high credibility on the issue of race.

The lesson was well learned. With undertakings that the politics of might would not challenge southern racial security, support on the basis of culture, politics, and economics for an active, internationalist response could be activated. In all, the South's emergent positions reprised the theme that took hold during World War I, to the effect there was no contradiction between being southern and being American. Jim Crow could continue to be defended as a means to keep the social peace, protect black as well as white citizens, and ensure equal status to all white southern citizens without negating the willingness to fight for democracy.[53]

III.

T HE FIRST big international issue Congress confronted was American neutrality.[54] By the summer of 1935, with 100,000 Italian troops mobilized and massed on the Ethiopian frontier, and with both Germany and the Soviet Union engaged in heavy rearmament, there was growing fear that the United States risked being drawn once again into a European war. Just as Congress was acting on Social Security, the Wagner Act, and other major pieces of domestic legislation, and on the eve of the September 15 Nuremberg Rally, something of a mass American antiwar movement was emerging. This impulse was supported by a wide array of groups, including the Federal Council of Churches and the National Council for the Prevention of War, to promote legislation that would guarantee strict and impartial American neutrality.[55] Much of the populace, perhaps as many as three in four, favored the resolution introduced by Democratic congressman Louis Ludlow of Indiana that called for a constitutional amendment requiring a referendum before Congress could approve any declaration of war.[56] The Neutrality Act signed by President Roosevelt on August 31, 1935, sought to remove the contingencies that might bring the United States, perhaps unwillingly, into war. It prohibited the export of arms to belligerent countries and forbade the transport of weapons for their use on American ships. It also required that producers and shippers of armaments be licensed, and it restricted travel by American citizens during war on the vessels of countries at war. These provisions were to be triggered when the president certified that a war had begun. No distinction was made between aggressors and victims.[57]

Both in Congress and in the country as a whole, the 1935 Neutrality Act was uncontroversial. To be sure, the president did not like the idea of mandatory neutrality, but, after hesitating, he backed the law's passage.[58] Weeks after he signed it, he told the country in a San Diego address that "despite what happens in continents overseas, the United States of America shall and must remain, as long ago the Father of our country prayed that it might remain—untangled and free."[59] Debate in both chambers took place in the midst of extensive hearings conducted by the Senate Munitions Investigating Committee, led by Gerald Nye, a progressive Republican from North Dakota, about armaments, financial capital, and war profits two decades earlier.[60] Driven by widespread agreement not to repeat the experience of World War I, which had taken 116,516 American lives and had cost more than thirty billion dollars, legislators passed the new law by a voice vote in the House, and by a margin of 79–2 in the Senate.[61] Less than a month before his assassination on September 10, Louisiana Democrat Huey Long reminded the Senate that "it has been 17 years since we ended the war with Europe," and remonstrated that "we have not done a thing in the world, have we, to keep from being drawn into another one? Seventeen years have gone by, and we are still just where we started."[62]

The 1935 Neutrality Act passed with a sunset provision stating that the law would expire on March 1, 1936. This condition kept skeptics on board, especially southerners concerned about potential restrictions on the cotton trade.[63] With the act set to expire and with large portions of Ethiopia having been seized by Italy, January and February of that year saw the introduction of three bills to ensure that the United States would not be without neutrality protection. Strikingly, Mussolini's brutal conquest in East Africa did not call neutrality into question, but quite the reverse. The legislation signed by President Roosevelt on February 28 extended the 1935 law, added a prohibition on the extension of loans, credit, or securities to belligerents, and included a stipulation that required payment in cash for American goods by countries at war. The 1936 act passed the Senate by voice vote, and carried the House by the overwhelming margin of 355–27.

Two features of the debate in both chambers are particularly interesting in light of later developments. First is the strong rhetorical support offered by many southern representatives. Serving his first term in the House at the start of a career, mainly in the Senate, that would last until 1978, Democrat John McClellan of Arkansas insisted, "We cannot underwrite the peace of the world; it would be suicidal folly for us to ever undertake it."[64] Another Democratic first-termer in the House, Georgia's Benjamin Whelchel, did "not think it fair, neither do I believe it right, for a Christian nation, as America is, to permit the spilling of American blood on foreign soil in furtherance of these conflicts that have raged since the beginning of the world, and, in my opinion, will continue to do so until the end of time."[65] Second is the emergence of an expressive minority—later to become the majority—concerned that neutrality legislation would ensure inaction in dangerous times. What mattered was to identify aggressors and protect the globe's democracies. This position garnered support primarily from Democrats, both southern and nonsouthern. Thus, in the House, William Colmer of Mississippi called for an "armed neutrality" that would make America "strong enough to demand the respect of those warlike nations who profess a desire for peace and at the same time are, with wanton abandonment, bent upon a policy of economic expansion and aggression," and he hoped to warn "those who would break that peace with her that there will inevitably and surely be but one result, the annihilation of that aggressor."[66]

The Seventy-fourth Congress adjourned on June 20, 1936. Less than a month later, the Spanish Civil War, which inflamed the American Left like no other international event, began. In mid-August, President Roosevelt pledged to "pass unnumbered hours thinking and planning how war may be kept from this Nation," and he reiterated how "we shun political commitments which might entangle us in foreign wars; we avoid connection with the political activities of the League of Nations. . . . We seek to isolate ourselves completely from war."[67] Because Spain was experiencing a civil war between the Republican government and the Nationalist rebels, not a war between two or more separate countries, the Neutrality Act of 1936 did not technically apply, nor would it have been unlawful for the United States or American citizens to send arms, ammunition, or implements of war to another country for transshipment to either side in the civil war. When the Seventy-fifth Congress came into session in January 1937, it immediately took up consideration of this issue. There was, the *New York Times* reported, "a race between the President of the United States and Congress on the one hand and some American dealers and American exporters of arms, munitions, and other implements of war, including airplanes and airplane parts." As Congress took up the neutrality question for Spain, the State Department was authorizing export licenses for machine guns, forty million rounds of ammunition, five hundred airplane engines, and forty-seven airplanes to Loyalist forces.[68]

Brought to the floor by Senator Key Pittman, the Nevada Democrat who chaired the Foreign Relations Committee, a resolution was quickly passed that "simply makes it unlawful to export arms, ammunition, or implements of war from the United States or any of its possessions, or to export to a foreign country for transshipment, to Spain, or for the use of either of the opposing parties in Spain during the present internal strife in that country."[69] Pittman explained that "two forms of government are fighting in Spain in what is called a 'civil war,' but it is a fight of foreign theories of government, not involving democracy, in which the opposing forces are aided and sympathized with by great, powerful governments who espouse one cause or another."[70] Tennessee's Samuel McReynolds, who chaired the Committee on Foreign Affairs in the House, expressed the overwhelming consensus on Capitol Hill: "I want to save this country from becoming involved in European wars," he explained, "and I shall not be a party to the carnage and crucifixion that is going on in Spain, and I want to see the eyes of the men in this House who will. That is the way I feel about it."[71] Narrow and targeted, this legislation passed on the day it was introduced, unanimously in the Senate and by a 411–1 vote in the House.[72] President Roosevelt swiftly signed the resolution. As he did, stopping the shipment of arms already loaded for export, J. Edgar Hoover opened an investigation of whether the recruitment of American volunteers to serve the Loyalist cause violated federal prohibitions on enlistments in foreign armed forces.[73]

The United States had no appetite for war. Neutrality continued to elicit overwhelming support across regional and party lines when Congress considered the first permanent legislation in 1937. This law was tougher and more restrictive than the earlier acts. During the prior two years, the global arms race had gathered pace.[74] Watching this acceleration of European military mobilization from afar, Congress extended the 1936 law by votes in March of 63–6 in the Senate, and 377–12 in the House.[75] With the exception of the cash-and-carry provisions that were to expire on May 1, 1939, there was no termination date. Crucially, this law broadened neutrality's scope to include all countries engaged in civil strife, and it applied equally to all belligerents once the president found they were in fact at war. It mandated the president to ban the shipment of all goods to belligerents, voided all export licenses for arms to countries at war, prohibited the arming of merchant ships, lest they attract attention by such nations, and widened the cash-and-carry provisions of the earlier law. The new statute, the *Los Angeles Times* reported, "serves notice on foreign countries that the United States will have nothing to do with their wars."[76]

Underlying the near unanimity that characterized voting on neutrality legislation between 1935 and 1937 were two sets of alliances whose members supported these various bills for somewhat different reasons. The first congressional group was concerned with matters of national and international security. Exponents in this camp were both isolationists, keen to shield the country from foreign entanglements, and supporters of collective security who strongly preferred multilateral cooperation to unilateral action in order to prevent war and deter potential aggressors.[77] The second group, equally interested in international political economy, joined representatives who were troubled about the prospects for global trade with others who wished to support humanitarian efforts during times of war. Both sets of representatives had to find common ground despite the diversity of motives. Their solution was cash and carry. The United States could safeguard its overseas commerce, protect its revenues, and provide access to necessary humanitarian supplies without taking sides in the conflict. California House Democrat Jerry Voorhis (later defeated by Richard Nixon in 1946) explained that this provision was "a compromise which we are compelled to accept because we believe we cannot succeed in cutting off all trade with belligerents, and it is a compromise because even if we could do so, we do not want to prevent even belligerents from getting food, medical supplies, and things like that. It is the best we can do."[78]

IV.

As circumstances altered, these partnerships grew increasingly difficult to sustain, especially when it became clear during the course of 1937 that efforts by law to secure the widespread popular preference for peace and avoid the human and fiscal costs that had been paid in World War I were premised on assumptions and arrangements about global security that were no longer viable.

President Roosevelt signed the permanent Neutrality Act on May 1, 1937, but the law was already in crisis by July, tested by developments it had not been created to confront in an altogether different place. Skirmishes between Japanese and Chinese troops at the Marco Polo Bridge southwest of Beijing began on July 7, and by late July the situation had escalated to a full-scale war on the Chinese mainland between these countries. By the end of the month, Beijing lay in Japanese hands; by mid-August, the battle for Shanghai had begun. China's government desperately appealed to the League of Nations in late August. It rightly asserted that Japanese aggression violated both the League's Covenant and the Kellogg-Briand Pact of 1928, championed by then Secretary of State Frank B. Kellogg, which had outlawed war as a means to settle international disputes by committing the signatory countries—including Great Britain, Germany, Italy, and Japan, as well as the United States and France—to "renounce" war as an "instrument of national policy." Although the Chinese representative was warmly received, the League took no meaningful action.

The implications of the Sino-Japanese War for American policy were unclear. Neither country had formally declared war, and the Neutrality Act would come into play only if President Roosevelt declared that a war had indeed begun. Writing in early August 1937, after Beijing had fallen to the Japanese (and just as Congress was considering Roosevelt's proposal for the Fair Labor Standards Act), Anne O'Hare McCormick summarized the case that would soon begin to be made about the emerging conflict in Europe. Noting that FDR had not triggered the Neutrality Act by proclaiming the existence of a state of war in China, even though "several Americans have already been killed in the hell which has been let loose at Shanghai," she made clear why "every day of fighting underlines the complications inherent in the neutrality policy." Ironically, only by not invoking neutrality could the United States actually stay neutral, for the operation of the law clearly would have worked to the benefit of Japan by making any help of arms or credit to China impossible. Within weeks of having come into force, in short, the law had turned into an imposing burden, satisfying virtually no one. "The extraordinary point about our neutrality policy," McCormick persuasively concluded, "is that practically nobody, at home or abroad, believes it will work."[79]

When, in February 1938, Japan finally declared war to exist, largely in order to force Roosevelt's hand, he continued to demur.[80] Two months later, in replying to critics about the conduct of his policies in the Far East, the president defended the policy of neutrality, maintaining that it had kept the United States out of both the Spanish Civil War and the Sino-Japanese War. But he conceded that while the law intended that the United States avoid giving aid or penalizing one side against the other when a foreign war broke out, that was proving "difficult of application."[81] Soon, isolationists in Congress were demanding that the president make a public accounting of this position, and a group of congressional anti-isolationists opened a drive to repeal the Neutrality Act.[82] The center no longer held.

Official neutrality was plagued by persistent practical and conceptual problems. The peace treaties of 1919 had envisaged global arrangements based on universality and the peaceful settlement of disputes among countries that were democratic, as well as disarmament and collective security. Such positive international law as the source of a decent peace had been shattered. All its assumptions became nullified as Europe and Asia became embroiled in hostilities in the 1930s. Crisp distinctions between peace and war and between international and domestic affairs had become indistinct.[83] Fascists did not include *peace* in their vocabulary, "except as a term of mockery or abuse."[84] Treaties were being violated without any sense of sanctity. Countries dissatisfied with the Versailles settlement announced that global law was merely a cynical cover for the vested interests of the victors of World War I. Wars, moreover, were being initiated without declaration, and they often were framed not as warfare but as police actions. And with changes to means and objects, the rules of warfare had become impossible to sustain, even though they continued to exist in numerous international documents.[85]

The world, in short, dramatically failed to conform to the neutrality legislation's conditions and expectations. It soon became increasingly difficult to sustain the hypothesis that the results of overseas wars would not imperil the United States.[86] It was, as one student of the period from 1937 to 1941 has put the point, a moment marked by "the reawakening" of the "dormant sense of fear."[87] Writing to introduce a 1939 volume of essays on "war in our time" by the refugee faculty at the New School's Graduate Faculty, Hans Speier and Alfred Kahler observed how "today the word 'war' connotes less a memory than an apprehension. It is tomorrow's war that governs the imagination."[88] The demise of collective security and "its graveyard of wishful resolutions,"[89] and the rise of international anarchy and militarism, made the neutrality strategy too abstract, and thus remote from particular conflicts. It was also too prescriptive, because it reduced the scope for judgment and action on behalf of principles and friends.[90]

The world's big conflicts were producing "less a war between nations than a war between ideologies."[91] Either by omission or commission, the United States would have to choose what stance to take. Assistant Secretary of State Francis Sayre pressed the American people in June 1938 to understand that "events have taken place which challenge the very existence of the international order," threatening "international anarchy."[92] With force having replaced law, only active participation in an arms race and only a rejection of older ideas about global arrangements would make it possible for the United States to pursue policies that would protect and enhance democratic power.

It was in this difficult context, with Americans, as Walter Lippmann was writing, "seized by deep uncertainty" and "sick with nervous indecision," that sharp congressional battles about neutrality and conscription unfolded.[93] A growing chorus of voices in the late 1930s and early 1940s began to argue, as the international relations scholar Frederick Schuman did, that it had become imperative to set aside "the dominant mood since 1931, and indeed, since 1919," which, in the United States, "has been one of fear and flight." The United States, he counseled, must overcome its aversion to a global role and develop "a design for power" in which its "central task" is not "passive defense or acquiescence to a world-environment created by others but to remake that environment . . . by the world-wide use of their own power."[94]

The chances for such policies of engagement did not seem promising. There were no guarantees that the United States would prove equal to "the cruel necessities" by which the balance of democracy and dictatorship would be decided.[95] Ideas about isolation, which later came to seem cranky, were based on historical traditions, global agreements, and an idealistic wish never to repeat the carnage of 1914–1918. Over the course of American political development, geopolitical isolation from European affairs arguably "formed our most fundamental theory of foreign policy." From the nation's founding until World War I, it was a truism in the country's political life that it was in the interest of the United States to stay clear of Europe's conflicts and, in turn, to keep European governments out of North and South America. What shifted during and after World War I was the status of isolation, which swung from being the fundamental premise of foreign affairs based on British sea power and global hegemony to being one policy possibility among others after the United States "became the decisive weight" in the global balance of power.[96] During the early Roosevelt years, the core premise of American foreign policy was the isolationist idea that the United States did not have a stake in European conflicts. It was just this view that former president Hoover articulated upon returning from a fourteen-nation tour of Europe in March 1938, when, speaking to the Council on Foreign Relations, he urgently warned the United States not to join the formation of any democratic alliance with Britain and France against the Fascist dictatorships. "We should have none of it," he cautioned, adding that "the forms of government which other peoples pass through in working out their destinies is not our business."[97]

Events would now make Hoover's position untenable. The Neutrality Acts of 1935, 1936, and 1937 had been designed to keep the United States out of war. What would happen, the administration began to ask, should powerful armed countries determine that it would be advantageous to violate American assertions of neutrality when "the only protection of the position and interests of a neutral in such a situation is its ability to make its possible entry into the war on one side or the other a serious factor in the military calculations of the belligerents?"[98] Ironically, it was the three powers—Germany, Italy, Japan—that had joined to form an Axis in 1937 which were most favorably disposed to U.S. laws on neutrality, because the provision for an automatic embargo on shipments of arms and ammunition sharply favored those who had militarized and who already possessed facilities to manufacture weapons. Yet ever since 1935, American policy had tried to insulate the United States from global warfare irrespective of how it evaluated the contending countries and their prospects for challenging American values and threatening national security.

The United States had steered itself, with good intentions, into a dead end. If a U-turn was required, its execution would not be easy. After all, the Neutrality Acts had done much to reassure Americans who, like mid-century Europeans, stood, as Denis Brogan put the point, "in the shadow of a great fear, and if the angel of death is not yet abroad in the land, we can hear the beating of his wings."[99] Threatening development after development in Ethiopia, Spain, central Europe, and the Chinese mainland was forcing new decisions, including rearmament and confrontation with the forces resisting even the possibility of war. As fear grew and a sense of drama heightened, the New Deal swiftly had to move into a zone of action it had long sought to keep at a remove. Neutrality provided the key first test. Could it be made compatible with taking sides?

V.

Pᴿᴱˢᴵᴰᴱᴺᵀ Rᴏᴏˢᴱᵛᴱʟᵀ delivered his State of the Union address to a joint
session of Congress on January 4, 1939. It was a charged moment. He
spoke nearly ten months after the Anschluss had swallowed an all-too-pliant
Austria into the Third Reich, nine months after both Mussolini and Hitler had rebuffed his call for a declaration of nonaggression to last for ten
years, some six months after the Evian Conference had failed to cope with
the growing problem of stateless Jewish refugees, just over three months
after the Munich agreement had conceded the Sudetenland to Germany,
two months after Kristallnacht, and in the context of alarming press reports
about growing Nazi influence in Latin America. Moreover, Adolf Hitler had
just greeted the New Year by pledging to accelerate the buildup of German
military might and by committing his government to "forging the complete
National-Socialist unity of the German people."[100]

The president's talk, which had been expected to avoid controversy and
focus primarily on the military buildup, made clear that he no longer stood
behind the neutrality laws he had once supported. "All about us rage unde-
clared wars—military and economic," President Roosevelt intoned. "All
about us grow more deadly armaments—military and economic. All about
us are threats of new aggression—military and economic." Organizing the
speech around contrasts between the dictatorships and the democracies, he
warned that the United States "cannot safely be indifferent to international
lawlessness anywhere," and "cannot forever let pass, without effective protest,
acts of aggression against sister nations." In addition to preparing the country
for an impending request to increase spending on defense radically, he signaled the need to deal with what had been learned about the country's neutrality legislation. "At the very least," he contended, "we can and should avoid
any action, or any lack of action, which will encourage, assist or build up an
aggressor." Underscoring how "when we deliberately try to legislate neutrality, our neutrality laws may operate unevenly and unfairly—may actually
give aid to an aggressor and deny it to the victim," he called on Congress "not
to let that happen any more."[101]

Now an alternative course to strict neutrality had to be considered: quar-
antining aggressor states. At a press conference on March 7, the president
"expressed the belief that neutrality legislation enacted in recent years had

encouraged war threats instead of contributing to the cause of peace."[102] Undeterred by the Munich agreement or world opinion, Germany marched into Czechoslovakia on March 15. The next day, Roosevelt told Texas senator Tom Connally that the correct response was an elimination of the arms embargo, for without that, "we will be on the side of Hitler by invoking the act."[103] By April, rumors were rife that Hitler soon planned to march against Poland.[104] With the cash-and-carry provisions of the 1937 act about to expire on May 1 in any event, vital decisions had to be made about the future character of neutrality. The law Congress passed at the urging of the president did not break with the notion that restrictions on the behavior of American citizens, prohibitions on their presence in zones of combat, and the preservation of neutrality in wars between foreign belligerents could help keep the United States at peace. The Neutrality Act was not repealed, as Democratic Representative Asa Allen of Louisiana proposed (garnering 68 votes, almost exclusively southern, against a majority of 195). But it was changed significantly by the elimination of the embargo on arms, a makeover that moved the United States "toward a more evident willingness to 'take sides' and to consider the cause and effect of American neutrality upon impending conflict."[105]

At first, the effort to change the law failed. The bill passed by the House included an amendment by John Vorys, an Ohio Republican, that renewed an embargo on arms and ammunition but, in a compromise gesture, permitted the export of other implements of war.[106] This proposal passed by a 159–157 vote on June 29. An attempt to reverse this decision by a maneuver led by Luther Johnson, the Texas Democrat, failed the next day on a 176–180 vote. The now-weakened bill, which still faced isolationist opposition because it had slightly relaxed the embargo, survived a vote to recommit the legislation by only a 194–196 margin[107] before it passed by a close 201–187 vote. The South was the driving force in securing this limited victory for a less isolationist policy. When the House voted on the measure, Republicans overwhelmingly sought to sink it, and nonsouthern Democrats were divided. Only the stalwart southern bloc made passage possible.[108]

A leading isolationist campaigner, Republican Hamilton Fish of New York, the ranking Republican on the House Foreign Affairs Committee, reacted strongly to the House action by using the imagery Denis Brogan had deployed three years earlier. "You can almost hear the beating of the wings of the angel of death as she hovers over England, France, Germany,

Italy, and Poland tonight. . . . To pass a law without an arms embargo, that
will put us exactly where we were 22 years ago, and launch us into another
World War."[109] Though Fish and his colleagues who favored a strict embargo
had not prevailed in the House, even the watered-down bill that chamber
had passed failed to emerge from the Senate Foreign Relations Committee,
which opted on a 12–11 vote to delay consideration on the floor until 1940
after it became clear that a bloc of more than forty senators was prepared to
mount a filibuster.[110] The absence of an invasion of Poland by July had made
it difficult to push the neutrality-repeal fight to success. Back from Europe,
Walter Lippmann told the president that the prospects for peace were favorable, that "France and Britain are much stronger," and "there is a growing
disgust with Hitler."[111] On July 18, at a three-hour White House meeting
with both Democratic and Republican congressional leaders marked by
angry exchanges, Roosevelt was told the cause was hopeless. The Senate
would not act. DEFEAT CONCEDED read the *New York Times* headline; PRESI-
DENT QUITS ARMS FIGHT shouted the *Chicago Daily Tribune*.[112]

Germany's lightening attack on Poland transformed legislative possibilities. Noting how "the unbelievable has become reality," and how "the
outcome . . . for everything we hold most dear is utterly unpredictable," the
Washington Post's page-one editorial of September 2 argued that neutrality
was no longer possible. This war, it claimed, differed from the prior global
conflict "not only because it threatens to be even more horrible" but even
more because "it is essentially an ideological war."[113] Not long thereafter, this
once-contentious view became common wisdom.

Naming Germany, Poland, France, and Britain as belligerents,[114] a presidential declaration of neutrality banning direct and indirect exports to these
countries was issued on September 5. But in the radio address announcing
that he would take this course as required by the 1937 Neutrality Act, a
law he termed "the so-called Neutrality Act," Roosevelt made clear that he
wanted an end to the arms embargo, a policy in which "our neutrality can
be made a true neutrality."[115] Six days later, he wrote to Neville Chamberlain, still Britain's prime minister: "I hope and believe that we shall repeal
the embargo next month, and this is definitely a part of the Administration's
policy."[116] On the twenty-first, the president addressed a joint session of Congress; special precautions were taken to protect his security.[117] Never once
speaking in his "solemn message" of the need to arm Britain and France,

he declared that all Americans belonged to the peace bloc, not just the supporters of existing neutrality legislation. He thus identified the reason to end the embargo on arms as a means to keep America out of the war. He called on Congress to prohibit American ships from entering war zones, and to require belligerents purchasing any American commodities to take possession of them before they left U.S. shores. He also endorsed the existing law's prohibitions on citizens traveling on belligerent ships, and on extending credit to nations at war. But the heart of the matter was his strong request to repeal the arms ban, the only nonnegotiable item in the president's package of suggestions.[118] Nazis Criticize, Britons Hail Roosevelt's Plea, ran the headline in the *Washington Post*.[119]

Southern Democrats in Congress quickly rallied. "A great speech," said Missouri senator Harry Truman. "It was a splendid statement of international policy," remarked Tom Connally of Texas. Alabama congressman George Grant reviewed how the speech had provided "convincing reasons why the Neutrality Act should be repealed," and his colleague Carl Vinson of Georgia, whose more than fifty-year tenure in Congress lasted until 1964, announced, "I favor repeal of the Neutrality Act. If we can't repeal it, I favor modifying it to eliminate the arms embargo." Even FDR's southern critics on domestic policy rallied around. Walter George of Georgia, a target of Roosevelt's electoral purge effort in 1938, thought the president had mounted "a very strong plea," a remark that heralded his emphatic endorsement. Virginia's Carter Glass pronounced the speech "very fine, very pungent, very conclusive. I don't see how anybody could take any other attitude."[120] These were popular views in the region. George Gallup quickly reported that support for the president, which was increasing overall, had grown especially in the South.[121]

But many others did take the opposite view. Anticipating the call to end the embargo, Roosevelt's isolationist opponents already were charging that such a retraction would lead directly to American intervention in Europe's war. Speaking less than a week before the president's speech, and just one day after he had left military service, Charles Lindbergh warned on September 15 in a speech carried by all three radio networks that "if we enter fighting for democracy abroad, we may end by losing it at home." Cautioning against letting sentiment or ideological sympathies set the course, he further cautioned that the United States stood to "lose a million men, possibly several millions—the heart of American youth. We will be staggering under the burdens of recovery during the rest of our lives."[122] Within days of the president's call, Lindbergh was joined by Charles Beard, Henry Ford, and Herbert Hoover to launch a "stay neutral" drive.[123]

With huge public mobilizations and mail campaigns under way on both sides, Congress proceeded to consider the question. On September 29, the Foreign Relations Committee voted 16–7 to send the bill to the Senate floor. A month later, on October 27, after protracted discussion, with more than one million words of debate in the *Congressional Record*,[124] that chamber passed a bill that decisively ended the embargo by a 63–30 margin. Eight Republicans supported the bill; twelve Democrats were opposed. A nearly unanimous South made victory possible, preventing a potential filibuster by what the *Wall Street Journal* was describing as a "formidable opposition."[125]

The House was embroiled in furious debate. The key vote concerned the Vorys amendment, which the chamber had passed in June. Would the House stand firm on this formulation that would keep the embargo intact when its representatives would be meeting in conference with delegates from the Senate? The House voted on this proposition on June 30; 196 voted to insist, but 228, including a nearly undivided southern bloc, voted no. The bill thus was returned from conference with the Senate's stipulations intact.

As the House prepared to endorse the end of the embargo, Hamilton Fish noted, "There is not a northern State, not one, that is not divided, that I know about, but in the South you will find Virginia and North Carolina and Georgia and Alabama all lined up to defeat the arms embargo. If this vote rested with the North and with the East and the West we would carry it by an overwhelming majority."[126] This bitter observation proved accurate. During the November 3 House vote of 243–181, "the solid Democratic South . . . delivered the decisive votes to repeal the arms embargo."[127] Southern voices, in fact, had been the most constant and determined in making the case. In just one of tens of interventions by southern members, Majority Leader Sam Rayburn of Texas asked the House, "When great governments, ambitious men who have a desire to control the earth, attempt to stamp out liberty and democracy, is there any immorality in supplying arms to a little weak country so that it may let the dictators and the autocracies of the earth know that it can somewhere, even though it does not have a factory within its own boundaries, get arms to protect its liberty?"[128]

Similar southern talk predominated in the Senate. Tom Connally of

Texas recalled, "We passed this embargo act unwittingly and with not the proper foresight, not with clear enough vision, not with a view away down the road; we passed it as a handsome and beautiful gesture of peace, but we now find that the operation of this domestic law ... has put us in a position where we are not neutral in this war, but to all intents and purposes we are aiding Stalin and Hitler." Long-serving Kenneth McKellar of Tennessee, who first had arrived in Washington two years before Vinson, in 1911, explained that he advocated "repeal of the embargo because it has the effect of aiding nazi-ism and communism, to neither of which 'isms' I subscribe, and both of which I abhor. . . . I am against the embargo because some time ago I read Hitler's book *Mein Kampf,* and after reading that book I believe it is Hitler's purpose to bring as much of the world as possible under his control during his lifetime."[129]

Fortune's projection that public opinion would shape what Congress would do was borne out. "The neutrality act of 1939," the historian Robert Divine observed, in fact "was a perfect expression of the contradictory mood of the American people. They strongly favored the cause of England and France, yet they did not want to risk American involvement in the European conflict."[130] Combining a softer version of cash and carry with an end to the arms embargo was something of a contradictory policy, and the other limitations that had been elements of earlier laws remained present. Still, this legislation provided a huge boost to Britain. The repeal, Neville Chamberlain told his country, "reopens for the Allies the doors of the greatest storehouse of supplies in the world."[131]

Tapping those reserves required hard currency, which Britain no longer had. With the Royal Navy pressed for ships, the United States agreed in September 1940 to send fifty destroyers of World War I vintage in exchange for British colonial basing rights, primarily in the Caribbean. But this was a limited option and an inadequate response as Nazi Germany conquered much of Europe, turning neutral yellow to German green, and Britain became ever more isolated. The answer, signed into law on March 11, 1941, was Lend-Lease. Building on the end of the arms embargo, the law permitted the United States to transfer huge stocks of weapons to any country whose military actions advanced the defense of the United States. Lend-Lease did not offer credit for purchases, much to the chagrin of the government in London, which faced a severe monetary crisis, but it did provide for a continuing flow of weapons once cash terms became impossible by implementing the formal fiction that these supplies were being loaned. As Britain fought for survival, steady consignments of ships, aircraft, tanks, and self-propelled guns began to cross the Atlantic. Observers and historians differ about how quickly this delivery of arms enhanced British capabilities, but even in the spring of 1941, the symbolic significance of Lend-Lease was impossible to miss.[132] As the *Washington Post* columnist Mark Sullivan observed, "the psychological factor" would have a powerful effect on German understanding. "Every agent Hitler has in America, every expert who follows the American press for him, and the actions of our Congress, must have already told him that Britain is going to be able to get practically unlimited war supplies from the United States."[133]

Congressional Lend-Lease roll calls followed the same course as the 1939 votes that had first rotated away from neutrality. When the House endorsed the program by a majority of 95 on February 8, southern Democrats offered overwhelming support, producing a decisive regional majority of 102. In the Senate, the majority of twenty-five southern members produced on March 8, voting 27–2, was smaller than the overall majority of twenty-nine (on a 62–33 division), but these votes were crucial, nonetheless, because they made the prospect of a filibuster by the bill's strong isolationist opponents impossible.[134] A pleased president cautioned the dictatorships not to confuse division in the legislature with a country whose citizens were at odds. "As a united nation," he declared on March 15, "our democracy has gone into action."[135]

The Lend-Lease votes proceeded, it should be recalled, in an atmosphere of acute fear. Writing in February 1941, Walter Lippmann offered up "a horrid subject to discuss," the entirely realistic and haunting prospect of a British defeat: "For there is at stake here—let us realize—not merely aid to Britain in the sense of supplying the British resistance. In the last analysis there is at stake also, should Britain fall, the dire possibility that the whole vast power of the British and French and Dutch empires will not only be lost to our defense but will be turned around and turned against us."[136]

The vote also followed a period in which the United States had begun to build up its military capacity. On May 16, 1940, President Roosevelt had urgently called for a special appropriation of nearly one billion dollars, bringing the annual total to an unprecedented $3,787,000,000 to bolster the army, navy, and marine corps, and produce an air force with fifty thousand planes. By month's end, labor had endorsed the buildup, and industry offered full cooperation. Extensive steps were taken to speed up production. Some were technical, including a decision that aircraft engines would be standardized. Others were organizational. These included sidestepping competitive bidding requirements for arms contracts, remaking the Reconstruction Finance Corporation as an instrument to finance the conversion of industry to defense production and the purchase of strategic materials, and suspending antitrust rules for such arms manufacturers. It also took in the appointment of a National Defense Advisory Commission, which included Sidney Hillman, the garment labor leader who was put in charge of manpower utilization and labor problems (a harbinger of the active role labor would play during the mobilization of the U.S. economy in World War II), and, to deal with strategic raw materials, Edward Stettinius Jr., chairman of the board of U.S. Steel, who had signed the first contract with the CIO, who had worked for the NRA, and who, in 1941, would be chosen to head up Lend-Lease.[137]

As moneys flowed (contracts for national defense were being awarded from June 1, 1940, to the end of the year at the rate of $1.5 billion each month[138]), American factories were booming, and weapons production began to provide a powerful antidote to a recurring economic depression. Government oversight of industry and labor, the type of intervention that had characterized the radical moment of the NRA during the early years of the New Deal, returned in a new form. Deepened in scope and capacity, it now was limited to matters of might. Like that of the NRA, the program of mobilization that reached its peak in 1943 harnessed civil society to public purpose. As Eliot Janeway put it in his classic study, "to Roosevelt, as the crisis deepened, as the battle over isolationism grew more embittered, the important question was the participation of the nation as a whole in its own defense."[139]

A remarkable national consensus developed among political leaders and the mass populace to build American strength. This policy was supported not just by those who backed energetic, direct help to the Allies but also by isolationists who had not, who were now worried about the country's abilities to protect its own shores and its own hemisphere. "I was astounded to learn," John Carl Hinshaw, a Republican isolationist, reported to the House, "that there were only three antiaircraft guns in the whole of southern California, and that those were accompanied by antiquated auxiliary equipment.

... We are 3,000,000 people in Los Angeles County with practically no defense against hostile attack if our fleet is disposed elsewhere."[140] Likewise, Hamilton Fish bitterly complained about the lack of preparedness, scoring partisan points:

> President Roosevelt has been in power ever since Hitler came into power in Germany. No man in America has had a better opportunity to observe the preparedness program in Germany during the last 7 years. President Roosevelt has had full advantage of the information that came through his military and naval aides at Berlin, but, nevertheless, knowing that Germany had modernized its army, the President of the United States has completely failed to take cognizance of these facts and has failed to modernize and properly equip the Army of the United States; and I say this without fear of contradiction from anyone.[141]

For the internationalists, by contrast, it was Hitler's advances that should motivate the dramatic increases in spending and production. Once again, southern voices dominated. Oklahoma's senator Joshua Lee sought to rejoin a common isolationist argument that Germany would be incapable of assaulting the United States after its victories in Europe. "There are those who say that the Nazis would be too exhausted. But has the victor exhausted? . . . On the contrary, like a beast, with every new fresh piece of meat he has gained strength. With new aggression his vision has widened, with every new conquest, until today he is on the pinnacle of success and world domination is in his mind."[142] During the same debate, Florida's Claude Pepper, who was the most assertive voice on the Democratic side of the aisle, similarly commented on the swift pace of German expansion. "We see in every headline evidence of the expanding power of the military machine of Hitlerism," he said, and insisted that Congress face up to "how it can most effectively and efficiently assure the country and this hemisphere that our soil will always be sacred against an invader's foot."[143]

Congress seemed uncharacteristically covered by a welter of unanimity. With this drumbeat of diverse but universally positive opinions, it opted for preparedness with uncommon solidarity: 392–1 in the House and 80–0 in the Senate in May and June of 1940 for "A Bill to Expedite the Strengthening of the National Defense"; and 401–1 in the House and 78–0 in the Senate in late May for naval expenditures.[144] At the start of June, the *New York Times* took note of how "there was unanimity over the need for expanded defense," but it also observed that "wide differences of opinion continued over where to draw the lines of defense." Despite agreement about a massive acceleration of defense spending and the production of weapons, these views were irreconcilable. The central choice posed by the newspaper's editorial was this: "Was it North America alone, with enough protection of the South American shore to assure defense of the Panama Canal? Or was it necessary, for American security, to prevent defeat of the Allies in Western Europe?"[145]

Despite the best efforts of Hinshaw, Fish, and the countrywide isolationist movement, Lend-Lease produced a decisive answer to this question, turning a remarkable, indeed unprecedented, peacetime mobilization into a means to stiffen British capacity and resolve. The United States was not yet at war, but neutrality had now been quarantined. Speaking on the Senate floor during a critical debate he was shepherding on conscription only months later, Lister Hill of Alabama reminded his colleagues that, in building America's military and extending arms overseas, "we have done that which perhaps no man in this Chamber 2 or 3 years ago even dreamed we might do, a thing 2 or 3 years ago would no doubt have seemed absolutely fantastic to any man in this Chamber; that is, we have given millions of dollars in arms and equipment and military supplies to England, China, and other countries. . . . We have given to every country that stands and helps hold the line against Adolf Hitler in his attempted conquest of this world, that helps keep Adolf Hitler from coming to the shores of the United States."[146]

If military preparedness elicited wide support, the same was not the case with respect to neutrality. Even after the end of the arms embargo, the United States faced barriers in its wish to help the British war effort, most notably the restriction on sending armed ships into combat zones. On October 7, 1941, President Roosevelt wrote to Winston Churchill to explain why he was about to ask Congress to legislate "sweeping amendments to our Neutrality Act," because "the Act is seriously crippling our means of helping you."[147] Two days later, he asked Congress to remove existing shipping prohibitions. The 50–37 November 7 vote in the Senate, exactly one month before Pearl Harbor, and the 212–194 vote that followed on November 13 in the House were uncomfortably close, the smallest majorities on war-related roll calls since the German invasion of Poland. With Republicans united and nonsouthern Democrats divided, it yet again took positive southern support to defeat the isolationist position.

VI.

RAISING QUESTIONS about consent and obligation at the most fundamental level of life, the issue of conscription[148] was a good deal less abstract to most Americans than neutrality or Lend-Lease. How to organize an army in a manner appropriate to a liberal democracy and to citizens guaranteed the right to be free from arbitrary coercion by political authorities had been long-standing puzzles.[149] In the early republic, the main solution had combined the development of a small professional military, recruited on a voluntary basis, and state militias that could be mobilized for national purposes in wartime. During the Civil War, the country established a draft not conducted through the militia system; it met with enormous resistance, much corruption, and opportunities for substitution, and World War I had witnessed the renewal of a draft.[150] But these were exceptions at times of total warfare. When those wars ended, conscription ceased. Even interventionists like Walter Lippmann worried at the start of the 1940s that the creation of a large conscripted army with its troubled associations could be "a cancer which obstructs national unity."[151]

Mandatory military service was closely identified with the dictatorships. In August 1930, the Soviet Union had adopted a sweeping compulsory military service law, which extended liability to women, who were accepted into the armed forces during peace and were made eligible for the draft during war. Italy had adopted a deep program of militarization, specifying that boys and girls at six should begin premilitary training; the draft was universal for men past the age of twenty-one. Germany had also made all citizens eligible and had entered teenagers into a rigorous training program. Japan, which first had adopted a national draft in 1873, owed much of its success in China in the 1930s, where it deployed more than 1.5 million soldiers, to its modernized conscript army. Britain, by contrast, opted for conscription only with the Emergency Powers Defense Bill of May 22, 1940.[152]

Not surprisingly, the Selective Service Act of 1940 was the subject of intense debate on Capitol Hill and beyond. Though the Republican Party's presidential candidate, Wendell Willkie, was to endorse the draft in mid-August and call for national unity even as he conceded the election, the party platform adopted in June rejected the idea of compulsory military service as unnecessary with the country at peace, and even the news headlines of the country's largest Republican paper called it the "Dictator-Draft Bill."[153] Taking the same position, the CIO announced that it opposed peacetime conscription.[154] On the other side of the question, at the start of hearings by the Senate Military Affairs Committee, Gen. John Pershing, who had led American Expeditionary Forces during World War I, wrote to argue that compulsory training in advance of war was essential to avoid repeating the experience he had faced when he had commanded only "partially trained boys."[155] Eleanor Roosevelt intervened to recognize that "this is a very unusual procedure for us, when we are not at war," but an urgent one, nonetheless, because the country had to confront a self-styled "chosen race" that "cannot be fought in our traditional ways."[156] No one who spoke on either side of the question in Congress disagreed with the exaggerated claim made by Mississippi's Wilmer Colmer that this was "the most important measure that has been before the American Congress in the last 50 years."[157]

In March 1938, the Department of War had prepared plans to put some two million men under arms within four months of a declaration of war.[158] A year later, the Joint Army and Navy Selection Service Committee published detailed plans to draft a military force of several million should the country find itself at war. But in 1940, there was no such declaration and no such situation. The United States was at peace, if precariously so, when a bill was introduced in the House on September 3, 1940, to require all male citizens between the ages of twenty-one and forty-five, unless exempted, to register as potential draftees. At issue was whether the country should train a reserve of military manpower for potential future deployment.

Even more than neutrality and Lend-Lease, conscription signaled to its opponents that the United States was gearing up for war. Its sponsors thought it no less than prudent to get ready to confront the militarized dictatorships, especially that of Nazi Germany, whose forces were storming through Europe and murdering civilians as they went. The first group thought a draft would make war more likely by providing the administration with the means to fight, and that, as North Dakota's Republican representative Usher Burdick argued, "there will be time enough for that when

we are threatened and war is inevitable."[159] The second group thought a draft
would help keep the peace by deterring aggressors. "We can be certain,"
Pennsylvania Democrat Herman Eberharter argued, "that if we remain in
such a state that we can easily be overcome by force that there will be no hesitation on the part of the dictators to attempt to subjugate us."[160]

Once again, southern members dominated the advocacy side in the
House and Senate. Across the region, people had gathered at mass meetings,
demanding that Congress act.[161] Support for the draft, Gallup reported, was
especially robust in the South.[162] In addressing the House, Colmer spoke of
"the object sought [as] the preparedness of this country. We all agree that
we ought to be prepared." Georgia's Malcolm Tarver warned that "unless
we are willing to sacrifice to build up our Army and our Navy, and our
national defenses generally, there lies before us not only the possibility but
the probability of our being subjected to aggression." Luther Patrick of Alabama advanced the claim that "America is preparing against one thing, and
one thing only—totalitarian spread." Robert Thomason of Texas called the
bill "a life insurance policy," and Andrew Jackson May of Kentucky, who
chaired the House Military Affairs Committee, cautioned that "if England
is conquered we will have a job on our own hands that will be much more
difficult than the one we have now."[163]

Southern members also insisted that the draft was fairer than any
other way to raise an army. They noticed that the rate of voluntary enlistment was highest in their region; approximately half of the seventy thousand young men who had enlisted from January to June of 1940 came from
the South. Southern members clearly believed their constituents had been
more than adequately satisfying their patriotic duty but that the rest of
the country had been shirking. Alabama's John Sparkman, then serving
his second term in the House (later the 1952 running mate for vice president on the Democratic ticket headed by Adlai Stevenson), maintained
that "this burden which equally belongs to every citizen of this Republic
should be equally distributed, and these people from other areas ought to
be required to do their share toward public defense."[164] Southern representatives composed the most cohesive and supportive bloc on the three key
votes in the House—recommital (171–241), final passage (263–149), and
agreeing to the conference report (233–124).[165]

The 1940 act was both revolutionary and limited. It was revolutionary because it broke with American traditions, especially a deep skepticism about having a large standing army, by promising to train millions of young Americans during its first half decade even if the country remained at peace. It was limited because it stipulated that no more than 900,000 men between the ages of twenty-one and thirty-six, of a cohort of 16,500,000, were to be drafted annually; each would be required to serve only a year in the armed forces (voluntary enlistment would be permitted for those over eighteen); and deployment was limited to the Western Hemisphere, where German subversion in Argentina, Brazil, Chile, Colombia, Ecuador, Mexico, Panama, and Venezuela caused major concerns.[166] This, indeed, was to be a "selective" system. Fully 44 percent of the men called for induction were rejected by board physicians for physical or mental deficiencies, and fully twelve million secured deferments because of their occupations, when deemed critical, marital status, or lack of literacy.[167]

Further, the manner in which the Selective Service System would be administered differed from every other arrangement for conscription both in the world's dictatorships and its democracies. The U.S. draft was decentralized. It was run by 6,442 local boards that were staffed not by paid government officials but by at least three civilian volunteers who were given wide discretion about which persons to enlist and which to defer. With the armed forces practicing racial segregation, and with draft boards overwhelmingly white (250 African-Americans served out of a total of at least 25,000 outside the South, and with the exception of a tiny number in Kentucky, North Carolina, and Tennessee, the South had none), the law provided the South with a buffer against racial challenge. Worried that "their" blacks, if drafted, would mix with nonsouthern African-Americans, and thus have their views about race contaminated by radical ideas, the members of southern boards simply did not conscript black civilians until American participation in the war later required more manpower. With the administrative and substantive assurances provided by military segregation and draft board decentralization, the white South could pursue its preferences about global affairs as if they had no consequences for their racial order.[168] Later, of course, this proved to have been a profound miscalculation.

By mid-1941, global desolation was accelerating. The tyranny inside occupied Poland included the erection of the Warsaw Ghetto. The German occupying force and the Vichy government presided in France.

Japan controlled roughly half of China, occupied the strategic ports of French Indochina, and closed the Burma Road. Massive air raids persisted in Britain. Italy invaded Greece. Yugoslavia had been bombed and occupied. North Africa and the Middle East were convulsed in bitter fighting. And on June 22, 1941, in the most momentous development of the war, Germany invaded the Soviet Union.

In light of these ongoing events, the impending truncation of service in mid-1941 by recently trained men unnerved the Department of War and frightened the White House. War was everywhere, and the fledgling U.S. Army was threatened with dissolution.[169] With Japan increasingly astride East Asia and much of the Pacific, with almost all of Europe under Nazi domination, and with the Soviet Union reeling, and thus with Britain at ever more risk, this hardly seemed a good time to return to a pre-1940 military. Echoing the urgent recommendation of the Department of War that limitations on the length of military service be dispensed, a shaken FDR warned, on July 4, that Americans must pledge their lives as well as their allegiance if freedom was to live, and, on July 21, he sent a message that cautioned Congress not to make a "tragic error" by permitting "the disintegration" of its newly expanded army."[170]

Congressional debate was fierce over what were technically the 1941 amendments to the Selective Training and Services Act of 1940, but in fact this was a great dispute about America's stance in the world. The House and Senate had to decide whether to extend soldiers' term of service by eighteen months, remove limits on the total number of conscripted troops, and take out the geographic restrictions that had been included to win over unsure votes in 1940. Following intensive hearings in both chambers, discussions in the House and the Senate were prolonged and tart. Senator Hill recalled how "those who opposed aid to England and China and other countries, in spite of their protestations that they believed in a strong America, an America well-armed and well-fortified, have opposed practically every measure . . . brought to this floor to the end that we might have a strong armed force and that we might have a strong America."[171]

Full of tension, they proceeded, with the outcome truly not known. The administration and internationally assertive members of Congress argued, as the Senate Military Affairs Committee put the point, that the "national interest is imperiled."[172] Hill elaborated on the fear that the Axis countries of Germany and Japan threatened to put the United States "in the jaws of a gigantic pincers movement, with one jaw in Japan, the other Jaw in Germany, and South America being used as the handle through which the pressure will be applied to us." In this context, he argued, the question was simple: "Shall we keep our Army? Shall we, if possible, make that Army stronger and better and more efficient for our safety and our protection? Or shall we do as 13 other nations did in Europe; disregard these rumblings and invite by default the destruction of all we cherish?"[173]

By contrast, those who opposed the extension of the draft beyond one year argued that there was little chance the army would disintegrate or that the national interest would be put in danger. America's position had actually strengthened during the past year. War production was proceeding at great speed. Weapons were reaching the Allies. The Italians had suffered defeat in Africa. Nazi forces were busy in Russia. The Germans had failed to invade England. Surely there was no need to lift territorial restrictions on the army, or even extend the period of service for draftees.[174] Alexander Wiley, a Wisconsin Republican senator, offered the most coherent argument along these lines, forcefully noting when the 1940 draft bill had been debated, Germany had "not lost a million men in the Russian campaign. . . . Singapore and the East Indies were almost defenseless. Now they are equipped and garrisoned . . . and before England got one American bomber she was able to bomb out practically all the ships and boats Hitler had assembled for an attempt on Britain. Hitler has not been able to cross the water with his troops."[175]

Building on this analysis, Republicans proposed to recommit the bill, with instructions to the Committee on Military Affairs to redo it by reiterating the twelve-month restriction on the service of those who had been drafted, allowing an exception only for those who would choose to stay on a voluntary basis. This proposal was rejected in the House by merely a 190–215 vote. With Republicans strongly opposing the draft and nonsouthern Democrats badly divided, the only cohesive bloc to support conscription was that of the southern Democrats.[176] Without a united South, the bill would have been gutted well before a vote on passage.

When the time came to vote on the bill itself on August 7, the Senate voted 45–30, a reasonably comfortable margin, buttressed once more by southern solidarity.[177] The House, by contrast, approved conscription five days later by just one vote, 203–202, "in an atmosphere of hushed tension alternating with clamorous uproar. . . . By that narrow margin," the *Los Angeles Times* conveyed, the House "saved the administration from a devastating defeat."[178] With fully sixty-five Democrats joining almost every Republican in voting no, only a nearly united South, voting 123–8 in favor, rescued the draft.[179] Lacking the 100-vote majority provided by the South, the measure would have failed.

On December 7, what the Japanese called the Hawaii Operation launched a successful attack at Pearl Harbor. One day after the event, Franklin Roosevelt reported to Congress that "the casualty list . . . included 2,335 servicemen and 68 civilians killed, and 1,178 wounded," and he conveyed to a stunned nation how "over a thousand crewmen aboard the *USS Arizona* battleship were killed after a 1,760 pound aerial bomb penetrated the forward magazine causing catastrophic explosions."[180]

By December 11, the United States was irrevocably at war with the three Axis powers. On December 17, the House approved by voice vote "a bill to amend the Selective Training and Service Act of 1940." The Senate followed the next day. With its vote of 79–2,[181] military service was extended to an indeterminate date, six months after the end of the war, and it became "the duty of every male citizen of the United States, and of every other male person residing in the United States . . . between the ages of 18 and 65 to present himself for and submit to registration," with those "between the ages of 19 and 45 at the time fixed for his registration . . . liable for training and service under this act." The law had been introduced at the behest of the Department of War by none other than North Carolina's Bob Reynolds. Even this long-committed isolationist and Nazi sympathizer voted yes.[182]

"Overnight," Lippmann wrote on December 9, "we have become . . . at long last a united people . . . an awakened people—wide awake to the stark truth that the very existence of the Nation, the lives, the liberties, and the fortunes of all of us are in the balance."[183] What once had been a southern cause at once became the nation's. With uncommon solidarity, America's first crusade had begun.

9 ▷ Unrestricted War

"WE ARE DETERMINED that before the sun sets on this terrible struggle," declared Gen. George C. Marshall, addressing a West Point graduating class in May 1942, "our flag will be recognized throughout the world as a symbol of freedom on the one hand and of overwhelming power on the other."[1] Liberty and might, America would soon learn in the decade that followed, did not always go comfortably hand in hand. Characterized by tense and often bewildering paradoxes and moral fluidity, the fight against the Axis nations demanded tough choices and exceptional powers that challenged so many of America's ethical, legal, and political tenets. The war inspired national unity, energetically committing Americans to the strong and appealing purposes declaimed by their leaders. In the process, extraordinary concentrations of executive power, evoking Lincoln's behavior during the Civil War, and actions that otherwise would have been judged to violate decent conduct and constitutional constraints frequently became routine.

The powerful crusade Marshall helped to lead stemmed from a global cause so compelling that more than one kind of compromise with the values and institutional conduct it was advancing seemed allowable, even necessary. With the ability of democracies to marshal might and wage war brought in question both by friends and foes, the fight against rampant militarism and oppressive dictatorships provoked decisions about allies, cruelty, and liberal democracy that often violated the very norms for which the global struggle was being waged. It would be facile simply to denounce, or even regret, such compromises. Nonetheless, it is important to assess their character and implications, especially because the challenges and questions posed by the requirements of the world war—a war in which, on average, 23,000 persons died every single day—did not end with the Allied victories in Europe and Asia.

Some of the country's leading thinkers were not unmindful of these grave issues in the late 1930s and early 1940s. Observing, even from a distance, Hitler's military mobilization and expansion, Japan's push into mainland Asia, Italy's plunge into Africa, the rearmament of the Soviet Union, coupled with the incapacity of the League of Nations, they began to ponder how attempts to defeat the nefarious dictators might compromise liberty at home. Some, of course, thought what was at stake was a choice between competing conceptions of the good, between which the United States should remain neutral. Others believed there existed a choice between right and wrong from which America could not abstain. Irrespective, they agreed, as one of the nation's leading military analysts, the Princeton Institute for Advanced Study's Edward Meade Earle, put the point in 1938, that "it is difficult to see how . . . the cherished heritage of Anglo-American freedom can be maintained in a world so thoroughly dominated by war and the war mentality."[2]

These dilemmas, of course, were not new. Federalist Paper No. 8 had famously commented as long ago as 1787 that "safety from external danger is the most powerful dictator of national conduct," and observed how "a state of continued danger will compel nations the most attached to liberty to resort for repose and security to institutions which have the tendency to destroy their civil and political rights." In states of "continual danger," its author, Alexander Hamilton, cautioned, "even the ardent love of liberty will after a time, give way to its dictates."[3] Watching the enemies of liberal democracy transforming their countries into armed camps, the New School's Emil Lederer, a German émigré, had warned shortly before Germany invaded Poland in early 1939 that democratic states could no longer choose a traditional way of life, for "the pressure of the totalitarian powers makes it daily more difficult for men and women . . . to pursue their accustomed way of living."[4] A year later, Earle called "tragic" the fact that military mobilization would inevitably cause the United States to "lose some of the values which it is essential to retain,"[5] and one of the country's most respected political scientists, Harold Lasswell, sought to understand "what democratic values can be preserved, and how," in light of growing demands for internal as well as external security.[6]

Almost weekly, confirmation of these alarms abounded, and the academics and policy specialists responded accordingly. One of the most visible and influential instances was a report on "mobilizing civilian America" published by the Council on Foreign Relations in late May 1940, just as Nazi troops were sweeping into the Low Countries and France. Chaired by Allen Dulles, a future director of the Central Intelligence Agency, the council's Committee on Research convened a study group in 1939 to judge how government should act "in this time of emergency when national defense is of paramount concern" and consider what would be at stake in "the direction and control of war by a democracy."[7] Following a review of the inadequate state of war planning, the document explored how America's political and economic institutions could be made fit for war. First on its list of proposals was "propaganda" to create "attitudes favorable to loyalty and sacrifice," and "censorship" that would aim "to keep out of the public press, the motion pictures, the radio and even oral communications, information and opinions which might weaken popular enthusiasm for war." The study also called for assertive procurement planning and the control of prices and profits, and it offered detailed mobilization plans for the armed forces, industrial labor, and business. To put this program into effect, the council called on Congress to confer "sweeping and complete control" to the president, as "mobilization depends upon concentration of authority," and "the logical place for its concentration is in the hands of the Executive." Should Congress balk, it added, the president already possessed "emergency powers" to restrain radio stations and manage the dissemination of news, to "commandeer any system of transportation," to speed up work by lifting restrictions in government contracts, and to fix the price of coal and "take control over the banks and stock exchanges."[8]

I.

THE SHOCK of Pearl Harbor was still fresh when Franklin Roosevelt addressed the nation from the Oval Office by radio on December 9, 1941. Casting the confrontation in principled terms, he explained why this would not be a traditional war between states about contested territory, but a fundamental battle between different ways of living and governing. Japan, which had come to possess virtually all the coastal areas of China, and had extended its control from Russia to French Indochina, had shown itself ready, the president reported, to embrace the "international immorality" and "international brutality" of the Rome-Berlin-Tokyo Axis. Led by "powerful and resourceful gangsters [who] have branded together to make war upon the whole human race," the Tripartite Pact of 1940[9] represented "immediate evil." The United States, he declared, would act on behalf of "the vast majority of the members of the human race" in order to combat a "world dominated by Hitler and Mussolini."[10]

The president adopted similar Manichean language on the eleventh, when Germany and Italy declared war on the United States two days after the Japanese strike force had taken out every battleship in America's Pacific Fleet.[11] "Never before has there been a greater challenge to life, liberty, and civilization," he proclaimed in asking Congress to reciprocate with an American war declaration. With "the forces endeavoring to enslave the entire world now . . . moving toward this hemisphere," only the "rapid and united effort by all of the peoples of the world who are determined to remain free" could "ensure a world victory of the forces of justice and of righteousness over the forces of savagery and of barbarism."[12]

Months earlier, well before the United States was formally at war, the president had enlisted the country in this principled cause. On May 27, 1941, he had described how "the whole world is divided, divided between human slavery and human freedom—between pagan brutality and the Christian ideal."[13] Concluding a conference off the coast of Newfoundland ten weeks later, on August 12, the very day the House of Representatives renewed America's peacetime draft by a one-vote margin, Roosevelt had joined Prime Minister Winston Churchill in issuing the Atlantic Charter, a declaration of shared "war and peace aims." With the horrors of war on the eastern front unfolding in Russia, and with Japanese assets recently frozen by the United States and diplomatic relations suspended, the two leaders identified the ideals—including self-determination, human dignity, multilateral peace-making, open seas, and "freedom from fear and want"—that would guide their quest to secure the "final destruction of the Nazi tyranny."[14]

Even at the beginning of hostilities, World War II came to be seen as a crusade that pit decency and freedom against malevolence. This proved to be a steady and persuasive American theme. During the war, America's Office of War Information (OWI) distributed hundreds of thousands of posters that reprinted this charter, and its standards were resonantly repeated time and again by the administration. The distinguished poet and playwright Archibald MacLeish, the librarian of Congress, who worked for the OWI before becoming the Department of State's first assistant secretary of state for cultural and public affairs, gave voice in just these terms to "the basic issue of the war" some four months after D-day, in October 1944. He declared that the global battle between the democracies and the dictatorships posed the choice of how "individual men and women would live under government for generations to come—and not only in fascist countries and in the countries conquered by the fascists but in other countries as well."[15]

The scope of this struggle both demanded and justified a new balance between its imperatives and the values for which the war was being waged. From the very start, President Roosevelt warned the country that pursuing the battle could not but restrict freedom. His fireside speech two days after the hammer blow at Pearl Harbor explained that Washington would provide information to the public only when it "will not prove valuable to the enemy directly or indirectly. . . . It must be remembered by each and every one of us that our free and rapid communication these days must be greatly restricted in wartime." He further cautioned the press that "you have no right in the ethics of patriotism to deal out unconfirmed reports in such a way as to make people believe they are the gospel truth."[16]

FDR also warned Americans against spreading rumors and untruths, though he had done much the same in July 1941, when he had reported the existence of secret German papers outlining plans to reorganize a conquered Latin America into five dependent states, despite having "made no effort to demonstrate the validity of the Nazi documents." Two months later, he willfully exaggerated an exchange of fire in the North Atlantic southeast of Greenland between an American ship and a German U-boat. His radio address of September 11 reported that the submarine had "fired first . . . without warning" on the destroyer *Greer*, whose "identity as an American ship was unmistakable." He also insisted that there had been a "deliberate design to sink her," notwithstanding a U.S. Navy report that had questioned whether the German commander had actually known the nationality of the ship that had been stalking it, or of the plane that had attacked it with depth charges.[17]

At best half-truths, these claims became rationalized through an enlarged conception of national security.[18] In a radio address from the White House on May 26, 1940, the president warned the country that within the United States the "undiluted poison" of "spies, saboteurs, and traitors" composed a "Fifth Column that betrays a nation unprepared for treachery."[19] Four months later, on September 23, J. Edgar Hoover, the director of the FBI, warned the American Legion, the country's leading veterans organization, that "a fifth column of destruction" was on the march in the United States.[20] Against the advice of Hoover's boss, Attorney General Robert Jackson, who would later lead the American prosecution team at Nuremberg, FDR authorized wiretaps against Americans thought to be Nazi spies, even though Congress had explicitly banned the practice in the Communications Act of 1934, and despite the fact that the Supreme Court had ruled that evidence obtained in this manner was inadmissible.[21] The Court, he argued, had not anticipated "grave matters involving the defense of the nation." Without legal sanction, Hoover also instructed the FBI to initiate a mail-opening program. In addition, he initiated a Bureau investigation of persons who had telegraphed their backing to Charles Lindbergh, who had been leading the opposition to the administration's program of military mobilization.[22] Further pressing against traditional boundaries, the administration in July 1941 charged William J. Donovan, later the head of the wartime Office of Strategic Services (OSS), to plan "covert offensive operations" as the country's coordinator of information (COI).[23]

These were but some of the institutional developments that would be part of the era's legacy, and that would later become long-run features of a crusading global state. Outside public view, the Department of War had been considering how to prepare for future conflicts ever since Congress had passed the National Defense Act of 1920, a law that established an Office of the Assistant Secretary of War (OASW) to guide supply and procurement without disrupting economic mobilization in any future emergency. In 1930, it had drawn up an "Industrial Mobilization Plan." Updated and revised in 1933, 1936, and 1939, these documents focused on the nation's industrial capacity and led to ever closer and more "numerous war department contacts with the business community" on much the same model as the NRA had convened for domestic economic affairs during its brief existence. At least fourteen thousand corporate executives and trade association representatives became reserve officers assigned to OASW to help draft the agency's designs for mobilization and to advance strong cooperation between business and the military.[24]

Building on this planning impulse, a slew of new national security agencies were fashioned in the run-up to the war. Together with an enlarged Department of War, including its Army and Navy Munitions Board and the OASW planning unit, the Office of Production Management, the War Resources Board, the National Defense Advisory Commission, and the Office of Scientific Research and Development, the federal government inaugurated an "apparatus . . . notable for its sophistication in planning over the long term and on a global scale."[25] It was, remarkably, as if the ABC programs of the domestic New Deal, which had been crafted to deal with an emergency as if the country were at war, had provided a fail-safe model. The sheer range, level of funding, quality of personnel, bureaucratic capacity, and degree of authority possessed by this constellation of institutions dwarfed all prior attempts to build a planning capacity for the federal government, including the establishment of similar agencies during World War I.[26]

As the United States confronted the war's rain of destruction and organized depravity, it had to consider the degree to which to respond to its enemies in kind. Facing a coven of dictators with contempt for liberal democracy and with immense capacities to mobilize and fight, three sets of questions loomed large: How should national will, unity, and purpose be maintained and policed? What limits, if any, of the traditional distinction between soldiers and civilians should be retained? How might "democracy's fight against world conquest"[27] be conducted alongside a key ally, the Soviet Union, that also was a brutal dictatorship, and whose unbearably great human sacrifices would be indispensable to the victory against Nazism?

II.

FDR RECOGNIZED THAT united, popular support was a condition of decisive military action. "Let me make the simple plea that partisanship and selfishness be adjourned; and that national unity be the thought that underlies all others."[28] "We Americans will contribute unified production and unified acceptance of sacrifice and of effort. That means a national unity that can know no limitations of race or creed or selfish politics."[29] "Every loyal American is aware of his individual responsibility. . . . This great war effort must be carried through to its victorious conclusion by the whole indomitable will and determination of the people as one great whole."[30]

With these speeches of September 3, 1939, February 23, 1942, and April 28, 1942, President Roosevelt stirringly rallied the nation with these assertions of national cohesion. His calls were heeded in Congress, which responded by setting aside the conflicts that had dominated prewar debate, when southern members had led the way to preparedness and conscription. Guarded during the war by southern-dominated defense committees (Andrew Jackson May of Kentucky and Carl Vinson of Georgia led the Military Affairs Committee and the Naval Affairs Committee, respectively, in the House, and Bob Reynolds of North Carolina chaired the Senate's Committee on Military Affairs), the region's global wishes became the nation's actions. During the war's first year, the House cast twenty-two votes that concerned international and military affairs. With one exception—a partisan debate in January 1942 about whether the civilian defense program should be lodged in the Department of War, as the president requested—both party voting and sectional divisions almost entirely disappeared. Typical votes split by lopsided 335–2, 398–0, 315–22, and 345–16 margins.[31]

The president's calls for collective mobilization often were accompanied by an undercurrent of concern for internal security and appeals for watchfulness. "Let us no longer blind ourselves to the undeniable fact that the evil forces which have crushed and undermined and corrupted so many others," he warned on December 29, 1940, "are already within our own gates. Your government knows much about them and every day is ferreting them out." The problem, he chillingly cautioned, did not lie exclusively with foreign agents. "There are also American citizens, many of them in high places who, unwittingly in most cases, are aiding and abetting the work of these agents." FDR was careful "not [to] charge these American citizens with being foreign agents. But," he added, "I do charge them with doing exactly the kind of work that the dictators want done in the United States."[32]

The quest for unity and security entailed watchfulness, surveillance, and investigations of loyalty. When disloyalty is suspected, central public principles and protected rights are placed in jeopardy, and the specter of official illiberal illegality is raised in the name of liberal obligation.[33] The language of loyalty, implying the possibility of disloyalty, was invoked by the president before the war when he declared an unlimited state of emergency on May 27, 1941. His proclamation called upon "all loyal citizens . . . to give precedence to the needs of the nation," and "to place the nation's needs first in mind and in action."[34]

The issue of wartime loyalty was not new. During World War I, the quest for internal security had generated fear, and fear had justified stark violations of civil liberty.[35] In 1917, Congress passed an Espionage Act that mandated sentences of up to twenty years for individuals who encouraged "disloyalty" in wartime. In November 1917, President Wilson ordered male German-Americans to register at local post offices and police stations; in April 1918, the directive was extended to women. In all, 482,000 ethnic German citizens "filled out forms, submitted photographs and fingerprints, and swore an oath of loyalty to the United States," and 4,000 were detained, if briefly. Enemy aliens were forbidden to live or work near military installations or arms factories.[36] The year 1918 witnessed the enactment of an Alien Act that authorized Washington to deport members of anarchist organizations. The same year, a Sedition Act made it illegal to use "disloyal, profane, scurrilous, or abusive language" about the flag, the armed forces, and the country during the war. There had been little public notice or concern regarding these actions; to the contrary, there was a widespread demand to violate the liberties of German-Americans.[37] Immediately following the war, in 1919, Attorney General A. Mitchell Palmer famously initiated widespread raids on some ten thousand suspected radicals, and he infamously deported 249 individuals on the SS *Buford* to the Soviet Union, where they did not meet a happy fate.[38]

In 1918 and 1919, Senator Lee Slater Overman of North Carolina led a subcommittee of the Committee on the Judiciary that was called on to investigate disloyalty among German-Americans in the brewery industry. Overman swiftly broadened its scope to probe all pro-German sentiments and propaganda. The committee's attention also turned to Communist subversion, which it identified with German interests. Its report summoned an image of a Bolshevik takeover in America by radical sympathizers of the Russian Revolution's "program of terror, fear, extermination, and destruction." Setting a template for future congressional initiatives, it recommended strengthening the powers of the FBI, passing a peacetime law against sedition, monitoring and registering private organizations, and establishing federal control of the foreign-language press.[39] In August 1919, the precursor to the FBI, the Bureau of Investigation, created a General Intelligence Division to monitor radical activity.[40]

During the interwar years, this type of congressional scrutiny went hand in hand with the growth of federal police powers. Two developments stand out. First was an extension of FBI activities beyond investigations of specific crimes. The Bureau would now take on intelligence gathering and surveillance of potentially subversive groups as a regular responsibility. On August 24, 1936, the FBI's director, J. Edgar Hoover, met with President Roosevelt.[41] They were joined by Secretary of State Cordell Hull, who asked that an inquiry into Fascist and Communist activities in the United States be undertaken, as these were international in character, with overseas inspiration and direction.[42] Endorsing this request, FDR directed Hoover to brief Attorney General Homer Cummings and initiate FBI field office work on subversive activities in conjunction with the Office of Naval Intelligence and the Military Intelligence Division.

Five years before American participation in World War II, Hoover put this program in motion on September 5 (five days before he informed his boss, the attorney general) by ordering monitoring of the fur, garment, steel, coal, and shipping industries, and by scrutinizing newspapers, labor unions, educational institutions, and the armed forces for potential subversives.[43] The federal government also began to mount extraconstitutional wiretaps and mail intercepts to disrupt the activities of pro-Nazi groups, especially the Friends of the New Germany (the German-American Bund).[44]

Less than a week after the German invasion of Poland, President Roosevelt asked the country's thousands of police jurisdictions to promptly provide the FBI with information about potential subversives, spies, and saboteurs. Hoover was more than well prepared, having sprung into action long before the outbreak of war in Europe. He reported to Congress on November 30, 1939, that with this material as well as the Bureau's own initiatives, the General Intelligence Division had "compiled extensive indices of individuals, groups, and organizations engaged in . . . subversive activities, in espionage activities, or in any activities possibly detrimental to the internal security of the United States," including domestic Nazis and Communists.[45] Significantly, the Bureau's investigations, beginning in 1938, also included a special "Negroes" category. Unlike other targets defined by group membership, "the investigations of Negroes, in contrast, were based on color, an entirely different sort of category, and on the assumption that black people posed special loyalty problems for the government."[46]

Lurking behind these activities was a racial shibboleth—that enemies can be "separated not by geographical boundaries but by hostile loyalties."[47] During his first term, in 1934, President Roosevelt asked the State Department to report on prospects for sabotage and spying by ethnic Japanese. That analysis had wrongly predicted that "when war breaks out, the entire Japanese population on the West Coast will rise and commit sabotage."[48] Five years later, in September 1939, Roosevelt again singled out Japanese nationals and Japanese-Americans for special attention. He commanded the intelligence units of the U.S. Army and Navy to watch those living on the Pacific Coast, and ordered the FBI to track individuals thought to be subversive. "The result was a master list of suspects maintained by the Justice Department," to which immigration matters had been transferred from the Department of Labor, "known as the ABC list (because individuals were assigned grades of A for 'immediately dangerous,' B for 'potentially dangerous,' and C for 'possible Japan sympathizer')."[49]

By 1940, Hoover was planning to have the Bureau "act," as he put it, "as the coordinating head of all civilian organizations furnishing information relating to subversive movements" in the United States, taking charge, he told the police chiefs who gathered for their annual convention in San Francisco, "of all investigative work in matters involving espionage, sabotage, subversive activities." The Bureau's field offices, which housed nine hundred agents in 1940 but fully five thousand by war's end, quickly shifted emphasis from crime fighting to internal security. It trained agents to protect defense plants, recruited workers in most of the country's industrial factories to "be on the alert for any evidence of sabotage, espionage, or subversive activities" (with the result that many thousands of false leads and rumors were reported), and developed an extensive network of informants, ultimately numbering some seventy thousand, with at least one in each county in the country, drawn primarily from fraternal and veterans organizations.[50] By nighttime on December 7, 1941, with the American fleet at Pearl Harbor enveloped in acrid smoke, the FBI detained 770 Japanese nationals it had targeted as dangerous; these raids soon took in one out of every eight Japanese citizens who resided in the United States.[51]

The second development of the interwar period was the increasing attention paid by Congress to matters of internal security. In 1930, the House voted 210–18 to appoint a special committee to investigate American Communism. Led by New York's Hamilton Fish, it identified a modest-size organization of twelve thousand dues-paying members, then with little influence, yet it recommended draconian measures. Arguing that more than 500,000 sympathizers who wished to overthrow the political and economic systems of the United States took direction from the Communist Party, it proposed outlawing the Party, annulling the citizenship of its members, denying citizenship to any Party member who had applied for naturalization, deporting alien members, barring from the mails publications that advocated revolutionary Communism, and prosecuting members for spreading false rumors about American banks. It also called on the United States to send inspectors to investigate labor conditions in the Soviet Union. These suggestions were opposed as examples of "hysteria" by the Maine Republican John Nelson but were endorsed by the committee's other four members—Chairman Fish, West Virginia Republican Carl Bachmann, and its two southern Democrats, Tennessee's Edward Eslick and Mississippi's Robert Hall.[52]

A newly elected member of the House, Martin Dies, fervently embraced the cause. Elected in 1930 from a predominantly rural and heavily black East Texas district once represented by his father,[53] Dies had won his 1930 primary contest when only twenty-nine, defeating a six-term incumbent by pushing racial questions. At a campaign stop in Port Arthur, he referred to the only African-American member of Congress, a Republican from Chicago's South Side, by declaring, "Had I been a member of congress when Oscar DePriest made a speech assailing the southern white man, I would have taken a swing at that nigger's jaw."[54]

Once in Washington, Dies's congressional career was fast-tracked by his fellow Texans, Speaker of the House John Nance Garner, a close friend of Martin Dies Sr. and soon to be Franklin Roosevelt's vice president, and by the chair of the Committee on Interstate Commerce, Sam Rayburn, a future Speaker of the House. By 1935, Dies was one of twelve members of the Rules Committee, the chamber's most important. Like almost all his fellow southern Democrats, Dies was an ardent New Dealer in his early congressional years, when he discerned no contradiction between his racism and progressive populism. With the spectacular growth of the labor movement after the passage of the Wagner Act in 1935, and with the first efforts by some non-southern Democrats after mid-decade to grapple with the worst excesses of southern racial patterns, Dies began to move away from his earlier declaration "I consider it my duty to support [the president and the New Deal] to the utmost."[55]

Though still vice president, Garner emerged as an antilabor, anti–civil rights guardian of southern prerogatives during FDR's second term. Using Dies as his public face, Garner successfully maneuvered to have the House create a Special Committee on Un-American Activities in 1938, with Dies as chair, by a vote, on May 26, of 194–41.[56] Most of the positive votes were cast by southern Democrats and Republicans, with a majority of northern Democrats not voting, caught between resisting what they believed to be an antilabor, anti-Roosevelt push and being accused of failing to investigate subversion.

The new committee succeeded a prior Special Committee on Un-American Activities, which had been led by a future Democratic Party Speaker of the House, John McCormack of Massachusetts, and New York Democrat Samuel Dickstein, who served as vice chair. But its focus was radically different. The McCormick-Dickstein committee investigated Nazi propaganda and exposed the direct financial aid and ideological direction Berlin was giving to the German-American Bund.[57] By contrast, the Dies committee paid only perfunctory attention to Nazism. Dies quickly appointed Edward Sullivan as chief investigator. Sullivan had worked for the country's largest labor espionage organization, was a strong supporter of right-wing Ukrainian nationalist groups with Fascist sympathies, and had been a prominent participant in an August 1936 conference of anti-Semitic organizations that met in Asheville, North Carolina. He also shared an office in the National Press Building in Washington with the journalist James True, a prominent anti-Semite, who later, in 1944, was indicated for pro-Nazi subversion.[58]

An early version of a southern Democratic–Republican alliance lay at the committee's core. The most aggressive questioning of witnesses was conducted by Dies and Alabama's Joe Starnes, who served as vice chair. They were assertively joined by "two Republicans of the distant right-wing," Noah Mason of Illinois and J. Parnell Thomas of New Jersey, "who pointed out that the Communist party was a greater threat than Nazi organizations since, according to his research, Communists outnumbered Nazis by more than five to one. Worse than both," Parnell underscored, "were the Communist-influenced agencies of the federal government." Together, these four directed committee business away from the Bund and Nazi testimony, limited to a single day, to focus on the role of Communists in unions and New Deal agencies, notably the Federal Theatre Project of the Works Project Administration (WPA).[59]

What most knit the southern Democrats and Republicans together was not simply their anathema of Communism but also a shared concern about the growing power of organized labor.[60] Featuring dramatic testimony by John Frey, a senior AFL union official, the committee spotlighted the role of Communists in the CIO, and made known the active role of the Communist Party in popular-front organizations. It also heard testimony from a former Hollywood Communist, who alleged that leading actors, including Humphrey Bogart and James Cagney, were secret Party members, a charge that even Dies found unconvincing. During the 1938 election season in Michigan, the committee called witnesses who "alleged Communist activity within that state, control over labor unions, Communist connections to Governor Frank Murphy, and Murphy's 'treasonous' handling of the wave of Michigan sit-down strikes." In advance of Murphy's defeat, President Roosevelt denounced the committee for its "flagrantly unfair and un-American attempt to influence an election."[61]

The Dies committee was a harbinger of things to come. As "the first congressional committee to take full advantage of its power to punish with subpoenas and contempt citations, and its ability to harm through insinuations and publicity,"[62] it established a pattern of threat, denunciation, and rancor that was adopted by its successor, the permanent standing House committee created in 1945, by the 1951-1952 Senate Internal Security Subcommittee, led by Nevada Democrat Pat McCarran, and most famously by the Senate Subcommittee on Investigations headed by Wisconsin Republican Joseph McCarthy after 1953. The Dies committee also witnessed the first use of the Fifth Amendment, the constitutional protection against self-incrimination, in testimony by Earl Browder, the secretary of the Communist Party, when he was asked whether he ever had traveled to Moscow on a forged passport.[63]

The Committee was a forerunner in another sense, as well. Roosevelt, Hoover, and other leaders of the executive branch, including those most willing to compromise civil liberties to fight subversion, were apprehensive about freewheeling congressional investigations they could not control, in part because they were institutional rivals, and in part because committee activities could undermine ongoing official investigations. Hoover regularly rebuffed calls by Dies for cooperation, thinking him to be afflicted by "great delusions of personal grandeur," and a competitor for attention and resources. With the FBI and the senior figures in the Department of Justice particularly concerned that Dies and his committee were prematurely disclosing evidence, the president pressured Dies at the White House in November 1940 to act in a more measured way.[64]

Dies self-referentially created the Dies Foundation for Americanism and became a widely sought-after speaker to promote his views about subversion and immigration. Despite apprehension about his committee's methods, its hearings were broadly popular, among both the mass public and leading commentators. A careful 1939 study demonstrated just how much the committee had altered public opinion.[65] A *New York Times* lead editorial in January of that year exemplifies the ambivalent but ultimately supportive position of elite views at the time. The paper cautioned that the committee's procedures were flawed, its members having "solemnly listened to a great deal of obviously hysterical tosh," and having been "genuinely guilty of red-baiting in the sense of overzealousness to pin a Communist label on every species of liberal thought." Yet the editorial also observed that the committee had "performed a useful and important service" by revealing "the disingenuous character of Communist tactics in this country."[66]

With widespread approval of its goals, the committee's mandate was renewed in February 1939 by a wide margin in the House, 344–35, and its annual budget was quadrupled, to $100,000. In February 1941, the committee was endorsed by an even wider margin, 354–6, with the budget set at $150,000. By contrast, once the United States was at war, and the Soviet Union had become a vital ally, congressional enthusiasm diminished. When the committee was extended yet again in February 1943, many nonsouthern Democrats changed sides, leading to a vote of 302–94.

The committee's work continued to push the boundary between inquiry and inquisition. It was, Walter Lippmann judged in 1940, "a kind of committee on public safety . . . official vigilantes . . . often lawless in spirit and disorderly in their methods." Yet, like most with an establishment opinion, Lippmann refused to call for a halt. "It is plain," he concluded, "that the Dies Committee cannot be abolished and must be continued since it offers a center of resistance to evils which could not otherwise be brought to light and checked."[67]

Before the country's wartime alliance with the Soviet Union caused it to lose steam, the committee demonstrated that even a president and an executive branch attuned to matters of subversion could not contain or control demagogic initiatives in Congress. It revealed that the lack of clear borders between open and closed politics and between liberal and Communist perspectives could cripple progressive politics. It established how indiscriminate speech and often careless and irresponsible charges based on self-interested testimony could mobilize public opinion. By so doing, it created a permissive climate for new federal legislation that constrained liberty for suspected classes of persons, those who held radical views, and especially those who lacked the status of citizenship.

Embracing the policies advocated by Dies and his committee, Virginia's Howard Smith ushered the Alien Registration Act (Smith Act) through Congress in June 1940. Passed by a voice vote in the Senate and by a nearly unanimous 382–4 vote in the House, this law mandated that all aliens older than fourteen register with federal authorities and get fingerprinted, required that alien subversives and criminals be deported, and defined as a federal crime speech intended "to reach and advocate the overthrow of the United States government by force and violence."[68] The vote affirmed that this was popular legislation. That month, a *Fortune* poll asked, "What if anything do you think should be done about Communists in the United States?" A third of the respondents did not know, and 10 percent responded, "Do nothing; let them alone." More predominant was the 43 percent that counseled drastic action, including 26 percent that supported deportation, 13 percent that backed finding "some way of getting rid of them," and 5 percent that favored jail, concentration camps, or even capital punishment. Another 8 percent supported curbs and controls, including a ban on having a Party.[69]

At first, some nonsouthern Democrats expressed hesitation and even opposition to Smith's proposal. Brooklyn's Emanuel Celler, who later chaired the House Judiciary Committee, initially resisted the bill, but ultimately he voted yes, explaining how "in fear of a worse bill, we must accept" this law. President Roosevelt quickly signed the legislation, announcing that it would "hardly . . . constitute an improper encroachment on civil liberties in the light of present world conditions."[70] Some five million aliens were soon registered in the first-ever inventory of foreigners residing in the United States.[71] Citing the new law in a memorandum to field agents, Hoover directed the FBI to develop a custodial detention list of persons who either "should be apprehended and interned immediately" after the start of war or should be "watched carefully" because their activities indicated they might harm the nation's interest.[72] Within days of Pearl Harbor and the declaration of war by Italy and Germany, 890,000 Italians, Germans, and Japanese were designated as enemy aliens; their travel was sharply restricted, and they were forbidden to enter the third of the country designated as military zones. They were not allowed to possess weapons, cameras, signal devices, codes, photographs of military installations, or shortwave radios.[73]

The first sedition trial under the Smith Act was conducted in Minneapolis from October to December 1941, ending one day after Pearl Harbor. Confiscated papers from the offices of the Trotskyist Socialist Workers Party (SWP) provided the evidence for charges against twenty-eight persons who either were members of the Party or of Local 544 of the Teamsters Union, what had been guided in part by the SWP. Eighteen were convicted of having violated the Smith Act. "The American people," the

Communist journalist Milton Howard argued in the *Daily Worker,* the Party newspaper, "can find no objection to the destruction of the Fifth Column in this country. On the contrary, they must insist on it." Clearly, he did not anticipate how, starting in 1946, this law would be used to prosecute Communist Party leaders.[74]

In 1944, a more spectacular Smith Act sedition trial of twenty-seven American Fascists relied on the defendants' pro-German, anti-Semitic, and anti-Communist writings, but the prosecution failed to present persuasive evidence that they had conspired, in concert with Nazi Germany and Fascist Italy, to promote the Axis cause. Upon the death of the presiding judge in November, a mistrial was declared. In December 1945, after the war had ended, the indictments were dismissed. Though what came to be known as the Great Sedition Trial "left no legal precedent and put no one behind bars," it did "set an important *political* precedent for the Smith Act prosecutions of Communists during the Cold War, which loomed just around the corner."[75]

Arguably an even more ominous practice was established when two German-Americans and six German nationals who lived in the United States were arrested for sabotage on June 6, 1942. Having landed by U-boat days earlier in Amagansett, New York, and south of Jacksonville, Florida, they had planned to attack rail terminals, chemical factories, and a hydroelectric plant at Niagara Falls. One of the would-be saboteurs betrayed the plot. All were arrested between the twentieth and the twenty-seventh. Their lawyers petitioned to have their case heard in civil court, and the habeas corpus petitions they filed were denied by the U.S. District Court of the District of Columbia. On July 2, acting as commander in chief, President Roosevelt declared them to be unlawful enemy combatants. He appointed a seven-person military commission to conduct a trial under procedural rules its members alone would set. The trial took place at the Department of Justice from July 8 to August 1. Attorney General Biddle led the prosecution team. Each defendant was convicted and sentenced to die. There was no process of appeal. Six were electrocuted on August 8. One, who had intended to defect, had his sentence commuted by Roosevelt to life in prison. The other, who had defected, had his term set at thirty years. President Truman deported both to occupied Germany in 1948.[76]

III.

EVEN BEFORE Pearl Harbor, President Roosevelt had declared states of emergency.[77] These edicts were controversial, because there existed no clear constitutional or statutory authority for such far-reaching expansions of executive power. Dating from the prewar period of 1941 into the first part of the war, these presidential orders and proclamations complemented action by Congress to change the Neutrality Acts, build military preparedness, and create a peacetime draft. These executive "forms of action taken by President Roosevelt under emergency conditions in the absence of definite statutory or constitutional authority," an approving 1949 study concluded, were premised on the idea that "when the need became apparent, legality, though considered, was secondary and subordinate to crisis demands."[78]

To be sure, Roosevelt did draw on a legacy of presidential practice and Supreme Court endorsement, or at least on a particular reading of this legal patrimony, dating from President Lincoln's invocation of presidential war power as singular and unified. Following World War I, Chief Justice Edward Douglass White declared, in *Northern Pacific Railway v. North Dakota*, in 1919, that "the complete and undivided character of the war power" is "indisputable."[79] Fifteen years later, the Court considered whether emergencies authorized constitutional exceptions in *Home Building and Loan Association vs. Blaisdell*. Writing for the majority, Chief Justice Charles Evans Hughes had determined that "emergency does not create power," nor does it "increase granted power or diminish restrictions imposed upon power granted or reserved" by the Constitution.[80] FDR's actions thus depended on interpreting the Constitution as authorizing presidents to take action that was implied but not specifically granted. This "inherent-power theory," the constitutional scholar Edward Corwin wrote just after World War II, "logically guarantees the *constitutional adequacy of the war power by equating it with the full actual power of the nation in waging war*. It makes the full power of the nation constitutionally available."[81]

FDR issued a military order on July 5, 1939, that removed the secretaries of war and the navy from the military chain of authority to his own supervision as commander in chief.[82] A week after the German invasion of Poland, his Proclamation 2352 announced, on September 8, what it called a limited national emergency, giving the president the powers he needed "for the proper observance, safeguarding, and enforcing of the neutrality of the United States and of strengthening our national defense within the limits of peacetime authorizations."[83] The concept of a limited emergency had never been used before.

On May 27, 1941, seven months before the conflagration in Hawaii, FDR issued Proclamation 2487, which affirmed the existence of an unlimited national emergency, thus placing the country on a war footing for the purposes he alone announced. "The war is approaching the brink of the Western Hemisphere itself," he informed the American people in that evening's radio address. He explained that he would act to keep sea-lanes open, prepare to repel potential German attacks, and "give every possible assistance to Britain and to all who, with Britain, are resisting Hitlerism or its equivalent with force of arms" in circumstances marked by Nazism's "military possession of the greater part of Europe" and much of North Africa, by an imminent threat to Egypt and the wider Middle East, and by Germany's growing capacity to attack American shipping in the Atlantic.[84]

Critics who disagreed argued that the president was seizing unlawful authority by way of on an uncommonly broad interpretation of his constitutional authority. During the war, such doubts largely remained unspoken because they seemed partisan, even illegitimate. Moreover, with a state of war declared, it was widely understood, as the *New York Times* put it on December 9, 1941, that a situation had come to exist that "lifts the limit from Presidential powers."[85]

To be sure, Roosevelt continued to ask Congress for legislation he thought necessary. But he also made clear that when he believed the crisis demanded action, he would give the House and Senate no choice, asserting a capacity to override or circumvent congressional power.[86] His fireside chat of September 7, 1942, "the high point in F.D.R.'s *explicit* claims for Presidential prerogative," and "the most exorbitant claim for Presidential power ever made by a President,"[87] called for the repeal of that part of the Price Control Act constraining regulatory action until farm prices had risen to a designated level. "I have told the Congress that inaction on their part" by the end of the month, he informed his listeners, "will leave me with an inescapable responsibility to the people of this country to see to it that the war effort is no longer imperiled by the threat of economic chaos," adding that "in the event that the

Congress should fail to act, and act adequately, I shall accept the responsibility, and I will act."[88]

Senator Robert Taft, the Republican leader, strongly objected, calling instead for more ordinary lawmaking. Warning about "a complete one-man dictatorship" and the prospect that "Congress would become" a shell of a legislative body, he argued that the president's assertion of a right to bypass Congress implied a doctrine "so revolutionary and so dangerous to the country" that disobedience should be considered: "If these powers are assumed without legislation, I should not hesitate to advise any man that his patriotic duty is to refuse obedience of any order issued by them—just as I should refuse to leave my duties here in Washington if the President attempted to suspend congress for the period of the war."[89] After the war, in 1946, Corwin observed that, in this instance, FDR had gone far beyond the assertions of any other in professing powers to disregard a manifestly lawful provision that had been passed by Congress and signed by him into law. Noting Roosevelt had declared that, after the war, these emergency powers would "automatically revert to the people," Corwin wryly noted "the implication . . . that the President owed the transcendent powers he was claiming to some peculiar relationship between himself and the people—a doctrine with a strong family resemblance to the Leadership principle against which the war was supposedly being fought."[90]

What is clear is that Roosevelt's assertions of entitlement extended well beyond those claimed in wars by Abraham Lincoln or Woodrow Wilson. But also striking is the acquiescence of the legislature, which was not always the case during the Civil War. Roosevelt's wartime powers were not simply proclaimed; many were explicitly delegated by Congress. The first such instance came a week after Pearl Harbor, when Congress passed the sweeping War Powers Act by voice vote, after only two hours of debate in each chamber. In addition to expanding the president's economic powers, and reorganizing governmental functions, the law authorized the president to order the surveillance and censorship of mail, telegraph cable communications, and radio broadcasts "when deemed necessary to the public safety."[91]

Active planning for wartime censorship had preceded American entry into the war. In early 1941, President Roosevelt had reviewed a plan devised by the Joint Army and Navy Board, the precursor to the Joint Chiefs of Staff, to put a navy officer in charge of censoring cables and radio broadcasts and an army officer to direct censorship of wire communications and the mail. He approved the plan on June 4, while asking the FBI to undertake a full review. As it turned out, the Bureau issued detailed recommendations on December 7, just as Pearl Harbor was coming under attack. Utilizing authority granted by the War Powers Act, Roosevelt issued an executive order on the nineteenth to establish the Office of Censorship, stating that "the Director of Censorship shall cause to be censored, in his absolute discretion, communications by mail, cable, radio, or other means of transmission passing between the United States and any foreign country." On January 27, 1942, the president wrote to the director of censorship, Byron Price, asking him "to coordinate the efforts of the domestic press and radio in voluntarily withholding from publication military and other information which should not be released in the interest of the effective prosecution of the war." Quickly, the Army, Navy, and Maritime Commission developed codes of conduct to preserve war security and to deal with such matters as how, if at all, to report on German submarine successes in sinking ships in the Atlantic or the shelling by a Japanese submarine of the southern coast of California.[92]

A tandem effort to distribute materials to rally the public was developed during the winter and spring of 1942. On March 7, the director of the Bureau of the Budget, Harold Smith, urged the president to create a central agency "to stimulate citizen understanding of the war effort." He argued that it was "imperative that some single agency be responsible for policy coordination and for providing centralized control over Government use of such media as the radio, motion pictures, and posters."[93] Following this advice, Roosevelt issued Executive Order 9182 on June 13, which established the Office of War Information (OWI).[94] The creation of this and a host of other wartime agencies by the president—including the Board of Economic Warfare (BEW), the Office of Civilian Defense (OCD), and the Office of Defense Transportation (ODT)—sidestepped the Constitution's provision that unless Congress provided otherwise, all civil offices except those of the president and vice president "shall be established by law."[95]

This, Congress did not do, but it did pass the remarkably expansive Second War Powers Act on March 27, 1942. Title XIV authorized the executive branch to carry out "special investigations and reports of census or statistical matters as may be needed in connection with the conduct of the war" and repealed the confidential status of census data, "notwithstanding any other provision in law."[96] These stipulations concerning "the utilization of vital war information" were adopted to underpin the policy of Japanese internment that had been announced on February 19. Arguing that "the successful prosecution of the war requires every possible protection against espionage and sabotage," Executive Order 9066 established military areas in Arizona, California, Oregon, and Washington from which every person with Japanese ancestry—112,000 in all, 79,000 of whom were citizens—was purged, notwithstanding the absence of treason or subversion.[97]

The Japanese Exclusion League of California and the Native Sons of the Golden West, organizations long preoccupied with Asian immigrants, had already led a vigorous nativist campaign prior to Pearl Harbor. Publicized by the Hearst newspaper chain, the drive to exclude this population was fueled by the Committee for the Investigation of Un-American Activities.[98] During the summer of 1941, Chairman Dies declared an intention to convene hearings to reveal subversion by Japanese living in California. He particularly targeted fishermen, whom he charged with arming their boats after meeting members of Japan's navy. Hoover and the FBI were utterly unconvinced.[99] Once the war began, Dies alleged in demagogic fashion that some fifteen thousand Japanese were spies who should have been apprehended well before the war.[100] Leading politicians, including California's full congressional delegation and Earl Warren, the state's Republican attorney general and future chief justice of the Supreme Court, as well as members of the West Coast Army Command and prestigious journalists, including Walter Lippmann, also campaigned for removal.[101]

Like other residents, Japanese in Hawaii were subjected to martial law, under whose terms jury trials, habeas corpus, and other constitutional protections were suspended from December 7, 1941, until October 1944.[102] On the mainland, they experienced mass confinement after they were removed from an area described by Lt. Gen. J. L. DeWitt, head of the Western Defense Command, as "particularly subject to attack, to attempted invasion, to espionage and acts of sabotage."[103] Placed under a curfew from 8:00 P.M. to 6:00 A.M., then expelled from their homes, they were first moved, starting on March 23, 1942, to overcrowded and rudimentary temporary centers located at racetracks and fairgrounds whose functions had been suspended during the war. Sanitation was poor, privacy minimal. Books and articles written in Japanese were banned. Transfers followed in antiquated and packed passenger trains to ten austere and isolated "relocation centers" built hastily in remote and inhospitable locations in the interior of the country. Here, too, facilities were rudimentary and privacy hard to secure. Food was modest, medical care uneven. Work was made available at wages below those of the lowest-paid army private. Though President Roosevelt twice referred to "concentration camps," the term was banned by the War Relocation Authority (WRA), the responsible agency first led by Milton Eisenhower, Dwight Eisenhower's brother, who later became president of Kansas State University, Pennsylvania State University, and Johns Hopkins University, and, still later, a candidate for vice president in Texas in 1980 on the third-party ticket led by Congressman John Anderson of Illinois.[104]

As subjects of an extraconstitutional "naked dictatorship,"[105] the internees were put through an interrogation process to determine their loyalty. All persons older than seventeen were asked whether they would "swear unqualified allegiance to the United States of America and faithfully defend the United States from any or all attack by foreign and domestic forces and forswear any form of allegiance or obedience to the Japanese emperor." Those deemed disloyal, less than 15 percent, were physically separated from the majority in what the *Washington Post* described in a headline as a JAP SEGREGATION PLAN.[106]

Until the order excluding persons with Japanese ancestry from the Pacific coast was lifted in January 1945, when the threat to U.S. security clearly no longer existed, Congress remained largely quiet but complicit. By voice vote in each chamber on March 21, 1942, it passed legislation that backed Executive Order 9066 by making it a federal crime to violate "the restrictions laid down by the President, the Secretary of War, or designated military subordinates."[107] Throughout the war, Congress continued to appropriate the funds, without debate, that made the camps possible.[108] The main exception to congressional silence came in hearings conducted by Martin Dies's committee. In June 1943, it featured wildly exaggerated testimony by a former WRA camp supply officer who alleged that the interned Japanese were being indulged by lax administrators who were supplying the interned with superior food and offering excessive latitude.[109]

With the United States fighting with a racially segregated military, with segregation and disenfranchisement the dominant forms of social and political organization in the South, and with national patterns of racism and discrimination rife in housing and jobs, the loyalty of African-Americans was also thought to be at issue. This was a particularly tumultuous period for black Americans. They debated the role they should play in the war, a discussion that was resolved in the main by strong participation, and they experienced massive demographic change, with more than three million African-Americans leaving the South for war-production jobs in the North and the West.

In June 1942, J. Edgar Hoover commissioned the *Survey of Racial Conditions in the United States* (RACON), a 730-page document that took nearly fifteen months to complete. It was part of a lKKarger effort, a monumental internal security investigation, the subject of which was labeled "Foreign-Inspired Agitation Among the American Negroes." The FBI sought both to assess black loyalty and to monitor racial unrest, especially after the three-day Detroit riot of June 1943, in which 34 were killed and 433 wounded, and the two-day August 1943 Harlem riot in New York, in which 6 were killed, and just under 400 wounded.[110]

By 1945, the project had taken on Herculean proportions, producing thirteen volumes in the process. Marked "Secret," each included newspaper clippings and reports by the Bureau's fifty-six field divisions that offered detailed accounts based on intelligence provided by FBI agents' paid informants, or "voluntarily supplied by various sources." The *Survey* especially targeted persistent Japanese efforts to influence black opinion, and it focused on the role of the Communist Party in exploiting black grievances and mobilizing protest, despite the Party's decision to downplay black rights during the war, lest it impede the war effort.[111] Other targets included "non-subversive" leaders of the NAACP, then undergoing a massive membership growth, from 50,000 in 1940 to almost 450,000 by 1946, and the 155 newspapers that composed the period's lively black press.[112]

Over the course of the war, these newspapers maintained a steady drumbeat of reports and editorials that highlighted racial injustice in the military and in civil society. The Justice Department, the Department of War, the various armed services, and specialized agencies such as the Office of War Information and the Office of Censorship kept persistent watch over African-American reporters and editors, worried that stories like that in the *Oklahoma City Black Dispatch* entitled "War Department Aids Hitler by Letting South Wreak Prejudice on Negro Soldiers" would produce disloyalty.[113]

Hoover sought to suppress that newspaper in the summer of 1942 for articles that complained about the conditions black soldiers faced on trains without food and in filthy segregated restaurants, even though he was advised by junior lawyers in the Department of Justice that there was no statutory basis for such censorship. He had to desist, but the army, by contrast, did ban African-American newspapers it thought to be subversive. The black press faced other hurdles. The U.S. Post Office Department conducted lengthy examinations before renewing their mailing permits, and its investigators decided not to mail issues they considered to be subversive. The person appointed to review the *Pittsburgh Courier,* for example, ruled that the issue published on May 2, 1942, exceeded proper bounds because its editorial projected the possibility the newspaper might be suppressed, and because it ran an article in which a future Harlem congressman, the Reverend Adam Clayton Powell Jr., compared the conditions experienced by blacks in the United States to those suffered by Jews in Germany. The examiner concluded that these articles "are designed to cause insubordination, disloyalty, mutiny or refusal of duty in the military or naval forces of the United States among Negroes.... This type of reading matter tends to cause persons of the colored race to advocate resistance or forcibly resist the laws of the United States and induces insurrection among these people."[114] In the name of national unity, racial distrust thrived.

IV.

THE FIRST and Second War Powers Acts delegated to President Roosevelt more power over American capitalism than he had achieved even during the New Deal's radical moment. The December 1941 law conferred authority to modify existing government contracts, speed up production without competitive bidding, seize foreign property for use in the war, and regulate all trade, credit, and economic transactions with other countries. The March 1942 law granted the president even more far-reaching discretionary power to control the nation's economy. Its provisions gave him the means to allocate resources for defense purposes "in such manner, upon such conditions and to such extent as he shall deem necessary in the public interest." These authorizations included the ability to seize immediately land and personal property for war purposes, set prices for government purchases, impose priorities on production and on the delivery of goods and services, violate prior contracts, and control all forms of transportation. Above all, the act furnished the president with "tremendous, effectively unrestrained power over resource allocation," including a provision that he could allocate any materials and direct any facility to produce for defense or export "as he shall deem necessary or appropriate in the public interest and to promote the national defense." This stipulation underpinned the all-encompassing economic control exercised by the War Production Board (WPB) during the duration of the war. "No greater economic power," the economist Robert Higgs has commented, "was ever delegated by Congress to the President."[115]

There was more. A National War Labor Board, created by executive order in January 1942, had granted the capacity to impose its will during labor disputes by enforcing its preferred settlements.[116] That month, Congress passed the Emergency Price Control Act of 1942, which established a new independent agency, the Office of Price Administration (OPA), to prevent wartime inflation by preventing "speculative, unwarranted, and abnormal increases in prices and rents" and eliminating "profiteering, hoarding, manipulation, speculation, and other disruptive practices." Mimicking the draft boards that had been formed by the Selective Service Act, the OPA created eight thousand local boards to police its price policies. When Congress passed the Economic Stabilization Act in October 1942 to amend the Price Control Act, the president was given the power to adjust all prices and wages as he thought necessary "to aid in the effective prosecution of the war or to correct gross inequities," including the ability to override wage agreements even when labor and business had come to an agreement through collective bargaining.

To achieve these purposes, Roosevelt immediately issued an executive order to create the Office of Economic Stabilization. To lead it, he directed James Byrnes, the former senator from South Carolina, Senate majority leader, and future secretary of state under Harry Truman, to step down from the Supreme Court, where he had served as an associate justice for just fifteen months. Seven months later, in May 1943, Byrnes also became the head of the Office of War Mobilization, thus effectively putting wartime capitalism in politically capable hands.[117] Roosevelt's "assistant president," as many called him, soon recruited the Wall Street banker Bernard Baruch to be his key policy adviser, fully knowing that when Baruch had led the War Industries

Board in World War I, he had testified that "in modern warfare, administrative control must replace the law of supply and demand."[118]

Like the peacetime NRA, this constellation of economic agencies rejuvenated early 1930s ideas about economic planning and identified a primary role for many of the country's leading industrialists to come to Washington and work hand in hand with the government's administrative cadres. Like the NRA, this mixed public-private system mobilized immense capacity to guide economic decisions. Tethered during the war to a massive, indeed unprecedented, program of military production and mobilization, this set of economic arrangements and tools was buttressed by an overwhelmingly united citizenry. Also like the NRA, the combination of public power and private recruitment elicited participation from the country's best-organized economic groups and guarded the prerogatives of the big firms represented by the National Association of Manufacturers, whose profits were protected by cost-plus contracts, and the unions of the AFL and CIO, which were authorized to count all new employees as dues-paying members in plants where unions had already achieved recognition.

Businessmen working for a dollar a year, while continuing to collect their corporate salaries, were brought into the federal government's agencies and onto boards that governed the nation's wartime economy. Headed by former Sears Roebuck executive Donald Nelson, these recruits dominated the WPB, with powers to "exercise general direction of the war procurement and production program."[119] Working in tandem with the Defense Plant Corporation (DPC), which spent nearly $10 billion to build and modernize a huge array of factories,[120] and with military planners, including the Army Service Forces, which tendered $32 billion in wartime contracts,[121] the WPB coordinated the federal government's strategy and logistics by scheduling production and keeping the flow of raw materials coming. This wartime mobilization also used federal authority to operate the civilian economy with controlled prices, restrictions on strikes, and the clear understanding that war needs and defense production must come first. In all, the federal government galvanized a planned economy whose enormous productive capacity was a key element in winning the war. Washington allocated materials and production facilities and cut off supplies to businesses not in compliance with its rules and regulations. Employers could not hire workers without authorization by the U.S. Employment Service.

Total war—a war unrestricted by limits on manpower, production, means, and ideological commitment—required unprecedented economic organization and mobilization. Many thousands of plants were converted to war production. A massive munitions industry was created. Over a thousand new factories were financed by the DPC, which provided fully two-thirds of all capital investment in the United States between 1940 and 1945. To support the air war, the DPC also built many other facilities, mainly in the Midwest and the South. New airfields sprouted across the country. Government-funded plants provided key raw materials, including aluminum for air frames and magnesium for incendiary bombs. One billion dollars of federal funds expanded the steel industry and modernized its aging facilities. The armed forces built their own plants. Many operated under contract with private firms to produce weapons, explosives, uniforms, and other defense needs. The Army Corps of Engineers oversaw the construction of massive military aircraft-assembly factories in Kansas, Nebraska, Oklahoma, and Texas. By war's end, the federal government owned fully 40 percent of the country's capital assets.[122]

Placed on a war footing, the American economy, in short, was directed by a system of planning and control that "managed almost every area of what effectively became a state-capitalist system." This second radical moment froze prices, capped profits, and rationed commodities, crops, and commercial goods. Government agencies and policies also controlled wages and rents, limited maximum salaries after taxation to $25,000, starkly reduced consumer credit, and, in 1942, utterly banned the sale of new automobiles. A transformation of public finance was ushered in by the Revenue Acts of 1941 and 1942, which dramatically increased income-tax rates and expanded the tax base by reducing exemption levels. After 1943, steeply progressive pay-as-you-go income taxes that withheld earnings as they were paid made income taxes the main source of government revenue.[123] There was also a victory tax of 5 percent on incomes higher than twelve dollars per week. These changes to public finance funded a radical increase in the federal budget, which grew from total expenditures of some $9.5 billion in 1940 to nearly ten times that amount, $92 billion, in 1945.

In all, the United States spent $350 billion on World War II, nearly half of which was funded by taxes, the remainder by borrowing.[124] Spending on defense jumped from 1.4 percent of the gross national product in 1939 to 43 percent in 1944.[125] In an unprecedented burst of productivity, the U.S. wartime political economy built 324,000 airplanes, 88,000 tanks, 1,060 ships, 1.5 million machine guns, 516,000 artillery pieces, and 2,400,000 military trucks. To the Allies, it sent 43,000 of these planes, 800,000 of the trucks, as well as enormous shipments of other military supplies.[126] The economic effects were profound. Overall, the economy surged and unemployment disappeared, dropping from a rate of 14.6 percent in 1940 to just 1.2 percent in 1944.[127] In this respect, at least, the dire years of economic suffering had come to a close.

V.

WARTIME MOBILIZATION witnessed dramatic changes to how the federal government organized a national capacity for technological innovation. During the 1930s, the New Deal had moved in fits and starts toward a society with a more enhanced scientific capacity.[128] With the war, the issue became infinitely more pressing. In 1940, Vannevar Bush, an applied mathematician and electrical engineer and a former MIT professor and dean of the School of Engineering who had just come to Washington to direct the Carnegie Institution and head the National Advisory Committee for Aeronautics, persuaded President Roosevelt to create a federal agency to guide the mobilization of American science and technology for military purposes. On June 27 of that year, FDR created the National Defense Research Committee (NDRC) and asked Bush to lead its five research divisions on patents and inventions, instruments and controls, communications and transportation, armor and ordnance, and chemistry and explosives.

Within a year, Bush was also directing the Office of Scientific Research and Development (OSRD), which could not only help initiate research but act as well as an operating agency to develop prototypes of weapons and techniques for industrial production. At OSRD, which included the NDRC, Bush worked with other talented science administrators, including Harvard University's president, James B. Conant, an organic chemist, who was put in charge of NDRC, and J. Robert Oppenheimer, the distinguished University of California theoretical physicist, to develop weapons that could be utilized as quickly as possible.[129] With the backing of the president, Bush became the "czar of research," with sufficient authority to dictate to the generals and civilians who led the Department of War. At a time when anti-Semitism was restricting Jewish opportunities in the humanities and social sciences at leading American universities, physics and chemistry were operating on more meritocratic grounds. As a result, American science was able to draw not only on native-born Jews of talent but also on a trove of Jewish scientists fleeing Nazism. Reinforced in this way, a talented community of natives and refugees joined together to fashion a cutting-edge large-project scientific research community at just the moment when German science had lost some of its key figures.[130]

During the course of the war, the OSRD and a new advisory group Bush headed, the Joint Committee on New Weapons and Equipment, blurred traditional lines. During World War I, the federal government had drafted scientists to build new military laboratories. By contrast, Bush and his colleagues launched projects and organized war-related research under contract to the country's universities and laboratories, thus changing the relationship among government, the armed forces, and civilian institutions of higher learning. In this way, the government could take advantage of existing facilities and personnel without losing time to new construction and recruitment. Conant's Harvard, as an example, quickly took up the task of conducting experiments to design more lethal explosives.[131] The NDRC and OSRD also fashioned close ties between the military and the staffs of scientists and engineers who worked for private firms by offering contracts to these companies, thus further eroding the division between civilians and soldiers. In all, the new federal science establishment deepened Washington's commitment to central military planning to unite and coordinate the military, corporations, and universities in a common endeavor for what Bush called "the preservation of civilization."[132]

These were no small ventures. There had never been anything like this in terms of mobilizing science in civil society for public purposes. During its first year, the NDRC "enlisted the services of about 2,000 scientists, including about 75 percent of the nation's top physicists and half of the leading chemists." Many millions were invested in university science facilities and in federal testing facilities. By 1944, the OSRD was spending three million dollars every week, while harnessing six thousand scientists and engineers who worked in more than three hundred university and industrial research labs.[133] Building what Bush boasted was a new intimacy between soldiers and scientists, these organizations directed a largely secret effort to assemble talented experts who could accelerate innovations in electronics, radar, and the destructive power of weapons. Together with the military services, the United States devoted some two billion dollars to military research and development between 1940 and 1945, based on the understanding that Conant had articulated two weeks after Pearl Harbor. "This war," he observed, "is in many ways a race of scientific developments and devices."[134]

The most important aspect of this race, the culmination of America's scientific mobilization, was the successful construction of atomic weapons. Writing to President Roosevelt on March 9, 1942, Bush reported that the "work is under way at full speed," adding, "The subject is more important than I believed when I last spoke to you about it." He went on to explain that "the stuff will apparently be more powerful than we thought, the amount necessary appears to be less, the possibilities of actual production appear more certain." The president responded two days later. Underscoring the need "for absolute secrecy," he declared, "I think the whole thing should be pushed not only in regard to development, but also with due regard to time. This is very much of the essence."[135] Crucially, the administrators, scientists, and engineers who forged the bomb did so before any other was built.[136] Whether by design, inexperience, or insufficient skill, their German counterparts did not manage this task, despite a common starting point.

Never questioning the ethics or necessity of the bomb, and drawing a sharp line dividing scientific from political decisions, the OSRD helped oversee advances that transformed nuclear physics into usable technology.[137] At first, like nonnuclear research and technology, the project was decentralized to university and corporate settings. By March 1942, contracts had been let to Standard Oil for work on the diffusion process and suitable catalysts, to Westinghouse Electric for an experimental centrifuge and a four-meter gas separator, and to ten university labs. The three largest recipients of these funds were the University of California, for research on the relationship between electromagnetic methods and chemical processes; Columbia University, for pure chemical substances prepared by physical means; and the University of Chicago, for physics aspects of the tube alloy program and to study the "possibility of producing volatile 'X' compounds."[138]

Soon, though, the scale of the program, and the need to conceal fissionable material, the technology of production, and testing placed the enterprise primarily at an immense purpose-built 45,000-acre secret research and development site in Los Alamos, New Mexico. Containing 37 technical buildings, 49 administrative structures, 620 apartment units, and 52 dormitories, this laboratory, and the larger Manhattan Project of which it was a part, was led administratively by Maj. Gen. Leslie Groves, of the Army Corps of Engineers, and directed intellectually by Oppenheimer. Together with a military contingent of two thousand, the civilian staff grew to nearly four thousand.[139] Drawing on mass spectroscopy, tracer techniques, and other advances, these scientists overcame great practical and technical barriers.[140] They did not work alone. Outside of Los Alamos, the Manhattan Project, which took its name from the Office of the Corps of Engineers in New York City, employed more than 125,000 scientists, engineers, construction personnel, and administrators in thirty-seven installations.[141]

When the first of two operational bombs literally wiped Hiroshima off the map on August 6, 1945, with an explosive force of at least 12,500 tons of TNT,[142] Oppenheimer expressed relief. "Thank God it wasn't a dud," he told a cheering crowd at Los Alamos. Adding that he was "proud" of their accomplishment, he regretted only that the bomb had not been available to use against Nazi Germany.[143] That day, President Truman proclaimed, "This is the greatest thing in history."[144] More soberly, Emperor Hirohito talked of "a most cruel bomb, the power of which to do damage is indeed incalculable."[145]

"It had been there just a few minutes before," a Japanese Catholic priest at Hiroshima testified, "but it was absolutely gone."[146] This triumph for atomic science certainly marked a fateful turning point, producing what Secretary of War Henry Stimson called, in May 1945, "a revolutionary change in the relations of man to the universe," and giving humans what the émigré physicist Leo Szilard called, in July 1945, the capability for "devastation on an unimaginable scale."[147] Fear became permanent. Writing about "the Bomb" three years later, the constitutional scholar Clinton Rossiter cautioned, "You can't go home again; the positive state is here to stay, and from now on the accent will be on power, not limitations."[148] Within five years, just after the Soviet Union exploded its first atomic bomb in August 1949, the United States possessed 298 bombs and 250 long-range bombers. By the time Dwight Eisenhower was inaugurated, the country's strategic nuclear weapons stock had grown to 1,005.[149]

On August 12, 1945, three days after Nagasaki was made to disappear by an even more powerful bomb, bringing the combined total of atomic death to 210,000 civilians, an official report written by the physicist Henry DeWolf Smyth, *A General Account of the Development of Methods of Using Atomic Energy for Military Purposes*, gave the public the first comprehensive account of what had been the world's most secret scientific project; secret, at least by intent, both from Axis enemies and America's Soviet ally.[150] Though short on details that remained classified, the sheer sweep of the story of unprecedented scientific capacity that it told "was startling even to the compartmentalized project scientists."[151]

Looking back seven months after Hiroshima and Nagasaki, Arthur Compton, the University of Chicago physicist who had headed the Manhattan Project's Chicago radiation lab, maintained that atomic weapons were not worse than conventional bombing, as each "was of about the same destructiveness as a raid by a fleet of B-29s using ordinary bombs."[152] Indeed, well before any atomic weapon had been tested or used, the intensity of the air campaign the United States and Britain were conducting had led Winston Churchill to wonder, at a June 1943 meeting of the war cabinet, "Are we beasts? Are we taking this too far?"[153] Rather than desist, the Allies accelerated the largest and most relentless bombing campaign ever directed against civilian targets, an operation that ultimately cost the lives of 140,000 American and British airmen.[154] By 1944, America's Eighth Air Force alone was dropping five thousand tons of incendiaries each month.[155] Firebombing in Germany reduced Cologne, Hamburg (Operation Gomorrah), Berlin, Nuremberg, and, notably, Dresden to charred rubble. When attention turned to Japan, all attempts at precision bombing were supplanted by the type of saturation bombing that had been more of a hallmark of British air campaigns. In 1942, the bomb tonnage of America's air force was just 6,123; in 1943, 154,117; and in 1944, fully 938,952. Likewise, the incidents of firepower from the air increased dramatically in the Pacific theater; 4,080 in 1942, 44,683 in 1943, 147,026 in 1944 and, before the atomic bombs, 1,051,714 in 1945.[156] Incendiary attacks directed by Gen. Curtis LeMay (assisted by his statistician assistant, Robert McNamara) killed 83,000 people during the Great Tokyo Air Raid of March 10, 1945, and another 37,000 when more than 750,000 bombs were let fall thirteen days later. More than a million of that city's residents were rendered homeless. Overall, fully 40 percent of the built area of sixty-six Japanese cities was destroyed.[157] These attacks, *Time* exulted in jingoistic rhetoric, were "a dream come true" and had demonstrated how, "properly kindled, Japanese cities will burn like autumn leaves."[158] By August, more than half of Tokyo's residential areas had been obliterated.[159]

These saturation campaigns combined strategic war aims with an impulse for revenge. These fantastic bombardments significantly reduced the ability of both Germany and Japan to hold out against Allied forces—given the scale and disruptive force of nearly 2.5 million tons of bombs, it could hardly be otherwise[160]—but there was more. "Hitler and Mussolini," the president told Congress at the start of 1943, "will understand the enormity of their miscalculation—that the Nazis would always have the advantage of superior war power as they did when they bombed Warsaw, Rotterdam, London, and Coventry. . . . Yes—the Nazis and Fascists have asked for it—and they are going to get it."[161] In March 1944, the *New York Times* justified "this hideous business" by recalling "what the Nazi fliers did in Rotterdam, on the roads of France and Belgium in 1940, in Poland in 1939, and to British cities in 1940 and 1941," and *The Nation,* though condemning any "indecent gloating," backed the bombing's "revolting necessity."[162]

By war's end, with three-quarters of a million German and Japanese civilians killed from the air,[163] it was hard to recall Cordell Hull's horrified reaction to the bombing of Barcelona by Franco's Nationalist air force from March 16–18, 1938, in which some thirteen hundred were killed and two thousand injured. "Speaking for the whole American people," he had proclaimed that "no theory of war can justify such conduct."[164] Nor was it easy to remember Franklin Roosevelt's own September 1, 1939, "urgent appeal" to the governments of Britain, France, Germany, Italy, and Poland to renounce "this form of human barbarism" and for each "publicly to affirm its determination that its armed forces shall in no event, and under no circumstances, undertake the bombardment from the air of civilian populations or unfortified cities."[165] Crusading for democracy, Washington had cast off such inhibitions to unleash terrifying and unconstrained expressions of American might.

Looking ahead in October 1945, Oppenheimer was asked about the future of atomic weapons. "If you ask: 'can we make them more terrible?' the answer is yes. If you ask: 'can we make a lot of them?' the answer is yes. If you ask, 'can we make them terribly more terrible?' the answer is probably," a projection that was to prove too modest.[166]

VI.

B Y COMBINING military know-how with scientific research and business leadership, the United States mastered the art of unrestricted war. Demonstrating that democracies could, in fact, solve the biggest problems, the country learned to act as if it were one great unified corporation, a cohesive company that superintended economic, social, and military mobilization on an almost unimaginable scale.[167] In all, the means that were utilized to propel the wartime effort to confront "the militaristic totalitarianism of the Roosevelt period"[168] spurred the economy, brought about remarkable advances in weaponry, and established a tightly constrained civil capitalism and a firmly directed national security state, which reinvigorated the early New Deal's emphasis on planning. The Soviet armed force was larger at the close of the war—the largest ever in global history—but America's was "the mightiest in the world."[169]

In critical ways, the war years interrupted normal lawmaking. During the conflict, the country fashioned an emergency polity whose various enabling acts, concentration of executive power, censorship, propaganda, surveillance, violations of due process, suspicion of disloyalty, planning and corporatism backed by coercion, and unrestrained violence resembled rather more the public policies of the country from which Italo Balbo's air armada had come to the United States than the early New Deal country where they had disembarked in 1933. The wartime national security state that built unprecedented military power and effectively mobilized civilian society began to fuse the United States into "one unified technical enterprise" in order to advance the well-being of liberal democracy across the globe. Preoccupied by danger, devoted to planning, and organized by "specialists on violence," this aspect of America's political order operated with vastly reduced constraints. So doing, it projected irresolvable and persistent tensions inside America's own democracy.[170] When Earl Michener, a Republican member of the House, announced in February 1942, "Under no condition would I vote to grant these additional powers if I did not realize the condition the country is in today," he and his colleagues in both political parties could not have anticipated either the full extent of the concentration of power over the course of the war or that an emergency sensibility would persist long after the Allied victory.[171]

Pursuing victory, the United States adopted a span and depth of executive power that surpassed those of prior wartime emergencies or the New Deal's first one hundred days. The war thus raised significant questions about the U.S. separation of powers system under crisis conditions. It also generated uncertainly about the proper balance between Washington and other units of government in the federal system, and between the federal government and the operation of markets in capital, labor, and ideas.

The war, however, did not simply challenge traditional democratic and constitutional rights and ideas. Central aspects of American democracy persisted. A robust press carried on. The House and Senate continued to meet, legislate, and, frequently clash with the president, especially after the 1942 elections produced significant Republican gains (the party won a majority of votes cast for the House, but a minority of seats, 209 of 435, and gained 8 Senate seats, thereby increasing to 38 members).

There was nothing in the United States that came close to the degree of mobilization, repression, and murder practiced over the course of the war by the governments in Berlin and Moscow. Total war in the United States was a good deal less total. The assaults on the civil liberties of Japanese-Americans, African-Americans, and persons tried under the Smith Act were not the rule, but targeted exceptions. The broad assaults on freedom of assembly, speech, and person in the name of loyalty and security that had characterized the Civil War and World War I were not reprised. Nor did state governments pass their own sedition acts as many had in 1917. Patriotism did not again become a reason to target German-Americans or dramatically enlarge the scope for charges of betrayal. Dissent was not made to disappear. In all, measured against other countries and times, "problems of civil liberty were . . . comparatively easy to solve" during World War II, as Clinton Rossiter observed, in part because the war was so broadly popular.[172]

Though he often pushed the Department of Justice to be more assertive in rooting out subversives, President Roosevelt established a tone that valued the freedoms that had been lost "in other continents and other countries." He made this point when, less than two weeks before Pearl Harbor, he announced that December 15, 1941, would be "Bill of Rights Day" to mark the sesquicentennial anniversary of the first ten amendments to the Constitution.[173] With the period's attorneys general even more committed to maintain as much liberty as possible under emergency conditions, the government promoted self-policing rather more than repression.[174] The Office of Censorship's Code of Wartime Practices was administered by the radio and press industries, not by executive authorities. Unlike Britain, moreover, the United States cancelled no elections. Further, in light of the central role played in the war by the Soviet Union, Washington suspended its restrictions and assaults on the civil liberties of American Communists.

At issue was not whether the United States would become a dictatorship, but, rather, what kind of democracy it would elect to possess during and after the war. The very nature of the wartime coalition made it difficult to address this issue frontally. When, two days after Pearl Harbor, FDR declared the war to be a "united effort by all of the peoples of the world who are determined to remain free," Leningrad was under siege and a German counteroffensive was under way outside Moscow. As the war did not crisply line up a democratic alliance against an alliance of dictatorships, the phrase "determined to be free" was charged with ambiguity—free from conquest or free more substantively? The Big Three coalition coalesced on the same basis, a "united front against fascism," that the Communist movement had adopted as its policy stance in the mid to late 1930s.[175] This basis for collaboration obscured how the partners radically differed with regard to the liberal and democratic commitments that had been announced as Allied war aims in the Atlantic Charter. The urgent high stakes of the war dictated that such questions be suspended.

It was the USSR, not Britain or the United States, that turned the tide against Hitler. Fighting on the eastern front took the lives of four out of every five German soldiers who perished in the entire conflict, and it was the Soviet army that pushed the Nazi force back to Berlin. It is an uncomfortable fact that when Germany's unparalleled invasion force of 2,758,000 soldiers, organized into 103 divisions, poured across the border on June 22, 1941, the Soviet capacity for endurance was galvanized by the brute authority of its relentless dictatorship.[176] Civilian life in the USSR simply ceased to exist in any normal sense, which was not the case in other Allied nations. Mixing appeals for the motherland with ruthless pressure, Moscow rallied the war effort by imposing conditions that the democracies would not have been able to enforce, first to resist, then defeat the Wehrmacht. In mobilizing the country as a single war camp, the Soviet government did not hesitate to use the unrestricted powers of its Party-led state to deport, jail, and kill as it enforced a tight regimen of censorship, austere rationing, and harsh labor conditions. Even for elites, it forced radical changes to daily life, as when, in 1942, Stalin commanded the full complement of scientists from the country's scattered seventy-six research institutes to come to Sverdlovsk, in the Urals, under the aegis of a compulsory State Science Plan.[177]

Much as the Axis forces failed to coordinate strategy between Germany and Japan, the Allies proceeded separately and unevenly. The Combined Chiefs of Staff of the United States and Great Britain planned grand strategy together, while Stalin and his generals separately coped with, then pushed back against, the massive German assault. But the two wars were interdependent. With the United States grappling with Japan, devoting immense resources to the war in the Pacific, and joining the British to do battle in North Africa and Italy while delaying the cross-Channel invasion in Normandy until mid-1944,[178] it fell to the Red Army to confront the central thrust of German military power directly. It was widely understood that only with a Communist victory, representing a Faustian bargain with enormous implications, could the United States and Britain succeed in Europe, and that only with Soviet forces freeing up resources could the democracies devote the means that were required to push back Japan's spectacular gains in the Pacific and on the Asian mainland.

Soviet agony dominated Allied suffering. The Red Army's resistance was achieved at an appalling price. After just seven months of fighting, the Soviet Union had lost 2,663,000 soldiers, with 3,000,000 captured. This was a ratio of twenty Soviet soldiers killed for every German. By war's end, fully 84 percent of the 34.5 million persons the USSR mobilized for war service, of whom 29.5 million were soldiers, had died or endured injury or detention. By contrast, of the 16,112,556 people who had served the United States during the course of the war, 405,399 died, and 671,846 were wounded, according to official figures. Moreover, the war never reached the North American mainland.[179]

Commencing on September 8, 1941, the Soviet Union experienced the longest siege in human history, in the once-fabled city of Leningrad. Over the course of nine hundred days, one million of the city's three million Russians perished, most by starvation. The country also endured the most punishing campaign in the long history of war, a 162-day battle for Stalingrad. During this turning point of the European war, the German army lost 200,000 men, but the victors paid a higher price. In pushing the Wehrmacht back, 479,000 Red Army soldiers and airmen were killed or captured, which amounted to much the same thing.[180] Overall, nearly 9 million Red Army soldiers were killed, and estimates of civilian wartime deaths range from just under 17 million to 24 million.[181] This rate was fully two hundred times higher than the combined civilian death toll for the United States and Britain, and twelve times higher than the pooled American and British military loss of life.[182]

Within the Soviet Union, censorship masked the true costs. Pain was excised from public speech. Starvation was transformed into heroism.[183]The alliance that had been formed between London and Washington on one side and Moscow on the other required the Allies to set aside conventional ethical standards. Thus, Stalin's command to massacre nearly 22,000 Poles at the Katyn Forest in April and May 1940 was treated in the indictment at Nuremberg as if it were a German war crime.[184] At Nuremberg, no mention was made of the Soviet Union's 1939 pact with Nazi Germany, or how Ribbentrop had been welcomed at the Moscow airport with swastika flags flying (taken from movie sets where anti-Fascist films had been made). Nothing was said about the massive Soviet territorial gains the agreement sanctioned in the Baltic states and in Poland, approximately half of which was taken over by the one million Soviet troops who arrived in mid-September 1939. Nothing was mentioned about the deportation of some 2,000,000 Polish families and 230,000 Polish soldiers to Siberia, or about the kangaroo courts organized by the NKVD secret police to try people accused of nationalist resistance and anti-Communist excess. While German leaders were being executed, a stone of silence was place on Soviet complicity with German anti-Semitism in the first phase of the war. Jews fleeing the Nazis in Poland had been summarily returned to face death, as had many who had come to the USSR in the 1930s. Within Poland, Stalin had ordered the repression of Jewish religious and cultural life. The Sabbath and the holidays as well as kosher slaughter were banned.[185]

Comradely amnesia succeeded in putting out of mind the regime of terror the USSR imposed on Estonia, Lithuania, and Latvia, which led to the deportation of more than 120,000 and the murder of thousands after 500,000 Soviet soldiers entered in June 1940. There was no Allied commentary on the growing Gulag prison camp network and its brutal conditions of wartime forced labor, or the persistent acts of repression within the Soviet

Union by the NKVD and Party authorities. The other Allied nations also took no notice of the relentless maltreatment of German prisoners of war and ethnic Germans in western Russia, or Stalin's Order 227 and Order 270, which authorized executions of Soviet soldiers thought to have hesitated or retreated. Nor was any fuss made about the widespread looting, mass rape, and wanton killing that characterized the behavior of Red Army troops in zones they liberated from German control. Barbaric reprisals echoed Nazi cruelty.[186]

Here lay the war's greatest irony. To ensure a future for Western democracies, and to pursue the war aims first announced in their Atlantic Charter, Britain and the United States could proceed only by ignoring, even shielding, the full range of action by their most important ally, thus compromising core tenets of liberal democracy. "Whenever anyone is heard saying . . . that we dare not trust Russia much, it is well to remember this is Nazi propaganda," the *Dallas Morning News* warned in October 1943. "No matter how honest and patriotic the American who repeats such statements, he proves himself gullible and a victim of enemy wiles."[187] The war's crusade thus was compromised by an ethos of unaccountability, especially when it concerned the Soviet Union. Whether this troubling pattern would prevail after the war was a question of paramount concern to the Allied powers.[188]

VII.

THESE DILEMMAS underpinned discussions at Yalta in early February 1945, when President Roosevelt, two months before his death at Warm Springs, traveled 4,883 miles by sea and 1,275 by air to the Crimean Peninsula in Ukraine to confer with Winston Churchill and summit host Josef Stalin. Like vast areas of the Soviet Union, the Crimea bore palpable signs of war. Its scarred green hills and Black Sea beaches had witnessed the mass murder of Jews and Gypsies. The Crimea had undergone extensive physical destruction, and, after liberation by the Red Army, had become party to the mass deportation of the indigenous Tatar population, an ethnic cleansing of nearly 200,000, to Uzbekistan, Kazakhstan, and other distant destinations, an action that was justified as a response to instances of local collaboration with Nazi Germany.[189] Protected from such unpleasantness in the restored grand ballroom of the white-stoned Livadia Palace, which had been built by Czar Nicholas II in 1910, the three leaders charted a course for the world war's uncertain aftermath.[190] "We had the world at our feet," Churchill recalled, "twenty-five million men marching at our orders by land and sea."[191]

As partners in a common cause, he added, "we seemed to be friends."[192] Marked by a spirit of give-and-take, the strange bedfellows appeared ready to guide future global relations. Expectations ran high. Writing in 1943, at the height of World War II, Walter Lippmann identified America's "primary interest" as that of ensuring that "no European power should emerge which is capable of aggression outside of the European continent. Therefore," he concluded, "our two natural and permanent allies have been and are Britain and Russia." He counseled that "combined action by America, Britain, and Russia is the irreducible minimum guarantee of the security of each of them, and the only condition under which it is possible even to begin to establish any wider order of security."[193] The war, it seemed, had been less a fight against dictatorship or totalitarianism than against a particular kind of repression, and its end would focus on finding a durable framework for global peace, not dwelling on past behavior.

Yalta concluded with a host of signed agreements. Some concerned how to "destroy German militarism and Nazism," defeat Japan, and exchange prisoners of war. Looking ahead, the Allies demarcated future European and Asian borders, designated zones of occupation to govern postwar Germany, and organized the troop movements that, in fact, would determine patterns of Soviet and Western control in Europe. They also came to an understanding about how to build the United Nations. The February 11 communiqué was nothing if not optimistic. Using the language of mutual understanding and cooperation, it argued that "victory in this war and establishment of the proposed international organization will provide the greatest opportunity in all history to create in the years to come the essential conditions of such a peace."[194]

Even with their divergent ideologies and values, and mutual suspicions about motives, Britain, the United States, and the USSR left the summit with a shared sense that prospects for future cooperation based on good-spirited compromises about territory, military affairs, and international governance had been secured. "I am profoundly impressed with the friendly attitude of Stalin and Molotov," Churchill cabled to the deputy prime minister of his coalition government, the Labour Party leader Clement Attlee. "It is a different Russian world to any I have seen hitherto."[195] Likewise, Vyacheslav Molotov, the Soviet Union's minister of foreign affairs, telegrammed his country's embassies that "the general atmosphere at the conference was of a friendly nature, and one could feel an effort to come to an agreement on contested questions." Harry Hopkins, FDR's closest long-term adviser, chimed in accordingly, reporting to Robert Sherwood, his biographer, how "we really believed in our hearts that this was the dawn of the new day we had all been praying for and talking about for so many years." The atmosphere, said Roosevelt at a mid-summit dinner, "was as that of a family."[196]

To be sure, each leader was most pleased by different, distinct outcomes.[197] Looking forward to a peace based on collective security, Roosevelt delighted in Stalin's agreement to embrace the UN project with a Security Council of the great powers as its core. He welcomed the USSR's decision to join the fight against Japan three months after victory over Germany. FDR was persuaded that the existence of the United Nations would make it impossible for the United States to return to an isolationist stance, and believed that it was imperative to integrate the Soviet Union into a stable postwar order.[198] He also thought Stalin to be a reasonable interlocutor, driven less by ideological passion than by traditional Russian interests, and thus willing to subordinate its ideological objectives to build an acceptable peace.[199] Even the more skeptical Churchill was confident that durable spheres of influence had been obtained through statecraft, with the Soviets, as a key example, conceding British power in Greece and promising to compromise the interests of that country's Communist comrades in exchange for a free hand in Bulgaria and Romania.[200] In this way, he was convinced, a mix of tacit and explicit understandings for a concert of power would fill the vacuum caused by a Nazi collapse.[201] Stalin, in turn, gained recognition for new borders of the USSR: The Soviet-Polish boundary was moved between one hundred and two hundred miles farther west than before the war, though not quite to the western limits of czarist Russia.[202] He also secured the annexation of the Baltic states, Western Ukraine, and Western Belarus. He also understood that within the scope of what was agreed at Yalta, the Soviet Union's overwhelming military presence in much of Germany and Eastern Europe would guarantee Communist domination, most notably in Poland, which had already been conquered from Germany by the Red Army. With ideological gains and a favorable security structure established for the Soviet Union, good relations with the country's wartime allies could be maintained.

The parties thus emerged from Yalta convinced that future stability was at hand. After all, the line that would soon come to separate Eastern Europe from Western Europe was already established by troop positions on the ground. They also could take satisfaction that Hitler had failed in his persistent attempts to divide the Allies during the war by playing on their inherent tension and wariness.[203] The balance between principles and the realities of global power the Big Three had found at the summit seemed, at the time, to confirm a position that had been advanced a year earlier, in 1944, by a leading international relations specialist, William T. R. Fox. Coining the term *superpower* to take account of the massive differences in power between the United States, Great Britain, and the Soviet Union, on the one side, and the rest of the world, on the other, Fox looked forward to "the high politics of the postwar world." He counseled policymakers to identify "a definition of the national interest of each in such terms that each will find it possible to collaborate with the others to maintain a stable and just postwar world." This goal could be achieved, he thought, despite the yawning ideological gap because the USSR's demand for new territory was unlikely to be extreme, and because, as he rightly predicted, "the British and American governments will not make war on the Soviet Union to prevent the creation of a near-communist vassal Poland."[204]

"This was," McGeorge Bundy wrote in 1949, "the high tide of the Grand Alliance." Unlike those of earlier wartime summits, Yalta's results were less "a council of war than . . . a clear harbinger of peacetime cooperation."[205] For participants and informed observers alike, it seemed almost inconceivable in early 1945 that within a short period the United States would move decisively away from Yalta's foreign policy orientation to the Soviet Union. Before Yalta, even the hardheaded Walter Lippmann was foretelling that "Russia's distrust of the Western Powers, which is the counterpart of their distrust of Russia, can be finally overcome by our support of a peace settlement which ends conclusively the German and Japanese threat to Russian security." He declared that "the fact is that Marshal Stalin has repeatedly affirmed the democratic principle in respect to his dealings with his neighbors within the Russian Orbit."[206]

Public opinion also backed U.S efforts to find a common basis of coop-

eration with this wartime ally.[207] At Yalta's conclusion, none of the participants or informed observers projected how the Grand Alliance would give
way to the Cold War, how quickly Soviet and Communist control of Eastern
Europe would become absolute, or how ambiguities about whether liberal
democracies or Soviet-dominated regimes would define the contours of liberated Europe would quickly underpin Manichean conflicts. None anticipated the retrospective malign assessments of Yalta's significance that later
became common, especially in the United States. None could know whether
the United States would maintain a long-term involvement in European
and Asian affairs. And none fully comprehended the ways in which World
War II would produce a legacy of perpetual fear.[208]

Yalta's agreements were inherently unstable because they combined two
radically different impulses. First was a set of principled guidelines consistent with liberal political values, including self-determination and national
independence, democratic rights, and multilateral global governance of the
kind that been embraced as Anglo-American values in the Atlantic Charter of 1941. Second was the impulse of international-relations realism based
on might, power, and interests. Looking back, Summer Welles, who had
served as undersecretary of state from 1937 to 1943, argued that because the
wartime decision to create the United Nations had not been accompanied by
a decision to settle outstanding territorial problems when the Soviet Union
was still being pressed by the Wehrmacht, the ambitions of collective global
security had been dangerously compromised.[209]

As it turned out, countervailing qualities did more than create zones of
suspicion and discord in world politics. It became clear within weeks that the
USSR would not permit Poland to be governed by a coalition of Communist and non-Communist parties, or allow Romania to have anything but a
Communist regime. By late spring 1945, with Roosevelt now dead, the comity
of Yalta had begun to dissolve. With the Soviet Union violating the broad
principles it had signed on to, the United States, now led by the erstwhile
Missouri haberdasher, senator, and vice president Harry Truman, began to
insist that Yalta had not given Moscow a blank check to proceed as it wished
within its zone of influence. By the time the Big Three next met at Potsdam's
Cecilienhof Palace from mid-July to early August, each, now "both friends
and enemies," had become more rigid, though still ready to negotiate in ways
that ratified Europe's divisions.[210] James Byrnes, who played a key role in the

negotiations, thought Potsdam "would provide a basis for the early restoration of stability in Europe," and concurrently observed that the American delegation returning from conquered Germany "probably was less sanguine than the one that had departed from Yalta."[211] Though there was no immediate confrontation, and though Truman still hoped for decent, if not warm, relations with the Soviet Union, Cold War clouds loomed.[212]

Within a year, the landscape was transformed. Flash points of conflict in Greece, Turkey, Yugoslavia, and Iran roiled the Middle East. The consolidation of Communist power in Poland and elsewhere in Eastern Europe, as well as revelations about Soviet atomic spying during the Manhattan Project, produced a baleful climate of conflict.[213] Soviet power, once viewed as analgesic, came to seem a potent threat to the West's democracies. By March 5, 1946, when Winston Churchill was announcing, in Harry Truman's Missouri, that "an Iron Curtain has descended across the Continent," it was clear that Stalin would not risk the possibility of non-Communist governments in the East for fear that they would almost inevitably gravitate toward the West.[214]

Four months later, on July 1 and July 25, the United States conducted atomic weapons tests at the Bikini Atoll in the Pacific, events that were witnessed not only by journalists and members of Congress but also by observers from the USSR. The fierce atomic capacity possessed by the United States was on public display.[215] By August, relations with the Soviet Union seemed too fraught to proceed with the third planned test. With its cancellation, the Joint Task Force in Washington held a farewell party, at the end of which an angel food cake in the form of an eighteen-inch-high mock-up of a bomb's mushroom cloud was wheeled out for all to view.[216]

VIII.

WITH YALTA already a failed relic of World War II diplomacy, and with the shift from anti-Communism, a new set of concerns appeared on America's political horizon. It was clear that the United States had decisively supplanted Britain as the West's global leader, and so, after the war, it fell primarily to Americans to manage a set of difficult problems and paradoxes. How should friends and enemies be adjudged? What degree of force ought to be mobilized to secure liberty? How might a national security state be organized within a liberal democracy? The questions, many reflecting grave concerns, mounted quickly. Which weapons and what strategies should the United States employ? When, and to what extent, could surveillance be conducted and secrecy permitted despite commitments to individual rights and the open procedures of democratic politics? At what point would a concern with subversion and espionage stray from a legitimate worry to a distorted patriotism, an excessive fear of conspiracy, and the inflation of popular anxieties?[217]

While international and civil liberties concerns proliferated, the country also had to decide how many of the economic powers it had concentrated in the executive branch should be maintained in order to guide demobilization and ensure that prewar Depression conditions would not return. Could U.S. capitalism learn to prosper without the stimulus provided by war production? What lessons should be learned from wartime prosperity? Should future policy rely on centralized economic power and planning, or on the fine tuning of spending and budgets?

Much as presidents and cabinet officers might have wished to address these questions without legislative encumbrances, Congress, we shall soon see, played a decisive role in determining the extent of federal power and the character of public policy. Building on decisions it was already formulating, Congress determined how peacetime capitalism would return once the conflict was over, especially by adjusting the role unions would play in American life. Its investigations, debates, and legislation established the physical reach of the country's armed forces, the scope and nature of America's postwar alliances, and the balance between civil liberty and internal security. Congressional lawmaking also resolved how much authority over military and foreign affairs should reside in the executive branch, and it shaped key solutions about atomic weapons.

As such postwar politics took hold, southern preferences continued to matter, especially after Republican congressional gains, first in 1942 and again in 1946, when Democratic Party losses in the North "increased the relative power of southern Democrats."[218] With their ever more pivotal role, these representatives helped conduct the transition to the postwar era, when peace often felt nearly as ominous as war. With their privileged position in Congress, they were able to promote the policies that established the basic terms of America's market economy, global presence, and patterns of democratic participation. In doing so, they guided the development of a new American state.

PART IV

DEMOCRACY'S
PRICE

10 ▷ Public Procedures, Private Interests

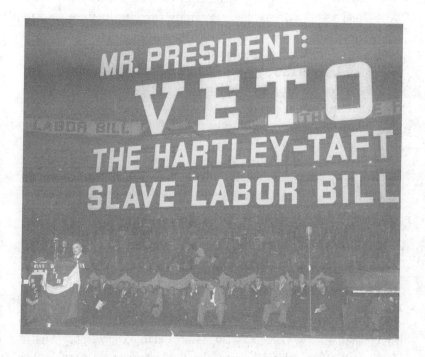

THE CAMPAIGNS AGAINST Japanese militarism, Italian Fascism, and German Nazism turned the war into what a history of American bombing rightly recalled as "a crusade" in which "America tended to justify its actions in universal terms and pursue its goals with idealistic zeal. There was," it concluded, "no limitation in the American way of fighting."[1] It would be folly to expect that normal market practices and democratic procedures would carry on as usual during this kind of struggle. What, though, would happen when the fighting stopped?

Unrestricted wartime mobilization was coordinated from the new, four-million-square-foot Pentagon building, situated just outside Arlington Cemetery. Opened in March 1943 after a crash construction effort that took just sixteen months, this massive structure was designed to be temporary.[2] Even as American troops spanned the globe, active planning was being conducted to ascertain how best to demobilize the armed forces, return the country to a prosperous peacetime economy, and recover normal democratic processes. With a fierce war being fought on two fronts, broad and detailed prescriptions for military discharges, readjustment centers, job placement, and veterans benefits were being developed in many federal agencies. So, too, were designs for terminating war contracts, disposing of stocks of supplies, scrapping weapons, and returning factories owned by the government to private ownership, control, and use.

Eager then to ready America for its journey back to peace and tranquillity, FDR, in the summer of 1943, enlisted Bernard Baruch to coordinate plans for postwar adjustment. Following a key recommendation made by the February 1944 policy guide he developed, President Roosevelt appointed a Contract Termination Board and a Retraining and Reemployment Administration. Working with these new agencies, the army and navy planned for an orderly release by creating a queue on the basis of a point system that relied on such criteria as time spent overseas and service in combat.[3]

Congress, too, impatient for a cessation to the hostilities, prepared for the war's aftermath. A Senate Special Committee on Postwar Economic Policy and Planning, led by Georgia's Walter George, and an equivalent committee in the House, directed by William Colmer of Mississippi, developed legislation that established how soldiers should be compensated upon leaving the service. Committees led by J. Bennett Clark of Missouri in the Senate and Mississippi's John Rankin in the House wrote the GI Bill, which offered unprecedented benefits to veterans, including moneys for schooling at the vocational and university levels, job-placement services, loans for small business, and mortgages for homes, but it also included key features of administrative decentralization that sharply disadvantaged southern black veterans.[4] Also in 1944, Congress passed the Contract Settlements Act, which defined fair compensation for war-contract terminations. That year, it legislated the Surplus Property Act to superintend the transfer of property back to private hands, and return more than five hundred airfields to local governments, thus establishing the basis for a national system of air travel. It also voted to bar any effort by the federal government to ask the armed services to hold on to its soldiers as a means to prevent postwar unemployment.

The frantic pace of all this planning and legislation was propelled by anxiety. If the war had brought an end to Depression conditions of investment and employment, what would happen when this unprecedented federal investment and spending, not to mention price controls and active manpower policies, were finally withdrawn?

The memory of the dire prewar economy lingered, especially the prewar economy before military spending and conscription first kicked in, and hung like a dark cloud over the nation. Americans could not fail to recall how 1938 had been an especially terrible year for American capitalism. During the first four years of the New Deal, economic growth had averaged a robust 9.6 percent. Though still uncommonly high, unemployment had begun to fall from a high of 25 percent to just over 14 percent of the labor force. By contrast, the U.S. gross national product declined by 5.3 percent by the end of 1938, and unemployment leapt to a shocking 19 percent. Tremors of fear were back. The American people, Walter Lippmann wrote at the start of June 1939, had once believed "with Roosevelt that they were organizing securely an abundant life for all the people." With those hopes dashed, "the generation to which we belong is now frightened."[5]

During the fraught spring of 1939, the New School's cohort of émigré scholars had gathered to consider "the struggle for economic security in democracy." They understood, arguably better than anyone else, that more was at stake than whether this or that adjustment to economic policy might make the economic crisis less severe. The central question was whether liberal democracy could achieve palatable economic results, a question, as Erich Hula put the point, made ever more pressing by "the stubborn fact . . . that the totalitarian dictatorships have more or less succeeded—so far, at least— in doing away with unemployment." Would equivalent results be possible within the framework of democratic institutions?[6]

A corollary puzzle had also vexed prewar commentators. The leap in organized class consciousness during the half decade before U.S. participation in World War II had been begun to reshape powers and possibilities in American life.[7] Contributing to a distinguished 1938 collection of essays assessing "civilization in the United States," which included chapters by

Jacques Barzun on race, John Cowles on journalism, and Karl Menninger on psychiatry, Louis Stark, the labor analyst, concluded in 1938 that the union surge might further "stimulate organization on a scale hitherto undreamt even by the most optimistic." By sowing the "formation of a new political orientation of labor and agriculture," union activity promised to reactivate the type of democratic corporatism and planning that had characterized the short-lived radical moment of the early New Deal.[8]

These challenges facing capitalism, labor, and the direction of American democracy returned to front and center as the war wound down. Tense, fearful uncertainty in the midst of unpredictable political horizons raised huge questions about the shape, control, and management of U.S. capitalism. Paramount among these concerns was the role that would be played by the country's burgeoning unions. Over the course of the 1940s, moreover, the important choices the federal government would have to make about economic management clarified. This process of selection produced two enduring outcomes for the direction of U.S. capitalism. Fiscal policy trumped other options, and shifts to labor law tightly constrained what unions could do and where they could expand. During this phase of the New Deal, key features of domestic economic policy—including democratic planning, central government management of sectors of the economy, and corporatist patterns of bargaining among business, labor, and government—were cast aside. Concurrently, the class-based labor movement that had mobilized so assertively after the passage of the Wagner Act in 1935 diminished and focused more narrowly on wages, benefits, and working conditions. As a result, the repertoire of policy instruments the New Deal had utilized during the NRA period and more intensively during the war no longer could serve as models for a long-term peacetime economy. Further, with a corporatist role for U.S. unions blocked as well, political life came to be dominated by a pattern of interest-group politics that the era's political scientists came to call "pluralist," a form of democracy marked more by competition among organizations and lobbyists than by a sense of the public interest.

The development of these policies was vehemently contested, notably in Congress. There, southern members critically shaped each of the key results. With the region's segregated social order coming under enormous stress, they acted to curtail Washington's capacity to direct investment and employment. Most important, they fought successfully to place tight reins on labor's ambitions. The South produced these results as the pivotal agent in two quite different congressional alliances, one with fellow Democrats, the other with Republicans.

Against the opposition of most Republicans, southern Democrats joined with party colleagues to promote an active fiscal role for the national government. But with what they believed to be a racial crisis under way, they no longer were willing to back more hands-on economic interventions. The Democratic Party could continue to come together only by endorsing active macroeconomic policies. Fearing the federal power that long-range planning required, southerners shied away from enhancing the government's capacities to intervene directly in capital and labor markets. Shunning such initiatives, southern members acted to strip Washington's planning institutions of their staffs and budgets. By contrast, they were happy to rely on budgeting—that is, on taxation and setting overall spending levels—as means to buttress the economy. Fiscal policies could support economic growth and development without licensing incursions into the South's economic arrangements and race relations. Because planning grew in importance during World War II as the federal government authoritatively deployed huge sums for investment and induced workers to move in massive numbers to defense production jobs, it became ever more important from a southern perspective to establish rules that sharply distinguished between the requirements for national security and the long-run domestic economy.

A different but equally effective alliance remade the framework within which organized labor could operate. A constellation of southern Democrats and Republicans affected the contours and limits of social class by altering the legal framework within which organized labor could make choices and deploy resources. As unions gained strength during the tight labor markets caused by World War II, their organizing efforts aggressively moved below the Mason-Dixon Line. These successes posed powerful, if mostly indirect, challenges to the southern hierarchy by threatening to undercut the labor market underpinnings of the racial order. In these circumstances, southern representatives shifted positions. Having gingerly supported lawmaking that enhanced and coordinated working-class action in the early and mid-1930s, the embattled South acted to disarm unions in order to diminish the threat it believed labor posed to the economic underpinnings of the region's racial order.

The contest between fiscal and planning instruments played out in more than one legislative battle. Each cluster of ideas and institutions grew stronger during World War II. The diverse group of wartime agencies utilized both sets to plan, bargain, target, cajole, tax, and spend. During the war, pay-as-you-go taxation was implemented, together with a dramatically increased income-tax scope and higher rates. Budgeting became more developed and complex. Equally, direct planned management of markets became a key feature of domestic mobilization, as the government authoritatively moved billions of dollars in capital from place to place and induced workers to travel in order to find work that would support the war effort. Markets in capital and labor were organized by direction, with key decisions being taken either by executive officials from the president on down or by a process of negotiation among representatives of business, labor, and government.

During the war, a domestic battlefront took shape that pitted against each other planning and fiscal policy as ways to manage capitalism. For sure, these were not pure opposing categories. Both possessed visions of an active state, and in this manner were very different from the market-centered laissez-faire that had been discredited by the Great Depression. Planning included fiscal instruments, and the advocates of fiscal policy in part had to plan. Notwithstanding, each was a distinct orientation, understood as such by key actors at the time. What was unclear was what mix of policies, arrayed in which hierarchy, would govern over the long haul.

Fiscal policy scored the decisive victory. Key decisions included the choice to do away with the National Resources Planning Board (NRPB) and thus make the Bureau of the Budget the central coordinating site for economic affairs. These choices also included the postwar creation of a Council of Economic Advisers, and a shift in responsibility for the U.S. Employment Service from the Department of Labor to each of the forty-eight states. Labor questions, too, were shaped not all at once but in a series of wartime and postwar legislative decisions, culminating in 1947 with the Taft-Hartley Act. Although unions remained an important source of influence as the best-funded mass-based constituency group within the nonsouthern wing of the Democratic Party, the new law confined their possibilities and prevented labor from becoming a fully national political force. As a result, organized labor became a good deal less than its advocates had hoped and its adversaries had feared.[9]

I.

A FTER THE death of the National Recovery Administration in 1935, democratic planning faced steep barriers. By contrast, with the publication by John Maynard Keynes of *The General Theory of Employment, Interest and Money* in 1936, interventionist fiscal ideas gained growing traction both within the academy and in public life. Yet the planning impulse did not disappear. During the late 1930s and early 1940s, policy intellectuals and politicians revived the idea that government could, indeed must, directly intervene in sectors of the economy, including their labor markets.

A symposium of economists, sociologists, and political leaders convened in 1937 to discern how "planning, so far from being inimical to the democratic way of life," might come to stand "as one of its chief justifications and ultimate fulfillments."[10] With these guiding words by the prolific urbanist Lewis Mumford, a group of twenty-nine other distinguished contributors—including the economist Wesley Clair Mitchell, the sociologist W. F. Ogburn, the anthropologist Margaret Mead, the political scientist Harold Lasswell, and the philosopher Sidney Hook—probed the prospects for democratic planning even before the economic downturn hit the country. Mitchell called on the social sciences to specify how government can be "a positive force for the public good" by identifying proper relations between government and business.[11] Ogburn appealed for the development of regulatory means consistent with democracy to exercise control over the pace and direction of social change ("the logical means to control is planning; and adequate control must be based on planning in and for a changing society").[12] Mead looked to primitive societies as sources of motivation to a reliance on cooperation rather than competition.[13] Lasswell cautioned about the dangers of propaganda even in nondictatorial systems of planning, which he thought to be inevitable.[14] Hook stressed the importance of a "*democratic* conception of a socially planned order."[15]

This diverse group captured both the sweep and the ambiguities that were inherent in the idea of democratic planning. As the decade was ending, the centrist Brookings Institution published an extended analysis of steps that could build effectively on the New Deal's "shifts in the relationships of government to industry." Running some thirteen hundred dry pages, its two volumes ambitiously called for "a considerable extension of government power over economic life" to mold business firms, provide knowledge for effective planning, mold labor markets, adjust labor disputes, manage natural resources, and organize a welfare state.[16]

The agency best suited for these tasks was the NRPB, "the most nearly comprehensive planning organization this country has ever known."[17] The board had been founded in 1933 as part of the Public Works Administration and was made a presidential board the next year by an executive order issued by Franklin Roosevelt. Assigned the task of advising the president on long-range planning, what then was called the National Planning Board announced its purpose in 1934, in its first report:

> The experience of our day shows that no system, political or economic, unless it faces frankly the grave realities of modern economic and governmental life and boldly takes the initiative in broad plans for a better day, can be protection against explosion that wrecks and twists, while social discontent struggles to build some new structure promising more to the body and soul of those who feel themselves disinherited by the existing order of things.[18]

Drawing on a national community of social scientists and policy experts, the board's wide remit included public works, transportation, electric power, housing, welfare concerns, technology, natural resources, and the structure of the economy.[19] Looking back from the vantage point of 1939, the economist Allan Gruchy observed how such distinguished colleagues as Gardiner Means and Wesley Clair Mitchell had been developing an appealing approach to planning that promised to improve economic efficiency and achieve social values. Like that of the defunct NRA, this type of planning sought to build cooperation between business and labor in the public interest.[20]

Guided by a commitment to social citizenship, its longtime member Charles Merriam observed how the NRPB was organized to "plan primarily for freedom," and he stressed that "democratic planning aimed not at curtailing but at enlarging liberty."[21] This, of course, was not a unanimous view. Just as Merriam was writing these words, Friedrich Hayek was publishing *The Road to Serfdom*, which presented planning as a tragic illusion for democrats.[22] What both Merriam's and Hayek's writings signify is that planning was a subject for vibrant debate about economic and social policy, and whether it could serve as an instrument to protect democratic freedoms from dictatorial models. To be sure, the NRPB's importance should not be overestimated. In the main, it did not plan but, rather, called for planning by gathering information and offering proposals. Moreover, as it was dismantled at the height of World War II, the NRPB proved short-lived.

Yet its role, both practical and symbolic, was significant nevertheless. In 1939, Congress simultaneously established the NRPB and the Bureau of the Budget (BOB) in the Executive Office of the President. These agencies were to be the president's "principal management arms."[23] They were designed to work together. "The planning function," the NRPB's report of 1939 insisted, "is the natural and twin companion of the budget function. Long range plans are necessary to budget making."[24]

From this vantage point, the NRPB was both a collaborator and a competitor with the BOB. From its founding in 1921, the BOB had largely been restricted to promoting and enforcing norms of efficiency within the public sector. The vast majority of its work until 1939 centered on collecting departmental budget requests, preparing the budget document, conducting studies of management techniques, and submitting proposals to make government more effective. This limited set of responsibilities continued during the early years of the New Deal. The BOB experienced only trivial growth during the first two Roosevelt terms, and it did not begin to grow substantially before the decade ended.

These two presidential agencies represented overlapping and potentially complementary but distinct impulses: planning and fiscal policy. The NRPB sought to facilitate what it hoped would be a more egalitarian nation, while the BOB emerged as a confident instrument of fiscal policy. What is clear when we follow the scale of their budgets and the size of their staffs is that, at first, there was an implicit tilt toward planning as the master idea. At the time, the NRPB's budget was twice that of the BOB ($709,827, compared with $362,484), and its staff was some 50 percent larger (143 employees, compared with 103).[25] In 1939, as a former staffer recalled, the Bureau of the Budget was "a very small, very hidebound organization which viewed its main function as a 'no man' or as a sort of green shade manipulator of the figures in the budget book."[26] Its forty-five professionals conducted their work with just one calculator and one adding machine.[27]

This balance altered dramatically in the next half decade. By 1943, the

BOB's budget grew to twice the size of the NRPB's ($1,194,575, compared with $1,035,370); its staff became three times larger (352, compared with 129). By 1944, the NRPB was reduced to a skeleton staff of six and a budget of a mere $75,132 (compared with 360 and $2,415,425). By war's end, it was gone.[28] By then, the BOB's budget was higher than $3,110,000 and its staffing, located in the Executive Building adjacent to the White House, stood at 512. With the death of the NRPB, the BOB swiftly became "the most vital part of the Executive Office," as Wayne Coy remarked shortly before joining the Federal Communications Commission, after having served as an assistant budget director during World War II.[29]

The start of the European war in 1939 had provided new goals for the agency. These included eliminating resource shortages and production bottlenecks, and creating emergency systems for transportation, manpower policy, energy, and industrial production. Understanding that defense spending could be a powerful means to revitalize depressed areas, the BOB encouraged targeting such investments to economically stagnant counties, taking note of how the location of "defense facilities raises social and economic problems."[30] The new federal agency that placed these production facilities, the Plant Site Board of the Office of Production Management, was guided by the BOB's recommendations.

The NRPB's most significant and assertive activities concerned planning for postwar America. The board's spate of writings during the early years of World War II remains the most comprehensive elaboration ever produced in the United States on the role democratic planning might play within the country's political and economic institutions. Well before the United States entered World War II, President Roosevelt directed the agency in November 1940 to initiate studies of postwar planning. Its Post-War Agenda Section was particularly concerned to prevent a return to prewar economic conditions, especially the country's high rate of unemployment. Taken together, the pamphlets and reports the board issued constituted an ambitious effort to articulate a vision of how the national state should direct markets, ensure high levels of employment, and provide comprehensive social welfare.[31] In a credo issued in 1942, the board announced the aim of cleansing capitalism from "irresponsible private power, arbitrary public authority, and unregulated monopolies." Through planning, it insisted, the federal government could help secure "a greater freedom for the American people."[32]

As the board pressed this case, the Bureau of the Budget also grew in stature and responsibility. With the shift of the BOB from the Treasury to the Executive Office of the President in 1939, the agency entered a vigorous stage of expansion under the aegis of its new director, Harold Smith. A capable Michigan reformer and state budget director, Smith often used the simile of a central nervous system in describing the BOB's role. Its dominant perspective was a Keynesian one, using budget surpluses and deficits as means to grapple with the business cycle, a position that members of the pivotal Fiscal Division and Smith often articulated. Speaking at Allegheny College in 1940, Smith characterized the federal government as "a great service enterprise which not only gives protection and care to individuals, but also undertakes to influence the business cycle in such fashion as to minimize its impact upon our citizens." The budget, he argued, was government's key tool, "the most accurate measure of this significant transition in the responsibility of government."[33] A key BOB manager, Donald Stone, who led the Division of Administrative Management, explained that this approach differed from that of the more interventionist NRPB. The board "mainly is concerned with long-range problems of the physical and human resources of the country," while the BOB is responsible for finding fiscal means with which to stabilize employment and prices in the here and now.[34]

The BOB developed the concept of a national budget to promote a low-inflation, high-employment economy. Its economists, including its chief fiscal analyst, the New School's Gerhard Colm, turned the budget into an economic policy instrument that utilized fiscal tools to deal with these fundamental macroeconomic issues. Of the agency's five increasingly capable divisions, the Fiscal Division grew most rapidly.[35] By mobilizing the expertise of those in the economics profession, and by incorporating their skills and knowledge into the heart of the bureau, this division's professional staff placed budgeting within the context of larger economic and financial trends. Prior to 1939, the professional service of the bureau had been staffed exclusively by lawyers. That year, Smith engineered a radical transformation by employing fifteen economists out of the total professional staff of nineteen; by 1946, thirty-nine full-time economists were on his staff.[36] Once simply the accounting arm of the federal government, the bureau became a crucial site of fiscal intelligence and policy.

As late as 1942, President Roosevelt continued to anticipate that the

NRPB and BOB would work in tandem to steer the U.S. economy during and after the war. In transmitting the board's *Report for 1942—National Resources Development* to Congress in January, he announced how this served as the first instance in "establishing the custom of an annual planning report as a companion document to the Budget of the United States."[37] Congress, however, imposed a different result. In a dramatic turn of events, the board was abolished and the BOB was placed in a position of commanding authority. Once again, the South's role in directing the nature of the debate and in determining legislative outcomes proved pivotal.

The key decision to starve the board of its funding was made in the spring of 1943. The November 1942 elections had produced significant gains for Republican representation when many Italian and German constituencies shifted their vote, and as many Americans had tired of the New Deal and yearned for change. The Democratic Party lost 45 seats in the House. Despite losing the overall popular vote, gaining just 46 percent, the Democrats maintained a modest majority of 222 to 209, based on their unyielding southern representation.[38] In the Senate, the Democrats lost 8 seats, but maintained a 20-seat, 57–37 majority. Though historians differ about the intensity of President Roosevelt's efforts to keep the agency,[39] it is clear that straight party-line voting in Congress would have preserved the NRPB and its budget.

The South, we have seen, had ample reasons to be partial to planning. Some southern voices expressed appreciation, if in muted terms, for "the very material service" the board had rendered the South and the country, as Alabama's Lister Hill put the point; for its "creditable . . . working in the right direction," in the words of Florida's Claude Pepper.[40] Yet for each of these southern Democrats, there were as many others who simply and silently voted no, or worried aloud about how planning threatened interference in matters best left to the states. Maryland Democrat Millard Tydings archly remarked that "the Board ought to be called the Board of Political Textbooks of a Certain Strain rather than the National Resources Planning Board."[41] Describing abolition of the agency as an issue of "major importance," Virginia's Senator Harry Byrd, who chaired the Joint Economic Committee, explained that a crucial consideration was the ability of Congress, rather than the executive branch, to control postwar planning. Conceding that "we must have post-war planning," he insisted that it must differ from the Washington-based, centralized "pre-war domestic planning that characterized the economic policies of the New Deal."[42] In May 1943, he declared, "I hope that the entire National Resources Planning Board will be abolished," and that Congress would end appropriations for the agency.[43]

This became a steady southern theme. "If we are to have Government planning," the *Baltimore Sun* editorialized, "it should be planning which assumes that the greater the field of postwar activity which can be trusted to private initiative and local and State governments, the better the chance that our freedom will survive."[44] In April 1943, a gathering of southern governors at the Southern Regional Conference of the Council of State Governments in Atlanta resolved that the end of the war must bring a close to federal domination of planning and a shift of primary responsibility to the states. Even the most progressive of these leaders, Ellis Arnall of Georgia, announced that he had to yield to the doctrine of states' rights even though "I don't subscribe, as most of the gentlemen here do, to the moth-eaten doctrine."[45] Hands off the South and its racial order was the dominant message.

The NRPB began the budget cycle for the 1944 fiscal year with a call by the president for $1,400,000, and authorization for a staff of 350. This request was rebuffed in the House by the Appropriations Committee, chaired by Clarence Cannon of Missouri; fourteen of its twenty-five Democrats were southern. With Republicans unanimously opposed to the NRPB, "some Democrats," Marion Clawson somewhat blandly reports, "teaming up" with Republicans, were able to defeat any appropriation for the agency.[46] This outcome was yet another instance, a reporter on Capitol Hill noted, that bore out "predictions that on many issues Southern Democrats would combine with the minority party and control the House."[47] A similar pattern prevailed in the Senate, where southern votes tipped the balance.

Lacking funds, the board had no choice but to dismantle its operations.[48] "Our swan song has been sung for us by Congress," its chairman, Frederic Delano (the president's uncle), lamented when he visited the White House to offer the president the agency's final report.[49]

II.

ALTHOUGH ITS staff was dispersed and its files sent to the National Archives, the NRPB's ideas did retain some currency. They resonated in President Roosevelt's call for a Second Bill of Rights in his January 1944

State of the Union address, which sought to renew a progressive—one might say radical—New Deal, and in his "Sixty Million Jobs" speech in that year's presidential campaign. They also informed President Truman's first major domestic policy message, "21 Points," in September 1945, and served as a centerpiece for Henry Wallace's ill-fated 1948 Progressive Party bid for the presidency.[50] Key legislative proposals tried to advance these goals. Notably, the original Senate full-employment bill of 1945 combined aspects of corporatism and planning, and gave the president the authority to organize advisory boards consisting of representatives of business, labor, and agriculture, as well as state and local governments, to assist in assuring robust economic growth and the creation of jobs for all who wished to work. It was understood that these goals would require a new steering mechanism, one more powerful then the NRPB, and closer to the intended capacities of the NRA of the early New Deal. One such candidate was the Office of War Mobilization and Reconversion.

But with the end of the agency and the concomitant rise of the Bureau of the Budget to the executive branch's central steering role, planning went into an eclipse. Its policy space was filled by fiscal ideas and policies. With this shift, both the ability and the willingness of the federal government to affect the details of the economy's sectors and regional qualities was replaced by a more remote and general manipulation of budget sums and by more decentralized policy capacities. Both trends appealed to southern representatives because they were far less menacing and far more compatible with local decision making about the region's entwined economic and racial affairs. A notable instance was the passage not of the planning-oriented Full Employment Bill, but the alternative, generated in the House by Mississippi's William Whittington, who recommended the "establishment of a permanent board, agency, or commission, to give to the President of the United States the best available expert advice" about fiscal policy without a tandem apparatus for planning or implementation. This proposal found its way into law as part of the 1946 Employment Act, a law that created a Council of Economic Advisers (CEA) in the office of the president as a partner to the Bureau of the Budget. Limited to an advisory function, the CEA was required to report both to the president and to a newly created Congressional Joint Committee on the Economic Report.[51]

The Employment Act was a contradictory piece of legislation. It called for maintaining the "conditions" for full employment and maximum levels of output and purchasing power while insisting on "promoting" free enterprise, untrammeled by government planning. As a result, there was competition for representation on the council during the Truman years between planning-oriented economists like Leon Keyserling, who wished to devise programs of direct adjustment, and business-oriented economists like John Clark, who put great faith in the capacity of markets to behave rationally. The compromise, and dominant position, was represented by its chair, the agricultural economist Edwin Nourse from the Brookings Institution, who favored using the federal government to modify economic aggregates while leaving major hiring and investment decisions in the hands of firms acting in accord with market criteria.

The CEA was deliberately kept small. Its spending in the Truman years averaged some $300,000 each year, and its average staff of thirty-eight was composed mainly of academic economists and clerks.[52] Its role, however, should not be underestimated, for its policy stance, like that of the larger BOB, was very different from that which was being advocated by many conservatives in the late 1940s. The CEA helped build a new kind of fiscal capacity, underpinned by a broad spectrum of opinion within the Democratic Party, that required a radical break from budget-balancing orthodoxy. The fiscal policies of the CEA represented nothing so much as an extension of the ideas that were motivating the Fiscal Policy Division of the Bureau of the Budget. In fact, three of the CEA's key staff members—Gerhard Colm, John Davis, and Frances James—were recruited from the bureau.[53]

Despite its many internal tensions, the Democratic Party was able to unite with enthusiasm to support this fiscal turn. While it promised an active role for government in managing the economy, its "hands-off" character, as distinct from planning, made it attractive to southern leaders. With interventionist planning taken out of the equation, straight party-line votes were typical. Thus, on a January 31, 1941, motion by a New York Republican to recommit a 1942 appropriations bill with instructions to substantially reduce nondefense spending, every Republican but one voted aye, while every southern member who cast a vote joined all other Democrats but three to vote nay. The conference report on the Employment Bill that created the CEA was supported on February 6, 1946, by nine out of ten southern members, and a 1949 proposal to increase spending on the CEA garnered the support of all but one southern senator. With the South in tow, policies that enhanced the fiscal capacities of the federal government routinely passed despite sharp Republican objections.

But, significantly, this cross-region Democratic Party coalition fell apart just as soon as economic action touched the South's labor markets. During the 1940s, national employment policy pivoted on two questions. Where in the federal system would responsibility be lodged, in Washington or in the states? Within the federal government, would responsibility for jobs belong to the Department of Labor or to some other unit of government less sympathetic to unions and the concerns of working people? Crucially, the willingness of southern representatives to join hands with congressional Republicans decentralized the U.S. Employment Service and removed it from the Department of Labor.

The country's first large-scale experiment with a federal employment service dated from World War I, a program of job placement that peaked with 832 offices and a budget of nearly $6 million in 1918.[54] With the end of the war, this version of the U.S. Employment Service (USES) essentially folded. By 1924, it had a budget of only some $79,000 and its functions were moved out of the Department of Labor to the various states.[55]

The rebirth of a federal system to manage the supply and job placement of labor came in 1933, with the passage of the Wagner-Peyser Act, which created a new employment service within the Department of Labor. Among other tasks, the new USES channeled the unemployed to public-works jobs.[56] It also provided grants to states to establish and maintain employment centers that both actively aided job placement by routing workers to available employment and determined eligibility to unemployment insurance once this national program was created under the aegis of the Social Security Act in 1935.[57]

The entry of the United States into World War II produced an enhanced version of the manpower policies of World War I when President Roosevelt recentralized the USES in January 1942 by executive order. Transferred to the War Manpower Commission, the agency placed more than twelve million workers in jobs that year through seventeen hundred local offices administered from Washington. In balancing wartime supply and demand for labor and in coordinating a national labor exchange of unprecedented scale, the USES reached a budget of $58 million in 1945, during the last year of the war, which rivaled that of the entire Department of Labor. It also had four times as many employees, 20,628 as compared with 5,662.[58]

During this period, the federal government developed an unprecedented capacity to intervene in labor markets to maintain an efficient distribution of labor. It was a form of intervention that was a good deal more focused and domineering than the fiscal policies pursued by the BOB, rather more like those that had been advocated by the NRPB. Instead of using tax incentives or other such devices to affect employment, the USES directly adjusted the labor supply to meet the needs of wartime production by acting as a national employment agency that matched workers with job openings posted by employers. To be sure, the USES never moved workers from place to place or compelled anyone to work. Nor did it engage in large-scale training programs or set the price of labor. Just the same, the agency represented the most assertive example of an intervention by the national government in the labor market, short of conscription, in American history.

Just as World War II was ending with atomic explosions over Hiroshima and Nagasaki, the Truman administration was determining how to keep these capacities within the federal government in order to guide a transition to the peacetime economy. "The task of helping this array of job seekers seeking to fit themselves into the peacetime economy," the president told Congress on September 6, 1945, soon after Japan's surrender, "is fully as difficult as the mobilization of manpower for war." In spelling out his twenty-one-point reconversion program, he argued that "any decided change in the machinery to handle this problem now would cause unnecessary hardship to workers and veterans." Accordingly, he continued, "I urgently recommend that the Congress not yet return the Employment Service to the States."[59]

Two weeks after his speech, the president transferred the USES from the War Manpower Commission to the Department of Labor by executive order under the authority of the War Powers Act.[60] This shift was part of a larger effort on his part to strengthen this cabinet agency, shifting its central purpose from collecting statistical data to policy initiatives and oversight, just as growing union strength was deepening the working-class electoral base of the Democratic Party. To lead a strengthened agency, the president selected a labor lawyer and former Washington State Democratic senator, the ardent New Dealer Lewis Schwellenbach.

Truman's administrative decision set off a heated congressional debate (the April 1946 *Congressional Digest* "controversy of the month") that focused on whether the federal government or the states should take responsibility for employment policy. The competing visions crystallized in a competition between two versions of how the Wagner-Peyser Act of 1933 should be amended. An administration bill, stoutly supported by President Truman, continued the full federal status of USES through June 1947. Crucially, it also authorized the strict oversight of state and local employment offices by the Department of Labor after their return to the states.[61]

An alternative to this administration bill proposed by Congressman Everett Dirksen, the Illinois Republican, favored full and unsupervised decentralization. It mandated a return of USES offices to the states a year earlier, by the close of June 1946. The House debated these options in January 1946. The arguments broke along clear party and sectional lines. Southern Democrats apprehensive about the implications of federal government control of labor policy for race relations joined the Republicans to favor the Dirksen option. Every Democrat who spoke against the administration bill was southern; every southerner but one who spoke in this debate opposed his party's position.[62]

Like their Republican allies, they feared that an additional year might lead to a decision to keep USES offices permanently in federal hands. Dirksen forcefully argued that if the federal government were allowed to retain control until June 30, 1947, "the effort will be unrelenting to Federalize this system. You can bet all the tea in China on the fact that there is a definite effort to keep this in federal hands."[63] Southern speakers echoed this argument.[64] They were concerned that the creation of new federal powers for the secretary of labor, which looked "mighty funny for anybody who wants to close out Federal activities," as Hatton Sumners of Texas put the point, might serve as an excuse for prolonged federal control. Arguing that "this proposed legislation . . . is one of the most important items of legislation that has come before this Congress in a long time," he cautioned, "Wait until this overload of federal power is turned loose, wait until this outfit turns loose its power and you will wait until doomsday."[65]

What most worried southern members was that new federal powers after the return of employment offices to the states would change the racial situation. Again and again, they insisted that both job placement and the supervision of unemployment claims must lie with state government, and thus opposed, as Ezekiel Gathings of Arkansas insisted, "legislation in which the Secretary of Labor and the Federal Government would maintain absolute control and domination over all phases of employment practices. . . . We only ask that we be permitted in the several States to solve our own employment problems."[66]

This plea for self-determination was explicitly grounded in qualms about the impact of federal control of labor markets for the South's economy, especially agriculture, for race, and for the growing power of organized labor. A truly national labor system threatened to erode the ability of plantations to hold on to low-paid field-workers. Making this point, Gathings put in the record an advertisement the USES had run in a local Arkansas newspaper in 1944 that read:

Unskilled labor: Work for one of the largest steel companies in Pennsylvania. Transportation paid by employer. Available housing. Forty-eight-hour workweek. Time and one-half after 40 hours. Representative will hire at United States Employment Service. Helena, Ark. September 21, 22, 23.

Lamenting that "one-fourth to one-third of the cotton produced in 1945 in Arkansas remains in the field unpicked," he announced how "we have not forgotten that our labor has been taken away from the agricultural sections of the country and transplanted in the metropolitan areas, leaving farm houses empty and an inadequate supply of labor to harvest the crops."[67] Gathings further suggested that federal control of the employment services had caused unemployment compensation to be paid in a way that was continuing to diminish the incentive for poor workers who remained in the South to participate in agricultural labor. He stated, "What little labor we have in the South available for farm work has stopped working and are drawing allotment checks, unemployment compensation or other Federal benefits."[68]

Setting what became a recurring theme, Gathings also attacked the bill for the authority it conferred on the secretary of labor to compel states to treat applicants equally, thus prohibiting racial discrimination. "Why this bill," he exclaimed, "goes so far as giving the Secretary of Labor the power to set all of the standards from Washington," and "to assure equal referral opportunities for equally qualified applicants and at wages and working conditions which are not less favorable to the individual than those prevailing on similar work in the locality."[69] In this objection, he echoed Robert Doughton of North Carolina, who, recalling the wartime Fair Employment Practices Committee, objected that the proposed law threatened to "establish at the whim of the Secretary of Labor a modified but nevertheless effective FEPC."[70] By contrast, the decentralization of employment offices would permit the maintenance of separate offices for black and white workers, a pattern that indeed did come to exist "at least through the 1960s."[71]

The South identified the burgeoning union movement as the force most central to the effort to maintain and enhance federal control over local labor markets. Recalling how both the president of the AFL, William Green, and the secretary-treasurer of the CIO, James Carey, had testified positively during the hearings conducted by the Committee on Labor on which he served, Randolph reported how "organized labor strongly urged that only a unified national system of offices could guide and place a mobile labor force without being restricted by state boundaries. . . ."[72] Paul Stewart of Oklahoma interpreted this with respect to "a bill that makes labor laws by labor union directives" as a result of labor's preferences and growing influence. The consequence, he complained, is that the USES acts as "a clearance house for the unions."[73]

Despite overwhelming support by nonsouthern Democrats, the votes of three-quarters of their southern colleagues, and a nearly unanimous Republican Party ensured the success of the Dirksen alternative.[74] Once more, a crucial decision about national power was shaped decisively by southern roll-call behavior. By this decision, the USES was reduced to becoming a funnel for funds for the states to use as they wished, which, for southern states, included the capacity to reinforce racial discrimination in employment.[75]

The success of their representatives in thwarting a federal USES was matched by their ability to prevent unemployment insurance from being administered from Washington, and especially by their skill in working with Republicans to alter essential features of national labor law. Both are stories of southern power.

Federal control over unemployment compensation was regarded by southern representatives as even a greater threat to their social system than federal control over employment services. In 1935, the Social Security Act had placed control over eligibility and benefit levels for unemployed workers in the hands of the states; southern benefits tended to be especially miserly. A decade later, as Congress considered the War Mobilization and Reconversion Act in September 1945, Senator Robert Wagner of New York led an attempt to create uniform national standards for unemployment insurance during the period of transition from a wartime to peacetime economy.[76] The legislation that was considered by the Finance Committee would have extended the duration and added federal payments to state benefit levels, and it stipulated that "Federal machinery" administer payments in order to overcome the country's widely divergent standards. This bill further alarmed the South because it would have extended unemployment insurance coverage for the first time to the primarily black labor force in agricultural processing.[77] While this was a temporary bill to deal with economic reconversion, Wagner made clear that this was to be a first step in implementing a federal system of unemployment insurance on a permanent basis that would replace the individual state systems.[78]

The Finance Committee was dominated by southern senators. Five of the six most senior members of the committee's Democratic majority were southern, including its chair, Georgia's Walter George. Joined by Maryland's more junior George Radcliffe, half of the twelve Democrats were southern. With the party possessing only a 12–9 committee majority, these southerners, who effectively controlled the committee, proceeded to gut the idea of national standards. Their committee rejected all the provisions Wagner had sponsored, including the coverage for agricultural-processing employees.[79] When an attempt was made on the Senate floor to reverse the committee's decisions by supplementing state payments with federal funds to bring them up to a uniform twenty-five dollars per week and extend the maximum period of eligibility to twenty-six weeks under all state systems, southern senators overwhelmingly joined the Republicans on September 19 to defeat the amendment.[80]

Despite such aggressive efforts, the issue simply would not disappear. As the Senate again debated a plan to transfer the administration of unemployment compensation to the Department of Labor in March 1948, the Texas Manufacturers Association and the South Carolina Chamber of Commerce vehemently lobbied to oppose the bill as an assault on the South's ability to discriminate on the basis of race. Titled "News and Views on Legislation: Action Required if FEPC by Default is to be Avoided—This Tells How," the letter, entered into the *Congressional Record,* argued that "permanent supervisory control over the unemployment compensation and employment service functions of the 48 states" by the Department of Labor "will mean the subjection of the State systems to carrying out, indirectly but nevertheless effectively, FEPC policies through the rule-making and purse-string-control powers of the Secretary of Labor."[81] Yet again, southern Democrats, voting with Republicans, succeeded in scuttling the change.[82]

III.

DURING WORLD War II, USES offices in many southern cities ran segregated, sometimes entirely separate, offices to serve whites and blacks. They routinely made referrals in accordance with employer requests for "whites only" skilled and clerical positions, and "blacks only" positions for laborers, janitors, and maids. They regularly did not refer skilled African-American workers to available and suitable skilled jobs in war industries. Further, following the war, some southern USES offices began working in conjunction with state unemployment compensation offices to deny benefits to skilled blacks if they refused to accept referrals to unskilled jobs.[83]

These and other discriminatory practices brought southern USES administrators into conflict with the FEPC. In June 1941, President Roosevelt had created the Fair Employment Practices Committee as a wartime agency by an executive order prohibiting the federal government from discriminating in its hiring practices on the basis of race, color, creed, or national origin, and further requiring federal agencies to negotiate contracts with private employers certifying they would abjure bias on any of those grounds. The FEPC was charged to probe and find remedies for complaints of hiring prejudice. Shortly after its inception, it began investigating defense industries in the South, holding hearings in Birmingham in May 1942 to make its findings of discrimination public. Moreover, in response to numerous complaints about the discriminatory practices of southern USES offices, it investigated and successfully pressured southern offices to cease advertising in "jobs for whites" and "jobs for colored" sections of local newspapers and to provide identical job listings for both whites and blacks searching for work.[84]

Nine months after Congress acted at the start of 1946 to decentralize the USES, Secretary of Labor Schwellenbach sought to ban such discrimination. On September 6, rules sent to USES field offices explicitly stated that it was the "policy of the USES to service all orders by referring workers on the basis of occupational qualifications, without regard to discriminatory qualifications concerning race, creed, color, national origin or citizenship (unless citizenship is a legal requirement) when such workers are available." This stipulation was short-lived. After the southern states strenuously objected later that month, on the twentieth, at a meeting held at the Department of Labor, the regulation was rescinded, but not before underscoring for the white South how labor market issues might undermine the economic underpinnings of the region's racial order.[85]

The link between labor market and civil rights questions quickly centered on unions. As a leading economist, Orme Phelps, observed in 1947, "no domestic issue exceeds in importance and no issue, domestic or foreign, has received more attention since World War II than that of the proper policy to be observed in labor disputes."[86] We have already seen how during World War II successful labor organization in the South and its implications for race relations had shocked southerners.[87] George Gallup discovered in 1943 that national labor policy, particularly the growth of unions under Wagner Act auspices, and thus "what they consider the poor handling of labor or the 'coddling of unions'" was "the chief complaint" in southern mass opinion about the New Deal.[88] During and just after the war, the coalition that southern members had begun to fashion with Republicans on labor union issues in 1939 grew to near-unanimous solidarity as southern legislators moved vigorously in Congress to alter the institutional rules within which unions could operate. Three such efforts stand out: the War Labor Disputes Act (WLDA, or the Smith-Connally Act) of 1943, which passed despite President Roosevelt's veto; the Case Bill of 1946, which passed both houses but was successfully vetoed by President Truman; and the Taft-Hartley Act of 1947, passed by Congress by overriding President Truman's veto.

As sponsors, House Democrat Howard Smith of Virginia in partnership with Senator Tom Connally of Texas gave the WLDA a southern pedigree. Union power, they insisted, had to be curbed. "We have permitted political organization, under the name of organized labor, to grow to such proportions," Albert Gore of Tennessee cautioned, "that they now threaten the sovereignty of the Government itself."[89] To bring unions under control, they and their southern colleagues supported increasing federal administrative authority over the labor relationship by giving statutory authority to a War Labor Board, authorizing the president to seize and operate struck plants, requiring a thirty-day notice to the NLRB prior to striking in a labor dispute that might interrupt war production, mandating a secret strike ballot on the thirtieth day, if the dispute had not been resolved, and prohibiting labor organizations from making national election political contributions, a move that would have weakened the national Democratic Party.[90] Almost every southern member of the House voted with Republicans to pass the WLDA.[91] In the Senate, southern and Republican voting patterns to override the president's veto were identical.[92] Much southern rhetoric was both anxious and inflammatory. Referring to labor organizers from northern industrial centers, Georgia's John Gibson, cited "the nefarious and dastardly attempts of the Communist to fool the lower classes, and especially the American Negro."[93] When a number of Republicans sought to introduce an amendment banning discrimination in employment and union membership, a quick objection by Senator Tom Connally of Texas saw the amendment defeated by voice vote; most Republicans understood that its passage would doom the bill.

Southern defections from Democratic Party positions in 1943 in effect constituted a declaration of war on their colleagues for whom labor unions had become the single most important source of money, political muscle, and votes. This party schism deepened in 1946 with the debate about the Case bill, sponsored by New Jersey Republican Clifford Case, which sought to curb strikes by mandating a sixty-day cooling-off period before a strike could begin, a prohibition against violence or conspiracy that interferes with the movement of goods in interstate commerce, monetary damages against unions for contract violations, and the proscription of secondary boycotts.[94] Once again, it was a nearly perfectly aligned coalition of southern Democrats and Republicans that passed the bill in both chambers.[95] The legislation failed only when the House narrowly failed to override the presidential veto by five votes (a vote on which southerners voted with Republicans).

Southerners were vocal supporters of the bill. During protracted floor debates, they expressed concern about the power of organized labor, especially the CIO, to bring the national economy to a grinding halt, and the potential impact of unions on the racial order. They also resurrected longstanding southern tropes about the colonial dominance of the North.[96] Responding to critics of the bill who had argued that it represented not just an antilabor but an antiurban bias by rural sectional interests, Paul Stewart, an Oklahoma Democrat, responded by arguing "that from the viewpoint of the big industrial cities, the agricultural states are just colonies." Using populist language, he went on to say that "the people are going to take over. . . . They are getting tired of this minority stuff, and labor is the predominant minority group that is trying to wreck the government." Labor, he continued, had become "stronger than the law or any political organization that has ever been in power in this country, a supergovernment within this great Government that we love so well."[97]

However exaggerated, such fears were accelerating in 1946. A special issue of *Fortune* fretfully described the country's rising industrial conflict. With labor "scarce, expensive, and rebellious," it chronicled the accelerating number of picket lines on the docks, and in the key industries of steel, coal, automobiles, and electrical products. It also wryly noted that even elevator operators, barbers, and bakers were taking strike action. In all, the magazine identified how "all the arguments and all the strikes of 1945–46 really boiled down to a single issue," which it identified as the vexing question of "the role of a strong labor movement in a democratic, capitalistic state." With a massive wave of strikes pummeling American industry—at one point, nearly 2,000,000 workers were on strike simultaneously; 3,470,000 workers struck in 1945 and 4,600,000 in 1946, when fully 116,000,000 "man days" were lost to the economy—and with union membership having tripled in the decade since the passage of the Wagner Act, the labor question had become "the most urgent of the country's domestic problems."[98] The country remained transfixed by the huge strikes of mine workers and railroad workers in the spring of 1946, and the seizure of the railroads by President Truman on May 17, just as the Case bill was being debated.[99]

What was especially notable, *Fortune* further commented, was how, in building on their quite stunning wartime gains, both the AFL and the CIO had set out to conquer the South, which it designated as "the last U.S. labor frontier." The CIO's executive board launched Operation Dixie in February 1946, an operation with headquarters in Atlanta and led by a long-time organizer Van Amberg Bittner, who had scored big successes in coal, steel, and meatpacking drives, and who commanded an initial budget of $1,250,000. This campaign was driven by a mix of necessity and opportunity. With the South far less integrated into national unions than the rest of the country, the CIO feared that low-wage unorganized southern firms would undercut national wages and induce companies to move away from centers of union strength. There also was a political factor, the wish to counteract southern congressional hostility to organized labor. In turn, the AFL responded by opening what its president, William Green, called "a crusade to organize the unorganized workers of the South" at the third Southern Labor Conference the AFL held in Asheville, North Carolina, in May 1946.[100]

In addition to menacing the region's traditional low-wage and racially inscribed cotton fields, textile firms, and mines, these union drives posed a more tangible, direct threat to southern patterns. During World War II, even before Operation Dixie, the Washington headquarters of the CIO was issuing widely circulated pamphlet materials opposing racism. "The CIO and the Negro Worker: Together for Victory" stressed, in 1942, "the great contribution" of the organization in acting "to break down the barriers which have existed in the past between Negro and white workers in labor organizations," a form of unity necessary for "the resistance of our own people to Hitler and his Japanese allies." It boasted how a "southern drive" was bringing "many thousands of Southern workers, Negro and white alike . . . under the protection of the CIO." In 1943, it underscored the need for "working and fighting together regardless of race, creed, color, or national origin." As the war drew to a close, its National CIO Committee to Abolish Discrimination called for equal treatment in employment and housing, and, after the war, this committee continued to press for a permanent FEPC.[101]

Fortune's report noted that "both the A.F. of L. and C.I.O. southern leaders are convinced that organizing in the South means organizing white and Negro workers." To be sure, the AFL largely kept white and black workers apart in segregated union locals, and the CIO, while placing blacks and whites in the same organization, often took care in the South to address larger questions of Jim Crow only very gingerly. But with both federations understanding "that southern whites and Negroes must be organized together if they work together," all the key actors understood how much was at stake, especially as the CIO often entered into alliances of cooperation to promote litigation on labor-related issues with the NAACP in the early years of the wartime and postwar civil rights movement.[102]

In these circumstances, both employers and politicians in the South proved "willing to fan the flames of race feeling" to prevent the organization of southern plants.[103] They understood just how deeply race and labor inter-twined. "Over the years," *Fortune* projected, "it may well be that the most important effect of southern unionism will be in the field of Negro-white relationships." Since Reconstruction, it recalled,

> segregation has so increased in efficiency that today, novel as the idea may seem to most Southerners, the South's two great popula-tion groups are almost strangers to each other. They live in different sections, go to different schools, worship in different churches, read different newspapers, shop in different stores, seek different places of amusement, live separate lives, and are buried in separate ceme-teries. *The only local institution that southern whites and Negroes have in common today is the labor union.*[104]

It was this recognition, coupled with the widespread sense that both the AFL and CIO were in a strong strategic position in the South, that led the magazine to conclude that "there is little doubt that eventually the South can be organized. . . . The question is not whether, but when."[105]

When never arrived.[106] The principal reason was the radical shift to labor law that the South, together with Republican congressional allies, succeeded in producing in 1947. This legislation transformed the prospects for U.S. unions—across the country and especially in the South. On June 23, 1947, the Labor-Management Relations Act, the Taft-Hartley law, passed over the veto of President Truman, who denounced it as a "slave labor bill." The act, which was technically a series of amendments to the National Labor Rela-tions Act (Wagner Act) of 1935, dramatically shifted power in favor of own-ers and managers. The major provisions of the Wagner Act had included exclusive union representation in any given bargaining unit, and restrictions on unfair labor practices by employers. Taft-Hartley dramatically relocated the vectors of labor and management bargaining capacities.

Taking note of the coalition of Republicans and southern Democrats, the editorial page of the *New York Times* celebrated how the bill "has been approved with a larger majority of both parties in both Houses than Con-gress has ever mustered . . . on other controversial measures of similar impor-tance which have aroused controversy—Lend-Lease, Selective Service, and the Hull Trade Agreements Act, for example."[107] Taft-Hartley's proponents and foes understood the legislation in the same terms, even as they evaluated its desirability in dramatically different ways. The law, its Senate sponsor, Republican Robert Taft of Ohio, argued, was passed "to restore justice and equality in labor relations . . . and to eliminate special privileges conferred on labor union officials by law and administrative regulation." The law, President Truman averred, would "go far toward weakening our trade union movement" by converting the National Labor Relations Act "from an instrument with the major purpose of protecting the right of workers to organize and bargain collectively into a maze of pitfalls and complex procedures."[108]

Truman's own 1947 State of the Union message had called for modest amendments to the Wagner Act to ban certain types of secondary boycotts, jurisdictional strikes, and strikes over contract interpretation; he also called for better machinery for mediation and arbitration. The bill introduced by Republicans Fred Hartley in the House and Taft in the Senate was far more sweeping. It narrowed the definition of who counted as an employer under the law, and it excluded independent contractors and foremen from the meaning of the term *employee*. To the rights of employees to join or assist unions, bargain collectively through representatives, and have the right to strike "for the purpose of collective bargaining," the new law appended new language. It stipulated that workers "shall also have the right to refrain from any or all such activities" unless an existing agreement compelled union membership. Acts by union members, moreover, were to be constrained by a redefinition of an unfair labor practice to include "interference with an employee's rights of non-membership." This stipulation effectively banned closed union shops that required union membership as a condition of being hired.

Crucially, the law authorized states to pass "right to work" laws. These could make it illegal by state action to require workers to pay union dues as a condition of their employment. And even where no right-to-work law existed, Taft-Hartley required union shop provisions to be approved by a majority of the membership in a secret ballot. These measures were aimed to promote open shops that made it voluntary to join a union even after it was recognized through Wagner Act procedures. As a result, union organizing was made dramatically more difficult, especially in right-to-work states. By the early 1950s, Alabama, Arkansas, Florida, Georgia, Mississippi, North Carolina, South Carolina, Tennessee, Texas, and Virginia had passed such laws, effectively bringing labor organization to a halt.[109]

Two other features are especially noteworthy. Taft-Hartley kept the exact language of the Wagner Act regarding the exemption of agricultural workers and maids, stipulating that the law "shall not include any individual employed as an agricultural laborer, or in the domestic service of any family or person at his home." But in fact the agricultural exclusion was substantially expanded. When the Wagner Act passed in 1935, this set of exclusions had not been the subject of open debate, since the Democratic Party then convened a compromise in which the South went along with the North on labor, and the North went along with the South on occupational exemptions in order to leave southern race relations untouched. But with the collapse of this arrangement, the legislative record contains open disagreement about what amounted to an even wider agricultural exclusion, of the extended kind nonsouthern Democrats had agreed to in the 1938 version of the Fair Labor Standards Act.

In the House, every Republican who served on the Labor Committee was joined by its four southern Democrats (Graham Barden of North Carolina, Ovie Clark Fisher of Texas, John Wood of Georgia, and Wingate Lucas of Texas) to support widening the exclusion to include workers who handled, dried, packaged, processed, froze, stored, or delivered crops, the vast majority of whom in the South were black. The six Democrats who opposed this extension notably included Harlem's African-American representative, Adam Clayton Powell Jr., and a future president of the United States, John F. Kennedy. In the Senate Committee, only Florida's Claude Pepper demurred, while Louisiana's Allen Ellender and Alabama's Lister Hill joined the Republican majority. There was little debate on the matter once the bill reached the floor, though Robert Wagner did excoriate fellow Democrats who voted with Republicans in favor of "excluding agricultural workers."[110]

A key element of the new law was its expansion of activities that it labeled "unfair labor practices," including secondary boycotts, picketing, or strikes that targeted companies doing business with a firm where the union was engaged in a labor dispute. But as the historian Hugh Davis Graham pointed out, despite this development, "racial discrimination as an unfair labor practice was expressly rejected by Congress when it passed Taft-Hartley."[111] As Senator Taft explained, "Let us take the case of unions which prohibit the admission of Negroes to membership. If they prohibit the admission of

Negroes to membership, they may continue to do so; but representatives of the union cannot go to the employer and say, 'You have got to fire this man because he is not a member of the union.'" Further, Florida's Spessard Holland successfully included an amendment specifying that unfair labor practice provisions "shall not impair the right of a labor organization to prescribe its own rules with respect to the acquisition or retention of membership therein."[112] With such reassurances, Virginia's Howard Smith reminded the House after the law had been signed that care had been taken to make sure that no FEPC requirements had been smuggled in.[113]

Republican support for Taft-Hartley was based on a variety of motives. Influenced not only by established big industry that had made a kind of peace with labor but wished to protect its traditional managerial prerogatives, but by upstart, strongly anti-union entrepreneurs who had extreme free-market commitments, congressional Republicans were concerned that union wages might make many firms uncompetitive. They also desired to roll back any remaining prospects for democratic planning and corporatism that would require effective union representation. Additionally, they sought to punish unions that had actively been mobilizing to elect Democratic Party candidates, and they hoped to eliminate Communist influence in some CIO unions by making the signature of a non-Communist affidavit mandatory for union officials.[114]

Southern Democratic purposes were different. They offered indispensable support for this law in order to restrict union penetration into their region, broaden the exclusion of farmworkers, and make it possible for unions to continue to practice racial discrimination without federal restriction. They understood that the legislation's key provisions would advance their efforts to insulate the South's employment relationships and labor markets from the effective reach of countrywide unions. Right-to-work laws would negate federal union protections and help the region build up the hungry new industries that had been spurred by the war, including independent oil, electronics, and aircraft, without having to worry about union demands. The prohibition of secondary boycotts would prevent such developments as the refusal by national unions to transport agricultural goods produced in the South by non-union labor. Clauses that bolstered independent and regional unions would aid organizations that were likely to understand and adapt to the southern circumstances, and be less interested in industry wide national bargaining.

The new law allowed the South to correct what it now viewed as a mistake. The only outspoken southern supporter of unions during the protracted debate was Florida's Claude Pepper.[115] "I come from the South," he remarked, "where I regret to say we have not yet gained as large an organized labor force as I hope we shall have, where our attitude toward labor organization is not always as sympathetic and understanding as I wish it were."[116] Rather more typical was Senator W. Lee "Pappy" O'Daniel of Texas, who "saw the need to take power away from labor," and "wanted to protect employees from 'goon squads' and 'labor racketeers.'"[117] In the House, Graham Barden of North Carolina explicitly referred to Van Bittner ("a little Caesar") and Operation Dixie to argue that unless action were taken to curb union power "we certainly cannot continue . . . and preserve our American economy and our American way of life."[118] His Mississippi colleague, William Whittington, likewise sought to take on Bittner and the CIO, arguing for "an amendment that would definitely ban the union shop" and stressing the importance, in deliberately ironic language, of "freedom from involuntary servitude."[119]

"As we all know," Congressman Hartley observed in his review of the process by which the Labor Management Relations Act of 1947 had become law, the Wagner Act's enactment "was made possible only through the support of a good many southern Democrats who were later to regret their action."[120] One such House member was Mississippi's John Rankin, who now spoke of how "some of the greatest injustices that have ever been wrought have been in some of the labor legislation that has been passed in the last 10 years."[121] Of all the lawmaking in the Truman years, Taft-Hartley represented the greatest triumph for the security of Jim Crow by creating a legal climate that was designed to inhibit a genuinely national labor movement. Not surprisingly, it mobilized overwhelming southern support in the House and Senate. If, in the late 1930s, southern Democrats had begun to be an essential partner in a new coalition with Republicans that then sought to reduce the administrative scope of the National Labor Relations Board and to enhance the relative position of employers as they faced organized labor, a decade later the southerners had become the pivot around which far-reaching antilabor initiatives could succeed even against the determined opposition of a Democratic president. In the early years of the Wagner Act, "the NLRB had 'tackled the Big Boys in every industry': the Aluminum Company of

America, Carnegie-Illinois, Wierton, Inland and Republic Steel, Swift, Standard Oil, Shell Oil, Western Union, Consolidated Aircraft, Goodyear, the Associated Press, Chevrolet, Ford, Remington Rand, the growers and shippers associations in California, United Fruit, and the East, West, and Gulf Coast shipping associations."[122] Taft-Hartley shifted the targets of federal concern to the AFL and CIO, which would now be attacked as "Big Boys" in an even more punitive way.[123]

The South made this happen. The country's profound change in law and attitude toward the circumstances of organized labor was the direct result of shifts in southern legislative behavior during the 1940s. Faced with the surprising rise of labor in their region, and with the union movement's increasing command of resources and issues in the Democratic Party, southern members of Congress came to believe that they no longer could afford to treat labor as an issue that should command party loyalty. Labor organizing, they saw, stimulated civil rights activism. A powerful labor movement that pressed against employment discrimination threatened to level wages across racial lines and directly challenge Jim Crow. It also encouraged blacks to leave the South, and diminished the southern establishment's control over those who stayed. Even the 1930s arrangements excluding the occupations in which the majority of southern blacks worked from federal social welfare and labor laws had become precarious. Agricultural workers had been included in the FEPC, and some were incorporated within Senator Wagner's proposed changes to unemployment compensation.

Distressed by these developments and keenly aware of the dangers that threatened the South's racial order, southern members closed ranks in Congress to reshape the framework within which unions and the labor market could operate. For their Republican partners, labor remained an issue of party and ideology. For southern legislators, labor had become race.

IV.

A SSESSING THE historical changes that had transformed the United States after World War II, the British economist Andrew Shonfield, the leading commentator on postwar capitalism in the West in the mid-1960s, underscored how, by the end of the Roosevelt and Truman years, with "public authority having been deliberately weakened," there was "no serious attempt to co-ordinate the various economic activities of the Government in the public sphere into a coherent policy endowed with purpose and direction." Such public power would have required an appropriate institutional ensemble within the federal government, and a capable national labor movement in the country. These the United States lacked. To be sure, Schonfield noted, "the central government can from time to time make its influence felt through the Bureau of the Budget," but apart from the BOB, there were no federal agencies with the authority and expertise to determine spending priorities or direct, plan, and coordinate capitalist development. Furthermore, he noted, American labor did "not extend—as it does on the continent of Europe—to those occupations in which workers' organizations happen to be weak." He observed how, in all, the postwar years did not revive the radical experimentation of the 1930s or build a domestic state that stood on the shoulders of the dramatic mobilization of the war economy.[124]

More than any other factor, we have seen, southern political power in Congress explains this unforeseen outcome. There was no lack of ambition or interest within the Roosevelt and Truman administrations for public policies to guide capitalism or advance union interests. Nor was there an absence of mass constituencies, or a lack of support among experts and politicians, that would have precluded such assertive government action and enhanced powers for working-class organizations.

With southern representatives being able to confine policies about capitalism and labor to the limited options consistent with their racial preferences, the Democratic Party and labor unions remade themselves. Seeking to bring its internecine warfare to a close, the party settled on an activist fiscal approach, supported across regional lines, which distinguished it from the more cautious orientation to spending and taxes backed by Republicans. Working with broad strokes, these impulses made it possible to find policy agreement within the Democratic Party across regional lines. Despite sharp differences about organized labor, the party's southern and nonsouthern representatives could agree to back significant spending based on revenue generated by progressive income taxes, and find sufficient, if often uneasy, harmony to garner the votes needed to pass federal programs for hospital construction, public housing, and urban renewal, each of which was crafted to conform to existing racial rules.[125] This new variation of Democratic Party liberalism came to be reflected in the hands-off racial policies of the Democratic Party's presidential nominee in 1952, Governor Adlai Stevenson of Illinois. Equally telling was the Democratic candidate for vice president, Alabama's segregationist senator John Sparkman, who, four years later, would be one of 101 southern members of the Senate and House to sign the Southern Manifesto, which promised to resist the Supreme Court's ruling against segregation in *Brown v. Board of Education.*

Bringing together restrictions on unions with generous fiscal policies, the combination of limited unions and active fiscal policy that the South successfully promoted created a distinctive kind of American economy. These policies set capitalism's outer boundaries. They defined the powers, strategies, and identities of key actors, and clarified the stakes over which they could conflict. This policy mix would foreclose the type of coordinated market economy that developed after World War II in much of Western Europe and Japan. It would rule out national patterns of bargaining among representatives of business, labor, and the state. Rather than use the powers of the national state to shape corporate patterns of investment, governance, and employment actively, the economy relied mainly on competitive market mechanisms, including financial instruments and price signals, to solve problems of coordination and induce collaboration among firms. In turn, the concerns of unions were restricted in the main to wage levels and working conditions in particular industries and firms. Especially after Taft-Hartley and the return of USES to the states, labor markets became uncommonly fluid, ever more weakly regulated, and not sustained by national labor policies or institutions for training and placement. Large swaths of the country lacked virtually any union presence or capacity.[126]

These policies and outcomes did more than remake and help shape the main features of U.S. capitalism or determine the vectors of union power. Together, fiscal and labor policy set the course for the country's political system. They fashioned, in effect, a new national state that was dramatically different from its crusading face. With debate focused on the scale and distribution of spending, and with organized labor as a critical interest group but not a national political class, U.S. politics increasingly came to be a politics of competitive bargaining among organized interests for the public purse. Under this system of pressure-group pluralism, lobbying grew. Groups pressing particular claims mobilized constituents, influenced public opinion, spent funds to elect favored candidates, penetrated regulatory agencies, swayed the legislative process, and built webs of influence to orient public policies in ways that would help them achieve their private ends.[127]

This form of democratic politics was largely procedural. By establishing and policing rules, Washington convened a game dominated by organized interests. Tens upon tens of organizations formed to pressure Washington to adopt policies to their advantage. Even before a later expansion of such groups, the Department of Commerce identified some four thousand civic, trade, and professional entities that engaged in lobbying in 1949.[128] Noting how that list "gives some idea of the tremendous number of groups operating in the American scene," the political scientist David Truman stressed, in 1951, how their astonishing range of types "from the Abrasive Grain Association and the American Bible Society to the Society for the Preservation and Encouragement of Barber Shop Quartet Singing in America (23,000 members) and the Zionist Organization of America" reflected an uncommonly open political system.[129]

The most striking feature of Truman's classic analysis of American politics at the end of the New Deal is how it underlines the absence of a public interest. The postwar arrangement of policies and procedures lacked "an interest of the nation as a whole." Many groups, he argued, claimed to represent the public interest, but such assertions "did not describe any actual or possible political situation" within the arrangements that were crafted by the procedural face of the national state. Thus, he concluded that observers of American politics "do not need to account for a totally inclusive interest, because one does not exist."[130]

Understandably, many observers, including David Truman, celebrated this combination of group diversity, multiple interests, and competitive politics as the polar opposite of the era's totalitarian regimes. There were no fixed outcomes, no guiding substantive principles, no ideological imperatives. Conducted within this process, this procedural state transported a market model to the political realm. More than a set of facts, but "an ideology about how a democratic polity ought to work," such interest-group liberalism represented a triumph for democracy.[131]

But just as planned administrative economic management or corporatist forms of political negotiation do not come without cost, neither did this pluralist model of procedural politics. Unchecked by the pursuit of a public interest, its formal neutrality opened the state to the distortions of private power. The new public philosophy of group competition abdicated any democratic, as distinct from dictatorial, notions of a civic interest. Placed under great stress, public authority to achieve common goals thus lacked means to articulate why private interests should not dominate decision making about public policy.

The resulting contest veered between an open and fair competition and a game with skewed rules and a syntax of inequality. The more diffuse an interest—that is, the more civic and public—the less it could be served by this organization of political influence. With planning replaced by bargaining, government, too, often came to be "captured by too-narrow a range of interests."[132] Especially notable was a pro-business bias. This outcome was a consequence of decision in Congress to set aside important controls over economic life and to constrain the capacity of organized labor to act as the only available countervailing national force. Of the 1,247 lobbying organizations in Washington that were identified by a House Select Committee in 1950, fully 825 were business associations. In all, the political scientist E. E. Schattschneider concluded, "the flaw in the pluralist heaven is that the heavenly chorus sings with a strong upper class accent."[133]

There was an additional cost, not a small one. The combination of a hands-off fiscal consensus for the Democratic Party and sharp constraints on the expansion of union labor protected the South's rotten-borough political system and its structure of racial domination. Without planning instruments and without unions as a fully national force, the procedural state offered a lifeline to the system of segregation. With labor—the one force best poised to mount an assault on Jim Crow—demobilized by Taft-Hartley, southern resistance stiffened. In turn, the era's still-nascent movement for civil rights proceeded in the main without active labor allies. As a result, the frontal attack on black civic and political exclusion advanced without focusing on social class, economic equality, or labor rights as essential features of racial justice.[134]

11 ▷ "Wildest Hopes"

THE FIRST ATOMIC BOMB exploded on American soil. At 11:00 P.M. on July 15, 1945, already morning in Potsdam as Churchill, Stalin, and Truman gathered for their victors' summit, a convoy of Manhattan Project scientists, administrators, and one journalist, William Laurence, a fifty-seven-year-old Lithuanian-born science reporter for the *New York Times,* set out for a secret destination 212 miles south of Los Alamos to observe the start of the atomic age. Stationed on a hill in the desert at the edge of New Mexico's remote and inaccessible Alamogordo Air Base, twenty miles from test site Zero,[1] they were cautioned not to look until the flash had ended and a mushroom cloud had risen. Manhattan Project leaders, among them Vannevar Bush, James Conant, Enrico Fermi, and Leslie Groves, waited in the control room for Robert Oppenheimer, who had named the test Trinity, to issue the command.

Some had participated in a betting pool about the size of the explosion.[2] The order was given at 5:30 A.M. on the sixteenth. A bomb, referred to as "the Gadget," with a plutonium core in the form of two small hemispheres, was to drop from the one-hundred-foot-high steel tower on which it stood poised. Laurence reported:

> There rose from the bowels of the earth, a light not of this world, the light of many suns in one. It was a sunrise such as the world had never seen, a great green super-sun climbing in a fraction of a second to a height of more than eight thousand feet, rising ever higher until it touched the clouds, lighting up earth and sky all around with a dazzling luminosity. Up it went, a great ball of fire a mile in diameter, changing colors as it kept shooting upward, from deep purple to orange, expanding, growing bigger, rising as it expanded, an elemental force freed from its bonds after being chained for billions of years. For a fleeting instant the color was unearthly green, such as one sees only in the corona of the sun during a total eclipse. It was as though the earth had opened up and the skies had split. One felt as though one were present at the moment of creation when God said: "Let there be light."[3]

Another eyewitness, Brig. Gen. T. F. Farrell, the chief of field operations for the Manhattan Project, described the event in more prosaic prose:

> Dr. Conant reached over and shook hands with General Groves. Dr. Bush, who was on the other side of the General, did likewise. Dr. Kistiakowsky[4] threw his arms around Dr. Oppenheimer and embraced him with shouts of glee. Others were equally enthusiastic. All pent-up emotions were released in those few minutes and seemed to sense immediately that the explosion had far exceeded the most optimistic expectations and wildest hopes of the scientists.[5]

Only animals, including a herd of antelope, disappeared that morning. That all was to change, of course, three weeks later, once three B-29s took off from Tinian Island in the Marianas, some fifteen hundred miles east of Japan, on August 6, 1945.[6] Laurence was permitted access to that air base, the home of what amounted to an air force, under the direction of Leslie Groves, exclusively for atomic warfare.[7] He observed the departure—and, hours later, the return—of the *Enola Gay,* the bomber that dropped "Little Boy" on Hiroshima. "Could it be," he wondered, "that this innocent-looking object, so beautifully designed, so safe to handle, could in much less time than it takes to wink an eye annihilate an entire city and its population?"[8]

"Results clear-cut successful in all respects" was how the Department of War informed President Truman by telegram that the weapon had obliterated Hiroshima. "Visible effects greater than any test."[9] Three days later, Laurence received authorization to fly with the second mission, this one carrying "Fat Man" in the *Bockscar* to Nagasaki. A midnight briefing closed with a prayer by the base chaplain, Capt. William B. Downey of the Hope Evangelical Lutheran Church in Minneapolis. "Almighty God, Father of all mercies . . . give to us all courage and strength for the hours that are ahead; give to them rewards according to their efforts." Twelve hours later, watching from a front-row seat in the cramped, transparent nose of an accompanying B-29, Laurence witnessed Nagasaki "in its last brief moments under the sun." As the city "stood out clearly in broad daylight," he observed the "black object that went downward."[10]

I.

FOURTEEN YEARS after Japan had conquered Manchuria, Emperor Hirohito addressed his nation by radio on August 15. His country lay in ruins. Some three million Japanese had died. Nearly five million servicemen were wounded or ill. Almost half the urban areas of the country had been destroyed. Nine million were homeless. With the enemy's use of "cruel bombs to kill and maim large numbers of the innocent," and with the casualties at Hiroshima and Nagasaki "beyond measure," a decision to continue the war further," he announced, "could lead in the end not only to the extermination of our race, but also to the destruction of all human civilization."[11]

With this announcement of capitulation, the United States witnessed an explosion of joy even before the arrival of the first U.S. occupation forces or Japan's formal surrender on the deck of the battleship *Missouri* on September 2, which the president declared as V-J Day. More than two million New Yorkers filled the Times Square area in a spontaneous celebration on August

14, once the electric news bulletin board on the *New York Times* annex reported President Truman's announcement that Japan had been defeated. "The greatest throng in New York's history goes wild in Times Square," *Life* reported. The scene was repeated in other parts of the city and, indeed, across the country as something of a national party began. Americans took to the streets to celebrate the end of wartime sorrow and the prospect of normal times.[12]

"Bring Back Daddy" clubs sprang up in something of a mass movement. Before long, the "greatest postwar demobilization of the American armed forces got underway."[13] Soldiers started to come home at great speed. When Japan laid down its arms, 8,020,000 U.S. Army soldiers and 3,400,000 U.S. Navy sailors were in service. Within months, by the start of 1946, the total had fallen to 3,024,000; by year's close, to just 1,582,000. U.S. combat forces in Europe numbered just twelve understrength combat divisions by mid-1947, down from the ninety-seven that had been in combat when Germany surrendered.[14] Defense spending also dropped drastically, from $81 billion to $13 billion between 1945 and 1947.[15] It did not go without notice that this decline seemed to confirm that the United States intended to leave Europe just as soon as it could, much as President Roosevelt had indicated at Yalta, and that the serious range of conventional American might had been reduced for the most part to a defense posture limited to the Western Hemisphere.[16]

Concurrently, Washington's war agencies began to ease their grip and close down. As early as August 18, Isaiah Berlin was reporting to London from the British embassy in Washington both about the public's "recklessly carefree mood" and how, "in clear response to the public mood, war agencies have been competing with one another in slashing of controls, and an impression is given that the gigantic and complex American war machine is being dismantled overnight."[17]

The effects on American society were immediate. Censorship was lifted. Gasoline was no longer rationed. Nylon would be in stockings by Christmas. The Office of War Information stopped functioning in late August 1945, and its overseas programs were transferred to the State Department. Within a month, the doors shut at the Foreign Economic Administration, the bureaucracy that managed Lend-Lease; that program came to an unequivocal end, notwithstanding the negative impact of its abrupt termination on Great Britain.[18] The Office of Strategic Services (OSS), which had conducted intelligence operations, was disbanded by an executive order issued on September 20.[19] Its research and analysis divisions were transferred to the Department of State, while its operational side was moved to the Department of War.[20]

At that moment, both the public and its leaders expected that a combination of international law, collective security, and the country's atomic shield would permit the United States to draw back from most of its global commitments. Not terribly worried about the Soviet Union, an "exhausted, devastated nation,"[21] the administration turned its attention to the home front's housing crisis and massive strike wave. It also superintended a speedy return to a civilian economy by overseeing the rapid termination of military contracts, the disposal of surplus goods, the removal of war-focused materials from American factories, and an end to price controls. For now, at least, President Truman left foreign affairs for the most part to his secretary of state, the former South Carolina senator James Byrnes.[22]

The *Cold War*—a term that would not be coined until 1947 by Bernard Baruch and popularized by Walter Lippmann[23]—was not anticipated. During World War II, Lippmann had not been alone in thinking that the alliance of the non-Axis countries would persist because the core strategic interest of the United States lay in not allowing any power in Europe to act with force outside that continent.[24] Likewise, President Roosevelt had believed the wartime coalition would continue, if for more prosaic reasons. "They have got a large enough 'hunk of bread' right in Russia to keep them busy for a great many years to come," he told the Advertising War Council Conference on March 8, 1944, "without taking on any more headaches."[25]

This was a widely shared view.[26] The armed forces, the office of the president, and Congress projected a continuing partnership of the Allies when they conducted planning efforts during the war for a smooth and rapid postwar demobilization.[27] They took heart not just from negotiations to establish the United Nations but also from the way American participation was beyond controversy. Drafted in San Francisco before the war ended, the United Nations Charter was signed on June 26, 1945, and ratified by a lopsided 89–2 margin in the U.S. Senate on July 28,[28] twenty-six years after American participation in the League of Nations had been rejected by that body. Three months later, on October 24, the United Nations Charter came into effect just as the war crimes trial of Nazi leaders was convening in Nuremberg under the collective auspices of the wartime alliance.

President Truman had every reason to expect the UN would advance Franklin Roosevelt's postwar vision.[29] When they returned from Alamogordo to Washington, Vannevar Bush and James Conant agreed that the best course forward would be to impart all available information about the bomb in order "to avoid a secret armament race." For that reason, they argued, efforts to build the capacity of the United Nations "must be the prime objective of every sane man."[30] Despite emerging tensions, the Soviet Union was not yet an enemy.[31] Even Mississippi's James Eastland, a fierce anti-Communist, told his Senate colleagues during the UN ratification debate in July 1945 that "we must cooperate with Russia."[32] When the first session of the UN General Assembly met in January 1946 at Church House in London, a collaborative relationship between the United States, whose delegation was led by former secretary of state Edward Stettinius, and the Soviet Union, whose delegation was led by Andrei Vyshinsky, the former Soviet purge trial prosecutor, still did not appear far-fetched, even though Iran charged the USSR with interference in its internal affairs, and the Soviet Union charged Britain with interference in Greece, both omens of disputes to come. Consistent with the euphoria and relief that had accompanied the end of the war, a tone of cooperation prevailed. It quickly seemed to take practical form. Within a fortnight, the United Nations' first resolution, unanimously adopted by the fifty-one member nations on January 24, initiated a process to secure a global treaty that would eliminate atomic weapons and guide the peaceful application of atomic science. Stalin soon expressed confidence that the UN was developing as a "serious instrument" for preserving world peace.[33]

A mere five years later, these expectations were in tatters. When the Brookings Institution considered America's position in global affairs in 1951 at the request of the Bureau of the Budget and the Executive Office of the President, it could only wistfully recall how, at war's end, almost no one had foreseen the impending collapse of security coordination with the Soviet Union, the rapid intensification of East-West suspicions, or the severity of the Cold War.[34] By contrast, the report recorded how the problems confronting the United States in foreign affairs had become more difficult than those that the country had confronted during the economic emergency of the 1930s. Global developments, it drily noted, if with a sense of wonder, entailed "a violation of traditional expectations, requiring a departure from historical principles of action."[35]

Most of the national security agencies the Brookings document discussed did not exist when the UN was being formed or when atomic weapons were first used. Put in place during the Truman administration, these institutions adjusted the structure and strategy of U.S. foreign policy. The Department of War was refashioned into a substantially different Department of Defense, a conglomerate that was "unique in its basic structure, differing from any other executive department."[36] The era also witnessed the creation of the National Security Council (NSC), the Central Intelligence Agency (CIA), the National Security Resources Board (NSRB), the National Science Foundation (NSF), and a good many other new agencies that managed postwar relief, foreign aid, and overseas information. The Department of State dramatically expanded. The Foreign Service grew from 4,000 overseas diplomats and support staff in 1940 to 24,000 by 1950, and the department's Washington workforce likewise jumped from 1,000 to 8,000.[37]

Shaped simultaneously to restrict Soviet power and to advance the West's political and economic models, the country's new organizational, fiscal, and military instruments made insistent global action possible. Acting with wide discretion, these specialized, often insular agencies built military might, oversaw the multiplication of atomic weapons, pursued intelligence, and practiced covert action, all in the name of liberal democracy. Premised on the assumption that the United States was freedom's indispensable guardian, these organizations extended American power as if the country were still engaged in total warfare.

This national security state—a state premised on the idea that the largest threats to American democracy were located outside the country's boundaries—offered a mirror image of the state of public procedures and private interests that had rejected economic planning and a national corporatist role for labor. Combining the activist impulses of the early New Deal with features of wartime mobilization and technology, it advanced scientific and military planning; built corporatist relationships among business, labor, and the national state; insisted on rigorous demands for secrecy; and was premised on the understanding that all loyal citizens should subscribe to a singular public interest. American citizens were summoned once again "to wage a war against the emergency," but an emergency dissimilar both from the kind Franklin Roosevelt had announced on his first Inauguration Day and from the time-bound emergency of World War II.

It did not take long for anxiety about the bomb to supplant the festive mood that dominated the late summer of 1945. Nor did it take long for a new climate of fear, with the bomb as the original impetus, to engender a crusading national security state. "The tragic truth," William Laurence wrote, "is that at present we really cannot be sure that the war is over. Twenty-five years from now, or even sooner, we may find out that what we thought was the end of the war was no more than merely another prolonged armistice, a period in which we took time out to stock up with bigger and better atomic bombs." Having seen the bomb firsthand, he shuddered at the prospect. "If that happens the end cannot be far away."[38] With palpable fear not only seizing the mass public but also the decision-making elite, the bomb informed every aspect of postwar military organization and strategy. It created suspicions about loyalty and promoted a zone of policymaking that valued secrecy and, at the same time, insulated the coercive capacity of the federal government from ordinary democratic processes and scrutiny. Both the Great Depression and World War II had promised a solution. Prosperity could be made to return. Enemies would be forced to surrender. But with the permanent existence of atomic weapons linked to a turbulent and global ideological conflict of uncertain duration, fear itself projected a meaning qualitatively different from that when Roosevelt first spoke the words in March 1933.

II.

BROADCASTING FIVE days after the explosion at Nagasaki, America's leading radio news commentator, H. V. Kaltenborn, urged his NBC listeners to "think of the mass murder which will come with World War III." That week, two rather different voices warned that history had just experienced a great moment of fracture. First was Gen. Henry Harley "Hap" Arnold, chief of the Army's Air Staff from March 1943 to February 1946, fourth in the army command behind Generals Marshall, MacArthur, and Eisenhower, and the person who had led the carpet-bombing campaigns of World War II. Arnold, who had advocated a post-Nagasaki "'grand finale' by a thousand fire-raising aircraft,"[39] outlined a postwar program of research and development that would improve the bomb, produce planes faster than sound, and build guided missiles that could hit any target on the globe from anywhere on Earth.[40] Second was the critic and noted author James Agee, whose *Time* article appeared under a picture of an atomic cloud in the first issue published since Nagasaki. Writing in "sorrow and doubt," he remarked how "the greatest and most terrible of wars ended, this week, in the echoes of an enormous event—an event so much more enormous that, relative to it, the war itself shrank to minor significance." The existence of "the bomb," he continued, "rendered all decisions made so far at Yalta and Postdam mere trivial dams across tributary rivulets." Fearful that even "the good uses of this power might easily bring disaster as prodigious as the evil," Agee concluded that "with the controlled splitting of the atom, humanity, already profoundly perplexed and disunified, was brought inescapably into a new age in which all thoughts and things were split—and far from controlled."[41]

By mid-September, Gallup was reporting that fully 27 percent of Americans believed that one day there would be a chain of atomic "explosions which will destroy the entire world."[42] Two months later, Leslie Groves was warning that the world "will be courting suicide if it permits the atomic bomb to get out of control," and the secretary of state, addressing a "Jimmy Byrnes Homecoming Day" in Charleston, South Carolina, was pronouncing how, "from the day the first bomb fell on Hiroshima, one thing has been clear to us: the civilized world cannot survive an atomic war."[43]

In a startling photo-essay in November 1945, "The 36-Hour War," *Life* chillingly portrayed a future global conflict as one that "begins with the atomic bombardment of key U.S. cities," even as its ends with "the U.S. wins the atomic war." Cautioning that attacks across the United States could not be stopped by defensive means, and projecting how "some 40,000,000 people have been killed and all cities of more than 50,000 populations have been leveled," the article opened with a realistic image showing, as the caption put it, "a shower of white-hot enemy rockets [falling] on Washington, D.C." Illustrated by vivid and credible drawings that depicted atomic bombs descending on the United States, and hidden radar centers tracking the fateful attack, it closed with a terrifying image that portrayed an utterly devastated Fifth Avenue under the description "By the Marble Lions of New York's Public Library, U.S. Technicians Test the Rubble of the Shattered City for Radioactivity."[44]

The only plausible enemy was the Soviet Union, but was it not still a collaborator, if not quite an ally? February 1946 stands out as the moment when the conditions that might actually produce *Life*'s imaginary rendering began to take rhetorical and practical form. On February 9, the eve of the USSR's first single-party general election of candidates for the Supreme Soviet since 1937, Josef Stalin broadcast from the Bolshoi Theater in Moscow. With his power, credibility, and appeal at an all-time high, Stalin argued that "victory means, first of all, that our Soviet social system has won," and that the war had demonstrated "that it is truly a popular system," rather than one "imposed on the people by the organs of the Cheka." Continuing, he underscored the "firmness and grit" of the Communist Party in breaking the "machinations of Trotskyites and Rightists, participating in the sabotage of the measures of our government," and went on to stress the quality and quantity of the country's munitions, and the pugnacious character of the Red Army. In a veiled but unmistakable reference to atomic weapons, he revealed that the USSR had adopted a plan to generate conditions for Soviet science "not only to overtake but also in the very near future to surpass the achievements of science outside the boundaries of our country."[45]

This strong rhetoric was embedded in an account of the origins of World War II that seemed to turn decisively from the spirit of Yalta and the peacemaking potential of the United Nations. War, Stalin contended, is an inherent feature of "world capitalism." That system "proceeds through crises and the catastrophes of war." The partnership between capitalist countries and the "progressive forces" led by the Soviet Union had merely been a situational convenience. In all, Stalin contended, the recent war had been "the inevitable result of the world economic and political forces on the basis of monopoly capitalism."[46]

Even though "no one familiar with Stalin's thinking," as John Lewis Gaddis has observed, "would have found much new in the speech," as it "reflected what he had long believed and often said," many in the West thought that his truculent talk—page-one news in all the major newspapers—represented a willful declaration that nothing was left of the wartime alliance.[47] This was how the Foreign Service officer Elbridge Durbrow (later the U.S. ambassador to South Vietnam from 1957 to 1961) saw things in Moscow. "It was just unbelievable how he threw it all out of the window." The Bolshoi speech, Durbrow believed, seemed to say "to hell with the rest of the world."[48]

Unlike Durbrow, George Kennan, who had been recruited to Moscow as Ambassador Averell Harriman's Russian expert, thought the talk had been a more routine reflection of Soviet distrust.[49] But it was Kennan's eight-thousand-word telegram to Washington from Moscow on February 22—the longest ever written within the Foreign Service—that established both the terms of analysis and the framework for U.S. foreign policy that endured throughout the Cold War. Sent in response to a request by Secretary of State Byrnes for an interpretation of what Stalin had said, Kennan's telegram analyzed the USSR as a regime that combined the traditional goals of Russian nationalism with a more "truculent and intolerant" ideological Bolshevism. This amalgam organized "a political force committed fanatically to the belief that with US there can be no permanent *modus vivendi*." Kennan further projected that the USSR would make strenuous efforts to undermine the West, weaken its hold on colonized peoples, and "work toward destruction of all forms of personal independence, economic, political, or moral."

He advised that, faced with this kind of enemy, American diplomacy be conducted with firmness, "calmly and with good heart," on the basis of an analytical assessment of the USSR and its goals. As the Soviet Union was "neither schematic not adventuristic," he predicted that its leaders would not gamble excessively. To the contrary, they would prudently retreat should the West build effective means to inhibit their policy choices. American leaders, he counseled, should educate the public, build "the health and vigor of our own society," and have "the courage and self confidence to cling to our own methods and conceptions of human society. After all," he concluded, "the greatest danger that can befall us in coping with this problem of Soviet communism, is that we shall allow ourselves to become like those with whom we are coping."[50] Together with his anonymous "Mr. X" July 1947 *Foreign Affairs* essay, "The Sources of Soviet Conduct," the "Long Telegram" combined caution with contention. "The main element of any United States policy toward the Soviet Union," Kennan advised, "must be that of a long-term, patient but firm and vigilant containment." This policy, he argued, could ultimately help produce the "gradual mellowing" or even "the break-up" of Soviet power.[51]

Kennan's telegraphed report from Moscow was immediately influential. "It came right at a moment," as the State Department officer Louis Halle recalled, "when the . . . Department was floundering about, looking for new intellectual moorings."[52] On February 28, 1946, soon after receiving the telegram, Secretary Byrnes delivered a policy speech to the Overseas Press Club in New York. Targeting Stalin's words, he denounced "loose talk about the inevitability of war." Calling for "patience and firmness," he appealed for military readiness so that America could effectively "act as a great power."[53]

Winston Churchill, too, had seen the Long Telegram. Famously declaring that "an iron curtain has descended across the Continent," his March 5 speech in Harry Truman's home state called for a stance of stern resistance.[54] Stalin quickly responded in a *Pravda* interview headlined, "On Churchill's Speech at Fulton." Appraising the talk "as a dangerous act," Stalin compared Churchill and his "friends in the United States" to "Hitler and his friends." There is nothing "surprising," he added "that in her desire to safeguard her future, Russia was trying to secure in neighboring countries governments loyal to the Soviet Union." Any person "who believes this orientation to be expansionist," he concluded, "has gone mad."[55]

This stiffening global climate coincided with an acceleration of public attention to nuclear danger. As Cold War talk accelerated, the usually sedate *Wall Street Journal*'s editorial writers were warning that "if another world war comes, so will atomic bombing."[56] In March 1946, a paperback published by the Federation of American Scientists cautioned that the combination of peril and vulnerability posed a stark choice of "one world or none." Subtitled "A Report to the Public on the Full Meaning of the Atomic Bomb," it quickly sold 100,000 copies. This was hardly a fringe effort. With contributions from leading physicists, including Albert Einstein, Robert Oppenheimer, Arthur Compton, Neils Bohr, Hans Bethe, Harold Urey, and Leo Szilard, and from Walter Lippmann and General Arnold, the volume projected an atomic arms race that "adds up to the most dangerous situation that humanity has ever faced in all history."[57]

Especially compelling was the description in the opening chapter of "the burned and the broken" city of Hiroshima by the Manhattan Project physicist Philip Morrison, who, on Tinian Island, had participated in the final assembly of the Hiroshima and Nagasaki bombs, then had joined the damage-assessment group sent to evaluate the aftermath. Reprising the testimony he had offered to a congressional committee in December 1945 on "the terror of the bomb," Morrison conveyed the surreal scene of "hundreds, even thousands, of fires [that] burned unchecked among the dead and the injured," and how doses of radiation had produced circumstances in which "the blood does not coagulate, but oozes in many spots through the unbroken skin, and internally seeps into the cavities of the body." He also projected the effects of a similar attack on New York, making palpable the threat of nuclear Armageddon. He described how close to the city center, "nothing much was left" but "men with burning clothing, women with terrible red and blackened burns, and dead children caught while hurrying home to lunch." The conclusion was even more frightening: "New York City had thus suffered under one bomb, and the story is unreal in only one way: The bombs will never again, as in Japan, come in ones or twos. They will come in hundreds, even in thousands."[58] Chilling, too, was the warning by the associate director of the Westinghouse Research Laboratory, Edward Condon, that sabotage by nonstate actors who possessed atomic weapons, what he called "the new technique of private war," would soon become possible.[59]

Few Americans could elude what the theologian Reinhold Niebuhr was calling "the very great apprehension" and "strange disquiet" that such horrifying representations were producing.[60] In early March 1946, the mass-circulation *Collier's* reported in detail on "what the atomic bomb really did," and showed graphically what an equivalent attack on New York would accomplish. In late March and early April 1946, Walter Lippmann published nine newspaper columns to caution that only "the union of mankind under universal law," and, ultimately, the formation of a world state out of the embryo of the United Nations, could prevent "the desolation of utter anarchy" in the atomic age.[61] Concurrently, wrote Joseph and Stewart Alsop, it was clear the international control of atomic weapons "is the issue most likely to decide the relationship between the Soviet Union and the rest of the world." The alternative, should agreement not be reached, is a "showdown," since it will not be possible to "keep the atom bomb for ourselves."[62]

That year, the August 31 issue of *The New Yorker* devoted all its editorial pages to John Hershey's riveting 31,000-word description of the noiseless flash and fire that had eliminated Hiroshima. Based on interviews with survivors, his "A Reporter at Large" essay presented an unsentimental, restrained account of the injuries and anguish of six individuals. It immediately became a national sensation. This eschatological text sold out. Quickly published as a book, it sold more than three million copies, and was sent, gratis, to every member of the Book of the Month Club. Newspapers across the country placed extracts on their front pages. Preempting all its usual programs, ABC radio broadcast the unedited manuscript to the nation in half-hour readings, at the 9.30 P.M. prime-time slot, for four consecutive nights.[63] Soon, the head of the country's Atomic Energy Commission, David Lilienthal, was lamenting how "public thinking is dominated by fear," how "fear is brother to panic," and how "unreasoning fear . . . is not going to get us anywhere . . . we want to go."[64]

III.

THE STARK portraits that so worried Lilienthal did more than shock, in fact. They captured quite accurately how the coming of atomic fission was transforming U.S. security. Even before the type of intercontinental rocket portrayed by *Life* was developed, the rise of the long-distance bomber made the map's traditional protections obsolete. The United States had been kept safe by distance. Protected by two great oceans, its homeland had remained secure even during the century's great global wars. "Distance no longer presents the same kind of barrier to effective strategic bombing with atomic bombs that it does with chemical weapons," the atomic bomb strategist Bernard Brodie explained in 1948.[65] Earth had become a "small apple," the military editor of the *New York Times,* Hanson Baldwin, argued four months before the USSR exploded its first atomic weapon, in August 1949, because the Soviet Union had begun to build and deploy advanced bombers similar to the type used by the Allies to smash Germany's and Japan's cities. With the United States "no longer a continent in a geographic or strategic sense," he cautioned that the "Atlantic and Pacific Oceans have shrunk in the modern terms of high-speed weapons to roughly the dimensions of the English Channel and the North Sea," and he recalled how those ramparts had proved completely inadequate to "protect Britain during the last war from frightful destruction."[66] Should the Soviet Union soon join the nuclear club, he warned, their atomic weapons—"so cheap and so destructive"—would "accomplish what had heretofore been beyond the means of any single foreign nation: the capacity to strike a mortal blow at the American continent."[67]

Before World War II, the United States could afford not to mobilize its military capacity. The balance of power in Europe so engaged "the interests and arms of the other Great Powers" that were so committed against one another, a leading scholar of defense reasoned, "that none was free to direct its strength against the United States."[68] America's remarkable military potential thus mostly lay dormant. It was activated during the first half of the twentieth century only when Germany twice used conquests and alliances to override the Continent's power balance.

All this changed irrevocably after World War II. With its absolute security eliminated by the existence of the bomb, the United States effectively became a European power just when economic and physical desolation in Germany, Italy, and France, together with the near-bankrupt status of Great Britain, made it impossible for the earlier great power balance in Europe to return. Instead, a new constellation emerged. Only the United States could fill the power vacuum in the West and confront the one truly great power in the East. In these circumstances, the USSR, now a superpower with unrivaled conventional military strength, potentially could accomplish what the Third Reich had sought, hegemony in Europe that might threaten the United States.[69]

In these circumstances, the mixed signals about collaboration and conflict that characterized the early postwar period were quickly supplanted by the unwillingness of either side to find compromises about such key issues as the future of Germany. Each, moreover, developed expansive conceptions of security. By late 1946, the adversaries began to meet in dangerous confrontations, direct and indirect. December witnessed Communist guerrilla movements in Greece and Turkey, a continuing civil war in China, and the start of the First Indochina War, which pitted France against the Vietminh. Three months thereafter, on March 12, in what he later recalled as "the turning point in America's foreign policy," President Truman declared that the United States would provide large-scale aid to Greece and Turkey to prevent their absorption into an emerging Communist bloc.[70]

This decision to have the United States hold the line against Soviet penetration was an alternative to letting events take their course or placing the issue on the docket of the United Nations. Truman cast his choice in terms of a battle between systems. The United States, he insisted, was engaged in a fight to preserve a "way of life" that "is based upon the will of the majority, and is distinguished by free institutions," from another political, economic, and social order that, by contrast, is "based upon the will of a minority forcibly imposed upon the majority" and that, instead, "relies upon terror and oppression."[71] Eight weeks later, on June 5, Secretary of State George Marshall cautioned at Harvard University that Europe "must have substantial additional help or face economic, social, and political deterioration of a very grave character," thus giving first notice of the administration's European Recovery Program.[72]

Both the Truman Doctrine and the Marshall Plan were viewed as threatening by the Soviet Union. Its policies grew more forceful. It founded the Cominform as a coordinating body for the international Communist movement loyal to Moscow and, in February 1948, initiated a Communist coup in Czechoslovakia that was undertaken despite the existence of a democratic government that had been friendly to the USSR. In June, the Soviet Union denied the Western powers access to Berlin by rail or road. The West responded with an airlift, which broke the blockade by May 1949, a month after the creation of the North Atlantic Treaty Organization (NATO), which pledged the United States, Canada, and ten other states (Belgium, Denmark, Great Britain, France, Iceland, Italy, Luxembourg, the Netherlands, Norway, and Portugal) to provide mutual military assistance should any member be attacked. Then there was the German question. Rather than find a resolution in an agreement among the occupying powers, the Federal Republic of Germany was created out of the American, British, and French zones from May to September 1949, followed in October by the founding of the German Democratic Republic in the Soviet zone.

Conflict was hardly confined to Europe. Asia also became a site of contention. The Chinese civil war ended with the September 1949 establishment of the People's Republic of China and the evacuation of the remnants of the Nationalist government to Taiwan. On June 22, 1950, the army of the People's Democratic Republic of North Korea, with Stalin's permission, crossed the thirty-eighth parallel. Within five days, advance units entered Seoul, the capital of South Korea. Fighting in Vietnam also began to escalate as French forces began to use napalm against the Vietminh for the first time in early 1951.

As these Asian conflicts accelerated, the United States joined with Australia and New Zealand in a Pacific security and defense pact, the September 1951 ANZUS Treaty. Three months later, NATO established an integrated defense force under the command of Gen. Dwight Eisenhower that directly faced Soviet forces in the heart of Europe. All the while, the Soviet Union was fastening the rule of orthodox, brutal, and compliant regimes in Eastern Europe, while tightening its ties to the Communist Party in other areas.

Over the course of this tense period, the hope that the United Nations would serve as an agent of global peace collapsed in unresolved contradictions. The young organization awkwardly combined a dedication to human rights and international law with a commitment to national sovereignty. As the victorious great powers sought to further their own ambitions for different kinds of empire, the UN became a setting for the expression and amplification of East-West conflicts.[73] Moreover, as all the great powers had demanded and secured the right to veto actions by the Security Council, the UN could act to prevent or check the use of force only when their interests were not directly involved or, as in the case of Korea, when one of these powers was absent.[74]

The failure of the United Nations to substitute collective security for confrontation was most acute in the realm of atomic weapons. During the immediate postwar period, the superpowers did explore whether the UN might actually contain the prospect of an atomic arms race, but not nearly with the seriousness with which they simultaneously undertook to build or develop the capacity to manufacture such weapons, and craft strategic options for a nuclear age.

Negotiations to develop an international arrangement that could halt an incipient atomic arms race were initiated in December 1945. Meeting in Moscow, the foreign ministers of Britain, the Soviet Union, and the United States agreed to seek "effective safeguards" under the auspices of the United Nations Atomic Energy Commission, "by way of inspection and other means," to secure the "elimination from national armaments of atomic weapons."[75] In practice, however, these discussions could not overcome the unwillingness of the United States to discontinue the production and stockpiling of atomic weapons, let alone disarm or share atomic secrets, in the absence of an agreement about compliance, or the Soviet Union's unwillingness to agree to a meaningful system of international scrutiny. Representing the United States, Bernard Baruch told the UN in June 1946 that international control was indispensable, as the globe faced "a choice between the quick and the dead." But he also made clear that in the absence of "a guarantee of safety" the United States would not, indeed could not, "relinquish" its "winning weapons."[76] In turn, the Soviet Union's Andrei Gromyko made no provision in his government's proposals for a regime of inspection. Rather, he stressed how, within three months from the conclusion of an agreement, "all stocks of atomic energy weapons, whether in a finished or semi-finished condition," would have to be destroyed. The USSR further insisted that the United States freely share all the information it had about atomic energy.[77]

The gulf proved impassable.[78] Anarchy's desolation beckoned, to be contained, perhaps, only by the half peace of deterrence. It was this prospect that five of the leading American scholars of international relations considered just as Baruch and Gromyko were sketching their incommensurable positions. Arguing that neither international agreements nor inspections could, in fact, prevent atomic warfare, this group of experts contended that only the fear of retaliation would keep the peace, albeit a peace of mistrust and suspicion. That course, they maintained, would require the United States to build bigger and better bombs so that even an enemy with the bomb would not be tempted to use it.[79]

This perspective almost existentially informed U.S. policy. With international regulation discussions at an impasse, the United States warned the UN Atomic Energy Commission in late August 1946 that "the remaining alternative is development of superior bombs and superior ways of delivering them to the target as counter-offensive weapons" that could "deter a nation from starting an aggressive war by making it apparent that victory is impossible."[80] On June 5, 1947, a closed meeting of the UN Atomic Energy Commission, held in Lake Success, New York, heard Frederick Osborn, the U.S. representative, declare that an "atomic race has started."[81] Within months, the United States closed the mid-Pacific atoll of Eniwetok, in the Marshall Island, to ships, planes, and visitors, especially journalists.[82] It placed the area "under full security restrictions" and moved "the native inhabitants of the coral islands" some 150 miles southwest in order to secure the area as a proving grounds to test new types of atomic bombs.[83]

A sense of gloom and danger continued to accelerate. "We are traveling to a land we cannot see," Robert Oppenheimer observed in 1948. He understood that "our atomic monopoly is like a cake of ice melting in the sun."[84] Noting with remarkable understatement that "the development of atomic energy" is not marked by "the otherworldliness normally characteristic of new developments in science," the physicist most responsible for harnessing the Manhattan Project advised Americans to prepare for "weapons even more terrifying, and perhaps vastly more terrifying," which, in all likelihood, would be built "in truly terrifying numbers." Any basis for cooperation between the United States and the Soviet Union, he concluded, had been "eradicated by a revelation of their deep conflicts of interest, the deep and apparently mutual repugnance of their ways of life, and the apparent conviction on the part of the Soviet Union of the inevitability of conflict—and not in ideas alone, but in force." With "the nature of atomic armament" coupled with "the political climate of the postwar world . . . there is the gravest danger," he warned, that "the fabric of civilized life . . . will not hold."[85]

IV.

AMERICA'S NATIONAL SECURITY state was incubated under the shadow of the bomb. The rupture this weapon inflicted on the human condition generated a sense of alarm and foreboding that accelerated as relations with the Soviet Union grew more fraught. The era's landmark decisions in Congress—including the adoption of the Atomic Energy Act of 1946, the National Security Act of 1947, the Defense Reorganization Act of 1949, and the Internal Security Act of 1950—all were motivated by this new source of fear itself.

A paradox became apparent. Every key building block of the national security state that was developed during the Truman years required and secured congressional approval. By shaping the national security state's agencies, Congress placed foreign and military policy within arrangements and processes consistent with its own purposes. The structures and procedures Congress brought into being allowed its members to build their own preferences into the substance of policy.[86] And yet, as Congress grappled with national security, it circumscribed its own long-term role. By delegating immense capacity to the executive branch, Congress effectively stepped aside, just as it had during World War II when it had restrained its own powers of investigation and provided the country's professional military leaders and President Roosevelt with all the means they requested.[87]

With mounting concern about Soviet ambitions and behavior, with Communism losing standing as a good, or at least well-intentioned, cause, and with global affairs increasingly understood as a fierce ideological battlefield, Congress was faced with choices that carried a huge responsibility. It had to decide when and how to assign authority, which security frameworks to adopt, and when to test the devotion and trustworthiness of American citizens.

It was congressional lawmaking, in short, that sorted not just the extent but also the manner in which powers held by the central government would be augmented. In so doing, members of the House and Senate had to consider the risks posed for representative government by the growth of concentrated and often concealed executive power as the country confronted the world's only other superpower. They had to determine whether and when programs created to advance U.S. safety and promote its commitment to democracy might contradict the country's liberal principles, humanitarian norms, and familiar procedures of government, and when such policies might endanger the country rather than promote its security.[88] As capacious security instruments were developed, it was by no means clear whether "the concentration of power, and the authoritarian control of it, [which] are inescapable in a military establishment," would characterize the national security state; that is, as Charles Merriam put the question in 1946, whether it would be possible to develop "security without militarism."[89]

Hugely motivated by fears of Communism, congressional decisions were guided by a more bipartisan approach to foreign affairs than had existed before Pearl Harbor, particularly those related to the control of atomic energy and the organization of the armed services. The U.S. delegation to the San Francisco conference that brought the UN into being included Tom Connally of Texas, who chaired the Senate Committee on Foreign Relations, and the ranking Republican member, Arthur Vandenberg of Michigan, who increasingly abjured his prewar isolationism. The fierce divisions and close votes that had marked lawmaking about neutrality and conscription in the late 1930s and the start of the 1940s did not reappear. Some of the most far-reaching laws passed with little or no recorded opposition. The Atomic Energy Act of 1946, which gathered great power in the hands of the Atomic Energy Commission, was approved without a roll call in the Senate, and by a large majority in the House, followed by a voice vote that endorsed the conference report. Similarly, the National Security Act of 1947, which redesigned the organizational architecture of the federal government in fundamental ways, was adopted in each chamber by voice vote. Joseph Wilson, a Texan, expressed a widely shared sentiment when he told the House, "It has been said here that this is a piece of 'must' legislation for both the Democrats and the Republicans. I say you can leave out 'Democrats' and 'Republicans' and say that this is a piece of 'must' legislation for America and its future."[90] Similarly, the Defense Reorganization Act of 1949, which fine-tuned the Pentagon, was confirmed by voice vote in the Senate, and approved in the House by a 356–7 margin after the ranking Republican on the House Armed Services Committee, Dewey Short, of Missouri, praised Georgia's Carl Vinson, the committee's Democratic chair, for his "capacity, energy, and sagacity" in moving the law to completion.[91] Fear for the country's survival as a robust democracy often placed national security above national politics.

Notwithstanding, controversy remained. There was much debate, often sharp and rancorous, inside congressional committee rooms and sometimes on the floor about policies and purposes, concepts and practices. When the regulation of atomic energy was considered, there was a well-defined division between the members of Congress who wanted the military to be in charge and those who insisted on civilian control. When the armed forces were reorganized, some preferred a unified military command under the auspices of a single senior general; others favored a more complex structure of leadership. When military manpower was discussed, there emerged severe differences dividing members who supported universal military training from those who wanted a draft that would only conscript persons who were needed for a current conflict.

We have already seen how the congressional power of the southern wing of the Democratic Party loomed large during the postwar years when crucial judgments were made about capitalism and labor. Regarding might and security, the southern position tended to be persistently expansive, just as it had been before World War II. Of all the blocs in Congress that backed the Truman administration's international policies, southern Democrats were the most steadfast; the great majority of state delegations that offered the highest level of support for its prodigious initiatives were southern.[92] As a whole, representatives from this region were the most consistently prepared to project U.S. military power and campaign for democracy overseas. Especially striking was how members of the House and Senate from the South who resisted the more vigorous parts of the domestic New Deal and a key role for organized labor forcefully backed the national security state. Maryland senator Millard Tydings, for example, gave Presidents Roosevelt and Truman fits as a congressional adversary on economic and social policy. He helped lead the frontal assault on organized labor that produced the Taft-Hartley Act. But he strongly backed policies and institutions that asserted global power. Americans, he counseled in November 1947, must unite, and be "willing to curtail our own enjoyment of wealth and possessions," and not "turn back from this sacrificial action" because "the risk is too great."[93] In this quest, he was happy to join with organized labor and liberal Democrats who were prepared to back his sense of an American crusade, including a new group, Americans for Democratic Action, whose founders included Walter Reuther, Eleanor Roosevelt, and Arthur Schlesinger Jr.

Republicans, by contrast, were less united.[94] Within the Republican Party, two distinct lines of criticism regarding President Truman's policies developed. The first, though hostile to the Soviet Union, wanted to sharply limit any continuing U.S. involvement in European affairs, restrict the country's defense perimeter to the Western Hemisphere, and confront Soviet power only when core U.S. interests were threatened directly. Supporters of this position also were concerned, as California's Donald Jackson told the House, that a powerful and centralized national security state could pose "a serious challenge to our national traditions" by creating "evils of concentration . . . more dangerous in its implications than anything now existent in the executive branch of government."[95] Harold Knutson of Minnesota, the chairman of the House Ways and Means Committee in the Eightieth Congress, which served during the critical moment for the formation of the national security state in 1947–1948, fought for tax reductions and against overseas spending on the grounds that "people are becoming fed up with all these foreign entanglements."[96] When plans were being made for a national intelligence agency, the country's leading Republican newspaper, the *Chicago Daily Tribune,* campaigned against it under the headline. NEW DEAL PLANS TO SPY ON WORLD AND HOME FOLKS; SUPER GESTAPO AGENCY IS UNDER CONSIDERATION.[97] Of this Republican group, Georgia Democrat Carl Vinson wryly argued, "They don't like Russia, they don't like Communism, but they don't want to do anything to stop it."[98]

By contrast, other Republicans (including the first-term California House member Richard Nixon, who had campaigned for a no-appeasement "realistic foreign policy" and was disappointed that President Truman's announcement of aid to Greece and Turkey was silent about China,[99] thought that the Truman administration was "weak on Communism," especially in Asia, and that its efforts to contain the Soviet Union were too hesitant. Their preference was a greatly more assertive American military stance, even to the point of initiating a showdown with the USSR before that country could level the playing field by coming to possess atomic weapons.[100]

The Senate's most important Republican, Robert Taft of Ohio, the majority leader in the Eightieth Congress, was forced to balance both schools of thought. In a speech to the Rhode Island Republican Club in January 1948, he argued that high military spending and mobilization for national security threatened to overcome the very "America we are trying to preserve."[101] But concurrently, he criticized the Democrats for practicing a policy of "appeasing Russia" and sacrificing "the freedom of many nations and millions of people."[102]

Most nonsouthern Democrats joined their southern colleagues to back President Truman's global policies, which they believed were successfully combining assertiveness with prudence. On those occasions when Congress did not vote to build a national security state with overwhelmingly bipartisan votes, the House and Senate largely split along party lines. From 1945 through 1952, southern and nonsouthern Democrats voted in the main with a similar commitment to back the Truman administration.[103]

Yet high Democratic agreement across regional lines should not obscure tensions about these issues within the party. Nonsouthern Democrats also found themselves often unable to speak with one voice. With nostalgia for the anti-Fascist alliance, a sense of sympathy with left-wing European movements, and hope for cooperation with the Soviet Union, more than a few Democrats thought that the Cold War had developed less as the result of Soviet behavior than of persistent American misjudgment and overextended ambition.[104] While others saw ominous signs in Soviet speech and behavior, this vocal minority, led before his defection in 1948 by former vice president and former commerce secretary Henry Wallace, focused on the fact that the Soviet Union had taken positions that were not unreasonable about reparations from Germany, the reconstruction of Italy and Japan, and other strategic issues.[105] When President Truman declared his doctrine of active engagement in Greece and Turkey, many liberal Democrats in Congress and outside it were either reserved or opposed at the outset.[106] Rather than follow a policy of active containment, they preferred negotiations and concessions to restore the spirit of Yalta.[107]

Faced with insecure support from the left side of his party and with complex divisions among Republicans, Truman and his administration came to rely heavily on southern legislators, especially in congressional committees and, where needed, on the floor of each chamber, to lead coalitions that would advance their preferred policies. The policy steadiness, seniority, and party leadership of southern representatives placed them in a pivotal role when the content of national security bills was crafted, when the amending process had to be controlled, and when votes had to be won when there were divisions on the floor. As the war was ending, sixteen Democrats served on the Military Affairs Committee in the House. The six with the most seniority were from Kentucky, Texas, Louisiana, Alabama, North Carolina, and Tennessee. Of the others, three more were southern. On the Committee on Naval Affairs, six of the most-senior nine Democrats were from the South, including the chair. The eight longest-serving Democrats on the Committee on Foreign Affairs included six southern members. Four of the six Democrats on the Committee on Un-American Activities were southern, including the three who were most senior. Much the same pattern prevailed in the Senate, where seven of the eleven Democrats on Naval Affairs were southern, and half the fourteen on Foreign Relations, including the two most senior. Even more striking was the role southern representatives assumed in the Republican Eightieth Congress, the one that adopted the National Security Act. Each of the six Democrats on the thirteen-person Senate Armed Services Committee was from the South; half of those on Foreign Affairs were southern, but these included the two longest-serving members. In the House, only two of the fourteen Democrats serving on Armed Services were not southern, and every Democrat on the Committee on Un-American Activities came from a southern district.[108]

This pattern of overrepresentation, which continued to prevail through all the Congresses that shaped the national security state in the Truman administration, placed southern Democrats in the most pivotal position. Though the South Dakota Republican John Chandler "Chan" Gurney, who chaired the Armed Services Committee during the Republican Eightieth Congress, introduced the National Security Act of 1947 and shepherded its passage, the three Democrats he brought to the House-Senate conference were influential southerners: Harry Byrd of Virginia, Millard Tydings of Maryland, and Richard Russell of Georgia. When the Defense Reorganization Act of 1949 went to conference, Tydings, then chair of Armed Services, again negotiated with Russell and Byrd by his side, along with the addition of Virgil Chapman of Kentucky. All the House conferees also were southern: Carl Vinson of Georgia, Overton Brooks of Louisiana, Paul Kilday of Texas, and Carl Durham of North Carolina.

The South's concerns about economic development and race, moreover, gave its representatives added reasons to lead in this way. The buildup of American military strength that had begun just before the war was most concentrated in this region, marking the start of a geopolitical propensity that has endured. "Defense Boom in Dixie" was how *Time* titled its report on the impressive increase in the construction of shipyards, military-base camps, plants for airplanes and ordnance, and oil refineries that led to accelerated economic development and urban growth.[109] Over the course of World War II, the South accounted for more than 60 percent of the country's new army bases, including the largest training camp at Fort Benning, Georgia. The region also benefited from some 40 percent of all spending on new military installations, and, despite its backward industrial structure, from 20 percent of the country's defense-industry expenditures.[110] During the second half of the decade, decisions to continue with such investments were critical to the South's efforts to close the large economic gap that existed between this region and the rest of the nation. An equation that correlated economic growth with military spending had taken hold in the South, and defense spending came to supplant in many ways the region's prior agricultural dependency.

We have also seen how the war and its aftermath accelerated racial conflict. Many scholars have emphasized how both the war against Nazism and the postwar confrontation with the Soviet Union advanced the emerging movement for civil rights because the United States could not credibly fight for liberty abroad while practicing Jim Crow at home.[111] But the relationship between white racial preferences and foreign affairs had another dimension, something of a countercurrent. With the American Communist Party "raising the red flag in the South" against segregation, southern legislators were sure that an affinity existed between their wish to resist black political advancement and their preference for a robust national security state.[112] Writing in 1947, a leading student of civil liberty observed how John Rankin of Mississippi, the ranking Democrat and "the guiding spirit" on the House Committee on Un-American Activities, had established a standard by which "anyone who favors the Fair Employment Practice Committee or who wishes to see the poll tax abolished in the South is a communist."[113]

V.

As LEGISLATORS turned to national security, the deep anxiety occasioned by the bomb marked every debate. The language frequently was tinged with alarm, often more of a tocsin than a logical argument. When the House deliberated about military organization in 1947, Mississippi's John Bell Williams, a World War II pilot who had been wounded in action, solemnly spoke about "the atomic bomb—the most devastating and powerful instrument of man."[114] Alabama's Lister Hill, his fellow southern Democrat, warned the Senate that "pilotless aircraft, homing rockets, supersonic planes, and atomic explosives will finish the demonstration that the Japanese Zero of 1941 so dramatically began" at Pearl Harbor. Republican senator John Chandler Chan Gurney likewise pointed out how, "with the development of supersonic planes and guided missiles with atomic warheads, the cushion of distance provided by the Atlantic, Arctic, and Pacific Oceans will no longer provide a corresponding cushion of time in which we may react to attack and mobilize our forces. It is not being an alarmist to point out that in the event of another global war hostilities will be initiated without prior warning, and by an attack as complete and devastating as lies within the capabilities of the nation which launches it."[115] With "another world war" conducted in these circumstances, Texas Democrat John Emmett Lyle Jr. warned the House, "it is highly probable that life on this star, as we know it, will be at an end."[116]

From the start of the atomic age, Washington was pressed to find legal, organizational, and strategic frameworks within which to superintend the revolutionary weapons that had devastated Hiroshima and Nagasaki. Adding to the widespread sense of fear was the absence of any precedents.[117] Starting with the Atomic Energy Act of 1946, and culminating in the decision in 1950 to pursue the greatly more powerful H-bomb (which was first tested in the South Pacific with the explosion of "Mike" at the start of November 1952[118]), the Truman administration sought to discover the means not only to create the bomb but also to manage this source of perpetual fear.

William Laurence ended his best-selling book on the birth of the atomic age with the urgent realization that as "mankind must now face the reality that atomic energy is here to stay . . . we must find means to control it."[119] It was just this goal that President Truman announced when he asked Congress on October 3, 1945, to create an Atomic Energy Commission in this "new era in the history of civilization" to grapple with the "potential danger" as well as the "full promise" of nuclear fission. With two months having "passed since the atomic bomb was used against Japan," it had become vital to adopt "drastic and far reaching" legislation beyond "any of our usual concepts" to regulate "the control, use and development of atomic energy within the United States."[120]

The stakes were immense. One of the country's top journalists, William S. White, published a report ten days later entitled "Bill for Atomic Control Is Expedited in Congress." His disquieting lead paragraph recorded how "Congress set out this week with anxiety and even foreboding on a task unique in the parliamentary history of the world, an attempt to control the well-nigh uncontrollable, atomic energy and the atomic bomb," and how the federal government would soon assume "powers unprecedented in the life of the country." Congress, he projected, was about to offer the executive branch a "grant of administrative power, vast and beyond anything in the history of this Government . . . to direct this fearsome force," a grant that would include the capacity to "nationalize atomic energy as nothing had ever been nationalized here before."[121]

As White was writing, Congress was taking up an atomic energy bill that was prepared inside the Department of War and offered by Kentucky's Andrew Jackson May, the Democrat who chaired the Military Affairs Committee in the House, and by Colorado Democrat Edwin "Big Ed" Johnson in the Senate. "Its aim," President Truman's memoirs recalled, "was to set up a kind of permanent 'Manhattan District' under military control."[122] Doing "what the armed forces wanted,"[123] as Congressman May put things, the May-Johnson bill proposed a part-time commission, to be composed by active military officers and atomic scientists who would oversee the work of a strong administrator and deputy administrator, each of whom could be a military officer. These commissioners would specify rules for the ownership of fissionable materials, the production of atomic bombs, the regulation of patents, the degree of secrecy that would be required, as well as decide how to police the loyalty of those with access to confidential information.

Despite endorsements by some leading physicists, including Oppenheimer, and despite vigorous support by Secretary of War Robert Patterson and Leslie Groves, for whom the administrator position seemed designed, key leaders quickly jettisoned this approach. Its Manhattan Project model could not overcome the resistance of administration figures in the Office of War Mobilization and Reconversion and the Bureau of the Budget who wanted civilians to be in control. Nor could it prevail over the active lobbying by "scores of atomic scientists [who] descended upon Washington to button-hole congressmen, lobby within the administration, and educate the public." These scholars and experts worried that the degree of rigidity and secrecy that "a military dictatorship over atomic energy" might impose would restrict effective scientific research.[124]

This was not, shall we say, a polite struggle. *Fortune* took note of how "the scientists of the country, backed by democratic forces, rose in fury and smashed the May-Johnson bill."[125] It was clear, the executive secretary of the American Association for the Advancement of Science, Howard Meyerhoff, conceded, that "so powerful a weapon as atomic energy calls for restriction of use, and restriction of use in turn demands certain restrictions upon freedom of research and freedom of publication," but military control seemed a step too far.[126] Leading Manhattan Project scientists denounced the May-Johnson bill. Some were appalled that even minor security violations might lead to long prison terms.[127] Harold Urey, the Manhattan Project physical chemist at Columbia University, told a group of one hundred scientists meeting on that campus on October 30, 1945, that this was the "first totalitarian bill ever written by Congress. . . . You can call it either a Communist bill or a Nazi bill, which ever you think is worse."[128]

With this opposition signaling that key physicists might refuse to collaborate in the future development of atomic weapons, the May-Johnson bill was buried in the House Rules Committee. Initiative shifted to the Senate, which voted to form a Special Committee on Atomic Energy. That committee began a first round of hearings in November 1945. Chaired by Connecticut Democrat Brien McMahon, who observed that "military control of atomic energy, though necessary and useful during war, is a form of direction to which scientists in peacetime will not willingly submit,"[129] the Atomic Energy Committee (AEC) soon began to craft a new version of atomic control legislation that was consistent with an early December statement by President Truman directing "that the entire program and operation should be under civilian control and that the government should have a monopoly of materials, facilities, and processes."[130]

In addition to McMahon and Michigan Republican Arthur Vandenberg, it was the committee's four southern Democrats—Senators Harry Byrd of Virginia, Tom Connally of Texas, Richard Russell of Georgia, and Millard Tydings of Maryland—who most shaped the Atomic Energy Act clause by clause. They understood that a framework had to be fashioned to facilitate advances in atomic weapons and assist the growth and security of the country's stockpile. The law they designed included a full-time civilian commission, advised by a military liaison committee (a compromise that satisfied the scientists and the armed forces) with nearly unrestricted authority to plan and organize all aspects of both peaceful and military applications of atomic energy.[131] The bill conferred to the commission the possession of all fissionable substances and all facilities required to produce atomic weapons. It was designated as the sole manufacturer of these bombs, subject to the ultimate assent of the president, who could authorize exceptions that would allow the armed forces to make atomic weapons in the public interest. The AEC was granted authority to investigate the loyalty of its employees in order to preserve atomic secrets, and alone determine which scientific and technical information should classified as secret, a restriction that it would define solely on the basis of how such a release would affect national security. Private patents that dealt with atomic energy were banned. Instead, the AEC was made the exclusive custodian of "all patents, plants, contracts and information related to atomic energy." In so doing, the law reflected the view articulated on the editorial page of the *New York Times,* which argued that "we cannot have free enterprise in a field which includes not only uranium but anything associated with it in utilizing atomic energy for peace. It is the price we have to pay if we want to avoid another catastrophic global war."[132]

With these provisions, the law established the commission as an unequaled bureaucratic planner of investment and production within the national state. The economic actor it created was "a very heavy property owner—one of the world's largest."[133] A 1951 overview observed that "today the Atomic Energy Commission's installations and grounds cover more area than the states of Delaware and Rhode Island combined," that "a new diffusion plant near Paducah will alone consume almost as much electricity as the city of Chicago," and that "the Savannah River project for tritium-plutonium production is just now commencing in a modest way by biting 250,000 acres out of South Carolina's farmland, sweeping villages and homes before it."[134] When it came time to appoint a chairman, President Truman chose David E. Lilienthal, who had served as one of the three directors of the Tennessee Valley Authority at its inception in 1933, and had led the TVA during World War II.[135]

Of course, the New Deal era had witnessed other instances of delegation to executive agencies, notably including the NRA, and to regulatory commissions such as the SEC. But the creation of the AEC, E. Blythe Stason, dean of the University of Michigan Law School, observed in 1947, was utterly without precedent in terms of the sweep of "powers to be exercised without effective guiding standards." With its remarkable capacities, the commission's "uncanalized power" placed it "outside the range of legal rules, principles, or standards." Perhaps, Stason concluded, "there is absolutely no alternative . . . no escape from conferring such powers," but he insisted that it was important to record the extraordinary degree to which planning for atomic power had replaced the market system, and to note the extent to which "the rule of law will be largely replaced over a considerable segment of human activity by control through the judgment of public administrators."[136]

A thorough 1948 review of the nine-month congressional process that generated the Atomic Energy Act underscored how it had been suffused with "emotions of fear and awe," and how, absent prior party positions, legislators did not divide along traditional lines.[137] Votes on amendments lacked named roll calls. The act itself passed the Senate by a voice vote. But as a complex and often heated process in the House revealed, there was no simple consensus. In that chamber, fully seventy-one amendments were offered. After much debate, each section of the bill was modified on the floor.

Though no roll calls were taken, an examination of the debate indicates that a southern switchboard often determined key outcomes when the House was divided, as it was, on the 121–57 division that passed an amendment offered by Texas Democrat Fritz Lanham to protect the AEC's power to oversee patents, in opposition to an alternative Republican proposal to strike any regulation of patents by the commission as an infringement on market competition. We can also see southern leadership on amendments when no divisions were recorded but the issue was controversial.[138]

Especially striking is the lead role played by southern members in promoting amendments, passed without recorded votes, that strengthened the AEC's ability to watch over the secrets of atomic energy and guard the loyalty of its employees. Any reservations were immediately equated with a leftist taint. The leak of a late June report by Ernest Adamson, the chief investigator for the House Committee on Un-American Activities, disclosed how security officers at the atom-bomb plant in Oak Ridge, Tennessee, feared that there had been contact between left-wing scientists, described as disposed positively both toward the CIO and world government, and "persons outside the United States."[139] Virginia's Howard Smith—the author of the 1940 Smith Act—followed up by successfully offering a proposal to oblige the FBI to investigate all individuals the commission planned to hire, and to certify that they would do no harm to the nation's security despite their access to sensitive information. Hatton Sumners of Texas followed with an amendment that included the death penalty as a punishment for divulging atomic secrets. Smith, in turn, claimed successfully that the minimum level of punishment for such acts should be specified as no less than ten years in prison. He also added language confirming that all other relevant language in the bill must be made to "conform to the amendment offered by the gentleman from Texas and the amendment offered by myself."[140]

When the Atomic Energy Act passed the House on July 20, 1946, it did so by a lopsided 265–79 margin. With the exception of a dozen Democrats, primarily southern, who held out for military control of the AEC, the negative votes were cast by members of a sharply divided Republican Party.[141] The main objection of those voting nay concerned the commission's control of atomic-energy patents. "If anything ever placed shackles on private industry it is the bill before you today," announced Charles Elston of Ohio. "Private industry under this bill cannot make a single experiment in the development of atomic energy for industrial purposes without a license from this Government bureau."[142] Republican Clare Boothe Luce of Connecticut likewise argued that the patent provisions of the bill "might have been written by the most ardent Soviet Commissar"; and Dewey Short, the Missouri Republican, remonstrated how "we are going to set up an Atomic Energy Commission and give it the power of life and death over private industry in this country," adding, "I do not like such a blanket, broad, delegation of powers run riot."[143]

Southern members secured a significant role in another dimension: congressional oversight. One of the most unusual features of the Atomic Energy Act was its directive mandating the establishment of a Joint Committee on Atomic Energy (JCAE), the first congressional committee in American history to be required by law. Because it dealt with a complicated and secret subject, and thus could not be challenged knowledgeably, and because, uniquely for joint committees, it was given the standing to consider bills for hearings and to vote on whether to bring them to the floor of the House and Senate, the JCAE garnered "more power than possessed by any congressional committee up to that time."[144] Its composition thus was uncommonly important. Of the eight Democrats in the initial committee, four southerners—from the House, North Carolina's Carl Durham and Texas's Lyndon Baines Johnson; from the Senate, Georgia's Richard Russell and Texas's Tom Connally—were key players.[145] Each was selected by the party's leaders, Sam Rayburn of Texas in the House and Alben Barkley of Kentucky (soon to be vice president of the United States) in the Senate, for their standing and for possessing positions consistent with the core features of the emerging national security state.

After holding more than forty secret sessions during its first eighteen months, the JCAE considered recommending an extension of the terms of members of the AEC to 1950 without revealing either the content of its reasoning, the substance of its deliberations, or the nature of disagreement within the committee.[146] The Democratic majority's report explained:

> Because of secrecy necessary to preserve knowledge essential to the production of atomic weapons, the operation of this vast setup is clothed with restrictions and mandates for security, and the opportunity for public examination and evaluation of its progress and of the impact of its activities upon the our normal peacetime or even potential wartime economy are non-existent. This situation is unique in administrative policy of our nation. It places solemn responsibility on your joint committee.[147]

Within days of the House's approval of the Atomic Energy Act, Soviet statesman Andrei Gromyko, speaking at the United Nations, rejected any plan for the supervision of atomic energy that did not vest its powers in the UN Security Council, where his country could exercise a veto.[148] Following final passage of the Atomic Energy Act in August 1946, President Truman signed an executive order the day before the commission's first day of operation that ordered the Department of War to hand over the Manhattan

Project and its atomic weapons, fissionable materials, and research labs in eighteen states to the AEC, despite the army's resistance to this transfer.[149] Chairman Lilienthal swiftly made clear that he would impose a tighter rein on information than had prevailed since the war. He denounced the publication of the Department of War's Smyth Report, *A General Account of the Development of Methods of Using Atomic Energy for Military Purposes under the Auspices of the United States Government 1940–1945,* which, he said during his Senate confirmation hearing, "has been the biggest breach of security since the beginning of the project," notwithstanding the fact that it had included only information that was otherwise in the public realm and had left out all the complicated details, vital to making the bomb, that concerned metallurgy, engineering, and industrial production.[150]

Within months, Robert Oppenheimer felt "some melancholy," having concluded on the basis of his service on the General Advisory Committee of the AEC, as he put things in 1954, "that the principal job of the Commission was to provide atomic weapons and good atomic weapons and many atomic weapons."[151] It was Section 6 of the act—the part that placed the commission in charge of developing this arsenal when "the express consent of the President of the United States has been obtained . . . for such use as he deems necessary in the interest of national defense"—that became the law's pivot, and the means to rectify the situation that the commission found when it came into being. As the law went into effect, there were no usable bombs in the stockpile; parts to build only a small number of these weapons; and no technology to construct them except by hand, the way Little Boy and Fat Man had been assembled. Notwithstanding the resolution of the conflict about civilian or military control, the commission thus primarily served strategic military purposes. More than anything else, it was "an off-budget subsidiary of the air force," a task it pursued with great success.[152]

Noticing this development in 1948, Byron Miller, the wartime associate general counsel of the Office of War Mobilization and Reconversion, recorded "a definite swing to military emphasis despite the victory for 'civilian control.'" With the Military Liaison Committee playing a significant role, the pendulum, he argued, had swung "way over toward military control in a period of war hysteria." In addition to taking note of the remarkable degree of central state power, including insulated planning abilities, economic ownership and control, and command of scientific research, Miller also underscored the difficulties that had been created for the scientific community by the demand for secrecy and intrusive loyalty procedures.[153] Looking back a decade later, the military staff writer for the *New York Herald Tribune,* Walter Millis, regretted how "the writing of the domestic atomic energy act, in the atmosphere of intense excitement, uncertainty and bewilderment which surrounded the subject in late 1945, contributed to the imprisonment of American atomic policy behind the bars of secrecy, rigidity and national-ist fears and bellicosity which were to hamper every subsequent effort at the solution of this gigantic world problem."[154]

VI.

THE DISAPPOINTMENTS of the postwar period, the rise of Cold War ten-sions, and the existence of atomic weapons made the question of how to organize America's central institutions of national security urgent and press-ing. In an emerging bipolar world with a growing number of flash points, it seemed imperative to arrange the federal government to overcome the incho-ate structures with which it had come out of the war. As the troops moved home, the country's strategic capacities were threatened by interservice rival-ries, a lack of clarity about what would supplant OSS intelligence, and a slackening of investments in military technology that came close to freez-ing the development of more-advanced strategic bombers and atomic weap-ons. Further, by 1947, the United States had taken on a remarkable range of worldwide commitments, some with boots on the ground. In addition to the country's responsibilities to defend the Western Hemisphere, an obligation that was formalized that year in the Inter-American Treaty of Reciprocal Assistance, U.S. soldiers were now stationed in Japan and South Korea, Ger-many and Western Europe, and the Eastern Mediterranean.

What was clear, yet again, was how no prior set of arrangements would quite do. As a result, the United States entered a remarkable period of inven-tion, a moment that witnessed the creation of a crusading state that would campaign—virtually without limit—on behalf of liberal democracy.

It had already become clear during the late stages of World War II that the increasing rift between the Department of War and the Department of the Navy—each with its own cabinet secretary, separate budget, and distinct congressional committees—had become a barrier to effective coordination.

Certainly this is how Vice President Truman saw the issue when he published "Our Armed Forces Must be Unified" in *Collier's* in August 1944.[155]

Truman, as it turned out, was something of an expert. No neophyte, he had served on the Military Affairs Committee as a member of the Senate, and had propelled his political career by chairing the Special Committee to Investigate the National Defense Program during World War II. He had also been attentive when Virginia Democrat Clifton Woodrum had led a House Select Committee from March to May of 1944 on "postwar military policy" that heard witness after witness, including Secretary of War Henry Stimson, make the case that the unification of the armed forces should be "the primary objective of the postwar period." There was only one witness who demurred, the new secretary of the navy, James Forrestal, who was "not prepared to say that the Navy believes that the consolidation into one department is desirable."[156]

One of President Truman's very first requests to Congress, on December 19, 1945, was an appeal for legislation to create "A Department of National Defense" that, combining the Departments of War and the Navy, would "be charged with the full responsibility for armed national security." He recalled how pathologies of division had hampered the war effort, and how it had been necessary not only to invent the Joint Chiefs of Staff but also to unify commands in the field. It thus was imperative, he urged, to "overcome permanently the present imperfections in our defense organization." The answer, he suggested, was a unified Department of National Defense with a single civilian leader. This form of organization promised to integrate strategic plans, achieve economies of control and supply, and line up military policy with larger national security objectives. It also projected an integrated training program for new troops, a leaner and more effective relationship between the military and the scientific community, and a single structure of command for the rising number of U.S. bases overseas, including those that were involved in reconnaissance and counterintelligence.[157]

Both the army and the navy, however, wanted something else.[158] The army's Department of War promoted "the idea of a single chief of staff at the top of the military hierarchy with over-all military and administrative responsibility."[159] This position was not new. The army had been promoting unification of this kind as early as 1943, when Gen. George Marshall had advocated a program of full military integration under his leadership. The

Department of the Navy resisted. Wishing to preserve its traditional prerogatives, it vigorously promoted an alternative plan, its leaders all too aware
that these developments posed a fundamental threat to the preeminence of
the navy, a position it had maintained since the beginning of the nineteenth
century. As a result, Secretary Forrestal recruited Ferdinand Eberstadt, his
Princeton classmate and a leading Wall Street banker, to design an alternative. Drawing on his wartime experiences as the head of the Army and
Navy Munitions Board and as vice chairman of the War Productions Board,
Eberstadt called for coordination between the Departments of War and the
Navy, not their consolidation. He explicitly rejected the army's ideas by arguing that a unified military command might overwhelm civilian governance,
especially if it installed "a military personage or hierarchy whose control over
the armed forces could dominate the civilian Secretaries."[160]

Ultimately, this dispute was resolved more to the navy's liking, despite
President Truman's tilt the other way in his Special Message to Congress
of December 19, 1945. Though the National Security Act, which he signed
on August 26, 1947, did create the Office of the Secretary of Defense, it also
continued with the Joint Chiefs, allowed each service to have its own civilian
secretary, and discarded the idea of a single supreme military commander.

Two other features of the 1947 National Security Act are noteworthy.
First, the "National Security Organization" it brought into being rested on a
much more extensive foundation than just the armed services. When Congress announced its purpose as that of providing "a comprehensive program
for the future security of the United States," its lawmaking conducted a
broad effort, as a contemporary observed, to also "establish and arrange civilian agencies in the executive branch to deal with the government's military
security functions."[161] Second was the creation of the air force as a coequal
branch, which reflected how sea power's role in U.S. strategic planning
had attenuated, with the military brass relying more and more on atomic
weapons.

Eberstadt had insisted in 1945 not only that the army was wrong to seek
to place the military under a single commander but also that a much broader
national security state was required "in the light of our new world power
and position, our new international commitments and risks." To meet these
tasks, he had envisioned a dense network of corporatist-style civil-military
coordinating boards that would culminate in a national security council, a

system not unlike that which had been convened by the NRA for the domestic economy in 1933 and by the wartime mobilization agencies with which he was intimately acquainted. Truman's December 1945 message concurred with this aspect of Eberstadt's recommendations. It strongly endorsed "a more comprehensive national security program," which he hoped would include "a coordinated, government-wide intelligence system," a new federal science agency to coordinate and sponsor research, and a mechanism that would be able to bring together all aspects of national security.

With the exception of the suggestion of an instrument to guide American science, which would have to wait until Congress created the National Science Foundation in 1950, the National Security Act fashioned these organizations. Most notable were the Central Intelligence Agency and the National Security Council (NSC), which continue to persist alongside the Department of Defense and the Department of State as the main "modern mechanisms of the national security state."[162] They were complemented by the National Security Resources Board (NSRB), to plan for civilian, industrial, and military mobilization in times of war; the Munitions Board, to coordinate the production and procurement of weapons; and the Research and Development Board, to maintain standards, rectify gaps, and oversee shifts of emphasis.[163]

When the OSS had been launched in 1942, Gen. William J. "Wild Bill" Donovan, its charismatic director, pronounced that "in a global and totalitarian war, intelligence must be global and totalitarian."[164] This credo lived on after the war when the navy, still smarting from the absence of proper intelligence warnings before Pearl Harbor, took the lead to push for a postwar organization that, as Adm. Samuel Robinson, who had served as the navy's production chief during the war, declared, should have a freedom of action based on lump sum appropriations that "would not be subject to accounting."[165]

Three principal alternatives presented themselves. One was simply to keep the OSS going, as Donovan was proposing. Another was to expand the FBI, which was conducting covert intelligence activities in Latin America, and whose budget had soared from $6 million in 1938 to $45 million in 1945.[166] Yet another was to lodge these functions in the Department of State, as Secretary Byrnes was suggesting. President Truman thought the first two smacked of a gestapo, and he worried that the State Department would prove inadequate to the task. At the start of 1946, he created the Central Intelligence Group (CIG) by executive order on January 22, to be led by Adm. Sidney Souers. The organization swiftly grew from a small staff of eighty at its founding to more than eighteen hundred by the time the CIA itself was brought into being by Congress in 1947.[167]

What this complex of organizations lacked was democratic legitimacy and an end to institutional uncertainty, achievements it could secure, its leaders and supporters understood, only if it were sanctioned by an act of Congress.[168] But even here secrecy prevailed. When the House and Senate considered whether to include a permanent intelligence agency in the National Security Act, it conducted hearings in camera and invited Allen Dulles, then a lawyer in private practice who had been OSS station chief in Berlin, then Bern, after World War II, and later directed the agency from 1953 to 1961, to lead an ad hoc seminar for a select group of members on how to obtain better foreign information and gain the ability to conduct secret operations overseas. He explained behind the closed doors of Room 1501 of the Longworth House Office Building that the "prime objectives today . . . are scientific—in the field of atomic energy, guided missiles, supersonic aircraft, and the like," as well as "political and social." Noting the "conflicting ideologies as democracy faces communism," not just in Russia but across Europe, Latin America, and Asia, Dulles declared that analytically parsed information based on systematic probes was essential to national security, and he called on Congress to create a CIA that would be "directed by a relatively small but elite corps of men with a passion for anonymity."[169]

With the establishment of the agency by Section 102 of the National Security Act, the CIA began to act. Its most notable early covert operations, directed by James Angleton, the counterintelligence expert who had served in the wartime OSS, were mounted in Italy, where Angleton had lived as a teenager. There, a Communist Party, the second-largest in the world, loomed as the potential victor in elections scheduled for April 1948. By subsidizing the Christian Democrats of the center-right, by deploying the American Federation of Labor to disburse assistance to non-Communist unions, and by influencing Italian opinion by planting false publications, the CIA enjoyed its first covert success when the Communists were defeated. It would hardly be the last time that the CIA would fail to recognize the sovereignty of borders. A new era had triumphantly begun.

The next month, the new National Security Council issued a directive, NSC 10/2, that formally set up an operations branch within the CIA. "Taking cognizance of the vicious covert activities of the USSR," it wrote, this unit, acting "in the interests of world peace and U.S. national security," was charged to undertake "propaganda; economic warfare; preventive direct action, including sabotage, anti-sabotage, demolition, and evacuation measures; subversion against hostile states, including assistance to underground resistance movements, guerillas and refugee liberation groups, and support of indigenous anti-communist elements in threatened countries of the free world," all of which had to be activities for which "the U.S. Government can plausibly disclaim any responsibility."[170]

Unlike the CIA, the National Security Council was hardly a secret organization, but its mandate to coordinate foreign and military policies in the White House reduced the scope of congressional authority. The 1947 Act specified that its members, in addition to the president as the presiding officer, must include the secretaries of state and defense, the civilian secretaries of the army, navy, and air force, and the directors of the National Security Resources Board and the CIA. Congress, by contrast, was tellingly not represented. Cut off from participation in this policymaking body, the legislature had to watch at a remove as the NSC's importance grew appreciably after the explosion of the first Soviet atomic bomb in August 1949 and the commencement of hostilities on the Korean peninsula the following summer.[171] In this, as in other areas of national security, members of Congress had actively consented to a reduction in its exercise of traditional, democratic controls; through these new structures, power was shifting from the legislature to the executive branch. Nuclear fear was fueling lasting changes to the American state.

12 ▶ Armed and Loyal

NOT SURPRISINGLY, THESE IMMENSE institutional innovations, so fundamental in their transformation of U.S.
foreign policy, experienced growing pains. It fell to
the Eighty-first Congress, the one elected when President Truman accomplished a surprising reelection in November 1948, to
make adjustments, and to the Eighty-second Congress to grapple with the new Soviet bomb and the Korean War. Not only
were Democrats back in control thanks to a remarkable gain
in 1948 of 75 seats in the House and 9 in the Senate—achieved
concurrently with the surprising reelection of Truman, who had
campaigned against the "do-nothing" Republican Congress—
but southern members composed the majority of this majority.

Of the 263 Democrats elected to the House, 140, or 53 percent, represented southern districts (alongside 8 Republicans).[1] In the Senate, where there were no southern Republicans, fully 63 percent, 34 of the 54 Democrats, were southern.

As this new majority considered how to fine-tune and further fashion the national security state, veteran southern representatives dominated the relevant committees. In the Senate, Armed Services, chaired by Millard Tydings, included seven Democrats; all but one, the most junior, were from the South. Their number included such key figures as Richard Russell, Lyndon Johnson, and Estes Kefauver. Four of the five most senior persons on Foreign Relations, led by Tom Connally, also were southern; a fifth southerner, the most junior, J. William Fulbright of Arkansas, was destined to be its chair from 1959 to 1974. Carl Vinson's Armed Services Committee in the House similarly was composed disproportionately of a senior southern cohort, eight of the most experienced ten. While Foreign Affairs, split between southern and nonsouthern members, was led by a New York Democrat, the next two in line were southern. Un-American Activities, about to enter its soon-to-be notorious heyday, was led by Georgia's John Wood; only one of its five committee Democrats was selected from the nonsouthern cohort.

Southern domination within the Democratic majority reached a peak in the Eighty-second Congress, elected in 1950. A Republican gain of five Senate seats, including one in the Southern border state of Maryland, left the Democrats with a teetering majority of 49–47. With this result, fully 67 percent of the party's senators came from below the Mason-Dixon Line. Likewise, the southern contingent grew as a proportion of the Democratic majority, to 58 percent of the party's seats.[2] Moreover, the South's hold on key committees was maintained and, in some cases, strengthened. It acted like nothing short of a legislative vise. Richard Russell chaired Armed Services in the Senate, thus placing the South's strongest leader in charge. In the House, Foreign Affairs was led by a southern member, John Kee of West Virginia, for the first time. There now also existed a Joint House and Senate Committee on Defense Production, chaired by Senator Burnet Maybank of South Carolina. Every Democrat, six of its ten members, was southern.

What is so striking is how the further ascension of southern Democrats strengthened the constellation of Washington's national security organizations. On their watch, Congress furnished the executive branch with enhanced capacities to coordinate military and diplomatic strategies, systematic intelligence, covert action, and tight relationships with large firms and leaders in science and technology. These decisions made permanent the planning and corporatist instruments similar to those employed during the New Deal's radical first period at home and during the recent global war. But there was a distinct fillip. This national security state was sealed off from the procedures and private interests that Congress was creating at the same time as a result of southern insistence. By contrast, central state planning and concentrated power were becoming hallmarks of the national security state, hand in hand with the rigorous policing of the loyalty of individuals and organizations.

I.

Congress reinforced the powers of the CIA and fashioned a full Department of Defense in 1949. In launching its various activities, the CIA had found itself hampered by the ill-specified terms in the 1947 legislation. Its director, Rear Adm. Roscoe Hillenkoetter, went to Capitol Hill in February 1949 to brief Chairman Vinson about what he believed to be imperative requirements for the CIA. Vinson soon convened another set of secret hearings, declaring that "when you are in the spy business you can't go shouting about it from the house tops." His Armed Service Committee produced the legislation that became the Central Intelligence Act of 1949, a law that passed by voice votes in both chambers on May 27 without any open debate.

This legislation conferred almost limitless powers.[3] It freed the CIA from ordinary procedures of many kinds, including the need to release its spending patterns or reveal its fiscal practices. CIA funds could be left unvouchered, and its administrative procedures, including its "organization, functions, officials, titles, salaries, or numbers of personnel employed," could remain undisclosed. This was the model that had been utilized for the Manhattan Project. In February 1944, Vannevar Bush and Secretary of War Henry Stimson had visited with the House Speaker, Sam Rayburn of Texas, to request an appropriation of $1.6 billion to build an atomic bomb without, as the Republican minority leader, Joe Martin, recalled, "a trace of evidence to show how it was spent."[4] Further, the new law allowed the CIA to bypass immigration rules and quotas in order to bring up to one hundred "essential aliens" to the United States each year. The first person to be admitted under this provision, a harbinger of future practices, was Mykola Lebed, a Ukrainian who had allied his paramilitary force with the invading Nazis and who had made his partisans available for anti-Soviet actions after they returned. Though "the Justice Department determined that he was a war criminal who had slaughtered Ukrainians, Poles, and Jews," its effort to deport him was halted when "Allen Dulles wrote to the federal immigration commissioner to insist that Lebed was 'of inestimable value to this Agency.'"[5] With activities like these, the CIA became complicit in cooperating with the "ratlines," especially the one directed by a Croatian Franciscan priest, Father Krunoslav Draganović, which furthered the model of recruitment that the OSS had used in Operation Paperclip to bring thousands of ex-Nazis to North and South America, including many scientists and military experts.[6]

This year also witnessed the passage of the Defense Reorganization Act. The Office of the Secretary of Defense fashioned two years earlier had not been a cabinet department, and it was quickly shown to possess insufficient clarity or authority with which to navigate among the military's competing interests and perspectives. Initiated in the House Armed Services Committee by Chairman Vinson and a fellow southern Democrat, Alabama's Overton Brooks, and ratified by President Truman on August 10, 1949, the reorganization legislation converted "the National Military Establishment" that had been created in 1947, the president explained, "into a new executive Department of Defense," which "gives the Secretary of Defense, under the direction of the President, direction, authority, and control over the Department of Defense."[7] By providing for a single cabinet officer secretary as well as a chairman of the Joint Chiefs of Staff to coordinate all the branches of the military, this law brought into being the structure that has persisted ever since. The Defense Department possessed no small dominion. During the 1949 fiscal year, this department commanded more than one-third of the peacetime federal budget, $15 billion of the $43 billion total, despite a wide-ranging consensus that it was desirable to rein in military spending.[8]

At the core of this burgeoning enterprise was the newly established independent air force that the National Security Act had detached from the army. Within the air force, lay the most significant new institution of all—the Strategic Air Command (SAC), which was responsible for the delivery of atomic weapons. Led, after 1948, by Gen. Curtis LeMay, a larger-than-life leader who would run for vice president on George Wallace's racist American Independent Party ticket in 1968, it had a distinctive structure of command within operational war planning. Unlike any other subordinate unit, it maintained a direct reporting relationship with the Joint Chiefs, for whom it prepared its own annual war plans, detailing how it would strike the Soviet Union.[9]

SAC compensated for the postwar decline in conventional U.S. forces. "Our military picture," Robert Lee Sikes, a Florida Democrat, informed the House in July 1947, shortly before the act passed, "is a sad spectacle compared to that magnificent fighting machine we had at the close of the war."[10] To be sure, his detailed assessment of military decline left out how, even after mass demobilization, the country still possessed an army and navy five times the size of the mid-1930s military, a force that was able to take on occupation duties in Germany and Japan successfully and place troops in distant military bases. After the devastation of the war, moreover, no other power could begin to equal the economic wealth and manufacturing capacity of the United States, or its extensive functioning oil reserves and productive farms. Nor, at the moment, had any other state yet demonstrated a comparable ability to build ever more advanced aircraft or manufacture a formidable arsenal of atomic weapons.

As America's postwar shield and sword, "the bomb was the heart of the matter."[11] "Now, after World War II," the editorial page of the *Los Angeles Times* observed in March 1947, "we have almost demobilized our Army. We have virtually deactivated our Air Forces. Our Navy is partly wrapped up. But we have the atomic bomb." From this, it took comfort. "What eminence would we have in world affairs of the moment," it asked, "if we did not have the atomic bomb?"[12] President Truman agreed. After the passage of the Atomic Energy Act, he institutionalized atomic weapons as a separate and primary part of the country's arsenal, thus putting into action the strategist Bernard Brodie's advice, dating from 1946, which had warned that "the force delegated to the retaliatory attack with atomic bombs will have to be maintained in rather sharp isolation from the national community. Its functions must not be compromised by the slightest demands for relief of struck areas."[13]

Before Truman approved research and development for a hydrogen bomb in January 1950, he authorized the accelerated rapid expansion of the atomic stockpile. When the Atomic Energy Act became law, the United States possessed nine atomic bombs. Under the management of the AEC, the country mobilized its industrial strength to build new reactors and mass-production plants. By the time the National Security Act was signed in August 1947, the arsenal had grown to twenty-nine. A year later, there were fifty-five bombs. By the start of July 1949, shortly after the first Soviet bomb, SAC could call on 240 that were ready for use. The following twelve months, taking the country to the start of the Korean War, witnessed a huge leap in numbers as the stockpile grew to 686. There also were technical gains. Each of the new bombs possessed a capacity for destruction that was considerably higher than that of Little Boy or Fat Man. By November 1952, when the United States had 1,000 atomic bombs, and the Soviet Union some 250, the largest was yielding five hundred kilotons, fully twenty-five times the explosive force that had wiped out Nagasaki.[14]

As this run-up was starting, and as SAC was taking shape as a potent "cocked weapon," the term General LeMay used to describe its purpose, the air force chief of staff, Gen. Hoyt Vandenberg, asked Bernard Brodie to comment on the target lists that had been prepared for a potential air offensive against the Soviet Union. Brodie fashioned his response by noting how the "admittedly temporary" American monopoly "makes possible *for the first time* decisive military action between the two great centers of power." He counseled that a policy of maintaining clear superiority should be pursued even after the end to America's exclusive possession, for "the fact remains that the atomic bomb is today our *only* means for throwing substantial power immediately against the Soviet Union in the event of flagrant Soviet aggression." As to targeting, Brodie recommended that in light of the bulky character of existing bombs, and the lack of sufficient numbers to take out fully the Soviet Union's widely dispersed military targets, the atomic arsenal should take aim exclusively at urban centers.[15]

So it was. A 1948 SAC emergency war plan prepared by General LeMay envisioned a thirty-day atomic war that would use 133 bombs to strike seventy urban targets in the USSR.[16] A 1949 Joint Chiefs war plan "called for attacks on 104 urban targets with 220 bombs, plus a re-attack reserve of 72 weapons."[17] But with what intention? On November 8, 1947, General Vandenberg had sent a memorandum to the first secretary of the air force, Stuart Symington, who later served as a Democratic senator from Missouri, from

1953 to 1976, where he continued to specialize in military affairs. "Is our purpose," Vandenberg asked, "to destroy the Russian people, industry, the Communist Party, the Communist hierarchy, or a combination of these?"

These were not questions an air force secretary could answer, but they swiftly defined a key aspect of the National Security Council's agenda, especially during the Berlin airlift crisis, when the balance of conventional forces was clearly seen to favor the USSR. Presented with the results of accelerated strategic planning, President Truman approved two policy documents. The first, NSC-30, "United States Policy on Atomic Weapons," the first official statement on the use of atomic weapons, instructed the military on September 18, 1948, to "be ready" in the event of war "to utilize promptly and effectively all appropriate means available, including atomic weapons," once the president directed that they be brought into play in order to reserve losses that were expected if a conventional war began. The second, NSC 20/4, defined "U.S. Objectives with Respect to the USSR to Counter Soviet Threats to U.S. Security" on November 23. Prepared by the State Department at the request of the Defense Department, it provided the answer that Vandenberg had been requesting, a change to the regime that governed the Soviet Union. The purpose of an atomic attack, it stated, "would be to reduce or eliminate Soviet or 'bolshevik' control inside or outside the Soviet Union."[18]

The prospective instrument of a war broadly undertaken for ideological reasons against civilian populations was the Strategic Air Command. First fashioned under Gen. George Kenney in March 1946, before airpower had been separated from the army, SAC was a small unit of just some twenty-five B-29s when Curtis LeMay took command in October 1948. LeMay's sense of the role atomic weapons should play was already on record. Following Operation Crossroads, the Pacific tests conducted in July 1946, he was asked to assess their results for the Joint Chiefs.[19] Summarizing the report's three main conclusions, he argued on July 28, 1947, that the bomb's utility and capacity had been underestimated:

> (1) Atomic bombs *in numbers conceded to be available in the foreseeable* future can nullify any nation's military effort and demolish its social and economic structures.
> (2) In conjunction with other mass destruction weapons *it is possible to depopulate vast areas of the earth's surface, leaving only vestigial remnants of man's material works.*

(3) The atomic bomb emphasizes the requirement for the most effective means of delivery. *In being there must be the most effective atomic bomb striking force possible.*[20]

The Berlin crisis, which had begun in June, had tremendously raised the chance of armed conflict. LeMay's announced goal was to build SAC's capabilities into an instrument that could deliver at least 80 percent of the country's stockpile of atomic bombs simultaneously in order to be able to strike a decisive blow against Soviet targets. By the start of the Korean War, June 1950, the fleet LeMay directed had grown to 250 B-29, B-39, and B-50 bombers that were manned by elite crews led by veterans of the strategic bombing campaigns of World War II. SAC also became an instrument of espionage. Unhappy at having to rely on captured German photographs of Soviet installations, it pioneered the use of photo spy missions from the air, initially flying air reconnaissance missions close to the Soviet Union while sending balloons with cameras across its borders.

By the close of the Truman administration, the air force was the fastest-growing unit in the armed services, commanding fully 40 percent of the military budget. As LeMay and his air force colleagues pushed for an ever larger force, they faced initial resistance from key congressional Republicans who wanted to keep the military budget in check. John Taber, who chaired the House Appropriations Committee during the Eightieth Congress, and Walter Andrews, who headed the Armed Services Committee, both of whom were from upstate New York, sharply criticized the scale of the air force's ambitions.[21] Their efforts at cost cutting were checked by key southern figures, especially Carl Vinson, who marshaled his fellow Democrats and some Republicans to press Taber to back an increase in that service's appropriations for fiscal year 1949 by $822 million, just $100 million less than the Defense Department had requested. Vinson argued on the floor that only airpower could counter the massive Soviet army of 175 divisions. Only in the air, he argued, was the United States "capable of competing with the Russians—and they are capable of competing with us. Preponderance of air power is in the balance. It is this element in which the decisive struggle is likely to take place."[22] Mississippi's John Rankin rose to endorse this view. Noting how "the next war will be an atomic conflict . . . fought with airplanes and atomic bombs," he contended that "this movement to increase our Air Force is to me the most encouraging step that has yet been taken on this floor. We have reached the time when our Air Force is the first line of defense."[23] Taber, meanwhile, was complaining that although it made sense to move more deliberately, "that seems impossible with the present feeling in the House."[24] The amendment offering the scale of appropriation that Vinson and Rankin championed was approved without opposition, 115–0, before the full defense appropriations bill was endorsed by an emphatic 343–3 vote.

With the Democrats back in control after the 1948 elections, such spending decisions were reviewed and sponsored by a single House Subcommittee on Armed Services Appropriations.[25] Given the new structure created by the National Security Act, it dealt for the first time with all the services together. Chaired by a Texan, George Mahon, it held eleven weeks of hearings. Among others, it heard from Vinson, who now led Armed Services, before it produced a budget that cut army appropriations, held the navy steady, and, most important, meaningfully increased the scale of the air force. The committee also received a briefing, off the record, about Soviet intentions from none other than George Kennan.[26] During the two days of floor debate— discussion that left almost all the members ignorant about why a certain level of spending was desirable and what it would buy—Mahon explained only in broad terms why this strategic posture was necessary. He argued that the United States must "prepare [itself] to strike a quick and deadly blow at the very heart of the potential enemy," and that "the only force under heaven that can now deliver the quick and devastating blow is the United States Air Force."[27]

With atomic weapons as its centerpiece, strategic planning took a turn toward making "a first strike on the Soviet Union's nuclear capability the highest priority in the event of war."[28] A key May 1949 review for the Joint Chiefs concluded that "from the standpoint of national security, the advantages of its early use would be transcending," and called urgently for a considerable increase in the atomic stockpile.[29] As war planning proceeded, it was understood that consultation with Congress would take place only "if time permitted."[30] But time, it was becoming clear, would not permit. With the Soviet Union's detonation of its first bomb and the war in Korea, U.S. strategic thinking took a turn toward the quick use of the superior American stockpile to first destroy the atomic capability of the USSR, even, perhaps, to the point of launching preventive bombing strikes at key targets.

On June 6, 1950, the sixth anniversary of D-day, General LeMay led a

SAC exercise that simulated a full-scale atomic attack on the Soviet Union.[31] As the Korean War remobilized the country, John Allison, the director of the State Department's Office of Northeast Asian Affairs, argued for a very assertive policy, one aimed at conquering North Korea by any means possible. "That this may mean war on a global scale is true," his memorandum of July 24, 1950, averred, "but when all legal and moral right is on our side why should we hesitate?" Using the term that had come to be widely used in the prior three years, he counseled that "the free world cannot any longer live under constant fear." In January 1951, air force secretary Symington was counseling a shift from the ground war in Korea to an air assault on China. If this course were to lead to the participation of the Soviet Union, the result, he advised, would be "the atomic bombardment of Soviet Russia itself."[32]

The development of an "early use" doctrine and the consideration of the possibility of overcoming inhibitions about the utilization of this terrible weapon raised questions about custody, which, under the terms of the Atomic Energy Act, belonged to the AEC. In 1949, after the Soviet Union developed the ability to strike the United States with atomic weapons, Maryland's Millard Tydings led a congressional effort to persuade President Truman to shift control to the armed forces. By April 1951, after Mao's two-year-old People's Republic of China had entered the war, and with the potential use of atomic weapons on the agenda as a pressing question, President Truman ordered the first exception to civilian custody of the bomb by transferring nine atomic weapons to the military command in Guam. By September 1952, as the Korean War raged on and fears for American vulnerability to Soviet attack grew, a new policy was put in place. Codified by the document "Agreed Concepts Regarding Atomic Weapons," it gave the Department of Defense, rather than the AEC, "custodial responsibility for stocks of atomic weapons outside of the continental United States and for such numbers of atomic weapons in the continental United States as may be needed to assure operational flexibility and military readiness."[33]

Hand in hand with this change was the exceptional buildup in both conventional and nuclear forces that began in the summer of 1950. Stimulated by the outbreak of war, a striking rationale for an energetic program of rearmament was sitting on the shelf as NSC-68, the landmark 1950 strategic assessment conducted jointly by the Departments of State and Defense at President Truman's request that they "undertake a reexamination of our objectives in peace and war and of the effect of these objectives on our strategic plans, in the light of the probable fission bomb capability and possible thermonuclear bomb capability of the Soviet Union."[34] Drafted from mid-February through March by a study group in the State Department led by Paul Nitze, this relatively brief document offered a hard-hitting, stern analysis that placed the incompatibility of the American and Soviet systems front and center. Unless spending on weapons were massively increased, and unless troop levels were substantially raised, this document counseled, the viability of the globe's democracies would be threatened by likely Soviet assaults. This was more than a standard geopolitical struggle for power; it was, rather, a battle for a particular way of life based on a "determination to maintain the essential elements of individual freedom, as set forth in the Constitution and Bill of Rights; our determination to create conditions under which our free and democratic system can live and prosper; and our determination to fight if necessary to defend our way of life, for which as in the Declaration of Independence, 'with a firm reliance on the protection of Divine Providence, we mutually pledge to each other our lives, our Fortunes and our sacred Honor.'" For this project to succeed, it concluded, "this Government, the American people, and all free peoples" must recognize "that the cold war is in fact a real war in which the survival of the free world is at stake."[35]

NSC-68 offered Americans four alternatives. They could continue to fund the military inadequately; undertake a preventive atomic war; withdraw to the Western Hemisphere; or do as the document proposed, ramp up American strength and preparedness through military investments and mobilize for a cold war of great range that would include the use of cultural and economic measures—that is, a crusade for freedom, with the United States at its center. Before the Korean War began, the document was yet to be approved. But with the outbreak of that fierce conflict, the country took the fourth course and broadly followed the document's directions.

With the adoption of NSC-68 as security policy in September, and with the quick adoption of a supplemental budget, U.S. defense spending ramped up very quickly, from an original projection of some $13 billion in fiscal year 1951 to an actual figure of $58 billion. Strikingly, while much of this expenditure was devoted to Korea, the bulk of it was directed elsewhere— to strengthen NATO and the European allies, to build a new class of aircraft carriers, and especially to enhance the air force's long-range capability to deliver atomic bombs. Military spending grew to $70 billion the next year, when expenditures on fighting in Korea reached their peak. Afterward, weapons and troop spending remained very high, just above $50 billion for fiscal 1953, never again to fall below $42 billion. A permanent war economy was born.[36]

Concurrently, the arms race took a more dramatic turn. Both the United States and the Soviet Union decided to develop and build a hydrogen bomb, a weapon based on plutonium fusion that could release one thousand times more energy than the bombs dropped over Japan, with each country's military and civilian leaders thinking it would be intolerable to have the other exclusively possess a thermonuclear weapon. This was a fateful instance of what specialists call "the security dilemma." Although the United States and the Soviet Union would have favored circumstances in which neither possessed hydrogen bombs, each was trapped by the desire, as a retrospective analysis recalled a decade later, "to avoid a world in which the other had the H-bomb and it did not." Thus both powers "rushed to make it, and they ended in a worse position than that in which they had begun."[37]

This had by no means been the only possibility. Famously, Robert Oppenheimer was deeply skeptical. Already in 1949, he had expressed ethical reservations, writing that "the use of this weapon will bring about the destruction of innumerable human lives," adding that this was "not a weapon which can be used exclusively for the destruction of material installations of military or semi-military purposes. Its use therefore carries much further than the atomic bomb itself the policy of exterminating civilian populations." He also had practical qualms. The H-bomb project faced formidable technological hurdles, and, he thought, had limited wartime purposes because it simply was too big for any strategic targets.[38] David Lilienthal and some other members of the Atomic Energy Commission thought that a decision to build a "Super" bomb either should be delayed until its strategic utility could be better assessed or the United States should opt for renunciation as a way to halt an accelerating nuclear competition, test anew the possibility of international agreements, and gain moral prestige in the cultural Cold War.[39]

Truman rejected this course. During a January 31, 1950, meeting with Chairman Lilienthal, Secretary of Defense Louis Johnson, and Secretary of State Dean Acheson that lasted just seven minutes, the president accepted the recommendation the AEC, the Joint Chiefs, the Defense Department, and the State Department had made, and he directed the AEC "to continue its work on all forms of atomic weapons, including the so-called hydrogen or super-bomb." By late February, Secretary of Defense Johnson received the "most urgent" appeal by the Joint Chiefs of Staff, who requested that the AEC move toward the "immediate implementation of an all-out development of hydrogen bombs and means for their production and delivery." On March 10, President Truman approved a National Security Council special committee report declaring that "the thermonuclear weapon program is regarded as a matter of the highest urgency."[40]

II.

DURING THE most confrontational moment of the Cold War, when the fate of the planet seemed literally to hang in the balance, the role of U.S. scientists as researchers and as citizens moved front and center. At stake was the control and funding of their research, and the certification of their loyalty. Both were adjudicated in an atmosphere suffused by nuclear fear.

At the very moment in 1945 when the original May-Johnson bill, which would have placed atomic energy under military control, was being resisted successfully by the organized scientific community, the Senate's Military Affairs Committee took up the closely related question of how to organize scientific research. The debate about the creation of the Atomic Energy Commission was a dispute about whether civilians or military officers would be in charge of an inherently guarded process. When a West Virginia Senator, Harley Kilgore, proposed during World War II that the federal government should create a National Science Foundation to actively plan priorities and provide oversight, he provoked conflict about the degree to which civilian government should direct research programs. His plan envisioned a director, to be appointed by the president, who would command a board composed of eight presidential nominees from American society, and nine from cabinet departments, including the Department of the Navy and the Department of War.

His explicit goal was that of linking research to social as well as military needs; to this end, he included a division for the social sciences. Kilgore's bill further ordered that funding be divided equally among the forty-eight states, plus some 15 percent to be distributed on the basis of each state's population, and that patents that resulted from federal funding remain in the public realm. In all, this approach combined populism with planning, an orientation that drew on early New Deal traditions and the left-of-center side of southern preferences. Over the course of the half decade of discussion that followed, his viewpoint was supported most ardently by some other southern members, including Claude Pepper and J. William Fulbright, who resisted what they believed to be elite control of science and sought instead to harness research in the spirit of their understanding of democracy.[41] Other southerners, by contrast, resisted strong federal planning capacity, including the control of patents, and thus often sided with Republicans during the various episodes in which this legislation was considered. For here was an issue in which the South's representatives were caught between their growing suspicion of federal bureaucracies in domestic affairs and their support for a strong federal role in national security.

Scientists lined up on both sides.[42] A minority, who backed progressive, popular-front organizations such as the American Association of Scientific Workers (AASW), which was founded in 1937, supported the Kilgore initiative. The leaders of the AASW first articulated this position in *Science,* the widely circulated and respected magazine, when Kilgore had first proposed a "Science Mobilization Bill" in 1943."[43]

Many other scientists, a considerable majority, demurred. Leading the opposition was Vannevar Bush, the director of the wartime Office of Scientific Research and Development (OSRD). His landmark report of July 1945, *Science: The Endless Frontier,* also called for a National Science Foundation, but of a rather different kind. He outlined principles and a program that called for assured long-term funding for basic research by an NSF to be "composed of citizens selected only on the basis of their interest in and capacity to promote the work of the agency." He called on government to provide the funding for research that would proceed "through contracts or grants to organizations outside the Federal Government," which "should not operate any laboratories of its own." Further, he argued, "support of basic research in the public and private colleges, universities, and research institutes must leave the internal control of policy, personnel, and the method and scope of the research to the institutions themselves." But this was more than just a plan for the autonomy of science. Bush, who persuaded Wilbur Mills, an

Arkansas House member in his fourth term, to sponsor a bill to his liking, also made clear that research was "absolutely essential for national security" and thus too important to leave entirely in military hands. As "modern war requires the use of the most advanced scientific techniques," he wrote, "a professional partnership between the officers in the Services and civilian scientists is needed."[44] When such legislation passed in 1946, President Truman vetoed it on the grounds that it took science out of the public realm and control by the president and Congress.

Following the creation of the other key institutions of the national security state, President Truman, in his budget message of January 1949, called on Congress to enact NSF legislation. After a circuitous process, the foundation was created in the spring of 1950, broadly along the lines that had been advocated by Bush, not Kilgore.[45] It was, finally, the combination of the acceleration of Cold War conflict and especially the explosion of the Soviet bomb that overcame the divisions that had prevented the adoption of a civilian federal science initiative ever since the war. As Oklahoma's George Howard Wilson emphasized in the House, the creation of the NSF no longer was a subject for debate about government planning versus civilian society, but about the ability of the United States to find "the slim margin of victory in a shooting or cold war."[46]

Between 1945 and 1950, the funding vacuum for basic research in the physical sciences had been filled by military and AEC patronage. "In the absence of a research foundation," Bush's biographer has observed, "the armed services would fill the breach, spawning a new breed of military technocrats that would dominate science funding for the next twenty years."[47] By 1949, fully 96 percent of federal funds for university-based research in physics, chemistry, and related fields came from the air force, the Office of Naval Research (ONR), the army, and the Atomic Energy Commission. The ONR was particularly attentive to the task of pursuing and recruiting talented academic scientists. As early as 1946, the navy spent $10 million on academic research and planned an expenditure of another $25 million for 1947.[48] When Truman was asking Congress to finally create an NSF, these sources were supporting more than thirteen thousand projects.[49]

In short, without a well-funded alternative to military sponsorship, American science developed an intimate relationship with military planners during the half decade following World War II, with little or no resistance by the scientific community. In 1946, General Eisenhower called on the Department of War to bring scientists into military planning, and create organizationally distinct units for research and development.[50] By the time the NSF finally appeared on the scene, its budget was tiny: $250,000 for start-up in the first year; $300,000, despite a request for $14 million, in the second. By contrast, "big science" basic research was amply funded by the national security state at a level approaching twenty-five times the federal government's investment on the eve of the European war in 1939.[51] During the course of the Korean War, NSF's funding was raised to $6.3 million, for fiscal 1952, but "the military remained the primary source for postwar funding for basic research in the physical sciences."[52]

Some scientists grew afraid as planning for scientific knowledge commanded the driver's seat under the closed and sheltered national security state auspices. Speaking to a rapt audience in April 1952 at Columbia University, the distinguished chemist and long-standing president of Harvard University, James Conant, remarked how "one must ponder on the consequences of the vast sums of money now being spent on secret military research and development undertakings." At stake, he believed, were "the traditions that have made science possible."[53] The mobilization of physics in particular made the discipline an adjunct of the military planning state that undergirded U.S. global policy, policy that combined a focus on defense in the face of vulnerability with an ideological offensive in the cause of liberal democracy.

It was this crusading aspect that Henry Stimson promoted in an influential article entitled "The Challenge to America," whom he wrote for *Foreign Affairs* in October 1947. Arguably more than any other figure, he symbolized the quest for a national consensus at a time of spiraling anxiety. Having served nearly four decades before as secretary of war for President Howard Taft from 1911 to 1913, as secretary of state for President Herbert Hoover from 1929 to 1933, and, in his mid-seventies, as secretary of war for President Roosevelt from July 1940 to September 1945, he stood above the political fray. Disappointed after having been "very patient with the Soviet Government, and very hopeful of its good intentions," he articulated a desire to orient U.S. global policy to "make freedom and prosperity real in the present world. If we can, Communism is no threat. If not, with or without Communism, our own civilization would ultimately fail."[54]

III.

A s SCIENTIFIC endeavor became increasingly defined in terms of its value to national security, America's crusading agenda raised concerns for the nation's principles of liberty. In his *Foreign Affairs* article, Stimson further advised that "those who now choose to travel in company with American Communists are very clearly either knaves or fools."[55] But he did not promote any policies or actions that would limit constitutional freedom. He was certainly aware of the spirited debate already under way about the character and range of civil liberty after the war. He had surely heard the increasingly full-bodied demands by many Republicans and southern Democrats in Congress to confront subversion, and he knew of the decision by President Truman to announce a "Federal Security-Loyalty Program" in March 1947, which created what the political scientist Andrew Grossman has called a "Ministry of Fear."[56]

Robert Cushman, a Cornell professor, had devoted his January 1944 presidential address to the American Political Science Association to ruminations about "civil liberty after the war." Worried that the United States might find itself confronted by a ruthless totalitarian enemy in peacetime that, like the Nazis, would be "bent upon destroying constitutional democracy as a system of government and replacing it by a brutal totalitarianism," he predicted that "peace will bring in its wake an unprecedented temptation to abridge some of our basic civil liberties." At home, it would be necessary to decide whether "to extend the full measure of our civil liberties to those who will seek to use them to destroy civil liberty." He was particularly concerned that Congress, in reflecting public anxiety, would take the lead in pressing for the removal of suspect government employees, and would define "un-American" so broadly as to take in a wide range of views that are "politically and economically unconventional."[57]

Three years later, Cushman returned to the subject. More than anything else, he argued, it was the bomb, and fears about the bomb, that had made it possible for anti-Communism to take the form of persecution. Writing in an urgent tone in January 1947, Cushman focused on the "revival of witch-hunting," the widening criteria of disloyalty, and a heightened willingness to proclaim guilt by association both in Congress, especially HUAC, and the wider society. Having "brought us fear," he concluded, "one of the questions the bomb poses for us is whether our security is more important to us than our freedom."[58]

On March 21 of that year, President Truman signed Executive Order 9835, which obligated every federal agency to use the FBI to investigate the trustworthiness and allegiance of all its employees.[59] This deed—described by Arthur Schlesinger Jr., then one of the key leaders of the new anti-Communist organization Americans for Democratic Action, as a "shocking action" that had been "motivated in great part by a desire to head off more extreme action from Congress"[60]—announced its purpose as that of producing "maximum protection" to "the United States against the infiltration of disloyal persons into the ranks of its employees." The core ideas, it declared, were, first, that every government employee "is endowed with a measure of trusteeship over the democratic processes which are the heart and sinew of the United States," and, second, that the presence within the Government service of any disloyal or subversive person constitutes a threat to our democratic processes."[61]

But how should such citizens be identified? How should loyalty be measured? The order followed the outline of recommendations put forth by President Truman's Temporary Commission on Employee Loyalty, which had been appointed in November 1946 on the recommendation of a subcommittee of the House Civil Service Committee, a group chaired by Robert Ramspeck of Georgia, all but one of whose six most senior Democrats represented southern districts.[62] The president's March 1947 order commanded that investigations to determine the loyalty of the nearly 2,400,000 government workers would be overseen by a permanent Loyalty Review Board, with an initial budget of eleven million dollars. The board would inspect files held by the FBI, HUAC, the military, the Civil Service Commission, and those held by "any other appropriate government investigative or intelligence agency," state and local police and courts, the individual's school and college, former employers, referees, or "any other appropriate source." "Reasonable grounds" for the "belief that the person involved is disloyal to the Government of the United States" were defined broadly. They included more than acts of spying or sabotage, or an explicit advocacy of treason, sedition, or revolution, or actions "to serve the interest of another government in preference to the interests of the United States," such as the intentional disclosure of confidential information. "Reasonable grounds" also took in, as the dry language of the executive order defined them, "membership in, affiliation with or sympathetic association with any foreign or domestic organization, movement, group, or combination of persons, designated by the Attorney-General as totalitarian, fascist, communist, or subversive."[63]

The order's broad scope reached well beyond the most sensitive positions. Its capacious standards for disloyalty included associations and states of mind, and the absence of procedural guarantees or traditional trial procedures effectively suspended both constitutional and conventional standards by chartering an extrajudicial process loaded in favor of the prosecution.[64] By December 1948, a professor and a graduate fellow at Yale Law School were writing an assessment of "the constant and intensive check on the loyalty of all government employees" that took note of how in circumstances of "struggle, uncertainty, fear, and confusion," the United States had been brought "to a critical point in the matter of political and civil rights," and had created "a rising threat to democratic institutions."[65]

In effect, they argued, "a veto power on Government employment" had been placed "in the hands of the FBI." Underscoring the Bureau's refusal to identify confidential sources, they asserted that it had moved in the direction of a "secret police" with an "ingrown tradition of militant police methods" that could develop into a "grave and ruthless menace to the democratic process."[66] J. Edgar Hoover felt compelled to write a response. He insisted that the FBI was confined by the scope of the president's directions and would simply "report facts ascertained during investigation of persons alleged to be disloyal."[67]

From the announcement of this process until the standard was further toughened in April 1953 by President Eisenhower from evidence of disloyalty to mere doubt about loyalty,[68] fully 4,765,705 federal employees had to fill out forms that initiated the loyalty investigation of each, a requirement that was unprecedented in American history. Of these, 26,236 were referred for further scrutiny, charges were issued in 12,589 cases, but just 560 were fired or not hired, and 1,776 cases were pending at the end of this period. These, a member of the Loyalty Review Board, assessed as "pretty small pickings for a program which in cost ran into the millions and which caused hardships and heartburns to many of those involved."[69] But this form of counting significantly understates the effect. Life in science became precarious. By 1949, at least twenty thousand, and perhaps as many as fifty thousand scientists, engineers, and technicians "were either not working or working with interim clearance because they were waiting to be cleared."[70]

Two groups were especially vulnerable. Homosexuals became particular targets of the security scare. A 1950 report by the Subcommittee on Investigations, entitled *Employment of Homosexuals and Other Sex Perverts by Government,* revealed that the committee had conducted executive sessions with psychiatrists, prosecutors, and police to understand how, because gays and lesbians lacked "the emotional stability of normal persons," they constituted a security risk and were vulnerable to blackmail. The federal government's chosen answer was expulsion. Taking note of how the Department of Defense had announced a policy of removal in 1949, and how the Department of State was following suit, the report concluded with a soon-to-be heeded general recommendation that "those who engage in acts of homosexuality and other perverted sex activities are unsuitable for employment in the Federal Government," noting that "it is in the public interest to get sex perverts out of Government and keep them out." Some five thousand federal employees soon lost their jobs to this Lavender Scare.[71]

Atomic scientists composed the second exposed group, especially theoretical physicists who had been political activists on the Left before World War II in such organizations as the American Association of Scientific Workers and the American Association for the Advancement of Science, some of whom remained engaged after the war in efforts to contain the destructive potential of the bomb they had helped create.[72] They founded local organizations like the Oak Ridge Scientists and the Atomic Scientists of Chicago; and some fashioned national lobby groups, most notably the Federation of American Scientists (which later became the Federation of Atomic Scientists, or FAS). Drawing on the legitimacy of their knowledge to affect public affairs, they were particularly interested in promoting the civilian control of atomic energy at home and international control abroad.[73]

With the turn to loyalty investigations, these scientists proved to be the most important targets, especially after the Soviet Union exploded its own atomic bomb. Many wondered how a country with a more primitive infrastructure, less advanced technology, and more insulated community of scientists than the United States could have developed this weapon unless it had had the critical assistance of subversive American scientists.[74]

Of course, scientists were not alone as objects of suspicion. Some of the most spectacular investigations during the late 1940s and early 1950s focused on labor leaders, Hollywood actors and screenwriters, and State Department officials. But scientists stood out because of their pivotal position and the demand for atomic security. Not just tens but "thousands of scientists were subjected to varying degrees of harassment concerning their loyalty, sometimes from HUAC, but more often from the federal government's loyalty and security program."[75] An irony was at work. "Partly because what they do is so important to the national military security," the sociologist Edward Shils wrote in a classic consideration of what he called "the torment of secrecy," and "partly, too, because although they have an enormous responsibility conferred on them, they are not trusted, scientists . . . have come to bear the brunt of the loyalty-security measures."[76] As a result, science itself was changed, shifting from an open system that policed itself to a profession marked by compartmentalization and classification.[77] Strikingly, the flagship publication *Science* began to carry articles not about its usual substantive topics, but on "loyalty clearance procedures in research laboratories" and the "loyalty and security problems of scientists."[78]

To be sure, a tiny minority did, in fact, spy for the Soviet Union.[79] Some, like Ted Hall, the youngest physicist at Los Alamos during the war, simply got away with it.[80] Others, notably including Morton Sobell, who received a thirty-year prison term, and Julius Rosenberg, who was executed with his wife, Ethel, on June 19, 1953, almost certainly assisted in the dissemination of scientific secrets.[81] But despite the overwhelming constancy and faithfulness of the country's vast scientific community, and even though Soviet atomic spying dated almost exclusively to the period before 1945, America's scientists were subject, more than any other group, to FBI surveillance and to investigations in Congress by HUAC and the Senate Internal Security Subcommittee.

Not their actions, but their ideological proclivities and political leanings often moved to center stage. Sources of suspicion that made their way into FBI reports, loyalty investigations, and congressional committee plans included the "failure to show enthusiasm for cold war foreign policy; open advocacy of U.S.-Soviet accommodation, arms control, greater U.S.-Soviet cooperation in science, civil rights for African Americans, and noncentrist labor politics; insufficient expressions of antipathy toward communism of the Soviet Union; vigorously stated opposition to loyalty investigations; display of interest in

Marxism or other radical political ideas; association with communist or radical family members, friends or acquaintances; attendance or participation in meetings of left-wing organizations or gatherings where supposed communists were present; [and] refusal to name and denounce friends and acquaintances."[82] Such information was frequently conveyed by confidential science informants, themselves often subjects of doubt and distrust. The line between the necessity for mechanisms to ensure probity and the creation of a climate of inhibition and fear was crossed repeatedly. As a result, the boundary between totalitarian and democratic loyalty became increasingly difficult to discern.[83]

All the while, Congress exerted more and more pressure for punitive internal security policies by conducting its own investigations, holding public hearings, and initiating legislation that defined limits and conditions of citizenship. The congressional committees that were concerned with national security mocked the rules of due process they seemed to follow, including the right to counsel and the right to respond to charges, by proceeding with inquiries and examinations of witnesses in which "conclusions are contained in its premises. The purpose of the investigation," Andrew Grossman and Guy Oakes have observed, "is to present evidence, the logical force and probity of which are not subject to cross-examination, which affirms that the premises are true."[84] The key presupposition was the existence of a "Fifth Column" seeking to undermine America's institutions and "way of life" that had to be combatted in order to keep loyal but naïve Americans from unknowingly becoming part of the plan of subversion. The purpose of these hearings was not to prove a case, as if this were a judicial proceeding, but to confirm the theory.[85]

One of the most visible instances was the way HUAC kept returning to Edward Condon as a security risk, despite acknowledging that he had never been a member of the Communist Party, and despite the absence of evidence of his culpability in espionage or any clandestine activity. Born, of all places, in Alamogordo, New Mexico, Condon was an important nuclear physicist who helped build the bomb and draft the Atomic Energy Act. He worked in quantum mechanics, served as president of the American Physical Society in 1946 after working in the Manhattan Project, and was appointed that year by President Truman to direct the National Bureau of Standards. He strongly advocated open science across borders with the fewest possible restrictions of secrecy, and civil rather than military control of scientific research and institutions. Those views, and his affiliations with the National Council of American-Soviet Friendship, a group that was placed on the attorney general's November 1947 list of "totalitarian, fascist, communist, or subversive" organizations, got him into trouble, ultimately leading to the loss of his security clearance in 1954.[86]

Not long after Wisconsin senator Joseph McCarthy's February 7, 1950, Lincoln Day speech to the Republican Women's Club of Wheeling, West Virginia, in which he dramatically, but falsely, proclaimed to have a list of 205 Communists working in the State Department, Congress passed the Internal Security Act of 1950. The product of legislation sponsored in the House by HUAC chair John Wood of Georgia and in the Senate by the chair of the Internal Security Subcommittee, Nevada's Pat McCarran,[87] both Democrats, this legislation's declared aim was "to protect the United States against certain un-American and subversive activities." The act required "Communist front" and "Communist action" organizations to register with the federal government. It tightened laws on sabotage and espionage, lifted any statute of limitations in cases punishable by death, and made political beliefs grounds for the exclusion and deportation of "subversive aliens." Most remarkably, it provided for the detention without trial of citizens who had joined organizations defined as seditious by a Subversive Activities Control Board during times of "an internal security emergency," subject only to an appraisal of the basis for probable cause by a Detention Review Board.

The source of these provisions, which had not been included initially in the legislation proposed by Woods and McCarran, was the substitute bill authored by West Virginia's Senator Kilgore. Instead of requiring the registration of suspected groups, this bill built on the model of Japanese internment during World War II "to provide for the detention of persons who may commit acts of espionage or sabotage."[88] Though intended as a means to defeat registration provisions, these detention specifications were added, as Title II, to the Internal Security Act, which was adopted by a 313–20 vote in the House and a 51–7 vote in the Senate.

President Truman vetoed the bill on September 22.[89] His objections, like those of the supporters of the Kilgore detention legislation, were to Title I, which contained the registration stipulations. Truman declared these to be unworkable, a waste of time and money, and a misguided sacrifice of liberty that "would put the Government of the United States in the thought control business." Further, having received an objection to the immigration regulations from the CIA, which had seen them as "deterrents to our intelligence activities," a point of view backed by the National Security Council, he argued that the bill "would deprive us of the great assistance of many aliens in intelligence matters," since it would seem to make it necessary to exclude persons who had once belonged to Communist or Nazi parties. About detention, he was silent, except to note that this course might not be effective because the title did not clearly provide for the suspension of habeas corpus, and to recommend study of the issue "along these lines."[90]

Within hours, an aggressively determined House overrode the president, voting 286–48, with the negative votes coming mainly from northern liberal Democrats. Likewise in the Senate, which voted to reject the veto by a 57–10 margin on September 23, with support for the president limited to such leading Democratic liberals as Paul Douglas of Illinois, Hubert Humphrey of Minnesota, and Herbert Lehman of New York—all of whom, however, had supported the Kilgore detention bill. Their position was much like the one Arthur Schlesinger Jr. had articulated three years earlier when he had searched for a liberal standpoint. While rejecting the simplistic approach of HUAC and the many demands for "more extreme action" by Congress, he conceded "that a serious problem for national security has been created by that fanatical group which rejects all American interests in favor of those of the Soviet Union." In circumstances characterized by "the grim dangers of foreign espionage," and with "Soviet totalitarianism" being "massive, well-organized, and on the march," he identified "an inescapable conflict between civil liberty and national security" and called on the country's political leaders to "face up to the problem of resolving the conflict."[91]

IV.

"THERE IS much to fear in the atomic age, and our fear is the more naked because it touches on the unknown." The political scientist Clinton Rossiter published these words two months after the detonation of the first Soviet atomic bomb in Kazakhstan in 1949. Recording the "brutal fact that within five years at the outside an atomic attack on the American continent will be a scientific-military-political possibility," he bluntly identified "distressing questions" he thought it would be irresponsible to evade by asking how the United States would be governed and what would happen to civil liberty should the country have to face a "hail of bombs," "cities laid waste," "a fear-crazed population," and "mass panic."[92] Faced with a collapse of normal government, the only option, he suggested, would be "dictatorship, military dictatorship under the direction, I hope, of the President or acting President of the United States." He must, of course, have seen the irony of projecting how "the absolute weapon" designed to preserve democracy "will have brought absolute government."[93]

He added, "almost completely." Rossiter's dystopian, almost science fiction, imagination anticipated "the one alternative to no Congress at all," a joint interim committee of some fifteen to twenty members "with a specific mandate to act for the whole Congress until a constitutional session is once again physically possible."[94] Strikingly, seven of the eleven Democrats he enumerated as the most significant younger representatives who might be tapped to serve were southern: Alben Barkley of Kentucky, Kenneth McKellar of Tennessee, and Millard Tydings of Maryland in the Senate; and A. S. "Mike" Monroney of Oklahoma, Sam Rayburn of Texas, Hugo Sims of South Carolina, and Carl Vinson of Georgia in the House.

This vision reflected and reinforced the country's unprecedented sense of unending vulnerability. It was no longer possible even in peacetime, he concluded, to imagine an American government that "can be strong enough to maintain its own existence without at the same time being so strong as to subvert the liberties of the people it has been instituted to defend." No longer was the strength of the federal government at issue. "It is going to be powerful or we are going to be obliterated."[95] Based on planning and secrecy, and designed to fight totalitarianism and crusade for democracy, American might had seeped homeward.[96]

G EN. DWIGHT EISENHOWER prepared for the White
House from his home at 60 Morningside Drive,
Columbia University's presidential residence, during the period between his election, on November 4, 1952,
and his inauguration, on January 20, 1953. At 4:30 A.M. on
November 19, he emerged, collar turned up. Entering a waiting sedan, he was quickly whisked away to Mitchell Air Base
on Long Island to begin a clandestine journey, starting with a

twelve-hour flight to Travis Field in California and quickly followed by a ten-hour journey to Hawaii's Hickam Field. Meanwhile, the press was told that Eisenhower was spending the afternoon in front of his television to watch the Army-Navy football game.

No one left the plane either in California or in Honolulu. On it flew to Midway, then Iwo Jima, adding another twelve hours. There, Ike paid homage to the Allied war dead at the war memorial on Mount Suribachi, where the American flag had been raised by five marines and one navy corpsman, an event that had been immortalized in an iconic photograph. Eisenhower stayed the night in a Quonset hut before leaving for Korea, where he arrived fully seventy-three hours after he had first left home.[1] Such was air travel in 1953.

Earlier that month, days before Americans would cast 34,075,529 ballots for the war hero Eisenhower and the young California senator Richard Nixon, who had been making his name as a congressional investigator of disloyalty, and 27,375,090 for the uncommonly intellectual Governor Adlai Stevenson of Illinois and his segregationist running mate, Alabama senator John Sparkman, the United States successfully tested "Ivy Mike," its first hydrogen bomb.[2] The secret was revealed when sailors who had witnessed the blast at the Pacific Eniwetok testing ground in the Marshall Islands wrote home, in violation of the secrets provisions of the Atomic Energy Act, to tell family members what they had seen. Reluctantly, the Atomic Energy Commission had confirmed the explosion shortly before Eisenhower departed for Korea. The blast generated by this new type of bomb produced a mushroom cloud twenty-seven miles high and eight miles wide, with a canopy that extended one hundred miles. The test island simply disappeared. "It would take at least ten suns," one navy navigator wrote, to equal the explosion's light." "I could hardly believe my eyes," another testified. "A flame about two miles wide was shooting five miles into the air. . . . Then we saw thousands of tons of earth being thrown straight into the sky. . . . You would swear that the whole world was on fire."[3]

Touring the Korean front, inspecting combat battalions, and visiting with the wounded in standard army-issue winter clothing with no insignia over the course of three days, Eisenhower witnessed the trials of a "long, dreary war."[4] Following a meeting with South Korea's president, Syngman Rhee, the president-elect stated that he had found "no panaceas, no trick ways of solving problems." He also made clear that he would not heed the advice he had received to extend the war to the Asian mainland. "How difficult it seems to be in a war of this kind," he announced, "to work out a plan that would bring a positive and definite victory without possibly running the grave risk of enlarging the war."[5]

We know that as a five-star general, Eisenhower was well informed about atomic weapons well before the H-bomb was detonated. In early December 1951, he had been briefed at the Allied Powers Supreme Headquarters in Rocquencourt, France, by Robert Oppenheimer, who reported, over the course of five days, on the state of the country's stockpile, the results of recent tests in Nevada, and Project Vista, a research enterprise at the California Institute of Technology that was exploring whether tactical nuclear weapons could repulse a conventional Soviet invasion of Western Europe. Their last meeting also included other scientists and military leaders to review how America's atomic capability might be deployed in the event of a European war.

This session was followed by a lunch, hosted by Eisenhower, with the commander of the Strategic Air Command, Gen. Curtis LeMay. Both Oppenheimer and LeMay, reported the *Washington Post,* "went into detail with Eisenhower and his staff on exactly what the United States can deliver from its atomic arsenal if war comes."[6] Later that month, Oppenheimer broadcast the last of his six Reith Lectures in London for the BBC on the topic "Science and the Common Understanding." Delivered on December 20, "The Sciences and Man's Community" was his concluding subject. Both rueful and hopeful, he closed the talk by contrasting a vision of the "open society" with the Communist idea that "all truth is one truth," and he articulated the faith that notwithstanding the birth of the atomic age "there is a harmony between knowledge in the sense of science, that specialised and general knowledge which it is our purpose to uncover, and the community of man."[7]

We can be less sure that Eisenhower had been comparably informed about how atomic diplomacy was being deployed in Korea, or how military planners were considering how to take advantage of U.S. nuclear superiority. In 1950, with the war just under way, the United States had more than 260 SAC bombers and 300 atomic weapons at the ready; the USSR, by contrast, could only threaten to strike American shores in one-way suicide missions with a very small stock of bombs. During especially grim moments—in July 1950, as North Korean troops moved south; in November 1950, as the Chinese crossed the Yalu River into Korea; and in April 1951, as Allied troops were pushed southward across the thirty-eighth parallel—the United States transferred B-29s and partially assembled atomic bombs to Guam, signaling their potential use. The National Security Council minutes of January 25, 1951, record how Missouri's future Democratic senator, Stuart Symington, then chairman of the National Security Resources Board, declared that the bomb was "America's ace," and how Walter Bedell Smith, director of the CIA, told his colleagues that the U.S. stockpile was a wasting asset, "best used before the Soviet stockpile grew to such a point that Moscow would be willing to risk atomic war."[8]

During the first two crises, the bombers sent into the Pacific were accompanied only by bomb parts. In April 1951, President Truman ordered that complete and ready atomic weapons accompany the bombers "for possible action" against Soviet forces that might join the battle in Korea or invade Japan. When North Korea and China renewed their offensive later that month, the president approved a second movement of bombs and bombers to the Pacific. There they stayed until June, when the Soviet Union announced its readiness to open armistice negotiations.

I.

TAKING HIS oath of office during this winter of heightened fear, General Eisenhower placed his hand on the Bible that George Washington had selected for his, and the nation's, first inauguration. Conducted in the Senate chamber on April 30, 1789, just days before France's Estates General convened in Versailles and less than three months before the Bastille was stormed, Washington had asserted that America's "new and free government," a republic of laws, rights, and the separation of powers, was ready to "auspiciously commence."[9] Eisenhower selected this Bible, which had been present at the funeral of President Lincoln, and at the laying of cornerstones for the White House, the U.S. Capitol, and the Statue of Liberty, as a symbol of American continuity following two decades of crisis.

President Washington had said that he would "dwell . . . with every satisfaction" on the prospect that Congress, a "great assemblage of communities and interests," would act with "tranquil deliberations and voluntary consent" to advance "the preeminence of free government" and "win the affections of its citizens and command the respect of the world." It was just this capacity to govern though a representative legislature that was in question when Franklin Roosevelt took his initial oath of office on March 4, 1933. Across the globe, President Woodrow Wilson's crusade for democracy was a spent force. Parliamentary governments were toppling. Many doubted the surviving democracies could effectively address the troubles of the time without modifying their basic commitments to individual rights and political representation. When FDR spoke of how "withered leaves of industrial enterprise lie on every side; farmers find no markets for their produce; the savings of many years in thousands of families are gone," and, "more important, a host of unemployed citizens face the grim problem of existence," his listeners understood that in that "dark hour of our national life" even more was at stake than whether capitalism's spectacular collapse could be rectified. If Roosevelt were to prove wrong in his claim that "our Constitution is so simple and practical that it is possible always to meet extraordinary needs by changes in emphasis and arrangement without loss of essential form," alternative models based on absolute executive power would beckon.

Over the course of the New Deal, that possibility had been quashed. America's system, and especially the central role played by Congress, persisted. Lawmaking flourished. Capitalism was managed in novel ways. Labor was given a place. American might grew by leaps and bounds. Prosperity returned. The country's cohesion was maintained. The Constitution held.

Fear, though, persisted, and palpably so. Breaches of rights within the United States included the internment of nearly eighty thousand citizens and assaults on due process, privacy, and civil liberty. Loyalty investigations produced a corrosive atmosphere of suspicion in the name of national security. The period was also marked by deplorable acts of omission, including the failure to rescue those desperate to evade Nazi persecution or, subsequently, to offer refuge to persons who somehow had survived the worst. Demagogic figures like Father Charles Coughlin and Huey Long appealed to many millions.[10] Across America's racial divide, battles for the future of white supremacy and black possibility gathered force. And at the core of the New Deal enterprise stood the segregated South and its representatives in Congress, whose partnerships with nonsouthern members of their Democratic Party and, on some issues, with Republicans, were, as we have seen, indispensable to the period's lawmaking.

Fear also gained intensity through perilous confrontations with the Soviet Union and the failure to prevent an atomic arms race. Many worried that Soviet unity, industrial strength, military power, and ideological appeal would gain adherents as the more tempting, formally egalitarian, alternative. What was clear on the eve of Eisenhower's inauguration was that the Soviet bloc was combining defensive repression with assertive threats in Europe and Asia. News reports talked of purged Czech Communists put on trial in Prague and sentenced to death; a Russian UN aide deported as a spy; and nine Jewish doctors who had been arrested in Moscow on charges of plotting to kill Soviet leaders at the behest of Zionists and British and U.S. intelligence. There were also reports of new Soviet pressure on West Berlin, with President Wilhelm Pieck of East Germany threatening a blockade should the government in Bonn ratify the European Defense Community Treaty.[11]

Speaking at the imposing East Portico of the Capitol, Eisenhower focused in his first presidential address on such global sources of alarm, dangers that "dwarfed . . . the preoccupations absorbing us at home." Speaking in plain tones, he invoked the dramatic battles "through the forests of the Argonne, to the shores of Iwo Jima, and to the cold mountains of Korea" on the very day combat was raging in the Mundung-ni Valley, northwest of Kansong and south of Kasong, and American Sabre jets were battling Chinese MiG fighters near the Yalu River in a war whose outcome was indeterminate.[12]

Calling on the country to "acquire proficiency in defense and display stamina in purpose," Eisenhower defined the stakes as more than geopolitical. "Freedom is pitted against slavery; lightness against the dark." The United States, he reported, was engaged in an encompassing crusade against a Communist enemy that knows "no god but force, no devotion but its use," a foe led by persons who "tutor men in treason," and who "torture, especially the truth." This struggle, he insisted, "confers dignity upon the French soldier who dies in Indo-China, the British soldier killed in Malaya, the American life given in Korea."[13]

The language of a crusade dominated the talk. With the wartime U.S.-Soviet relationship having dissolved in acrimony, with atomic weapons at the ready, and with the United States having assumed "the responsibility of the free world's leadership," he exhorted America's citizens to "be willing, individually and as a Nation, to accept whatever sacrifices may be required of us . . . to dare all for our country." Speaking as the strategic store of nuclear weapons had reached 800 warheads deliverable by bomber and 1,005 in the country's stockpile, and as American schoolchildren were preparing for the possibility of an atomic attack on the United States by practicing duck-and-cover drills in their schools and by wearing metal "dog tags" that were identical to those American soldiers carried (I recall both vividly), the president soberly observed how "science seems ready to confer upon us, as its final gift, the power to erase human life from this planet."[14]

This severe speech closed the New Deal era with silences as telling as its emphases. Together, what was said and what was not sanctioned the central features of the national state that had been brought into being during the prior two decades. The new president was offering no frontal challenge either to the state of procedures and competing private interests or to the crusading state that was conducting a worldwide campaign for liberal democracy. Rather, as the *Wall Street Journal* reluctantly acknowledged, his talk was an act of "reaffirmation."[15]

Across the political spectrum, the nation's press quickly focused on what the *Detroit Free Press* celebrated as "the call to the crusade," the renewal of the "battle cry which launched the forces of freedom against the foe on the plains of Normandy," and the *Chicago Tribune* lamented an address that "might have been written at Mr. Truman's order for it amounted to little more than an endorsement of the foreign policies of the outgoing administration."[16] The "conjunction of an immense military establishment and a large arms industry," which President Eisenhower would later identify in his farewell address of January 17, 1961, as a reality charged with "grave implications,"[17] was embraced at his 1953 inaugural rostrum as "the strength that will deter the forces of aggression."

Concurrently, the new leader's silence about the New Deal's programs and policies at home tacitly sanctioned the domestic state that had been fashioned in the Roosevelt and Truman years. The long-gone radical moment of the early New Deal would not be revived; that was hardly a surprise from the leader of a political party that had fiercely resisted efforts to use the federal state to direct U.S. capitalism through democratic planning and shape a strong national role for organized labor. But with his silences, Eisenhower also signaled a break with the conservative wing of his own Republican Party. Wall Street would remain regulated. Markets would not be unfettered. Social Security would endure, and soon expand. Labor, though limited by Taft-Hartley, would not be squeezed further. The New Deal's program of fiscal management and interest-group competition would not be rolled back, either.

At the depths of the Great Depression in 1932, few could have anticipated how an economically prostrate and militarily feckless United States would revamp capitalism, deal with social class, build might, and solve issues of national security. Few could have predicted that the New Deal would craft effective policies when faced by the despair generated by a failed economic system, the pressures of mass disaffection, and the availability of alternative models that wished liberal democracy ill. When the curtain finally came down on the era after a twenty-year run, Fascism and Nazism had crumbled, while Bolshevism was being confronted. In 1953, the country was prosperous and internationally dominant. Washington had been transformed from a sleepy southern town to a great international capital. No longer perceived as a global backwater, the United States led what soon would be called the "free world," offering an appealing model for postwar designs in Europe and occupied Japan.[18] Less apparent but no less important were its democratic achievements, which inspired anticolonial struggles abroad and early civil rights efforts at home.

In the fall 1952 election, it was no longer debated whether liberal democracy would carry on. The existence of competitive interest-group politics and the fiscal framework within which it operated were taken for granted. There was broad agreement that the United States should take the fight to the globe's only other superpower. Across party lines America's leaders concurred with Arthur Schlesinger Jr.'s judgment of 1949 that in mid-century's "time of troubles" in which "Western man . . . is tense, uncertain, adrift," it was "only the United States," having come through the New Deal, that "still has buffers between itself and the anxieties of the age."[19]

At last, the protracted New Deal ended, but the new political era opened with more continuity than change. The combination of a procedural and crusading national state that Eisenhower's Republicanism chose to approve as the framework for America's resurgent democracy represented, not without irony, the last, but enduring, triumph for an expiring Jim Crow South.

Motivated to save their threatened racial order, the region's representatives had repeatedly proved during the Roosevelt and Truman years that they composed the legislature's most pivotal bloc. Their strategic position allowed them to halt disliked initiatives and advance preferred lawmaking. When Eisenhower concluded his remarks, Virginia senator Harry Byrd swiftly lauded the president's commitment to "policies that encourage productivity and profitable trade," which implied an acceptance of open world commerce buttressed by low tariffs, long a southern preference. House Minority Leader Sam Rayburn of Texas immediately praised Eisenhower for standing tall, like his immediate predecessors, in confronting "international desperadoes and aggressors" who, faced with massive military power, "will fear to attack us," also a southern preference. Senator Lyndon Johnson, his fellow Texan, almost giddily affirmed that, overall, Ike's opening manifesto offered "an inspiring statement of Democratic programs for the past 20 years," and celebrated how these policies were those that his region had propelled in Congress.[20]

II.

Looking back to the French Revolution, Alexis de Tocqueville warned that as great revolutions succeed it is important not to let "the causes which produced them disappear," or to miss the chance to ask a series of fundamental questions. "Was the event really as extraordinary as it appeared to contemporaries? As tremendous, as earth-shattering, and as rejuvenating as they supposed? What was its real meaning, what was its real character, what were the permanent effects of this strange and terrible revolution? What exactly did it destroy? What has it created?"[21]

Fear Itself has been devoted to comparable questions about a moment that was "something close to a revolution."[22] Rightly designated this way in David Truman's classic 1951 study of the process of government, the New Deal dramatically altered the context within which American politics operated. In making a state of procedures that organized political life at home, and in creating an assertive state that crusaded almost without limit for American power and values, the New Deal proved to be a rejuvenating triumph. By refashioning the context within which subsequent political strategies, decisions, and conflicts have unfolded, these relatively permanent boundary conditions bestowed an enduring legacy, and effectively demonstrated that a once-struggling and fearful democracy could, in fact, address the great issues of the time.[23]

Writing in 1944, the Hungarian émigré Karl Polanyi took note in one of the great books at mid-century of "how the very possibility of freedom is in question," adding that at issue was not only whether freedom would prevail but "the meaning of freedom itself." Over the course of two decades, the New Deal answered both questions. With "the political *and* the economic system of the planet [having] disintegrated conjointly," and with laissez-faire and many parliamentary democracies discredited, only "fascism, socialism, and the New Deal" were left standing as Polanyi finished his account of the origins of his time. Notably, he did not designate "liberal democracy" as the third option, because, at the time, only the New Deal's resurgent version of democracy could claim high legitimacy and achieve wide support.[24]

Having gained this standing, it was Roosevelt's and Truman's New Deal—more particularly, the New Deal that Congress sculpted in law—that rejoined the era's widespread claims that representative democracy was obsolete and incapable, a type of government paralyzed by division and indecision. Its decisions comforted constitutional democracy's anxious supporters, who, like Gilbert Murray, Oxford's Regius Professor of Greek, were concerned, as he wrote in 1938, that that it would be difficult "to keep alive liberal thought and feeling in a world which seems to have turned anti-liberal."[25] Combining audacity and imagination, the New Deal successfully initiated a durable shift in governing authority that brought a new national state into being.[26] Though the Constitution remained unamended, a "Second Republic of the United States"[27] was created, quite unlike the one that existed when Franklin Roosevelt first was inaugurated, and has governed the United States ever since. In so doing, this new republic has continued to define the meaning and character of freedom.

Ever since the inauguration of George Washington, American democracy had relied on tenets of constitutionalism—a structure of civic authority that prevents those who govern from limiting individual freedom; that protects persons and property from searches and seizures; that constrains government by law; and that offers elections as the means to give citizens a choice among officeholders whose positions differ on key issues of the day. Working to secure this framework, the New Deal did more than adjust policies. More fundamentally, its efforts to manage capitalism and assert global power changed the nature of the national state. It did so by emplacing a politics of groups, and competition among their interests, at the center of the procedural state it fashioned. It also did so by permanently embracing military and diplomatic might as instruments of democratic advantage. The manner in which these dramatic reorientations were accomplished—with congressional coalitions anchored by southern representatives who safeguarded racial segregation—both rescued and distorted American democracy.

Replacing the Progressive vision of a strong-minded state that pursued a widely backed common good as the hallmark of a healthy democracy, the domestic state the New Deal created substituted an institutional framework within which political pressure could operate. The result was a more fluid, more balkanized, understanding of how things did, and should, work. Stability was maintained not by sharing a communal sense of a singular public interest but by the fact that individuals are likely to have many overlapping memberships and commitments, thus making difficult the emergence of a single fault line across which citizens would confront one another. What counted in this vision was neither such oversized categories as capitalists and workers or individuals acting alone. What mattered most was how a plethora of groups pursuing their particular interests could compete within well-established rules of the game. The only national interest lies in these rules and the habits supporting them. These shape an open democratic game.

In the dictatorships, where fanatical emotion was tethered to confidence that a resplendent future could be grasped by mass vanguard parties, the state was everything, truth was unitary, and rights, the rule of law, political representation, and an open political process counted for nothing. In America's procedural democracy, the very sense of state dissolved into the process convened by officially neutral rules. With the state disinterested, the regime was understood to be fair. Any given set of policy outcomes represented a legitimate public interest because it had resulted from the play of politics governed by impartial procedures. Rather than being known in advance or imposed by fiat, the public interest was discovered only within the game. Outcomes were provisional. As the game continued, results could differ. No fixed end beckoned.

During the radical phase of the New Deal in the early and mid-1930s, the National Recovery Administration had singled out business, labor, and agriculture as the fundamental units of competition, bargaining, and collaboration. By the late 1940s, with laws having been passed under the joint aegis of Republicans and southern Democrats that limited the national scope of organized labor, this kind of political economy became impossible. Instead, the procedural side of the American state that Eisenhower inherited invited the competition and pressure activities of many hundreds of organized lobby groups, not just those associated with farmers, workers, and, capitalists. This structure of influence brought them directly into the legislative process by enhancing the place of congressional hearings that "quickly turned into a forum for the interested, organized associations to have their say . . . bid for influence, and act out in the open the fragmented nature of the social will."[28] There, pressure group politics gained force. Those who rail at the preponderance of lobbyists in Washington today or the uneven impact of organization and money in American politics must examine the 1930s and 1940s to understand these origins.

The vision that underpinned this procedural state was not "radically decentralized and democratized down to the grass roots and the shop floor," as once had been imagined by early twentieth-century and some New Deal political thinkers. Rather, as the historian Daniel Rodgers has acutely observed, "the New Deal realists . . . accepted the basic social interests pretty much as given; the benefits of government-sponsored 'counterorganization' bypassed most farm laborers, black sharecroppers, and the poorest of the poor. Their essential job, as the New Dealers increasingly saw it, was to keep the craft of state, leaky and unevenly loaded, in balance."[29]

The social whole, and with it the idea of a common good based on shared goals, disappeared. There was no attempt to galvanize agreement about the ends of government. That orientation served democracy by building a barrier against excessive ambitions of those who rule and as a means to constrain any potential tyranny of the majority. With government possessing no inherent goals of its own, the potential to abuse power is moderated. This procedural state thus advanced a robust version of democracy. In now classic studies, leading scholars writing in the early to mid-1950s celebrated what the political scientist Robert Dahl called "the American hybrid," a democratic regime based on a plurality of independent and relatively autonomous organizations, and agreed with David Truman, who approved its rejection of a national or public interest, "because one does not exist."[30]

But this particular type of democratic state opened the door to three kinds of deep problems that have persisted. First is a narrowing of politics to thin, confined, restricted, and potentially polarized interests. This contraction of civic sensibility to a politics without public purpose or norms can heighten conflict over limited matters and lead to gridlock or the rule of intense minorities.

Second is how putatively neutral rules favored those with more resources.[31] Open rules can lead to the capture of key policies, agencies, congressional committees, even political parties, by outside interests with focused goals and concentrated means. A state without substance is a state ripe for special interests to grab hold of key elements of government.[32] Although the procedural face of government did not officially recognize particular private interests as more privileged than any others, it effectively reduced the scope of labor as a national class, and in so doing helped enhance the power of capitalist firms and business ideology. This was quite an achievement, even a surprising one, in light of how much the Depression had shattered business prestige and had put market capitalism's legitimacy in question.[33] Especially with limits placed on organized labor, indeed with the steady decline in union membership since the mid-1950s, the political system has failed to counterbalance economic power. From time to time, efforts have been made to counter the imbalance of money, organization, and access, but unless strong counterpressures can be mobilized, inequality grows, poverty is neglected, and equal citizenship is compromised.[34]

Third is how, with "sovereignty . . . parceled out among the groups" and with public values trumped by private-regarding goals and power, the procedural state generates recurring crises of public authority and civic trust.[35] Disillusionment and cynicism result when a system declared to be impartial and just by definition is found to be unfair. The result is either too little political participation or episodic and volatile participation by enraged citizens who are convinced that the putatively neutral rules of the game are rigged. Once the New Deal's more assertive projects for managing capitalism ended and the prospects of a national labor movement diminished, both the result of actions by fearful southern representatives, the longer-term prospects of American democracy were sharply constrained, and the range of feasible options narrowed to a conservative return to business capitalism or a liberal defense of the fiscal policies that the New Deal ultimately fashioned.

If this domestic state was designated as dispassionate and disinterested, Washington's other face was remarkably different. Fighting on behalf of a keen sense of national interest—itself an amalgam of power considerations and liberal democratic ideals—this crusading national security state did not shy away from being cruel, cunning, and faithless. These were the three harsh adjectives the leading realist theorist of international relations, Hans Morgenthau, used in December 1952 to designate how all nations, including the United States, must act when their interests are at stake in a world persistently threatened by "continuous conflict and the threat of war." For the United States, such an orientation and such behavior, he argued, was both reasonable and rightful. When American security and liberty are jeopardized, he wrote, "the cause of liberty everywhere will be impaired."[36]

With the United States shedding illusions and embracing a hardheaded assessment of its global adversary, this combination of power and value dominated the diplomatic, military, and clandestine activities of the postwar crusading state. A week after his November 4, 1952, landslide, General Eisenhower addressed the country. EISENHOWER HAILS FREEDOM CRUSADE, the New York Times headlined. Calling for public support of the Crusade for Freedom campaign that "carries the message of freedom into all countries behind the Iron Curtain by means of Radio Free Europe and Radio Free Asia," the president-elect endorsed a war of ideas as an aspect of the larger struggle for the indivisibility of freedom, a concept that he insisted applied to "any nation, no matter how powerful."[37] The president-elect was joined in this appeal by Adlai Stevenson, a signal that this aspect of U.S. policy crossed partisan boundaries.

This side of the new American state projected might to advance democracy, but, in so doing, it often traduced liberty at home, and promoted authoritarian, often repressive, and sometimes murderous regimes elsewhere. It did not so much supplant Congress as live off powers delegated to it by a mostly compliant House and Senate, creating a sensibility that opposition to American military expansion was simply un-American. It celebrated military virtues, promoted private armies, conducted foreign subversion even of legitimate and democratic governments, and planted hundreds of military bases around the world. Many of its key decisions were made by small groups of actors, often in secret. When the sociologist C. Wright Mills published the controversial book The Power Elite in 1956, every decision he singled out as having been made in this manner concerned violence and military might.[38]

Though a critic of Mills's writing for underestimating America's procedural state, Robert Dahl had already shown how, in the vital area of international and military affairs, especially atomic energy policy, "the political processes of democracy do not operate." He cited as distinguishing characteristics the "*significantly* smaller" policymaking elite in this area, and the practice of secrecy. These traits, he cautioned, which diminish opportunities for popular control, had begun to produce "a kind of indigestible element in the operation of American democratic politics." He concluded by stating that "atomic energy appears to be one of a growing class of situations for which the traditional democratic processes are rather unsuitable and for which traditional theories of democracy provide no rational answer."[39]

This insulated state also stood guard at home, often exercising highly autonomous executive powers, all the while effecting profound changes on society at large. It watched closely over those who were thought to support external enemies, and it demanded a strong sense of unity, loyalty, and obligation from American citizens. This assertive state prized the kind of cohesion that was announced in 1940 by Justice Felix Frankfurter, writing for the 8–1 majority in *Minersville School District v. Gobitis,* a Supreme Court ruling that public schools could compel Jehovah's Witnesses to salute the American flag and recite the Pledge of Allegiance despite their view that such actions signify idolatry. Though this decision was reversed three years later, the language he used to reject their claim of First Amendment rights anticipated the increasingly common understanding that "national unity is the basis of national security."[40] Not the full-blown garrison state famously feared in 1941 by the political scientist Harold Lasswell,[41] the crusader state was partially contained by constitutional rules and congressional oversight, and by concern for international rights.[42] But its ambitions, reach, and abilities were, and remain, astonishing.[43]

National security crowded individual freedom. Lasswell, a friend of civil liberty, opened his 1950 assessment by stating that "the central problem . . . is how to maintain a proper balance between national security and individual freedom in a continuing crisis of national defense."[44] This continuing crisis generated perpetual fear, especially atomic fear, that sometimes led not to the reasoned assessment Lasswell sought to promote but to hysterical witch-hunts marked by a quest for disciplined unity, suspicious about loyalty, distrust of privacy, limitations on dissent, and an obsession with safety. As the country faced predatory enemies who wished it ill, it became all too tempting to compromise constitutional guarantees and confine the democratic character of the procedural state to issues far from questions of might and global power. Conflict, diversity, open expression, and the representative process itself, in these circumstances, often fell victim to the zealous defense of liberty and democracy, to loyalty as a supreme value, and to an obsessive search for treason.[45] A sense of permanent emergency governed by agencies specializing in security developed corrosive habits of enclosure that often eluded democratic accountability.[46] Civil society, moreover, came to be bruised by these circumstances and demands. A leading example is how the physical sciences came to be defined as an instrument of the state, and owed more and more of their research capability to military support, and faced intense scrutiny about loyalty and obligation in an atmosphere of frenzied political pressure.[47]

In the early 1950s, Robert Oppenheimer offered a vivid example of how even a most important architect of American national security could fall prey to such suspicions and practices. Well before he led the Manhattan Project, he had been attracted by various popular-front organizations on the left periphery of the New Deal. He never joined the Communist Party, but his brother had, and so had his wife before they married. When he was accused by former Communists Paul and Sylvia Crouch of having hosted a secret Party meeting at his home in 1941, his effective denial, based on compelling evidence that he had been in New Mexico at the time, persuaded even Richard Nixon, then a member of the House Committee on Un-American Activities, to report that he had "complete confidence" in Oppenheimer's loyalty. "I am convinced that Dr. Oppenheimer has been and is a completely loyal American, and further, one to whom the people of the United States owe a great debt of gratitude for his tireless and magnificent job in atomic research."[48] When an effort had been made in 1943 to turn Oppenheimer into a source of secret information for Soviet science, he had refused, and, after a period of reflection, he reported the effort.[49]

As it turned out, the FBI opened an investigation on Oppenheimer before Los Alamos, and had been tapping his phone and opening his mail ever since he had taken a lead role in building the bomb. With the end of the war, the Bureau renewed its surveillance, including more wiretapping, on the basis of his prewar associations. An intensive period of surveillance in 1947 turned up nothing, and Oppenheimer was assessed as loyal. In 1948, he openly recalled his former left-wing orientation, "with lots of Communist friends." This, he wrote, had been a quite typical product of concern for the Depression and hatred of Nazi Germany, a country he had come to know well when he had done graduate work at Göttingen in the mid-1920s.[50]

It was this blemished past combined with his mostly persistent opposition to the development of the H-bomb that generated fresh suspicions and investigations, with such suspicions reinforced by the arrest of Soviet atomic spies in Britain and the United States. Most important was the search for evidence of subversion and disloyalty by the executive director of the Joint Committee on Atomic Energy, William Borden. Based on the argument that Oppenheimer had contributed to the Communist Party before the war, had been in contact with Soviet agents, had weakened in his support of the atomic program after the war, and had opposed building the new bomb— arguments based on deeply flawed information and mere supposition; at most, the evidence was charged with ambiguity—Borden wrote to J. Edgar Hoover on November 7, 1953, to report his "exhaustively considered opinion, based upon years of study, of the available classified evidence that more probably than not J. Robert Oppenheimer is an agent of the Soviet Union."[51] Hoover, who had become a paradigmatic reflection of the worst aspects of the crusading state, followed up by warning the White House, and opened his own investigation. Though it found many of Borden's charges to be "distorted," its assessment concluded with the statement that Oppenheimer was "a serious security risk."[52] With this report, the White House was confronted with a political problem, and possibly with a security one. And with Senator Joseph McCarthy traveling a destructive and tortured path, the young Eisenhower administration decided to take no chances. At the start of December 1953, President Eisenhower ordered Oppenheimer's security clearance to be lifted.

Oppenheimer demanded a hearing to be conducted by the Atomic Energy Commission. Now led by Adm. Lewis Strauss, a strong supporter of the H-bomb who wanted to marginalize Oppenheimer for policy and political reasons, this process proved to be much like a criminal trial, but without the usual protections and guarantees. The FBI flagrantly monitored conversations between Oppenheimer and his lawyers, thus presenting Strauss in advance with the defense they would offer. On May 27, 1954, the hearing board decreed by a 2–1 vote that this leading scientist was, in fact, a security risk, largely because of his opposition to the hydrogen bomb, and thus lifted all his access to classified information. He was not found to have been disloyal, but there was no affirmation of his loyalty. Ironically, the one hearing judge, Ward Evans, who had made anti-Semitic comments about Oppenheimer, "about Jewish scientists usually being guilty," voted in his favor.[53] Following an appeal, the Board of Review declared that it had "been unable to arrive at the conclusion that it would be clearly consistent with the security interests of the United States to reinstate Dr. Oppenheimer's clearance, and, therefore, we do not so recommend."[54]

Remarkably, Wernher von Braun, the physicist and engineer who had developed the V-1 and even more devastating V-2 ballistic rockets for Nazi Germany, and who had utilized slave labor drawn from the Mittelbau-Dora concentration camp, was swiftly put to work to develop U.S. guided missiles. With his wartime compromises forgotten, he emerged as the single most important leader of American rocketry, and the incipient space program with headquarters in Huntsville, Alabama. His five-year citizenship clock concluded just as Oppenheimer was egregiously extruded from America's atomic program.[55]

III.

L IKE THOSE of Janus, who watched over the crossroads, gates, and doorways of Rome, the two faces of America's post–New Deal state were charged with the particular tasks of liberal guardianship. Both were rejoinders to the era's global tyrannies. The disunity that marked the procedural state's loose and messy political marketplace contrasted with totalitarianism's nightmarish political system, which permitted no discord or abrasion, and promoted "no interest but that of the state itself."[56] The crusading state's zealous global politics confronted the era's antiliberal dictatorships.

These two faces of the new national state were inextricably fused. Each side proved integral to the other, forming a practical and symbolic marriage that continues to define the United States today. The procedural model of freedom was tethered to its forceful defense and promotion. Without garrisons, the country would not have had the time or freedom to protect its constitutional practices and address its pressing problems through democratic institutions and norms. In turn, without its representative political order, America's global forcefulness could not have earned the necessary popular suspension of disbelief. The era's accomplishments keenly reflected this dualism, in effect the creation of a dual constitution—the one open and public, the other covert and far less inhibited by democratic oversight. As a campaigner for liberalism, the United States defeated or contained those who wished liberal democracy ill. As a procedural state, it advanced lawmaking that incorporated and balanced interests in a complex, diverse society, giving the large majority of Americans a stake both in the process of government and in the outcomes such legislation produced. This two-sided state, a state characterized by democratic advantages yet marked by antidemocratic pathologies, continues to constitute the world Americans inhabit. This, ultimately, is the legacy of the New Deal's southern cage.

From start to finish, the New Deal flourished with ethical compromise. These were not the kinds of compromises that constitute the ordinary content of bargaining, in which each side makes concessions in order to move ahead, reduce tensions, or achieve some other desirable goal. Democratic political life cannot proceed without such give-and-take. But as the tales of Italo Balbo, Iola Nikitchenko, and Theodore Bilbo signify, key New Deal compromises were of a wholly different order, various choices of the lesser evil.[57]

To be sure, they were not all the same. The Roosevelt administration's engagement with Fascist Italy, a more palatable form of Fascism than Nazism, was relatively benign. It was largely an attempt to absorb lessons about policy models that could be adapted to democratic conditions, and it lasted only until Mussolini decided to cast his lot entirely with Hitler and adopt anti-Jewish policies. The wartime alliance with the Soviet Union was more complicated. Stalin was a much more corrosive despot than Mussolini. Yet without this partnership, Nazism would have triumphed. The choice between Hitler and Stalin, the moral philosopher Avishai Margalit has rightly observed, was a "choice between radical evil and evil" once Germany had invaded the Soviet Union, with Nazi Germany representing the former.[58] Decisions at Yalta and Potsdam at war's end to concede large swaths of Europe and millions of European to tyrannical Soviet control was arguably more deeply flawed. But at stake was the creation of the new possibility for global security represented by the United Nations, the hope that international law could become a powerful constraint on malevolence, and a recognition that only more war could reverse the division of Europe. In all, the Soviet absorption of Eastern Europe oscillated between a genuine trade-off and a recognition of the inevitability of Russian domination.

The most deeply inscribed compromise—one that qualifies for Margalit's definition of a "rotten compromise," which he identifies as "an agreement to establish or maintain an inhuman regime, a regime of cruelty and humiliation"[59]—was the one the New Deal made with America's then–white supremacist South. With it, human suffering on the most existential scale was sanctioned. With it, eyes were averted when callousness and brutality proceeded, and black citizenship was traduced. Yet with it, the New Deal became possible. Only with a Faustian terrible compromise could lawmaking have stayed at center stage. There was no American enabling act. Productive legislation proceeded to grapple with the largest issues of the day in familiar democratic terms. In that painfully ironic way, the New Deal secured democracy, perhaps against the odds. Taking an even longer view, we now know that lawmaking ironically shaped by the southern bloc modernized in a manner that ultimately undermined Jim Crow's prospects. The New Deal—the New Deal of the CIO and the welfare state—produced at first mere chinks, then whole openings for social change that were grasped by an incipient, soon powerful, movement for equal rights for blacks.

The world the New Deal made thus did not preclude racial transformation or, in reaction, the radical realignment of southern white partisanship. It did not exclude big democratic gains or losses of liberty. Thus in establishing the boundary conditions of American life, the New Deal did more than define the origins of our time. It molded the institutions, conventions, and habits that continue to demand thoughtful choices in a world scored by fear.

NOTES

INTRODUCTION · TRIUMPH AND SORROW

1   Charles Beard, "The Historical Approach to the New Deal," *American Political Science Review* 28 (1934): 11. In this essay, Beard called for an approach that could place the New Deal in the context of other crises in American history. Roosevelt's first use of the term came in his July 2, 1932, acceptance speech at the Democratic National Convention in Chicago. "Ours must be a party of liberal thought, of planned action, of enlightened international outlook, and of the greatest good to the greatest number of our citizens," he argued, concluding with this promise: "I pledge you, I pledge myself, to a new deal for the American people. Let us all here assembled constitute ourselves prophets of a new order of competence and of courage. This is more than a political campaign; it is a call to arms. Give me your help, not to win votes alone, but to win in this crusade to restore America to its own people." Writing in 1950, John Gunther thought the origins of the term to be obscure. See Gunther, *Roosevelt in Retrospect: A Profile in History* (New York: Harper and Brothers), p. 124. Alan Brinkley credits the term to a 1931 cartoon by John Baer. See Brinkley, "Dilemmas of Modern Liberalism," *Prologue* 22 (1990): 288. Calling for "a drastic change in our economic system," Stuart Chase, an economist and student of semantics, published *A New Deal* (New York: Macmillan, 1932), which extended the four-part series "A New Deal for America" (Chase wrote three of the four contributions) that appeared in *The New Republic*. The first of these essays provided the cover story for the June 29, 1932, issue, just days before FDR's acceptance speech. Any link, however, remains speculative.

2   A quarter of a century ago, an influential survey observed that "while there remains a research agenda on the New Deal, it is secondary, not fundamental—the broad outlines and terms of appraisal are known." See John Braeman, "The New Deal: The Collapse of the Liberal Consensus," *Canadian Review of American Studies* 20 (1989): 76–77. "Energy brought to despair" is the way Alfred Kazin, in 1942, described the central theme of *USA*, the epic novel published in 1937 by John Dos Passos. See Kazin, "All the Lost Generations,"

reprinted in *Alfred Kazin's America: Critical and Personal Writings*, ed. Ted Solotaroff (New York: HarperCollins, 2003), p. 154.

3   Morton Keller, "The New Deal: A New Look," *Polity* 31 (1999): 662, 663.

4   Most notably, *The Aspern Papers* (1888) and *The Wings of the Dove* (1902). Henry James, *Italian Hours*, ed. John Auchard (London: Penguin, 1995), pp. 52, 76.

5   James, *Italian Hours*, pp. 7, 10. For the "brooding tourist" reference, see ibid., pp. 61, 63. The usage is discussed in Scott Byrd, "The Spoils of Venice: Henry James's 'Two Old Houses and Three Young Women' and *The Golden Bowl*," *American Literature* 43 (1971): 373. A useful overview of his fourteen trips to Italy is provided by Robert L. Gale, "Henry James and Italy," *Nineteenth-Century Fiction* 14 (1959): 157–70.

6   James, *Italian Hours*, pp. 7, 10.

7   Benito Mussolini, *Fascism: Doctrine and Institutions* (New York: Howard Fetig, 1935), p. 10. This book was first published in Italian in 1932. For a discussion of these issues in Gentile's own voice, see Giovanni Gentile, "The Philosophic Basis of Fascism," *Foreign Affairs* 6 (1928): 290–304.

8   "If I had the tragic honor of being German," Jorge Luis Borges wrote from the vantage of Argentina in October 1939, one month after the German invasion of Poland, "I would not resign myself to sacrificing to mere military efficiency the intelligence and integrity of my fatherland; if I were English or French, I would be grateful for the perfect coincidence of my country's particular cause with the universal cause of humanity. . . . I hope the years will bring us the auspicious annihilation of Adolf Hitler, this atrocious offspring of Versailles." See Borges, "An Essay on Neutrality," in *Jorge Luis Borges: Selected Non-Fictions*, ed. Eliot Weinberger (New York: Viking, 1999), p. 203.

9   Jawaharlal Nehru, "President Roosevelt to the Rescue," August 4, 1933; reprinted in Nehru, *Glimpses of World History: Being Further Letters to His Daughter, Written in Prison, and Containing a Rambling Account of History for Young People* (New Delhi: Penguin, 2004), pp. 1077-82.

10   John Maynard Keynes, "An Open Letter," *New York Times,* December 31, 1933.

11   Cited in Erika Mann and Klaus Mann, *Escape to Life* (Boston: Houghton Mifflin, 1939), p. 124.

12   Previously, American thinkers and politicians had looked across the ocean for answers to problems of urban planning, workplace protection, and social welfare. A feature of the extended New Deal is how "the surge of policy energy and initiative . . . reversed overnight the Progressive-era pattern of transatlantic political influences. . . . As Americans had once set off for social-political laboratories in Germany, Denmark, or New Zealand, John Maynard Keynes, William Beveridge, H. G. Wells, Gunnar Myrdal, and others now came to the United States to take the New Deal's measure." See Daniel T. Rodgers, *Atlantic Crossings: Social Politics in a Progressive Age* (Cambridge: Harvard University Press, 1998), p. 410.

13   "The beginning, then, is the first step in the intentional creation of meaning. ... a beginning is often that which is left behind." See Edward Said, *Beginnings: Intention and Method* (New York: Basic Books, 1975), pp. 5, 29.

14   This point is forcefully made by Albert Hirschman in *The Rhetoric of Reaction: Perversity, Futility, Jeopardy* (Cambridge: Harvard University Press, 1991). He stresses how public instruments in open political systems can outweigh any jeopardy they create.

15   "The New Deal in Review, 1936–1940," *New Republic,* May 20, 1940, p. 706.

16   Hubert H. Humphrey, *The Political Philosophy of the New Deal* (1940; reprint, Baton Rouge: Louisiana State University Press, 1970), p. 120.

17   E. H. Carr, "Vital Democracy," *Times* (London), November 13, 1940; cited in Charles Jones, *E. H. Carr and International Relations: A Duty to Lie* (Cambridge: Cambridge University Press, 1998), p. 83.

18   John Gunther, *Roosevelt in Retrospect: A Profile in History* (New York: Harper and Brothers, 1950), p. 289. All this was accomplished, he claimed, "without ever resorting to police power or terror," and "without any violation whatsoever of civil liberties."

19   Isaiah Berlin, "Roosevelt through European Eyes," *Atlantic Monthly,* July 1955, p. 71.

20   Arthur M. Schlesinger Jr., *The Politics of Hope: Some Searching Explorations into American Politics and Culture* (Boston: Houghton Mifflin, 1962), pp. 124, 125.

21   Hannah Arendt, "Home to Roost: A Bicentennial Address," *New York Review of Books,* June 26, 1975, p. 3.

22   Fernando Pessoa, *The Book of Disquiet* (London: Penguin, 2002), p. 247.

23   Reinhart Koselleck, "Crisis," *Journal of the History of Ideas* 67 (2006): 338.

24   Alexander Gerschenkron, *Bread and Democracy in Germany* (Berkeley: University of California Press, 1943), p. 224.

25   E. Pendleton Herring, *Presidential Leadership: The Political Relations of Congress and the Chief Executive* (New York: Farrar and Rinehart, 1940), pp. x–xi.

26   "To make the literary field longer, larger, and deeper" is how the literary critic Franco Moretti describes his parallel goal in Franco Moretti, ed., *The Novel,* vol. 2, *Forms and Themes* (Princeton, NJ: Princeton University Press, 2006), p. x.

27   For a discussion, see Richard Hofstadter, "History and the Social Sciences," in *The Varieties of History: From Voltaire to the Present,* ed. Fritz Stern (New York: Meridian Books, 1956), p. 363. Also see T. J. Clark, *The Sight of Death: An Experiment in Art Writing* (New Haven: Yale University Press, 2006). Day after day, Clark returned to a gallery at the Getty Museum that displayed two paintings by Nicolas Poussin—*Landscape with a Man Killed by a Snake* and *Landscape with a Calm*—to record how his perceptions shifted over time, and as conditions for viewing, such as the character of natural light, altered. The objects remained fixed, yet understandings and perceptions varied.

28   Many histories tend to truncate the New Deal, noting, as one student of the era put it, that "as a vital reform effort the New Deal lasted but five years." See Richard Polenberg, "The Decline of the New Deal, 1937–1940," in *The New Deal: The National Level*, ed. John Braeman, Robert H. Bremner, and David Brody (Columbus: Ohio State University Press, 1975), p. 263. See also David L. Porter, *Congress and the Waning of the New Deal* (Port Washington, NY: Kennikat Press, 1980).

29   I first was guided in this direction by reading the classic study by Lawrence H. Chamberlain, *The President, Congress, and Legislation* (New York: Columbia University Press, 1946). Chamberlain studied ninety major laws that had been enacted since the early twentieth century to discern the relative contribution made by Congress and the president. His central finding was that the role of Congress had been widely underestimated. "It does not detract from the importance of the President," he wrote, "to point out that [the] tendency to magnify his participation to the exclusion or neglect of Congress distorts the facts and creates impressions that are not only false but dangerous" (p. 15).

30   The classic statement is Michael Walzer, "Political Action: The Problem of Dirty Hands," *Philosophy and Public Affairs* 2 (1973): 160–80. An illuminating recent discussion can be found in János Kis, *Politics as a Moral Problem* (Budapest: Central European University Press, 2008).

31   Arthur Schlesinger Jr., *The Age of Roosevelt*, 3 vols. (Boston: Houghton Mifflin, 1957–1960).

32   Arthur Schlesinger Jr., "History and National Stupidity," *New York Review of Books,* April 27, 2006, p. 14. Historians, of course, have good reason to worry about any search for a usable past. Concerned by the potential for facile comparisons that lose the particularity of each moment, they are also troubled by the temptation to map the past as a road that must have led inexorably to the present. Such warnings are valuable admonitions, not blanket proscriptions. All good history is interested in explaining outcomes, whether recent or distant. And the significance of which outcomes to try to account for necessarily varies across time and experience. It was for this reason that the rumination that "we can truly understand the past only if we read it by the light of the present" by the outstanding historian Marc Bloch (whose fate it was to be executed by the Gestapo in 1944 after being caught and tortured as a member of the French Resistance) is a good deal more than a simple banality. Recognizing that there is no single correct map of the past, historians seek to craft a variety of maps that portray social reality with different levels of detail. See Marc Bloch, *Strange Defeat: A Statement of Evidence Written in 1940* (New York: W. W. Norton, 1968). Mapping is how John Lewis Gaddis describes the goals of the historical profession in *The Landscape of History* (New York: Oxford University Press, 2002), pp. 33, 48.

33   Alexis de Tocqueville, *The Old Regime and the French Revolution* (1856; reprint, Chicago: University of Chicago Press, 1998), p. 95.

34 Ibid., pp. 95, 83, 86. His passion, he explained, consisted of a "strong ... taste for freedom."

35 They were "historical moments when the basic metaphors of politics were up for grabs." See Daniel T. Rodgers, *Contested Truths: Keywords in American Politics since Independence* (New York: Basic Books, 1987), pp. 11–12.

36 Bernard Bailyn, "Political Experience and Enlightenment Ideas in Eighteenth-Century America," *American Historical Review* 67 (1962): 339.

37 George Steiner, writing about the complex friendship of Gershom Scholem and Walter Benjamin, observes how both the "minute particular" and the "generalizing interference" might "alter the whole landscape of our historical, literary, and social perceptions." See Steiner, "The Friend of a Friend," in *George Steiner at the New Yorker,* ed. Robert Boyers (New York: New Directions, 2009), p. 208.

38 Studs Terkel, "Hard Times," *Pen America* 10 (2009): 39, 43.

39 For the distinctions between acute and chronic fear, and between "the direct object of the fear and the effects of being frightened by it," see John Hollander, "Fear Itself," *Social Research* 71 (2004): 865, 868.

40 One of England's leading historians, Lewis Namier, collected his essays on the 1936–1940 period under the title, *Europe in Decay: A Study of Disintegration* (London: Macmillan, 1950).

41 *Congressional Record,* 72d Cong., 1st sess., May 5, 1932, p. 9644.

42 *Barron's* is cited in Ronald Steel, *Walter Lippmann and the American Century* (Boston: Little, Brown, 1980), p. 299. It is mistakenly attributed to Walter Lippmann by Jonathan Alter, *The Defining Moment: FDR's Hundred Days and the Triumph of Hope* (New York: Simon & Schuster, 2006), p. 187.

43 Denis W. Brogan, *Democratic Government in an Atomic World: A Lecture Delivered under the Auspices of the Walter J. Shepard Foundation, April 24, 1956* (Columbus: Ohio State University, 1956), pp. 15, 31.

44 Ibid., p. 21.

45 Ibid., p. 20.

46 Ibid., pp. 20, 32.

47 Richard Wright, "The Ethics of Living Jim Crow: An Autobiographical Sketch," in *American Stuff: An Anthology of Prose and Verse by Members of the Federal Writers' Project* (New York: Viking, 1937), p. 45.

48 Milton had backed a successful fusion movement of Tennessee Republicans and prohibition Democrats in 1910. George Fort Milton, "Also There Is Politics," in *Culture in the South,* ed. W. T. Couch (Chapel Hill: University of North Carolina Press, 1934), pp. 117, 118.

49 W. E. B. Du Bois, "Black North," *New York Times Magazine,* November 17, 1901.

50 An excellent appraisal of national race relations that makes these points, if also underplaying differences between the South and the rest of the United States, is Desmond King and Stephen Tuck, "De-Centering the South: America's

Nationwide White Supremacist Order after Reconstruction," *Past and Present*, no. 194 (2007): 213–53.

51   For a representative sample of the copious work of Du Bois, see Eric J. Sundquist, ed., *The Oxford W. E. B. Du Bois Reader* (New York: Oxford University Press, 1996); Charles S. Johnson, *Growing Up in the Black Belt: Negro Youth in the Rural South* (New York: American Council on Education, 1941); Charles S. Johnson, *Patterns of Negro Segregation* (New York: Harper and Brothers, 1943); St. Clair Drake and Horace Cayton, *Black Metropolis: A Study of Negro Life in a Northern City* (New York: Harper and Brothers, 1945); Allison Davis, *Deep South: A Social Anthropological Study of Caste and Class* (Chicago: University of Chicago Press, 1941); Gunnar Myrdal, *An American Dilemma: The Negro Problem and American Democracy* (New York: Harper and Brothers, 1944).

52   Ralph J. Bunche, *The Political Status of the Negro in the Age of Age of FDR* (Chicago: University of Chicago Press, 1973), 66.

53   Braeman, "The New Deal," p. 72.

54   "In order to change policies . . . a certain number of individual or collective actors have to agree to the proposed change. I call such actors *veto players*." See George Tsebelis, *Veto Players: How Political Institutions Work* (New York: Russell Sage Foundation; Princeton, NJ: Princeton University Press, 2002), p. 2.

55   Stephen A. Grant, *Conscience and Power: An Examination of Dirty Hands and Political Leadership* (New York: Palgrave Macmillan, 1996), p. viii. Roosevelt apologized to Stalin for dealing with Darlan; Stalin replied that the policy was "perfectly correct." See Susan Butler, ed., *My Dear Mr. Stalin: The Complete Correspndence of Franklin D. Roosevelt and Joseph V. Stalin* (New Haven: Yale University Press, 2005), p. 62.

56   See Norbert Frei, *Adenauer's Germany and the Nazi Past: The Politics of Amnesty and Integration* (New York: Columbia University Press), 2002.

57   Of the era's strange bedfellow collaborations, one of the most surprising was the decision of the Republican Party to advertise its own opposition to war during the period of the Hitler-Stalin pact in the *Daily Worker,* America's Communist newspaper. Noted in Gunther, *Roosevelt in Retrospect,* p. 311.

58   Reinhold Niebuhr, *Moral Man and Immoral Society: A Study in Ethics and Politics* (New York: Charles Scribner's Sons, 1932), p. 4.

59   Unusual but not entirely unprecedented in the way it governed as a liberal state at home and as a unitary state projecting might abroad; such, of course, had been the character of the nineteenth- and early-twentieth-century states of Britain and Third Republic France.

60   Rodgers, *Contested Truths,* p. 175. He elaborates on this observation in chapter 6, "Interests," pp. 176–211.

61   Juan J. Linz, "Crisis, Breakdown, and Reequilibration," in Juan J. Linz and Alfred Stepan, *The Breakdown of Democratic Regimes* (Baltimore: Johns Hopkins University Press, 1978), p. 48.

62 Theodore J. Lowi, *The End of Liberalism: Ideology, Policy, and the Crisis of Authority* (New York: W. W. Norton, 1969), p. 97.

63 Ibid., p. 71.

64 C. Wright Mills, *The Power Elite* (New York: Oxford University Press, 1956); Michael J. Sandel, *Democracy's Discontent: America in Search of a Public Philosophy* (Cambridge: Harvard University Press, 1996); Lowi, *The End of Liberalism*. For similar critiques, see also E. E. Schattschneider, *The Semisovereign People: A Realist's View of Democracy in America* (New York: Holt, Rinehart and Winston, 1960); Grant McConnell, *Private Power and American Democracy* (New York: Alfred A. Knopf, 1966).

65 Lowi argues that "the most important difference between liberals and conservatives, Republicans and Democrats—however they define themselves—is to be found in the interest groups they identify with. Congressmen are guided in their votes, Presidents in their programs, and administrators in their discretion by whatever organized interests they have taken for themselves as the most legitimate; and that is the measure of the legitimacy of demands." See Lowi, *End of Liberalism*, p. 72.

66 Walter A. McDougall, *Promised Land, Crusader State: The American Encounter with the World since 1776* (Boston: Houghton Mifflin, 1997).

67 For a discussion of how the postwar enemy was understood and represented, see Marc Silverstone, *Constructing the Monolith: The United States, Great Britain, and International Communism, 1945–1950* (Cambridge: Harvard University Press, 2008).

68 Cordell Hull, "Europe's Democratic Future," *American Journal of Economics and Sociology* 4 (1945): 542.

69 See Steve Vogel, *The Pentagon—A History: The Untold Story of the Wartime Race to Build the Pentagon—and to Remove It Sixty Years Later* (New York: Random House, 2007).

70 In 1953, fully $56 billion of the country's $80 billion budget was spent on defense. Office of Management and Budget, "Historical Tables," *Budget of the United States Government Fiscal Year 2005* (Washington, DC: U.S. Government Printing Office, 2005), pp. 45–52; available at http://www.usgovernmentspending.com/us_military_spending_30.html#usgs302.

71 See Elias Canetti, *Crowds and Power* (New York: Farrar, Straus and Giroux, 1960).

72 "The key problem, however, is that Sicily does not exist in isolation but rather forms part of the *modern* Italian nation." See Nelson Moe, *The View from Vesuvius: Italian Culture and the Southern Question* (Berkeley: University of California Press, 2002), p. 245.

73 There are partial exceptions, to be sure, including Frank Freidel, *F.D.R. and the South* (Baton Rouge: Louisiana State University Press, 1965). Yet in the larger compass of his work, this remains a peripheral theme.

74 Jean Edward Smith, *FDR* (New York: Random House, 2007), p. 374.

75 Toni Morrison, *Playing in the Dark: Whiteness and the Literary Imagination* (New York: Random House, 1992), pp. 18, 11.

76 W. E. B. Du Bois famously opened each chapter of *The Souls of Black Folks* with a sorrow song. He explained:

> They that walked in darkness sang songs in the olden days—Sorrow Songs—for they were weary at heart. And so before each thought that I have written in this book I have set a phrase, a haunting echo of these weird old songs in which the soul of the black slave spoke to men. Ever since I was a child these songs have stirred me strangely. They came out of the South unknown to me, one by one, and yet at once I knew them as of me and of mine. . . . Little of beauty has America given the world save the rude grandeur God himself stamped on her bosom; the human spirit in this new world has expressed itself in vigor and ingenuity rather than in beauty. And so by fateful chance the Negro folk-song—the rhythmic cry of the slave—stands to-day not simply as the sole American music, but as the most beautiful expression of human experience born this side the seas. It has been neglected, it has been, and is, half despised, and above all it has been persistently mistaken and misunderstood; but notwithstanding, it still remains as the singular spiritual heritage of the nation and the greatest gift of the Negro people.

See Du Bois, *The Souls of Black Folk* (1903; reprint, New York: Penguin, 1996), pp. 204–5. For a discussion of this "electrifying manifesto," see David Levering Lewis, *W. E. B. Du Bois: Biography of a Race, 1868–1919* (New York: Henry Holt, 1993), pp. 277–91.

77 Hajo Holborn, *The Political Collapse of Europe* (New York: Alfred A. Knopf, 1965); Gregory M. Luebbert, *Liberalism, Fascism, or Social Democracy: Social Classes and the Political Origins of Regimes in Interwar Europe* (New York: Oxford University Press, 1991); Joseph Rothschild, *East Central Europe between the Two World Wars* (Seattle: University of Washington Press, 1994); MacGregor Knox, *To the Threshold of Power, 1922/33: Origins and Dynamics of the Fascist and National Socialist Dictatorships,* vol. 1 (Cambridge: Cambridge University Press, 2007).

78 Dietrich Rueschemeyer, Evelyne Huber Stephens, and John D. Stephens, *Capitalist Development and Democracy* (Cambridge: Cambridge University Press, 1992); Linz and Stepan, *The Breakdown of Democratic Regimes;* Lois E. Athey, "Democracy and Populism: Some Recent Studies," *Latin American Research Review* 19, no. 3 (1984): 172–83; Leslie Bethell, ed., *The Cambridge History of Latin America,* vol. 7, *1930 to the Present* (Cambridge: Cambridge University Press, 1990); Ruth Berins Collier and David Collier, *Shaping the Political Arena: Critical Junctures, The Labor Movement, and Regime Dynamics in Latin*

America (Princeton, NJ: Princeton University Press, 1991); Evelyne Huber and Frank Safford, eds., *Agrarian Structure and Political Power: Landlord & Peasant in the Making of Latin America* (Pittsburgh: University of Pittsburgh Press, 1995); Thomas E. Skidmore and Peter H. Smith, *Modern Latin America*, 6th ed. (New York: Oxford University Press, 2005), pp. 51–54.

79 Anthony J. Badger, "Huey Long and the New Deal," in Badger, *New Deal/New South* (Fayetteville: University of Arkansas Press, 2007), p. 1. Like Thurmond and Wallace, Long was a plausible presidential candidate before his assassination in September 1935.

80 When the Socialist Party leader Norman Thomas implored President Roosevelt to back an antilynching bill that had been introduced in the Senate in January 1934, FDR explained why he could not risk offending southern leaders, and added, "Now come, Norman. I'm a damned sight better politician than you are. I know the South, and there is arising a new generation of leaders and we've got to be patient." Cited in David M. Kennedy, *Freedom from Fear: The American People in Depression and War, 1929–1945* (New York: Oxford University Press, 1999), p. 210.

81 D. W. Brogan, "American Liberalism Today," in *British Essays in American History*, ed. H. C. Allen and C. P. Hill (New York: St. Martin's Press, 1957), p. 326.

82 Ira Katznelson, *When Affirmative Action Was White: An Untold History of Racial Inequality in Twentieth-Century America* (New York: W. W, Norton, 2005).

83 Anthony J. Badger, *FDR: The Hundred Days* (New York: Hill and Wang, 2008), p. 161.

84 Ackerman, *We the People*, 2 vols. (Cambridge: Harvard University Press, 1991–1998).

CHAPTER 1 ▪ A JOURNEY WITHOUT MAPS

1 Donald M. Frame, ed., *The Complete Essays of Montaigne* (Stanford, CA: Stanford University Press, 1958), pp. 52–53.

2 Edmund Burke, *A Philosophical Enquiry into the Origin of Our Ideas of the Sublime and Beautiful* (1757; reprint, South Bend, IN: University of Notre Dame Press, 1968), p. 57; Francis Bacon, *De Augmentis Scientiarum,* Book II (1623); Henry David Thoreau's journal entry for September 7, 1851. Henry David Thoreau, *Writings of Henry David Thoreau*, vol. 2 (Boston: Houghton Mifflin, 1906), p. 468.

3 Kenneth Finegold and Theda Skocpol, *State and Party in America's New Deal* (Madison: University of Wisconsin Press, 1995); Michael Goldfield, "Worker Insurgency, Radical Organization, and New Deal Labor Legislation," *American Political Science Review* 83 (1989): 1257–82; Theda Skocpol, Kenneth Finegold, and Michael Goldfield, "Explaining New Deal Labor Policy," ibid., 84 (1990): 1297–315; Alan Brinkley, *The End of Reform: New Deal Liberalism in Recession and War* (New York: Alfred A. Knopf, 1995); Thomas Ferguson,

"From Normalcy to New Deal: Industrial Structure, Party Competition, and American Public Policy in the Great Depression," *International Organization* 1 (1984): 41–94.

4   I take the title of this chapter from Graham Greene, *Journey without Maps* (London: William Heinemann, 1936).

5   For the distinctions between acute fear and chronic fear, and between "the direct object of the fear and the effects of being frightened by it," see John Hollander, "Fear Itself," *Social Research* 71 (2004): 865, 868.

6   Paul Berben, *Dachau: 1933–1945, the Official History* (London: Norfolk Press, 1975); Nikolaus Wachsmann, "Looking into the Abyss: Historians and the Nazi Concentration Camps," *European History Quarterly* 36 (2006): 247–78.

7   Walter Lippmann, *A New Social Order* (New York: John Day, 1933), pp. 7–8, 9–10. Lippmann's description of modern politics as defined by the emergence of the mass state heralded an account of masses and groups in the dictatorships by the sociologist Emil Lederer, who served as the first dean of the Graduate Faculty at the New School for Social Research. His book *State of the Masses: The Threat of the Classless Society* (New York: W. W. Norton, 1940) contrasts the enforced unity of the masses in the Soviet, Italian, and German dictatorships with the heterogeneous plurality of persons and interests in the mass democracies.

8   Lippmann, *A New Social Order,* pp. 10–11.

9   Albert Camus, "Speech of Acceptance upon the Award of the Nobel Prize for Literature, Delivered in Stockholm on the Tenth of December, 1957," in *Fifty Years,* ed. Clifton Fadiman, New York: Alfred A. Knopf, 1965, p. 723.

10   James W. Garner, "Proposed Rules for the Regulation of Aerial Warfare," *American Journal of International Law* 18 (1924): 56.

11   Greene, *Journey without Maps,* p. 11. Greene's *Ministry of Fear* (London: William Heinemann, 1943), one critic has noted, invokes fear as "the terror that arises when ordinary men become murderers, when the world of organized destruction and murder on a massive scale begins to seem admirably fitted to the minds of men." Robert Hoskins, "Greene and Wordsworth: 'The Ministry of Fear,'" *South Atlantic Review* 48 (1983): 34.

12   Karl Loewenstein, "Militant Democracy and Fundamental Rights," *American Political Science Review* 31 (1937): 417.

13   William E. Dodd, "Can Democracy Be Preserved?," *Public Opinion Quarterly* 2 (1938): 26. Dodd's diaries record how, when the phone rang in his University of Chicago Department of History office, Franklin Roosevelt recruited him, stating, "I want an American liberal in Germany as a standing example." See William E. Dodd, Jr., and Martha Dodd, eds., *Ambassador Dodd's Diary, 1933–1938* (New York: Harcourt, Brace, 1941), p. 3. A native of North Carolina and a scholar of the Old South, Dodd had just been selected president of the American Historical Association for 1934. A useful biography is Fred Arthur Baily, *William Edward Dodd: The South's Yeoman Scholar* (Charlottesville: University

of Virginia Press, 1997). For a treatment of the experience of the Dodd family in Berlin, one that focuses on daughter Martha's affairs with Nazi officials, see Erik Larson, *In the Garden of Beasts: Love, Terror, and an American Family in Hitler's Berlin* (New York: Crown, 2011).

14 Pitirim A. Sorokin, "A Neglected Factor of War," *American Sociological Review* 3 (1938): 483.

15 Cited in David Mayers, *George Kennan and the Dilemmas of US Foreign Policy* (New York: Oxford University Press, 1990), pp. 53, 54. Kennan's book was never completed or published, and he did not refer to it in his memoirs.

16 Frank Hyneman Knight, *Risk, Uncertainty, and Profit* (Boston: Houghton Mifflin, 1921), pp. 225, 233; see also Paul Davidson, "Is Probability Theory Relevant for Uncertainty? A Post-Keynesian Perspective," *Journal of Economic Perspectives* 8, no. 1 (1991): 129–43. The theme of Knightian uncertainty is highlighted in Mark Blyth, *Great Transformations: Economic Ideas and Institutional Change in the Twentieth Century* (Cambridge: Cambridge University Press, 2002).

17 An excellent overview of this scholarship is provided in Tom Pyszczynski et al., "Experimental Existential Psychology: Coping with the Facts of Life," in ed. S. T. Fiske, D. T. Gilbert, and G. Lindzey, *Handbook of Social Psychology*, 5th ed. (New York: Wiley, 2010), pp. 724-57. On attempts to make estimates about uncertain and shifting parameters internal to choices, see Robert W. Klwein et al., "Decisions with Estimation Uncertainty," *Econometrica* 46 (1978): 1363–87.

18 Walter Lippmann, *Interpretations, 1933–1935,* ed. Allan Nevins (New York: Macmillan, 1936), p. 27.

19 This concern about the use, and misuse, of fear is a central theme in Corey Robin, *Fear: The History of a Political Idea* (New York: Oxford University Press, 2004).

20 Franklin D. Roosevelt, "Acceptance for Renomination," June 27, 1936, in *The Public Papers and Addresses of Franklin D. Roosevelt*, vol. 5 (New York: Random House, 1938), p. 231. This speech is most remembered for its attack on "the economic royalists," "the privileged princes of economic dynasties," and for its famous statement of how "this generation has a rendezvous with destiny." The swift movement from fear to faith is echoed by Leuchtenburg. His book ends before World War II, just after the 1938 Fair Labor Standards Act established a minimum wage and set maximum hours of work. See William E. Leuchtenburg, *Franklin D. Roosevelt and the New Deal: 1932–1940* (New York: Harper & Row, 1963), pp. 345-346.

21 Alfred Kazin, "Arthur Schlesinger, Jr.: The Historian at the Center," in *Alfred Kazin's America: Critical and Personal Writings*, ed. Ted Solotaroff (New York: HarperCollins, 2003), pp. 223, 227, 224, 227-28. This is the "truth" that Kazin thought Schlesinger had sacrificed. But he does recognize that "Schlesinger's book, which becomes thin in its complacent New Deal references, is actually exciting and moving whenever, in seeking to render the facts, it hints of the permanent crisis that is the truth of our times" (p. 228). This text, written in 1959, was first published in Alfred Kazin, *Contemporaries* (Boston: Little, Brown, 1962).

22 Arthur Meier Schlesinger, *The New Deal in Action: A Continuation of A. M. Schlesinger's Political and Social Growth of the United States to the Special Session of the United States Congress, November 15, 1937* (New York: Macmillan, 1938).

23 A useful summary can be found in Theodore J. Lowi, "The Roosevelt Revolution and the New American State," in *Comparative Theory and Political Experience,* ed. Peter J. Katzenstein, Theodore J. Lowi, and Sidney Tarrow (Ithaca, NY: Cornell University Press, 1990), pp. 188–212.

24 Hubert H. Humphrey, *The Political Philosophy of the New Deal* (1940; reprint, Baton Rouge: Louisiana State University Press, 1970), p. v.

25 Harold Stearns, *Liberalism in America: Its Origin, Its Temporary Collapse, Its Future* (New York: Boni and Liveright, 1919).

26 Richard Hofstadter, *The Age of Reform: From Bryan to F.D.R.* (New York: Alfred A. Knopf, 1955), pp. 319, 302.

27 It is important to give comparable status to both the reality and the representation of fear, and to assess their fit with each other. For a discussion of this relationship, see John Lewis Gaddis, *The Landscape of History* (New York: Oxford University Press, 2002), pp. 104, 123.

28 Leuchtenburg, *Franklin D. Roosevelt and the New Deal, 1932–1940,* pp. 1–40.

29 Arthur Schlesinger Jr., *The Age of Roosevelt,* 3 vols. (Boston: Houghton Mifflin, 1957–1960).

30 Department of Commerce figures cited in Jean Edward Smith, *FDR* (New York: Random House, 2007), p. 241.

31 Arthur M. Schlesinger Jr., *The Age of Roosevelt,* vol. 1, *The Crisis of the Old Order, 1919–1933* (Boston: Houghton Mifflin, 1957), pp. 1, 3.

32 A partial exception is Alonzo Hamby, *For the Survival of Democracy: Franklin Roosevelt and the World Crisis of the 1930s* (New York: Free Press, 2004). This fine book firmly emplaces the New Deal within global affairs and the challenge to liberal democracy by the dictatorships, but its narrative structure is more traditional than its central theme projects.

33 An important example with a somewhat different time frame is James Patterson's *Grand Expectations: The United States, 1945–1974* (New York: Oxford University Press, 1996). That book's prologue introduces the reader to the explosion of joy on V-J Day in August 1945, when Japan surrendered, though tempered by the wartime experience of death and injury, and other grounds for concern—President Truman's inexperience, the uncertain capacities of a peacetime economy, and atomic weapons. And yet, the dominant mood was upbeat, Patterson reports, vastly different from the agonies of early Depression uncertainties. "The enemies had been defeated; the soldiers would soon return; families would reunite; the future promised a great deal more than the past. In this optimistic mood millions of Americans plunged hopefully into the new post-war world" (p. 9).

34 Arthur Schlesinger Jr., *The Age of Roosevelt,* vol. 3, *The Politics of Upheaval: 1935–1936* (Boston: Houghton Mifflin, 1960), p. 656.

35   Schlesinger Jr., *The Politics of Upheaval,* p. 656; Schlesinger Jr., *Crisis of the Old Order,* p. 8. For the past half century, this portrayal of how an active presidency overcame hard times has set the tone, established the agenda, and defined the range of most New Deal histories, including William Leuchtenburg's classic account of "Roosevelt's Reconstruction," and David Kennedy's magisterial tale of how the New Deal liberated "freedom from fear." "The Politics of Hard Times" and the "Winter of Despair" open Leuchtenburg's *Franklin D. Roosevelt and the New Deal,* pp. 1–40. David M. Kennedy, *Freedom from Fear: The American People in Depression and War, 1929–1945* (New York: Oxford University Press, 1999).

36   See Louise Young, *Japan's Total Empire: Manchuria and the Culture of Wartime Imperialism* (Berkeley: University of California Press, 1998). She traces the impact of colonization, including a massive settlement project, on Manchuria and on Japan.

37   Anne Applebaum, "A History of Horror," *New York Review of Books,* October 18, 2001, p. 41; Applebaum was reviewing Joel Kotek and Pierre Rigoulot's excellent book, *Le Siècle des camps* (Paris: J. C. Lattès, 2001).

38   For an excellent consideration, see Sarah T. Phillips, *This Land, This Nation: Conservation, Rural America, and the New Deal* (Cambridge: Cambridge University Press, 2007).

39   A nuanced treatment can be found in Alan Brinkley, *Voices of Protest: Huey Long, Father Coughlin, and the Great Depression* (New York: Alfred A. Knopf, 1982); especially useful is the balanced discussion in Appendix I, "The Question of Anti-Semitism and the Problem of Fascism." A contemporary view of the status of anti-Semitism in the 1930s and 1940s is provided in Carey McWilliams, *A Mask for Privilege: Anti-Semitism in America* (Boston: Little, Brown, 1948).

40   Stephen Spender, *Forward from Liberalism* (London: Gollancz, 1937).

41   Franz Neumann, *The Democratic and the Authoritarian State* (Glencoe, IL: Free Press, 1957), p. 236.

42   R. J. B. Bosworth, "Explaining 'Auschwitz' after the End of History," *History and Theory* 38 (1999): 84.

43   Harold Laski, "The Challenge of Our Times," *American Scholar* 8 (1939): 387, 391.

44   Michael Howard, "A Thirty Years War? The Two World Wars in Historical Perspective," *Transactions of the Royal Historical Society* 3 (1993): 177.

45   Richard Vinen, *The Unfree French: Life under the Occupation* (London: Allen Lane, 2006); Hanna Diamond, *Fleeing Hitler: France 1940* (New York: Oxford University Press, 2007). In June 1940, as the Third Republic government abandoned Paris, fully "a quarter of the French population was on the run." By the time the Germans arrived in Paris, only some three-quarters of a million of its three million residents remained in the city. See Geert Mak, *In Europe: Travels through the Twentieth Century* (New York: Vintage, 2008), pp. 356, 357. Retrospectively, the Vichy government portrayed "the exodus as a journey through suffering to patriotic enlightenment. . . . Pétain's genius in the wake of defeat was to insist not on the humiliating nature of the occasion for the government and the military but on the hardships of the exodus for the millions who had been on the roads." See Jeremy Harding, "In Order of Rank," *London Review of Books,* May 8, 2008, pp. 16, 17.

46   I am indebted to Matthieu Leimgruber for directing me to this text, and for his translation.

47   Gilbert Murray, *Liberality and Civilization: Lectures Given at the Invitation of the Hibbert Trustees in the Universities of Bristol, Glasgow, and Birmingham in October and November 1937* (London: George Allen and Unwin, 1938), p. 59.

48   Mak, *In Europe,* pp. 379–80; J. G. Ballard, *The Drowned World* (New York: Liveright, 2012).

49   Mark Mazower, *Hitler's Empire: Nazi Rule in Occupied Europe* (London: Allen Lane, 2008).

50   Timothy Snyder, "The Forgotten Holocaust," *IWM Post* 97 (2008): 26–27. See also Timothy Snyder, "Holocaust: The Ignored Reality," *The New York Review of Books,* July 16, 2009, pp. 14–16; Omer Bartov, "Eastern Europe as the Site of Genocide," *Journal of Modern History* 80 (2008): 557–93. Bartov designates this area as marked by "sites of forgetting" (p. 557).

51   Peter Fritzsche, *Life and Death in the Third Reich* (Cambridge: Harvard University Press, 2008), pp. 200, 196–97, 195.

52   For discussions, see Michael A. Barnhart, *Japan Prepares for Total War* (Ithaca, NY: Cornell University Press, 1987); Meirion Harns and Susie Harries, *Soldiers of the Sun: The Rise and Fall of the Imperial Japanese Army* (New York: Random House, 1991); Peter Duus, Ramon H. Myers, and Mark R. Peattie, eds., *The Japanese Wartime Empire, 1931–1945* (Princeton, NJ: Princeton University Press, 1996).

53   David Riesman, "Civil Liberties in a Period of Transition," *Public Policy* 4 (1942): 46.

54   Niall Ferguson, *The War of the World: Twentieth-Century Conflict and the Descent of the West* (New York: Penguin, 2006), p. 503.

55   Jeremy Black, *War and the World: Military Power and the Fate of Continents, 1450–2000* (New Haven: Yale University Press, 1998), p. 258.

56   In February 1945, "U.S. Air Force General Curtis 'Iron Ass' LeMay, ably assisted by a young statistician named Robert McNamara, decided to 'bomb and burn em till they quit.' He was talking about the citizens of Tokyo, Osaka, Nagoya, Fukuoka, and scores of other cities and towns, culminating in Hiroshima and Nagasaki." See Ian Buruma, "The Cruelest War," *New York Review of Books,* May 1, 2008, p. 24.

57   In terms of the 1941 typology of Hans Speier, World War II can be characterized as an example of "absolute war," an "unrestricted and unregulated war

... characterized, negatively, by the absence of any restrictions and regulations imposed upon violence, treachery, and frightfulness." See Hans Speier, "The Social Types of War," *American Journal of Sociology* 76, no. 4 (1941): 445. Not all observers thought the shift to civilian victimization to be morally more heinous than warfare conducted in more traditional ways. In a startling essay, for example, George Orwell observed in May 1944 that as "war is not avoidable at this stage of history, and since it has to happen it does not seem to me a bad thing that others should be killed besides young men." See George Orwell, "As I Please," *Tribune*, May 19, 1944, p. 603. This essay was a rejoinder to Vera Brittan's pamphlet *Seed of Chaos*, in which she had bravely condemned "obliteration" bombing for subjecting "thousands of helpless and innocent people in German, Italian, and German-occupied cities ... to agonising forms of death and injury comparable to the worst tortures of the Middle Ages" (cited in Orwell, "As I Please," p. 602).

58   Well before the killings began, Wolf Jobst Siedler described the reaction of his fellow Germans to November 1938's Kristallnacht: "On the very evening of the burning of the synagogues, an event which brought the Eastern Europe of the Middle Ages into the Germany of the twentieth-century, everywhere in the cities of our country festively clad people went to operetta, theatres, and symphony halls, and that, six hours after the deportation wagons left the station platforms in Berlin, the trains for the seaside left also." Cited in Clive James, *Cultural Amnesia: Necessary Memories from History and the Arts* (New York: W. W. Norton, 2007), p. 716.

59   Eric Hobsbawm, *The Age of Extremes: A History of the World, 1914–1991* (New York: Pantheon, 1994), p. 51.

60   Black milk of daybreak we drink it at sundown
         we drink it at noon in the morning we drink it at night
         we drink it and drink it ...

61   John Morton Blum, "World War II," in C. Vann Woodward, *The Comparative Approach to American History* (New York: Oxford University Press, 1968), p. 320. Also note A. J. P. Taylor's assessment that "if the Americans would not divide the world with the Russians, the only alternative would have been to impose a free Eastern Europe on the Russians in 1945 by superior force. This was ... too logical for the Americans. They hoped vaguely for a Russian change of heart.... This was a clash between two fundamental conceptions of the world—the one logical and ruthless, the other benevolent and muddled and undefined." See Taylor, *Europe: Grandeur and Decline* (London: Penguin, 1967), p. 318.

62   Tony Judt, *Postwar: A History of Europe since 1945* (New York: Penguin, 2005), p. 40.

63   Leszek Kolakowski, *My Correct Views on Everything* (South Bend, IN: St. Augustine's Press, 2005), p. 133.

64 Howard W. Odum, "Orderly Transitional Democracy," *Annals of the American Academy of Political and Social Science* 180 (1935): 37–39.

65 Joseph P. Kennedy, *I'm for Roosevelt* (New York: Reynal and Hitchcock, 1936), pp. 102, 103.

66 Franklin D. Roosevelt, "Radio Address on Electing Liberals to Office," November 4, 1938, in *The Public Papers and Addresses of Franklin D. Roosevelt,* vol. 7 (New York: Macmillan, 1941), pp. 585–86.

67 Walter Lippmann, "The American Destiny," *Life,* June 5, 1939, p. 47; reprinted in Walter Lippmann, *The American Destiny* (New York: Life Magazine Press, 1939), p. 4. Lippmann on the New Deal has to be read with caution, given his strong anticollectivist views and his preference to reinvigorate laissez-faire. See his polemic, *Inquiry into the Principles of the Good Society* (Boston: Little, Brown, 1937).

68 Lewis Mumford, *Faith for Living* (New York: Harcourt, Brace, 1940), pp. 56–57. Mumford was particularly exercised by the lead role Communists had been playing within the country's Left during the popular-front moment that had been initiated in 1935. "The truth," he wrote, "is the liberals no longer dared to act. In America, during the period of the United Front, the liberal accepted the leadership of a small communist minority, fanatical, unscrupulous, deeply contemptuous of essential human values, incredibly stupid in tactics and incredibly arrogant in matters of intellectual belief; they accepted this leadership simply because the communists alone among the political groups had firm convictions and the courage to act on them" (pp. 57–58).

69 Harold Lasswell, "The Garrison State," *American Sociological Review* 46 (1941): 459, 467.

70 Riesman, "Civil Liberties in a Period of Transition," pp. 47, 46, 45, 51, 93, 90, 96.

71 Morris Raphael Cohen, *The Faith of a Liberal* (New York: Henry Holt, 1946), p. 448. See also, Horace Kallen, *The Liberal Spirit: Essays on Problems of Freedom in the Modern World* (Ithaca, NY: Cornell University Press, 1948).

72 The Kennedy and *Fortune* citations are from Leuchtenburg, "The Great Depression," in Woodward, ed., *Comparative Approach,* p. 311.

73 Paul Meadows, "The New Tasks of the Liberal State," *American Journal of Economics and Sociology* 7 (1948): 257, 263.

74 For thorough histories, see Clay Blair, *The Forgotten War: America in Korea, 1950–1953* (Annapolis MD: Naval Institute Press, 2003), David Halberstam, *The Coldest Winter: America and the Korean War* (New York: Hyperion, 2007), which includes a useful discussion of the dismissal of General MacArthur and of the congressional hearings that followed.

75 Richard Hofstadter, "The Patrician as Opportunist," *The American Political Tradition and the Men Who Made it* (New York: Alfred A. Knopf, 1948), p. 352.

76 Nathaniel Peffer, "Democracy Losing by Default," *Political Science Quarterly* 63 (1948): 322, 321, 328.

77 Archibald MacLeish, "The American State of Mind," *American Scholar* 19 (1950): 406.

78 Robert Musil, *The Man without Qualities* (London: Secker and Warburg, 1953), p. 8.

79 Reinhart Kosselleck, "Crisis," *Journal of the History of Ideas* 67 (2006): 358. This essay brilliantly follows the concept, tracing a lineage from the way the ancient Greeks utilized it to connote the need to choose between stark alternatives to present usage, which is focused on special historical moments that connote the intensification of time and the actual or potential end of an epoch, tending toward something significantly different.

80 Hans Morgenthau, "The Evil of Politics and the Ethics of Evil," *Ethics* 56 (1945): 1–18.

81 "Intransigence, difficulty and unresolved contradictions" is how Edward Said describes the "late style" of musicians, writers, and artists. See Edward W. Said, *On Late Style: Music and Literature against the Grain* (New York: Pantheon, 2006), p. 7. For Said, such a style combines a sense of ending with an acute alertness about the present.

82 Alvin Johnson, in *Political and Economic Democracy*, ed. Max Ascoli and Fritz Lehmann (New York: W. W. Norton, 1937), p. 7.

83 Hans Simons, ibid., p. 192. Other contributors to this volume reporting on the 1935–1936 General Seminar include the public finance specialist Gerhard Colm, who later served on President Truman's Council of Economic Advisers; the social policy expert and psychologist Frieda Wunderlich; the economic theorist Eduard Heimann; the economist and sociologist Emil Lederer; and the sociologist Hans Speier. See also Eduart Heimann, *Communism, Fascism or Democracy?* (New York: W. W. Norton, 1938).

84 This New School seminar continues today.

85 Thomas Mann, *The Coming Victory of Democracy* (New York: Alfred A. Knopf, 1938), pp. 15, 48, 52–53, 43, 24–25.

86 Arendt described the orientation of the refugees as "thankful but unhappy." Cited in James, *Cultural Amnesia,* p. 566.

87 For discussions of this exceptional group, see Laura Fermi, *Illustrious Immigrants: The Intellectual Migration from Europe, 1930/1941* (Chicago: University of Chicago Press, 1968); H. Stuart Hughes, *The Sea Change: The Migration of Social Thought, 1930–1965* (New York: Harper & Row, 1975); Anthony Heilbut, *Exiled in Paradise: German Refugee Artists and Intellectuals in America from the 1930s to the Present* (New York: Viking, 1983).

88 Stefan Zweig, *The World of Yesterday* (New York: Viking, 1943), p. 436.

89 Jan-Werner Müller, "Research Note: The Triumph of What (If Anything?): Rethinking Political Ideologies and Political Institutions in Twentieth-Century Europe" (unpublished manuscript, 2008).

90 This is the perspective offered in Stephen Kotkin's superb "Modern Times:

The Soviet Union and the Interwar Conjuncture," *Kritika: Explorations in Russian and Eurasian History* 2 (2001): 111–64.

91 For acute assessments, see Naum Jasny, *Soviet Industrialization, 1928–1952* (Chicago: University of Chicago Press, 1961); Holland Hunter, "Priorities and Shortfalls in Prewar Soviet Planning," in *Soviet Planning: Essays in Honor of Naum Jasny*, ed. Jane Degras (New York: Praeger, 1964), pp. 1–45.

92 For a pithy statement of this view, see Edward Hallett Carr, *The New Society* (London: Macmillan, 1951).

93 Richard Overy, *The Dictators: Hitler's Germany, Stalin's Russia* (New York: W. W. Norton, 2004), pp. 450–51, 453.

94 See http://www.usgovernmentspending.com/us_military_spending_30.html# usgs.302.

95 Their democracies were more theatrical than real, what Tzvetan Todorov has called "pseudo-democracy" in "Stalin Close Up," *Totalitarian Movements and Political Religions* 5, no. 1 (2004): 94–111.

96 Kotkin, "Modern Times," p. 159.

97 Giovanni Gentile, "The Philosophic Basis of Fascism," *Foreign Affairs* 6 (1928): 302–3.

98 Cited in Erik van Ree, *The Political Thought of Joseph Stalin: A Study in Twentieth-Century Revolutionary Patriotism* (New York: Routledge, 2002), p. 131.

99 Kotkin, "Modern Times," pp. 129–130.

100 "The Depression triggered among key players in the North Atlantic economy much common watchfulness of one another's policy moves and a wide array of common responses." See Daniel T. Rodgers, *Atlantic Crossings: Social Politics in a Progressive Age* (Cambridge: Harvard University Press, 1998), pp. 416–17; Louis Brownlow, *Report of the President's Committee on Administrative Management* (Washington, DC: U.S. Government Printing Office, 1937); Peri E. Arnold, *Making the Managerial Presidency: Comprehensive Reorganization Planning, 1950–1980* (Princeton, NJ: Princeton University Press, 1986); Barry Karl, *The Uneasy State: The United States from 1915 to 1945* (Chicago: University of Chicago Press, 1985), pp. 156–58.

101 The most compelling overview I know of how the "democratic" dictatorships combined institutional innovations, the arts of ruling, and finding answers to domestic and global challenges is provided in Overy, *The Dictator*. For a discussion of the capacities of democracies, in comparison with the dictatorships, to build military machines, see Talbot Imlay, "Democracy and War: Political Regime, Industrial Relations, and Economic Preparations for War in France and Britain Up to 1940," *Journal of Modern History* 79 (2007): 1–47.

102 Kotkin, "Modern Times," p. 129.

103 Kiran Klaus Patel, *Soldiers of Labor: Labor Service in Nazi Germany and New Deal America, 1933–1945* (Cambridge: Cambridge University Press, 2005); Nor-

bert Götz and Kiran Klaus Patel, "Facing the Fascist Model: Discourse and the Construction of Labour Services in the USA and Sweden in the 1930s and 1940s," *Journal of Contemporary History* 41, no. 1 (2006): 57–73; Wolfgang Schivelbusch, *The Three New Deals: Reflections on Roosevelt's America, Mussolini's Italy, and Hitler's Germany, 1933–1939* (New York: Metropolitan Books, 2006).

104 For discussions, see Harvey Klehr, *The Heyday of American Communism: The Depression Decade* (New York: Basic Books, 1984); Fraser M. Ottanelli, *The Communist Party of the United States: From the Depression to World War II* (New Brunswick, NJ: Rutgers University Press, 1991). On the popular front, see the account by Earl Browder, the Communist Party's general secretary: Earl Browder, *The People's Front* (New York: International Publishers, 1938). In the struggle against Fascism, he wrote, "the camp of progress and peace finds its stronghold in the Soviet Union, the country of socialist prosperity" (p. 19).

105 Walter Duranty, *I Write as I Please* (New York: Simon & Schuster, 1935), pp. 301–2.

106 Richard Crossman, ed., *The God That Failed: Six Studies in Communism* (London: Hamish Hamilton, 1950). In addition to Fischer, the contributors were Arthur Koestler, Ignazio Silone, André Gide, Richard Wright, and Stephen Spender.

107 "Soviet Democracy," *New Republic,* June 17, 1936, pp. 762, 761; Sidney Webb and Beatrice Webb, *Soviet Communism: A New Civilization,* 2 vols. (London: Longmans, Green, 1935), p. 337. See also Peter G. Filene, *Americans and the Soviet Experiment, 1917–1933* (Cambridge: Harvard University Press, 1967).

108 He concluded this way: "And if American champions of civil liberties could all think of economic freedom as the goal of their labors, they too would accept 'workers democracy' as *far superior to what the capitalist world offers to any but a small minority. Yes, and they would accept—regretfully, of course—the necessity of dictatorship while the job of reorganizing society on a socialist basis is being done."* See Roger N. Baldwin, "Freedom in the U.S.A. and the U.S.S.R.," *Soviet Russia Today,* September 1934; available at http://www.law.ucla.edu/volokh/blog/baldwin.pdf. I thank Robert Amdur for guiding me to this essay. Five years earlier, Baldwin published *Liberty under the Soviets* (New York: Vanguard Press, 1928) in a book series, *Vanguard Studies of Soviet Russia,* edited by Yale's Jerome Davis, that "is designed to meet the need for reliable, accurate information on the major aspects of present-day Russia" (p. ix).

109 Edmund Wilson, *Travels in Two Democracies* (New York: Harcourt, Brace, 1936).

110 See Stephen A. Norwood, *Third Reich in the Ivory Tower* (Cambridge: Cambridge University Press, 2011), especially chapters 2 and 3, which deal with Harvard and Columbia. See also "Fascism at Columbia University," *Nation,* November 7, 1934, pp. 530–31; Harry F. Ward, "The Development of Fascism in the United States," *Annals of the American Academy of Political and Social Sci-*

ence 180 (1935): 55–56; Ido Oren, "Uncritical Portrayals of Fascist Italy and of Iberic-Latin Dictatorships in American Political Science," *Comparative Studies in Society and History* 42 (2000): 87–118.

111 Richard Washburn Child, *The Saturday Evening Post,* June 28, 1924, pp. 157–58; cited in W. Y. Elliott, "Mussolini, Prophet of the Pragmatic Era in Politics," *Political Science Quarterly* 41 (1926): 168. For a discussion of the pro-Fascist role of *The Saturday Evening Post,* see John P. Diggins, "Mussolini and America: Hero-Worship, Charisma, and the 'Vulgar Talent,'" *The Historian* 28 (1966): 564–66.

112 Richard Washburn Child, in Benito Mussolini, *My Autobiography* (New York: Charles Scribner's Sons, 1928), pp. xi, xv, xix.

113 Lawrence Dennis, "Fascism for America," *Annals of the American Academy of Political and Social Science* 180 (1935): 62.

114 Mario A. Pei, "Freedom under Fascism," *Annals of the American Academy of Political and Social Science* 180 (1935): 13.

115 I draw these distinctions from Edna Ullman-Margalit and Sidney Morgenbesser, "Picking and Choosing," *Social Research* 44, no. 4 (1977): 757-85; and Edna Ullman-Margalit, "Big Decisions: Opting, Converting, Drifting" (unpublished paper, Center for the Study of Rationality, Hebrew University of Jerusalem, November 2005). For an account of the history of statistics in terms of the ambition to produce tolerable risk, see Ian Hacking, *The Taming of Chance* (Cambridge: Cambridge University Press, 1990).

CHAPTER 2 · PILOT, JUDGE, SENATOR

1 Mussolini had preceded Balbo as a minister of aviation, one of the many cabinet posts the party leader held, and was fascinated by flight as a symbol of reactionary modernism, a position he held in common with Herman Göring and Charles Lindbergh. Balbo had been fascinated by flying since early adolescence. See R. J. B. Bosworth, *Mussolini* (London: Arnold, 2002), pp. 142–43. For a survey of Fascist political culture, see Mabel Berezin, *Making the Fascist Self: The Political Culture of Interwar Italy* (Ithaca, NY: Cornell University Press, 1997); and for a discussion of the Italian regime's objectives, see Edward R. Tannenbaum, "The Goals of Italian Fascism," *American Historical Review* 74 (1969): 1183–204.

2 Robert Wohl, *The Spectacle of Flight: Aviation and the Western Imagination, 1920–1950* (New Haven: Yale University Press, 2005), p. 89.

3 "No institution did Stalin's bidding more than the Military Collegium of the USSR Supreme Court." See Michael Parrish, *The Lesser Terror: Soviet State Security, 1939–1953* (Westport, CT: Praeger, 1996), p. 206. Just before the trial opened, *Pravda* editorialized on August 13, "The slightest liberalism towards these filthy double-dealers is a crime against the people, against socialism"; and

once the trial had concluded, it signaled, on August 27, that there was more to come, observing, "Unfortunately we still have quite a number of liberals" in the Party. Cited in Jonathan Haslam, "Political Opposition and the Origins of the Terror in Russia, 1932–1936." *Historical Journal* 29 (1986): 417–18.

4   On his early political career, see Vincent A. Giroux, Jr., "The Rise of Theodore G. Bilbo," *Journal of Mississippi History* 43 (1981): 180–209.

5   U.S. Congress, *Memorial Services Held in the House of Representatives and Senate of the United States, Together with Remarks Presented in Eulogy of Theodore Gilmore Bilbo, Late a Senator from Mississippi* (Washington, DC: U.S. Government Printing Office, 1950), p. 19.

6   For a rich and multilayered consideration, see Alan Brinkley, *The Publisher: Henry Luce and His American Century* (New York: Alfred A. Knopf, 2010).

7   *Time,* June 26, 1933, p. 33.

8   Ibid., pp. 50, 49, 18.

9   Its absence was widely thought responsible for contributing to the economic meltdown of 2008.

10   *Time,* June 26, 1933, p. 9.

11   One possibility is that his synagogue would not allow him to appear onstage.

12   *Time,* June 26, 1933, pp. 33–34. The Madonna of Loreto is the patron saint of aviators. The priest, Monsignor Carlo Ferrari, also greeted the fliers "with embraces and tears" on their return. "Bishop Paolo Galeazzi of Grosseto held a Te Deum at the cathedral, and the town authorities declared a holiday." See *New York Times,* August 15, 1933.

13   Balbo strongly encouraged the Fascist identity of the air force. In December 1927, he circulated a paper entitled "Moral and Political Education of Airmen" which urged his men, as exemplars, to speak out for Fascism. See the discussion in the sympathetic biography: Claudio G. Segré, *Italo Balbo: A Fascist Life* (Berkeley: University of California Press, 1987), p. 177. Balbo was strongly influenced by Giulio Douhet, the Italian supporter of air power (and of Mussolini) and a prophet of strategic bombing, who believed that, in future, war from the air could most effectively decimate civilian areas. "The prevailing forms of social organization," Douhet wrote, "have given war a character of national totality—that is, the entire population and all the resources of the nation are sucked into the maws of war. And since society is now definitely evolving along this line, it is within the power of human foresight to see now that future wars will be total in character and scope." Cited in Mark E. Neely Jr., "Was the Civil War a Total War?," in *On the Road to Total War: The American Civil War and the German Wars of Unification, 1861–1871,* ed. Stig Förster and Jörg Nagler (Cambridge: Cambridge University Press, 1997), p. 33. In 1936, Balbo wrote the preface for a posthumous collection of Douhet's articles on total war.

14   Benito Mussolini, *My Autobiography* (New York: Charles Scribner's Sons, 1928), p. 291.

15   Wohl, *The Spectacle of Flight*, pp. 63, 51.

16   Cited ibid., p. 51. "I can say with pride," Mussolini stated, "that I am an aviator, a title that I earned by flying at a time when few people flew, and by crashing; because I was determined to be a pilot at 37 years of age, and, naturally, continued to fly after I crashed" (p. 105).

17   Ibid., p. 49.

18   Cited ibid., p. 70.

19   These mass flights were intended in part to advance Douhet's conception of the effectiveness of attack by massive aerial formations. *The United States Air Force Dictionary* defines *balbo* as "a large flight or formation of planes." Air University, Aerospace Studies Institute, *The United States Air Force Dictionary* (Washington, DC: U.S. Government Printing Office, 1956), p. 69; cited in Segré, *Italo Balbo*, p. 146. Reporting on his trip to Odessa, Balbo noted (Milan: Fratelli Treves, 1929) in *Da Roma a Odessa* that he had found common purpose with much-hated Bolshevism in its contempt, like that of Fascism, for liberal democracy, which he characterized as "rotten to the bone, lying and false, with all the wiles of a superior civilization." Cited in Segré, *Italo Balbo,* p. 207. See also James J. Sadkovich, "The Development of the Italian Air Force prior to World War II," *Military Affairs* 51 (1987), which gives a detailed account of the Aeronautica's scope, equipment, and organization.

20   Wohl, *The Spectacle of Flight,* p. 77.

21   John Gooch, *Mussolini and His Generals: The Armed Forces and Fascist Foreign Policy, 1922–1940* (Cambridge: Cambridge University Press, 2007), p. 75; Herman Finer, *Mussolini's Italy* (New York: Henry Holt, 1935), p. 145.

22   Reviewing the publication of Balbo's *Diario 1922* (Milan: Mondadori, 1932), Muriel Currey observed how in that year "the largest part of the armed forces of Fascism was under the command of General Balbo in what he calls the great quadrilateral, Ferrara, Mantova, Bologna, and Modena, and with them he fought pitched battles in Ravenna, Parma, and Bologna, against the Communists and their allies, while the Government and the local authorities looked on with mingled fear and indifference." Currey's review appeared in *International Affairs* 12 (1933): 681. In May 1922, five months before the March on Rome, Balbo's forces had occupied Ferrara: his Blackshirts mobilized some forty thousand agricultural workers in a show of force that displayed the impotence of governmental forces, and "at the end of July Balbo led a second march on Ravenna that secured the Po Valley's southeast exit for Fascism." See MacGregor Knox, *To the Threshold of Power, 1922/33: Origins and Dynamics of the Fascist and National Socialist Dictatorships,* vol. 1 (Cambridge: Cambridge University Press, 2007), pp. 364, 365.

23   Segré, *Italo Balbo*, p. 114. The other three were Cesare De Vecchi, Michele Bianchi, and Emilio De Bono. For an overview of pre-Fascist Italy focused on matters of political economy, see Douglas J. Forsyth, *The Crisis of Liberal Italy: Monetary and Financial Policy, 1914–1922* (Cambridge: Cambridge University Press, 1993).

24 Cited in Finer, *Mussolini's Italy*, p. 139. The source is Balbo, *Diario 1922*. There is a brief but telling portrait of Balbo in John Gunther, *Inside Europe, Again Completely Revised* (New York: Harper and Brothers, 1938), pp. 209–11. Gunther describes him as "tall, copper-bearded, a picturesque as well as arrogant figure . . . a vivacious and accomplished ruffian, reportedly the inventor of the castor oil treatment for recalcitrant non-Fascists, a 'Fascist from the first hour,' and Mussolini's 'right hand'" (pp. 210, 209).

25 Cited in Tannenbaum, "The Goals of Italian Fascism," pp. 1186–87.

26 Cited in Finer, *Mussolini's Italy*, p. 140.

27 Zara Steiner, *The Lights That Failed: European International History, 1919–1933* (Oxford: Oxford University Press, 2005), pp. 500–501; Gooch, *Mussolini and His Generals*, p. 373; MacGregor Knox, *Common Destiny: Dictatorship, Foreign Policy, and War in Fascist Italy and Nazi Germany* (Cambridge: Cambridge University Press, 2000), p. 136. Together with the SA and SS, "Göring's Prussian police ruled the streets" in Germany after Hitler's selection as chancellor on January 30, 1933. See Knox, *To the Threshold of Power, 1922/33*, p. 404.

28 "It was not polite," the *New York Times* (June 30, 1940) obituary reported, to recall "that the natty flier was the inventor of Fascism's 'castor oil treatment' for its enemies." On the February to April exercises, see Gooch, *Mussolini and His Generals*, p. 169. For overviews, see Giorgio Rochat, *Italo Balbo aviatore e ministro dell'Aeronautica, 1926–1933* (Ferrara: Bovolenta, 1979); Giorgio Rochat, *Italo Balbo* (Turin: UTET, 1986); and Carlo Maria Santoro, ed., *Italo Balbo: Aviazione e potere aereo* (Rome: Aeronautica Militare, 1998).

29 *New York Times*, July 13, 1933.

30 Ibid., July 3, 1933.

31 Ibid., July 14, 1933. Four days later, Balbo's counterpart, aviation minister Hermann Göring, suspended the publication of *Deutsche Zeitung*, a pan-German nationalist newspaper, for alleging that Balbo was "a baptized Jew," an allegation taken from a Nazi Party publication, *The Handbook of the Jewish Question*. The three-month ban was lifted the next day, when the paper apologized for its "editorial blunder." See *New York Times*, July 18, 1933; July 19, 1933. In August 1938, Balbo, then governor of Libya, flew from Tripoli to Berlin "on a non-stop flight intended to emphasize Italo-German collaboration." See *New York Times*, August 9, 1938.

32 Cited in Knox, *To the Threshold of Power, 1922/33*, p. 377.

33 *New York Times*, July 15, 1933.

34 Ibid., July 16, 1933. The cable was written by Assistant Secretary of Commerce Ewing Y. Mitchell, who was dismissed in 1935 by President Roosevelt after refusing to resign following his allegations of corruption in the department. He reports on these matters in *Kicked In and Kicked Out of the President's Little Cabinet* (Washington, DC: Andrew Jackson Press, 1936).

35 *New York Times*, July 16, 1933.

36 Wohl, *The Spectacle of Flight*, p. 93.

37   *New York Times,* July 24, 1933.

38   Ibid., July 16, 1933.

39   The Stevens, which had opened in 1927, was then the world's largest hotel, with three thousand guest rooms, multiple ballrooms, and conference facilities. During the Depression, it went into receivership.

40   *New York Times,* June 30, 1940.

41   Segré, *Italo Balbo,* pp. 243–44; *New York Times,* July 16 and July 17, 1933.

42   *New York Times,* July 16, 1933.

43   Ibid., July 20, 1933.

44   Ibid., July 21, 1933.

45   Ibid., July 20, 1933.

46   Ibid., July 21, 1933.

47   Ibid., July 24, 1933.

48   Long contributed the fifth largest sum to Wilson's 1916 presidential campaign. See "Report Campaign Fund; $1,006,283 Raised by Democrats to Reelect Wilson," *Washington Post,* October 28, 1916. Only four individuals donated more than the $5,000 donated by Long. The biggest supporter was Bernard Baruch, at $25,000. In 1920, Long was an unsuccessful Senate candidate from Missouri, and, later, he became an outspoken isolationist before rejoining the Department of State as the official responsible for refugee policy, where he actively opposed any relaxation of quotas that might help admit threatened Jews in Europe.

49   *New York Times,* July 25, 1933.

50   *New York Times,* August 20, 1933; Finer, *Mussolini's Italy,* p. 305.

51   *New York Times,* August 14, 1933.

52   Cited in Amos Elon, "A Shrine to Mussolini," *New York Review of Books,* February 23, 2006, p. 33.

53   *New York Times,* April 18, 1934 and October 12, 1927.

54   Ibid., August 30, 1934.

55   Ibid., April 5 and May 14, 1935. "The expedition was bid Godspeed by Pope Pius XI. In the Cathedral of Milan, Cardinal Alfred Schuster blessed the banners which would 'bear the cross of Christ to Ethiopia.'" Geert Mak, *In Europe: Travels through the Twentieth Century* (New York: Vintage, 2008), p. 294.

56   Congress voted this honor in early April 1935. See *New York Times,* April 15 and May 14, 1935. Balbo then was governor of Libya, something of an exile arranged by Mussolini, who feared Balbo's popularity, because Balbo was widely touted as "the next Duce." Breckenridge Long was an important force in the administration's promoting of cordial relations with the Italian regime, which, he believed, offered both useful economic models similar to that of the New Deal's National Recovery Administration (NRA) and the chance to moderate Hitler's geopolitics.

57   *Time,* June 26, 1933, p. 37.

58 John Whitaker, the European correspondent of the *New York Herald Tribune,* recorded the popularity of the Ethiopian war in Italy. "I went to Rome thinking the Italian people were duped and dragooned into war; I left believing that the war had become a popular war of the people." On October 2, 1935, the population, "mobilized in every Italian city, village, and hamlet, roared the country's solidarity from Sicily to the Alps." See John T. Whitaker, *And Fear Came* (New York: Macmillan, 1936), pp. 233, 255. For an overview of the brutal and efficient campaign conducted by Italian forces in Ethiopia, see Gooch, *Mussolini and His Generals*, pp. 252–314. The air force, he notes, dropped 1,853,000 kilos of bombs and 1,074,000 of supplies, while losing only 8 of some 250 aircraft (p. 372).

59 *Chicago Daily Tribune,* July 1, 1936.

60 A. J. Barker, *The Civilizing Mission: The Italo-Ethiopian War, 1935–36* (London: Cassell, 1936).

61 *New York Times,* February 12, 1937.

62 Cited in Scott Berg, *Lindbergh* (New York: Berkley, 1998), pp. 360, 361.

63 *New York Times,* December 22, 1936.

64 Ibid., October 20, 1938. Anne Morrow Lindbergh recorded in her diary, "C. came back late from his dinner, with a German decoration presented him quite unexpectedly by General Göring. Henry Ford is the only other American to get it. The parchment is signed by Hitler." On October 25, Lindberg wrote Göring, "I want to thank you especially for the honor which you conferred on me at the dinner given by Ambassador Wilson. I hope that when the opportunity presents itself, you will convey my thanks to the Reichschancellor. It is difficult for me to express adequately my appreciation for this decoration, and for the way you presented it that evening. It is an honor which I shall always prize highly." Both are cited in Max Wallace, *The American Axis: Henry Ford, Charles Lindbergh, and the Rise of the Third Reich* (New York: St. Martin's Press, 2003), pp. 185, 186. Shortly thereafter, the week following Kristallnacht, Lindbergh was reported to be considering a move to Berlin to conduct aviation research with German partners. The *New York Times* noted (November 16, 1938) that "the Colonel's German friends were particularly anxious to find a house with a garden for him so his two small sons might have a place to play. . . . Friends said that the recent abandonment of many Jewish homes might make available apartments for rent."

65 *New York Times,* August 10, 1940.

66 Ibid., July 2, 1941.

67 The rally was on September 11, 1941; cited in Berg, *Lindbergh,* pp. 378, 427.

68 *New York Times,* August 11, 1941.

69 Ibid., July 1, 1940.

70 Ibid., July 2, 1940. Italian armed forces invaded Egypt in November under Graziani's command and were repulsed in January in Operation Compass.

British forces, with Australian and Indian troops, captured Tobruk later that month. In June 1942, the Germans took the city, which was retaken by the Allies in November.

71   Ibid., July 4, and July 3, 1940.

72   Ibid., July 1, 1940. In 2002, the forecourt at Ciampino Airport, just south of Rome, was renamed Piazza Balbo. Gen. Leonard Ticarico, then military adviser to Prime Minister Silvio Berlusconi, defended the naming, saying it was a response to a demand by air force pilots to honor a person who continued to be a point of reference for them. "It is an act consistent with our tradition," he said, "which acknowledges the merits of Italo Balbo in the history of the Italian Air Force." See *Times* (London), August 1, 2002. Balbo has not been forgotten in the United States. By chance, I discovered an obituary of a ninety-year-old seamstress, Tomasina Grella Armoian, who had served as president of the Italo Balbo Women's Club of Everett, New Hampshire. See *Boston Globe,* March 30, 2006.

73   The Russians wanted the trial to be held in their zone of Berlin; the other delegations opted for Nuremberg, in the American occupation zone. As a compromise, Berlin was designated as the "permanent seat of the Tribunal." See Ann Tusa and John Tusa, *The Nuremberg Trial* (London: Macmillan, 1983), p. 84. For a discussion of the continuing importance of the trial, see Richard Wasserstein, "The Relevance of Nuremberg," *Philosophy and Public Affairs* 1 (1971): 22–46.

74   István Deák, *Essays on Hitler's Europe* (Lincoln: University of Nebraska Press, 2001), p. xvii. Deák thoughtfully took note of the contradictory impact of the trial and subsequent proceedings: "A few dozen Nazi leaders were actually executed, but most others, including thousands of mass murderers, were soon released or were never even charged. They were all allowed to continue and to thrive as if nothing had happened" (pp. 17–18). A useful summary of subsequent trials of accused Nazis is provided in Adalbert Rückerl, *The Investigation of Nazi Crimes, 1945–1978.* (Hamden, CT: Archon Books, 1980).

75   The appointment of Nikitchenko raised issues of judicial propriety, as he had been the Soviet negotiator in setting the terms of the tribunal.

76   Bradley F. Smith, *Reaching Judgment at Nuremberg* (New York: Basic Books, 1963), p. 4; Patrick Dean, cited in Tusa and Tusa, *The Nuremberg Trial*, p. 207.

77   Joseph E. Persico, *Nuremberg: Infamy on Trial* (London: Penguin, 1994), p. 133.

78   Robert H. Jackson, *The Case against the Nazi War Criminals: Opening Statement for the United States of America by Robert H. Jackson, and Other Documents* (New York: Alfred A. Knopf, 1946).

79   Robert Gellately, ed., *The Nuremberg Interviews* (New York: Alfred A. Knopf, 2004), p. xv.

80   A summary of RAF bombing attacks on German cities appears in A. C. Grayling, *Among the Dead Cities: The History and Moral Legacy of the WWII Bomb-*

ing of Civilians in Germany and Japan (New York: Walker, 2006), pp. 283–328. The basic work regarding this subject for Berlin is Reinhard Rurup, *Berlin 1945: Eine Dokumentation* (Berlin: W. Arenhövel, 1995).

81 Richard G. Davis, *Bombing the European Axis Powers: A Historical Digest of the Combined Bomber Offensive, 1939–1945* (Maxwell Air Force Base, AL: Air University Press, 2006), pp. 511–12; see also Ian Buruma, "The Destruction of Germany," *The New York Review of Books,* October 21, 2004, pp. 8–12.

82 Joseph E. Persico, *Nuremberg,* p. 128. Incredibly, the city's best hotel, the Grand, also was sufficiently unscathed to house the members of the tribunal and the press.

83 In all, Allied bombing raids killed some 300,000 and injured some 800,000 Germans, and destroyed one in five German homes. Mak, *In Europe,* pp. 561, 563.

84 Peter De Mendelssohn, "The Two Nuernbergs," *Nation,* December 1, 1945, p. 569.

85 Nikitchenko originally had led the Soviet team of prosecutors. Called back to Moscow in September, he returned to the trial as the Soviet judge, taking his oath with the others on October 18. See Robert E. Conot, *Justice at Nuremberg* (New York: Harper & Row, 1983), p. 65. For his role in suggesting Nuremberg as the site, see Arieh H. Kochavi, *Prelude to Nuremberg: Allied War Crimes Policy and the Question of Punishment* (Chapel Hill: University of North Carolina Press, 1998), p. 240. Some iconic places met a different fate. The Soviet occupation force, for example, kept Buchenwald open to house suspect social democrats. See Clive James, *Cultural Amnesia: Necessary Memories from History and the Arts* (New York: W. W. Norton, 2007), p. 721.

86 Marion A. Kaplan, *Between Dignity and Despair: Jewish Life in Nazi Germany* (New York: Oxford University Press, 1998), pp. 17–49. The new regulations originated in a process that began in July 1933 when a Ministry of Interior Advisory Committee for Population and Race Policy was asked to draw up proposals concerning Jewish citizenship rights in the new Reich. See Saul Friedländer, *Nazi Germany and the Jews*, vol. 1, *The Years of Persecution, 1933–1939* (New York: HarperCollins), p. 146.

87 Cited in Avraham Barkai, "Exclusion and Persecution: 1933–1938," in *German-Jewish History in Modern Times*, vol. 4, *Renewal and Destruction, 1918–1945*, ed. Michael A. Meyer (New York: Columbia University Press, 1998), p. 211.

88 Robert H. Jackson, *The Nürnberg Case as Presented by Robert H. Jackson, Chief of Counsel for the United States Together with Other Documents* (New York: Alfred A. Knopf, 1947), p. 31.

89 Elizabeth Borgwardt, *A New Deal for the World: America's Vision for Human Rights* (Cambridge: Harvard University Press, 2005), p. 203.

90 Grayling, *Among the Dead Cities,* pp. 12–13.

91 Frederick Taylor, *Dresden: Tuesday, 13 February 1945* (London: Bloomsbury,

2004), pp. 373, 375. For a powerfully realized account of Allied bombing during World War II, see Randall Hansen, *Fire and Fury: The Allied Bombing of Germany, 1942–1945* (Toronto: Doubleday, 2009).

92 For useful discussions of the ethical issues, see the essays in Paul Addison and Jeremy Craig, eds., *Firestorm: The Bombing of Dresden, 1945* (London: Pimlico, 2006); Grayling, *Among the Dead Cities.*

93 Cited in Arieh J. Kochavi, *Prelude to Nuremberg,* p. 57.

94 An excellent discussion of "The London Conference and the Nuremberg Indictment," including the give-and-take among the four powers, can be found in Smith, *Reaching Judgment at Nuremberg,* pp. 46–73.

95 Cited in Telford Taylor, "The Nuremberg Trials," *Columbia Law Review* 55 (1955): 500.

96 Cited in Jackson, *The Nürnberg Case,* p. xv. For a discussion, see Jonathan A. Bush, "Nuremberg: The Modern Law of War and Its Limitations," *Columbia Law Review* 93 (1993): 2022–86.

97 Jackson, *The Nürnberg Case,* p. 33.

98 For an uncommonly thoughtful discussion, see Borgwardt, *A New Deal for the World,* pp. 196–248. Genocide was recognized as an international crime in the December 1946 Resolution of the United Nations General Assembly, and codified by the 1948 Convention on the Prevention and Punishment of the Crime of Genocide as the targeting for elimination of a group on the basis of its racial, religious, ethnic, or national characteristics.

99 Borgwardt, *A New Deal for the World,* p. 247.

100 Cited in Taylor, "The Nuremberg Trials," p. 499.

101 Smith, *Reaching Judgment at Nuremberg,* p. 103.

102 Cited in Tusa and Tusa, *The Nuremberg Trial,* p. 449; James Owen, *Nuremberg: Evil on Trial* (London: Headline Review, 2006), p. 317; Norbert Ehrenfreund, *The Nuremberg Legacy* (New York: Palgrave, 2007), p. 87. Ehrenfreund covered the trial for *Stars and Stripes,* the army newspaper.

103 Cited in Taylor, "The Nuremberg Trials," p. 499.

104 Persico, *Nuremberg,* p. 94. Writing when the tribunal was in session, Max Radin, a retired law professor from the University of California at Berkeley, noted how "the utmost care has been taken to enable all the defendants to present the fullest defense for themselves." They had access to all charges and counsel of their choosing, were offered simultaneous translation of all testimony irrespective of its language, could cross-examine prosecution witnesses and call witnesses of their own, and were to be allowed final statements. See Max Radin, "Justice at Nuremberg," *Foreign Affairs* 24 (1946): 383.

105 International Military Tribunal, *Trial of the Major War Crimes before the International Military Tribunal,* vol. 1 (Nuremberg, Germany: International Military Tribunal, 1947), p. 26; some members of the American delegation came to believe that "Nikitchenko was a decent chap and a covert liberal, but a man

imprisoned behind the ideological bars of the regime he served." See Persico, *Nuremberg*, p. 182.

106 William Taubman, *Khrushchev: The Man and His Era* (New York: W. W. Norton, 2002), p. 99. Addressing the Twentieth Party Congress in the 1956 secret speech, Khrushchev denounced Stalin for originating "the concept 'enemy of the people.' This term automatically rendered it unnecessary that the ideological errors of a man or men engaged in controversy be proven; this term made possible the most cruel repression, violating all norms of revolutionary legality, against anyone who in any way disagreed with Stalin, against those who were only suspected of evil intent." Nikita Sergeevich Khrushchev, *Khrushchev Remembers* (New York: Little, Brown, 1971), p. 510.

107 Cited in Robert Gellately, *Lenin, Stalin, and Hitler: The Age of Social Catastrophe* (New York: Vintage, 2008), p. 273.

108 Richard Overy, *The Dictators: Hitler's Germany, Stalin's Russia* (New York: W. W. Norton, 2004), pp. 128, 182.

109 See Nicolas Werth, "Strategies of Violence in the Stalinist USSR," in *Stalinism and Nazism: History and Memory Compared,* ed. Henry Russo (Lincoln: University of Nebraska Press, 1999), pp. 73–95.

110 For a powerful discussion of the fear-inducing effects of nighttime raids and nighttime interrogations, see Stephen Kotkin, *Magnetic Mountain: Stalinism as a Civilization* (Berkeley: University of California Press, 1995), pp. 344–48.

111 Niall Ferguson, *The War of the World: Twentieth-Century Conflict and the Descent of the West* (New York: Penguin, 2006), p. 210. During the Great Terror, some 800,000 Soviet citizens were put to death. For discussions of death estimates during this period, see Robert Conquest, *The Great Terror: A Reassessment* (New York: Oxford University Press, 1990); Alec Nove, "Victims of Stalinism: How Many?," in *Stalin's Terror: New Perspectives,* ed. J. Arch Getty and Roberta T. Mannings (Cambridge: Cambridge University Press, 2003). For a discussion of the process of setting, securing, and increasing quotas, see Nicholas Werth, "The Red Terror," in Stéphane Courtois et al., *The Black Book of Communism: Crimes, Terror, Repression* (Cambridge: Harvard University Press, 1999), 71–80. A concise discussion of debates among historians about the sources and meaning of the Great Terror can be found in Kotkin, *Magnetic Mountain,* pp. 280–86. "Moscow's Communist boss, Nikita Khrushchev, had already been presented with a quota of 35,000 'enemies' to arrest, 5,000 of whom were to be shot." See Mak, *In Europe,* p. 452.

112 J. Arch Getty and Oleg Naumov, *The Road to Terror: Stalin and the Self-Destruction of the Bolsheviks, 1932–1939* (New Haven: Yale University Press, 2002), p. 588; Anne Applebaum, *Gulag: A History* (New York: Doubleday, 2003), p. 93. During Stalin's reign from 1929 to 1953, some 29 million Soviet citizens were imprisoned in the Gulag. See Mak, *In Europe,* p. 453.

113 Kotkin, *Magnetic Mountain,* p. 300.

114 Cynthia A. Ruder, *Making History for Stalin: The Story of the Belomor Canal* (Gainesville: University Press of Florida, 1998). Clive James has sardonically observed that the ballet company, "when on tour outside Russia, is still called the Kirov, presumably on the assumption that the ballet audience abroad remains clueless enough to believe that Kirov had once had some sort of background in the fine arts. . . . Kirov's background was one of unrestricted power and the extermination of blameless human beings. A measure of our slowness to face up to the real history of the Soviet Union is that the expression 'Kirov Ballet' does not strike us as obscene." See James, *Cultural Amnesia,* p. 548.

115 "Of the 394 members of the Comintern's executive committee in January 1936, only 171 were still alive in April 1938." During the Great Terror, leading generals were killed and some 100,000 officers were put on trial; in all, "more Russian officers with a rank superior to colonel died at Stalin's hand than at Hitler's." See Mak, *In Europe,* pp. 454, 455.

116 For an account of this trial, see Donald Rayfield, *Stalin and His Hangmen: The Tyrant and Those Who Killed for Him* (New York: Random House, 2004), pp. 254–57. When the presiding judge, Vasili Ulrikh, sought to refer the case for further inquiry, Stalin responded, "No further investigation, finish the trial . . . they must all have the same sentence—shooting" (pp. 255–56). Kamenev's brother, Nikolai Rosenfeld, a painter married to a doctor inside the Kremlin, testified against him at the trial.

117 Like Trotsky, Kamenev and Zinoviev were among the most prominent Jews in the leadership of the Communist Party. For a discussion that touches on the role of anti-Semitism in the purges, see Alfred A. Greenbaum, "Soviet Jewry during the Lenin-Stalin Period," *Soviet Studies* 16 (1965): 84–92.

118 Report of Court Proceedings. *The Case of the Trotskyite-Zionvievite Terrorist Centre* (Moscow: People's Commisariat of Justice of the U.S.S.R., 1936), p. 18. An overview of "The Russian Trials," with more than a tinge of sympathy and tendentiousness, can be found in Gunther, *Inside Europe,* pp. 489–99. Gunther sought to remind his readers that "an important point to keep in mind is the peculiarity of the Russian legal procedure . . . where the real 'trial' is the preliminary investigation; the final court session does not so much determine guilt as decide what penalty should be attached to the guilty. . . . Within the circumspections of Russian procedure the trials were perfectly fair. . . . The attitude of the court was severe but not coercive," he wrote, noting that "the confessions were genuine, of which there can be little sincere doubt" (pp. 490, 496).

119 Conquest, *The Great Terror,* pp. 91–92.

120 Cited in Overy, *The Dictators,* p. 292. See also Z. I. Zile, ed., *Ideas and Forces in Soviet Legal History: A Reader on the Soviet State and the Law* (Oxford: Oxford University Press, 1992); Piers Beirne, ed., *Revolution in Law: Contributions to the Development of Soviet Legal Theory, 1917–1938* (Armonk, NY: M. E. Sharpe, 1990).

121   Cited in Stéphane Courtois, "Why?," in Stéphane Courtois et al., *The Black Book of Communism*, p. 750. For his role in the 1930s, see Arkady Vaksberg, *The Prosecutor and the Prey: Vyshinsky and the 1930s Moscow Show Trials* (London: Weidenfeld and Nicolson, 1990).

122   The fifteen victims of the second trial included Grigori Piatakov and Karl Radek; at the third, the convicted included Nikolai Bukharin and Genrikh G. Yagoda, the former director of the Secret Police, who had been instrumental in organizing the first two trials. These proceedings brought to a close the often credulous perspectives on Soviet justice that had been offered by Western friends of the regime. Writing in April 1933, for example, on the eve of a Soviet trial in Moscow of English engineers accused of espionage, the barrister D. N. Pritt wrote, "The method of investigation and trial of criminal charges in Soviet Russia, in sober truth, bears an unexpectedly close resemblance in its main features to that prevailing in many non-Communist countries; indeed, the distinctions between the methods of Russia and those of, say, Denmark are perhaps smaller than the distinctions between those of England and Denmark." See D. N. Pritt, "Procedures in a Soviet Court," in *The Moscow Trial (April, 1933)*, comp. W. P. Coates (London: Anglo-Russian Parliamentary Committee, 1933), p. 11.

123   Piers Brendon, *The Dark Valley: A Panorama of the 1930s* (New York: Alfred A. Knopf, 2000), p. 472.

124   Cited in Simon Sebag Montifiore, *Stalin: The Court of the Red Tsar* (New York: Phoenix, 2004), p. 192.

125   Report of Court Proceedings, *The Case of the Trotskyite-Zinovievite Terrorist Centre*, p. 171.

126   Ibid., pp. 165–73.

127   Ibid., p. 119.

128   Alan Bullock, *Hitler and Stalin: Parallel Lives* (New York: Alfred A. Knopf, 1992), p. 480.

129   Alexander Orlov, *The Secret History of Stalin's Crimes* (New York: Random House, 1953), pp. 168–69.

130   Cited in Rayfield, *Stalin and His Hangmen*, p. 317. Bukharin's confession at his trial in March 1938 inspired Arthur Koestler to break with Communism and write *Darkness at Noon* (New York: Macmillan, 1940).

131   *History of the Communist Party of the Soviet Union (Bolsheviks): Short Course* (New York: International Publishers, 1939), pp. 346–48.

132   Vaksberg, *The Prosecutor and the Prey*, p. 101.

133   Tusa and Tusa, *The Nuremberg Trial*, p. 232.

134   Vyshinsky chaired a secret "Government Commission on the Nuremberg Trial" set up by Stalin, on which Nikitchenko served. See Parrish, *The Lesser Terror*, pp. 62–63. The Soviet prosecution had alleged German responsibility for Katyn. Against Nikitchenko's objections, the Germans were allowed to call

witnesses in July to refute these charges. See Conot, *Justice at Nuremberg,* pp. 452–55. More broadly, he enforced Stalin's wishes at the trial.

135   After a two-day hearing, the tribunal decided not to pursue the matter. See Tusa and Tusa, *The Nuremberg Trial,* p. 412.

136   Persico, *Nuremberg,* p. 451; Tusa and Tusa, *The Nuremberg Trial,* p. 476; Owen, *Nuremberg,* p. 327. In 2005, Anthony Marreco, the only surviving member of the British prosecution team at Nuremberg, recalled, "I felt sorry for Nikitchenko, the main Russian judge. He was a tremendous chap and widely respected, but after the sentencing, he was cast into the wilderness because he'd failed to secure the 100 per cent death sentences Stalin expected. Nikitchenko was last seen pushing his wife in a wheelchair along some drab, forsaken Black Sea resort." See *Evening Standard* (London), November 23, 2005.

137   *New York Times,* April 23, 1967.

138   U.S. Congress, *Memorial Services Held,* p. 19.

139   Chester M. Morgan, "Senator Theodore G. Bilbo, the New Deal, and Mississippi Politics (1934–1940)," *Journal of Mississippi History* 47 (1985): 149, 151, 152, 161.

140   See William D. McCain, "Theodore Gilmore Bilbo and the Mississippi Delta," *Journal of Mississippi History* 31 (1969): 1–27.

141   William F. Holmes, *The White Chief: James Kimble Vardaman* (Baton Rouge: Louisiana State University Press, 1970), pp. 77–87.

142   Vincent Giroux Jr., "The Rise of Theodore G. Bilbo (1908–1932)," *Journal of Mississippi History* 43 (1981): 198–99; Daniel M. Robison, "From Tillman to Long: Some Striking Leaders of the Rural South," *Journal of Southern History* 3 (1937): 208. For overviews that help set Bilbo in context, see Cortez A. M. Ewing, "Southern Governors," *Journal of Politics* 10 (1948): 385–409; Robert L. Fleegler, "Theodore G. Bilbo and the Decline of Public Racism," *Journal of Mississippi History* 68 (2006): 1–27.

143   Harrison wanted Bilbo, a potential political rival, kept away from Mississippi's electoral politics. See R. G. Tugwell, "The Compromising Roosevelt," *Western Political Quarterly* 6 (1953): 338–39.

144   *New York Times,* September 20, 1934.

145   U.S. Congress, *Memorial Services Held,* pp. 71, 74, 76. These House speeches were delivered exactly a year before the memorial service, on November 17, 1947, and were included in the service volume.

146   Joseph D. Kennan to Bilbo, August 28, 1940; cited in Morgan, "Senator Theodore G. Bilbo," p. 162.

147   Campaign press release, October 29, 1940, in Bilbo papers; cited in Chester M. Morgan, *Redneck Liberal: Theodore G. Bilbo and the New Deal* (Baton Rouge: Louisiana State University Press, 1985), p. 230. With this record, two critical students of "Dixie demagogues" concluded in 1939 that he was "the least destructive representative of Dixie in either House of Congress." See Allan A.

Michie and Frank Ryhlick, *Dixie Demagogues* (New York: Vanguard Press, 1939), p. 107. In his fine synthetic history, David Kennedy, writing about President Roosevelt's decision to intervene actively in a series of 1938 primary elections, mistakenly notes that the campaign was aimed at producing "fewer reactionaries like . . . Bilbo." See David M. Kennedy, *Freedom from Fear: The American People in Depression and War* (New York: Oxford University Press, 1999), p. 346. By contrast, Arthur Schlesinger Jr. rightly underscored Bilbo's progressive inclinations, especially in agriculture, in his discussion of the Bankhead Act. See Arthur Schlesinger Jr., *The Age of Roosevelt*, vol. 2, *The Coming of the New Deal, 1933–1935* (Boston: Houghton Mifflin, 1959), pp. 380–81.

148 Dewey W. Grantham, *The Life and Death of the Solid South: A Political History* (Lexington: University of Kentucky Press, 1988), p. 113.

149 William G. Carleton, "The Southern Politician—1900 and 1950," *Journal of Politics* 13 (1951): 221.

150 A biographer aptly described him as the "archangel of white supremacy," who represented a constituency where "white supremacy was an unquestioned fact." See A. Wigfall Green, *The Man Bilbo* (Baton Rouge: Louisiana State University Press, 1963), pp. 104, 98, 99.

151 U.S. Congress, *Memorial Services Held,* pp. 59, 72.

152 *Chicago Defender,* July 12, 1919.

153 *Congressional Record,* 75th Cong., 3d sess., February 1, 1940, p. 894.

154 Ibid., p. 1554.

155 *Newsweek,* August 6, 1945; cited in Green, *The Man Bilbo,* p. 105.

156 Victor Riesel, "New Bilbo Blast Revives Old Ku Klux Klan Techniques," *New York Post,* July 30, 1945. During the Fair Employment debate, Bilbo "told the Senate Agriculture Committee that if fair employment is to be guaranteed to every individual regardless of race, color, or creed as provided by the President's Executive Order 8802, 'then you had better not disband your army when the war is over—you'll need it.'" See *Chicago Defender,* February 24, 1945.

157 Cited in Benjamin E. Mays, "Veterans: It Need Not Happen Again," *Phylon* 6 (1945): 208.

158 *Congressional Record,* 79th Cong., 1st sess. 1945, 91, pt. 3, p. 6898.

159 *Chicago Defender,* November 10, 1945.

160 Raymond Gram Swing, "Bilbo the Rabble Rouser," *Nation,* January 30, 1935, p. 124.

161 *Chicago Defender,* February 12, 1944.

162 Ibid.

163 Morgan, *Redneck Liberal*, pp. 251–52; *Chicago Defender,* July 7, 1945; Flora Bryant Brown, "NAACP Sponsored Sit-Ins by Howard University Students in Washington, D.C.," *Journal of Negro History* 85 (2000): 274–86. A multiracial group in the city, whose meeting was addressed by Charles Houston, the noted Howard University civil rights lawyer and law school dean, formed to try to

remove Bilbo from his D.C. chairmanship, and sent him a telegram demanding that he step down in light of his racial views, all to no avail.

164   *Chicago Defender,* February 19, 1944.

165   Cited in Hodding Carter, "'The Man' from Mississippi—Bilbo: Portrait of a Senator on the Home Grounds Making His Plea for Another Term in Office," *New York Times Magazine,* June 30, 1946, p. 7.

166   Garry Boulard, "'The Man' versus 'The Quisling': Theodore Bilbo, Hodding Carter, and the 1946 Democratic Party," *Journal of Mississippi History* 51 (1989): 201–17; Richard D. Ethridge, "The Fall of the Man: The United States Senate's Probe of Theodore G. Bilbo in December 1946 and Its Aftermath," *Journal of Mississippi History* 38 (August 1976): 241–62.

167   Senate Special Committee to Investigate Senatorial Campaign Expenditures, *Hearings, Mississippi* (Washington, DC: U.S. Government Printing Office, 1946), p. 13.

168   *New York Times,* June 23, 1946; *Chicago Defender,* June 29, 1946; Boulard, "'The Man,'" p. 211; Senate Special Committee, *Hearings, Mississippi,* pp. 7–11. In an editorial, the *New York Times* noted that "it is now assured that Senator Theodore G. Bilbo of Mississippi will not take his seat in the next Senate without a full-dress investigation of his qualifications to serve. . . . The real issue is what has come to be known as 'Bilboism,' a combination of racial hatred, Ku Klux Klannery, intimidation at the polls and a narrow parochialism to which all national interests are subordinate." See *New York Times,* November 18, 1946. See also F. Ross Peterson, "Glen H. Taylor and the Bilbo Case," *Phylon* 31 (1970): 344–50.

169   Theodore G. Bilbo, *Take Your Choice: Separation or Mongrelization* (Poplarville, MS: Dream House Publishing Company, 1947), pp. 8, 5, 6, 7.

170   Senate Special Committee, *Hearings, Mississippi,* p. 23.

171   Ellender emphasized that he intended the word *nigger.* Cited in Ethridge, "The Fall of the Man," p. 255.

172   Floyd M. Riddick, "American Government and Politics: The First Session of the Eightieth Congress," *American Political Science Review* 42 (1948): 679; L. W. Jr., "The Right of Congress to Exclude Its Members," *Virginia Law Review* 33 (1947): 323.

173   *Time,* September 1, 1947, p. 14.

174   See James Q. Whitman, "Of Corporatism, Fascism, and the First New Deal," *American Journal of Constitutional Law* 39 (1991): 747–78.

175   John P. Diggins, "Flirtation with Fascism: American Pragmatic Liberals and Mussolini's Italy," *American Historical Review* 71 (1966): 498. See also, John P. Diggins, "American Catholics and Italian Fascism," *Journal of Contemporary History* 2 (1967): 51–68; David F. Schmitz, *The United States and Fascist Italy* (Chapel Hill: University of North Carolina Press, 1988); Ido Oren, "Uncritical Portrayals of Fascist Italy and of Iberic-Latin Dictatorships in American

Political Science," *Comparative Studies in Society and History* 42 (2000): 87–118. Maurizio Vaudagna, "The New Deal and Corporativism in Italy," *Radical History Review* 4 (1977): 3–35. Support for Mussolini in the liberal democracies was not limited to the United States. "Winston Churchill, who applauded the fascist struggle against the 'bestial appetite and passions of Leninism,' was quick to recognize the Duce's accomplishments. Just weeks before the Italian attack on Abyssinia, he was still praising Mussolini, 'so great a man, so wise a ruler,' who was presiding over 'a revivified Italian nation.'" Steiner, *The Lights That Failed,* pp. 331–32.

176 John Garraty, "The New Deal, National Socialism, and the Great Depression," *American Historical Review* 78 (1973): p. 914. See also James Q. Whitman, "Of Corporatism, Fascism, and the First New Deal," *The American Journal of Comparative Law* 39 (1991): 747–78; available at http://digitalcommons.law.yale.edu/fss_papers/600. Devoting a full 1934 issue, mostly approvingly, to Italian corporatism, *Fortune* described how "the Corporate State is to Mussolini what the New Deal is to Roosevelt" (cited on p. 748).

177 See Vaudagna, "The New Deal and Corporativism in Italy."

178 Peri E. Arnold, *Making the Managerial Presidency: Comprehensive Reorganization Planning, 1905–1980* (Princeton, NJ: Princeton University Press, 1986), chap. 4.

179 Louis Brownlaw, *Report of the President's Committee on Administrative Management* (Washington, DC: U.S. Government Printing Office, 1937), p. 4; cited in Arnold, *Making the Managerial Presidency,* p. 104.

180 It was Hannah Arendt's insight that there was an internal relationship between relatively moderate popular-front policies and the deepening of repression at home. "Stalin has carried this art of balance, which demands more skill than the ordinary routine of diplomacy, to the point where a moderation in foreign policy or the political line of the Comintern is almost invariably accompanied by radical purges in the Russian party. It was certainly more than coincidence that the Popular Front policy and the drafting of the comparatively liberal Soviet constitution were accompanied by the Moscow Trials." See Arendt, *The Origins of Totalitarianism* (London: George Allen and Unwin, 1951), p. 415.

181 François Furet, *The Passing of an Illusion: The Ideal of Communism in the Twentieth Century* (Chicago: University of Chicago Press, 1999), p. 279.

182 Ibid., p. 282.

CHAPTER 3 · "STRONG MEDICINE"

1 "Nine Lynchings Reported for 2 Months in 1933," *Chicago Defender,* March 18, 1933. The place-name abbreviations in the original text have been expanded. An earlier *Defender* report of March 4 had detailed how "some 40 local white business men and landowners" had carried out the Nash lynching. "Undeterred by [a] lack of identification, the posse took Nash into the woods and strung him up from a tree, after first attempting to burn him at the stake but finding the brush too wet to accommodate that form of lingering death and torture."

2   The photograph is dated March 10, 1933. Geert Mak, *In Europe: Travels through the Twentieth Century* (New York: Vintage, 2007), p. 244.

3   For a discussion of "the demise of party government," and how the influence of political parties and politicians declined rapidly following the assassination of Prime Minister Inukai in May 1932, see James L. McClain, *Japan: A Modern History* (New York: W. W. Norton, 2002), pp. 422, 423, 424, 426–31. Of the twelve prime ministers in office between May 1932 and August 1945, four were admirals and four were generals. See W. Beasley, *The Japanese Experience: A Short History of Japan* (Berkeley: University of California Press, 1999), p. 243. For a discussion of implications of this assassination, and how it led to the steady growth of military power within the subsequent compromise "National Governments," see Edwin O. Reischauer, *Japan: Past and Present*, 3d. ed., rev. (New York: Alfred A. Knopf, 1965), p. 171. A useful treatment of the Japanese military is Meirion and Susie Harries, *Soldiers of the Sun: The Rise and Fall of the Imperial Japanese Army, 1868–1945* (London: Heinemann, 1991).

4   Alan Bullock, *Hitler and Stalin: Parallel Lives* (New York: Alfred A. Knopf, 1992), p. 316. The Nationalist and Center parties supported the Enabling Act, thinking it would be directed only against Communists and Social Democrats, "failing to realize that once the act was passed, they too would be vulnerable and Hitler free to dispense with them" (p. 315). The 81 Communist representatives were barred from the session (most were in concentration camps, in hiding, or had been killed), and only 94 of the 120 Social Democrats were admitted.

5   An early draft of the speech read, more flaccidly, "This is no occasion of soft speaking or the raising of false hopes." The record of who wrote the famous sentence is unclear. Samuel Rosenman, who edited the Roosevelt papers, attributes it to FDR, noting how Eleanor had given her husband a copy of Henry David Thoreau's writings shortly before his inauguration, and that the text, containing the sentence "Nothing is so much to be feared as fear," was in his hotel suite when the speech was put in final form. By contrast, Raymond Moley, who had penned the first draft, believes Louis Howe rewrote the text, adding the first paragraph, having read a newspaper advertisement that used the expression "fear itself." We will never know. For a summary of the controversy, see William Safire, *Safire's Political Dictionary* (New York: Oxford University Press, 2008), pp. 481–82.

6   John Gunther, *Roosevelt in Retrospect: A Profile in History* (New York: Harper and Brothers, 1950), p. 19.

7   William E. Leuchtenburg, "The Great Depression," in *The Comparative Approach to American History*, ed. C. Vann Woodward (New York: Oxford

University Press, 1997), pp. 296–97. Until the eve of World War II, the cumulative rate of unemployment in the United States was two and a half times the level in France, more than one and a half times those of Britain and Sweden, and 20 percent higher than that of Germany, where the Depression originally hit nearly as hard. See Daniel T. Rodgers, *Atlantic Crossings: Social Politics in a Progressive Age* (Cambridge: Harvard University Press, 1998), p. 412. On the banks, in comparative perspective, see Barry Eichengreen, *Golden Fetters: The Gold Standard and the Great Depression, 1919–1939* (New York: Oxford University Press, 1992), especially pp. 222–86.

8   John Shuckburgh Risley, *The Law of War* (London: A. D. Innes, 1897), pp. 73–74. Risley's text continues to have some resonance. It was cited, for example, in the habeas petition of David Hicks in October 2004. Hicks, an Australian citizen detained at Guantánamo Bay, was the first person to be tried and convicted by a Military Commission for persons held there. He was returned to Australia in April 2007, where he served the last nine months of his sentence, and was released in December of that year.

9   A. W. Ward, G. W. Prothero, and Stanley Leathes, eds., *The Cambridge Modern History,* vol. 12, *The Modern Age* (Cambridge: Cambridge University Press, 1910). The series was first planned by Lord Acton in 1898. He is widely remembered for pronouncing in an 1887 letter to Bishop Mandell Creighton that "power tends to corrupt, and absolute power corrupts absolutely." After Acton's death in 1902, the series was edited by the Cambridge University historians A. W. Ward, G. W. Prothero, and Stanley Leathes.

10 Eric Hobsbawm, *The Age of Empire, 1875–1914* (New York: Pantheon, 1987), pp. 307–8. "In Germany," he notes, "Krupp, the king of cannons, employed 16,000 in 1873, 24,000 around 1890, 45,000 around 1900, and almost 70,000 in 1912 when the fifty-thousandth of Krupp's famous guns left the works. In Britain Armstrong Whitworth employed 12,000 men at their main works in Newcastle, who had increased to 20,000—or over 40 per cent of all metalworkers on Tyneside—by 1914, not counting those in the 1500 smaller firms who lived by Armstrong's sub-contracts" (p. 308).

11 Stanley Leathes, "Modern Europe," in *The Modern Age*, ed. Word, Prothero, and Leathes, pp. 7–8.

12 Cited in MacGregor Knox, *To the Threshold of Power, 1922/33: Origins and Dynamics of the Fascist and National Socialist Dictatorships,* vol. 1 (Cambridge: Cambridge University Press, 2007), p. 170. Max Weber's emphasis is in his original text.

13 Alan Kramer, *Dynamics of Destruction: Culture and Mass Killing in the First World War* (Oxford: Oxford University Press, 2007), pp. 2, 34, 35; John Keegan, *The First World War* (London: Hutchinson, 1998), pp. 3, 6, 7.

14 For World War I casualties, see Hew Strachan, *World War I: A History* (New York: Oxford University Press, 1991); Alan Kramer, *Dynamic of Destruction:*

Culture and Mass Killing in the First World War (New York: Oxford University Press, 2007); T. J. Mitchell, *Casualties and Medical Statistics of the Great War* (1931; reprint, London: Battery Press, 1997).

15　Knox, *To the Threshold of Power,* p. 167; Mark Thompson, *The White War: Life and Death on the Italian Front 1915–1919* (New York: Basic Books, 2009).

16　Robert Gellately, *Lenin, Stalin, and Hitler* (New York: Alfred A. Knopf, 2007), p. 4. For overviews, see Charles Messenger, *Call to Arms: The British Army, 1914–1918* (London: Weidenfeld and Nicolson, 2005); Michael S. Neibeft, *Fighting the Great War: A Global History* (Cambridge: Harvard University Press, 2005).

17　James W. Garner, "Proposed Rules for the Regulation of Aerial Warfare," *American Journal of International Law* 18 (1924): 65; Joanna Bourke, *Fear: A Cultural History* (London: Virago, 2005), p. 195.

18　Kramer, *Dynamics of Destruction,* p. 31.

19　Garner, "Proposed Rules," p. 69.

20　On what he calls the Armenian catastrophe, see Norman M. Naimark, *Fires of Hatred: Ethnic Cleansing in Twentieth-Century Europe* (Cambridge: Harvard University Press, 2001), pp. 17–56.

21　Raphael Lemkin, *Axis Rule in Occupied Europe* (Washington, DC: Carnegie Endowment for International Peace, 1944), pp. 79–95; United Nations, General Assembly Resolution 260, "Convention on the Prevention and Punishment of the Crime of Genocide," December 1948; the text may be found at http://www.hrweb.org/legal/genocide.html. For a discussion, see John Cooper, *Raphael Lemkin and the Struggle for the Genocide Convention* (New York: Palgrave Macmillan, 2008). See also Donald Bloxham, "Modernity and Genocide," *European History Quarterly* 38 (2008): 294–311.

22　This is how Hannah Arendt assessed such programs of killing. See Arendt, *The Origins of Totalitarianism* (London: George Allen and Unwin, 1951), pp. 437–59. In anticipation of worse to come, anti-Soviet White Army contingents murdered more than 100,000 Jews in Ukraine and Belarus at war's end, between 1918 and 1922. The peak year was 1919. A contemporaneous account is Elias Haifetz, *Slaughter of the Jews in the Ukraine in 1919* (New York: Thomas Seltzer, 1921). "Systematically, methodically, step by step, house by house, street by street, the Jewish population was killed, violated, and exterminated." This is a report of the pogrom in Kiev, p. 120. See also Zvi Y. Gitelman, *A Century of Ambivalence: The Jews of Russia and the Soviet Union, 1881 to the Present* (Bloomington: Indiana University Press, 2001).

23　Cited in John T. Whitaker, *And Fear Came* (New York: Macmillan, 1936), p. 40.

24　For a useful discussion of the crisis in Manchuria, see Zara Steiner, *The Lights That Failed: European International History, 1919–1933* (Oxford: Oxford University Press, 2005), pp. 707–51. On Shanghai, see Christian Henriot and Wen-Hsien Yeh, eds., *In the Shadow of the Rising Sun: Shanghai under Japanese*

Occupation (Cambridge: Cambridge University Press, 2004). A broader overview is provided in Akira Iriye, ed., *The Chinese and the Japanese: Essays in Political and Cultural Interaction* (Princeton, NJ: Princeton University Press, 1980).

25   Hajo Holborn, *The Political Collapse of Europe* (New York: Alfred A. Knopf, 1951), pp. 110, 137; Steiner, *The Lights That Failed,* pp. 800, 810.

26   And looking ahead, Steiner noted that "American economic and political isolationism would reach a new peak." See Steiner, *The Lights That Failed,* p. 807.

27   Denis W. Brogan, *Democratic Government in an Atomic World: A Lecture Delivered under the Auspices of the Walter J. Shepard Foundation, April 24, 1957* (Columbus: Ohio State University, 1956), pp. 6–7.

28   Steiner, *The Lights That Failed,* p. 826; Italy's population in 1930 was 40,900,000; that of the United States was 123,200,000. Of the 140,000 soldiers in the professional army, only some 4,000 were black. In this interwar period, "most blacks were assigned, on paper, to the congressionally mandated four black regiments: the 9th and 10th Cavalry, and 24th and 25th Infantry. In practice, however, most blacks were consigned to demeaning post duties such as collecting garbage, policing lawns, operating the laundries, driving trucks, providing senior officers domestic help ('orderlies'), or entertaining the troops with gospel songs. As in the civilian sector, blacks were denied opportunities for schooling and advancement. Black officers were a rarity." See Clay Blair, *The Forgotten War: America in Korea, 1950–1953* (New York: Anchor Books, 1989), p. 148.

29   Stefan Zweig, *The World of Yesterday: An Autobiography* (New York: Viking, 1943), p. 316.

30   Leathes, "Modern Europe," pp. 1–2.

31   James Harvey Robinson, *The Last Decade of European History and the Great War* (Boston: Ginn and Company, 1918), p. i. This text was a supplement to James Harvey Robinson and Charles Beard, *The Development of Modern Europe: An Introduction to the Study of Current History* (Boston: Ginn and Company, 1907–1908).

32   Leathes, "Modern Europe," pp. 6–7.

33   Cited in Mark Mazower, *Dark Continent: Europe's Twentieth Century* (London: Allen Lane, 1998), p. 2.

34   Ibid., p. 2.

35   Cited in Niall Ferguson, *The War of the World: Twentieth-Century Conflict and the Descent of the West* (New York: Penguin, 2006), p. 227.

36   For an incisive treatment of this collapse in the context of a larger cultural and social history, see Eric D. Weitz, *Weimar Germany: Promise and Tragedy* (Princeton, NJ: Princeton University Press, 2007), pp. 331–60; for a powerful contemporaneous account, written in 1933, see Franz L. Neumann, "The Decay of German Democracy," in *The Rule of Law under Siege: Selected Essays of Franz L. Neumann and Otto Kirchheimer,* ed. William Scheuerman (Berkeley: University of California Press, 1996), pp. 29–43.

37 Jonathan Bell, *The Liberal State on Trial: The Cold War and American Politics in the Truman Years* (New York: Columbia University Press, 2004).

38 W. Y. Elliott, "Mussolini, Prophet of the Pragmatic Era in Politics," *Political Science Quarterly* 41 (1926): 161. Elliott identified Italian Fascism as a bastard offspring of the pragmatism of William James.

39 "Triumphant in 1918, it was virtually extinct twenty years on." See Mazower, *Dark Continent,* pp. 2, 3. "Of twenty-eight European countries—using the broadest credible definition of Europe—nearly all had acquired some form of representative government before, during or after the First World War. Yet eight were dictatorships by 1925, and a further five by 1933. Five years later, only ten democracies remained." See Ferguson, *The War of the World,* p. 228.

40 Arthur Moeller van den Bruck, *Germany's Third Empire* (London: George Allen and Unwin, 1934), pp. 77–114. For a discussion, see Fritz Stern, *The Politics of Cultural Despair: A Study in the Rise of the Germanic Ideology* (New York: Doubleday, 1965), pp. 236–66.

41 Carl E. Schorske, "Politics in a New Key: Schönerer," in *The Responsibility of Power: Historical Essays in Honor of Hajo Holborn,* ed. Leonard Krieger and Fritz Stern (New York: Doubleday, 1967), p. 236.

42 Karl Loewenstein, "Autocracy versus Democracy in Contemporary Europe, II," *American Political Science Review* 29 (1935): 755, 769.

43 Dan Diner, *Cataclysms: A History of the Twentieth Century from Europe's Edge* (Madison: University of Wisconsin Press, 2008), p. 130.

44 Karl Loewenstein, "Autocracy versus Democracy in Contemporary Europe, I," *American Political Science Review* 29 (1935): 571, 574.

45 Karl Loewenstein, "Militant Democracy and Fundamental Rights, I," *American Political Science Review* 31 (1937): 417.

46 Karl Loewenstein, "Militant Democracy and Fundamental Rights, II," *American Political Science Review* 31 (1937): 657.

47 For a discussion, see Michael Geyer and Sheila Fitzpatrick, eds., *Beyond Totalitarianism: Stalinism and Nazism Compared* (Cambridge: Cambridge University Press, 2009), p. 21.

48 José Ortega y Gasset, *The Revolt of the Masses* (New York: W. W. Norton, 1932), p. 11. This book was first published in Madrid in 1930 as *La rebelión de las masas.*

49 Cited in Richard Overy, *The Dictators: Hitler's Germany and Stalin's Russia* (New York: W. W. Norton, 2004), pp. 294–95. The literature on Carl Schmitt is immense. Influential appraisals include John P. McCormick, *Carl Schmitt's Critique of Liberalism: Against Politics as Technology* (Cambridge University Press, 1997); William E. Scheuerman, *Carl Schmitt: The End of Law* (Lanham, MD: Rowman & Littlefield, 1999); Raphael Gross, *Carl Schmitt and the Jews: The "Jewish Question," the Holocaust, and German Legal Theory* (Madison: University of Wisconsin Press, 2007), showing how Schmitt's radical democratic

illiberalism was entwined with his anti-Semitism; Andreas Kalyvas, *Democracy and the Politics of the Extraordinary: Max Weber, Carl Schmitt, and Hannah Arendt* (Cambridge: Cambridge University Press, 2008).

50 Overy, *The Dictators,* p. 175.

51 I take the phrase from Gellately, *Lenin, Stalin, Hitler,* p. 298. A superb account of such consent, and its mechanisms, in Nazi Germany can be found in Peter Fritzsche, *Life and Death in the Third Reich* (Cambridge: Harvard University Press, 2008), especially chaps. 1 and 2. Similarly, Richard Overy's monumental study of the USSR and Germany concluded that "the Stalin and Hitler dictatorships were populist dictatorships, nourished by mass acclamation and mass participation, and by fascination with unrestricted power." See Overy, *The Dictators,* p. 650. For Italy, see Victoria De Grazia's fine monograph, *The Culture of Consent: Mass Organization of Leisure in Fascist Italy* (New York: Cambridge University Press, 1981).

52 Hans J. Morgenthau, *The Purpose of American Politics* (New York: Alfred A. Knopf, 1960), p. 115.

53 So doing, these dictatorships assertively combined two types of modern states, what the refugee political scientist Ernst Fraenkel labeled a "dual state"—a "normative state" marked by regard for law, rules, and procedures; and an extralegal "prerogative state" that was charged with unfettered and relentless violence, intimidation, terror, and secret police. They thereby made emergency permanent and expanded the scope of moral and political possibility. See Fraenkel, *Dual State: A Contribution to the Theory of Dictatorship* (London: Oxford University Press, 1941).

54 Overy, *The Dictators,* p. 58.

55 Konrad Heiden, *Der Fuehrer: Hitler's Rise to Power* (Boston: Houghton Mifflin, 1944), p. 579.

56 Cited in Bullock, *Hitler and Stalin,* p. 316; Ian Kershaw, *Hitler, 1889–1936: Hubris* (New York: W. W. Norton, 1999), pp. 465–68.

57 Karl Loewenstein, "Dictatorship and the German Constitution," *University of Chicago Law Review* 4 (1937): 544.

58 Cited in Gellately, *Lenin, Stalin, Hitler,* p. 301. An overview of the relationship between the Enabling Acts of the Weimar Republic and the Nazi Enabling Act of 1933 can be found in Peter L. Lindseth, "The Paradox of Parliamentary Supremacy: Delegation, Democracy, and Dictatorship in Germany and France, 1920s–1950s," *Yale Law Journal* 113 (2004): 1361–71.

59 Charles S. Maier, *Recasting Bourgeois Europe: Stabilization of France, Germany, and Italy in the Decade after World War I* (Princeton, NJ: Princeton University Press, 1975), p. 344.

60 John Locke, *Second Treatise of Government* (1690; reprint, Indianapolis: Hackett Publishing, 1980), p. 75; cited in Lindseth, "The Paradox of Parliamentary Supremacy," p. 1356.

61   I draw these distinctions from Andrew Rehfeld, "Representation Rethought: On Trustees, Delegates, and Gyroscopes in the Study of Political Representation and Democracy," *American Political Science Review* 103 (2009): 214–15.

62   In rejecting the idea that the only legitimate power is controlled power, "dictatorial government," Loewenstein aptly summarized, "facilitates the legislative process in that the legislative will of the state encounters no obstacle from the parliamentary deliberation and compromise involved in parties and in the free functioning of public opinion." See Karl Loewenstein, "Law in the Third Reich," *Yale Law Journal* 45 (1936): 779, 787.

63   Cited ibid., pp. 803, 815.

64   Karl Loewenstein, "The Balance between Legislative and Executive Power: A Study in Comparative Constitutional Law," *University of Chicago Law Review* 5 (1938): 581.

65   A year after Hitler's ascent to power, on January 30, 1934, the Reichstag passed the Reconstruction Act, declaring that "the government of the Reich may enact new constitutional law," thus eliminating any remaining distinction between ordinary legislation and constitutional amendments.

66   Richard J. Evans, *The Third Reich in Power, 1933–1939* (New York: Penguin, 2005), p. 13.

67   Fritzsche, *Life and Death in the Third Reich,* p. 122.

68   Cited in Stephen A. Norwood, *The Third Reich in the Ivory Tower: Complicity and Conflict on American Campuses* (Cambridge: Cambridge University Press, 2009), p. 75.

69   Ferguson, *The War of the World,* p. 241; Knox, *To the Threshold of Power,* p. 404.

70   Mussolini, *Fascism: Doctrine and Institutions* (New York: Howard Fertig, 1935), pp. 93–94. See also Eric Hobsbawm, *The Age of Extremes: A History of the World, 1914–1991* (New York: Pantheon, 1994), pp. 109–41.

71   "Nineteenth-century thought, the principle of government by consent, of decision by the expressed will of the majority was being subordinated. . . . Within a few years after the peace it was already fair to raise the question whether democracy as a principle and an institution could survive. . . . The parliamentary system, which was both its embodiment and symbol, was losing the faith of men in most of Europe. At best, it was on the defensive. Certainly it was being steadily beaten back. Mostly it seemed futile. . . . More and more it was becoming associated with reaction. It was becoming associated with the status quo, just when the status quo was unbearable to more and more people. . . . At the same time and for the same reason, the idea of dictatorship, whether of the Left or of the Right, was steadily advancing." See Nathanial Peffer, "Democracy Losing by Default," *Political Science Quarterly* 63 (1948): 324, 326, 325.

72   "From 1920 through 1925, the liberals' attempt to make use of fascism as a force for order, as they traditionally conceived it, formed a major theme of Italian politics." See Maier, *Recasting Bourgeois Europe,* p. 322.

73 For a discussion, see R. J. B. Bosworth, "The English, the Historians, and the Età Gioliggiana," *Historical Journal* 12 (1969): 353–67. For an excellent overview, see Donald Sassoon, *Mussolini and the Rise of Fascism* (London: Harper Press, 2008).

74 Knox, *To the Threshold of Power*, pp. 78, 230, 233, 257, 281.

75 Various German Writers, *Modern Germany in Relation to the Great War* (New York: Mitchell Kennerley, 1916), pp. 10, 14–15.

76 Sanford Levinson and Jack M. Balkin, "Constitutional Dictatorship: Its Dangers and Its Design," paper presented at the American Political Science Association Meeting, September 2009, p. 12. Article 48 further stipulated that the president could "suspend, in whole or in part, the fundamental rights provided in [various] Articles" of the Constitution, "intervening if need be with the assistance of the armed forces."

77 For a discussion of these trends, see Carl J. Friedrich, "The Development of the Executive Power in Germany," *American Political Science Review* 27 (1933): 185–203. This is a particularly poignant essay by an émigré scholar, who ended by projecting, in prose written just before Hitler had come to power, how "in any case, Germany will remain a constitutional, democratic state with strong socializing tendencies whose backbone will continue to be its professional civil service" (p. 203).

78 Mussolini, *Fascism,* p. 10. For a discussion of Mussolini's search for an alternative to parliamentarianism, see R. J. B. Bosworth, *Mussolini* (London: Arnold, 2002), pp. 180–83.

79 Josef Stalin, "On the Draft Constitution of the U.S.S.R.," November 25, 1936, in Josef Stalin, *Problems of Leninism* (Moscow: International Publishers, 1947), p. 557.

80 Cited in Knox, *To the Threshold of Power*, p. 335.

81 Norman H. Baynes, ed., *The Speeches of Adolf Hitler, April 1922–August 1939* (New York: Howard Fertig, 1969), p. 427. The talk took place on April 5, 1933.

82 These aspects of his career emerge even in the (too) balanced and sympathetic assessment by Joseph W. Bendersky, "Carl Schmitt's Path to Nuremberg: A Sixty-Year Reassessment," *Telos* 139 (2007): 6–34; see also Bendersky's *Carl Schmitt: Theorist for the Reich* (Princeton, NJ: Princeton University Press, 1983).

83 James Bryce, "The Decline of Legislatures," in *Modern Parliaments: Change or Decline?* ed. Gerhard Loewenberg (1921; reprint, Chicago: Aldine Press, 1971), pp. 21–32; Carl Schmitt, *The Crisis of Parliamentary Democracy* (1923; reprint, Cambridge: MIT Press, 1988 [the translation is based on the revised 1926 edition]); Carl Schmitt, *The Concept of the Political* (1927; reprint, New Brunswick, NJ: Transaction Books, 1976). In these works, as one commentator notes, liberalism is "problematic. It is the ideology behind which bourgeois capitalist nations conceal their hegemony.... Its duplicity regarding the political allows Allies to dominate nations, like Germany, that wish to

be honest about the political. International liberalism uses universal morality, pacifism, perpetual peace, and human rights to subdue nations that are
just being honest about their concrete specificity." See John P. McCormick,
"Irrational Choice and Mortal Combat as Political Destiny: The Essential
Carl Schmitt," *Annual Review of Political Science* 10 (2007): 333. In addition to the works cited in note 49, the large literature on Schmitt and his
assault on liberalism and parliamentarism includes Otto Kirchheimer's 1933
essay, "Remarks on Carl Schmitt's *Legality and Legitimacy*," in Scheuerman,
ed., *The Rule of Law under Siege,* pp. 69–98; Paul Edward Gottfried, *Carl
Schmitt: Politics and Theory* (Westport, CT: Greenwood Press, 1990); David
Dyzenhaus, ed., *Law as Politics: Carl Schmitt's Critique of Liberalism* (Dur-
ham, NC: Duke University Press, 1998); Chantal Mouffe, *The Challenge of
Carl Schmitt* (London: Verso, 1999); Jeffrey Seitzer, *Comparative History and
Legal Theory: Carl Schmitt in the First German Democracy* (Westport, CT:
Greenwood Press, 2001); Gopal Balakrishnan, *The Enemy: An Intellectual
Portrait of Carl Schmitt* (London: Verso, 2002); Jan-Werner Muller, *A Dan-
gerous Mind: Carl Schmitt in Post-War European Thought* (New Haven: Yale
University Press, 2003); Ellen Kennedy, *Constitutional Failure: Carl Schmitt
in Weimar* (Durham, NC: Duke University Press, 2004). The decay of parliamentary democracy became a theme, too, in contemporary Marxist works,
notably including Frankfurt School theorists in the 1930s. For an example,
see Franz Neumann, *The Democratic and the Authoritarian State* (Glencoe,
IL: Free Press, 1957), pp. 101–41.

84   Max Weber, *Economy and Society* (New York: Bedminster Press, 1968), pp.
1381–97.

85   Reinhold Niebuhr, *Reflections on the End of an Era* (New York: Charles
Scribner's Sons, 1934), pp. 23, 3, ix, 19, 56.

86   William Ernest Hocking, "The Future of Liberalism," *Journal of Philosophy*
32 (1935): 230–31.

87   This strand of thought dates back at least to Italy's 1922 March on Rome, when
the question arose as to whether the "unknown quantity" of Fascism might be
exported to overcome the limitations of liberal states with legislatures at their
core. See Alan Cassels, "Fascism for Export: Italy and the United States in the
Twenties," *American Historical Review* 69 (1964): 707.

88   Hans. J. Morgenthau, *The Purpose of American Politics* (New York: Alfred A.
Knopf, 1960), p. 52.

89   Cited by Ronald Steel, *Walter Lippmann and the American Century* (Boston:
Little, Brown, 1980), p. 299.

90   Lindsay Rogers, *Crisis Government* (New York: W. W. Norton, 1934), pp. 61,
165, 112.

91   Arnold Toynbee, *Survey of International Affairs, 1931* (London: Oxford University Press, 1932), p. 1. For just this reason, Clive James's observation is com-

pelling to the effect that a book about the twentieth century that "does not deal constantly with just how close culture came to being eradicated altogether would not be worth reading." See James, *Cultural Amnesia: Necessary Memories from History and the Arts* (New York: W. W. Norton, 2007), p. 3.

92   F. J. C. Hearnshaw, "Democracy or Dictatorship?," *Contemporary Review* 146 (1934): 434–36.

93   Paul H. Douglas, *The Coming of a New Party* (New York: McGraw-Hill, 1932), p. 224.

94   The most important study of this question, placing the United States in a historical and comparative universe, is Clinton L. Rossiter, *Constitutional Dictatorship: Crisis Government in the Modern Democracies* (Princeton, NJ: Princeton University Press, 1948). Rossiter believed such government to be inevitable under modern conditions, and thus he sought to stipulate normative and practical conditions for the use of its instruments. See also The Editors, "Introduction" to "Symposium: Emergency Powers and Constitutionalism," *International Journal of Constitutional Law* 2 (2004): 207–10.

95   Stuart Chase, "A New Deal for America, IV: Survey for a Third Road," *The New Republic,* July 27, 1932, p. 282. This article was reprinted as chapter 9 of Stuart Chase, *A New Deal* (New York: Macmillan, 1932).

96   Cited in Arthur M. Schlesinger Jr., "Walter Lippmann: The Intellectual v. Politics," in *Walter Lippmann and His Times,* ed. Marquis Childs and James Reston (New York: Harcourt, Brace, 1959), p. 211. Adams, who had a successful career in business before turning to history, was best known for *Our Business Civilization: Some Aspects of American Culture* (New York: A&C Boni, 1929) and *The Epic of America* (Boston: Little, Brown, 1931).

97   Following his 1910 graduation from Harvard, where he had focused on philosophy, studying with William James, who proved a lasting influence, and serving as an assistant to George Santayana, a philosopher of aesthetics, and a poet and novelist, Lippmann had helped found *The New Republic* in 1913, and he later served as a columnist and editor of the *World,* arguably the country's most stimulating newspaper before it folded in the late 1920s. His books included *Drift and Mastery: An Attempt to Diagnose the Current Unrest* (New York: Mitchell Kennerley, 1914); *Liberty and the News* (New York: Harcourt, Brace and Howe, 1920); *Public Opinion* (New York: Macmillan, 1922); *The Phantom Public* (New York: Harcourt, Brace, 1925); and *A Preface to Morals* (New York: Macmillan, 1929).

98   These columns of January 17, January 24, February 10, February 14, and February 24 are gathered in Walter Lippmann, *Interpretations, 1933–1935,* ed. Alan Nevins (New York: Macmillan, 1936), pp. 1–13.

99   Cited by Steel, *Walter Lippmann and the American Century,* p. 300; Jonathan Alter, *The Defining Moment: FDR's Hundred Days and the Triumph of Hope* (New York: Simon & Schuster, 2006), pp. 5, 187.

100 Clinton L. Rossiter, ed., *The Federalist Papers* (New York: Mentor Books, 1999), p. 225.

101 Bryce is cited in Arthur M. Schlesinger Jr., "War and the Constitution: Abraham Lincoln and Franklin D. Roosevelt," in *Lincoln the War President: The Gettysburg Lectures*, ed. Gabir S. Borrett (New York: Oxford University Press, 1992), p. 159.

102 "Do We Need a Dictator?," *Nation* March 1, 1933, p. 220.

103 Herbert Hoover, *The Memoirs of Herbert Hoover: The Great Depression, 1929–1941* (New York: Macmillan, 1952), pp. 336, 351, 357. An example of the critique from the Right for how the New Deal was overriding classical liberalism during FDR's first term is Arthur A. Ekirch Jr., *The Decline of American Liberalism* (New York: Longmans, Green, 1955). See also Marquis Childs, "They Hate Roosevelt," in *The New Deal: The Critical Issues,* ed. Otis L. Graham Jr. (Boston: Little, Brown, 1971).

104 A revised version of James's talk first appeared in a 1910 pamphlet of the Association for International Conciliation, and was published as William James, "The Moral Equivalent of War," *McClure's Magazine,* August 1910, pp. 463–68. This phrase, which has been often deployed, was utilized by President Jimmy Carter to advocate a new federal energy policy. See "Carter Asks Strict Fuel Saving; Urges 'Moral Equivalent of War' to Bar a 'National Catastrophe,'" *New York Times,* April 19, 1977. President Carter did not credit William James; a column by James Reston, "Moral Equivalent War," *New York Times,* April 20, 1977, probed the continuing relevance of James's views.

105 William James, *The Varieties of Religious Experience: A Study in Human Nature* (New York: Longmans, Green, 1902); reprinted in William James, *Writings, 1902–1910,* ed. Bruce Kuklick (New York: Library of America, 1987), pp. 332–33.

106 In this phrase, I follow the spoken record rather than the written one.

107 The Editors, "Introduction" to the "Symposium: Emergency Powers and Constitutionalism," p. 207.

108 Franklin D. Roosevelt, "Inaugural Address," March 4, 1933, in *The Public Papers and Addresses of Franklin D. Roosevelt,* vol. 2 (New York: Random House, 1938), pp. 11–16.

109 Karl Loewenstein, "Militant Democracy and Fundamental Rights, I," p. 432.

110 For a discussion of democratic emergency powers as conservative, see John Ferejohn and Pasquale Pasquino, "The Law of the Exception: A Typology of Emergency Powers," *International Journal of Constitutional Law* 2 (2004): 210–39.

111 This parallelism has been noted by Giorgio Agamben, *State of Exception* (Chicago: University of Chicago Press, 2005), pp. 21–22.

112 He reviewed President Wilson's constitutional writings as well as Edward S. Corwin's *The President's Control of Foreign Relations* (Princeton, NJ: Prince-

ton University Press, 1917); and he surveyed the *Congressional Record* of the 65th Congress, meeting from April 2, 1917, to November 21, 1918. See Lindsay Rogers, "Presidential Dictatorship in the United States," *Quarterly Review* 231 (1919): 127–48.

113 His son, James C. Hagerty, later served as press secretary during Dwight Eisenhower's two White House terms.

114 *New York Times,* March 5, 1933.

115 Frank Freidel, *Franklin D. Roosevelt: A Rendezvous with Destiny* (Boston: Little, Brown, 1990), p. 205.

116 "One of the central characteristics of the state of exception [is] the provisional abolition of the distinction among legislative, executive, and judicial powers." Agamben, *State of Exception,* p. 7.

117 Anne O'Hare McCormick, "Vast Tides That Stir the Capital: Behind the Revolutionary Experiments in Washington There Is an Impetus That Derives Directly from a People Demanding Immediate Steps to Meet the Crisis," *New York Times Magazine,* May 7, 1933, pp. 1–3. McCormick was awarded the Pulitzer Prize for her reporting in 1937.

　　Commenting on the government's economic plans, she wrote that "one is dazed by the dimensions of this program" that "envisages a federation of industry, labor and government after the fashion of the corporative state as it exists in Italy." For a contemporaneous assessment, see Carmen Haider, "The Italian Corporate State," *Political Science Quarterly* 46 (1931): 228–47. A useful overview is Edward R. Tannenbaum, "The Goals of Italian Fascism," *American Historical Review* 74 (1969): 1183–1204.

118 Clinton L. Rossiter, *Constitutional Dictatorship: Crisis Government in Modern Democracies* (Princeton, NJ: Princeton University Press, 1948), pp. 257–58.

119 Ibid., p. 259.

120 Ibid., p. 260.

121 Ibid., p. 262.

122 During the interwar years, the sense of delegation as despotism was influentially argued by Lord Hewart of Bury, *The New Despotism* (London: E. Benn, 1929).

123 Anthony J. Badger, *FDR: The Hundred Days* (New York: Hill and Wang, 2008), pp. 169–71; see also Alter, *The Defining Moment,* p. 8.

124 Franklin D. Roosevelt, "Second Fireside Chat," Washington, DC, May 7, 1933, in Franklin Delano Roosevelt, *Great Speeches* (New York: Dover Publications, 1999), p. 41.

125 Joseph M. Bessette, *Mild Voice of Reason: Deliberative Democracy and American National Government* (Chicago: University of Chicago Press, 1994).

126 Rossiter, *Constitutional Dictatorship,* p. 263.

127 These are criteria identified by Frederick Watkins, Robert Dahl's most important teacher, in "The Problem of Constitutional Dictatorship," in *Public Policy,*

ed. Carl Friedrich and Edward Mason (Cambridge: Harvard University Press, 1940), p. 329, and by Arend Lijphart, "Emergency Powers and Emergency Regimes: A Commentary," *Asian Survey* 18 (1978): 404.

128 Ferejohn and Pasquino, "The Law of Exception," p. 217.

129 C. Vann Woodward, *Origins of the New South, 1877–1913* (Baton Rouge: Louisiana State University Press, 1951), pp. 373–74.

130 William A. Link, "The Social Context of Southern Progressivism, 1880–1930," in *The Wilson Era: Essays in Honor of Arthur S. Link,* ed. John Milton Cooper Jr. and Charles E. Neu (Arlington Heights, IL: Harlan Davidson, 1991), p. 77; Arthur S. Link, "The Progressive Movement in the South, 1870–1914," *North Carolina Historical Review* 23 (1946): 172, 179–92, 194–95.

131 V. O. Key Jr., *Southern Politics in State and Nation* (New York: Alfred A. Knopf, 1949), pp. 315, 5.

CHAPTER 4 ▪ AMERICAN WITH A DIFFERENCE

1 The number of registered blacks did not fall to zero, even in the Deep South. In 1940, for example, estimates place black registration at two thousand each in Alabama, Mississippi, and Louisiana, three thousand in South Carolina, and twenty thousand in Georgia, primarily in Atlanta. These, of course, were tiny proportions of the adult black population. See Steven F. Lawson, *Black Ballots: Voting Rights in the South, 1944–1969* (New York: Columbia University Press, 1976), p. 134.

2 For a detailed description of the operation of rules and practices aimed at depressing the franchise, see Ralph J. Bunche, *The Political Status of the Negro in the Age of FDR* (Chicago: University of Chicago Press, 1973), pp. 47–68, 181–378, and the discussions in Lawson, *Black Ballots*; Alexander Keyssar, *The Right to Vote: The Contested History of Democracy in the United States* (New York: Basic Books, 2000); Michael Perman, *Struggle for Mastery: Disfranchisement in the South, 1888–1908* (Chapel Hill: University of North Carolina Press, 2001); Richard M. Valelly, *The Two Reconstructions: The Struggle for Black Enfranchisement* (Chicago: University of Chicago Press, 2004).

3 Quoted by Virginius Dabney, *Liberalism in the South* (Chapel Hill: University of North Carolina Press, 1932), p. 247. See also Ray Stannard Baker, *Following the Color Line: American Negro Citizenship in the Progressive Era* (New York: Doubleday & Page, 1908); Desmond King and Stephen Tuck, "De-Centering the South: America's Nationwide White Supremacist Order after Reconstruction," *Past and Present,* no. 194 (2007): 219–57.

4 Richard Bensel, *Yankee Leviathan: The Origins of Central State Authority in America, 1859–1877* (Cambridge: Cambridge University Press, 1990), p. 425.

5 Taft understood that without a federal withdrawal from the racial affairs of the South, the Republican Party's prospects would be dim, and the chance either

"to effect a change in the electoral vote of the Southern States," or develop "a respectable political opposition in every State" would be unsuccessful.

6   Five years after Taft spoke, Maurice Evans, a South African segregationist, visited the American South. His remarkable travel account reports amazement at the parallels and similarities, despite the difference between the colonized status of blacks in South Africa and the formal citizenship status of blacks in the United States. See Maurice S. Evans, *Black and White in the Southern States* (Columbia: University of South Carolina Press, 2001). For a retrospective view covering this period, see Anthony J. Marx, *Making Race and Nation: A Comparison of the United States, South Africa, and Brazil* (Cambridge: Cambridge University Press, 1998).

7   For a discussion, see Leo Damrosch, *Tocqueville's Discovery of America* (New York: Farrar, Straus and Giroux, 2010), pp. 165–81.

8   Alexis de Tocqueville, *Democracy in America*, trans. George Lawrence (1835; reprint, New York: Anchor Books, 1969), p. 345.

9   Ulrich B. Phillips, "The Central Theme of Southern History," *American Historical Review* 34 (1928): 30. An important volume of essays that stresses how the South has both been southern and American is Charles Grier Sellers Jr., ed., *The Southerner as American* (Chapel Hill: University of North Carolina Press, 1960).

10   U.S. Bureau of the Census, *United States Census of Population, 1960. United States Summary, Number of Inhabitants, PC(1)-1A* (Washington, DC: U.S. Government Printing Office, 1964), p. 52.

11   The South, of course, was more than a place or a racial system. It was, as Marian Irish put things in 1952, "a myth, a dream, a sentiment, a prejudice." See Marian D. Irish, "Recent Political Thought in the South," *American Political Science Review* 46 (1952): 121. See also Michael O'Brien, *The Idea of the South, 1920–1941* (Baltimore: Johns Hopkins University Press, 1979). O'Brien shows how a southern culture was shaped by social perceptions that were developed by an indigenous intellectual class, albeit one that has often hidden its own intellectuality. For a discussion of the book's reception, and for a consideration of this argument that the South "is a relationship, not a thing," see Michael O'Brien, *Rethinking the South: Essays in Intellectual History* (Baltimore: Johns Hopkins University Press, 1988), pp. 207–18.

12   Tocqueville, *Democracy in America*, pp. 345–46.

13   Ulrich Bonnell Phillips, "The Plantation as a Civilizing Factor," *Sewanee Review* 12 (1904): 257–67. His core arguments anticipated econometric studies of plantation life, notably including Robert William Fogel and Stanley L. Engerman, *Time on the Cross*, 2 vols. (Boston: Little, Brown, 1974). Key works by Phillips include *American Negro Slavery: A Survey of the Supply, Employment, and Control of Negro Labor as Determined by the Plantation Régime* (New York: Appleton, 1918); *Life and Labor in the Old South* (Boston: Little, Brown,

1928). Phillips defended the antebellum southern system as having effectively combined racial paternalism with economic dynamism. He considered the plantation to have been "a civilizing factor" that "drilled" and "controlled" "heathen savages," making them fit "for life in civilized, Christian society." To record his admiration, Phillips dedicated his second book, *History of Transportation in the Eastern Cotton Belt* (New York: Columbia University Press, 1908), "To the Dominant Class of the South." For summaries and evaluations, see Fred Landon and Everett E. Edwards, "A Bibliography of the Writings of Professor Ulrich Bonnell Phillips," *Agricultural History* 8 (1934): 196–218; Richard Hofstadter, "U. B. Phillips and the Plantation Legend," *Journal of Negro History* 29 (1944): pp. 109–24; Daniel Joseph Singal, "Ulrich B. Phillips, The Old South as the New," *Journal of American History* 63 (1977): 871–91; John David Smith and John C. Inscoe, eds., *Ulrich Bonnell Phillips: A Southern Historian and His Critics* (Westport, CT: Greenwood Press, 1990).

14   Charles S. Sydnor, "The Southerner and the Laws," *Journal of Southern History* 6 (1940): 2.

15   Janet Hudson's excellent study of World War I–era South Carolina takes note of how white supremacy was the South's "nonnegotiable cultural value." See Janet G. Hudson, *Entangled by White Supremacy: Reform in World War I–Era South Carolina* (Lexington: University Press of Kentucky, 2009), p. 4; Phillips, "The Central Theme of Southern History," *American Historical Review* 34 (1928): 31.

16   Ulrich B. Phillips, "The Central Theme of Southern History," p. 30.

17   Ibid., p. 31. On southern political styles, see Allan Michie and Frank Ryhlick, *Dixie Demagogues* (New York: Vanguard Press, 1939).

18   Gunnar Myrdal, *An American Dilemma: The Negro Problem and American Democracy* (New York: Harper and Brothers, 1944).

19   Bunche, *The Political Status of the Negro in the Age of FDR,* p. 10. The very idea of southern distinctiveness is sometimes contested by underscoring the region's diversity, on the one hand, and its various similarities to other regions, on the other. A good example is Jack Temple Kirby, "The South as Pernicious Abstraction," in *Perspectives on the American South*, vol. 2, ed. Merle Black and John Shelton Reed (New York: Gordon and Breach, 1984), 167–79. Both aspects of this position contain a good deal of truth, but they do not ultimately contradict both the self-consciousness of the region or the compelling reasons to treat it as a coherent, and sometimes cohesive, entity in American life.

20   W. T. Couch, "The Negro in the South," in *Culture in the South*, ed. W. T. Couch (Chapel Hill: University of North Carolina Press, 1934), p. 434.

21   Rayford Logan, "The Negro Wants First-Class Citizenship," in *What Does the Negro Want?* ed. Rayford W. Logan (Chapel Hill: University of North Carolina Press, 1944), p. 7.

22   James Weldon Johnson, *Negro Americans, What Now?* (New York: Viking, 1935), pp. 98–99.

23 W. T. Couch, "Publisher's Introduction," in *What Does the Negro Want?* ed. Logan, p. xxiii.

24 Ibid., pp. xii–xiii.

25 Charles Wallace Collins, *Whither Solid South? A Study in Politics and Race Relations* (New Orleans: Pelican, 1947), pp. 77, 75. For an uncommonly thoughtful discussion of Collins, see Joseph E. Lowndes, *From New Deal to the New Right: Race and the Southern Origins of Modern Conservatism* (New Haven: Yale University Press, 2009), pp. 11–44.

26 Rather than being designated by color, as "any person in the United States is known to have any trace of Negro blood, he is classified as a Negro," not just culturally but in census reports.

27 Collins, *Whither Solid South?* pp. 75, 76.

28 Ibid., pp. 83, 84, 85.

29 Ibid., p. 80.

30 Nancy MacLean, *Behind the Mask of Chivalry: The Making of the Second Ku Klux Klan* (New York: Oxford University Press, 1994), p. 165.

31 H. C. Brearly, "The Pattern of Violence," in *Culture in the South,* ed. Couch, p. 679.

32 Ralph Ginzburg, *100 Years of Lynching* (Baltimore: Black Classic Press, 1962), pp. 211–15. See also, Arthur F. Raper, *The Tragedy of Lynching* (Chapel Hill: University of North Carolina Press, 1933); Michael J. Pfeifer, *Rough Justice: Lynching and American Society, 1874–1947* (Urbana: University of Illinois Press, 2004); Philip Dray, *At the Hands of Persons Unknown: The Lynching of Black America* (New York: Modern Library, 2003); Christopher Waldrep, *Lynching in America: A History in Documents* (New York: NYU Press, 2006).

33 Barbara Sinclair, *Congressional Realignment, 1925–1978* (Austin: University of Texas Press, 1992), p. 9.

34 Anne O'Hare McCormick, "The Promise of the New South," *New York Times,* July 20, 1930; reprinted in *The World at Home: Selections from the Writing of Anne O'Hare McCormick,* ed. Marion Turner Sheean (New York: Alfred A. Knopf, 1956), p. 60; Marian D. Irish, "The Southern One-Party System and National Politics," *Journal of Politics* 4 (1942): 80. Additional characteristics making southern politics distinctive, Irish added, were the section's "pronounced nativism," "fervid evangelism," and a pronounced rural makeup, with only a slight degree of industrialization and urbanization, the very forces that had propelled economic growth in most of the country.

35 J. Morgan Kousser, *The Shaping of Southern Politics: Suffrage Restriction and the Establishment of the One-Party South, 1880–1910* (New Haven: Yale University Press, 1974), p. 261.

36 Bunche, *The Political Status of the Negro in the Age of FDR,* p. 28; V. O. Key Jr., *Southern Politics in State and Nation* (New York: Alfred A. Knopf, 1949), pp. 578–618. See also Frederic D. Ogden, *The Poll Tax in the South* (Tuscaloosa: University of Alabama Press, 1958).

37 This data is recorded in Michael J. Dubin, *United States Congressional Elections, 1788–1997: The Official Results* (Jefferson, NC: McFarland, 1998), pp. 522–25.

38 Not every southern state elected a senator in 1938. In those that did, Lister Hill of Alabama secured 113,413 votes; Hattie Caraway of Arkansas, 122,883; Claude Pepper of Florida, 145,757; Walter George of Georgia, 66,897; Alben Barkley of Kentucky, 346,735; John Overton of Louisiana, 151,585; Bennett Champ Clark of Missouri, 757,587; Robert Reynolds of North Carolina, 316,685; Elmer Thomas of Oklahoma, 307,936; and Ellison "Cotton Ed" Smith of South Carolina, just 45,751. In part, of course, these numbers reflected the population size of their states; unlike those in the House, not all Senate seats are designed to be demographically equivalent. But southern voting rates were well below the national norm. Missouri, by far the best turnout achiever, had a population of 3,784,664 in the 1940 census and a total vote of 1,248,278. A comparable state, Indiana, with a smaller population—3,427,796—and with a southern section that had much in common with the more formally racist South, turned out 1,581,490, its electorate casting nearly four votes for every three cast in Missouri. Most everywhere in the South, disparities were far larger.

39 Collins, *Whither Solid South?* pp. 77, 81. "The dire racial problem of the South," Ralph Bunche noted, "puts the liberal there to a severe trial. Quite understandably, he has a deep-seated emotional inheritance on the Negro question that cannot be easily overcome. There is a violent conflict between this emotional inheritance from the traditional regional background and the more rational demands of the newly-acquired liberal social philosophy." See Bunche, *The Political Status of the Negro in the Age of FDR*, p. 39.

40 R. Charlton Wright, "The Southern White Man and the Negro," *Virginia Quarterly Review* 9 (1933): 179, 182, 179, 177.

41 Cited in Collins, *Whither Solid South?* p. 81; cited and discussed in Michael J. Klarman, *From Jim Crow to Civil Rights: The Supreme Court and the Struggle for Racial Equality* (New York: Oxford University Press, 2004), p. 180.

42 *Congressional Record*, 75th Cong., 1st sess., August 12, 1937; cited in William E. Leuchtenburg, *The White House Looks South: Franklin D. Roosevelt, Harry S. Truman, Lyndon B. Johnson* (Baton Rouge: Louisiana State University Press, 2005), p. 59.

43 A superb overview of the southern position on these issues is provided by the treatment of the agrarian program in Elizabeth Sanders, *Roots of Reform: Farmers, Workers, and the American State, 1877–1917* (Chicago: University of Chicago Press, 1999). This treatment of the agrarian model and the role of the South in promoting it, however, is curiously silent about matters of race. Also downplaying race and region is the otherwise-useful study by David Sarasohn, *The Party of Reform: Democrats in the Progressive Era* (Jackson: University Press of Mississippi, 1989). A portrait of the interplay between sectionalism, agriculture, and labor is provided in Arthur N. Holcombe, *The Political Parties of To-Day: A Study in Republican and Democratic Politics* (New York: Harper and Brothers, 1924).

44 Benjamin F. Long to Walter Page Hines, March 15, 1913; cited in Dewey W. Grantham Jr., "An American Politics for the South," in *Southerner as American,* ed. Sellers, p. 159.

45 A measured account of Wilson's racism and his "failure of moral conscience" can be found in John Milton Cooper, *Woodrow Wilson: A Biography* (New York: Alfred A. Knopf, 2009). For further discussions, see Henry Blumenthal, "Woodrow Wilson and the Race Question," *Journal of Negro History* 48 (1963): 1–21; Nancy J. Weiss, "The Negro and the New Freedom: Fighting Wilsonian Segregation," *Political Science Quarterly* 84 (1969): 61–79; Arthur S. Link, "Woodrow Wilson: The American as Southerner," *Journal of Southern History* 36 (1970): 3–17; Stephen Skowronek, "The Reassociation of Ideas and Purposes: Racism, Liberalism, and the American Political Tradition," *American Political Science Review* 100 (2006): 385–401.

46 This point is underscored persuasively in Skowronek, "The Reassociation of Ideas and Purposes," pp. 309–10.

47 Arthur S. Link, "The South and the 'New Freedom': An Interpretation," *American Scholar* 20 (1951): 316. An article with reservations about this claim, usefully showing internal tensions within the southern wing of the Democratic Party about the degree of Wilsonian radicalism, is Richard M. Abrams, "Woodrow Wilson and the Southern Congressmen," *Journal of Southern History* 4 (1956): 417–37. In all, Abrams showed that Link may have exaggerated southern radicalism but that he did not contradict the homologous relationship between southern and Wilsonian progressivism. A thoughtful adjudication of this dispute is offered by Morton Sosna, "The South in the Saddle: Racial Politics during the Wilson Years," *Wisconsin Magazine of History* 54 (1970): 35. See also George Brown Tindall, *The Emergence of the New South, 1915–1945* (Baton Rouge: Louisiana State University Press, 1967), whose discussion of the character of southern representation stresses the often central role played by the region in crafting and enacting key legislation (pp. 4–18).

48 Michael Perman, *Pursuit of Unity: A Political History of the American South* (Chapel Hill: University of North Carolina Press, 2009), p. 215.

49 Still, this consideration was not neglected. A comprehensive overview of southern congressional voting patterns during World War I concluded that, in addition to religious questions, "even more limiting to the southern vision was the racial question. . . . The outcome of roll calls on woman suffrage, prohibition, and perhaps selective service might well have been different had the racial issue been ignored." See Richard L. Watson, "A Testing Time for Southern Congressional Leadership: The War Crisis of 1917–1918," *Journal of Southern History* 44 (1978): 37.

50 W. Elliot Brownlee, *Federal Taxation in America: A Short History* (New York: Cambridge University Press, 1996), p. 62.

51 This discussion relies on the report in Sosna, "The South in the Saddle," pp. 42–45. See also Philip A. Grant Jr., "Senator Hoke Smith, Southern Congressmen, and Agricultural Education, 1914–1917," *Agricultural History* 60 (1986): 111–22.

52   *New York Tribune,* February 6, 1914; *Washington Post,* February 8, 1914.

53   Gilbert Hitchcock of Nebraska and Atlee Pomerene of Ohio.

54   *New York Times,* February 8, 1914.

55   "Soak-the-rich remained," but at the behest of the Harding and Coolidge administrations, "with progressiveness reduced, major loopholes added, and its sharp anticorporate edge dulled" despite the best efforts of the southern progressives. See Brownlee, *Federal Taxation in America,* p. 65.

56   Battles over taxation took place as "the nation found itself in the midst of a great transition from customs and excises to the income tax as a major source of federal revenue for peacetime as well as for war." See Kenyon E. Poole, "The Problem of Simplicity in the Enactment of Tax Legislation, 1920–1940," *Journal of Political Economy* 49 (1941): 900. On Sheppard-Tower and race, see the superb study by Deborah E. Ward, *The White Welfare State: The Racialization of U.S. Welfare Policy* (Ann Arbor: University of Michigan Press, 2005).

57   Lodge is best known, of course, for his successful leadership three decades later, when he chaired the Senate Foreign Relations Committee, in defeating participation by the United States in the fledgling League of Nations.

58   Gregory J. Wawro and Eric Schickler, *Filibuster: Obstruction and Lawmaking in the U.S. Senate* (Princeton, NJ: Princeton University Press, 2006), pp. 76–87. For a superb account of how debate about the federal elections bill intertwined with fundamental changes to the rules of the House, see Richard M. Valelly, "The Reed Rules and Republican Party Building: A New Look," *Studies in American Political Development* 23 (2009): 115–42.

59   These included John Townsend Jr., Philips Lee Goldsborough, Roscoe Patterson, and Henry Hatfield, largely forgotten Republican names, oddities in an overwhelmingly Democratic region, who represented Delaware, Maryland, Missouri, and West Virginia, respectively, in the U.S. Senate at the start of the New Deal. Each had been elected in 1928, when much of the South recoiled from the presidential candidacy of New York governor Alfred E. Smith, a Catholic and an opponent of Prohibition. A fifth southern Republican, Daniel Hastings of Delaware, was appointed to his seat in December 1928 to fill the vacancy caused by the resignation of Senator T. Coleman du Pont. Hastings was elected to a full term in November 1930, but he lost his seat in 1936 to the Democrat James Hughes. During the 1930s, Smith emerged as a leading critic of the New Deal. He criticized Roosevelt's program for opportunism, constitutional transgressions, and class discord, among other sins, in a series of speeches in the winter and fall of 1936. See Charles W. Calhoun, *Concerning a New Republic: The Republican Party and the Southern Question, 1869–1900* (Lawrence: University Press of Kansas, 2006); Vincent DeSantis, *Republicans Face the Southern Question: The New Departure Years, 1877–1897* (Bloomington: Indiana University Press, 1962); Richard M. Valelly, "Partisan Entrepreneur-

ship and Policy Windows: George Frisbie Hoar and the 1890 Federal Elections Bill," in *Formative Acts: American Politics in the Making,* ed. Stephen Skowronek and Matthew Glassman (Philadelphia: University of Pennsylvania Press, 2007), pp. 126–52.

60 Robert L. Zangando, *The NAACP's Crusade against Lynching, 1909–1950* (Philadelphia: Temple University Press, 1980), p. 69. See also Ira Katznelson, *Black Men, White Cities: Race, Politics, and Migration in the United States, 1900–1930, and Britain, 1948–1968* (London and New York: Oxford University Press, 1973), pp. 55–60; Jeffrey A. Jenkins, Justin Peck, and Vesla M. Weaver, "Between Reconstructions: Congressional Action on Civil Rights, 1891–1940," *Studies in American Political Development* 24 (2010): 61–63, 66–77. These authors treat the 7–6 vote favoring the bill by northern Democrats as a harbinger of the influence of black northern voters on the party's later turn to civil rights. But at this moment, the final passage roll call in the House on the Dyer antilynching bill was a party-line and sectional vote. "The anti-lynching measure was finally taken up in the Senate when it reconvened (after the Congressional elections) in late November. The Southerners, as predicted, filibustered. The filibuster, led by Senator Underwood of Alabama, was unexpectedly brief. On Saturday night, 2 December, a caucus of Republicans decided to implement the agreement reached by the leadership in July to have the Senate abandon the Bill and move on to other pending business" (Katznelson, *Black Men, White Cities,* p. 59).

61 In the early New Deal, the Finance Committee was particularly important. That committee, guided by Harrison, nurtured and reported the National Industrial Recovery Act in 1933, the Reciprocal Trade Act in 1934, and the Social Security Act of 1935—together, the very heart of the New Deal.

62 Irish, "The Southern One-Party System and National Politics," pp. 84–85. For a discussion and relevant data on the role of southern Democrats in Congress, see David W. Brady, *Critical Elections and Congressional Policy Making* (Stanford, CA: Stanford University Press, 1988); Sinclair, *Congressional Realignment,* especially the useful table on regional composition on p. 19. See also the discussion on the advantages that accrued to the South over the long term in Richard L. Watson Jr., "From Populism through the New Deal: Southern Political History," in *Interpreting Southern History: Historiographical Essays in Honor of Sanford W. Higginbotham,* ed. John B. Boles and Evelyn Thomas (Baton Rouge: Louisiana State University Press, 1987).

63 Republicans tended to be more competitive in Senate races than in House ones, yet even in that chamber victorious Democratic Party candidates secured 86.4 percent of the vote from 1912 to 1930, dipping below 85 percent only in 1920. The mean percentage of the two-party vote for all candidates in this period outside the South was 58 percent. See Donald Gross and David Breaux, "Historical Trends in U.S. Senate Elections, 1912–1988," *American Politics Quarterly* 19 (1991): 295, 300.

64 In the Senate, 70 percent in the 67th Congress; 66 in the 68th; 63 in the 69th; 65

in the 70th; 67 in the 71st; and 64 in the 72nd. The percentages for the House were 86, 66, 71, 69, 72, and 63. These proportions were calculated from data drawn from Kenneth C. Martis, *The Historical Atlas of Political Parties in the United States Congress, 1789–1989* (New York: Macmillan, 1989), pp. 174–85.

65   There were five Farmer-Labor Party members, as well. This was the composition of the House on March 4, 1933.

66   There was also one Farmer-Labor Party member. This was the composition of the Senate on March 4, 1933.

67   Milton Plesur, "The Republican Congressional Comeback of 1938," *Review of Politics* 24 (1962): 525–62; Clyde P. Weed, *The Nemesis of Reform: The Republican Party during the New Deal* (New York: Columbia University Press, 1994).

68   The pre–New Deal situation is summarized in Theodore J. Lowi, "The Roosevelt Revolution and the New American State," in *Comparative Theory and Political Experience: Mario Einaudi and the Liberal Tradition*, ed. Peter J. Katzenstein, Theodore J. Lowi, and Sidney Tarrow (Ithaca, NY: Cornell University Press, 1990), pp. 192–95. This essay stands on the shoulders of Mario Einaudi, *The Roosevelt Revolution* (New York: Harcourt, Brace, 1959).

69   Southern congressional power peaked during the New Deal era's second decade, from 1943 to 1952. Republicans averaged 43 members (45 percent) in the Senate, compared with 30 (31 percent) for southern Democrats and just 23 (24 percent) for nonsouthern Democrats. In the House, on average, the Republicans held 203 seats (47 percent), while southern Democrats had 133 (31 percent), and nonsouthern Democrats only 97 (23 percent). As a result, the region's representatives became a good deal more than a veto group. Commanding the Democratic Party, the South effectively controlled what Congress would, and would not, accomplish. More than once in his landmark treatment of the growth of congressional conservatism during the New Deal, James Patterson stressed that "too much can be made of the fact" that much of the emergent opposition to the New Deal within the Democratic Party was southern, and he cautioned that "it is easy to simplify the southern role in the conservative bloc" and said that "this factor should not be overemphasized." He rightly noted that outside of explicit race issues or those that elicited racial fears, the South hardly was solid, and, most often, continued to back the New Deal. But that is just the point I wish to stress. The South moved from a core initiator and supporter of the New Deal in the early years to a voting bloc that had to manage to find its way within a two-dimensional map with both party and regional coordinates. I fully agree with Patterson that the South was not the center of a sure and predictable conservative coalition. See James T. Patterson, *Congressional Conservatism and the New Deal* (Lexington: University of Kentucky Press, 1967), pp. 132, 278, 322–23. Patterson first put forth his arguments in the following two articles: "The Failure of Party Realignment in the South, 1937–1939," *Journal of Politics* 27 (1965): 602–617; "A Conservative Coalition Forms in Congress, 1933–1939," *Journal of American History* 52 (1966): 757–72.

70 The simple measure of "likeness" to gauge the behavior of legislative groups was first introduced by Stuart A. Rice in 1925, then widely adopted by congressional scholars. As summarized by David Mayhew, the "likeness index gauges the similarity of outlook among two voting blocs. For a given motion, an index of likeness is calculated by subtracting from 100 the difference between the percentages of 'aye' votes cast by two blocs. Thus, if blocs of Republican 'farm' and 'nonfarm' congressmen both unanimously support a motion, their index of likeness is 100. If each bloc unanimously opposes the other, their index of likeness is zero. If one bloc divides 90–10 and the other 70–30, their likeness index is 80." Conventionally, the cutoff dividing high from low likeness is a score of 70. See Stuart A. Rice, "The Behavior of Legislative Groups: A Method of Measurement," *Political Science Quarterly* 40 (1925): 63–64; David R. Mayhew, *Party Loyalty among Congressmen: The Difference between Democrats and Republicans, 1947–1962* (Cambridge: Harvard University Press, 1966), p. 9.

71 This count includes procedural roll calls that clearly were linked to a substantive policy issue. After a review of the *Congressional Record* for each procedural roll call, a determination was made as to whether a roll call was purely procedural, as in a vote to elect the Speaker of the House, or was clearly linked to a particular public policy area that was under discussion, as in a vote to adjourn during fierce debate about a substantive bill.

CHAPTER 5 · JIM CROW CONGRESS

1 The appointment was controversial. Lamar's nomination was confirmed by a vote of 42–38.

2 John F. Kennedy, *Profiles in Courage* (New York: Harper and Brothers, 1956), p. 273. On April 25, 1874, Lamar famously delivered a eulogy in the House of Representatives for Charles Sumner, abolitionist and Radical Republican senator from Massachusetts that called for an end to bitter divisions. Kennedy named Lamar "the most gifted statesman given by the South to the nation from the close of the Civil War to the turn of the century" (p. 188).

3 Twelve Southerners, *I'll Take My Stand* (New York: Harper and Brothers, 1930).

4 This was the assessment of Frank Owsley, one of the group's main figures. See Richard H. King, *A Southern Renaissance: The Cultural Awakening of the American South, 1930–1955* (New York: Oxford University Press, 1980), p. 58.

5 Virginius Dabney, *Liberalism in the South* (Chapel Hill: University of North Cardina Press, 1932), pp. 265, 428; Hans L. Trefousse, *Historical Dictionary of Reconstruction* (New York: Greenwood Press, 1991), pp. 126–27. See also Wirth Armisted Cate, *Lucius Q. C. Lamar: Secession and Reunion* (Chapel Hill: University of North Carolina Press, 1935); James B. Murphy, *L. C. Q. Lamar: Pragmatic Patriot* (Baton Rouge: Louisiana University Press, 1973).

6 Cited in Elizabeth Sanders, "Ballots and Bounty: Suffrage Expansion and Pol-

icy Change in the South" (Ph.D. dissertation, Cornell University, 1978), p. 217. A useful consideration of the role of economic development, in tandem with segregation, in southern politics and policy is Edward L. Ayers, *The Promise of the New South: Life after Reconstruction* (New York: Oxford University Press, 1992).

7   William N. Parker, "The South in the National Economy, 1865–1870," *Southern Economic Journal* 46 (1980): 1045.

8   Ibid., p. 1032. See also George B. Tindall, *The Emergence of the New South, 1913–1945* (Baton Rouge: Louisiana State University Press, 1967), pp. 111–42.

9   Calvin B. Hoover and B. U. Ratchford, *Economic Resources and Policies of the South* (New York: Macmillan, 1951); Clarence Heer, *Income and Wages in the South* (Chapel Hill: University of North Carolina Press, 1930); Richard Sterner, *The Negro's Share: A Study of Income, Consumption, Housing and Public Assistance* (New York: Harper and Brothers, 1943); B. B. Kendrick, "The Colonial Status of the South," in *The Pursuit of Southern History: Presidential Addresses of the Southern Historical Association, 1935–1963,* ed. George Brown Tindall (Baton Rouge: Louisiana State University Press, 1964), pp. 90–105. This was Professor Kendricks's presidential address, delivered in Atlanta on November 7, 1941.

10   Maury Maverick, "The South Is Rising," *Nation,* June 17, 1936, p. 772. "For all his progressivism, the feisty Texan was slow to abandon his traditionally paternalistic views about blacks. . . . Maverick sometimes went to extremes to keep blacks out of party politics—and thus he presented an embarrassing contradiction as a liberal defender of the Texas white primary until it was ruled unconstitutional in 1944." See John Egerton, *Speak Now against the Day: The Generation before the Civil Rights Movement in the South* (Chapel Hill: University of North Carolina Press, 1995), p. 223.

11   Howard W. Odum, *The Way of the South: Toward the Regional Balance of America* (New York: Macmillan, 1947), pp. 229–30.

12   Southern reticence went hand in hand with "the absence of any effective attack on southern racial practices remotely comparable to the earlier abolitionist or Radical Republican offensives." See George B. Tindall, "The Central Theme Revisited," in *The Southerner as American,* ed. Charles Grier Sellers Jr. (Chapel Hill: University of North Carolina Press, 1960), p. 114.

13   There was one Republican, Oscar DePriest, who was first elected from the South Side of Chicago in 1928. He lost his seat to Arthur Mitchell, a black Democrat, in 1934. For a discussion of race and Chicago politics, see Ira Katznelson, *Black Men, White Cities: Race, Politics, and Migration in the United States, 1900–1930, and Britain, 1948–1968* (New York: Oxford University Press, 1973).

14   See J. B. Shannon, "Presidential Politics in the South," *Journal of Politics* 10 (1948): 464–89.

15   William E. Leuchtenburg, *The White House Looks South: Franklin D. Roosevelt,*

Harry S. Truman, Lyndon B. Johnson (Baton Rouge: Louisiana State University Press, 2005), p. 56. Alan Brinkley has astutely observed that "Roosevelt was a coalition-builder," with an inclination "to conciliate, to broaden his base of support, to win the loyalties of existing leaders. In the South, that meant not only remaining solicitous of political elites in the distribution of patronage and the administration of programs. It meant avoiding issues altogether when those issues seemed likely to create regional antagonisms. Hence the New Deal's reluctance to challenge segregation in the South, its willingness to tolerate racial discrimination in the administration of its own relief programs, its acceptance of racial wage differentials, its refusal to endorse antilynching legislation, its notable lack of enthusiasm for supporting union-organizing in the South." See Brinkley, "The New Deal and Southern Politics," in *The New Deal and the South,* ed. James C. Cobb and Michael Namorato (Jackson: University of Mississippi Press, 1984), pp. 101–2.

16   Egerton, *Speak Now against the Day,* p. 115.

17   David Levering Lewis, "The Appeal of the New Deal," *Reviews in American History* 12 (1984): 554. Lewis notes that "FDR's administration appears to have been significantly preoccupied with discussing how to avoid civil rights discussions" (p. 556).

18   Walter White, *A Man Called White: The Autobiography of Walter White* (Athens: University of Georgia Press, 1995), pp. 168–69. Notwithstanding, White "left the meeting in fine fettle, believing victory was within his grasp," because he had understood Roosevelt to have "promised White that he would consult with Senator Wagner to spur passage and that he would tell Senate Democrats that he wanted the bill passed." There is no evidence he ever did so. See Kenneth Robert Janken, *White: The Biography of Walter White, Mr. NAACP* (New York: New Press, 2003), p. 210. It is not as if Roosevelt had much choice in the matter. "If the president assaulted the barriers of Jim Crow," Leuchtenburg remarks, "neither southern blacks, few of whom could even go to the polls, nor white liberals, who were in a decided minority on racial issues, could have given him the backing he would have needed." See Leuchtenburg, *The White House Looks South,* p. 59.

19   Leuchtenburg, *The White House Looks South,* pp. 56–57. See also Raymond Wolters, "The New Deal and the Negro," in *The New Deal: The National Level,* ed. John Braeman, Robert H. Bremner, and David Brody (Columbus: Ohio State University Press, 1975).

20   Frank Freidel, *F.D.R. and the South* (Baton Rouge: Louisiana State University Press, 1965), p. 41. "As for the Southern leadership in Congress, "he notes, "Roosevelt presumably gave it almost complete freedom during these months because he did not want to disturb the unified support he could expect from it" (p. 45).

21   Odum, *The Way of the South,* p. 231.

22   On September 8, 1945, Long was shot by an assassin in Baton Rouge, Louisiana; he died four days later.

23   Carter Glass to Walter Lippmann, August 10, 1933; cited in James T. Patterson, *Congressional Conservatism and the New Deal* (Lexington: University of Kentucky Press, 1967), p. 13.

24   Freidel, *F.D.R. and the South,* p. 46; "Rather forlornly voicing their complaints against the New Deal," the impact of the southern rejectionists "upon legislation was negligible." See James T. Patterson, *Congressional Conservatism and the New Deal* (Lexington: University of Kentucky Press, 1967), p. 31.

25   Patterson, *Congressional Conservatism and the New Deal,* pp. 57, 58.

26   Richard Hofstadter, *The Age of Reform: From Bryan to F.D.R.* (New York: Vintage, 1955), p. 302.

27   Southern intellectuals often were in the vanguard of efforts to legitimate planning as consistent with liberal democracy, and to urge its application especially to their own destitute region. For an example, see the Vanderbilt economist John V. Van Sickle's *Planning for the South: An Inquiry into the Economics of Regionalism* (Nashville: Vanderbilt University Press, 1943). This volume contrasts "liberal planning" with "total planning."

28   See Ira Katznelson, *When Affirmative Action Was White: An Untold History of Racial Inequality in Twentieth-Century America* (New York: W. W. Norton, 2005).

29   Bureau of the Census, U.S. Department of Commerce, Fifteenth Census of the United States: 1930 (1933); Bureau of the Census, U.S. Department of Commerce, Sixteenth Census of the United States: 1940 (1943).

30   African-Americans were confronted with a Hobson's choice. Unregulated hours and wages for farmworkers meant peonage; regulation to raise wages and limit hours often meant the loss of employment and deep poverty.

31   Travis M. Adams, "The Arkansas Congressional Delegation during the New Deal, 1933–1936" (master's thesis, Vanderbilt University, 1962), pp. 248–49; cited in Patterson, *Congressional Conservatism and the New Deal,* p. 65.

32   Hofstadter, *The Age of Reform,* p. 307.

33   Leuchtenburg, *The White House Looks South,* p. 2.

34   Broadus Mitchell, "Southern Quackery," *Southern Economic Journal* 3 (1936): p. 143. Mitchell called on the South to support a program that combined ending the worst racial practices, such as lynching, with a recognition that "what we have is the general problem of capitalist exploitation" (p. 145). A denial of that central fact, he believed, constituted southern quackery.

35   There had been earlier legislative proposals by President Benjamin Harrison in 1891 and 1892, after a mob had lynched eleven Italians in New Orleans, producing an international hue and cry. His first proposal protected aliens, but his second would have extended the law to African-Americans. See Will Maslow and Joseph B. Robinson, "Civil Rights Legislation and the Fight for Equality, 1862–1952," *University of Chicago Law Review* 20 (1953): 380.

36   Howard W. Odum, "Lynchings, Fears, and Folkways," *Nation,* December 30, 1931, pp. 719–20.

37   See http://www.law.umkc.edu/faculty/projects/ftrials/shipp/lynchingyear.html.

38   Philip Dray, *At the Hands of Persons Unknown: The Lynching of Black America* (New York: Random House, 2002), p. 335.

39   *New York Times,* October 28, 1934. Walter White, *The Lynching of Claude Neal* (New York: NAACP, 1934). This pamphlet was widely circulated. For an account of the lynching, see also Robert L. Zangrando, "The NAACP and a Federal Anti-Lynching Bill, 1934–1940," *Journal of Negro History* 50 (1965): 110.

40   The attorney general claimed that Washington had no jurisdiction because federal laws against kidnapping presumed a monetary motive. Tindall, *The Emergence of the New South,* p. 551.

41   Eleanor Roosevelt to Walter White, March 19, 1936, ER Correspondence, Franklin D. Roosevelt Library, Hyde Park, NY; cited in Dray, *At the Hands of Persons Unknown,* p. 344.

42   Arthur Krock, the *New York Times* columnist, praised the southern argument for its constitutional soundness. See *New York Times,* May 2, 1935. A learned defense of the southern position can be found in William D. Ford, "Constitutionality of Proposed Federal Anti-Lynching Legislation," *Virginia Law Review* 34 (1948): 944–53.

43   The debate is analyzed in George C. Rable, "The South and the Politics of Antilynching Legislation, 1920–1940," *Journal of Southern History* 51 (May 1985): 201–20. When Black was appointed to the Court in 1938, he was succeeded by Lister Hill, "a liberal for poor whites, but a racist to poor blacks." See Gary Boulard, "The Failure of the Southern Moderates," *American Quarterly* 40 (1988): 416.

44   *New York Times,* April 26, 1935. The paper was quoting Josiah Bailey of North Carolina.

45   Rable, "The South and the Politics of Antilynching Legislation," p. 212.

46   *New York Times,* April 28, 1935.

47   Ibid., April 29, 1935.

48   *Congressional Record,* 74th Cong., 1st sess., May 1, 1935, p. 6687; *Chicago Daily Tribune,* May 2, 1935.

49   Jeffrey A. Jenkins, Justin Peck, and Vesta M. Weaver, "Between Reconstructions: Congressional Action on Civil Rights, 1891–1940," *Studies in American Political Development* 24 (2010): 81.

50   Rable, "The South and the Politics of Antilynching Legislation," p. 210.

51   Odum, *The Way of the South,* p. 229.

52   Ella Lonn, "Reconciliation between the North and the South," in *The Pursuit of Southern History: Presidential Addresses of the Southern Historical Association,* ed. George Brown Tindall (Baton Rouge: Louisiana State University Press, 1964), pp. 207, 208. See Carol Bleser's "Tokens of Affection: The First

Three Women Presidents of the Southern Historical Association" in *Taking Off the White Gloves: Southern Women and Women Historians*, ed. Michele Gillespie and Catherine Clinton (Columbia: University of Missouri Press, 1998), pp. 145–57.

53   This was an approach "less concerned with racial justice than with the elevation of the region's people without regard for race." See "Introduction: The *Report* in Historical Perspective," in *Confronting Southern Poverty in the Great Depression: The Report on Economic Conditions of the South with Related Documents*, ed. David L. Carlton and Peter A. Coclanis (Boston: Bedford Books, 1996), p. 26.

54   The central work of the regional studies movement was Howard W. Odum, *Southern Regions of the United States* (Chapel Hill: University of North Carolina Press, 1936). Odum was an important national scholarly figure who served as president of the American Sociological Association in 1930.

55   "Request for Report," June 22, 1938, and "The President's Letter," July 5, 1938, in The National Emergency Council, prepared for the president, *Report on Economic Conditions of the South,* p. 1; the report is reprinted in Carlton and Coclanis, *Confronting Southern Poverty in the Great Depression,* pp. 41–82; the original document was published in a pamphlet that was widely distributed, with an initial press run of more than 100,000 copies. A useful discussion can be found in Leuchtenburg, *The White House Looks South,* pp. 102–12.

56   B. B. Kendrick, "The Colonial Status of the South," in Tindall, *The Pursuit of Southern History,* p. 90. For a discussion of colonial imagery in the South, and in studies about the region, see Numan Bartley, "Beyond Southern *Politics*: Some Suggestions for Research," in *Perspectives on the American South*, Vol. 2, ed. Merle Black and John Shelton Reed (New York: Gordon and Breach, 1984), pp. 40–41.

57   For a discussion, see Katznelson, *When Affirmative Action Was White*, pp. 25–52.

58   National Emergency Council, *Report on Economic Conditions of the South,* p. 22.

59   Ibid., 28. In 1930, South Carolina spent $5.20 per black pupil but $52.89 for each white student. The comparable figures for Mississippi, Georgia, Alabama, and Louisiana, respectively, were $5.94 and $31.33; $6.98 and $31.52; $7.16 and $37.50; and $7.84 and $40.64. See W. T. Couch, "The Negro in the South," in *Culture in the South,* ed. W. T. Couch (Chapel Hill: University of North Carolina Press, 1934), p. 459.

60   *Report on Economic Conditions of the South,* pp. 29–32. "Negro men and women who need to go to a hospital may or may not be permitted to go to a white one; they will not find Negro doctors or surgeons there to treat them. In many instances they are not admitted to white hospitals even though the case may be one of certain death if treatment is not promptly given. Hospitals run exclusively or partly by Negroes are scattered through the South, but only Negroes are treated in them and it happens they are not so well equipped that

whites ever tend to break over the well imposed self-restraint that keeps them out." See Couch, "The Negro in the South," p. 472.

61   *Report on Economic Conditions of the South,* pp. 33–36. For more extended treatments of data about the South in this era, see Richard Sterner, *The Negro's Share: A Study of Income, Consumption, Housing, and Public Assistance* (New York: Harper and Brothers, 1943); Rupert B. Vance, *All These People: The Nation's Human Resources in the South* (Chapel Hill: University of North Carolina Press, 1945); Maurice R. Davie, *Negroes in American Society* (New York: McGraw Hill, 1949). For a longer-term view, see John C. McKinney and Edgar T. Thompson, *The South in Continuity and Change* (Durham, NC: Duke University Press, 1965). A rich source for qualitative reviews of agriculture, industry, and urbanization that are embedded in a much broader survey of the South at the start of the New Deal is Couch, *Culture in the South.*

62   Robert H. Zieger, *The CIO, 1935–1955* (Chapel Hill: University of North Carolina Press, 1995), pp. 32–34.

63   Sidney Fine, *Sit-Down: The General Motors Strike of 1936–1937* (Ann Arbor: University of Michigan Press, 1969).

64   Edward Levinson, *Labor on the March* (1938; reprint, Ithaca, NY: Cornell University Press, 1995), p. 169.

65   Richard B. Freeman, "Spurts in Union Growth: Defining Moments and Social Processes," in *The Defining Moment: The Great Depression and the New American Economy in the Twentieth Century,* ed. Michael D. Bordo, Claudia Goldin, and Eugene N. White (Chicago: University of Chicago Press, 1998), p. 282.

66   Levinson, *Labor on the March,* p. 236; Michael Goldfield, *The Decline of Organized Labor in the United States* (Chicago: University of Chicago Press, 1987), p. 10.

67   American Federation of Labor, *Next Steps in Social Insurance* (Washington, DC, 1939); Congress of Industrial Organizations, *Security for the People* (Washington, DC, April 1940). Both plans included comprehensive national health programs.

68   Hofstadter, *The Age of Reform,* p. 308.

69   "Defeat in textiles . . . prefaced a dormant period in southern unionism." See Tindall, *The Emergence of the New South,* p. 512.

70   J. Wayne Flynt, "The New Deal and Southern Labor," in *The New Deal and the South,* ed. Cobb and Namorato, p. 71. Milton Derber estimated southern union membership in the eleven ex-Confederate states in 1938 to have been approximately half a million. See Milton Derber, "Growth and Expansion," in *Labor and the New Deal,* ed. Milton Derber and Edwin Young (Madison: University of Wisconsin Press, 1957), p. 28.

71   Herbert R. Northrup, *Organized Labor and the Negro* (New York: Harper and Brothers, 1944), pp. 3–8.

72   Harvard Sitkoff, *A New Deal for Blacks: The Emergence of Civil Rights as a National Issue* (New York: Oxford University Press, 1978), p. 169. Similarly,

Flynt noted how "the organizing drive launched by labor in the 1930s and supported by New Deal legislation fundamentally challenged southern society at four points. First, industrial unionism posed a serious threat to the major unorganized industries which repeatedly had defeated AFL offensives. Secondly, the CIO challenged the racial shibboleths underlying southern society. Thirdly, congressional and intellectual allies of the CIO attacked repeated and historic denials of civil liberties. And finally, labor in the 1930s broadened its political involvements." See Flynt, "The New Deal and Southern Labor," p. 72. "Prior to 1935," Northrup concluded, "unionism was probably more of a hindrance to than a help to Negroes. The most completely organized industries—railroads, building and printing trades—were those in which union policies are discriminatory and/or the proportion of Negroes small. Since 1936, the pendulum has swung the other way, and thousands of Negro workers have benefited from increased wages, improved working conditions, and job security as a result of collective agreements." See Northrup, *Organized Labor and the Negro,* p. 255.

73   See Robert K. Carr, *Federal Protection of Civil Rights: Quest for a Sword* (Ithaca, NY: Cornell University Press, 1947); Kevin J. McMahon, *Reconsidering Roosevelt on Race: How the Presidency Paved the Road to Brown* (Chicago: University of Chicago Press, 2004), especially chapters 3–5.

74   Glenda Gilmore is too generous, however, in her assessment that after FDR's "reelection in 1936, he tried to pry Democratic political power out of the hands of southern industrialists who thrived on cheap labor, exploited poor whites and African Americans, and held enormous political power." See Glenda Elizabeth Gilmore, *Defying Dixie: The Radical Roots of Civil Rights, 1919–1950* (New York: W. W. Norton, 2008), p. 233.

75   Franklin D. Roosevelt, "Address at the Dedication of the New Chemistry Building, Howard University, Washington, D.C.," October 26, 1936, in *The Public Papers and Addresses of Franklin D. Roosevelt,* vol. 4 (New York: Random House, 1938), p. 537.

76   Frank R. Kent, "The Swing of the Negroes," *Baltimore Sun,* November 12, 1936; citied in Nancy J. Weiss, *Farewell to the Party of Lincoln: Black Politics in the Age of FDR* (Princeton, NJ: Princeton University Press, 1983), p. 208. Whereas Weiss stressed how economic change motivated a shift of black support to the Democratic Party, others have also underscored the limited but real symbolic and practical racial changes ushered in by the administration's actions. For this view, see Sitkoff, *A New Deal for Blacks,* and John B. Kirby, *Black Americans in the Roosevelt Era: Liberals and Race* (Knoxville: University of Tennessee Press, 1980).

77   "Most black people knew that they were getting less economic assistance than whites, and most of them needed more than they were getting. But the point was that they got something, and that kept many families from starving." Weiss, *Farewell to the Party of Lincoln,* p. 211.

78 Tindall, *The Emergence of the New South,* p. 557. See also Shannon, "Presidential Politics in the South," p. 469.

79 John A. Salmond, *The Civilian Conservation Corps, 1933–1942: A New Deal Case Study* (Durham, NC: Duke University Press, 1967), pp. 91–101.

80 Leuchtenburg, *The White House Looks South,* p. 62.

81 See http://www.gwu.edu/~erpapers/teachinger/lesson-plans/notes-er-and-civil-rights.cfm.

82 Freidel, *F.D.R. and the South*, p. 80; Lewis, "The Appeal of the New Deal," p. 558; Tindall, *The Emergence of the New South,* p. 556.

83 In 1940, as it turned out, "the potential negro vote exceeded Roosevelt's plurality in each of these states except in Ohio which was carried by Dewey but by a margin considerably smaller than the potential negro vote." Shannon, "Presidential Politics in the South," p. 470.

84 See the discussions of southern activism in Egerton, *Speak Now Against the Day;* Patricia Sullivan, *Days of Hope: Race and Democracy in the New Deal Era* (Chapel Hill: University of North Carolina Press, 1996); and Gilmore, *Defying Dixie.*

85 For a discussion, see Sean Farhang and Ira Katznelson, "The Southern Imposition: Congress and Labor in the New Deal and Fair Deal," *Studies in American Political Development* 19 (2005): 1–30. See also Michael Goldfield, *The Color of Politics: Race and the Mainsprings of American Politics* (New York: New Press, 1997), pp. 176–261.

86 Cited in Leuchtenburg, *The White House Looks South,* p. 128.

87 "We have been moving deeper and deeper into confusion, as the New Deal became less and less new," the poet and essayist Donald Davidson, who had helped found the Southern Agrarians and later came to lead Tennessee's version of a White Citizens Council, wrote in 1938. Donald Davidson, "An Agrarian Looks at the New Deal," *Free America* 2 (1938): 4; reprinted in *The Southern Agrarians and the New Deal: Essays after "I'll Take My Stand,"* ed. Emily S. Bingham and Thomas A. Underwood (Charlottesville: University Press of Virginia, 2001), p. 125.

88 Cited in Egerton, *Speak Now against the Day,* p. 117.

89 For a systematic treatment of the era's party coalitions and electoral dynamics, see Alan Ware, *The Democratic Party Heads North, 1877–1962* (New York: Cambridge University Press, 2006), especially chaps. 6 and 7.

90 *Fayette Chronicle,* September 28, 1937; cited in Leuchtenburg, *The White House Looks South,* p. 127.

91 The occasion was a consideration of antilynching legislation. *Congressional Record,* 76th Cong., 3d sess., January 10, 1940, p. 248.

92 Patterson, *Congressional Conservatism and the New Deal,* pp. 98–99, 111–13. After the Court issued a series of pro–New Deal decisions in late March, April, and May 1937, which included upholding the constitutionality of the National

Industrial Relations Act and the Social Security Act, Roosevelt's plan was rejected by a 70–20 July recommittal vote in the Senate.

93 For a discussion of discharge petitions and civil rights legislation, see Eric Schickler, Kathryn Pearson, and Brian D. Feinstein, "Congressional Parties and Civil Rights Politics from 1933 to 1972," *Journal of Politics* 72 (2010): 672–89. I thank Eric Schickler for sharing their data on discharge petitions.

94 *Congressional Record*, 75th Cong., 3d sess., January 27, 1938, p. 1165.

95 These views are reported in Jenkins, Peck, and Weaver, "Between Reconstructions," p. 85.

96 Michael Perman observes that the strategy the South's congressmen constructed for the defense of their segregated society seems to have been similar to the formula developed a century earlier when slavery was first attacked during the Missouri Crisis. "On that occasion, it may be recalled, they took an unyielding stand at the margins of the system.... Likewise, by defending lynching, which a majority of southerners actually deplored ... they were taking a stand at the outermost limits of the system of white supremacy." Michael Perman, *Pursuit of Unity: A Political History of the American South* (Chapel Hill: University of North Carolina Press, 2009), p. 244.

97 *Congressional Record,* 75th Cong., 1st sess., April 15, 1937, p. 3550.

98 Ibid., 3d sess., January 26, 1938, pp. 1101–02; January 11, 1938, p. 310.

99 Ibid., January 21, 1938, p. 873.

100 Ibid., January 14, 1938, pp. 506–7; February 2, 1938, pp. 1391–99, 1390; ibid., 1st sess., April 13–14, 1937, pp. 3447–48, April 15, 1937, p. 3524; ibid., 3d sess., January 11, 1938, p. 305. Referring to Walter White and to Majority Leader Alben Barkley, Byrnes is quoted as having complained that "Barkley can't do anything without talking to that nigger first." Cited in Rable, "The South and the Politics of Antilynching Legislation," p. 218.

101 *Congressional Record,* 75th Cong., 1st sess., April 13, 1937, p. 3437.

102 Ibid., p. 3444; April 15, 1937, p. 3547.

103 Ibid., 1st sess., April 15, 1937, p. 3550.

104 Ibid., 3d sess., January 24, 1938, p. 973.

105 For a discussion of these shifting patterns, see John Robert Moore, "The Conservative Coalition in the United States Senate, 1942–1945," *Journal of Southern History* 33 (1967): 370–72.

106 David Brion Davis, *Challenging the Boundaries of Slavery* (Cambridge: Harvard University Press, 2003), p. 77.

107 See http://www.census.gov/population/www/documentation/twps0056/twps 0056.html.

108 Eric Schickler, "Public Opinion, the Congressional Policy Agenda, and the Limits of New Deal Liberalism, 1935–1945," paper prepared for the Congress and History Conference, University of Virginia, May 2009.

109 Brian D. Feinstein and Eric Schickler, "Platforms and Partners: The Civil

Rights Realignment Reconsidered," *Studies in American Political Development* 22 (2008): 1–31.

110 For discussions, see Neil R. McMillan, *Remaking Dixie: The Impact of World War II on the American South* (Jackson: University of Mississippi Press, 1997); Pamela Tyler, "The Impact of the New Deal and World War II on the South," in *A Companion to the American South,* ed. John B. Boles (Oxford: Blackwell, 2002); Morton Sosna, "More Important Than the Civil War? The Impact of World War II on the South," in *Perspectives on the American South: An Annual Review of Society, Politics and Culture,* ed. James C. Cobb and Charles Reagan Wilson (New York: Gordon and Breach, 1987).

111 For an overview of demographic and related changes, see Numan Bartley, *The New South: 1945–1980* (Baton Rouge: Louisiana State University Press, 1995), pp. 1–12.

112 There is a good compact discussion in Tindall, *The Emergence of the New South: 1913–1945,* pp. 318–53.

113 Derber, "Growth and Expansion," p. 28.

114 Frank Traver De Vyver, "The Present Status of Labor Unions in the South," *Southern Economic Journal* 5 (1939): 485–98; Frank T. De Vyver, "The Present Status of Labor Unions in the South—1948," ibid., 16 (1949): 1–22. Likewise, a survey of union membership in the South between 1939 and 1953 found that "for the entire period . . . union membership increased more rapidly in the South than in the rest of the country," noting that most of the growth had come in wartime. See Leo Troy, "The Growth of Union Membership in the South, 1939–1953," ibid., 24 (1958): 407–20. See also Derber, "Growth and Expansion," p. 34.

115 H. M. Douty, "Development of Trade-Unionism in the South," *Monthly Labor Review* 63 (1946): 581. There is a very large literature debating the character and extent of union multiracialism in the South, but there can be no doubt that measured against then-current practices, the labor movement, and especially the CIO, despite lingering racist practices, constituted the most widespread and effective popular force across racial lines in the 1940s.

116 Ibid., pp. 576–79.

117 For overviews of the southern transformation, see Rupert B. Vance, *All These People: The Nation's Human Resources in the South* (Chapel Hill: University of North Carolina Press, 1945); John M. Maclachlin and Joe S. Floyd, *The Changing South* (Gainesville: University of Florida Press, 1956); McKinney and Thompson, eds., *The South in Continuity and Change.*

118 James C. Cobb, *The Selling of the South: The Southern Crusade for Industrial Development, 1936–1980* (Baton Rouge: Louisiana State University Press, 1982); Bruce J. Schulman, *From Cotton Belt to Sunbelt: Federal Policy, Economic Development, and the Transformation of the South, 1938–1980* (Durham: Duke University Press, 1994).

119 Carl Brent Swisher, "The Supreme Court and the South," *Journal of Politics*

10 (1948): 291–92, 298–99. The state's 1923 law provided that "in no event shall a negro be eligible to participate in a Democratic primary election held in the State of Texas, and should a negro vote in a Democratic primary election, such ballot shall be void and election officials shall not count the same." Following a court challenge, the law was repealed in 1927 and replaced by a statute authorizing "every political party in this State through its State Executive Committee . . . to prescribe the qualifications of its own members." See V. O. Key Jr., *Southern Politics in State and Nation* (New York: Alfred A. Knopf), pp. 621–22.

120   Alexander Keyssar, *The Right to Vote: The Contested History of Democracy in the United States* (New York: Basic Books, 2000), p. 249.

121   Kimberley S. Johnson, *Reforming Jim Crow: Southern Politics and State in the Age before Brown* (New York: Oxford University Press, 2010), especially chaps. 3 and 4. For an uncommonly thoughtful consideration of the impact of the New Deal on the South, see Anthony J. Badger, *New Deal/New South: An Anthony J. Badger Reader* (Fayetteville: University of Arkansas Press, 2007), especially chaps. 2 and 3.

122   Maslow and Robison, "Civil Rights Legislation and the Fight for Equality," p. 394.

123   Lois Ruchames, *Race, Jobs, and Politics: The Story of the FEPC* (New York: Columbia University Press, 1953); Merl E. Reed, *Seedtime for the Modern Civil Rights Movement: The President's Committee on Fair Employment Practice, 1941–1946* (Baton Rouge: Louisiana State University Press, 1991); Anthony S. Chen, *The Fifth Freedom: Jobs, Politics, and Civil Rights in the United States, 1941–1972* (Princeton, NJ: Princeton University Press, 2009); Kenneth M. Schultz, "The FEPC and the Legacy of the Labor-Based Civil Rights Movement of the 1940s," *Labor History* 49 (2008): 71–92.

124   Richard Hofstadter, "From Calhoun to the Dixiecrats," *Social Research* 16 (1949): 135.

125   Tindall, *The Emergence of the New South*, p. 716; Egerton, *Speak Now against the Day*, p. 201.

126   Howard Odum, *Race and Rumors of Race: Challenge to American Crisis* (Chapel Hill: University of North Carolina Press, 1943), pp. 3, 6, 7, 9, 13, 11.

127   Egerton, *Speak Now against the Day*, 365, 358–63.

128   Charles Wallace Collins, *Whither Solid South? A Study in Politics and Race Relations* (New Orleans: Pelican Publishing Co., 1947), p. 254. Collins plays a central role in Hofstadter's "Calhoun to the Dixiecrats." An insightful discussion of Collins can be found in Joseph E. Lowndes, *From the New Deal to the New Right: Race and the Southern Origins of Modern Conservatism* (New Haven: Yale University Press, 2009), pp. 11–44.

129   Ibid., pp. 264, 256. For a similar view, see also Peter Molyneaux, *The South's Political Plight* (Dallas: Calhoun Clubs of the South, 1948).

130 Andrew Edmund Kersten, *Race, Jobs, and the War: The FEPC in the Midwest, 1941–1946* (Urbana: University of Illinois Press, 2000).

131 Merl E. Reed, "FEPC and Federal Agencies in the South," *Journal of Negro History* 65 (1980): 43–56.

132 Or even more far-reaching than the provisions concerning employment that came to be embedded in the Civil Rights Act of 1964. That landmark law covered employers with fifty or more employees; 1972 amendments extended coverage to employers with fifteen or more employees.

133 *Congressional Record*, 79th Cong., 2d sess., January 23, 1946, p. 251.

134 Ibid., January 22, 1946, p. 179; January 21, 1946, p. 158; January 28, 1946, pp. 455, 457; February 1, 1946, p. 723.

135 Ibid., January 29, 1946, p. 492; January 24, 1946, p. 321; January 31, 1946, p. 655.

136 Ibid., January 23, 1946, p. 253; January 30, 1946, p. 563; January 31, 1946, p. 632.

137 Ibid., January 23, 1946, p. 242.

138 Ibid., January 23, 1946, p. 252; January 30, 1946, p. 565; January 23, 1946, p. 245; February 1, 1946, p. 696; January 30, 1946, p. 565.

139 In 1949 and 1950, Congress returned to the FEPC after President Truman used his 1949 State of the Union address to propose a civil rights agenda that included the repeal of the poll tax and antilynching legislation. Following the Dixiecrat revolt, these proposals produced a particularly acrimonious debate. It was during this successful southern filibuster that the newly elected Texas senator, Lyndon Baines Johnson, offered an eloquent maiden speech, which lasted one and a half hours and was punctuated with the phrase "We of the South." Johnson defended southern prerogatives and autonomy, arguing that federal civil rights law would "keep alive the old flames of hate and bigotry." The speech is discussed in Katznelson, *When Affirmative Action Was White*, pp. 8–9.

140 Hofstadter, "Calhoun to Dixiecrats," p. 150.

141 Ibid., p. 141.

142 *Congressional Record*, 79th Cong., 2d sess., February 1, 1946, p. 719; February 4, 1946, p. 813; February 1, 1946, p. 708; January 31, 1946, p. 632.

CHAPTER 6 · BALLOTS FOR SOLDIERS

1 Roosevelt, "who considered this one of his most important messages," had planned to deliver the State of the Union address in person. "He himself labored hard and long on it, a good part of the work was done with us [Samuel Rosenman and Robert Sherwood] sitting around his bed, to which he was confined with a bad cough." Rosenman commented on how "the Teheran Conference must have been a terrific strain. . . . The President developed some kind of bronchial affliction in Teheran which gave him a racking cough. . . . It took him a long time to shake it off. While Teheran was a high point in the President's career as Commander-in-Chief of our armed forces and as our leader in foreign affairs, it seemed to me to be also the turning point of his physical career. I think his physical decline can be dated from Teheran, although at the time we did not see it." Samuel I. Rosenman, *Working with Roosevelt* (New York: Harper and Brothers, 1952), pp. 417–18, 411–12.

2   Franklin D. Roosevelt, "Annual Message to Congress," January 11, 1944, in *Nothing to Fear: The Selected Addresses of Franklin Delano Roosevelt, 1932–1945,* ed. B. D. Zevin (Boston: Houghton Mifflin, 1946), pp. 388–97. The call to the right to vote is on p. 395. Cass Sunstein has offered a detailed consideration of this speech in *The Second Bill of Rights: FDR's Unfinished Revolution and Why We Need It More Than Ever* (New York: Basic Books, 2006). Soldier voting usually merits only brief mention in histories of Franklin Roosevelt's third term. Useful descriptive summaries are Boyd A. Martin, "The Service Vote in the Elections of 1944," *American Political Science Review* 39 (1945): 720–32; Michael Anderson, "Politics, Patriotism, and the State: The Fight over the Soldier Vote, 1942–1944," in *Politics and Progress: American Society and the State Since 1865,* ed. Andrew E. Kersten and Kriste Lindenmeyer (Westport, CT: Praeger, 2001), pp. 84–100; Christopher DeRosa, "The Battle for Uniform Votes: The Politics of Soldier Voting in the Elections of 1944," in *Beyond Combat: Essays in Military History in Honor of Russell F. Weigley,* ed. Edward G. Longacre and Theodore J. Zeman (Philadelphia: American Philosophical Society, 2007), pp. 129–52.

3   P. Orman Ray, "Military Absent-Voting Laws," *American Political Science Review* 12 (1918): 461, 469; *New York Times,* May 19, 1918.

4   "Should Soldiers Have the Vote? They Say Yes, Congress Maybe," *Newsweek,* December 4, 1943, p. 54.

5   Additionally, New Jersey sent out some 58,000 ballots on the initiative of the state. See *New Republic,* September 6, 1943, p. 803.

6   Anderson, "Politics, Patriotism, and the State," p. 90; Martin, "The Service Vote in the Elections of 1944," pp. 725–26. The Census Bureau, Anderson reports, summarized the reasons for the restricted use as including an insufficient time for states to devise good procedures, and for soldiers, especially those abroad, to get and return ballots. The bureau also noted that "in the South the November elections traditionally drew less interest than the primaries, particularly in off year elections." See Anderson, "Politics, Patriotism and the State," p. 90. A Department of Defense report written thirty-five years later noted that the law had "had almost no impact at all," as it was enacted just weeks before the general election. See U.S. Department of Defense, *The Federal Voting Assistance Program, 11th Report* (Washington, DC: U.S. Government Printing Office, 1977), p. 2. A 1952 report by the Special Committee on Service Voting of the American Political Science Association, a study that had been commissioned by President Harry Truman, found that the legislative efforts in 1942 "to facilitate voting in the Armed Forces came too late." The

act "had almost no effect on the number of servicemen who were able to vote in the general election." See "Findings and Recommendations of the Special Committee on Service Voting," *American Political Science Review* 16 (1952): 513. The committee was chaired by Paul David. Its other members included Robert Cutler, Samuel Eldersveld, Bertram Gross, Alexander Heard, Edward Litchfield, Kathryn Stone, and William Prendergast. Truman thanked APSA, observing that "people need an organization like this to study government and politics in a scientific way, without a lot of drumbeating and headline-hunting" (p. 512).The president made the report the basis for his message to Congress on March 28, 1952, suggesting how soldier voting should be conducted during the Korean War.

7   I. C. B. Dear, ed., *The Oxford Companion to World War II* (New York: Oxford University Press, 2001), pp. 931, 936, 938. A detailed overview can be found in Russell F. Weigley, *History of the United States Army* (New York: Macmillan, 1967), pp. 421–50.

8   Franklin D. Roosevelt, "Christmas Eve Speech—Report on the Teheran Conference," December 24, 1943, in *Nothing to Fear*, ed. Zevin, pp. 378–87.

9   In all, American forces suffered 291,557 battle deaths and 113,182 deaths from other causes. See U.S. Bureau of the Census, *Historical Statistics of the United States: Colonial Times to 1970,* part 2. (Washington, DC: Bureau of the Census, Department of Commerce, 1976), p. 1140.

10 Franklin D. Roosevelt, State of the Union address, January 1944, in *Nothing to Fear,* ed. Zevin, p. 395.

11 Article 1, Section 2, of the Constitution stipulates that for elections to the House of Representatives "Electors in each state shall have the Qualifications requisite for Electors of the most numerous Branch of the State Legislature." The identical language is used with regard to the Senate in the Seventeenth Amendment. Further, Article I, Section 4, stipulates, "The Times, Places and Manner of holding Elections for Senators and Representatives, shall be prescribed in each State by the Legislature thereof"; but it also stipulates that "the Congress may at any time by Law make or alter such Regulations, except as to the Places of chusing Senators," which then were the state legislatures. The Supreme Court regularly upheld congressional supremacy over federal elections, including in *Smiley v. Holm,* a Minnesota redistricting case, when it held, referring to this feature of the Constitution, that

> [it] cannot be doubted that these comprehensive words embrace authority to provide a complete code for congressional elections, not only as to times and places, but in relation to notices, registration, supervision of voting, protection of voters, prevention of fraud and corrupt practices, counting of votes, duties of inspectors and canvassers, and making the publication of election returns; in short, to enact

the numerous requirements which experience shows are necessary in order to enforce the fundamental right involved.

See *Smiley v. Holm,* 285 U.S. 355 (1932). For a contemporaneous overview of the constitutional issues during the period of soldier-voting debates, see Charles M. Boynton, "A Study of the Elective Franchise of the United States," *Notre Dame Lawyer* 20 (1945): 230–302.

12 Roosevelt, State of the Union address, January 1944, in *Nothing to Fear,* ed. Zevin, p. 395.

13 *New York Times,* April 1, 1944.

14 Frank Freidel, *Franklin D. Roosevelt: A Rendezvous with Destiny* (New York: Little, Brown, 1990), p. 503. "The conference bill," Michael Anderson concluded, "amounted to a victory for opponents of a meaningful federal ballot." See Anderson, "Politics, Patriotism, and the State," p. 94.

15 *Congressional Record,* 78th Cong., 2d sess., March 15, 1944, p. 2623.

16 Franklin D. Roosevelt, *The Public Papers and Addresses of Franklin D. Roosevelt,* vol. 13 (New York: Macmillan, 1945), pp. 111–15.

17 *New York Times,* April 1, 1944. The earliest advocacy of an assertive standardizing federal role in shaping state regulations for absentee voting during World War II that I have found is the proposal made in May 1942 by Urban Lavery, a Chicago lawyer who was prominent in the Democratic Party; he later authored a leading volume on administrative law. He urged Congress to draft "a uniform legislative program to lift rigid restrictions in many states" that would be superintended by a nonpartisan national elections commission. See *Chicago Daily Tribune,* May 1, 1942.

18 "Should Absentee Soldier Voting Be Federally Controlled?," *Congressional Digest,* January 1944, p. 4. "The laws of politics being what they are," *The Nation* editorialized, "a Congressman would no more dream of opposing the right of soldiers and sailors to vote than he would of sponsoring a measure for compulsory polygamy." "Let Them Vote, But—" *Nation,* December 4, 1943, p. 655.

19 *Chicago Daily Tribune,* April 18, 1942.

20 "No—should not" garnered support of 5 percent, with 3 percent undecided. See "Public Opinion Polls," *Public Opinion Quarterly* 8 (1944): 131. Three in four thought such a plan to be feasible. Fifty-eight percent preferred a "federal law providing for the Army and Navy to give ballots to all men and women over 21 in the armed forces"; 30 percent favored "each state send ballots to men and women over 21 in the armed forces who will be eligible to vote under the laws of their states." A January 16, 1944, NORC survey asked, "Do you think Negroes over 21 in the armed forces should be allowed to vote or not (in the Presidential election of November 1944)?" An unqualified yes was offered by 77 percent of respondents, and another 2 percent endorsed voting for blacks

if they qualified in their home state. Opposed were 12 percent, and another 5 who were against soldier voting irrespective of race (p. 131).

21 When these votes were taken, on July 23 and August 25, 1942, less than a third of the House was present, and just over half of the Senate. In the pre-air-conditioning age, many members fled Washington's oppressive summer heat and humidity. For an account of the difference to practices and partisanship that air conditioning later made, see Nelson Polsby, *How Congress Evolves: Social Bases of Institutional Change* (New York: Oxford University Press, 2003), pp. 84–86.

22 *Congressional Record,* 78th Cong., 2d sess., March 15, 1944, p. 2617.

23 An exception is David Kennedy's brief treatment of soldier voting, stressing the limits of the 1944 legislation. David M. Kennedy, *Freedom from Fear: The American People in Depression and War, 1929-1945* (New York: Oxford University Press, 1999).

24 In *Breedlove v. Suttles,* a 1937 challenge to Georgia's poll tax by a white citizen, the Supreme Court found that the poll tax was a legitimate means of raising revenue, not an instrument of disenfranchisement violating the Fourteenth, Fifteenth, and Nineteenth Amendments to the Constitution. See *Breedlove v. Suttles* 320 U.S. 277 (1937).

25 "The present law," Senator Green observed in discussing the 1942 act, "has nothing to do with the constitutionality of the poll tax anywhere. It is perfectly logical for anyone who voted for it . . . and still oppose the repeal of the poll tax. This bill has nothing whatever to do with that. The question is simply whether the collection of such a tax from men in the armed forces in time of war can be used to prevent their voting; that is all." See *Congressional Record,* 78th Cong., 1st sess., November 22, 1943, p. 9794.

26 Joseph E. Kallenbach, "Constitutional Aspects of Federal Anti-Poll Tax Legislation," *Michigan Law Review* 45 (1947): 719.

27 The report was dated November 29, 1943. Isaiah Berlin, *Washington Despatches, 1941–45: Weekly Political Reports from the British Embassy,* ed. H. G. Nicholas (Chicago: University of Chicago Press, 1981), p. 280. Wendell Willkie, it might be noted, endorsed Roosevelt's proposed legislation in January 1944, stating, "I do not believe it is possible as a practical matter under State statutes for every member of the armed forces to be given opportunity to vote. . . . I would not wish to be elected President without every member of the armed services having an opportunity to decide whether I should be." See *New York Times,* January 20, 1944. Ohio senator Robert Taft, by contrast, warned that the soldier-vote bill "might throw the whole election into a legal tailspin." See *New York Times,* January 24, 1944.

28 Recalling his role in drafting soldier-voting legislation just before his appointment as assistant attorney general in charge of the War Division of the Department of Justice during World War II, Wechsler remembered this as his

"toughest assignment . . . in anticipation of the presidential election of 1944 . . . to formulate a solution to the potential disenfranchisement of the ten million Americans who were overseas or otherwise out of reach of the ordinary absentee ballot provisions of the state voting laws." See Norman Silber and Geoffrey Miller, "Toward 'Neutral Principles' in the Law: Selections from the Oral History of Herbert Wechsler," *Columbia Law Review* 93 (1993): 879. Informative appreciations by Ruth Bader Ginsburg, "In Memory of Herbert Wechsler," and Henry Paul Monaghan, "A Legal Giant Is Dead," appeared in the *Columbia Law Review* 100 (2000): 1359–61 and 1370–76, respectively.

29   *New York Times,* September 2, 1942. Brown, who also founded and led the National Negro Council, was the author of *What the Civilian Conservation Corps Is Doing for Colored Youth* (Washington, DC: Federal Security Agency, Civilian Conservation Corps, 1940).

30   Ronald R. Krebs, "In the Shadow of War: The Effects of Conflict on Liberal Democracy," *International Organization* 63 (2009): 190–92. See also Ronald R. Krebs, *Fighting for Rights: Military Service and the Politics of Citizenship* (Ithaca, NY: Cornell University Press, 2006). Michael Sherry writes of the "militarization of social change" during the war, but he does not discuss soldier voting as an instance of how the war affected the place of black soldiers in American society. See Michel Sherry, *In the Shadow of War: The United States since the 1930s* (New Haven: Yale University Press, 1995), pp. 101–2. Likewise, there is no mention of the issue in John Morton Blum, *V Was for Victory: Politics and American Culture during World War II* (New York: Harcourt Brace Jovanovich, 1974).

31   David Mayhew, "Wars and American Politics," *Perspectives on Politics* 3 (2005): 479; see also David Mayhew, "Events as Causes: The Case of American Politics," *Political Contingency: Studying the Unexpected, the Accidental, and the Unforeseen,* ed. Ian Shapiro and Sonu Bedi (New York: NYU Press, 2007), p. 114. There, Mayhew writes how "World War II brought another dose of small but real progress for southern blacks by way of the Soldier Voting Act of 1942."

32   Reeve Huston, "Battling over the Boundaries of the American Electorate," *Reviews in American History* 29 (2001): 632. A recent positive assessment of the Roosevelt administration and race relations underscores how the Soldier Voting Act the president had signed in 1942 "set up the machinery to allow qualified servicemen to file absentee votes in federal elections without paying a poll tax, thereby allowing many southern soldiers (including African-Americans) to vote for the first time." See Kevin J. McMahon, *Reconsidering Roosevelt on Race* (Chicago: University of Chicago Press, 2004), p. 158. Another important study of race in American history, in commenting on the 1942 act, finds that "just as in the Revolution and the Civil War, black military service had proven instrumental for obtaining black political rights," observing that "the law provided the first legislative expansion of black voting rights since the 1870s."

See Philip A. Klinker and Rogers M. Smith, *The Unsteady March: The Rise and Decline of Racial Inequality in America* (Chicago: University of Chicago Press, 2002), pp. 174–75. Similarly, a history of southern segregation and voting restrictions stresses the "advance" made for civil rights by the Soldier Voting Act of 1942. "Though Southerners held any tampering with the notorious poll tax—a device designed almost solely to keep blacks from the ballot box—to be an assault of the 'Southern way of life and on white supremacy,' the federal legislature passed the Soldier Vote Act in 1942, giving service members an absentee ballot and the right to cast it without having to pay any tax. For the first time since Reconstruction, voting had been made easier or freer for African-Americans." See Jerrold M. Packard, *American Nightmare: The History of Jim Crow*, rev. ed. (New York: Macmillan, 2002), p. 202.

33 Alexander Keyssar, *The Right to Vote: The Contested History of Democracy in the United States* (New York: Basic Books, 2000), p. 246.

34 A Proquest Historical Newspapers search yielded ninety-four instances of "soldier voting" or "soldier vote" described as "controversial" or as a matter of "controversy" between the start of 1942 and the end of 1944.

  John W. Malsberger, *From Obstruction to Moderation: The Transformation of Southern Conservatism, 1838–1952* (Selingsgrove, PA: Susquehanna University Press, 2000), p. 107; Martin, "The Service Vote in the Elections of 1944," p. 727; *Newsweek,* December 6, 1943, p. 59; Allen Drury, *A Senate Journal, 1943–1945* (New York: McGraw Hill, 1963), pp. 11–12; Rosenman, *Working with Roosevelt,* p. 28; *Chicago Daily Tribune,* July 24, 1942; Arthur Brody, "Soldiers' Votes and 1944," *Nation,* February 19, 1944, p. 207; *New York Times,* January 30, 1944; *New York Times,* February 22, 1944. Drury's diary, written when he covered the Senate for the United Press, was published in 1963 to take advantage of his fame as the author of *Advise and Consent* (1959) and *A Shade of Difference* (1962), both best-selling novels. A retrospective treatment of the era's "Congressional Blues" that also devotes attention to the war's rancorous debates about soldier voting is David Brinkley, *Washington Goes to War: The Extraordinary Story of the Transformation of a City* (New York: Alfred A. Knopf, 1988), pp. 220–23.

35 Franklin D. Roosevelt, "Annual Message to Congress," January 6, 1941, in National Archives and Records Administration, *Our Documents: 100 Milestone Documents from the National Archives* (New York: Oxford University Press, 2006), pp. 170–71.

36 *Chicago Daily Tribune,* April 17, 1942.

37 Steven F. Lawson, *Black Ballots: Voting Rights in the South, 1944–1969* (New York: Columbia University Press, 1976), p. 74.

38 The statement, drafted by Samuel Rosenman, also predicted that the Eastland bill "would not enable any soldier to vote with any greater facility than was provided by Public Law 712 (the 1942 act) under which only a negligible

number of soldiers' votes were cast." See Memorandum, Samuel I. Rosenman to President Roosevelt, January 21, 1944, Samuel I. Rosenman Papers, box 25, Soldier Vote Folder, Franklin D. Roosevelt Library, Hyde Park, NY; *New York Times,* January 27, 1944.

39   Anderson, "Politics, Patriotism, and the State," p. 94.

40   Boynton, "A Study of the Elective Franchise of the United States," p. 301.

41   The voting tally is reported in APSA, "Findings and Recommendations," p. 513; the estimate is by Edward G. Benson and Evelyn Wicoff, "Voters Pick Their Party," *Public Opinion Quarterly* 8 (1944): 172.

42   Harry S. Truman, "Special Message to the Congress on Absentee Voting by Members of the Armed Forces," March 28, 1952, in *Public Papers of the Presidents of the United States: Harry S. Truman, 1952–53* (Washington, DC: U.S. Government Printing Office, 1966), 217–20.

43   Cited in "Findings and Recommendations of the Special Committee on Service Voting," pp. 512–13.

44   Ibid., pp. 513–14. This pattern was consistent with broader southern turnout rates. In 1940, when "no state above the Mason-Dixon Line had a less than 65 per-cent turnout of voters," the percentage of citizens over twenty-one who voted in Mississippi and South Carolina was under 15 percent, under 25 percent in Alabama, Arkansas, Georgia, and Virginia, under 35 percent in Louisiana, Tennessee, and Texas, under 45 percent in Florida and North Carolina, and under 65 percent in Kentucky, Maryland, and Oklahoma. Of the southern states, only Missouri, Delaware, and West Virginia performed above the 65 percent rate. See Gordon M. Connelly and Harry H. Field, "The Non-Voter— Who He Is, What He Thinks," *Public Opinion Quarterly* 8 (1944): 176.

45   *Congressional Record,* 78th Cong., 2d sess., March 15, 1944, p. 2619. LeCompte, a supporter of the bill, immediately noted that the two sections of the 1942 act that "are very definitely the sections that provide for the suspension of the poll tax" still stood, and thus "if the Federal Government has not suspended the poll tax and the registration features, it is because the Federal Government is not able to do so. That is my frank and honest opinion" (p. 2619).

46   Lucas served as majority leader in the 81st Congress.

47   For a discussion of Rankin's role and the impact of southern congressional power on the Servicemen's Readjustment Act of 1944, see Ira Katznelson, *When Affirmative Action Was White: Am Untold History of Racial Inequality in Twentieth-Century America* (New York: W. W. Norton, 2005), pp. 113–41.

48   These citations are drawn from the useful overview by Kenneth W. Vickers, "John Rankin: Democrat and Demagogue" (M.A. thesis, Mississippi State University, 1993). In regard to his authoring the administration's bill, Herbert Wechsler remembered, "My principal opponent was one of the most miserable characters I think I have ever experienced in this life, a congressman from Mississippi by the name of John Rankin. John Rankin was certainly one of the

most totally racist, prejudiced people to come to Congress, even in those days, from anywhere in the country." When Wechsler was nominated to the Department of Justice post in February 1944, Rankin denounced the appointment. "He said I was that fellow 'Wechsler, who calls himself Wechsler.' . . . There was a family in Washington, Adam Wechsler, which was not a Jewish family, and the implication was that I had changed my name from a Jewish-sounding name to a non-Jewish sounding name." See Silber and Miller, "Toward 'Neutral-Principles' in the Law," pp. 881, 882. Rankin also stressed the similarity of the name with that of "James Wechsler, author of an article in today's PM, attacking yesterday's House vote." *See New York Times,* February 3, 1944. For documentation of Rankin's anti-Semitism, see Russell Whelan, "Rankin of Mississippi," *American Mercury* 49 (1944): 31–37.

49 *Washington Post,* September 4, 1942.

50 *Congressional Record,* 78th Cong., 1st sess., November 17, 1943, p. 9629.

51 Ibid., 2d sess., March 15, 1944, p. 2620. Rankin's one departure from his uncommonly cool talk came during his summary statement just before final passage of the conference version of soldier voting in 1944. Attacking "Sidney Hillman, the foreign-born, communistic crackpot" for his support of a federal ballot, he recalled, "I have been here through the long lean years when the southern Democrats held the party together. We went down the line and fought the battles during all those years, and all the Frankfurters and all the Hillmans and all the Winchells and all the radicals of the C.I.O. cannot run us out of the Democratic Party now." New York's Charles Buckley interrupted to ask, "Is the gentleman from Mississippi insinuating that the Democratic Party is made up entirely of the Jewish race?" Rankin replied, "Nobody intimated such a thing but the gentleman from New York" (pp. 2638–39.

52 *Congressional Record,* 78th Cong., 2d sess., January 31, 1944, pp. 908, 911. Eastland had previously served for eighty-eight days in 1941, having been appointed to fill out the term left vacant by the death of Senator Pat Harrison. Eastland declined to run in the special election, which was won by Wall Doxey, the member of Congress from the state's Second District. Defeating Doxey (who had the support of President Roosevelt and Senator Theodore Bilbo) in the Democratic Party primary of 1942, and winning an unopposed general election, Eastland began his service in the Senate in January 1943. For an illuminating discussion of Mississippi's politics "as a battle between the delta planters and the rednecks" of the hill country, see V. O. Key Jr., *Southern Politics in State and Nation* (New York: Alfred A. Knopf, 1949), pp. 229–53. In the 1950s, Eastland endorsed massive resistance to desegregation, counseling his constituents that they were free not to obey the Supreme Court's *Brown* decision because it was based on political imperatives and sociological evidence, rather than on constitutionally sanctioned jurisprudence.

53 *Congressional Record,* 77th Cong., 2d sess., September 9, 1942, pp. 7073–74.

54   Ibid., 68th Cong., 1st sess., April 9, 1924, pp. 5961–62.

55   Ibid., 78th Cong., 1st sess., November 29, 1943, p. 10067.

56   Key, *Southern Politics in State and Nation,* pp. 311, 664–75.

57   For an acute analysis of the character and limitations of southern modera-
      tion, see Anthony J. Badger, *New Deal/New South* (Fayetteville: University of
      Arkansas Press, 2007), pp. 102–26.

58   Gunnar Myrdal, *An American Dilemma: The Negro Problem and Modern
      Democracy* (New York: Harper and Brothers, 1944).

59   For a discussion, see chapter 12.

60   *Atlanta Daily World,* May 27, 1942.

61   *The Pittsburgh Courier,* June 13, 1942. In 1938, Governor Johnston had justi-
      fied the white primary as a means to keep racial demagoguery out of Demo-
      cratic Party campaigns. "Inasmuch as these changes in our rules have definitely
      eliminated even the possibility of Negroes' voting in the primary elections of
      South Carolina, any further mention of the Negro question by any candidate
      only serves to show that he is endeavoring to evade the real issues of the cam-
      paign, and appeal to the ignorance, the prejudices, and the emotions, rather
      than to the intelligence of the people of South Carolina." See *Pittsburgh Cou-
      rier,* August 13, 1938. Later, when he served in the Senate, "Senator Olin John-
      ston of South Carolina announced that he would filibuster any FEPC bill for
      three weeks—talking about the South's 'Negro problem' from the reconstruc-
      tion period down, so that the Nation could understand what it is all about." See
      Pittsburgh Courier, May 26, 1945.

62   *Congressional Record,* 77th Cong., 2d sess., July 23, 1942, p. 6552.

63   *New York Times,* July 23, 1942.

64   *Washington Post,* August 15, 1942.

65   *Congressional Record,* 77th Cong., 2d sess., August 17, 1942, p. 6859.

66   Ibid., August 20, 1942, p. 6901; September 9, 1942, p. 7074.

67   Ibid., July 13, 1942, p. 6553.

68   For discussions, see Lawson, *Black Ballots,* p. 66; *New York Times,* July 24, 1942.
      There was no roll call. Kefauver demanded a division on the vote. Following
      the vote, a Republican, John Martin Vorys of Ohio, demanded tellers, but the
      chairman, after counting, stated that "nine members have arisen—not a suf-
      ficient number. Tellers are refused." See *Congressional Record,* 77th Cong., 2d
      sess., July 13, 1942, p. 6561.

69   This was a standing vote, with the individual ayes and nays not recorded by
      name in the *Congressional Record,* but counted by tellers as members literally
      stood to record their positive or negative preference.

70   *Congressional Record,* 77th Cong., 2d sess., July 23, 1942, p. 6451; *Washington
      Post,* July 24, 1942; *New York Times,* August 18, 1942.

71   Rankin and other opponents of the poll tax suspension argued that the Con-
      stitution vested the power to determine suffrage qualifications in the states,
      that the poll tax constituted a reasonable exercise of state power over voting,

and that any suspension or repeal would require a constitutional amendment. The advocates of wartime suspension argued that the poll tax was not a suffrage qualification, that the Supreme Court had regularly found that the right of citizens to vote in congressional elections derived from the Constitution, not the states, and that the poll tax both restricted the franchise unduly and had been established to counteract the Fifteenth Amendment.

72   A thoughtful contemporary discussion of competition for black votes in the North is Louis Martin, "The Negro in the Political Picture," *Opportunity: Journal of Negro Life,* July 1943, pp. 104–7, 137–42. This issue of the Urban League journal was devoted to "The Negro and His Government."

73   There was a comical aspect to this: "Brooks beat Senator Pepper (Democrat), of Florida, to the gun in offering the amendment. Pepper charged the Illinois Republican had 'unfairly' used the substance of an antipoll tax amendment he had previously sponsored, but Brooks refused to withdraw in favor of Pepper's." See *Washington Post,* August 23, 1942. "Mr. Brooks submitted an amendment which was in almost the same language as Mr. Pepper's, and the two Senators engaged in a heated interchange over their prerogatives before Senator Herring, who was presiding, ruled that the Brooks amendment was in order." See *New York Times,* August 25, 1942.

74   *Chicago Daily Tribune,* September 12, 1942; *Chicago Daily Tribune,* October 25, 1942; *Atlanta Daily World,* November 10, 1942; Horace R. Cayton, "Negro Vote: New Deal Conservatism Delivered the Race Vote to Reactionary GOP," *Pittsburgh Courier,* November 21, 1942. McKeough, it might be noted, was a Chicago machine Democrat who defeated Paul Douglas in the Democratic primary.

75   "Doubt was widespread at the Capitol, however, that the Senate's expanding of the absentee balloting program to service men abroad as well as to the Continental United States would be much more than a gesture." See *New York Times,* September 2, 1942; *Congressional Record, 77th* Cong., 2d sess., September 9, 1942, p. 7075.

76   On this vote, the Democrats achieved a Rice likeness score of 85, one significantly different from the low likeness of 41 marking the relationship of nonsouthern Democrats to Republicans, and the even lower score of 22 characterizing how southern Democratic and Republican voting corresponded.

77   The editorial page thought it to be "a pity that Congress has not been able to disentangle these issues." See "Votes for Soldiers," *Washington Post,* August 28, 1942.

78   William M. Brewer, "The Poll Tax and Poll Taxers," *Journal of Negro History* 29 (1944): 260–99.

79   With a Rice score of 80.

80   With a Rice score of 55.

81   Indicated by a Rice score of 33.

82   *Washington Post,* August 27, 1942.

83   *Chicago Daily Tribune,* September 2, 1942.

84   *Washington Post,* September 1, 1942.

85   "By 1944, the African American vote in key northern states could decide a close presidential election." See Simon Topping, "'Never Argue with the Gallup Poll: Thomas Dewey, Civil Rights, and the Election of 1948," *Journal of American Studies* 38 (2004): 179. A detailing of voting by African-Americans in the 1944 election is provided by Topping in "The Republicans and Civil Rights, 1928–1948" (Ph.D. dissertation, University of Hull, 2002), pp. 315–38.

86   An excellent discussion of the poll tax can be found in Key, *Southern Politics in State and Nation,* pp. 578–618.

87   McCloy's July 2, 1942, memorandum to William Hastie, the African-American civilian aide to the secretary of war who had been appointed in response to organized black pressure, and the October 8, 1940, memo written for the president's approval, then disseminated to the army on October 16, are cited in Ulysses Lee, *The Employment of Negro Troops* (Washington, DC: U.S. Army, 1994), pp. 158–59, 76. This invaluable book appears as the eighth "Special Study" in the army's Center of Military History series, *United States Army in World War II.*

88   Charles P. Howard Sr., "The Observer," *Atlanta World,* May 9, 1942.

89   *Chicago Daily Tribune,* April 17, 1942.

90   Memorandum, FDR to General Fred Osborn, May 14, 1942, Franklin D. Roosevelt Papers, Official File 1113, box 4, Soldier Vote 1940–1943, Franklin D. Roosevelt Library, Hyde Park, NY. Likewise, a Department of War circular issued a week later, on May 21, counseled soldiers wishing to vote to "write to the Secretary of State of their home state requesting information under the laws of each state." See "Summary of War Department Actions and Policy," Franklin D. Roosevelt Papers. The memo was attached to a letter written to the President's Secretary, M. H. McIntyre, by Robert Patterson, under secretary of war.

91   When, with the administration's concurrence, Ramsay introduced a bill in July to fashion procedures to distribute and record absentee ballots, a few states— Kentucky, Mississippi, Florida, and Louisiana—lacked any such provision. One reporter wryly observed that in these locations "not only all colored, but all white soldiers are deprived of a vote in national and state elections and primaries." See Arthur Shears Henning, "Few Southern States Permit Soldier Votes," *Chicago Daily Tribune,* April 2, 1942.

92   *New York Times,* September 2, 1942.

93   *Congressional Record,* 77th Cong., 2d sess., August 25, 1942, p. 6959.

94   Richard N. Chapman, *Contours of Public Policy, 1939–1945* (New York: Garland Publishing, 1981), p. 266.

95   *Newsweek,* February 14, 1944, p. 39. When the Eastland version passed the Senate in December 1943, Smith declared, "I have one platform on which I

shall live and die—my loyalty to the Constitution, my loyalty to states' rights, and my loyalty to white supremacy." See *Nation,* December 25, 1943, p. 748.

96 For an analysis along these lines about the importance of absent soldier voters, see "Why Soldiers Votes Are Feared," *New Republic,* December 13, 1943, pp. 837–38.

97 Barry D. Karl, *The Uneasy State: The United States from 1915 to 1945* (Chicago: University of Chicago Press, 1983), p. 181.

98 George Gallup, "Soldiers' Ballots May Name President in '44," *Los Angeles Times,* December 5, 1943.

99 Benson and Wicoff, "Voters Pick Their Party," pp. 167, 170, 172.

100 *Newsweek,* December 13, 1943, pp. 44–45.

101 This was an American Institute of Public Opinion estimate. See "Public Opinion Polls," *Political Science Quarterly* 8 (1944): 439.

102 Franklin D. Roosevelt, "'Four Freedoms' Speech," January 6, 1941, in *Nothing to Fear,* ed. Zevin, pp. 258–67.

103 Franklin D. Roosevelt, Annual Message to Congress, January 6, 1942, *The Public Papers and Addresses of Franklin D. Roosevelt,* vol. 11. (New York: Macmillan, 1943), p. 39. Thus well before the Cold War, worries about how racial discrimination at home would harm the pursuit of American foreign policy goals were already present. For the postwar period, see Mary Dudziak, *Cold War Civil Rights: Race and the Image of American Democracy* (Princeton, NJ: Princeton University Press, 2000); Thomas Borstelmann, *The Cold War and the Color Line: American Race Relations in the Global Arena* (Cambridge: Harvard University Press, 2001).

104 Blum, *V Was for Victory,* p. 208. The campaign was launched by the *Pittsburgh Courier.*

105 Lee, *The Employment of Negro Troops,* p. 366.

106 For an overview, see Harvard Sitkoff, "Racial Militancy and Interracial Violence in the Second World War," *Journal of American History* 58 (1971): 661–81. Writing for an *American Mercury* symposium, "The Negro Problem Reaches a Crisis," that reflected on this violence, Archibald Rutledge, the South Carolina poet and author of fiction about nature and the South, argued that "it is nowhere apparent that the Negro as a race has been especially helped by the laws passed presumably in his behalf, including the law giving him the right to vote," and he reflected sadly how the "sagacity" and "kindness of heart" that "brought some order out of racial chaos . . . by establishing a caste system" in which "the white man has to govern" was being assaulted "by an intrusive, hostile spirit." See Archibald Rutledge, "What if the South Should be Right?" *American Mercury* 59 (1944): 681, 684. "There has been much foggy talk about democracy," he concluded, "that we have completely forgotten that this country is a republic; and if a democracy, a very limited one" (p. 686).

107 Myrdal, *An American Dilemma.*

108 Berlin, *Washington Despatches, 1941–45,* p. 280.

109   *Congressional Record,* 78th Cong., 1st sess., November 22, 1943, p. 9796; November 29, 1943, p. 10064.

110   Ibid., 2d sess., February 1, 1944, p. 1012.

111   Ibid., p. 1007.

112   Ibid., p. 1008.

113   *Congressional Record,* 78th Cong., 2d sess., March 14, 1944, p. 2567.

114   Remarkably, Democrat Malcolm Tarver of Georgia, who had opposed the 1942 act because it had included such elections, complained how "in my State . . . the election occurs in the primary and any bill which fails to make adequate provision for cooperation on the part of the responsible Federal authorities with State election officials in providing a method by which members of our armed services may vote in their State primaries carries to those men and women from my State as well as those from many other sections of the country no substantial aid in having their votes cast and counted in an effective way." See ibid., p. 1029.

115   In two of many interventions of this kind, Nebraska Republican Carl Thomas Curtis told the House that "there is something involved here . . . beside the right of a State. It is the right of the soldier, the right of a citizen soldier, to cast a complete ballot on precinct officers, county officers, State officers, Members of the House and of the Senate, and the President"; and North Dakota Republican Gerald Nye complained that "the bill carries only a limited voting privilege to the servicemen . . . only a blank ballot without names of candidates upon it, and it confines soldiers to a chance to vote only for President and Members of Congress." See *Congressional Record*, 78th Cong., 2d sess., February 8, 1944, p. 1404.

116   "Senator James O. Eastland [D. Miss.] who is serving his first term in the senate, received credit for rallying the forces against the Lucas-Green bill. He and 13 others of the 16 senators from the poll tax states, all Democrats, joined 10 other Democrats and 18 Republicans in voting to toss out the Lucas-Green bill." See *Chicago Daily Tribune,* December 4, 1943.

117   The act restricted, at first quite severely, access overseas to magazines or books "containing political argument or political propaganda of any kind designed or calculated to affect the result of any election for Federal officers," an amendment designed by Ohio senator Robert Taft to thwart Franklin Roosevelt's control, as commander in chief, of the flow of information to overseas voters. For discussions, see John Jamieson, "Censorship and the Soldier," *Public Opinion Quarterly* 11 (1947): 367–84; William M. Leary Jr., "Books, Soldiers, and Censorship during the Second World War," *American Quarterly* 20 (1968): 237–45; Betty Houchin Winfield, *FDR and the News Media* (New York: Columbia University Press, 1994), pp. 182–84. Two months after its enactment, this provision was relaxed by Congress after significant public protest and a press campaign generated by librarians.

118   Republican and southern Democratic likeness scored a remarkable 84 on the

Rice scale; by contrast, the score for the two parts of the Democratic Party was just 51, and the degree of likeness between Republicans and non-southern Democrats scored 64.

119 Cohesive at a level of 93.

120 With a Rice cohesion score of 96, all but unanimous.

121 Who were quite divided, with a very low cohesion score of just 11.

122 The Republican–southern Democratic coalition exhibited a likeness score of 98, fully fifty points higher than the intraparty Democratic score of 48.

123 "The vote in the house in favor of the bill to give soldiers and sailors valid ballots next November," the paper editorialized, "was a victory, and a magnificent victory." It called on the Senate to show "itself equally zealous in defense of the Constitution." See *Chicago Daily Tribune,* February 5, 1944. Vigorous editorials supporting an active federal role, while denouncing the southern Democrats, by contrast, ran in the paper on May 4, July 18, August 3, September 16, and October 18, 1942. A representative editorial underscored how "the New Deal party is going to the country in next month's election with the argument that only its adherents can be trusted to make good the promises of liberty 'everywhere in the world.' Yet the southern Democrats who are the mainstay of their party fought to the last ditch against the amendment waiving a poll tax qualification which Sen. Brooks succeeded in writing into the soldiers' vote law. . . . Dead men in India and boys hanged from a Mississippi bridge have had no comfort from the rhetoric, and the rhetoric will have no meaning to men and women anywhere until there is an end to death at the hands of those whose lips speak meaningless words about justice." See "The Words and the Music," *Chicago Daily Tribune,* October 18, 1942.

124 "Soldier Voting Deal," *Pittsburgh Courier,* January 29, 1944.

125 *Chicago Daily Tribune,* February 9, 1944.

126 *Congressional Record,* 79th Cong., 2d sess., April 1, 1946, p. 2914. That very week, Ms. Brazilla Carroll Reece, a long-serving Tennessee member of the House of Representatives, later an admiring biographer of President Andrew Johnson, and the most conservative candidate in the race, succeeded Herbert Brownell Jr., later President Eisenhower's attorney general, to lead the Republican National Committee. See "GOP Names Southerner as National Chairman," *Pittsburgh Courier,* April 6, 1946. See also B. Carroll Reece, *The Courageous Commoner: A Biography of Andrew Johnson* (Charleston: West Virginia Education Foundation, 1962).

CHAPTER 7 * RADICAL MOMENT

1 Five days before the event, Maj. Gen. Dennis Nolan, who chaired the parade committee, announced "that he had never met with such enthusiasm in a similar undertaking, not excepting even inaugural parades." See *New York Times,* September 8 and; September 10, 1933.

2   Christy is best known to New Yorkers as the artist who painted the six panels of wood nymphs that were installed at the Café des Artistes on West Sixty-seventh Street in 1934. His more chaste and immense 1940 painting, *Scene at the Signing of the Constitution of the United States,* hangs along the east stairway of the U.S. House of Representatives.

3   *New York Times,* September 14, 1933.

4   *Wall Street Journal,* September 15, 1933.

5   Franklin D. Roosevelt, *The Public Papers and Addresses of Franklin D. Roosevelt,* vol. 2 (New York: Random House, 1938), p. 246.

6   For an important essay on the use of wartime metaphors by President Roosevelt and other New Dealers, see William E. Leuchtenburg, *The FDR Years: On Roosevelt and His Legacy* (New York: Columbia University Press, 1995), pp. 35–75.

7   Radio appeal for the NRA, July 24, 1933; available at http://teachingamericanhistory.org/library/index.asp?document=2562.

8   Arthur Schlesinger Jr., *The Age of Roosevelt,* vol. 2, *The Coming of the New Deal, 1933–1935* (Boston: Houghton Mifflin, 1959), p. 116.

9   See http://www.mhric.org/fdr/chat3.html.

10   Frank Freidel, *Franklin D. Roosevelt: A Rendezvous with Destiny* (Boston: Little, Brown, 1973), p. 105.

11   Rexford G. Tugwell, "Design for Government," *Political Science Quarterly* 48 (1933): 323.

12   *New York Times,* June 15 and June 17, 1933. For a discussion of the business conservatism of the NIRA, a law, he claims, that gave American capitalists what they wanted, see Colin Gordon, *New Deals: Business, Labor, and Politics in America, 1920–1935* (New York: Cambridge University Press, 1994), pp. 166–203. This view elaborates the perspective advanced earlier by Ellis W. Hawley, *The New Deal and the Problem of Monopoly* (Princeton, NJ: Princeton University Press, 1966).

13   *New York Times,* June 18, 1933.

14   T. H. Watkins, *The Hungry Years: A Narrative History of the Great Depression in America* (New York: Holt, 2000), p. 188.

15   Overall, the best analysis of the law's character and implications remains Donald R. Brand, *Corporatism and the Rule of Law: A Study of the National Recovery Administration* (Ithaca, NY: Cornell University Press, 1988). For a discussion of the price goals of the Recovery Act, and how it was embedded within an economic analysis about the role of underconsumption in the Depression, see Meg Jacobs, *Pocketbook Politics: Economic Citizenship in Twentieth-Century America* (Princeton, NJ: Princeton University Press, 2005), p. 107.

16   Frank Freidel, *Franklin D. Roosevelt: Launching the New Deal* (Boston: Little, Brown, 1973), p. 428. Oklahoma's Democratic representative Ernest Marland had introduced a bill in mid-May that became the basis for the oil provisions of the National Industrial Recovery Act. See *New York Times,* May 20, 1933.

At the start of June, Secretary of the Interior Harold Ickes recommended the inclusion of this set of special oil-control provisions within the Recovery Act with the support of President Roosevelt. See ibid., June 2, 1933.

17   Melvyn Dubofsky and Warren Van Tine, *John L. Lewis: A Biography* (Urbana: University of Illinois Press, 1986), p. 133. Lewis declared that "organized labor is a single unit in its approval of the objectives of the National Industrial Recovery Act . . . the support of organized labor, in a fundamental sense, is without reservation." See John L. Lewis, "Labor and the National Recovery Administration," *Annals of the American Academy of Political and Social Science* 172 (1934): 58. Green is cited by Marjorie R. Clark, "Recent History of Labor Organization," ibid., 184 (1936): 161. Likewise, Sidney Hillman, who led the Amalgamated Clothing Workers of America, underscored how the NRA had successfully regulated the hours of work and secured a legal means to undercut competition that had cut wages below a decent minimum. See Hillman, "The NRA, Labor, and Recovery," ibid., 172 (1934): 70–71. See also Edwin E. Witte, "The Background of the Labor Provisions of the N.I.R.A.," *University of Chicago Law Review* 1 (1934): 572–79. Witte stressed the ambiguous quality of labor rights, including some opacity about whether business could satisfy the bill's labor provisions by creating and recognizing company unions.

18   Cited in Ruth L. Horowitz, *Political Ideologies of Organized Labor: The New Deal Era* (New Brunswick, NJ: Transaction Books, 1977), p. 101. Looking back, we might judge that these provisions did not do quite as much for unions as some labor leaders had anticipated, in part because the statute was charged with ambiguity about how workers might be represented.

19   Schlesinger, *The Coming of the New Deal, 1933–1935,* pp. 116–18.

20   For a comparative discussion, see J. P. Mayer, *Political Thought: The European Tradition* (London: J. M. Dent, 1939), pp. 407–14. Otto Nathan, an economist (and close friend of Albert Einstein) who had advised the Weimar government and who specialized in analyses of the Nazi economic system, offered a thoughtful evaluation of how the Recovery Act contributed to economic stabilization in the United States in "The N.I.R.A. and Stabilization," *American Economic Review* 25 (1935): 44–58. For an account of how the NRA drew not only on overseas models but also on homegrown experiences, see Glenn Lowell Clayton, "The Development of the Concept of National Planning in the United States" (Ph.D. dissertation, Ohio State University, 1948).

21   "The Washington Alphabet: New Deal Agencies," *New York Times,* March 4, 1934.

22   Tugwell, "Design for Government," pp. 327, 328, 325.

23   Donald R. Richberg, "Progress under the National Recovery Act," *Proceedings of the American Academy of Political Science* 15 (1934): 25.

24   A compact and largely positive contemporary overview was provided by the American Institute of Banking, *Anti-Depression Legislation, 1933* (New York: American Institute of Banking, 1934). On conservation, see Sarah T. Phillips,

This Land, This Nation: Conservation, Rural America, and the New Deal (New York: Cambridge University Press, 2007).

25 *New York Times,* July 7, 1933.

26 Daniel T. Rodgers, *Atlantic Crossings: Social Politics in a Progressive Age* (Cambridge: Harvard University Press, 2000).

27 Richard Hofstadter, *The American Political Tradition and the Men Who Made It* (New York: Alfred A. Knopf, 1949), p. x.

28 For a discussion, see Ellis W. Hawley, "Herbert Hoover, Associationalism, and the Great Depression Relief Crisis of 1930–1933," in *With Us Always: A History of Private Charity and Public Welfare,* ed. Donald T. Critchlow and Charles M. Parker (New York: Rowman & Littlefield, 1998), pp. 161–90.

29 Candidate Franklin Roosevelt took up the theme of budget balance, likening the federal budget to that of a family, in a campaign address in Pittsburgh on October 19, 1932. See http://www.presidency.ucsb.edu/ws/index.php?pid =88399#axzz1sJL6a7rt.

30 Cited in Julian E. Zelizer, "The Forgotten Legacy of New Deal Fiscal Conservatism and the Roosevelt Administration, 1933–1938," *Presidential Studies Quarterly* 30 (2000): 335. This article underscores this aspect of New Deal policy until 1938, and stresses the roles played by Lewis Douglas, who directed the Bureau of the Budget from March 1933 to August 1934, and Secretary of the Treasury Henry Morgenthau Jr., who served from 1934 to 1945. For further discussions, see James D. Savage, *Balanced Budgets and American Politics* (Ithaca, NY: Cornell University Press, 1988); Michael K. Brown, *Race, Money, and the American Welfare State* (Ithaca, NY: Cornell University Press, 1999).

31 Roosevelt, *The Public Papers and Addresses of Franklin D. Roosevelt,* vol. 2, p. 50.

32 Tugwell, "Design for Government," pp. 326, 330.

33 Herbert Hoover, "The Challenge to Liberty," *Saturday Evening Post,* September 8, 1934, pp. 6, 69.

34 *Congressional Record,* 73d Cong., 1st sess., May 26, 1933, p. 4333.

35 Ibid., May 25, 1933, p. 4188.

36 Ibid., May 5, 1933, p. 4217.

37 Ibid., May 25, 1933, p. 4211.

38 Ibid.

39 Cited in Freidel, *Franklin D. Roosevelt: Launching the New Deal,* p. 433.

40 *Congressional Record,* 73d Cong., 1st sess., May 25, 1933, p. 4207.

41 Alonzo L. Hamby, *For the Survival of Democracy: Franklin Roosevelt and the World Crisis of the 1930s* (New York: Free Press, 2004), p. 116.

42 Patrick D. Reagan, *Designing a New America: The Origins of New Deal Planning, 1890–1943* (Amherst: University of Massachusetts Press, 1999), pp. 6–7.

43 *Washington Post,* June 21, 1933.

44 *New York Times,* July 7, 1933.

45 Richberg, "Progress under the National Recovery Act," p. 25. This analysis anticipated how John Dewey would distinguish totalitarian from democratic

economics later in the decade. See John Dewey, *Freedom and Culture* (New York: G. P. Putnam's Sons, 1939), pp. 74–102.

46   Richberg, "Progress under the National Recovery Act," pp. 6, 29. In this summary of New Deal values and positions, Richberg anticipated the "radical distinction" between state corporatism, which relies primarily on constraints, and societal corporatism, which relies primarily on inducements, famously put forward by the political scientist Philippe Schmitter some four decades ago. See Philippe Schmitter, "Still the Century of Corporatism?," *Review of Politics* 36 (1974): 103, 93, 103–4, 105. See also Ruth Berins Collier and David Collier, "Inducement versus Constraints: Disaggregating 'Corporatism,'" *American Political Science Review* 73 (1979): 967–86.

47   Richberg, "Progress under the National Recovery Act," pp. 28, 30. See also Roger Shaw, "Fascism and the New Deal," *North American Review* 238 (1934): 559, 562, 561, 560, 562; Lewis L. Lorwin, "The Plan State and the Democratic Ideal," *Annals of the American Academy of Political and Social Science* 180 (1935): 114–18. This article was a contribution to a special issue on "Socialism, Fascism, and Democracy."

48   Lewis L. Lorwin, "Some Political Aspects of Economic Planning," *American Political Science Review* 26 (1932): 727.

49   *Congressional Record,* 73d Cong., 1st sess., June 7, 1933, p. 5306.

50   Ibid., May 25, 1933, p. 4188.

51   Ibid., May 26, 1933, p. 4358.

52   Ibid., May 25, 1933, p. 4223.

53   Ibid., June 10, 1933, p. 5700.

54   Ibid., June 7, 1933, p. 5185.

55   Ibid., May 25, 1933, p. 4202.

56   For a discussion of this "alternative philosophy," see Anthony J. Badger, *FDR: The First Hundred Days* (New York: Hill and Wang, 2008), pp. 95–98.

57   The party's likeness scores were, respectively, 96, 99, 96, and 93. For a discussion of the vote concerning the allocation of subsidies for road construction, see Richard Bensel, *Sectionalism and American Political Development: 1880–1980* (Madison: University of Wisconsin Press, 1984), pp. 155–56.

58   With a likeness score of 92. Inside the Finance Committee, all but the public works provisions of the bill had nearly been defeated by a coalition that included two nonsouthern Democrats (William King of Utah and William McAdoo of California), two conservative southern Democrats (Josiah Bailey of North Carolina and Harry Byrd of Virginia), and three southern Democrats who wanted the bill to be tougher on business (Champ Clark of Missouri, Tom Connally of Texas, and Thomas Gore of Oklahoma).

59   *Congressional Record,* 73d Cong., 1st sess., May 25, 1933, p. 4202.

60   Roger K. Newman, *Hugo Black: A Biography* (New York: Pantheon, 1994), pp. 159–61.

61   Senator Black thus proposed an amendment that would have allowed all states to have representation and equal voting power in any industry code group. The amendment would also have granted equal representation to firms within an industry regardless of their size or their relative power. He explained that "seventy-five percent [of industry] is in 134 of over 3,000 counties. Fifty percent of it is in 34 counties out of over 3,000 counties. It means that unless we provide legislatively for equal representation of the States in those new law-making trade associations, the great majority of States will have no voting chance at all." The amendment was rejected 25–41, with supporters coming from the economically less developed states in the West as well as the South. See *Congressional Record,* 73d Cong., 1st sess., June 8, 1933, pp. 5285–5286.

62 These were Hattie Caraway of Arkansas, Huey Long of Louisiana, Matthew Neely of West Virginia, and Robert Reynolds of North Carolina.

63 The majority was constituted by twenty southern Democrats, twenty-one non-southern Democrats, and five Republicans.

64 *Congressional Record,* 73d Cong., 1st sess., June 8, 1933, 5241.

65 Ibid., 5243.

66 Ibid., 5241.

67 This discussion, including the Roosevelt citation, draws on the excellent overview by Marc Linder, "Farm Workers and the Fair Labor Standards Act: Racial Discrimination in the New Deal," *Texas Law Review* 65 (1987): 1354–61.

68 *New York Times,* September 14, 1933.

69 Ibid., September 13, 1933.

70 Clair Wilcox, Herbert F. Fraser, and Patrick Murphy Malin, eds., *America's Recovery Program* (New York: Oxford University Press, 1934), pp. 42, 65, 85, 196, 180, 102.

71 *A. L. A. Schechter Poultry Corp. v. United States,* 295 U.S. 495 (1935).

72 Charles Frederic Roos, *NRA Economic Planning* (Colorado Springs: Cowles Commission for Research in Economics, 1937), p. 472.

73 Hawley, *The New Deal and the Problem of Monopoly,* p. 135.

74 David M. Kennedy, *Freedom from Fear: The American People in Depression and War, 1929–1945* (New York: Oxford University Press, 1999), pp. 184, 179. For Alonzo Hamby, the NRA was "a definable culprit" whose "unrealistic expectations about its capacities, built-in contradictions among the interests it attempted to harmonize, and its fundamental unsuitability to an American environment" made it "fall short as an instrument of economic rescue." According to the economic journalist Amity Shlaes, the NRA made a terrible situation worse by mistaking challenges facing the economy as a whole for challenges specific to individual sectors and firms. A leading social science appraisal by Kenneth Finegold and Theda Skocpol likewise argues that "the National Recovery Administration did not contribute to recovery and probably actually hindered it." See Hamby, *For the Survival of Democracy,* p. 165; Amity Shlaes, *The Forgotten Man: A New History of the Great Depression* (New York: HarperCollins, 2007), pp. 150–52; Kenneth Finegold and Theda Skocpol,

State and Party in America's New Deal (Madison: University of Wisconsin Press, 1995), pp. 10, 12. These various citations hardly exhaust the negative literature on the NRA. One of the more measured considerations in this vein is George McJimsey, *The Presidency of Franklin Delano Roosevelt* (Lawrence: University Press of Kansas, 2000), pp. 55–84.

75   Jonathan Alter, *The Defining Moment: FDR's Hundred Days and the Triumph of Hope* (New York: Simon & Schuster, 2006), p. 303. There has been a loud drumbeat of retrospective criticism.

76   U.S. Bureau of the Census, *Historical Statistics of the United States, Colonial Times to 1970, Part 2* (Washington, DC: Bureau of the Census, Department of Commerce, 1976), pp. 226–27, 135. For a contemporaneous assessment, see Arthur Robert Burns, "The First Phase of the National Recovery Act, 1933," *Political Science Quarterly* 49 (1934): 161–94. A retrospective assessment commissioned by President Roosevelt in March 1936 found that the NRA's policies to spread work, increase purchasing power, limit ruthless and anarchic competition, control child labor, and advance the capacities of organized labor had in fact made positive contributions both to recovery in the short term and to a secure and evenhanded capitalism in the long term. See House, *The National Recovery Administration: Report of the President's Committee of Industrial Analysis,* 75th Cong., 1st sess., 1937, H. Doc. 138, pp. 1–240. Even more independent and skeptical economists highlighted the NRA's positive effects, even though it was difficult to disentangle its role from other factors. See Leonard Kurvin, "Effect of N.R.A. on the Physical Volume of Production," *Journal of the American Statistical Association* 31 (1936): 58–60.

77   Brand, *Corporatism and the Rule of Law,* pp. 229–89; for a more negative assessment, see Bernard Bellush, *The Failure of the NRA* (New York: W. W. Norton, 1975), a book that primarily focuses on labor and whose unremitting critique is ultimately less convincing than Brand's deeper and more measured assessment.

78   Basil Rauch, *A History of the New Deal: 1933–39* (New York: Creative Age Press, 1944), p. 97.

79   Louis Galambos and Joseph Pratt, *The Rise of the Corporate Commonwealth: United States Business and Public Policy in the 20th Century* (New York: Basic Books, 1988), p. 107.

80   *Wall Street Journal,* June 21, 1933.

81   Cited in Alan Brinkley, *The Publisher: Henry Luce and His American Century* (New York: Alfred A. Knopf, 2010), p. 162.

82   Gerard Swope, "Planning and Economic Organization," *Proceedings of the Academy of Political Science* 15 (1934): 455.

83   John Dickinson, "The Recovery Program," in *America's Recovery Program,* ed. Wilcox, Fraser, and Malin, p. 32. This chapter was based on the William J. Cooper Foundation Lecture he presented at Swarthmore College on October 22, 1933.

84   René de Visme Williamson, *The Politics of Planning in the Oil Industry under the Code* (New York: Harper and Brothers, 1936), p. 81.

85   A thoughtful overview can be found in Donald R. Brand, "Corporatism, the NRA, and the Oil Industry," *Political Science Quarterly* 98 (1983): 99–118; a revised version can be found in Brand, *Corporatism and the Rule of Law,* pp. 175–206.

86   Theda Skocpol and Kenneth Finegold, "State Capacity and Economic Intervention in the Early New Deal," *Political Science Quarterly* 97 (1982): 255–256. For an assessment that contrasts the NRA with prior economic policies after World War I, see Robert F. Himmelberg, *The Origins of the National Recovery Administration: Business, Government, and the Trade Association Issue, 1921–1933* (New York: Fordham University Press, 1976).

87   Brand, *Corporatism and the Rule of Law,* p. 288.

88   Alan Brinkley, *The End of Reform: New Deal Liberalism in Recession and War* (New York: Alfred A. Knopf, 1995), p. 38.

89   Rexford G. Tugwell, *In Search of Roosevelt* (Cambridge: Harvard University Press, 1972), p. 299.

90   Brinkley, *The End of Reform,* pp. 40, 39.

91   For an argument along these lines, see Anne-Marie Burley, "Regulating the World: Multilateralism, International Law, and the Projection of the New Deal Regulatory State," in *Multilateralism Matters: The Theory and Praxis of an Institutional Form,* ed. John Gerard Ruggie (New York: Columbia University Press, 1993).

92   James T. Patterson, *Congressional Conservatism and the New Deal* (Lexington: University of Kentucky Press, 1967), p. 37.

93   Arthur Schlesinger Sr., *The New Deal in Action, 1933–1937: A Continuation of A. M. Schlesinger's Political and Social Growth of the United States to the Special Session of the United States Congress, November 15, 1937* (New York: Macmillan, 1938).

94   Arthur Schlesinger Jr., *The Age of Roosevelt,* vol. 3, *The Politics of Upheaval, 1935–1936* (Boston: Houghton Mifflin, 1960), p. 385.

95   Rauch, *A History of the New Deal.* It was in his evaluation of the relative conservatism and assertiveness of the two moments that Schlesinger took note of how Rauch's "conception . . . differs from the one presented here" (p. 690). For a discussion of Rauch and the broader character of New Deal periodization, see Otis L. Graham Jr., "Historians and the New Deal, 1944–1960," *Social Studies* 54 (1963): 133–40.

96   Schlesinger Jr., *The Politics of Upheaval,* p. 397.

97   Ibid., p. 385.

98   Leon Keyserling to Arthur Schlesinger Jr., April 9, 1958; cited in Schlesinger Jr., *The Politics of Upheaval,* pp. 690–92. An analysis by economists arguing that the radical "political shocks" across this period, including the NRA, AAA, TVA, and Wagner Act, impeded business confidence and slowed the recovery rejects any distinction between the First and Second New Deal. See Thomas Mayer and Monojit Chatterji, "Political Shocks and Investment: Some Evidence

from the 1930s," *Journal of Economic History* 45 (1985): 913–24. For a rejoinder building on analysis by Joseph Schumpeter, see Antony Patrick O'Brien, "Were Businessmen Afraid of FDR? A Comment on Mayer and Chatterji," ibid., 50 (1990): 936–41.

99 Carl N. Degler, *Out of Our Past: The Forces That Shaped Modern America* (New York: Harper and Brothers, 1959), p. 416. Chapter 3 is called "The Third American Revolution."

100 Brinkley, *The End of Reform.*

101 See http://www.americanrhetoric.com/speeches/fdrcommonwealth.htm.

102 *Los Angeles Times,* June 29, 1934; http://www.mhric.org/fdr/chat5.html.

103 See http://www.austincc.edu/lpatrick/his2341/fdr36acceptancespeech.htm.

104 Franklin D. Roosevelt, "Annual Message to Congress," January 6, 1937; "Second Inaugural Address," January 20, 1937, in *Nothing to Fear: The Selected Addresses of Franklin Delano Roosevelt, 1932–1945,* ed. B. D. Zevin (Boston: Houghton Mifflin, 1946), pp. 79–87.

105 Ibid.

106 Roosevelt, "Annual Message to Congress," in *Nothing to Fear,* ed. Zevin, p. 81.

107 Franklin D. Roosevelt, "A Rendezvous with Destiny," June 27, 1936, in *The Public Papers and Addresses of Franklin D. Roosevelt,* vol. 7 (New York: Macmillan, 1941), p. 235.

108 Roosevelt, "Annual Message to Congress," in *Nothing to Fear,* ed. Zevin, p. 86.

109 Ibid.

110 The law also banned stock trading in unregulated markets; regulated credit and restricted borrowing and lending for stock purchases; regulated stockbrokers by providing powers to censure, penalize, and bar them from trading; prohibited the manipulation of stock prices, insider trading, and deceptive practices; mandated regular and transparent reporting; and established rules for securities litigation. In 1936, Congress further enlarged the SEC's responsibilities to include over-the-counter securities.

111 *New York Times,* June 28, 1933; "Comments: The Tennessee Valley Authority Act," *Yale Law Journal* 43 (1934): 815–26.

112 *Congressional Record,* 73d Cong., 1st sess., April 24, 1933, p. 2273.

113 *New York Times,* April 11, 1933.

114 *Congressional Record,* 73d Cong., 1st sess., April 24, 1933, pp. 2257, 2273.

115 Ibid., p. 2276.

116 Ibid., 73d Cong., 1st sess., April 22, 1933, p. 2202.

117 Ibid., April 24, 1933, p. 2255.

118 Marked on passage and agreement to the conference report by intra–Democratic Party likeness scores of 99 and 94 in the House and 98 and 97 in the Senate. See *Washington Post,* March 1, 1934; *New York Times,* March 25, 1934. For a contemporaneous overview, see also Thomas R. Henry, "Muscle Shoals: Proving Ground of the New Deal," *Los Angeles Times,* April 28, 1934.

119 For a retrospective evaluation of this collaboration by an official of the TVA, see Lawrence L. Durisch, "Local Government and the T.V.A. Program," *Public Administration Review* 1 (1941): 326–34.

120   Grandfather of the novelist Gore Vidal.

121   Philip Selznick, *TVA and the Grass Roots: A Study in the Sociology of Formal Organization* (Berkeley: University of California Press, 1949), p. 112.

122   Daniel R. Goldfield, *Black, White, and Southern: Race Relations and Southern Culture, 1940 to the Present* (Baton Rouge: Louisiana State University Press, 1991), p. 29. For a powerful and comprehensive overview, see Nancy Grant, *TVA and Black Americans: Planning for the Status Quo* (Philadelphia: Temple University Press, 1991). For studies that largely elide these issues, see Walter L. Creese, *TVA's Public Planning: The Vision and the Reality* (Knoxville: University of Tennessee Press, 1990); and Erwin C. Hargrove, *Prisoners of Myth: The Leadership of the Tennessee Valley Authority, 1933–1990* (Princeton, NJ: Princeton University Press, 1994).

123   In 1928, when northern Alabama's political leaders mobilized evangelical fervor to oppose the Democratic presidential nominee, Alfred E. Smith, for his views about Prohibition, "South Alabama Democratic loyalists," led by Steagall, "trumped this rebellious nativism and temperance enthusiasm with racism, sectionalism, Jacksonian defense of the right to have a drink when a man (or woman) felt like it, and their own brand of religious bigotry. . . . Rep. Henry B. Steagall even blasted Smith's Republican opponent, Herbert Hoover, as an evolutionist and wondered how orthodox Protestant ministers could support such a man." See Wayne Flint, *Alabama in the Twentieth Century* (Tuscaloosa: University of Alabama Press, 2004), p. 46.

124   Carter Glass to Walter Lippmann, August 10, 1933; cited in Patterson, *Congressional Conservatism and the New Deal*, p. 13. His letters, archived at the University of Virginia, are full of such judgments.

125   *Congressional Record,* 73d Cong., 1st sess., June 13, 1933, p. 5896.

126   Ibid., May 22, 1933, pp. 3930, 3935.

127   His amendment to include state banks was defeated by a 20–68 margin. Steagall explained that at issue was the security of depositors, and that all banks, including state banks, would have to be examined for solvency by federal authorities. See ibid., May 23, 1933, pp. 4034–36.

128   Ibid., May 22, 1933, p. 3925.

129   Ibid., May 25, 1933, p. 4170.

130   Wth Democratic Party likeness scores of 95 and 99.

131   *Congressional Record,* 73d Cong., 2d sess., April 30, 1934, pp. 7695, 7696.

132   Ibid., May 2, 1934, p. 7926; May 4, 1934, p. 8097.

133   Ibid., p. 7941; May 4, 1934, p. 8090. Opponents of this bill, as with other New Deal legislation, emphasized, as the Kansas House Republican Harold McGugin insisted, that "this bill bears the same tyranny which is found in much of our-so-called 'emergency legislation.' Russia, Germany, and Italy are not

the only countries in which citizens are being imprisoned for the violation of edicts." See ibid., May 3, 1934, p. 8012.

134 For a discussion, see Michael Goldfield, "Worker Insurgency, Radical Organization, and New Deal Labor Legislation," *American Political Science Review* 83 (1989): 1257–82.

135 National Labor Relations Act of 1935, §§ 7–9, as passed, reprinted in *Legislative History of the National Labor Relations Act, 1935,* comp. National Labor Relations Board (Washington, DC: U.S. Government Printing Office, 1959); 74th Cong., 1st sess., 1935, H. Doc. 1147, pp. 15–23; William B. Gould, *A Primer on American Labor Law* (Cambridge: MIT Press, 1993), pp. 45–46. The standard history is James A. Gross, *The Making of the National Labor Relations Board: A Study in Economics, Politics, and Law: 1933–1937,* vol. 1 (Albany: State University of New York Press, 1974). His discussion of implementation is found in James A. Gross, *The Reshaping of the National Labor Relations Board: National Labor Policy in Transition, 1937–1947,* vol. 2 (Albany: State University of New York Press, 1981). See also Murray Edelman, "New Deal Sensitivity to Labor Interests," in *Labor and the New Deal,* ed. Milton Derber and Edwin Young (Madison: University of Wisconsin Press, 1957), 157–91; David Plotke, "The Wagner Act, Again: Politics and Labor, 1935–1937," *Studies in American Political Development* 3 (1989): 104–56; Mark Barenberg, "The Political Economy of the Wagner Act: Power, Symbol, and Workplace Cooperation," *Harvard Law Review* 106 (1993): 1379–406.

136 National Labor Relations Act of 1935, § 8(a)(2), reprinted in *Legislative History of the National Labor Relations Act, 1935,* comp. National Labor Relations Board, 74th Cong., 1st sess., 1935, H. Doc. 1147, pp. 17–19; Gould, *A Primer on American Labor Law,* p. 47.

137 National Labor Relations Act of 1935, §§ 3–6, 10–12, reprinted in *Legislative History of the National Labor Relations Act, 1935,* comp. National Labor Relations Board; 74th Cong., 1st sess., 1235, H. Doc. 1147, pp. 11–15; 23–25. See Frank W. McCulloch and Tim Bornstein, *The National Labor Relations Board* (New York: Praeger, 1974). Gross, *The Reshaping of the National Labor Relations Board,* pp. 132–36, discusses the relatively greater power and independence of the NLRB under the NLRA than previous labor boards had held.

138 For an early assessment, see Lois MacDonald, "The National Labor Relations Act," *American Economic Review* 26 (1936): 412–27.

139 Despite their focus on the relationship of price changes and union growth, Ashenfelter and Pencavel acknowledge the importance of what they rather blandly refer to as "a favorable political environment." See Orley Ashenfelter and John H. Pencavel, "American Trade Union Growth: 1900–1960," *Quarterly Journal of Economics* 83 (1969): 446.

140 Leo Wolman, "Concentration of Union Membership," *Proceedings of Fifth Annual Meeting of the Industrial Relations Research Association* (Madison:

University of Wisconsin Press, 1952); cited in Milton Derber, "Growth and Expansion," in *Labor and the New Deal,* ed. Milton Derber and Edwin Young (Madison: University of Wisconsin, 1957), p. 17.

141 Levels and durations varied, as these were set by the states.

142 Kennedy, *Freedom from Fear,* p. 261.

143 At a likeness level of 85.

144 For a compelling analysis of the filibuster pivot in this Congress, see Brian R. Sala, "Time for a Change: Pivotal Politics and the 1935 Wagner Act," unpublished paper presented at the Midwest Political Science Association Annual Meeting, April 2002.

145 *Congressional Record,* 74th Cong., 1st sess., May 16, 1935, p. 7657.

146 With a likeness level of 88.

147 U.S. Committee on Economic Security, *Report to the President* (Washington, DC: U.S. Government Printing Office, 1935), p. 49; cited in Robert Lieberman, *Shifting the Color Line: Race and the American Welfare State* (Cambridge: Harvard University Press, 1998), p. 31.

148 Congressional Research Service, "Legislative History of the Exclusion of Agricultural Employees from the National Labor Relations Act, 1935, and the Fair Labor Standards Act of 1938" (Washington, DC: Library of Congress, 1966), pp. 1, 4.

149 Southerners joined other Democrats in the Senate with a likeness level of 92 to pass the labor bill, and with an identical level of 98 in the House and Senate votes to pass the Social Security Act. In these cross-partisan votes, southern Democrat–Republican likeness on labor scored 72 in the Senate and 86 in the House, and 75 in the Senate vote on Social Security.

150 *Congressional Record,* 74th Cong., 1st sess., April 19, 1935, p. 6041.

151 Michael Anthony Butler, *Cordell Hull and Trade Reform, 1933–1937* (Kent, OH: Kent State University Press, 1998), p. 7.

152 House, "Amend Tariff Act of 1930: Reciprocal Trade Agreements," 73rd Cong., 2nd sess., 1934, H. Doc. 1000, pp. 1–3.

153 The classic study, based on a close analysis of the process that produced the Smoot-Hawley tariff revision law of 1930, is E. E. Schattschneider, *Politics, Pressures, and the Tariff* (Englewood Cliffs, NJ: Prentice-Hall, 1935). A recent thoughtful consideration is Douglas A. Irwin, *Peddling Protectionism: Smoot-Hawley and the Great Depression* (Princeton, NJ: Princeton University Press, 2011).

154 About this there was "tremendous predictability," as the tariff was "a defining issue of partisan politics in the late nineteenth and early twentieth centuries." See Michael A. Bailey, Judith Goldstein, and Barry R. Weingast, "The Institutional Roots of American Trade Policy: Politics, Coalitions, and International Trade," *World Politics* 49 (1997): 311.

155 John Mark Hansen, "Taxation and the Political Economy of the Tariff," *International Organization* 44 (1990): 543.

156 During the go-go decade that preceded this statute, America's imports dropped by 31 percent and its exports by 44 percent as high tariffs took hold. See Judith Goldstein, *Ideas, Interests, and American Trade Policy* (Ithaca, NY: Cornell University Press, 1994), p. 94. For her incisive accounts of the protectionist era, which she dates from 1870 to 1930, and the subsequent liberalization of trade, see pp. 81–182. For a table of tariff legislation partisanship, see Michael J. Hiscox, "The Magic Bullet? The RTAA, Institutional Reform, and Trade Liberalization," *International Organization* 53 (1999): 692.

157 Schattschneider, *Politics, Pressures, and the Tariff,* p. 7.

158 For party-oriented accounts of trade legislation, see Robert Pastor, *Congress and the Politics of United States Foreign Economic Policy, 1929–1977* (Berkeley: University of California Press, 1980; Colleen M. Callahan, Judith A. McDonald, and Anthony Patrick O'Brien, "Who Voted for Smoot-Hawley?" *Journal of Economic History* 54 (1994): 683–90.

159 The jury is still out. A strongly argued revisionist case to the effect that Smoot-Hawley has an undeserved harsh reputation can be found in Alfred E. Eckes Jr., *Opening America's Market: U.S. Foreign Trade Policy since 1776* (Chapel Hill: University of North Carolina Press, 1995), pp. 100–139. A careful study attributing 25 percent of America's trade loss between 1930 and 1932 to Smoot-Hawley is Douglas A. Irwin, "The Smoot-Hawley Tariff: A Quantitative Assessment," *Review of Economics and Statistics* 80 (1998): 326–34.

160 *Congressional Record,* 71st Cong., 1st sess., May 10, 1929, p. 1134.

161 Ibid., May 11, 1929, p. 1159.

162 Ibid., May 13, 1929, p. 1208.

163 House, "Amend Tariff Act of 1930," p. 5.

164 The fullest statement of Cordell Hull's reasoning, including the claim that active trade is a force for world peace as well as for economic recovery, is the statement he read to the House Ways and Means Committee on March 8, 1934, printed in full in the *New York Times,* March 9, 1934.

165 Susanne Lohmann and Sharyn O'Halloran, "Divided Government and U.S. Trade Policy: Theory and Evidence," *International Organization* 48 (1994): 595–632.

166 Bailey, Goldstein, and Weingast, "The Institutional Roots of American Trade Policy," p. 318.

167 *Congressional Record,* 73d Cong., 2d sess., March 27, 1934, p. 5547.

168 Ibid., March 26, 1934, p. 5451.

169 Ibid., March 23, 1934, p. 5258.

170 V. O. Key Jr., *Southern Politics in State and Nation* (New York: Alfred A. Knopf, 1949), p. 353.

171 Party likeness reached 94 in the Senate, 96 in the House. Southern Democratic–Republican likeness was a mere 3, and overall Democratic-Republican likeness stood only at 6.

172 Lester J. Dickinson, "What's the Matter with Congress?," *American Mercury*

37 (1936): 129; cited in Patterson, *Congressional Conservatism and the New Deal,* pp. 69–70.

173 *New York Times,* January 5, 1937.

174 To a total of 193 in the House and 43 in the Senate.

175 Patterson, *Congressional Conservatism and the New Deal,* p. 160.

176 He continued to serve through 1940, when a Democrat, James Tunnell, took the seat, putting only Democrats in the Senate across the South.

177 Patterson, *Congressional Conservatism and the New Deal,* pp. 97–99, 110, 156–57. Patterson is right to point out that Democratic defections were not limited to the South, and that none of the Republican opponents was southern; but, as he observes, this voting pattern heralded a growing sectional division within the party, one that was to become more fateful during the mid- and late 1940s.

178 Bruce J. Schulman, *From Cotton Belt to Sunbelt: Federal Policy, Economic Development, and the Transformation of the South, 1938–1980* (Raleigh, NC: Duke University Press, 1994), pp. 57–58, 63–87.

179 Lee J. Alston and Joseph P. Ferrie, "Paternalism in Agricultural Contracts in the U.S. South: Implications for the Growth of the Welfare State," *American Economic Review* 83 (1993): 852–76. In itself, sharecropping was not simply racial. Every census from 1880 to 1940 shows more white than black sharecroppers and tenants in the South, but a significantly higher proportion of black farmers fell into these categories.

180 *Congressional Record,* 75th Cong., 2d sess., December 13, 1937, p. 1404. Representative Martin Dies, a Texas Democrat, articulated the same concern, stating that a "racial question" was implicated by the FLSA because under its minimum-wage provisions "what is prescribed for one race must be prescribed for the others, and you cannot prescribe the same wages for the black man as for the white man." Echoing Wilcox and Dies, Georgia Democratic representative Edward Cox complained that "organized Negro groups of the country are supporting [the FLSA] because it will . . . render easier the elimination and disappearance of racial and social distinctions, and . . . throw into the political field the determination of the standards and the customs which shall determine the relationship of our various groups of people in the South." See Patterson, *Congressional Conservatism and the New Deal,* p. 195. *Congressional Record,* 75th Cong., 2d sess., 1937, p. 442 (appendix).

181 John W. Tait, "The Fair Labor Standards Act of 1938," *University of Toronto Law Journal* 6 (1945): 193.

182 See http://publicpolicy.pepperdine.edu/faculty-research/new-deal/roosevelt-speeches/fr052437.htm.

183 Tait, "The Fair Labor Standards Act of 1938," p. 197.

184 "Ghost of the NRA" is the title of chapter 4 in the excellent history by George E. Paulsen, *A Living Wage for the Forgotten Man: The Quest for Fair Labor Standards, 1933–1941.* (London: Associated University Presses, 1996), pp. 68–81.

185 With a likeness score of 80.

186 Suzanne Mettler, *Dividing Citizens: Gender and Federalism in New Deal Public Policy* (Ithaca NY: Cornell University Press, 1998), pps. 185, 204, 209.

187 Congressional Research Service, "Legislative History of the Exclusion of Agricultural Employees," p. 11.

188 With a likeness score of 60.

189 Patterson, *Congressional Conservatism and the New Deal,* pp. 152–53. On Court packing, see Jeff Shesol, *Supreme Power: Franklin Roosevelt vs. the Supreme Court* (New York: W. W. Norton, 2010).

190 Edward Cox of Georgia, J. Bayard Clark of North Carolina, Martin Dies of Texas, William Driver of Arkansas, and Howard Smith of Virginia.

191 See http://www.mhric.org/fdr/chat10.html.

192 *Congressional Record,* 75th Cong., 2d sess., December 17, 1937, pp. 1786, 1812–13, 1832, 1834.

193 *Chicago Daily Tribune,* December 18, 1937.

194 Democratic Party likeness, previously in the 90s when top-tier bills about the economy were voted on, dropped to 55. For a discussion, see James MacGregor Burns, *Congress on Trial: The Politics of Modern Law Making* (New York: Harper and Brothers, 1949).

195 *Los Angeles Times,* December 18, 1937.

196 Fair Labor Standards Act of 1938, § 6, reproduced in Irving J. Sloan, ed., *American Landmark Legislation: The Fair Labor Standards Act of 1938* (Dobbs Ferry, NY: Oceana, 1984). By contrast, the original bill had mandated a level of forty cents at once.

197 Fair Labor Standards Act of 1938, § 7, reproduced in Sloan, ed., *American Landmark Legislation.* Rather than actually setting maximum allowable workhours, these "maximum"-hours provisions established a threshold above which overtime wages (time and a half) had to be paid.

198 Fair Labor Standards Act of 1938, § 12, reproduced in Sloan, ed., *American Landmark Legislation.*

199 Patterson, *Congressional Conservatism and the New Deal*, p. 246. In light of this history, Landon Storrs has called this an "ambiguous victory." See the instructive chapter "Ambiguous Victory: The Fair Labor Standards Act of 1938," in Landon R. Y. Storrs, *Civilizing Capitalism: The National Consumers' League, Women's Activism, and Labor Standards in the New Deal Era* (Chapel Hill: University of North Carolina Press, 2000), pp. 177–206. This book focuses on the role of the National Labor Committee in bringing pressure over a long period to curb sweatshops and raise labor standards.

200 John S. Forsythe, "Legislative History of the Fair Labor Standards Act," *Law and Contemporary Problems* 6 (1939): 19.

201 Robert F. Koretz, ed., *Statutory History of the United States: Labor Organization* (New York: Chelsea House, 1970), p. 401.

202 Forsythe, "Legislative History of the Fair Labor Standards Act," p. 21.

203   Fair Labor Standards Act of 1938, § 2 ("Findings and Declaration of Policy"), as passed, reproduced in Sloan, ed., *American Landmark Legislation.*

204   Paulsen, *A Living Wage for the Forgotten Man,* pp. 126–27.

205   An excellent systematic analysis confirming the centrality of the South to the legislative history of the FLSA is Robert K. Fleck, "Democratic Opposition to the Fair Labor Standards Act of 1938," *Journal of Economic History* 62 (2002): 25–54. This article was written to address a prior analysis that had minimized the role of the South, stressing the character of the political economy of constituencies irrespective of region: Andrew J. Seltzer, "The Political Economy of the Fair Labor Standards Act of 1938," *Journal of Political Economy* 103 (1995): 1302–42. Fleck won this argument hands down, as Seltzer's unconvincing rejoinder indicates: "Democratic Opposition to the Fair Labor Standards Act: A Comment on Fleck," *Journal of Economic History* 64 (2004): 226–30.

206   That just crossed the high likeness threshold of 70.

207   Intrasouthern likeness measured only 54.

208   Voting with a likeness level across the 7–10 state divide of 98.

209   With a likeness score of 56.

210   J. David Greenstone, *Labor in American Politics* (New York: Alfred A. Knopf, 1969), p. 408.

211   James A. Gross, *The Reshaping of the National Labor Relations Board,* pp. 5–6.

212   Ibid., pp. 17–18. A useful overview of the Smith committee, set in the larger context of the relationship between labor unions and the Democratic Party, including its southern wing, is Gilbert J. Gall, "CIO Leaders and the Democratic Alliance: The Case of the Smith Committee and the NLRB," *Labor Studies Journal* 14 (1989): 2–27.

213   Eric Schickler, "Entrepreneurial Defenses of Congressional Power," in *Formative Acts: American Politics in the Making,* ed. Stephen Skowronek and Matthew Glassman (Philadelphia: University of Pennsylvania Press, 2007), p. 302.

214   *Congressional Record,* 76th Cong., 3d sess., June 6, 1940, p. 7715.

215   With a likeness score of just 55.

216   At the high likeness level of 80.

217   Edward Frederick Lindley Wood, Earl of Halifax, *Fullness of Days* (New York: Dodd Mead, 1957), p. 215.

218   See http://www.airforce-magazine.com/MagazineArchive/Documents/2009/June%202009/0609fullkeeper.pdf.

CHAPTER 8 ▪ THE FIRST CRUSADE

1   *Fortune,* October 1939, folded insert, "The War of 1939."

2   Cited in Alan Brinkley, *The Publisher: Henry Luce and His American Century* (New York: Alfred A. Knopf, 2010), pp. 243, 247.

3   The survey was conducted for *Fortune* by the Roper Organization.

4   7 percent for the former, 23 for the latter.

5   Just 2 percent of nonsouthern Americans supported immediate participation in the war, and another 12 percent if such participation were needed to prevent a German victory. Nor did any other section enlist as many volunteers in the armed forces before the passage of the Selective Service Act in 1940; so much so that Alabama's Luther Patrick, a member of the House, wryly commented that "they had to start selective service to keep our Southern boys from filling up the army." Cited in John Temple Graves, "The Fighting South," *Virginia Quarterly Review* 18 (1942): 61.

6   George F. Kennan, *American Diplomacy, 1900–1950* (Chicago: University of Chicago Press, 1951), p. 66.

7   The United States had 301 bombers. See Eliot Janeway, *The Struggle for Survival: A Chronicle of Economic Mobilization in World War II* (New Haven: Yale University Press, 1951), p. 25.

8   Robert Dallek, *Franklin D. Roosevelt and American Foreign Policy, 1932–1945* (New York: Oxford University Press, 1995), p. 222.

9   Ibid., p. 221; Ross Gregory, *America 1941: A Nation at the Crossroads* (New York: Free Press, 1989), p. 27; Robert Woito, "Between the Wars," *Wilson Quarterly* 11 (1987), p. 108; Andrew Roberts, *Masters and Commanders: The Military Geniuses Who Led the West in World War II* (London: Penguin, 2008), pp. 26, 32.

10   Michael S. Sherry, *In the Shadow of War: The United States since the 1930s* (New Haven: Yale University Press, 1995), p. 27.

11   Harold J. Tobin and Percy W. Bidwell, *Mobilizing Civilian America* (New York: Council on Foreign Relations, 1940), p. 1.

12   Kennan, *American Diplomacy,* pp. 66–67.

13   The results found by Roper for *Fortune* were consistent with the findings of many other polls at the time. "By any measure, the South was more committed to a vigorous assertion of American leadership overseas than any other part of the country. Opinion polls consistently showed southerners to be more internationalist and interventionist than nonsoutherners." See Peter Trubowitz, *Defining the National Interest: Conflict and Change in American Foreign Policy* (Chicago: University of Chicago Press, 1998), p. 126. More than citizens in other regions, from 1938 to Pearl Harbor, southerners routinely favored increasing the size of the military, the development of a plan for total mobilization, and paying higher taxes to support preparedness. They were more likely than residents of other regions to recall American participation in World War I favorably, to believe that events in Europe were vital to American national interests, more hostile to appeasement, more willing to risk war to help the Allies, more prepared to change existing neutrality laws, and more inclined to support Russia than Germany in case of a war between these two powers. These findings were consistent over tens of opinion polls. For an overview of this poll data, see Alfred D. Hero Jr., *The Southerner and World Affairs* (Baton Rouge: Louisiana State University Press, 1965), pp. 80–103.

14   A consideration stressing such powers can be found in Harry Wilmer Jones,

"The President, Congress, and Foreign Relations," *California Law Review* 29 (1941): 565–85.

15 In his monograph on the 76th Congress, David Porter has observed how that Congress, which sat in 1939–1940, "determined the course of American foreign policy more than I anticipated." This finding, he noted, supplements the usual view of historians who "picture the executive rather than the legislative branch as the significant controller of American diplomacy." See David L. Porter, *The Seventy-sixth Congress and World War II* (Columbia: University of Missouri Press, 1979), pp. 174–75.

16 Overall, debate filled 21,846 pages of the *Congressional Record*. For an overview, see Floyd M. Riddick, "American Government and Politics: Third Session of the Seventy-sixth Congress, January 3, 1940, to January 3, 1941," *American Political Science Review* 35 (1941): 284–303.

17 Charles O. Lerche Jr., *The Uncertain South: Its Changing Patterns of Politics in Foreign Policy* (Chicago: Quadrangle Books, 1964), p. 41; on the role of regionalism in congressional voting about assistance to America's allies, see Leroy N. Rieselbach, "The Demography of the Congressional Vote on Foreign Aid, 1939–1958," *American Political Science Review* 58 (1964): 577–88. A useful companion piece, especially for its maps, which show the absence of the South from locations that produced roll-call votes for isolationist measures, is Ralph H. Smuckler, "The Region of Isolation," *American Political Science Review* 47 (1953): 386–401. There is a systematic discussion of congressional behavior during the 1940–1942 period, which includes regional data, in John W. Malsberger, *From Obstruction to Moderation: The Transformation of Senate Conservatism, 1938–1952* (Selinsgrove, PA: Susquehanna University Press, 2000), pp. 61-99. See also George L. Grassmuck, *Sectional Biases in Congress on Foreign Policy* (Baltimore: Johns Hopkins Press, 1951).

18 On the sometimes-competing pressures of ethnicity and party, see Leroy N. Rieselbach, "The Basis of Isolationist Behavior," *Public Opinion Quarterly* 24 (1960): 652–55.

19 For a discussion of President Roosevelt's engagement with southern members on foreign policy questions, see James T. Patterson, "Eating Humble Pie: A Note on Roosevelt, Congress, and Neutrality Revision in 1989," *Historian* 31 (1969): 407–14.

20 It proved fitting that the new army's first training exercises were conducted in the Carolinas, Louisiana, and Tennessee. See Michael Burleigh, *The Third Reich: A New History* (London: Macmillan, 2000), p. 733.

21 The historian Alexander DeConde rightly observed that "with very little dissent in their ranks on foreign policy," southern members of the House and Senate "gave President Franklin D. Roosevelt the essential political power he needed to carry out his foreign policy. . . . It is clear that without their votes no legislation on foreign policy could have survived in either house." See DeConde,

"The South and Isolationism," *Journal of Southern History* 24 (1958): 340. In the Senate, James Byrnes of South Carolina (later secretary of state) and Claude Pepper of Florida were especially vocal in and out of Congress in mobilizing support for an active American role. See Marian D. Irish, "Foreign Policy and the South," *Journal of Politics* 10 (1948): 306; Joan E. Denman, "Senator Claude D. Pepper: Advocate of Aid to the Allies, 1939–1941," *Florida Historical Quarterly* 83 (2004): 121–48.

22 See Selig Adler, *The Isolationist Impulse: Its Twentieth Century Reaction* (New York: Abelard-Schuman, 1957). At Yale, the campus chapter of America First was led by Kingman Brewster, later that university's president and ambassador to Great Britain during the Carter administration. One member was R. Sargent Shriver, then a student at Yale Law School. See Woito, "Between the Wars," pp. 114–115.

23 Wayne S. Cole, "America First and the South, 1940–1941," *Journal of Southern History* 22 (1956): 37, 38, 43, 47. See also Wayne S. Cole, *America First: The Battle against Intervention, 1940–1941* (Madison: University of Wisconsin Press, 1953), p. 31.

24 Virginius Dabney, "The South Looks Ahead," *Foreign Affairs* 19 (1940): 178.

25 The following paragraphs draw on the excellent article by Johnpeter Horst Grill and Robert L. Jenkins, "The Nazis and the American South in the 1930s: A Mirror Image?," *Journal of Southern History* 58 (1992): 668, 671, 674, 675, 676, 673, 677.

26 Cited in Hermann Rauschning, *The Voice of Destruction* (New York: Putnam, 1940), p. 69.

27 Margaret Mitchell, *Vom Winde verweht* (Hamburg: Claassen Verlag, 1937).

28 John Haag, "*Gone with the Wind* in Nazi Germany," *Georgia Historical Quarterly* 73 (1989): 279–304.

29 "That night, Goebbels had invited guests to watch David Selznick's *Gone With the Wind*, a film not yet released, but which Goebbels admired for its depiction of a morally strong armed Confederacy." See Peter Fritzsche, *Life and Death in the Third Reich* (Cambridge: Harvard University Press, 2008), p. 182.

30 These were circumstances he had witnessed after his own regiment had been captured. See Hans Habe, "The Nazi Plan for Negroes," *Nation,* March 1, 1941, p. 233.

31 Ibid., p. 234.

32 Germany's active propaganda program directed at the United States paid particular attention to the South, but it also directed its appeals more broadly. A curious example is Charlie and His Orchestra, a band located in Berlin that broadcast familiar swing and jazz songs to the United States, with their lyrics altered, over shortwave radio. A striking example is their rewriting of Ella Fitzgerald's 1938 recording of "F.D.R. Jones" (also famously sung by Judy Garland), whose middle stanzas observed:

It's a big holiday everywhere
For the Jones family has a brand new heir
He's the joy Heaven sent
And they proudly present Mister Franklin D. Roosevelt Jones

The Nazi version was adjusted to make more than one point:

It's a Hebrew holiday everywhere
All the Jewish family has a brand new heir
He's their joy Heaven sent
And they proudly present Mister Franklin D. Roosevelt Jones

These lyrics can be found today on white-supremacy Web sites.

33   Grill and Jenkins, "The Nazis and the American South in the 1930s," p. 670; the report by Pierre van Paassen appeared in the May 4, 1934, issue of the *Atlanta Constitution.* "By 1937," Glenda Gilmore reports, "Germans imagined the Klan as the perfect launching pad in the United States. That year Baron Manfred von Killinger, the Nazi general counsel in San Francisco, directed a woman using the alias Mrs. Leslie Fry to buy the Ku Klux Klan outright. At least part of her seventy-thousand dollars in purchase money came from the German Ministry of Propaganda and Public Enlightenment. She planned to unify domestic Fascist groups under the KKK cross and recruited a member of the Silver Shirts, an organization that attracted many former Klansmen, to approach the KKK's Imperial Wizard. The FBI chased her out of the country before she could succeed." See Glenda Elizabeth Gilmore, *Defying Dixie: The Radical Roots of Civil Rights, 1919–1950* (New York: W. W. Norton, 2008), p. 172.

34   For discussions, see Julian M. Pleasants, *Buncombe Bob: The Life and Times of Robert Rice Reynolds* (Chapel Hill: University of North Carolina Press, 2000), pp. 158–79; Irish, "Foreign Policy and the South," p. 309. Reynolds chaired the Senate Military Affairs Committee. In July 1943, with the country at war, he proclaimed, "I was an isolationist, and I am a thousand times more isolationist today than I was before we became engaged in this war." Cited in Alexander DeConde, "On Twentieth-Century Isolationism," in *Isolation and Security,* ed. DeConde (Durham, NC: Duke University Press, 1957), p. 5.

35   These instances are cited in Grill and Jenkins, "The Nazis and the American South in the 1930s," p. 685.

36   *Charleston News and Courier,* February 4, 1938.

37   Grill and Jenkins, "The Nazis and the American South in the 1930s," p. 669. There were some southern chapters of the German-American Bund in Memphis, Tennessee; Miami, Florida; Shreveport, Louisiana; and San Antonio and Taylor, Texas; the German veterans organization newspaper, the *Texas Herald,*

in Taylor, praised the Third Reich and promoted anti-Semitism. But overall, "the German-American community in the South simply did not support the *Bund*, and most of that community's newspapers, such as the *German Echo* in Miami, Florida, attacked the Nazi regime" (p. 681).

38 Ibid., pp. 685–86.

39 "Out of tune with the sentiment of his constituency, Senator Reynolds found it inexpedient to seek re-election in 1944." See V. O. Key Jr., *Southern Politics in State and Nation* (New York: Alfred A. Knopf, 1949), p. 363. It should be noted that Reynolds was returned to office in 1938 with 64 percent of the vote, having first been elected in 1932 by a 68–32 margin. Clearly, it was his extreme isolationism that cost him his career. His successor, the Democrat Clyde Hoey, secured 70 percent of the vote in 1944.

40 Grill and Jenkins, "The Nazis and the American South in the 1930s," p. 688.

41 Ibid., pp. 669, 683, 684.

42 Ibid., p. 693. The black press, by contrast, regularly and bitterly returned to this theme, with obvious justification. When the nation's most important black paper, the *Pittsburgh Courier,* published an article by George Schuyler, the well-regarded African-American journalist, in response to the report by Hans Habe, it underscored how "the Nazi plan for Negroes approximates so closely what seems to be the American plan for Negroes." The relatively liberal *Richmond Times-Dispatch* quickly rejoined. It is "dangerously misleading," even "absurd," it stated, to treat these instances as counterparts. Segregation, it argued, "is essential for the well being of the white race." Cited in ibid., pp. 690, 688.

43 George B. Tindall, "The Central Theme Revisited," in *The Southerner as American*, ed. Charles Grier Sellers, Jr. (Chapel Hill: University of North Carolina Press, 1960), p. 114.

44 John Hope Franklin, "As for Our History . . ." in *Southerner as American,* ed. Sellers, Jr., p. 18.

45 On the South's internationalism after World War I, see Dewey W. Grantham Jr., "The Southern Senators and the League of Nations, 1918–1920," *North Carolina Historical Review* 26 (1949): 187–205. For a discussion stressing the episodic character of southern internationalism, see DeConde, "The South and Isolationism,"

46 John Temple Graves, *The Fighting South* (New York: G. P. Putnam's Sons, 1943), p. 5.

47 Ibid., pp. 246–47.

48 Irish, "Foreign Policy and the South," pp. 312–13.

49 Anthony Gaughan, "Woodrow Wilson and the Rise of Militant Interventionism in the South," *Journal of Southern History* 65 (1999): p. 775.

50 Ibid., 778–83.

51 *Jackson Daily News,* August 15, 1918, cited in ibid., p. 804.

52   Gaughan, "Woodrow Wilson and the Rise of Militant Interventionism in the South," pp. 806, 807.

53   What John Calhoun had said about slavery resonated as an animating feature of the mid-twentieth-century southern system: "With us," he told the Senate on August 12, 1849, "the two great divisions of society are not the rich and poor, but white and black; and all the former, the poor as well as the rich, belong to the upper class, and are respected and treated as equals." Cited in Harry V. Jaffa, *A New Birth of Freedom: Abraham Lincoln and the Coming of the Civil War* (New York: Rowman & Littlefield, 2004), p. 283.

54   The most comprehensive treatment remains Robert A. Divine, *The Illusion of Neutrality* (Chicago: University of Chicago Press, 1962). For overviews of the prewar period, see Waldo Heinrichs, *Threshold of War: Franklin D. Roosevelt and American Entry into World War II* (New York: Oxford University Press, 1988); Richard M. Ketchum, *The Borrowed Years, 1938–1941: America on the Way to War* (New York: Random House, 1989); David Reynolds, *From Munich to Pearl Harbor: Roosevelt's America and the Origins of the Second World War* (Chicago: Ivan Dee, 2001).

55   For a discussion, see Dallek, *Franklin D. Roosevelt and American Foreign Policy*, pp. 103–08; he notes how the impending Italo-Ethiopian war helped shift the administration's views about neutrality legislation.

56   Ernest C. Bolt, *Ballots before Bullets: The War Referendum Approach to Peace in America, 1914–1941* (Charlottesville: University of Virginia Press, 1977), pp. 152–85.

57   The law was underpinned by an intellectual rationale that had been advanced by Charles Warren, an international lawyer who had been assistant attorney general of the United States from August 1914 to April 1918, when the United States entered World War I. His widely read April 1934 article in *Foreign Affairs* argued that technical neutrality was not enough; the experience of that war had shown that such formal and thin neutrality risked producing situations that could lead to military participation, however unwanted. Impartiality was insufficient; active policies of abstention and prevention were required. See Charles Warren, "Troubles of a Neutral," *Foreign Affairs* 12 (1934): 377. The 1935 Neutrality Act closely tracked his specific proposals. The next issue of the journal carried a sharp rejoinder by Allen Dulles, who later served as the director of the CIA from 1953 to 1961. Dulles argued, "We should not delude ourselves that like Perseus of mythology we can put on neutrality as a helmet and render ourselves invisible and immune to a world in conflict around us." See Allen W. Dulles, "The Cost of Peace," *Foreign Affairs* 12 (1934): 578.

58   More broadly, Roosevelt's views about foreign affairs in the 1930s remain opaque and contested among historians. A useful, if now dated, overview can be found in Brian McKercher, "Reaching for the Brass Ring: The Recent His-toriography of American Foreign Relations," in *Paths to Power: The Historiog-*

raphy of American Foreign Relations to 1941, ed. Michael J. Hogan (Cambridge: Cambridge University Press, 2000), pp. 176–223.

59 Franklin D. Roosevelt, "Address at San Diego Exposition," October 2, 1935, in *The Public Papers and Addresses of Franklin D. Roosevelt,* vol. 4 (New York: Random House, 1938), p. 410.

60 The committee reported its findings on February 24, 1936, after hearing from more than two hundred witnesses at ninety-three hearings. Nye's career was marked by a passion for agrarian reform and a suspicion of big business. A thoughtful consideration can be found in Wayne S. Cole, *Senator Gerald P. Nye and American Foreign Relations* (Minneapolis: University of Minnesota Press, 1962). The committee's chief investigator was Dorothy Detzer, the head of the Women's International League for Peace and Freedom (WILPF); her key aide was Alger Hiss. See Woito, "Between the Wars," p. 113; Divine, *The Illusion of Neutrality,* pp. 66–67.

61 At San Diego, Roosevelt had noted, "It is not surprising that many of our citizens feel a deep sense of apprehension lest some of the Nations of the world repeat the folly of twenty years ago and drag civilization to a level from which world-wide recovery may be all but impossible." See Roosevelt, "Address at San Diego Exposition," p. 410.

The nay votes were cast by two Democrats—Peter Gerry of Rhode Island, and John Bankhead of Alabama. Of the fifteen senators who did not vote, three were from the South: Theodore Bilbo of Mississippi, Harry Byrd of Virginia, and John Overton of Louisiana.

62 *Congressional Record,* 74th Cong., 1st sess., August 20, 1936, p. 13782.

63 This worry was articulated most strongly by Democratic senators Thomas Connally of Texas and Thomas Gore of Oklahoma. See ibid., August 23 and 24, 1935, pp. 14283, 14433.

64 Ibid., 2d sess., February 17, 1936, p. 2247.

65 Ibid., p. 2256.

66 Ibid., March 19, 1936, p. 4055.

67 This "I Hate War" speech in Chautauqua, New York, on August 14, 1936, did cautiously place limits on the administration's stance. "We are not isolationists except insofar as we seek to isolate ourselves completely from war" was how he put the point, adding, "We must remember that so long as war exists on earth there will be some danger that even the Nation which most ardently desires peace may be drawn into war." See William D. Pederson, *The FDR Years* (New York: Facts on File, 2006), p. 352

68 *New York Times,* January 6, 1937. Most of this shipment, which left New York a day before Congress acted, was sunk by Nationalist forces some ninety miles from Spain in early March. See *Washington Post,* March 9, 1937.

69 *Congressional Record,* 75th Cong., 1st sess., January 6, 1937, p. 73.

70 Ibid., p. 74.

71   Ibid., pp. 92–93.

72   The single negative vote was cast by John Bernard, a Farmer-Labor representative from Minnesota.

73   *Washington Post,* January 8, 1937.

74   The Foreign Policy Association reported in February that, having doubled between 1934 and the end of 1936, world expenditures on weapons stood "at three times the figure on the eve of the World War." Nazi Germany's 1936 expenditure of $2,660,000,000 was seven times that of 1934, and the Soviet Union's $2,983,100,000 represented a tripling during that period. U.S. spending had remained nearly flat, increasing from $710,000,000 in 1934 to $964,000,000 in 1936, roughly the same as Italy's $871,000,000, itself a jump from the $272,000,000 in 1934. See *Washington Post,* February 15, 1937. In all, global arms expenditures between 1931 and 1936 had topped $60 billion, a spending rate four times as great as on the eve of World War I, and "about 8 billion dollars more than the world production of gold since Columbus discovered America." See *Chicago Daily Tribune,* May 23, 1937.

75   The House passed the conference report on April 29 by a voice vote; the Senate passed it by a 41–15 margin.

76   *Los Angeles Times,* April 30, 1937.

77   For discussions, see Dallek, *Franklin D. Roosevelt and American Foreign Policy,* p. 102; Divine, *The Illusion of Neutrality,* p. 95. For a contemporaneous consideration of the era's heterogeneous peace movement, see Arthur Deerin Call, "The Contribution of the War Policies Commission to the Peace Movement," *Advocate of Peace through Justice* 93 (1931): 87–94.

78   *Congressional Record,* 75th Cong., 1st sess., March 16, 1937, p. 2298. For an extended discussion, see Divine, *The Illusion of Neutrality,* pp. 162–99.

79   Anne O'Hare McCormick, "Foreign Policy: The Neutrality Act and the Reciprocal Trade Compact," *New York Times,* August 9, 1937.

80   *Los Angeles Times,* February 3, 1938. There had been much speculation that the president would be unable to avoid an absolute ban on arms shipments under the terms of the act once Japan had declared war. *Los Angeles Times,* January 11, 1938.

81   *New York Times,* April 23, 1938.

82   Ibid., March 20, 1938.

83   Emil Lederer, "Domestic Policy and Foreign Relations," in *War in Our Time,* ed. Hans Speier and Alfred Kahler (New York: W.W. Norton, 1939), pp. 43–57.

84   Michael Howard, *The Invention of Peace: Reflections on War and International Order* (London: Profile Books, 2000), p. 68.

85   A superb account of these changes that was written at the time can be found in W. Friedmann, "International Law and the Present War," *Transactions of the Grotius Society* 26 (1940): 211–33.

86   For this formulation, I am indebted to John Thompson's views about conceptions of American security before World War II.

87   Frank Ninkovich, *The Wilsonian Century: U.S. Foreign Policy since 1900* (Chicago: University of Chicago Press, 1999), p. 119.

88   Hans Speier and Alfred Kahler, "Introduction," in *War in Our Time,* ed. Speier and Kahler, p. 11.

89   As an indicator of how completely the hopes for collective security, especially by smaller states, had been dashed, the Oslo Powers (Denmark, Norway, Sweden, Finland, the Netherlands, Belgium, and Luxemburg), which met in Copenhagen in July 1938, "expressed their willingness to cooperate in the work of the League of Nations, but made it understood at the same time that . . . the provisions of Article XVI concerning the sanctions to be applied against an aggressor state to have acquired a non-compulsory character." See Eric Hula, "The European Neutrals," *Social Research* 7, no. 1 (1940): 151, 157.

90   With Nazi domination in Europe and Japanese domination in Asia, "present actuality," the émigré legal scholar Eric Hula remarked in an article written in 1939, "is the abuse of the word neutrality, whenever and wherever an outrageous act is committed and tolerated." See Hula, "The European Neutrals," p. 168.

91   Friedmann, "International Law and the Present War," p. 229.

92   Cited in Georg Schwarzenberger, "The Rule of Law and the Disintegration of the International Society," *American Journal of International Law* 33 (1939): 57–58.

93   Walter Lippmann, "The American Destiny," *Life,* June 5, 1939, p. 47.

94   Frederick L. Schuman, "World Politics and America's Destiny," in *The Future of Government in the United States: Essays in Honor of Charles E. Merriam,* ed. Leonard D. White (Chicago: University of Chicago Press, 1942), pp. 245, 250, 251.

95   "If we merely *want* victory, making no great effort to find the price or disputing the bill," Denis Brogan, the Scottish student of the United States, wrote in 1942, "we go the way of admirable societies which died because they were politically inadequate to the cruel necessities of the times in which their fate was decided." See D. W. Brogan, "A Political Scientist and World Problems," *Annals of the American Academy of Political and Social Science* 222 (1942): 20.

96   DeConde, "On Twentieth-Century Isolationism," pp. 3–4, 8.

97   *Washington Post,* April 1, 1938.

98   Lawrence Preuss, "The Concepts of Neutrality and Nonbelligerency," *Annals of the American Academy of Political and Social Science* 218 (1941): 101.

99   D. W. Brogan, "Omens of 1936," *Edinburgh Review* 139 (1936): 1–2; cited in Richard Overy, *The Morbid Age: Britain and the Crisis of Civilization, 1919–1939* (London: Penguin, 2009), p. 315.

100   Cited in Martin Gilbert, *A History of the Twentieth Century,* vol. 2, *1933–1951* (New York: William Morrow, 1998), p. 225.

101   Franklin D. Roosevelt, "Annual Message to Congress," January 4, 1939, in *Nothing to Fear: The Selected Addresses of Franklin Delano Roosevelt, 1932–1945,* ed. B. D. Zevin (Boston: Houghton Mifflin, 1946), pp. 163, 165. These themes

were not entirely new. In an October 5, 1937, Chicago speech, FDR had recommended a "quarantine" of aggressor nations in circumstances of growing lawlessness and military buildup by the dictatorships.

102   *Washington Post,* March 8, 1939.

103   Tom Connally (as told to Alfred Steinberg), *My Name Is Tom Connally* (New York: Thomas Y. Crowell, 1954), p. 226.

104   *Atlanta Constitution,* April 9, 1939.

105   Francis O. Wilcox, "American Government and Politics: The Neutrality Fight in Congress 1939," *American Political Science Review* 33 (1939): 825.

106   It excluded more remote implements of war, a move Congressman Vorys argued was a fair compromise.

107   With a southern Democratic-Republican likeness score of just 6, a nonsouthern Democratic-Republican likeness score of 22, and intraparty likeness for all Democrats at the level of 84.

108   When the House voted on the proposal to recommit, Republicans were unanimous, achieving a maximum cohesion score of 100, but nonsouthern Democrats were divided, with a cohesion score of just 57. By contrast, southern Democratic cohesion scored a high 88. When the bill passed, Republican cohesion was at a lofty level of 93, but nonsouthern Democrats remained divided at 56. Passage required southern cohesion in favor, scored at 92.

109   *Congressional Record,* 76th Cong., 1st sess., June 30, 1939, p. 8509.

110   *New York Times,* July 8, 1939; *Chicago Daily Tribune,* July 12, 1939.

111   *Washington Post,* July 13, 1939.

112   *New York Times,* July 19, 1939; *Chicago Daily Tribune,* July 19, 1939.

113   "Is Neutrality Possible?" *Washington Post,* September 2, 1939. The importance to congressional action of the start of the European phase of World War II is discussed in Porter, *The Seventy-sixth Congress and World War II,* pp. 173–74.

114   Australia and New Zealand as well, for they went to war when Britain did.

115   *Washington Post,* September 4, 1939. He spoke of the "proclamation required by the existing neutrality act. I trust that in the days to come our neutrality can be made a true neutrality."

116   Franklin D. Roosevelt to Neville Chamberlain, in *F.D.R.: His Personal Letters,* vol. 2, *1928-1945,* ed. Elliott Roosevelt (New York: Duell, Sloan, and Pearce, 1950), p. 919.

117   *Los Angeles Times,* September 21, 1939.

118   *New York Times,* September 22, 1939; *Los Angeles Times,* September 25, 1939.

119   *Washington Post,* September 22, 1939.

120   *New York Times,* September 22, 1939. On Senator George, see *Atlanta Constitution,* September 26, 1939.

121   The percentage of voters approving Roosevelt's performance stood at 52 percent in the mid-Atlantic and 53 percent in the Midwest, but at 72 percent in the South. See *Atlanta Constitution,* September 22, 1939.

122   *Chicago Daily Tribune,* September 16, 1941.

123 Ibid., September 23, 1939.

124 *New York Times,* October 28, 1939.

125 *Wall Street Journal,* October 2, 1939.

126 *Congressional Record,* 76th Cong., 2nd sess., November 2, 1939, p. 1339.

127 Divine, *The Illusion of Neutrality,* p. 330. The positive vote gained support from 220 Democrats, 21 Republicans, 1 Farmer-Labor member, and 1 American Laborite. The negative vote was backed by 36 Democrats, 143 Republicans, and 2 Progressives.

128 *Congressional Record,* 76th Cong., 1st sess., June 30, 1939, p. 8059.

129 Ibid., 2d sess., October 14, 1939, p. 438; October 20, 1939, pp. 653, 654.

130 Divine, *The Illusion of Neutrality,* p. 334.

131 *New York Times,* November 10, 1939; for an overview of the act, see Guerra Everett, "The Neutrality Act of 1939," *Annals of the American Academy of Political and Social Science* 211 (1940): 95–101.

132 Edward R. Stettinius Jr., *Lend-Lease: Weapon for Victory* (New York: Macmillan, 1944), pp. 89–108; Warren F. Kimball, *The Most Unsordid Act: Lend-Lease, 1939–1941* (Baltimore: Johns Hopkins University Press, 1969), pp. 57–118; Max Hastings, *Winston's War: Churchill, 1940–1945* (New York: Vintage, 2011), pp. 147–49; Roberts, *Masters and Commanders,* p. 46.

133 Mark Sullivan, "Lend-Lease Status," *Washington Post,* February 1, 1941.

134 Kimball, *The Most Unsordid Act,* pp. 207, 217.

135 See http://historicalresources.wordpress.com/2009/01/01/franklin-delano -roosevelt-on-land-lease-march-15-1941/.

136 Walter Lippman, "Today and Tomorrow: If the Worst Happens," *Washington Post,* February 6, 1941.

137 *Wall Street Journal,* May 24, 1940, p. 1; Stettinius succeeded Cordell Hull as secretary of state in 1944, chaired the American delegation to the United Nations Conference on International Organization in the spring of 1945, and served as the country's first ambassador to the UN. In August 1939, President Roosevelt had created a War Resources Board (WRB), which was chaired by Stettinius and included Walter Sherman Gifford, the head of AT&T; John Lee Pratt, who served on the board of General Motors; Robert E. Wood, the chairman of Sears Roebuck; Harold Moulton, president of the Brookings Institution; and the physicist Karl Compton, who was president of MIT. This group was short-lived; on November 24, the president thanked its members for their service, bringing it to a close. For a discussion, see Paul A. C. Koistinen, "The Industrial-Military Complex in Historical Perspective: The Interwar Years," *Journal of American History* 56 (1970): 836–38.

138 Janeway, *The Struggle for Survival,* p. 100.

139 Ibid., p. 12.

140 *Congressional Record,* 76th Cong., 3d sess., May 24, 1940, p. 6837.

141 Ibid., p. 6829.

142 Ibid., June 10, 1940, p. 7823.

143 Ibid., June 6, 1940, p. 7650.

144 This near unanimity fell apart in votes on naval appropriations, which included a big investment in facilities in Guam. Republicans balked, proposing amendments to confine naval spending closer to home. In the House debate, Arthur Jenks of New Hampshire found it "beyond me to understand why we would want or need to have either Navy or Army planes scouting for purposes of protection some 5,000 miles away from the Pacific coast line of our country," and Robert Rich of Pennsylvania complained about the "item in the bill to improve Guam, near the Chinese coast. Let us give the island away before our improvements and fortification gets us into war. Let us stay away from Europe, Asia, and Africa in any possessions of real estate." See *Congressional Record,* 76th Cong., 3d sess., February 13, 1940, pp. 1437, 1421. On a straight party-line vote, the House rejected isolationist amendments by votes of 158–230 and 156–234.

145 "Arming America," *New York Times,* June 2, 1940.

146 *Congressional Record,* 77th Cong., 1st sess., August 1, 1941, p. 6590.

147 Cited in Dallek, *Franklin D. Roosevelt and American Foreign Policy,* pp. 290–91.

148 The term comes from the Latin *conscribere milites.* For a discussion of the history of the conscript system, including how it had become common in Continental Europe before World War I, see Herman Beukema, "Social and Political Aspects of Conscription: Europe's Experience," *Military Affairs* 5 (1941): 21–31.

149 For discussions, see George Q. Flynn, *The Draft, 1940–1973* (Lawrence: University Press of Kansas, 1993); George Q. Flynn, "Conscription and Equity in Western Democracies, 1940–1975," *Journal of Contemporary History* 33 (1998): 5–20; Harrop A. Freeman, "The Constitutionality of Wartime Conscription," *Virginia Law Review* 31 (1944), 40–82; Elliot Jay Feldman, "An Illusion of Power: Military Conscription as a Dilemma of Liberal Democracy in Great Britain, the United States, and France" (Ph.D. dissertation, MIT, 1972).

150 Ira Katznelson, "Flexible Capacity: The Military and Early American State-building," in *Shaped by War and Trade: International Influences on American Political Development,* ed. Ira Katznelson and Martin Shefter (Princeton, NJ: Princeton University Press, 2002), pp. 82–110; Margaret Levi, *Consent, Dissent, and Patriotism* (Cambridge: Cambridge University Press, 1997), pp. 58–66, 96–102.

151 Cited in Sherry, *In the Shadow of War,* p. 45.

152 Beukema, "Social and Political Aspects of Conscription," p. 29; Philip Jowett, *The Japanese Army, 1931–1945* (Oxford: Osprey Publishing, 2002); *New York Times,* May 10, 1940.

153 *Washington Post,* August 18, 1940; *Chicago Daily Tribune,* June 20 and August 29, 1940; *Los Angeles Times,* November 7, 1940.

154 *Los Angeles Times,* July 9, 1940.

155 *Washington Post,* July 4, 1940. Harvard University president James Conant tes-

tified that there is "no method of building an army in a free democracy more efficient and more just than that of compulsory selective service." Another visible university president, Henry Wriston of Brown, opposed conscription as "the tragic prelude to war." See ibid., September 9, 1940.

156 *Atlanta Constitution,* September 19, 1940.
157 *Congressional Record,* 76th Cong., 2d sess., September 3, 1940, p. 11363. Similarly, a front-page *Washington Post* editorial described the conscription bill as "the most important measure to come before Congress in a long time." See *Washington Post,* August 4, 1940. Passions ran high. During the House debate, Martin Sweeney, an isolationist Democrat from Ohio, "landed a hard right" to the nose of Beverly Vincent of Kentucky, who had called Sweeney a "traitor" for his views. See Ibid., September 5, 1940.
158 *Atlanta Constitution,* March 21, 1938.
159 *Congressional Record,* 76th Cong., 2d sess., September 3, 1940, p. 11381.
160 Ibid., September 4, 1940, p. 11482.
161 *New York Times,* August 26, 1940.
162 "States where conscription sentiment has reached the greatest peaks are Mississippi (87 percent), Texas (80 percent), Georgia (79 percent), and Florida (75 percent), well above the national average of 66 percent, and a good deal higher than in skeptical Indiana (55 percent)." See *Atlanta Constitution,* August 11, 1940.
163 *Congressional Record,* 76th Cong., 2d sess., September 3, 1940, pp. 11363, 11387, 11401; September 4, 1940, p. 11426; September 3, 1940, p. 11400.
164 Ibid., September 4, 1940, p. 11489.
165 Their cohesion scores were a nearly unanimous 98, 94, and 93. By contrast, Republicans and nonsouthern Democrats were internally divided, with cohesion scores, respectively, of 76, 37, and 31, and 70, 58, and 55.
166 For an overview, see J. Garry Clifford and Samuel R. Spencer Jr., *The First Peacetime Draft* (Lawrence: University Press of Kansas, 1986). When the Senate voted overwhelmingly to restrict draftees to the Western Hemisphere (67–4, on an amendment proposed by Massachusetts Republican Henry Cabot Lodge, who later was one of eight Republicans who supported conscription in that chamber), it rejected a more restrictive measure advanced by one of the few southern Democratic isolationists, Bennett Champ Clark of Missouri, that would have limited the use of conscripts to the United States and its possessions. That vote was close, 32–39, and would have passed without overwhelming southern opposition. See *Washington Post,* August 27, 1940. On reports of German subversion in the Western Hemisphere, see Dallek, *Franklin D. Roosevelt and American Foreign Policy,* p. 233.
167 The largest category of rejected persons was declared ineligible because of defective teeth. See *Chicago Daily Tribune,* February 17, 1941; Sherry, *In the Shadow of War,* p. 48. On literacy, see *Atlanta Constitution,* May 4, 1941.

168   For a discussion, see Ira Katznelson, *When Affirmative Action Was White: An Untold History of Racial Inequality in Twentieth-Century America* (New York: W. W. Norton, 2005), pp. 95–102.

169   On how the new army was put together, and the difficulties it faced, see Gregory, *America 1941,* pp. 25–49.

170   *Atlanta Constitution,* July 5, 1941; *New York Times,* July 22, 1944; Dallek, *Franklin D. Roosevelt and American Foreign Policy,* p. 277.

171   *Congressional Record,* 77th Cong., 1st sess., August 1, 1941, p. 6579.

172   On July 26, 1941.

173   *Congressional Record,* 77th Cong., 1st sess., August 1, 1941, p. 6591.

174   For a summary of these arguments, see Elias Huzar, "Selective Service Policy, 1940–1942," *Journal of Politics* 4 (1942): 221.

175   *Congressional Record,* 77th Cong., 1st sess., August 7, 1941, p. 6851.

176   The least cohesive bloc was that of nonsouthern Democrats, who scored only 37. By contrast, both Republicans, at 71, and southern Democrats, at 83, exhibited significant cohesion.

177   The majority was composed of less than half the chamber's members; twenty-one chose not to vote. Fully "thirty percent of the Democrats, including mainly members from states west of the Mississippi River," voted no, as they "equated the peacetime draft with forced regimentation and preferred voluntary enlistment." Democratic aye votes were predominantly southern. They were joined by Republicans, "particularly those from New England and the Middle Atlantic states" who "supported peacetime selective service." See Porter, *Seventy-sixth Congress and World War II,* p. 179.

178   *Los Angeles Times,* August 13, 1941. This was not a popular bill. "Strong popular opposition to this revision of the draft law almost gave the anti-militarist forces a belated victory as the House approved the extension by a margin of only one vote. While the people wanted the boys back home, the soliders who had been promised a one-year tour of duty were often the most bitter of all." See Arthur A. Ekirch Jr., *The Civilian and the Military* (New York: Oxford University Press, 1956), p. 261.

179   From within the South, only Missouri's Democrats, four of six, voted in the negative. They were joined by the state's three Republicans.

180   See http://www.historyplace.com/speeches/fdr-infamy.htm.

181   Both negative votes were cast by California's senators Sheridan Downey, a Democrat, and Hiram Johnson, a Republican.

182   *Congressional Record,* 77th Cong., 1st sess., December 17, 1941, p. 9943; December 18, 1941, p. 9985.

183   Walter Lippmann, "Today and Tomorrow: Wake Up, America," *Washington Post,* December 9, 1941, p. 19.

CHAPTER 9 · UNRESTRICTED WAR

1   George Catlett Marshall, *The Papers of George Catlett Marshall,* vol. 3, *"The Right Man for the Job," December 7, 1941–May 31, 1943* (Baltimore: Johns Hopkins University Press, 1991), p. 214. This sentence is carved on the Washington Mall's National World War II Memorial. Marshall was appointed to his chief of staff post on September 1, 1939.

2   Edward Meade Earle, "American Military Policy and National Security," *Political Science Quarterly* 53 (1938): 2.

3   Clinton L. Rossiter, ed., *The Federalist Papers* (New York, Mentor Books, 1999), p. 35.

4   Emil Lederer, "Domestic Policy and Foreign Relations," in *War in Our Time,* ed. Hans Speier and Alfred Kähler (New York: W. W. Norton, 1939), p. 56.

5   Edward Meade Earle, "National Defense and Political Science," *Political Science Quarterly* 55 (1940): 487, 495. A useful overview that considers the pioneering work by Earle and other scholars in the late 1930s and early 1940s concerning liberal democracy and matters of might and international relations is Gene M. Lyons, "The Growth of National Security Research," *Journal of Politics* 25 (1963): 489–508. See also Gene M. Lyons, *The Uneasy Partnership: Social Science and the Federal Government in the Twentieth Century* (New York: Russell Sage Foundation, 1969).

6   Harold D. Lasswell, "The Garrison State," *American Journal of Sociology* 46 (1941): 467.

7   General Frank R. McCoy, "Foreword," in *Mobilizing Civilian America*, by Harold J. Tobin and Percy W. Bidwell (New York: Council on Foreign Relations, 1940), pp. vi, vii. McCoy, who had served in the Spanish-American War, including the Battle of San Juan Hill; the Philippine-American War, where he was an aide to Governor-General Leonard Wood; and World War I, where he was a member of the General Staff of the American Expeditionary Forces.

8   Tobin and Bidwell, *Mobilizing Civilian America,* pp. 75–222, 226, 225, 227–30.

9   Other countries joined before Pearl Harbor. These included Hungary, Romania, Bulgaria, Slovakia, Yugoslavia, and Croatia.

10   See http://www.presidency.ucsb.edu/ws/index.php?pid=16056#axzz1OTlT29Jg.

11   Hitler, at this moment, was expressing contempt for the United States. "I don't see much future for the Americans," he told a gathering at his headquarters on January 7, 1942. "It's a decayed country. . . . My feelings against Americanism are feelings of hatred and deep repugnance. . . . Everything about the behavior of American society reveals that it's half Judaized, and the other half Negrified. How can one expect a State like that to hold together—a country where everything is built on the dollar." See William Shirer, *Rise and Fall of the Third Reich* (New York: Simon & Schuster, 1960), p. 895.

12   See http://www.ibiblio.org/pha/timeline/411211awp.html.

13 See http://www.mhric.org/fdr/chat17.html. After the outbreak of the European war, Roosevelt had issued a proclamation of limited emergency, on September 8, 1939, declaring "that a national emergency exists in connection with and to the extent necessary for the proper observance, safeguarding, and enforcing of the neutrality of the United States and the strengthening of our national defense within the limits of peacetime authorizations." See http://www.lawandfreedom.com/site/executive/execorders/Roosevelt.pdf.

14 For an important discussion that highlights the significance of the Atlantic Charter as the moment when a global quest for human rights was born, see Elizabeth Borgwardt, *A New Deal for the World: America's Vision for Human Rights* (Cambridge: Harvard University Press, 2005).

15 Archibald MacLeish, "The People Are Indivisible," *Nation,* October 28, 1944, p. 509.

16 See http://www.mhric.org/fdr/chat19.html.

17 Robert Dallek, *Franklin D. Roosevelt and American Foreign Policy, 1932–1945* (New York: Oxford University Press, 1995), p. 287.

18 Writing a decade later, Arnold Wolfers offered a particularly thoughtful consideration of "'National Security' as an Ambiguous Symbol," *Political Science Quarterly* 67 (1952): 481–502. He stressed how "decision makers are faced with the moral problem . . . of choosing first the values which deserve protection, with national independence ranking high not merely for its own sake but for the guarantee it may offer to values like liberty, justice and peace. He must further decide which level of security to make his target. . . . Finally, he must choose the means" (p. 500).

19 See http://docs.fdrlibrary.marist.edu/052640.html. "The term 'fifth column' was coined by a Fascist general who boasted of his strength: General Mola, when he was closing in on Madrid with four columns of his army, declared that he had a fifth one within the gates of the city." See Hans Speier, "Treachery in War," *Social Research* 7 (1940): 258.

20 *New York Times,* September 24, 1940.

21 Athan G. Theoharis and John Stuart Cox, *The Boss: J. Edgar Hoover and the Great American Inquisition* (Philadelphia: Temple University Press, 1988), pp. 169–71.

22 Dallek, *Franklin D. Roosevelt and American Foreign Policy,* p. 225; Michael S. Sherry, *In the Shadow of War: The United States since the 1930s* (New Haven: Yale University Press, 1995), pp. 51–52.

23 Dallek, *Franklin D. Roosevelt and American Foreign Policy,* p. 290.

24 Paul A. C. Koistinen, "The 'Industrial-Military Complex' in Historical Perspective: The InterWar Years," *Journal of American History* 56 (1970): 823–24, 826, 827.

25 Sherry, *In the Shadow of War,* p. 43.

26 W. Eliot Brownlee, "Social Investigation and Political Learning in the Financ-

ing of World War I," in *The State and Social Investigation in Britain and the United States*, ed. Michael Lacey and Mary O. Furner (Cambridge: Cambridge University Press, 1993); Grosvenor B. Clarkson, *Industrial America during the World War: The Strategy behind the Line, 1917–1918* (Boston: Houghton Mifflin, 1923); Robert D. Cuff, *The War Industries Board: Business-Government Relations during World War I* (Baltimore: Johns Hopkins University Press, 1971); Paul A. C. Koistinen, *Mobilizing for Modern War: The Political Economy of American Warfare, 1865–1919* (Lawrence: University Press of Kansas, 1997).

27   Fireside chat, December 29, 1940; available at http://www.mhric.org/fdr/chat16.html.

28   See http://www.mhric.org/fdr/chat14.html.

29   See http://www.mhric.org/fdr/chat20.html.

30   See http://www.mhric.org/fdr/chat21.html.

31   The only issue that generated significant Republican opposition, in a 249–86 roll call, was the proposal to create a Women's Auxiliary Corps in the army. In the Senate, questions about agricultural draft deferments generated some controversy, but otherwise cross-partisanship also easily prevailed. Even matters like price control, which ordinarily would have been resisted by Republican members, passed the Senate in January 1942 by a vote of 84–1.

32   See http://www.mhric.org/fdr/chat16.html.

33   Here I draw on Judith N. Shklar, "Obligation, Loyalty, Exile," *Political Theory* 21 (1993): 181–97.

34   See http://www.lawandfreedom.com/site/executive/execorders/Roosevelt.pdf.

35   For an overview, see Clinton Rossiter, *Constitutional Dictatorship: Crisis Government in Modern Democracies* (Princeton, NJ: Princeton University Press, 1948), pp. 240–54.

36   Christopher Capozzola, *Uncle Sam Wants You: World War I and the Making of the Modern American Citizen* (New York: Oxford University Press, 2008), p. 188.

37   John Sparks, "Civil Liberties in the Present Crisis," *Antioch Review* 2 (1942): 134; James R. Mock, *Censorship, 1917* (Princeton, NJ: Princeton University Press, 1941). Writing about the public's response to the Sedition Act of 1918, Mock observed how "the war was the center of national attention," and how "questions of freedom of speech and of the press were not newsworthy" (p. 54).

38   Capozzola's *Uncle Sam Wants You* is the best treatment of repression during World War I. See also William Preston Jr., *Aliens and Dissenters: Federal Suppression of Radicals, 1903–1933* (Cambridge: Harvard University Press, 1963), which is particularly useful in its account of postwar deportations and the anti-Communist Palmer Raids.

39   John Andrew Costello, "Congress and Internal Security: The Overman Committee, 1918–1919" (M.A. thesis, American University, 1965), Richard L. Watson, "Principle, Party, and Constituency: The North Carolina Congressional

Delegation, 1917–1919," *North Carolina Historical Review* 56 (1959): 298–323; Regin Schmidt, *Red Scare: FBI and the Origins of Anti-Communism in the United States, 1919–1943* (Copenhagen: Museum Tusculanum Press, 2000), pp. 136–46.

40   It collected published and unpublished materials, created files on some 60,000 persons within four weeks (200,000 within four months), and began to infiltrate the Communist Party USA, which was founded that year. See Max Lowenthal, *The Federal Bureau of Investigation* (New York: William Sloane Associates, 1950), pp. 83–93; Cappozola, *Uncle Sam Wants You,* p. 202. See also Preston Jr., *Aliens and Dissenters.*

41   Hoover had been serving as director of the Bureau since 1924. It was designated as the FBI in 1935.

42   By getting the State Department into the act, it became possible to bypass existing statutory limitations on the activities of the FBI, since the wartime Appropriations Act of 1916, "which was still on the books, allowed the bureau to use its funds for investigations requested by the secretary of state, even if no violations of law had yet occurred." See Jay Feldman, *Manufacturing Hysteria: A History of Scapegoating, Surveillance, and Secrecy in Modern America* (New York: Pantheon, 2011), p. 151.

43   Athan Theoharis, *The FBI and American Democracy: A Brief Critical History* (Lawrence: University Press of Kansas, 2004), p. 45–47.

44   Robert Edwin Herzstein, *Roosevelt and Hitler: Prelude to War* (New York: Paragon House, 1989).

45   Cited in Jeffrey R. Stone, *Perilous Times: Free Speech in Wartime, from the Sedition Act of 1798 to the War on Terrorism* (New York: W. W. Norton, 2004), p. 285.

46   Kenneth O'Reilly, "The Roosevelt Administration and Black America: Federal Surveillance Policy and Civil Rights during the New Deal and World War II Years," *Phylon* 48 (1987): 20.

47   Speier, "Treachery in War," p. 259.

48   Bob Kumamoto, "The Search for Spies: American Counterintelligence and the Japanese-American Community, 1931–1943." *Amerasia Journal* 6 (1979): 49.

49   Greg Robinson, *A Tragedy of Democracy: Japanese Confinement in North America* (New York: Columbia University Press, 2009), p. 47.

50   Rhodri Jeffreys-Jones, *The FBI: A History* (New Haven: Yale University Press, 2007), p. 107; Lowenthal, *The Federal Bureau of Investigation,* p. 425; James T. Sparrow, *Warfare State: World War II Americans and the Age of Big Government* (New York: Oxford University Press, 2011), p. 83. For an overview of anti-Communism in the 1930s, see Richard Gid Powers, *Not without Honor: The History of American Anti-Communism* (New York: Free Press, 1995), pp. 117–54.

51   Stone, *Perilous Times,* p. 285.

52 *New York Times,* January 18, 1931.

53 Martin Dies Sr., who represented Texas's Second District from 1909 to 1919, was best known for his nativist views. He spoke often about the wrong kind of foreigners, Catholic and Jewish, who were coming to America. The son's political life came to reflect many of the father's ideas. Both were haunted by southern parochialism, nativism, and an isolationism that, in retrospect, made the father look wise indeed during World War I but that led the son (along with a lot of other people) to support a disastrous isolationism in the 1930s. See Dennis McDaniel, "The First Congressman Martin Dies of Texas," *Southwestern Historical Quarterly* 102 (1998): 156.

54 He continued, "That burr-headed wife of DePriest may be good enough for Mrs. Herbert Hoover, but I'll tell you here and now that she's not good enough for you and your wife nor me and mine." See *Chicago Defender,* July 26, 1930.

55 Cited in Ted Morgan, *Reds: McCarthyism in Twentieth-Century America* (New York: Random House, 2003), p. 186. In 1942, Dies ran unsuccessfully in a June 1941 special election for an open Senate seat following the death of Morris Sheppard, a contest, won by Governor Wilbert Lee "Pappy" O'Daniel, in which the winner was trailed by Congressman Lyndon Johnson by just over a thousand votes.

56 Its full name was the Special Committee to Investigate Un-American Activities and Propaganda in the United States.

57 For a discussion of the McCormick-Dickstein committee, see Walter Goodman, *The Committee: The Extraordinary Career of the House Committee on Un-American Activities* (New York: Farrar, Straus and Giroux, 1968), pp. 3–23. A contemporaneous and adulatory treatment of Dickstein can be found in Dorothy Waring, *American Defender* (New York: Robert Speller, 1935). Though a Tammany Hall Democrat, he was supported when he first ran for the House in 1922 by the local Republican Party in order to defeat the Socialist House member, Meyer London. For a consideration of the largely unsuccessful attempt by the Nazi movement to rally German-Americans to their cause, see Sander A. Diamond, *The Nazi Movement in the United States, 1924–1941* (Ithaca, NY: Cornell University Press, 1974). Dickstein, we now know from the Venona transcripts, was almost certainly a Soviet spy between 1937 and 1940, having volunteered his services at Washington's Soviet embassy. His monthly stipend of $1,250 in exchange for mostly useless information led Soviet authorities to assign "Crook" as his code name. See Allen Weinstein and Alexander Vassiliev, *The Haunted Wood: Soviet Espionage in America— the Stalin Era* (New York: Random House, 1999), pp. 142–48. Dickstein, who had been born in Lithuania, represented the Lower East Side of New York City in Congress.

58 D. A. Saunders, "The Dies Committee: First Phase," *Public Opinion Quarterly* 3 (1939): 229–30.

59   Michael Wreszin, "The Dies Committee 1938," in *Congress Investigates: A Documented History, 1792–1974,* vol. 4, ed. Arthur M. Schlesinger Jr. and Roger Bruns (New York: Chelsea House, 1975) pp. 2930, 2929. The two nonsouthern liberal Democrats on the committee, John Dempsey of New Mexico and Arthur Healey of Massachusetts missed most of the committee's hearings, "compelled by the exigencies of seeking re-election to be absent." See *New York Times,* January 8, 1939.

60   This theme emerges in the contemporaneous overview by Father August Raymond Ogden, *The Dies Committee: A Study of the Special House Committee for the Investigation of Un-American Activities, 1938–1943* (Washington, DC: Catholic University of America Press, 1945). See also Nancy Lynn Lopez, "Allowing Fears to Overwhelm Us: A Re-Examination of the House Special Committee on Un-American Activities" (Ph.D. dissertation, Rice University, 2002).

61   Saunders, "The Dies Committee," p. 233. Murphy, who had served as the last governor-general of the Philippines between 1933 and 1935, and the first U.S. high commissioner from 1935 to 1936, before his election as governor of Michigan, served as attorney general of the United States in 1939 and 1940, the year he became a justice of the Supreme Court, where he served until his death in July 1949. A strong supporter of civil liberties, Murphy delivered the keynote address to the Conference on Civil Liberties in the National Emergency, which was organized in 1939 by the American Civil Liberties Union. See Sidney Fine, *Frank Murphy: The Washington Years* (Ann Arbor: University of Michigan Press, 1984).

62   Morgan, *Reds,* p. 188.

63   Ibid., p. 206.

64   Ibid., pp. 214–16. During the run-up to the 1940 campaign, the future Republican candidate, Wendell Willkie, spoke out in defense of civil liberties and criticized the committee's handling of Earl Browder and Fritz Kuhn, the leader of the German-American Bund, in an article entitled "Fair Trial," *New Republic,* March 18, 1940, pp. 370–73. Willkie argued that "among the so-called great powers . . . the United States stands alone in its practice of the belief that the State is designed to serve and protect the liberties of the individual," and that "even a Nazi is still entitled—in America—to fair treatment under the law" (pp. 370, 371).

65   Stewart Henderson Britt and Selden C. Menefee, "Did the Publicity of the Dies Committee in 1938 Influence Public Opinion?," *Public Opinion Quarterly* 3 (1939): 449–57.

66   *New York Times,* January 5, 1939.

67   Walter Lippmann, *New York Post,* January 11, 1940; cited in Benjamin Ginzburg, *Rededication to Freedom* (New York: Simon & Schuster, 1959), p. 89.

68   Only Vito Marcantonio, who represented East Harlem in New York and had switched from the Republican Party to the American Labor Party before his

election to the House in 1938 (he had previously served from 1935 to 1937), spoke against the bill in the House.

69 Hadley Cantril, *Public Opinion, 1935–1946* (Westport, CT: Greenwood Press, 1951), p. 130. Strikingly, fully 40 percent of CIO union members backed drastic action.

70 Stone, *Perilous Times,* pp. 251–52.

71 By early 1941, the Department of Justice's press releases of January 10, 13, and 14 were reporting that a total of 4,912,817 aliens had registered under the provisions of the Smith Act. See *Monthly Labor Review,* March 1941, p. 666.

72 Athan Theoharis, "The Truman Administration and the Decline of Civil Liberties: The FBI's Success in Securing Authorization for a Preventive Detention Program," *Journal of American History* 64 (1978): 1012–13.

73 Stone, *Perilous Times,* p. 286; *Washington Post,* December 10, 1941.

74 Cited in Goodman, *The Committee,* p. 99.

75 Stone, *Perilous Times,* p. 275 (italics in original). The constitutional scholar Mark Graber has rightly reminded us that while wars in the United States have put restrictions on individual liberty, "some civil rights and liberties have been unaffected by war," and these can vary under different circumstances. The more the country requires mobilization, and the more its enemies stand for the elimination of rights, the more likely it is that citizen liberties will be preserved. Crucially, he adds, "the beneficiaries of the civil right or liberty are . . . identified as loyal Americans." This was precisely what was at stake in the civil liberties violations in World War II. See Mark A. Graber, "Counter-Stories: Maintaining and Expanding Civil Liberties in Wartime," in *The Constitution in Wartime: Beyond Alarmism and Complacency,* ed. Mark Tushnet (Durham, NC: Duke University Press, 2005), pp. 95, 97.

76 Michael Dobbs, *Saboteurs: The Nazi Raid on America* (New York: Alfred A. Knopf, 2004).

77 An important study is Louis W. Koenig, *The Presidency and the Crisis* (New York: King's Crown Press, 1944).

78 Albert L. Sturm, "Emergencies and the Presidency," *Journal of Politics* II (1949): 135.

79 Rebecca S. Shoemaker, *The White Court: Justices, Rulings, and Legacy* (Santa Barbara, CA: ABC-CLIO, 2004), p. 152.

80 Cited in Sturm, "Emergencies and the Presidency," pp. 121–44. This decision upheld the use of emergency power by the state of Minnesota to deal with housing's foreclosure crisis, despite the fact that emergencies do not create power for the state. The basis for government's violating existing contracts, the Court argued, is that emergency situations can justify the usage of already-existing powers that are not used in more settled times.

81 Edward Samuel Corwin, *Total War and the Constitution* (New York: Alfred A. Knopf, 1947), p. 37 (italics in original).

82   Matthew J. Dickinson, *Bitter Harvest: FDR, Presidential Power, and the Growth of the Presidential Branch* (New York: Cambridge University Press, 1999), pp. 172–73; Brian Waddell, *The War against the New Deal: World War II and American Democracy* (DeKalb: Northern Illinois University Press, 2001), p. 55.

83   See http://www.presidency.ucsb.edu/ws/index.php?pid=15806#axzz1aHyjbUYi.

84   See http://www.usmm.org/fdr/emergency.html.

85   *New York Times,* December 9, 1941.

86   For a discussion, see Arthur Schlesinger Jr., *The Imperial Presidency* (Boston: Houghton Mifflin, 1973), p. 113.

87   Corwin, *Total War and the Constitution,* p. 65 (italics in original). Christopher H. Pyle and Richard M. Pious call this event "the most aggressive assertion of the 'stewardship theory.'" See Pyle and Pious, *The President, Congress, and the Constitution: Power and Legitimacy in American Politics* (New York: Free Press, 1984), p. 72.

88   Sturm, "Emergencies and the Presidency," p. 134. The threat to act without congressional approval was not carried out. The mandate he wanted in order to stabilize prices and wages was conferred by passage, on October 2, of the Stabilization Act of 1942. The Office of Economic Stabilization and the fixing of prices and wages were announced the next day in the president's Executive Order 9250.

89   *New York Times,* September 8, 1942; *Chicago Daily Tribune,* September 8, 1942; *Los Angeles Times,* September 8, 1942.

90   Corwin, *Total War and the Constitution,* pp. 64, 65. This claim was identical to the definition of prerogative power that John Locke had offered in his *Second Treatise of Civil Government*: "This Power to act according to discretion, for the publick good, without the prescription of the Law, and sometimes against it." See John Locke, *Two Treatises of Government,* ed. Peter Laslett (Cambridge: Cambridge University Press, 1990), p. 375.

91   *Wall Street Journal,* December 16, 1941; *Washington Post,* December 17, 1941. Two days earlier, the president had celebrated the 150th anniversary of the ratification of the Bill of Rights, and contrasted its guarantees of freedom with Nazism's goal to "overthrow throughout the earth the great revolution of human liberty of which our American Bill of Rights is the mother charter." See *New York Times,* December 16, 1941.

92   Committee of Records of War Administration, Bureau of the Budget, *The United States at War: Development and Administration of the War Program by the Federal Government* (Washington, DC: U.S. Government Printing Office, 1946).

93   Ibid., pp. 220–21.

94   For histories of the agency, see Allen Irving Safiano, *The Office of War Information* (Ithaca, NY: Cornell University Press, 1968); Constance Ruth Lael, "The Office of War Information: The Integration of Foreign Policy and Foreign Propaganda, 1942–1945" (Ph.D. dissertation, Wake Forest University, 1978).

95 U.S. Constitution, Article 2, Section 2. For an overview, see Luther Gulick, "War Organization of the Federal Government," *American Political Science Review* 38 (1944): 166–79.

96 See https://pantherfile.uwm.edu/margo/www/govstat/secwpa.htm.

97 See http://historymatters.gmu.edu/d/5154. J. R. Minkel, "Confirmed: The U.S. Census Bureau Gave Up Names of Japanese Americans in WWII," *Scientific American,* March 30, 2007, p. 3; "Papers Show Census Role in WWII Camps," *USA Today,* March 30, 2007.

98 Roger Daniels, *The Politics of Prejudice: The Anti-Japanese Movement in California and the Struggle for Japanese Exclusion* (Berkeley: University of California Press, 1962), pp. 85–88, 91, 97, 105.

99 Robinson, *A Tragedy of Democracy,* p. 54.

100 Goodman, *The Committee,* pp. 128–29.

101 Morton Grodzins, *Americans Betrayed: Politics and the Japanese Evacuation* (Chicago: University of Chicago Press, 1949), pp. 19–128. For a discussion of the hardening of West Coast opinion in favor of removing all Japanese, including citizens, see *New York Times,* March 1, 1942.

102 Before the war, Japanese-Americans vigorously protested their second-class status, especially the unwillingness of the Pearl Harbor naval yard to hire them. See *Washington Post,* July 28, 1940. Some functions of civilian government were restored in March 1943. Under martial law, the government conducted tens of thousands of military trials, numbering 22,000 in 1942 alone, with convictions rates exceeding 99 percent. See Fred I. Israel, "Military Justice in Hawaii, 1941–1944," *Pacific Historical Review* 36 (1967): 243–67.

103 *Chicago Daily Tribune,* March 4, 1942.

104 See Stephen E. Ambrose and Robert H. Immerman, *Milton S. Eisenhower: Educational Statesman* (Baltimore: Johns Hopkins University Press, 1983). For a discussion of Canadian internment policies, see John Stanton, "Government Internment Policy, 1939–1945," *Labour/Le Travail* 31 (1993): 203–41.

105 "The government of the American Republic was a naked dictatorship for its 70,000 Japanese-American citizens of the Pacific Coast." See Rossiter, *Constitutional Dictatorship,* p. 283. By contrast, Italians and Germans were not removed from their homes because there was no equivalent pressure to do so from below, since political leaders, including President Roosevelt, thought the Japanese posed the greater danger as a racially inassimilable group, and because the number of potential internees numbered in the millions. For a discussion, see Feldman, *Manufacturing Hysteria,* pp. 179–80. Small numbers of Italian and German detainees were held during the war at Justice Department detention camps in Idaho, Montana, Texas, and New Mexico.

106 *Washington Post,* July 8, 1943. In addition to Robinson, *A Tragedy of Democracy,* which offers a comprehensive overview, see Roger Daniels, *Concentration Camps USA: Japanese Americans and World War II* (New York: Holt, Rinehart

and Winston, 1972); Roger Daniels, *Prisoners without Trial: Japanese Americans in World War II* (New York: Hill and Wang, 1993); Richard Drinnon, *Keeper of Concentration Camps: Dillson S. Meyer and American Racism* (Berkeley: University of California Press, 1987); and the discussion in David M. Kennedy, *Freedom from Fear: The American People in Depression and War, 1929–1945* (New York: Oxford University Press, 1999), pp. 748–60. A justification, written in the context of the recent "war on terror," is Michelle Malkin, *In Defense of Internment: The Case for 'Racial Profiling' in World War II and the War on Terror* (Washington, DC: Regnery Press, 2004).

107   Rossiter, *Constitutional Dictatorship,* p. 282.

108   There were challenges that reached the Supreme Court, which ruled in 1943 in *Hirabayashi v. United States* that curfews could be imposed on a national group that originated from a country at war with the United States; and in 1944 in *Korematsu v. United States* that the exclusion order of Executive Order 9066 was constitutional. Fred Korematsu had resisted the deportation order by fleeing with his girlfriend, an Italian-American. Caught, he was arrested in May 1942. Though freed on bail, he was sent to an internment camp in Utah. He then sued the government with the help of the American Civil Liberties Union, but he was unsuccessful. The case was decided by a 6–3 margin. Justice Hugo Black wrote for the majority, while Justice Frank Murphy, the former Michigan governor and U.S. attorney general, issued a notable dissent, referring to the internment as an instance that "falls into the ugly abyss of racism." For discussions, see Eugene V. Rostow, "The Japanese American Cases—A Disaster," *Yale Law Journal* 54 (1945): 489–535; Roger Daniels, "*Korematsu v. US* Revisited: 1944 and 1983," in *Race on Trial: Law and Justice in American History,* ed. Annette Gordon-Reed (New York: Oxford University Press, 2002). Korematsu was awarded the Presidential Medal of Freedom by President Clinton in 1998; he died in March 2005.

109   *Sparrow, Warfare State,* pp. 100–104. For a discussion of the paucity of focused debate at the time about Japanese internment and the absence of empirical attention to charges of treachery, see David Riesman, "The Present State of Civil Liberty Theory," *Journal of Politics* 6 (1944): 327–28. Though German nationals and German-Americans were not rounded up en masse, the Justice Department's Enemy Alien Control Program, whose remit extended to those of "enemy ancestry," interned 11,507 ethnic Germans, some citizens, and evicted others from coastal areas. See Timothy J. Holian, *The German Americans and WW II: An Ethnic Experience* (New York: Peter Lang, 1996); John Eric Schmitz, "Enemies among Us: The Relocation, Internment, and Repatriation of German, Italian, and Japanese Americans during World War Two" (Ph.D. dissertation, American University, 2007).

110   The FBI report was released after a Freedom of Information request by Robert A. Hill, who compiled and edited it in *The FBI's RACON: Racial Condi-*

tions in the United States during World War II (Boston: Northeastern University Press, 1995). A brief but useful overview written at the time is Florence Murray, "The Negro and Civil Liberties during World War II," *Social Forces* 24 (1945): 211–16.

111 Maurice Isserman, *Which Side Were You On? The American Communist Party during the Second World War* (Urbana: University of Illinois Press, 1983), p. 119.

112 The newspapers were the *Baltimore Afro-American* (said to have numerous "Communist connections"), *New York Amsterdam Star News* (the only one to escape criticism), *People's Voice* ("a very helpful transmission belt for the Communist Party"), *Oklahoma City Black Dispatch* (thought to be sympathetic to Communist-front organizations), *Chicago Defender* (two of whose employees had attended Communist Party meetings), *Michigan Chronicle* (whose editor had been active, when a student at the University of Michigan, in the National Student League, a front organization), and the *Pittsburgh Courier* (deemed insufficiently critical of Japan). Though "Negroes as a whole" were "not "subversive or . . . influenced by anti-American forces," it concluded that "a number of Negroes and Negro groups" were found to have acted "in a manner inimical to the Nation's war effort," a category it treated expansively to include "a new militancy and aggressiveness" in the North, as "old boundaries are crossed by the lifting of many restrictions to these people who have heretofore been subjected in other sections," and "a general change in attitude of Negroes" in the South "as well as a new militancy on their part" that had led to "numerous reports and complaints of individual members of the Negro race expressing un-American sentiments." See Hill, ed., *The FBI's Racon,* pp. 445–53, 77, 254, 255.

113 U.S. Army, "Inflammatory Propaganda," undated (dealing with the black press from December 1941 through February 1942), cited in Patrick Scott Washburn, "The Federal Government's Investigations of the Black Press during World War II" (Ph.D. dissertation, Indiana University, 1984), p. 99.

114 Washburn, "The Federal Government's Investigations of the Black Press during World War II," pp. 161, 205, 217.

115 Robert Higgs, *Crisis and Leviathan: Critical Episodes in the Growth of American Government* (New York: Oxford University Press, 1987), p. 206.

116 Andrew A. Workman, "Creating the National War Labor Board: Franklin Roosevelt and the Politics of State Building in the Early 1940s," *Journal of Policy History* 12, no. 2 (2000): 233–64.

117 Byrnes was a stalwart, if relatively moderate, segregationist. When governor of South Carolina from 1951 to 1955, he strongly opposed the *Brown v. Board of Education* decision late in his term. He became disillusioned with his party's increasingly pro–civil rights stance. Byrnes endorsed Dwight Eisenhower for president in 1952 and 1956, supported Richard Nixon in 1960 and 1968, and backed Barry Goldwater in 1964. Late in life, in the mid-1960s, he switched to

the Republican Party after Senator Strom Thurmond, his state's leading politician, did just that in 1964. See David Robertson, *Sly and Able: A Political Biography of James F. Byrnes* (New York: W. W. Norton, 1980), pp. 526–48.

118   Eliot Janeway, *The Struggle for Survival* (New Haven: Yale University Press, 1951), p. 185. Janeway writes that "more than any other factor, Byrnes' involvement with the unpleasantness of manpower administration provoked the opposition which persuaded Roosevelt to make his famous last-minute decision not to run with his Assistant President in 1944," but with Harry Truman instead. For an overview of the role played by Eliot Janeway, see Michael Janeway, *The Fall of the House of Roosevelt: Brokers of Ideas and Power from FDR to LBJ* (New York: Columbia University Press, 2004). For an overview of the mobilization effort under Byrnes, see Herman Miles Somers, *Presidential Agency: The Office of War Mobilization and Reconversion* (Cambridge: Harvard University Press, 1950); on Baruch, see Jordan A. Schwartz, "Baruch, the New Deal, and the Origins of the Military-Industrial Complex," in *Arms, Politics, and the Economy: Historical and Contemporary Perspectives*, ed. Robert Higgs (New York: Holmes and Meier, 1990), pp. 1–21.

119   Waddell, *The War Against the New Deal*, p. 89.

120   Gerald T. White, *Billions for Defense: Government Financing by the Defense Plant Corporation during World War II* (Tuscaloosa: University of Alabama Press, 1980), especially pp. 67–87.

121   John D. Millett, *The Organization and Role of the Army Service Forces* (Washington, DC: Office of the Chief of Military History, 1954); Russell E. Weigley, *History of the United States Army* (New York: Macmillan, 1967), pp. 442–50.

122   For an overview, see Ralph J. Watkins, "Economic Mobilization," *American Political Science Review* 43 (1949): 556–67. On the federal government's investments and patterns of ownership, see Gregory Hooks, "The Weakness of Strong Theories: The U.S. State's Dominance of the World War II Investment Process," *American Sociological Review* 58 (1993): 37–53.

123   John F. Witte, *The Politics and Development of the Federal Income Tax* (Madison: University of Wisconsin Press, 1985), p. 123.

124   Andrew Roberts, *Storm of War: A New History of the Second World War* (London: Penguin, 2010), pp. 197–98; Higgs, *Crisis and Leviathan,* pp. 220–25; R. Elbertson Smith, *The Army and Economic Mobilization* (Washington, DC: U.S. Department of Defense, 1959); Gregory Hooks, *Forging the Military-Industrial Complex: World War II's Battle of the Potomac* (Urbana: University of Illinois Press, 1991); Bartholomew H. Sparrow, *From Outside In: World War II and the American State* (Princeton, NJ: Princeton University Press, 1996), p. 107; http://www.whitehouse.gov/omb/budget/Historicals. For a discussion of the financing of wartime deficits, see Marshall A. Robinson, "Federal Debt Management: Civil War, World War I, and World War II," *American Economic Review* 45 (1955): 388–401.

125 George Horwich and David J. Bjornstad, "Spending and Manpower in Four U.S. Mobilizations: A Macro/Policy Perspective," *Journal of Policy History* 3, no. 2 (1991): 175.

126 This productivity, Richard Overy argues, was at the core of Allied victory. See Overy, *Why the Allies Won* (New York: W. W. Norton, 1997). It counteracted the superior fighting capacity of the German and Japanese armed forces. For detailed production figures, see http://www.taphilo.com/history/WWII/Production -Figures-WWII.shtml.

127 See http://www.bls.gov/cps/cpsaat1.pdf.

128 For a discussion, see Robert Kargon and Elizabeth Hodes, "Karl Compton, Isaiah Bowman, and the Politics of Science in the Great Depression," *Isis* 76 (1985): 301–18. For the larger context of scientific discovery, see Helge Kragh, *Quantum Generations: A History of Physics in the Twentieth Century* (Princeton, NJ: Princeton University Press, 1999).

129 For a discussion of Oppenheimer's role at this prewar moment, see Kai Bird and Martin J. Sherwin, *American Prometheus: The Triumph and Tragedy of J. Robert Oppenheimer* (New York: Alfred A. Knopf, 2005), pp. 179–94.

130 Daniel J. Kevles, *The Physicists: The History of a Scientific Community in Modern America* (New York: Alfred A. Knopf, 1978), pp. 287–301, 277–84.

131 James G. Hershberg, *James B. Conant: Harvard to Hiroshima and the Making of the Nuclear Age* (Stanford, CA: Stanford University Press, 1993), p. 128.

132 "For the next thousand years," he wrote to former president Herbert Hoover in April 19, 1943, "I expect that the preservation of civilization will be based on force if it is preserved at all." See G. Pascal Zachary, *Endless Frontier: Vannevar Bush, Engineer of the American Century* (New York: Free Press, 1997), p. 164.

133 Zachary, *Endless Frontier,* pp. 138, 183.

134 David M. Hart, *Forged Consensus: Science, Technology, and Economic Policy in the United States, 1921–1953* (Princeton, NJ: Princeton University Press, 1998), pp. 122–29. Conant's talk, "What Victory Requires," was delivered on December 22, 1941; See Hershberg, *James B. Conant,* p. 135.

135 The letter and response are reproduced in Michael B. Stoff, Jonathan F. Fanton, and R. Hal Williams, eds., *The Manhattan Project: A Documentary Introduction to the Atomic Age* (New York: McGraw-Hill, 1991), pp. 21–26; see also Garry Wills, *Bomb Power: The Modern Presidency and the National Security State* (New York: Penguin, 2010), pp. 10–23.

136 As early as May 5, 1940, the *New York Times* was reporting, on page 1, that German scientists were "feverishly" working to build an atomic bomb; cited in Hershberg, *James B. Conant,* p. 140. See Malcolm C. MacPherson, *Time Bomb: Fermi, Heisenberg, and the Race for the Atomic Bomb* (New York: E. P. Dutton, 1986).

137 Zachary, *Endless Frontier,* pp. 205, 214.

138 Stoff, Fanton, and Williams, eds., *The Manhattan Project,* pp. 24–25.

139   William L. Laurence, *Dawn over Zero: The Story of the Atomic Bomb* (New York: Alfred A. Knopf, 1946), p. 181.

140   For an account of Los Alamos from the vantage point of Oppenheimer's role, see Bird and Sherwin, *American Prometheus,* pp. 223–309.

141   Joel Davidson, "Building for War, Preparing for Peace: World War II and the Military-Industrial Complex," in *World War II and the American Dream,* ed. Donald Albrecht (Cambridge: MIT Press, 1995), p. 213; Max Hastings, *Retribution: The Battle for Japan, 1944–1945* (New York: Alfred A. Knopf, 2007), p. 452. For an official history, see Vincent C. Jones, *Manhattan: The Army and the Atomic Bomb* (Washington, DC: U.S. Army Center of Military History, 1985). On Groves, see William Lawren, *The General and the Bomb: A Biography of Leslie R. Groves, Director of the Manhattan Project* (New York: Dodd Mead, 1988).

142   Of the city's 90,000 buildings, 62,000 simply disappeared, and 6,000 others were damaged beyond repair. See Edward Teller (with Allen Brown), *The Legacy of Hiroshima* (New York: Doubleday, 1962), p. 4.

143   Cited in Bird and Sherwin, *American Prometheus,* p. 316. Three days later, just before the second bomb was dropped on Nagasaki, President Truman stated, "When you have to deal with a beast you have to treat him as a beast. It is most regrettable but nonetheless true." See Paul Boyer, "'Some Sort of Peace': President Truman, the American People, and the Atomic Bomb," in *The Truman Presidency,* ed. Michael J. Lacey (New York: Cambridge University Press, 1989), pp. 176, 177. From the moment that President Roosevelt met with Secretary of War Henry Stimson and other members of a "top policy group" on October 9, 1941, to launch a process to develop an atomic bomb, the weapon was conceived as a legitimate tool that, if developed in time, would be used. Only for reasons of timing—the bomb was not ready—was it not used against Germany, the target against which it was primarily directed. See Martin J. Sherwin, "The Atomic Bomb and the Origins of the Cold War: U.S. Atomic Energy Policy and Diplomacy, 1941–1945," *American Historical Review* 78 (1973): 946; Barton J. Bernstein, "Roosevelt, Truman, and the Atomic Bomb, 1941–1945: A Reinterpretation," *Political Science Quarterly* 90 (1975): 32. Bernstein cites some evidence that FDR, at least for a time in 1944, considered not dropping the bomb on Japan but using it only as a threat (pp. 32–33).

144   So he recalled a decade later. See Harry S. Truman, "Greatest Thing in History,'" *Life,* October 24, 1955, p. 103. He was on the *Augusta,* sailing back from the Potsdam Conference.

145   Charles R. Reyher, *Memoirs of a B-29 Pilot* (Bennington, VT: Merriam Press, 2008), p. 153. Operating from Guam, Reyher flew thirteen missions against Japan between June and September of 1945. He believed the war could have been won without using atomic weapons and without an invasion of mainland Japan. Before Hiroshima, two key members of the Scientific Advisory Panel,

Arthur Compton, the chair of the University of Chicago Physics Department, who directed the Manhattan Project's Chicago laboratory, and Ernest Lawrence, the head of the California Radiation (Rad) Lab in Berkeley, proposed that the bomb be first used in a noncombat demonstration. Compton argued that the bomb's use in Japan constituted "more serious implications than the introduction of poison gas," and that at issue was "more a political than ... military question" because the bomb "introduces the question of mass slaughter, really for the first time in history." Oppenheimer disagreed, arguing that "no demonstration ... would be sufficiently spectacular to convince the Japs that further resistance was useless," Lawrence recalled. That view carried the day. See Barton J. Bernstein, "Four Physicists and the Bomb: The Early Years, 1945–1950," *Historical Studies in the Physical and Biological Sciences* 18, no. 2 (1988): 2365–36.

146   Father Tadashi Hasegawa, cited in James Carroll, *House of War: The Pentagon and the Disastrous Rise of American Power* (Boston: Houghton Mifflin, 2006), p. 77.

147   Hastings, *Retribution,* p. 455; Spencer R. Weart and Gertrud Weiss Szilard, eds., *Leo Szilard: His Version of the Facts* (Cambridge: MIT Press, 1978), p. 211. Szilard had been among the first to recommend to President Roosevelt that he initiate an atomic bomb program, but by 1945 he was trying to persuade FDR, then Truman, not to use the weapon. See Bird and Sherwin, *American Prometheus,* p. 291.

148   Rossiter, *Constitutional Dictatorship,* p. 314. "The second World War," he wrote, "was not to be the last" of the "great national crises. The possibility of an atomic war only establishes emergency government a little more prominently in the array of this nation's problems. Not that martial law is going to save us from an atomic attack; still, it may be the only glue available when it comes time to pick up the pieces" (p. 307).

149   Table Ed223–227, "U.S. Strategic Nuclear Weapons, 1945–1996," United States Bureau of the Census, *Historical Statistics of the United States* (New York: Cambridge University Press, 2006); available at https://hsus.cambridge.org.ezproxy .cul.columbia.edu/HSUSWeb/search/searchessavpdf.do?id=Ed223-227.

150   John W. Dower, *Cultures of War: Pearl Harbor, Hiroshima, 9–11, Iraq* (New York: W. W. Norton, 2010), p. 161; Henry DeWolf Smyth, *A General Account of the Development of Methods of Using Atomic Energy for Military Purposes* (Princeton, NJ: Princeton University Press, 1945). In August 1943, Britain and the United States signed an agreement at a summit in Quebec that promised nuclear cooperation and banned giving atomic information to the Soviet Union. See Hershberg, *James B. Conant,* pp. 172–93; Zachary, *Endless Frontier,* p. 212; Andrew Roberts, *Masters and Commanders: The Military Geniuses Who Led the West to Victory in World War II* (London: Penguin, 2009), p. 189. The secret was not kept because scientific communities, diplomatic agencies,

and military organizations in the United States and Great Britain were penetrated by Soviet agents. See Bird and Sherwin, *American Prometheus,* pp. 285–86; Max Hastings, *Winston's War: Churchill, 1940–1945* (New York: Vintage, 2011), p. 259; Hershberg, *James B. Conant,* pp. 158–59. The key figures who provided the USSR with reports from Los Alamos included Theodore Hall, a talented nineteen-year-old from Harvard who arrived in January 1944, and Klaus Fuchs, German by birth, who was part of the British team that came seven months later, in August.

151   H. H. Goldsmith, "The Literature of Atomic Energy of the Past Decade," *Scientific Monthly* 68 (1949): 295.

152   Cited in Bernstein, "Four Physicists and the Bomb," p. 241.

153   Cited in Martin Gilbert, *The Second World War* (London: Stoddart, 1989), p. 440.

154   Overy, *Why the Allies Won,* p. 128.

155   Edmund Russell, *War and Nature: Fighting Humans and Insects with Chemicals from World War I to Silent Spring* (New York: Cambridge University Press, 2001), p. 131.

156   General H. H. Arnold, "Air Force in the Atomic Age," in *One World or None,* ed. Dexter Masters and Katharine Way (New York: McGraw Hill, 1946), p. 27.

157   Overy, *Why the Allies Won,* p. 126; Ian Buruma, "The Cruelest War," *New York Review of Books,* May 1, 2008, p. 24.

158   *Time,* March 19, 1945, p. 32.

159   These campaigns were popular with the American and the British publics, serving as boosters of morale. See George E. Hopkins, "Bombing and the American Conscience during World War II," *Historian* 28 (1966): 451–73. For overviews, see Randall Hansen, *Fire and Fury: The Allied Bombing of Germany, 1942–1945* (New York: New American Library, 2009); Roberts, *Storm of War,* pp. 429–60.

160   "Japan's military economy was devoured in flames; her population desperately longed for escape from bombing. German forces lost half of the weapons needed at the front, millions of workers absented themselves from work, and the economy gradually creaked almost to a halt. . . . For all the arguments over the morality or operational effectiveness of the bombing campaigns, the air offensive was one of the decisive elements of Allied victory." See Overy, *Why the Allies Won,* p. 133.

161   See http://www.let.rug.nl/usa/P/fr32/speeches/su43fdr.htm.

162   *New York Times,* March 18, 1944; *The Nation,* March 18, 1944, p. 323.

163   Hastings, *Retribution,* p. 473.

164   "Barcelona Horrors," *Time,* March 28, 1938, p. 16.

165   Dower, *Cultures of War,* p. 160.

166   *Time,* October 29, 1945, p. 30.

167   D. W. Brogan, *The American Character* (New York: Alfred A. Knopf, 1944),

pp. 163–64; Brian Waddell, "The Dimensions of the Military Ascendancy during U.S. Industrial Mobilization for World War II," *Journal of Military and Political Sociology* 23 (S 1995): 81–98. For an account of the problems faced by such a mobilization, see E. J. B. Foxcroft, "Planning and Executing Resources Allocation—A Phase of War Administration," *Public Policy* 4 (1955): 158–81.

168 Janeway, *The Struggle for Survival,* p. 361. Janeway, who was close to a range of important war administrators, including James Forrestal, Ferdinand Eberstadt, and Abe Fortas, stressed how FDR's patterns of mobilization were meant to lean on and advance "the unorganized momentum of American democracy" (p. 361).

169 Weigley, *History of the United States Army,* p. 475. The U.S. Navy, though, was the largest in the world; larger than all the other navies combined. See John Lukacs, *The Legacy of the Second World War* (New Haven: Yale University Press, 2010), p. 48. For an overview of governmental planning and centralization during World War II, compared with that during World War I, the Korean War, and the Vietnam War, showing the extraordinary scale and growth in government spending and capacity between 1941 and 1945, see Arthur A. Stein, *The Nation at War* (Baltimore: Johns Hopkins University Press, 1980), pp. 54–71.

170 Government as a unified technical enterprise led by specialists in violence, distinguished from politicians who were specialists in bargaining, were key themes in Lasswell's landmark essay, "The Garrison State," pp. 464, 455.

171 *Congressional Record,* 78th Cong., 2d sess., February 24, 1942, pp. 1570–71.

172 Rossiter, *Constitutional Dictatorship,* p. 276.

173 Mark Tushnet, "Civil Liberties after 1937—The Justices and the Theories" (unpublished manuscript, 2011), pp. 51–52.

174 See the "Defending Civil Liberties" chapter in the memoir by former attorney general Francis Biddle, *In Brief Authority* (New York: Doubleday, 1962), pp. 152–60.

175 For an official statement of "the position of the Communist International on the basic issues of our time," see Georgi Dimitroff, *The United Front against Fascism* (New York: International Publishers, 1938).

176 John France, *Perilous Glory: The Rise of Western Military Power* (New Haven: Yale University Press, 2011), p. 329.

177 Richard Overy, *Russia's War: A History of the Soviet War Effort, 1941–1945* (New York: Penguin, 1998), p. 223.

178 In April 1942, Soviet Foreign Minister Vyacheslav Molotov was assured on a visit to the White House that a second front would be opened in France later that year in an effort to pull forty German divisions away from the USSR. See Roberts, *Masters and Commanders,* p. 175.

179 Table Ed1–5, "Military Personnel and Casualties, by War and Branch of Service: 1775–1991," United States Bureau of the Census, *Historical Statistics of*

the United States; available at https://hsus.cambridge.org.ezproxy.cul.columbia
.edu/HSUSWeb/toc/showTablePdf.do?id=Ed1–5.

180   See the discussion in "Prisoners of the Reich," in Max Hastings, *Armageddon:
The Battle for Germany, 1944–1945* (New York: Vintage, 2005), especially pp.
393–396. Hastings observes how, "by 1945, the custody, exploitation, and murder of prisoners had become the largest activities in Germany beyond the military struggle" (p. 381).

181   B. V. Sokolov, "The Cost of War: Human Losses of the USSR and Germany,
1938–1945," *Journal of Slavic Military Studies* 9 (1996): 156–71; V. E. Korol,
"The Price of Victory: Myths and Realities," *Journal of Slavic Military Studies* 9
(1996): 417–24. Estimates have varied widely, with some as high as 47 million,
but such losses seem exaggerated.

182   Compared with Soviet, Japanese, and German military forces, relatively small
numbers of American and British soldiers served on the front lines. Their support troops, backing up mechanized units, were far greater in number than the
soldiers most at risk to suffer casualties. Soviet units, by contrast, "lacked mechanization, and relied on horse-drawn transport, as did something like 75 per
cent of the German divisions." See France, *Perilous Glory,* pp. 346, 348. During
the war, the Soviet Union was devastated. It lost 32,000 factories, 40,000 miles
of railway track, 1,700 towns, and 70,000 villages. See Catherine Merridale,
Ivan's War: Life and Death in the Red Army, 1939–1945 (New York: Metropolitan Books, 2006), pp. 147, 190; Timothy Snyder, *Bloodlands: Europe between
Hitler and Stalin* (New York: Basic Books, 2010), pp. 171–75; Roberts, *Storm of
War,* pp. 172, 345, 565; I. C. B. Dear and M. R. D. Foot, eds., *The Oxford Com-
panion to World War II* (New York: Oxford University Press, 2001), pp. 823–25.
This summary of Russian costs also relies on the comprehensive overview in
Overy, *Russia's War.*

183   Merridale, *Ivan's War,* pp. 188–91.

184   George Sanford, *Katyn and the Soviet Massacre of 1940: Truth, Justice, and Memory* (New York: Routledge, 2005). The tribunal heard conflicting testimony,
and reached no conclusion about culpability at Katyn.

185   Once the USSR was invaded, the status of Jews changed, as they were mobilized to fight the Nazi invader. Notably, the Jewish Anti-Fascist Committee
was formed, led by the famous Yiddish actor Solomon Mikhoels, which sought
to rally Jewish support both within the country and outside, especially among
Jews in the United States.

186   Atina Grossman, "A Question of Silence: The Rape of German Women by
Occupation Soldiers," *October* 72 (1995): 42–63; Mark Naimark, *The Russians
in Germany: A History of the Soviet Zone of Occupation, 1945–1949* (Cambridge:
Harvard University Press, 1995); Ian Kershaw, *The End: The Defiance and
Destruction of Hitler's Germany, 1944–45* (New York: Penguin, 2011).

187   *Dallas Morning News,* October 24, 1943, cited in Hopkins, "Bombing and the
American Conscience During World War II," p. 461.

188 Soviet troops were advancing in East Prussia after a successful winter offensive, though suffering great numbers of casualties, and were preparing to move on to Berlin, where they would arrive first; American and British troops had just repulsed the German counteroffensive in the Ardennes, at high cost.

189 For a discussion that comments on the character of pro-German military activity and the scale and often horrific results of the deportation, see V. Stanley Vardys, "The Case of the Crimean Tartars," *Russian Review* 30 (1971): 101–10; Grégory Dufaud, "La déportation des Tatars de Crimée et leur vie en exil (1944–1956): Un ethnocide?" *Vingtième Siècle. Revue d'histoire*, no. 96 (2007): 151–62.

190 The reconstruction of the severely damaged palace was undertaken in a month under the direction of Lavrentiy Beria, the commissar of internal affairs, who directed the Gulag and would soon direct the successful postwar effort to build a Soviet atomic bomb.

191 Cited in Martin Gilbert, *Road to Victory: Winston S. Churchill, 1942–1945* (London: Heinemann, 1986), p. 1174.

192 Ibid.

193 Walter Lippmann, *U.S. Foreign Policy: Shield of the Republic* (Boston: Little, Brown, 1943), p. 164.

194 "The Crimean Conference: Text of the Communiqué Issued by President Roosevelt, Prime-Minister Churchill, and Premier Stalin on February 11, 1945," *World Affairs* 108 (1945): 54.

195 On his return to Britain from Yalta, Churchill reported to his war cabinet that it was "impossible to convey the true atmosphere of discussions between the [Big] Three. Stalin I'm sure means well to the world and Poland." Cited in Roberts, *Masters and Commanders,* p. 557.

196 Cited in S. M. Plokhy, *Yalta: The Price of Peace* (New York: Viking, 2010), pp. 331–32, 328, 238.

197 The classic study remains Diane S. Clemens, *Yalta* (New York: Oxford University Press, 1970), a book that persuasively stresses how each of the three leaders gained his most significant objectives.

198 There had been two Soviet compromises concerning the United Nations. The USSR retracted its initial insistence on an absolute Security Council veto and accepted the U.S. proposal that the veto could not be exercised by any party to a given dispute. It also reduced its demand for sixteen seats in the General Assembly for its various republics, to three—Russia, White Russia, and Ukraine. For a discussion, see Townsend Hoopes and Douglas Brinkley, *FDR and the Creation of the U.N.* (New Haven: Yale University Press, 1997), pp. 174–75. Roosevelt believed it crucial to offer "Moscow a prominent place" in the new organization, "by making it, so to speak, a member of the club" in order to effect "containment by integration." See John Lewis Gaddis, *Strategies of Containment* (New York: Oxford University Press, 1982), p. 9.

199 In August 1942, William Bullitt, who had served as the first U.S. ambassador

to the Soviet Union (1933–1936) after Roosevelt initiated diplomatic relations, cautioned the president about the "domination of Europe by Stalin's Communist dictatorship." FDR replied, "I just have a hunch that Stalin is not that kind of man. . . . I think that if I give him everything I possibly can and ask nothing in return, noblesse oblige, he won't try to annex anything and will work with me for a world of democracy and peace." Cited in Wilson D. Miscamble, *From Roosevelt to Truman: Potsdam, Hiroshima, and the Cold War* (New York: Cambridge University Press, 2007), p. 52.

200 Just two weeks after Yalta, Andrei Vyshinsky traveled to Bucharest to enforce a change to a pro-Soviet government. See Lukacs, *Legacy of the Second World War,* pp. 80–81.

201 An emphasis on Anglo-Soviet relations, as distinct from U.S. interests, is a central theme in Fraser J. Harbutt, *Yalta 1945: Europe and America at the Crossroads* (Cambridge: Cambridge University Press, 2010), a book that emphasizes the existence of "two distinct systems of behavior and styles of diplomacy as the two great political arenas, non-Nazi Europe and the United States, moved uneasily together toward victory" (p. 237). This view, underscoring British-U.S. tensions, provides a useful corrective to positions stressing tensions between the USSR and the democracies, but its place within a larger frame is hard to grasp. For a more measured view of British and American wartime cooperation and tension, see Roberts, *Masters and Commanders.* See also the discussions of Yalta in Warren F. Kimball, *The Juggler: Franklin Roosevelt as Wartime Statesman* (Princeton: Princeton University Press, 1991), pp. 170–77; Hastings, *Winston's War,* pp. 441–49.

202 W. Gordon East, "The New Frontiers of the Soviet Union," *Foreign Affairs* 29 (1951): 597.

203 For a discussion, see Lukacs, *The Legacy of the Second World War,* pp. 170–74.

204 William T. R. Fox, *The Super-Powers: The United States, Britain, and the Soviet Union—Their Responsibility for Peace* (New York: Harcourt, Brace, 1944), pp. 3, 9, 119.

205 McGeorge Bundy, "The Test of Yalta," *Foreign Affairs* 27 (1949): 618–19. At the time, Bundy was a member of the Council on Foreign Relations Study Group that was considering the history and effectiveness of the Marshall Plan. After serving as dean of the Faculty of Arts and Sciences at Harvard University (1953–1960), he became national security adviser to Presidents Kennedy and Johnson from 1961 to 1966, when he joined the Ford Foundation as its president.

206 Walter Lippmann, *U.S. War Aims* (Boston: Little, Brown, 1944), p. 142.

207 In 1944, eight out of every ten Americans thought the United States should cooperate with the USSR after the war, surveys conducted by Princeton University's Office of Public Opinion Research reported. See Jerome S. Bruner, *Mandate from the People* (New York: Duell, Sloan and Pearce, 1944), p. 109. See

also Ralph B. Levering, *American Opinion and the Russian Alliance, 1939–1945* (Chapel Hill: University of North Carolina Press, 1976). Levering shows how, by 1943, harsh opinion about the Soviet Union had mitigated and was replaced by strong sentiments of solidarity.

208 For an assessment of how the character and interactions of the three key personalities at Yalta affected the end of the wartime Grand Alliance and the start of the Cold War, see Frank Costigliola, *Roosevelt's Lost Alliances: How Personal Politics Helped Start the Cold War* (Princeton, NJ: Princeton University Press, 2012).

209 Sumner Welles, "Two Roosevelt Decisions: One Debit, One Credit," *Foreign Affairs* 29 (1951): 182–204.

210 Dimitri Antonovich Volkognov, *Stalin: Triumph and Tragedy* (New York: Random House, 1996), p. 501. For overviews of the summit, see J. Robert Moskin, *Mr. Truman's War: The Final Victories of World War II and the Birth of the Postwar World* (New York: Random House, 1996), pp. 197–242; Miscamble, *From Roosevelt to Truman,* pp. 191–217.

211 James F. Byrnes, *Speaking Frankly* (New York: Harper and Brothers, 1947), pp. 86–87.

212 Perhaps emblematic of the new ambivalence was the way Truman informed Stalin about "a new weapon of unusual destructive force," without specifying that it was an atomic weapon. See Bernstein, "Roosevelt, Truman, and the Atomic Bomb," p. 47.

213 See Bruce Kuniholm, *The Origins of the Cold War in the Near East: Great Power Conflict and Diplomacy in Iran, Turkey, and Greece* (Princeton, NJ: Princeton University Press, 1980); Jamil Hasanli, *Stalin and the Turkish Crisis of the Cold War, 1945–1953* (Lanham, MD: Lexington Books, 2011).

214 See http://en.wikisource.org/wiki/Sinews_of_Peace. For a history of the concept, which originated in the fire curtain used in British theaters, see Patrick Wright, *Iron Curtain: From Stage to Cold War* (New York: Oxford University Press, 2009).

215 The bombs were exploded underwater, contaminating some ten million tons of seawater, which was blown in the air, thus transporting lethal radiation. See A. G. L. McNaughton, "National and International Control of Atomic Energy," *International Journal* 3 (1947/1948): 12.

216 Lloyd T. Graybar, "The 1946 Atomic Bomb Tests: Diplomacy or Bureaucratic Infighting," *Journal of American History* 72 (1986): 904, 905.

217 For a discussion along these lines, see Edward A. Shils, *The Torment of Secrecy: The Background and Consequences of American Security Policies* (Glencoe, IL: Free Press, 1956), pp. 61–62.

218 David Brody, "The New Deal and World War II," in *The New Deal—The National Level*, vol. 1, ed. John Braeman, Robert H. Bremner, and David Brody (Columbus: Ohio State University Press, 1975), p. 272.

CHAPTER 10 ▪ PUBLIC PROCEDURES, PRIVATE INTERESTS

1   George E. Hopkins, "Bombing and the American Conscience during World War II," *Historian* 28 (1966): 472.

2   For an overview, see Joel Davidson, "Building for War, Preparing for Peace: World War II and the Military-Industrial Complex," in *World War II and the American Dream,* ed. Donald Albrecht (Cambridge: MIT Press, 1995), pp. 195–217. See also Donald M. Nelson, *Arsenal of Democracy: The Story of American War Production* (New York: Harcourt, Brace, 1946), Gerald T. White, *Billions for Defense: Government Financing by the Defense Plant Corporation during World War II* (Tuscaloosa: University of Alabama Press, 1980); Gregory Hooks, *Forging the Military-Industrial Complex: World War II's Battle of the Potomac* (Urbana: University of Illinois Press, 1991).

3   A summary, "Planning for the Great Demobilization," can be found in James Stokes Ballard, *The Shock of Peace: Military and Economic Demobilization after World War II* (Washington, DC: University Press of America, 1983), pp. 27–72. See also John C. Sparrow, *History of Personnel Demobilization in the United States Army* (Washington, DC: Department of the Army, 1952).

4   On the GI Bill, see Ira Katznelson, *When Affirmative Action Was White: An Untold History of Racial Inequality in Twentieth-Century America* (New York: W. W. Norton, 2005), pp. 113–41. See also Suzanne Mettler, *Soldiers to Citizens: The G.I. Bill and the Making of the Greatest Generation* (New York: Oxford University Press, 2007); Kathleen Frydl, *The G.I. Bill* (Cambridge: Cambridge University Press, 2011).

5   Walter Lippmann, "The American Destiny," *Life,* June 5, 1939, p. 47; reprinted in Walter Lippmann, *The American Destiny* (New York: Life Magazine Press, 1939), p. 4.

6   Erich Hula, "Constitutional and Administrative Readjustments," *Social Research* 6 (1939): 284, 245–46.

7   For an overview, see the essay written for the British Foreign Office in 1942 by the socialist intellectual R. H. Tawney, "The American Labour Movement," in *The American Labour Movement and Other Essays,* ed. J.M. Winter (New York: St. Martin's Press, 1979), pp. 1–110.

8   Louis Stark, "The New Labor Movement," in *America Now: An Inquiry into Civilization in the United States,* ed. Harold E. Stearns (New York: Charles Scribner's Sons, 1938), p. 145.

9   For important scholarly accounts of the political role of unions, especially the CIO, within the Democratic Party, see J. David Greenstone, *Labor in American Politics* (New York: Alfred A. Knopf, 1969), William H. Riker, "The CIO in Politics, 1936–1946" (Ph.D. dissertation, Harvard University, 1948). For a summary by a union activist, see Joseph Gaer, *The First Round: The Story of the CIO Political Action Committee* (New York: Duell, Sloan, and Pearce, 1944).

10   Lewis Mumford, "Foreword," in *Planned Society: Yesterday, Today, Tomorrow: A Symposium of Thirty-Five Economists, Sociologists, and Statesmen,* ed. Findlay Mackenzie (New York: Prentice-Hall, 1937), p.x. See also the attempt by the Frankfurt School émigré economist Karl W. Kapp to develop criteria "for distinguishing between different types of economic control . . . by a classification according to their compatibility with the free market economy" in Kapp, "Economic Regulation and Economic Planning," *American Economic Review* 29 (1939): 768.

11   Wesley C. Mitchell, "The Social Sciences and National Planning," in *Planned Society,* ed. Mackenzie, p. 108.

12   William F. Ogburn, "Social Change," in *Planned Society,* ed. Mackenzie, p. 603.

13   Margaret Mead, "Primitive Society," in *Planned Society,* ed. Mackenzie, pp. 3–25.

14   Harold D. Lasswell, "Propaganda in a Planned Society," in *Planned Society,* ed. Mackenzie, pp. 639–40.

15   Sidney Hook, "The Philosophical Implications of Economic Planning," in *Planned Society,* ed. Mackenzie, p. 677.

16   Leverett S. Lyon, Myron W. Watkins, and Victor Abramson, *Government and Economic Life: Development and Current Issues of American Public Policy,* 2 vols. (Washington, DC: Brookings Institution, 1939, 1940); citation is from vol. 1, p. 3.

17   Marion Clawson, *New Deal Planning: The National Resources Planning Board* (Baltimore: Johns Hopkins University Press, 1981), p. xvi.

18   Cited in Charles E. Merriam, "The National Resources Planning Board: A Chapter in American Planning Experience," *American Political Science Review* 38 (1944): 1076. Merriam, who was a distinguished political scientist, served on the NRPB from its founding to its end.

19   Following the encouragement of President Roosevelt to study and plan the relationship between natural and human resources, the NRPB, taking a broad approach to its mandate, divided into three divisions—on economic security, health, and nutrition; on transportation, energy, and land; and on public works and water resources. Each sought to connect planned interventions in markets to key economic goals, including stabilization and growth, and central social goals, including urban development, income redistribution, and the reduction of poverty. The NRPB was not a line agency, but a combination of intelligence, coordination, and guidance enabled it to help shape the political agenda of the executive branch.

20   Allan G. Gruchy, "The Economics of the National Resources Committee," *American Economic Review* 29 (1939): 60.

21   Merriam, "The National Resources Planning Board," p. 1086.

22   Friedrich A. Hayek, *Road to Serfdom* (Chicago: University of Chicago Press, 1944).

23   Together with the Liaison Office for Personnel Management. To carry out the authority Congress provided, President Roosevelt issued Executive Order 8248 on September 8, 1939: "Establishing the Divisions of the Executive Office of the President and Defining Their Functions and Duties." The Bureau of the Budget was directed "to assist the President in the preparation of the Budget and the formulation of the fiscal program of the Government," while the National Resources Planning Board was instructed to collect data and recommend "long term plans and programs" for human and natural resources, propose measures to improve and stabilize the economy and "the social, economic, and cultural advancement of the people of the United States," and "act as a clearing house and means of coordination for planning activities, linking together various levels and fields of planning." Cited in Clawson, *New Deal Planning,* pp. 314–18.

24   National Resources Planning Committee, *Progress Report* (Washington, DC: U.S. Government Printing Office, 1939); cited in L. G. Rockewell, "National Resources Planning: The Role of the National Resources Planning Board in the Process of Government" (Ph.D. dissertation, Princeton University, 1942), p. 95.

25   See Ira Katznelson and Bruce Pietrykowski, "Rebuilding the American State: Evidence from the 1940's," *Studies in American Political Development* 6 (1991): 312.

26   This former staff member, Roger W. Jones, described the agency to Daniel A. Biderman. See Biderman, *Harold Smith and the Growth of the Bureau of the Budget* (senior thesis, Princeton University, 1975), p. 11; cited in Andrew Rudalevige, "Inventing the Institutionalized Presidency: Entrepreneurship and the Rise of the Bureau of the Budget, 1939–1949," in *Formative Acts: American Politics in the Making,* ed. Stephen Skowronek and Matthew Glassman (Philadelphia: University of Pennsylvania Press, 2007), p. 316. The bureau had been established by the Budget and Accounting Act of 1921, which created the BOB to assist the president to prepare a unified and comprehensive annual budget. For a discussion, see Stephen Skowronek, *Building a New American State: The Expansion of National Administrative Capacities, 1877–1920* (New York: Cambridge University Press, 1982), pp. 206–09.

27   Rudalevige, "Inventing the Institutionalized Presidency," p. 323.

28   These data are culled from *The Budget of the United States Government Fiscal Years 1941 to 1947* (Washington, DC: U.S. Government Printing Office).

29   Wayne Cox, "Federal Executive Reorganization Re-Examined: Basic Problems," *American Political Science Review* 40 (1946): 1134.

30   National Resources Planning Board, "Industrial Location and National Policy" (Interim Report), May 1941, p. 23; cited in Philip W. Warken, *A History of the National Resources Planning Board, 1933–1943* (New York: Garland, 1979), p. 108.

31 Key NRPB documents included *After Defense—What?* (1941); *Security, Work, and Relief Policies* (1941); *After the War—Full Employment* (1942); *Demobilization and Readjustment* (1943); and *National Resources Development Report* (1943).

32 National Resources Planning Board, *Post-War Planning* (Washington, DC: U.S. Government Printing Office, 1942), p. 32. For strong endorsements, see "A New Bill of Rights," *Nation,* March 20, 1943, pp. 402–03; "Introduction: Charter for America," special section, *New Republic,* April 19, 1943, pp. 523–24. A surprisingly sympathetic summary can be found in "New Deal Plans Industry Control," *Business Week,* March 20, 1943, pp. 15–18.

33 Harold D. Smith, "The Budget in Transition," in *Material on Budgeting: An Instrument of Planning and Management, Unit I: The Evolution of the Budgetary Concept in the Federal Government,* ed. Catheryn Seckler-Hudson (Washington, DC: American University, 1944), p. 73. Smith left the Bureau in 1946 to become the first vice president of the World Bank; he resigned later that year when it became clear that he would not succeed in gaining the organization's presidency after Eugene Meyer left office after six months. Instead, the post went to John J. McCloy.

34 Donald C. Stone, "Planning as an Administrative Process," in *Material on Budgeting,* ed. Seckler-Hudson, pp. 116–18.

35 The other divisions were Estimates, whose work became more pressing as military spending ballooned during the war; Administrative Management, which sought to make a burgeoning federal government more organizationally rational and efficient; Statistical Standards; and Legislative Reference, which served as a clearinghouse for federal agency requests to Congress.

36 For discussions, see Stephen Kemp Bailey, *Congress Makes a Law: The Story behind the Employment Act of 1946* (New York: Columbia University Press, 1960), p. 25; Marion Fourcade, *Economists and Societies: Discipline and Profession in the United States, Britain and France, 1890s to 1990s* (Princeton, NJ: Princeton University Press, 2009), pp. 102–6.

37 Cited in Clawson, *New Deal Planning,* p. 183.

38 Plus one Farmer Labor Party member, one American Labor Party member, and two Progressive Party members.

39 Clawson, *New Deal Planning,* p. 238; Barry D. Karl, *Charles E. Merriam and the Study of Politics* (Chicago: University of Chicago Press, 1974) p. 279.

40 *Congressional Record,* 78th Cong., 1st sess., May 27, 1943, pp. 4961, 4962.

41 Ibid., p. 4953.

42 *New York Times,* February 19, 1943; *Christian Science Monitor,* February 19, 1943.

43 *Congressional Record,* 78th Cong., 1st sess., May 27, 1943, p. 945.

44 *Baltimore Sun,* February 18, 1943.

45 Ibid., April 18, 1943.

46 Clawson, *New Deal Planning,* p. 229.

47 *Baltimore Sun,* February 18, 1943.

48 *New York Times,* June 19, 1943.

49 *Washington Post,* July 1, 1943. A significant sector of the economics profession lamented the NRPB's demise, "a national misfortune" in the judgment at the time by Glenn E. Hoover. See Hoover, "National Planning within the Free Enterprise System," *American Journal of Economics and Sociology* 3 (1944): 410. Hoover's article called for a new national planning agency to manage the transition from war to peace. For an earlier attempt by Hoover to define a role for democratic planning, see Hoover, "Government Intervention in the Post-War Economy," *American Journal of Economics and Sociology* 1 (1942): 381–402.

50 See http://www.presidency.ucsb.edu/ws/index.php?pid=16518#axzz1Ppxp04m0; Cass R. Sunstein, *The Second Bill of Rights: FDR's Unfinished Revolution and Why We Need It More Than Ever* (New York: Basic Books, 2006); Alonzo L. Hamby, *Beyond the New Deal: Harry S. Truman and American Liberalism* (New York: Columbia University Press, 1973), pp. 11–13; Henry Wallace, *Sixty Million Jobs* (New York: Reynal and Hitchcock, 1945), pp. 8–9.

51 Edward S. Flash, *Economic Advice and Presidential Leadership: The Council of Economic Advisers* (New York: Columbia University Press, 1965), p. 16.

52 David Naveh, "The Political Role of Economic Advisers: The Case of the U.S. President's Council of Economic Advisers, 1946–1976," *Presidential Studies Quarterly* 11 (1981): 493.

53 Katznelson and Pietrykowski, "Rebuilding the American State," p. 327.

54 Philip Broughton, *Man Meets Job—How Uncle Sam Helps* (New York: Public Affairs Committee, 1941), p. 7.

55 Katznelson and Pietrykowski, "Rebuilding the American State," p. 328.

56 Leonard P. Adams, *The Public Employment Service in Transition, 1933–1968* (Ithaca, NY: New York School of Industrial Relations, Cornell University, 1969), p. 27. For a fine overview of the Department of Labor during the 1930s, see Hilda Kessler Gilbert, "The United States Department of Labor in the New Deal Period" (Ph.D. dissertation, University of Wisconsin, 1942).

57 "The Question of Federal or State Control of the Employment Services," *Congressional Digest* 25 (1946): 104.

58 *The Budget of the United States Government*; cited in Katznelson and Pietrykowsi, "Rebuilding the American State," p. 330.

59 Cited in "The Question of Federal or State Control of the Employment Services," p. 107.

60 In late 1945, Truman vetoed an appropriations bill after Congress added a rider that would have returned the employment services to the states within one hundred days. In his veto message, he essentially said that while he believed the employment offices should be returned to the states eventually, the immediate postwar reconversion period was the worst-possible time. See *Congressional Record,* 79th Cong., 2d sess., January 28, 1946, pp. 466, 445–46.

61   The bill delegated to the secretary of labor the capacity to fashion national rules regarding how state-level employment service and unemployment compensation offices should operate. Its "recapture clause" specified that the secretary could take over should they not comply with these regulations. Further, the department could open federal offices where no state employment service existed. The legislation also required states to maintain "reasonable referral standards" and "assure equal referral opportunities for equally qualified applicants." In addition, states were required to cooperate with the federal government and one another to maintain a system of "clearing labor" between the states, thus helping to fashion a truly national labor market. See ibid., January 28, 1946, p. 473; January 29, 1946, p. 540; January 28, 1946, pp. 474, 478.

62   The one exception was Representative Randolph (D, WVa), who said that while he opposed permanent federalization, he supported the administration bill because continued federal control was necessary during the reconversion period. See ibid., January 28, 1946, pp. 471–72; January 29, 1946, p. 544.

63   Ibid., January 29, 1946, p. 530.

64   This was not an imagined worry. Many nonsouthern Democrats did favor permanent federal control. Arizona's Richard Harless contended, "Our unified national system of public employment offices is now, under present Federal administration, being administered back home to an extent never equaled by a State-operated system; but administered under a system which assures the free interchange of labor market data and the free movement of workers from area to area and State to State wherever their skills are needed or can best be utilized." Similarly, Michigan's Frank Hook claimed that federal control was desirable for the way it promoted uniform standards in unemployment compensation systems. See ibid., p. 538; January 28, 1946, p. 475.

65   Ibid., January 29, 1946, p. 539.

66   Ibid.

67   Ibid., p. 540.

68   Ibid.

69   Ibid.

70   Ibid., January 28, 1946, pp. 477, 478.

71   Robert C. Lieberman, *Shifting the Color Line* (Cambridge: Harvard University Press, 1998), p. 189.

72   *Congressional Record*, 79th Cong., 2d sess., January 28, 1946, pp. 475, 472; January 29, 1946, p. 530.

73   Ibid., January 29, 1946, p. 540.

74   In adopting this substitute on January 29, the southerners voted with Republicans with a high likeness score of 76 (and with only a likeness of 38 with nonsouthern Democrats). The vote on passage records a southern Democratic–Republican likeness of 82, and intra–Democratic Party likeness of just 35.

75   In 1946, the USES spent $61,747,899, all in Washington or in federally controlled state and local employment offices. By 1949, only $5,735,812 was being

expended on the USES by the Department of Labor, as compared with fully $176,169,096 that was spent on grants to states. See Federal Security Agency, *Annual Report* (Washington, DC: U.S. Government Printing Office, 1946–1949); cited in Katznelson and Pietrykowski, "Rebuilding the American State," p. 333.

76 *Congressional Record*, 79th Cong., 1st sess., September 19, 1945, p. 8737.

77 Ibid., p. 8735.

78 Ibid., pp. 8737, 8743.

79 Ibid., p. 8735.

80 This coalition was marked by a high likeness score of 86 (by contrast, southern and nonsouthern Democratic likeness scored an uncommonly low 14).

81 *Congressional Record,* 80th Cong., 2d sess., March 16, 1948, p. 2904.

82 With a likeness score of 81. Following President Truman's election in 1948, and a gain of seventy-five southern Democrats in the House and nine in the Senate, the 81st Congress failed to veto a presidential reorganization plan that included transferring responsibility for unemployment insurance to the Department of Labor, where it has remained ever since.

83 For a discussion, see Sean Farhang and Ira Katznelson, "The Southern Imposition: Congress and Labor in the New Deal and Fair Deal," *Studies in American Political Development* 19 (2005): 25.

84 For discussions, see Lois Ruchames, *Race, Jobs, and Politics: The Story of the FEPC* (New York: Columbia University Press, 1953); Merl E. Reed, *Seedtime for the Modern Civil Rights Movement: The President's Committee on Fair Employment Practice, 1941–1946* (Baton Rouge: Louisiana State University Press, 1991); Anthony S. Chen, *The Fifth Freedom: Jobs, Politics, and Civil Rights in the United States, 1941–1972* (Princeton, NJ: Princeton University Press, 2009); Kenneth M. Schultz, "The FEPC and the Legacy of the Labor-Based Civil Rights Movement of the 1940s," *Labor History* 49 (2008): 71–92.

85 In a debate over a reorganization plan, Senator Elbert Duncan Thomas, a Utah Democrat, read into the record a letter from both the Texas Manufacturers Association and the South Carolina Chamber of Commerce that contained this information. See *Congressional Record,* 80th Cong., 2d sess., March 16, 1948, p. 2904.

86 Orme W. Phelps, "Public Policy in Labor Disputes: The Crisis of 1946," *Journal of Political Economy* 55 (1947): 189–211.

87 For a study of the late 1930s, see Marian D. Irish, "The Proletarian South," *Journal of Politics* 2 (1940): 231–58; and for data on union growth, see Leo Troy, "The Growth of Union Membership in the South, 1939–1953," *Southern Economic Journal* 24 (1958): 407–20. The key work remains Ray F. Marshall, *Labor in the South* (Cambridge: Harvard University Press, 1967).

88 *New York Times,* July 7, 1943.

89 *Congressional Record,* 78th Cong., 1st sess., June 2, 1943, p. 5228.

90   Harry A. Mills and Emily Clark Brown, *From the Wagner Act to Taft-Hartley: A Study of National Labor Policy and Labor Relations* (Chicago: University of Chicago Press, 1950), pp. 354–56. See also James B. Atleson, *Labor and the Wartime State: Labor Relations and Law during World War II* (Urbana: University of Illinois Press, 1998); Patrick Renshaw, "Organized Labor and the United States War Economy, 1939–1945," *Journal of Contemporary History* 21 (1986): 3–22.

91   With a likeness score of 84.

92   With a likeness score of 100. The head of the AFL, William Green, and the head of the CIO, Philip Murray, together with Donald Robertson, who led the Brotherhood of Locomotive Firemen and Engineers, sent a long memorandum to President Roosevelt, asking him to veto this "wicked, vicious bill," which they said was "born of malice" and represented "the very essence of fascism." See *New York Times,* June 18, 1943. The president's motives for issuing a veto were less ideological and more instrumental. As Nelson Lichtenstein has written:

> FDR had vetoed the bill, not because he or his advisers opposed its punitive sections—many thought them inadequate and maladroit—but because this particular effort to curb the unions promised only instability and disaffection within labor ranks. Ickes told FDR that the bill would make [John] Lewis [the head of the United Mine Workers, which had struck for the third time in six weeks] a martyr, and William Davis feared that if Roosevelt signed the measure, it would drive "responsible and loyal labor leaders into Lewis' corner." The section of the bill mandating rank-and-file strike votes forecast even more trouble. After talking to Philip Murray, domestic affairs aide Wayne Coy warned FDR that the Smith-Connally Act would "encourage local leaders to submit strike notices on their own responsibility. . . . Such a tendency can only weaken the authority and influence of responsible international officers over their constituencies, thereby increasing rather than diminishing the danger of widespread stoppages."

See Nelson Lichtenstein, *Labor's War at Home: The CIO in World War II* (New York: Cambridge University Press, 1982), pp. 167–68.

93   *Congressional Record,* 78th Cong., 1st sess., June 3, 1943, p. 5312.

94   Mills and Brown, *From the Wagner Act to Taft-Hartley*, pp. 360–62.

95   Southerners voted in favor of passage with Republicans at a remarkable likeness score of 100 in the House and 89 in the Senate.

96   For a discussion, see Farhang and Katznelson, "The Southern Imposition," p. 24.

97 *Congressional Record,* 79th Cong., 2d sess., February 6, 1946, p. 993; February 5, 1946, p. 922.

98 "The Labor Situation," *Fortune,* November 1946, p. 125. An important overview can be found in United States Department of Labor Bureau of Labor Statistics, Bulletin No. 898, *Labor in the South* (Washington, DC: U.S. Government Printing Office, 1947).

99 That crisis passed when the engineers and trainmen returned to work.

100 "Labor Drives South," *Fortune,* November 1946, pp. 134, 135.

101 Congress of Industrial Organizations, "The CIO and the Negro Worker: Together for Unity" (1942); "Working and Fighting Together Regardless of Race, Creed, Color or National Origin" (1943); "Report of the National CIO Committee to Abolish Discrimination" (1945); "A Legal Informational Guide to State Civil Rights Statutes and FEPC Legislation, and Procedures for Processing Court Cases" (1947).

102 Risa Lauren Goluboff, "Let Economic Equality Take Care of Itself: The NAACP, Labor Litigation, and the Making of Civil Rights in the 1940s," *UCLA Law Review* 52 (2005): 1393–1486.

103 "Labor Drives South," p. 230.

104 Ibid., pp. 230, 232 (italics in original). Discussions of the entwining of race and labor during this period include Robert Korstad and Nelson Lichtenstein, "Opportunities Found and Lost: Labor, Radicals, and the Early Civil Rights Movement," *Journal of American History* 75 (1988): 786–811; Michael Goldfield, *The Color of Politics: Race and the Mainsprings of American Politics* (New York: New Press, 1997), pp. 240–49; Philip Foner, *Organized Labor and the Black Worker, 1916–1973* (New York: Praeger, 1974), pp. 238–74; Ray Marshall, "The Negro in Southern Unions," Marc Karson and Ronald Radosh, "The American Federation of Labor and the Negro Worker," and Sumner N. Rosen, "The CIO Era, 1935–55," in *The Negro and the American Labor Movement,* ed. Julius Jacobson (New York: Doubleday, 1968), pp. 128–208; Paul Frymer, *Black and Blue: African Americans, the Labor Movement, and the Decline of the Democratic Party* (Princeton, NJ: Princeton University Press, 2008), pp. 54–63; Judith Stein, "Southern Workers in National Unions: Birmingham Steelworkers, 1936–1951," in *Organized Labor in the Twentieth-Century South,* ed. Robert H. Zieger (Knoxville: University of Tennessee Press, 1991), pp. 183–222.

105 "Labor Drives South," pp. 234, 237.

106 The collapse of Operation Dixie was a key development. For a discussion, see Michael Goldfield, "The Failure of Operation Dixie: A Critical Turning Point in American Political Development?" in *Race, Class, and Community in Southern Labor History,* ed. Gary M. Fink and Merl E. Reed (Tuscaloosa: University of Alabama Press, 1994), pp. 166–89.

107 "The Labor Bill Becomes Law," *New York Times,* June 24, 1947.

108 Robert A. Taft, "The Taft-Hartley Act: A Favorable View," *Annals of the*

American Academy of Political and Social Science 274 (1951), p. 195; http://www
.presidency.ucsb.edu/ws/index.php?pid=12675#axzz1Q7QXfGtV.

109 By 1954, the only nonsouthern states to pass such laws included Arizona, Iowa,
Nebraska, Nevada, and South Dakota. For a listing of right-to-work states,
see Erwin S. Mayer, "Union Security and the Taft-Hartley Act," *Duke Law
Journal* 4 (1961): 515. For fuller discussions of Taft-Hartley, see Katznelson,
When Affirmative Action Was White, pp. 61–65; Sumner H. Slichter, "The Taft-
Hartley Act," *Quarterly Journal of Economics* 63 (1949): 1–31; and especially R.
Alton Lee, *Truman and Taft-Hartley: A Question of Mandate* (Lexington: Uni-
versity of Kentucky Press, 1966). A rich nonpartisan contemporaneous source
is the 335-page report by the Bureau of National Affairs, *The Taft-Hartley Act
after One Year* (Washington, DC: BNA, 1948).

110 *Congressional Record,* 80th Cong., 1st sess., April 28, 1947, p. 4150.

111 Hugh Davis Graham, *The Civil Rights Era: Origins and Development of National
Policy* (New York: Oxford University Press, 1990), p. 37.

112 *Congressional Record,* 80th Cong., 1st sess., April 29, 1947, p. 4317–18, 4399.

113 Ibid., June 18, 1947, p. 906.

114 For a discussion, see Nelson Lichtenstein, "Taft-Hartley: A Slave Labor Law?,"
Catholic University Law Review 47 (1998): 770–72, 782–85.

115 In the Senate, Minority Leader Alben Barkley of Kentucky and Harley
Kilgore of West Virginia also spoke up for unions, although in far more measured terms than Pepper.

116 *Congressional Record,* 80th Cong., 1st sess., March 10, 1947, p. 1171.

117 Ibid., p. 1322.

118 Ibid., April 3, 1947, p. 632.

119 Ibid., April 26, 1947, p. 698.

120 Fred A. Hartley, *Our New National Labor Policy* (New York: Funk & Wag-
nalls, 1948), p. 12.

121 *Congressional Record,* 80th Cong., 1st sess., April 17, 1947, p. 857.

122 James A. Gross, *The Reshaping of the National Labor Relations Board: National
Labor Policy in Transition, 1937–1947* (Albany: State University of New York
Press, 1981), p. 16.

123 Had southern Democratic voting been patterned like that of other Democrats,
Taft-Hartley would not have been passed into law. On the legislation's five key
votes in the House, southern Democratic and Republican likeness averaged 89;
on the fourteen roll calls in the Senate, a nearly as high 81. When the House
voted to override President Truman's veto, the likeness score of this coalition
reached 91; in the Senate, it was a high 79. On the labor question, southern
defection was nearly total.

124 Andrew Schonfield, *Modern Capitalism: The Changing Balance of Public and
Private Power* (New York: Oxford University Press, 1965), pp. 357, 313, 322,
319, 115, 308.

125 The degree to which a strong interregional coalition on social policy could form varied by issue area. Likeness within the party fell below 70, to the mid-60s, on questions of housing and urban renewal; yet agreement was sufficiently strong to pass important legislation. See David R. Mayhew, *Party Loyalty among Congressmen: The Differences between Democrats and Republicans, 1947–1962* (Cambridge: Harvard University Press, 1966), especially pp. 57–90.

126 An important framework within which to assess these matters can be found in Peter A. Hall and David Soskice, eds., *Varieties of Capitalism: The Institutional Foundations of Comparative Advantage* (New York: Oxford University Press, 2001).

127 The classic study of interest-group pluralism written at the time is David B. Truman, *The Governmental Process: Political Interest and Public Opinion* (New York: Alfred A. Knopf, 1951).

128 U.S. Department of Commerce, *National Associations of the United States* (Washington, DC: U.S. Government Printing Office, 1949).

129 Truman, *The Governmental Process,* p. 59.

130 Ibid., pp. 50–51.

131 Theodore J. Lowi, *The End of Liberalism: Ideology, Policy, and the Crisis of Public Authority* (New York: W. W. Norton, 1969), p. 72.

132 Ibid., p. 123.

133 E. E. Schattschneider, *The Semi-Sovereign People: A Realist's View of Democracy in America* (New York: Holt, Rinehart and Winston, 1960), p. 35.

134 This occurred despite the first preference of black leaders to refuse this choice. See Dona C. Hamilton and Charles V. Hamilton, *The Dual Agenda: Race and Social Welfare Policies of Civil Rights Organizations* (New York: Columbia University Press, 1997). For a superb consideration of the broken link between labor and civil rights, see Risa L. Goluboff, *The Lost Promise of Civil Rights* (Cambridge: Harvard University Press, 2010).

CHAPTER 11 · "WILDEST HOPES"

1 The site is now part of the White Sands Missile Range.

2 James G. Hershberg, *James B. Conant: Harvard to Hiroshima and the Making of the Nuclear Age* (Stanford, CA: Stanford University Press, 1993, pp. 231–32.

3 Quickly, "the cloud reached a height of 41,000 feet, 12,000 feet higher than the earth's highest mountain," and the silence was broken by a "mighty thunder" and "a wave of hot wind." See William L. Laurence, *Dawn over Zero: The Story of the Atomic Bomb* (New York: Alfred A. Knopf, 1946), pp. 10–11. The test went forward only after Edward Teller was able to reassure the leaders of the Manhattan Project that it would not set off a chain reaction that might engulf the world. See Edward Teller (with Allen Brown), *The Legacy of Hiroshima* (New York: Doubleday, 1962), p. 16.

4   George Kistiakowsky was a Harvard University chemist who had participated in the Manhattan Project by leading a team that developed the lenses that compressed plutonium uniformly in order to achieve a critical mass.

5   This report to the Department of War is cited in Laurence, *Dawn over Zero,* pp. 193–94. Oppenheimer was far more reserved. Conant's eight-page handwritten account records how, upon the detonation, Oppenheimer cited the Bhagavad Gita: "I am become Death, the destroyer of worlds." Farrell also reported how "the lighting effects beggared description. The whole country was lighted by a searing light with the intensity many times that of the midday sun. It was golden purple, violet, gray, and blue. It lighted every peak, crevasse and ridge of the nearby mountain range with a clarity and beauty that cannot be described but must be seen to be imagined. It was that beauty that the great poets dream about but describe most poorly and inadequately." Both Oppenheimer and Farrell are cited in Hershberg, *James B. Conant,* p. 233.

6   These islands, as well as the Marshalls and the Carolines, had been mandated to Japan by the League of Nations after World War I.

7   Robert S. Norris, *Racing for the Bomb: General Leslie R. Groves and the Manhattan Project's Indispensable Man* (Hanover, NH: Steerforth Press, 2002), pp. 313–24; see also Gary Wills, *Bomb Power: The Modern Presidency and the National Security State* (New York: Penguin, 2010), p. 43.

8   Laurence, *Dawn over Zero,* p. 224.

9   Gregor Dallas, *1945: The War That Never Ended* (New Haven: Yale University Press, 2005), p. 571.

10   Laurence, *Dawn over Zero,* pp. 229, 241, 236–37.

11   John W. Dower, *Embracing Defeat: Japan in the Wake of World War II* (New York: W. W. Norton, 1999), pp. 45–46, 36.

12   *New York Times,* August 15, 1945; *Life,* August 27, 1945, pp. 25, 21.

13   Samuel P. Huntington, *The Common Defense: Strategic Programs in National Politics* (New York: Columbia University Press, 1961), p. 35.

14   TABLE Ed26–47, "Military Personnel on Active Duty, by Branch of Service and Sex: 1789–1995," *Historical Statistics of the United States* (New York: Cambridge University Press, 2006); Tony Judt, *Postwar: A History of Europe since 1945* (New York: Penguin, 2005), p. 109. Army readiness dropped even further, to seven active duty divisions, by the time the Korean War broke out in June 1950. See Stetson Conn, "Changing Concepts of National Defense in the United States, 1937–1947," *Military Affairs* 28 (1964): 7.

15   John Lewis Gaddis, "Comment," in the *AHR* Forum on Melvyn P. Leffler, "The American Conception of National Security and the Beginnings of the Cold War, 1945–48," *American Historical Review* 89 (1984): 383.

16   Judt, *Postwar,* p. 109.

17   Isaiah Berlin, *Washington Despatches, 1941–1945: Weekly Political Reports from*

632 Notes to Pages 406–407

the British Embassy, ed. H. G Nicholas (Chicago: University of Chicago Press, 1981), pp. 613–14.

18   See Peter Clarke, *The Last Thousand Days of the British Empire* (London: Penguin, 2008), pp. 400–403.

19   Rhodri Jeffreys-Jones, *The CIA and American Democracy* (New Haven: Yale University Press, 1989), p. 28.

20   It took nearly a year for the United States to abolish its blacklist of individuals and companies forbidden to trade with the United States because they had traded with one or more of its enemies during World War II. The Truman administration took this step on July 8, 1946.

21   On the toll of the war and the absence of American worry about the USSR as an enemy, see Melvyn P. Leffler, *A Preponderance of Power: National Security, the Truman Administration, and the Cold War* (Stanford, CA: Stanford University Press, 1992), p. 5.

22   A 1947 Council on Foreign Relations report observed that from the time President Truman appointed Byrnes to lead the State Department on July 3, 1945, until the spring of 1947, "save for the brief experience of the Potsdam Conference, which his position as chief executive required him to attend, Truman left foreign affairs largely to his Secretary of State." See John C. Campbell, *The United States in World Affairs, 1945–1947* (New York: Harper and Brothers, 1947), p. 17.

23   On April 16, 1947, Baruch spoke to the legislature of his home state South Carolina when his portrait was being unveiled in the chamber. He proclaimed, "We are today in the midst of a cold war. Our enemies are to be found abroad and at home." See *Washington Post,* April 17, 1947. Walter Lippmann, *The Cold War: A Study in U.S. Foreign Policy* (New York: Harper and Brothers, 1947).

24   Walter Lippmann, *U.S. Foreign Policy: Shield of the Republic* (Boston: Houghton Mifflin, 1943), p. 164.

25   Lippmann's and Roosevelt's views are discussed, and both cited, in John Lewis Gaddis, "The Insecurities of Victory: The United States and the Perception of the Soviet Threat after World War II," in *The Truman Presidency,* ed. Michael J. Lacey (Cambridge: Cambridge University Press, 1989), p. 243.

26   In October 1945, Adm. Samuel Robinson, who had served as the navy's production chief during the war and who was advocating the creation of a capable postwar intelligence unit on the model of the OSS, identified the USSR as just one of six leading potential enemies, the others being Germany and Japan, but also, remarkably, Brazil, France, and Great Britain. See Jeffreys-Jones, *The CIA and American Democracy,* p. 35.

27   Samuel P. Huntington, *The Common Defense: Strategic Programs in National Politics* (New York: Columbia University Press, 1961), p. 14. For a comprehensive overview, see Jack Stokes Ballard, *The Shock of Peace: Military and Economic Demobilization after World War II* (Washington, DC: University Press of America, 1983), pp. 27–72. America's wartime pattern is placed in a com-

parative frame in E. J. B. Foxcroft, "Planning and Executing Resources Allocation—A Phase of War Administration," *Public Policy* 6 (1955): 158–81.

28 The only negative votes were cast by two midwestern Republicans, William Langer of North Dakota and Henrik Shipstead of Minnesota.

29 For a discussion, see Wilson D. Miscamble, *From Roosevelt to Truman: Potsdam, Hiroshima, and the Cold War* (New York: Cambridge University Press, 2007), pp. 259–61.

30 Cited in Hershberg, *James B. Conant,* pp. 236–37. President Truman rejected the idea of sharing atomic secrets, a decision he reported on October 8, 1945. See G. Pascal Zachary, *Endless Frontier: Vannevar Bush, Engineer of the American Century* (New York: Free Press, 1997), p. 299.

31 Melvyn P. Leffler, *For the Soul of Mankind: The United States, the Soviet Union, and the Cold War* (New York: Hill and Wang, 2008), pp. 65, 59.

32 *Congressional Record,* 79th Cong., 1st sess., July 26, 1945, p. 8085.

33 Cited in Campbell, *United States in World Affairs, 1945–1947,* p. 523.

34 Brookings Institution, International Study Group, *The Administration of Foreign Affairs and Overseas Operations: A Report Prepared for the Bureau of the Budget and Executive Office of the President* (Washington, DC: U.S. Government Printing Office, June 1951), p. 5. For a contrary view, arguing that "long before the war in Europe ended in May of 1945, it was clear there would be no peace," see Theodore H. White, *Fire in the Ashes: Europe at Mid-Century* (New York: William Sloane Associates, 1953), p. 393.

35 Brookings Institution, *The Administration of Foreign Affairs and Overseas Operations,* pp. 1, 9.

36 Ibid., p. 55.

37 Ibid., p. 35.

38 Laurence, *Dawn over Zero,* pp. 270–71.

39 Max Hastings, *Inferno: The World at War, 1939–1945* (New York. Alfred A. Knopf, 2011), p. 628.

40 *Washington Post,* August 18, 1945. Arnold suffered five heart attacks during the course of the war.

41 James Agee, "The Bomb," *Time,* August 20, 1945, p. 175.

42 *Washington Post,* September 16, 1945.

43 *New York Times,* November 8, 1945, November 17, 1945.

44 "The 36-Hour War," *Life,* November 19, 1945, pp. 27–35. For an overview of how atomic weapons and nuclear war were portrayed by American artists after Hiroshima and Nagasaki, see Denise M. Rompilla, "From Hiroshima to the Hydrogen Bomb: American Artists Witness the Birth of the Atomic Age" (Ph.D. dissertation, Rutgers University, 2008).

45 The full text can be found in the *New York Times,* February 10, 1946. The Soviet quest to gain an atom bomb was hardly a secret. In November 1945, Foreign Minister Molotov declared that the USSR "would have atomic energy, too." Embassy of the U.S.S.R., Washington, *Information Bulletin,* November

17, 1945, p. 8; cited in Campbell, *United States in World Affairs, 1945–1947,* p. 40. For an overview of "Stalin and the Shattered Peace," see Vladislov Zubok and Constantine Pleshakov, *Inside the Kremlin's Cold War: From Stalin to Khrushchev* (Cambridge: Harvard University Press, 1997), pp. 36–77. We now know that Stalin made the bomb a high-priority project within a month of Hiroshima. See Zachary, *Endless Frontier,* p. 293.

46   *New York Times,* February 10, 1946. For a discussion of the speech placed in the wider context of the decline of prospects for positive East-West relations, see Robert Dallek, *The Lost Peace: Leadership in a Time of Horror and Hope, 1945–1953* (New York: HarperCollins, 2010), pp. 182–83.

47   John Lewis Gaddis, *George F. Kennan: An American Life* (New York: Penguin, 2011), p. 216. Stalin, in this period, "was vacillating, saying contradictory things, pursuing divergent policies. Historians violently argue about Stalin's motivations and his goals precisely because his rhetoric and his actions were so inconsistent." See Leffler, *For the Soul of Mankind,* p. 33.

48   Cited in Gaddis, *George F. Kennan,* p. 217.

49   For a useful discussion, see Judt, *Postwar,* pp. 103–4.

50   See http://www.trumanlibrary.org/whistlestop/study_collections/coldwar/documents/pdf/6-6.pdf. An incisive critique of the Long Telegram—"one of the two or three most important texts of the early cold war"—can be found in Anders Stephanson, *Kennan and the Art of Foreign Policy* (Cambridge: Harvard University Press, 1989), pp. 45–53; see also H. W. Brands, *What America Owes the World: The Struggle for the Soul of Foreign Policy* (New York: Cambridge University Press, 1998), pp. 144–56.

51   X [George Kennan], "The Sources of Soviet Conduct," *Foreign Affairs* 25 (1947): 575, 582.

52   Louis J. Halle, *The Cold War as History* (New York: Harper & Row, 1967), p. 105.

53   *New York Times,* March 1, 1946.

54   See http://www.fordham.edu/halsall/mod/churchill-iron.asp. For a discussion of the iron curtain metaphor, see Patrick Wright, *Iron Curtain: From Stage to Cold War* (New York: Oxford University Press, 2007). By 1948, Churchill was making the case for a preemptive war against the Soviet Union. Arguing that he thought eight more years would be required for the USSR to obtain the bomb, he proposed that "we ought not to wait until Russia is ready." Seeking a showdown when the United States still possessed a monopoly, he asked the House of Commons to imagine what the behavior of the Soviets would be like "when they got the atomic bomb and accumulated a large store. . . . No one in his senses can believe we have a limitless period before us." He thus counseled the Truman administration to offer an ultimatum to the Russians: Withdraw from East Germany or face an American atomic assault. See Marc Trachtenberg, "A 'Wasting Asset': American Strategy and the Shifting Nuclear Balance, 1949–1954," *International Security* 13 (1988/1989): 9–10.

55   Martin Gilbert, *A History of the Twentieth Century, Vol. 2, 1933–1951* (New York: William Morrow, 1998), p. 740; the text of the March 13, 1946, interview can be found at http://marxism.halkcephesi.net/Stalin/volume%2014%20 to%2018/pravda031346.htm.

56   *Wall Street Journal,* February 25, 1946.

57   Dexter Masters and Katharine Way, eds., *One World or None* (New York: McGraw Hill, 1946). The first quotation appears in the inside front cover; the second in the contribution by Harold C. Urey, "How Does It All Add Up?," p. 59.

58   Philip Morrison, "If the Bomb Gets Out of Hand," in ibid., pp. 1–6.

59   E. U. Condon, "The New Technique of Private War," in ibid., pp. 39–42; Condon was a key target of attention for HUAC, one of whose subcommittes, composed of the Republican Richard Vail of Illinois and the Georgia Democrat John S. Wood, labeled him in 1948 as "one of the weakest links in our atomic security." For a fair-minded consideration of the attack on Condon based on his associations with left-wing organizations alleged to be Communist fronts, see Jessica Wang, "Science, Security, and the Cold War: The Case of E. U. Condon," *Isis* 83 (1992): 238, 246.

60   Reinhold Niebuhr, "Our Relations with Japan," *Christianity and Crisis,* September 17, 1945, p. 5. This is a theme he continued to develop; see the "Foreword" he wrote for Harrison Brown and James Real, *Community of Fear* (Santa Barbara, CA: Center for the Study of Democratic Institutions, 1960). During the year following Hiroshima and Nagasaki, popular books that explained the principles of the atomic bomb began to appear. Two examples are Gessner G. Hawley and Sigmund W. Leifson, *Atomic Energy in War and Peace* (New York: Reinhold, 1946); and J. K. Robertson, *Atomic Artillery and the Atomic Bomb* (New York: D. Van Nostrand, 1946). In May 1946, a committee of the American Psychological Association warned that the effects of nuclear fears were indeterminate, as they might lead either to escapist thinking that minimized the problem or to a sense of desperation that would increase the prospects of atomic warfare. See *New York Times*, May 26, 1946.

61   This analysis appeared in a nine-part series on "Control of Atomic Energy" published by Walter Lippmann in his syndicated column between March 27 and April 6, 1946. For his conclusions about the choice facing the world, see the last two essays, *Los Angeles Times,* April 5 and April 6, 1946. He had first advanced his ideas about atomic energy, including the idea that agreements about the bomb be binding not only on nations but on individual leaders, in his "Today and Tomorrow" column half a year earlier. See *Washington Post,* November 17, 1945.

62   *Washington Post,* April 3, 1946. Later that year, Joseph Alsop urged Washington to use its period of monopoly to "seek an understanding with the Soviet Union," for once they catch up, he warned, "war will then be almost certain," and "the military advantage will be all on the Soviet side." See *Washington Post,* September 25, 1946.

63   John Hersey, *Hiroshima* (New York: Alfred A. Knopf, 1946); *Billboard,* September 14, 1946, p. 10. The editors explained, "The *New Yorker* this week devotes its entire editorial space to an article on the almost complete obliteration of a city by one atomic bomb, and what happened to the people of that city. It does so in the conviction that few of us have yet comprehended the all but incredible destructive power of this weapon, and that everyone might take time to consider the terrible implications of its use." See *The New Yorker,* August 31, 1946, p. 15. A Japanese translation of *Hiroshima* was not permitted until 1949 by the U.S. occupation administration. See Matthew Jones, *After Hiroshima: The United States, Race and Nuclear Weapons in Asia, 1945–1965* (New York: Cambridge University Press, 2010), p. 33.

64   Paul S. Boyer, *By the Bomb's Early Light: American Thought and Culture at the Dawn of the Atomic Age* (New York: Pantheon, 1985), p. 74.

65   Brodie clarified why this is the case:

> The reasons why the same plane can be effective over much greater distances with atomic bombs than with chemical bombs concern basically the intricate relationships between such factors as the amount of bombs which a plane can carry over any given distance, the total military effort expended in carrying it over that distance, and the tolerable rate of loss of attacking planes. Since the atomic bomb does enormously more damage than an equivalent load of chemical bombs, the cost per sortie which is acceptable with atomic bombs is also proportionately greater—great enough, in fact, to include 100 percent loss of planes on successful attacks. The greater acceptable cost; the fact that the plane itself need not be retrieved (whatever the arrangements made for the rescue of the crew); and the additional fact that a single atomic bomb, whatever its weight, is always a sufficient payload for any distance which the plane is capable of carrying it, will have the effect of at least doubling the maximum effective bombing range of any plane of B-29 size or greater.

See Bernard Brodie, "The Atom Bomb as Policy Maker," *Foreign Affairs* 27 (1948): 25.

66   Hanson W. Baldwin, *Power and Politics: The Price of Security in the Atomic Age* (Claremont, CA: Claremont University, 1950), pp. 66, 68. For an earlier statement, see Baldwin, "Two Great Delusions about the A-Bomb," *New York Times,* July 10, 1949.

67   Warner R. Schilling, "The H-Bomb Decision: How to Decide without Actually Choosing," *Political Science Quarterly* 76 (1961): 27. Gen. A. G. L. McNaughton, who served as Canada's representative to the United Nations Atomic Energy Commission in 1946 and 1947, explained, at the start of his service as a perma-

nent delegate to the UN in early 1948, why changes in weight and explosiveness had made it possible for bombers to achieve a radius of some five thousand miles and why defense against their attacks, as well as those by guided missile, approached the impossible. McNaughton, "National and International Control of Atomic Energy," *International Journal* 3 (1947/1948): 14–16. McNaughton and Baruch clashed at the UN over the insistence by the United States that the USSR forgo its veto rights in the Security Council regarding the enforcement of inspections of atomic facilities and programs. See *New York Times,* December 20, 1946.

68 Schilling, "The H-Bomb Decision," p. 25.

69 These points are made by Brodie, "The Atom Bomb as Policy Maker," pp. 26, 33.

70 Harry S. Truman, *Memoirs,* vol. 2, *Years of Trial and Hope* (Garden City, NY: Doubleday, 1956), p. 106. For the development of the Truman Doctrine, see Richard M. Freeland, *The Truman Doctrine and the Origins of McCarthyism* (New York: NYU Press, 1985), pp. 71–114.

71 See http://www.historyguide.org/europe/truman1947.html.

72 For an assessment of the Truman Doctrine as "a policy that might be as important for America as the Monroe Doctrine of 1823 and the Roosevelt Lend Lease Program of 1941," see the *New York Times,* March 16, 1947. On Marshall's commencement talk, see ibid., June 6, 1947. The text of his speech can be found at http://www.oecd.org/document/10/0,3746,en_2649_201185 _1876938_1_1_1_1,00.html. At a Paris gathering of the foreign ministers of Britain, France, and the USSR, Vyacheslav Molotov opposed the Marshall Plan, warning of "grave consequences" if the program of aid went ahead. No Soviet-bloc country joined in, and the French Communist Party, under pressure from Moscow, withdrew from the country's postwar coalition government.

73 For a bracing discussion, stressing often surprising organizational and normative continuities with the League of Nations, see Mark Mazower, *No Enchanted Palace: The End of Empire and the Ideological Origins of the United Nations* (Princeton, NJ: Princeton University Press, 2009); see also Townsend Hoopes and Douglas Brinkley, *FDR and the Creation of the UN* (New Haven: Yale University Press, 2000).

74 The inherent limits of the United Nations are underscored in F. H. Hinsley, *Power and the Pursuit of Peace* (Cambridge: Cambridge University Press, 1963), pp. 335–45. When the United Nations Security Council voted on July 7, 1950, to recommend that member states join a unified military command under the leadership of the United States to aid the Republic of Korea, the USSR was boycotting the council for not having admitted the People's Republic of China.

75 *New York Times,* December 28, 1945. The Moscow meeting followed the mid-November gathering of President Truman and Prime Ministers Clement Attlee of Great Britain and W. L. Mackenzie King of Canada. After five days

of discussion at the White House, they had declared on behalf of the "three countries which possess the knowledge essential to the use of atomic energy" the need to find "a constructive solution to the problem of the atomic bomb." Their declaration included the offer to share the secrets of atomic energy under the auspices of the United Nations, but only with the establishment of "effective, reciprocal, and enforceable safeguards acceptable to all nations." See *New York Times,* November 16, 1945.

76   *New York Times,* June 15, 1946. The U.S. position in the UN on controls and inspections was guided in part by *A Report on the International Control of Atomic Energy* (Washington, DC: U.S. Government Printing Office, March 16, 1946). The report was sent to Secretary of State James Byrnes by the Secretary of State's Committee on Atomic Energy, which he had appointed on January 7, 1946. The committee, chaired by Dean Acheson, and whose members included Vannevar Bush, James Conant, Leslie Groves, and John J. McCloy, designated a board of consultants (Chester I. Barnard, J. Robert Oppenheimer, Charles A. Thomas, Henry Winner, and, as chair, David Lilienthal), which did the bulk of the work. The Department of War fought an internal administration battle against the internationalization of atomic energy. A leaked departmental assessment in the early spring of 1947 warned that "other nations could wage atomic war on equal footing with the United States within six years after the adoption of the United States plan for international control of atomic energy." See *New York Times,* April 9, 1947.

77   *New York Times,* June 20, 1946; *Washington Post,* June 20, 1946. In March 1947, in a seventy-eight-minute speech to the Security Council, Gromyko denounced the American proposals as "thoroughly vicious and unacceptable" and "incompatible with state sovereignty." See *Chicago Daily Tribune,* March 6, 1947. On May 19, 1947, Gromyko once again flatly rejected an inspection regime, and he warned against the "illusion" that the United States would long keep its atomic bomb monopoly. See *Los Angeles Times,* May 20, 1947. In turn, the head of the U.S. Atomic Energy Commission, David Lilienthal, told the UN's Atomic Energy Commission that absent a "foolproof" system of inspection, the United States intended to maintain and improve its atomic weapons stockpile. See *New York Times,* June 3, 1947. Two days later, the country's deputy spokesman in the UN commission, Frederick Osborn, called the Soviet plan a "fraud on the peoples of the world." See *Washington Post,* June 5, 1947. Looking back at the situation when at the Truman Library in 1974, Osborn recalled that "there was a great deal of talk" among American officials "about how long it would be before Russia had atomic weapons." Estimates then ranged up to twenty-five years. "Of course, they were well along. This we didn't know during our negotiations. The Russians were almost at the point of exploding an atomic bomb during the negotiations. None of us had any idea of this. We all thought that this was a long way off." See http://www.trumanlibrary.org/oralhist/osbornf.htm#transcript.

78 For a thoughtful overview, see Campbell, *The United States in World Affairs, 1945–1947,* pp. 391–99.

79 Bernard Brodie, ed., *The Absolute Weapon: Atomic Power and World Order* (New York: Harcourt, Brace, 1946). The other contributors were Percy E. Corbett, Frederick Dunn, William T. R. Fox, and Arnold Wolfers.

80 *Chicago Daily Tribune,* August 29, 1946.

81 *Washington Post,* June 5, 1947.

82 In 1974, the official spelling was changed to Enewetak to better reflect local pronunciation. Sixteen years later, in 2000, the people of the atoll were awarded some $340 million by the Marshall Island Nuclear Claims Tribunal for the harms they had incurred as a result of the nuclear tests that had been conducted between 1948 and 1958.

83 *Washington Post,* December 2, 1947.

84 "The Eternal Apprentice," *Time,* November 8, 1948, p. 71.

85 J. Robert Oppenheimer, "International Control of Atomic Energy," *Foreign Affairs* (1948): 240, 241, 243, 244, 248, 250–51, 249, 252.

86 For a consideration of these issues, see James M. Lindsay, "Congress, Foreign Policy, and the New Institutionalism," *International Studies Quarterly* 38 (1994): 281–304.

87 For a discussion, see Samuel P. Huntington, *The Soldier and the State* (Cambridge: Harvard University Press, 1957), pp. 324–25.

88 This is the central theme of the magisterial treatment of congressional debates about global affairs by Michael J. Hogan, *A Cross of Iron: Harry S. Truman and the Origins of the National Security State, 1945–1954* (New York: Cambridge University Press, 1998).

89 William Frye, "The National Military Establishment," *American Political Science Review* 43 (1949): 544; Charles Merriam, "Security without Militarism: Preserving Civilian Control in American Political Institutions," in *Civil-Military Relationships in American Life,* ed. Jerome G. Kerwin (Chicago: University of Chicago Press, 1948) pp. 156–72.

90 *Congressional Record*, 80th Cong., 1st sess., July 19, 1947, p. 9414.

91 Ibid., 81st Cong., 1st sess., August 2, 1949, p. 10603.

92 During the 80th Congress, analyzed by Peter Trubowitz in just this way, the states that recorded more than 87 percent support for the administration's program included Alabama, Arkansas, Florida, Georgia, Kentucky, South Carolina, Texas, and Virginia. Only three nonsouthern states—Arizona, New Mexico, and Rhode Island—exhibited this very high degree of backing. The next tier of at least two-thirds support included the delegations from Louisiana, Maryland, Mississippi, and Tennessee. In all, the South dominated the internationalist bloc. See Peter Trubowitz, *Defining the National Interest: Conflict and Change in American Foreign Policy* (Chicago: University of Chicago Press, 1998), pp. 185–90.

640 Notes to Pages 424–425

93   The speech, delivered in Towson, Maryland, on November 28, 1947, is cited in Jonathan Bell, *The Liberal State on Trial* (New York: Columbia University Press, 2004), p. 51.

94   For an overview of comparatively low Republican cohesion in foreign affairs in the 81st Congress, see David B. Truman, *The Congressional Party: A Case Study* (New York: Wiley, 1959), pp. 78–82.

95   *Congressional Record*, 80th Cong., 1st sess., July 16, 1947, p. 9110.

96   Letter from Harold Knutson to Robert Taft, November 3, 1947; cited in Bell, *The Liberal State on Trial,* p. 91.

97   *Chicago Daily Tribune,* February 9, 1945.

98   Cited in Robert David Johnson, *Congress and the Cold War* (New York: Cambridge University Press, 2006), p. 20.

99   Irwin F. Gellman, *The Contender, Richard Nixon: The Congress Years, 1946–1952* (New York: Free Press, 1999), pp. 120–23.

100   The most important role within the Republican Party to manage these wings and maintain a significant degree of foreign policy bipartisanship fell to Senator Taft, a potential presidential nominee in both 1948 and 1952. For discussions, see Vernon Van Dyke and Edward Lane Davis, "Senator Taft and American Security," *Journal of Politics* 14 (1952): 177–202; William S. White, *The Taft Story* (New York: Harper and Brothers, 1954); and James T. Patterson, *Mr. Republican: A Biography of Robert A. Taft* (Boston: Houghton Mifflin, 1972).

101   Hogan, *A Cross of Iron,* p. 100.

102   Cited in Julian E. Zelizer, *Arsenal of Democracy: The Politics of National Security—From World War II to the War on Terrorism* (New York: Basic Books, 2010), p. 66.

103   They did so with high likeness on roll calls that concerned defense, geopolitics, and international political economy, scoring 89 in the House and 90 in the Senate. By contrast, Democrats and Republicans, in aggregate, voted together with lower likeness, scoring 63 in the House and 60 in the Senate.

104   Wallace effectively broke with the administration by denouncing its "Get tough with Russia" policy at a National Citizens Political Action Committee (NCPAC) rally in New York on September 12, 1946. This was the key paragraph:

> To achieve lasting peace, we must study in detail just how the Russian character was formed—by invasions of Tartars, Mongols, Germans, Poles, Swedes, and French; by the czarist rule based on ignorance, fear and force; by the intervention of the British, French and Americans in Russian affairs from 1919 to 1921; by the geography of the huge Russian land mass situated strategically between Europe and Asia; and by the vitality derived from the rich Russian soil and the

strenuous Russian climate. Add to all this the tremendous emotional power which Marxism and Leninism gives to the Russian leaders— and then we can realize that we are reckoning with a force which cannot be handled successfully by a "Get tough with Russia" policy. "Getting tough" never bought anything real and lasting—whether for schoolyard bullies or businessmen or world powers. The tougher we get, the tougher the Russians will get.

See http://newdeal.feri.org/wallace/haw28.htm. NCPAC was listed as a subversive organization by HUAC after its participation in the Scientific and Cultural Conference for World Peace, arranged by the Communist Party USA, which was held from March 25 to 27, 1949, at the Waldorf-Astoria Hotel in New York. Wallace resigned his post as secretary of commerce at the president's request on September 20, 1945.

105 Robert Jervis, "The End of the Cold War on the Cold War?," *Diplomatic History* 17 (1993): 658.

106 Zelizer, *Arsenal of Democracy*, p. 68.

107 Huntington, *The Common Defense*, pp. 16–17, 15. Writing on October 5, 1947, about "the kind of containment we need," I. F. Stone argued that "the 'containment' we need for world peace" is a recognition "that socialism is coming everywhere" by the "neurotic . . . American capitalist class," a group that possesses "almost hysterical fears." On November 23, 1947, Stone sought to counter the growing East-West split by arguing against the assumption that "Russian control in Eastern Europe, as in the USSR itself, is based merely on ruthless terror." See I. F. Stone, *The Truman Era, 1945–1952: A Nonconformist History of Our Times* (Boston: Little, Brown, 1953), pp. 42, 41, 32–33.

108 This information is drawn from the annual publication of the *Official Congressional Directory*, published by the U.S. Government Printing Office at the start of each congressional session.

109 "Defense Boom in Dixie," *Time*, February 17, 1941, pp. 75–80.

110 Dewey W. Grantham, *The South in Modern America: A Region at Odds* (New York: HarperCollins, 1994), pp. 170–75; see also George Brown Tindall, *The Emergence of the New South, 1913–1945* (Baton Rouge: Louisiana State University Press, 1967), pp. 694–704.

111 Brenda Gayle Plummer, *Rising Wind: Black Americans and U.S. Foreign Affairs, 1935–1960* (Chapel Hill: University of North Carolina Press, 1996); John David Skrentny, "The Effect of the Cold War on African American Civil Rights: America and the World Audience, 1945–1968," *Theory and Society* 27 (1998): 237–85; Mary L. Dudziak, *Cold War Civil Rights: Race and the Image of American Democracy* (Princeton, NJ: Princeton University Press, 2002); Carol Anderson, *Eyes off the Prize: The United Nations and the African American Struggle for Human Rights, 1944–1955* (New York: Cambridge University Press, 2003);

Thomas Borstelmann, *The Cold War and the Color Line: American Race Relations in the Global Arena* (Cambridge: Harvard University Press, 2003).

112 The phrase is from Glenda Gilmore's *Defying Dixie: The Radical Roots of Civil Rights* (New York: W. W. Norton, 2008), where it serves as the title of chapter 2.

113 Robert E. Cushman, "Civil Liberties in an Atomic Age," *Annals of the American Academy of Political and Social Science* 249 (1947): 61.

114 *Congressional Record,* 80th Cong., 1st sess., July 19, 1947, p. 9412.

115 Ibid., July 7, 1947, p. 8299.

116 Ibid., July 19, 1947, p. 9427.

117 "It was obvious," a classic study has recalled, "that in the future management of this appalling new force, political and military considerations must be closely integrated. But there was absolutely no existing pattern to indicate how this might be accomplished." See Walter Millis, *Arms and the State: Civil-Military Elements in National Policy* (New York: Twentieth-Century Fund, 1958), p. 143.

118 The pivotal moment for the scientific community came at a conference held at the Institute for Advanced Study in Princeton, New Jersey, on June 19 and 20, 1951, where consensus was reached on the technical aspects of a thermonuclear device. One of the bomb's key developers and advocates, Edward Teller, later recalled both the ingenious science that preceded and followed this meeting and how "everyone who worked on the hydrogen bomb was appalled by its success and by its possible consequences," yet "was driven by the knowledge that the work was necessary for the safety of our country." See Teller, *The Legacy of Hiroshima,* pp. 52–53, 56.

119 Laurence, *Dawn over Zero,* p. 272.

120 See http://universityhonors.umd.edu/HONR269J/archive/Truman451003.htm. Truman was able to draw on wartime planning on how to regulate atomic weapons after the war. The first sketch was produced by Vannevar Bush, then director of the Office for Emergency Management at the Office of Scientific Research and Development (OSRD), and James Conant, Harvard University's president and a key player in the Manhattan Project. "Their plan consisted of a twelve-man commission on atomic energy that would regulate all transfers of special nuclear materials, the construction of production plants, and all nuclear experiments. The commission would consist of five scientists or engineers appointed by the National Academy of Science, three other civilians appointed by the president, and two army and two navy officers." See Peter Douglas Feaver, *Guarding the Guardians: Civilian Control of Nuclear Weapons in the United States* (Ithaca, NY: Cornell University Press, 1992), p. 90.

121 William S. White, "Bill for Atomic Control Is Expedited in Congress," *New York Times,* October 14, 1945.

122 Truman, *Memoirs,* vol. 2, p. 2. This course was consistent with the Manhattan Project, an army operation directed by an army leader.

123 Cited in Millis, *Arms and the State,* p. 162.

124 Donald J. Kevles, *The Physicists: The History of a Scientific Community in Modern America* (New York: Alfred A. Knopf, 1978), p. 151; Marquis Childs, "Washington Calling: Atoms during Peace," *Washington Post,* January 9, 1946. Childs wrote five influential, much-discussed articles in early January that argued the case against military control of atomic energy.

125 Daniel Bell, "The Great Science Debate," *Fortune,* June 1946, p. 116. This was the first article Bell, a sociologist, wrote for the magazine.

126 Howard A. Meyerhoff, "Domestic Control of Atomic Energy," *Science* 103 (1946): 133.

127 Kai Bird and Martin J. Sherwin, *American Prometheus: The Triumph and Tragedy of J. Robert Oppenheimer* (New York: Alfred A. Knopf, 2005), p. 326.

128 *New York Times,* October 31, 1945.

129 Cited in Millis, *Arms and the State,* p. 166.

130 Truman, *Memoirs,* vol. 2, p. 3. The *Wall Street Journal* objected, calling for "an atomic energy control commission" that would "include in its membership a strong and even dominating representation of the armed services." See *Wall Street Journal,* February 25, 1946.

131 For a summary of why this "compromise is satisfactory," see Ernest Lindley, "Atomic Legislation," *Washington Post,* April 4, 1946. Lindley specialized in foreign affairs, and he later joined the Department of State as special assistant to Secretary Dean Rusk in 1961, and served as a member of the department's Policy Planning Council until 1969. This arrangement, the *New York Times* agreed, "is about the best that can be expected at this time." See *New York Times,* June 2, 1946.

132 *New York Times,* February 10, 1946. As the legislation unfolded, the Soviet Union denounced what it called a reprise of "the Japanese system" and argued that this approach showed that "the United States are not seeking the establishment of international collaboration in the sphere of atomic energy." See *Chicago Daily Tribune,* March 21, 1946.

133 E. Blythe Stason, "Law and Atomic Energy," *Annals of the American Academy of Political and Social Science* 249 (1947): 94.

134 Walter Gellhorn, "Security, Secrecy, and the Advancement of Science," in *Civil Liberties under Attack,* ed. Clair Wilcox (Philadelphia: University of Pennsylvania Press, 1951), pp. 85–86.

135 The other four members were Robert Bacher, a Cornell University physicist who had worked closely with Robert Oppenheimer at Los Alamos; Sumner Pike, director of the Fuel Price Division of the Office of Price Administration since 1942; Lewis Strauss, a New York lawyer who served as assistant to the secretary of the navy during World War II; and William Waymack, editor of the *Des Moines Register and Tribune.* On Lilienthal's views, see R. L. Duffus, "Lilienthal Charts a Fateful Course," *New York Times,* November 17,

1946. Lilienthal's association with the TVA and his reputation as a planner led to charges during his confirmation hearings in early 1947 by the Republican majority leader, Ohio's Robert Taft, that he was "a New Dealer," and by New Hampshire Republican Styles Bridges that he was "an appeaser of Russia." The main opponent was Tennessee's Democratic senator Kenneth McKellar, who had long resented Lilienthal for protecting civil service rules at the TVA. The *New York Times* commented that the reasons for this opposition, primarily by Republicans, included worries by oil interests "that the ex-head of the TVA would be inclined to push atomic energy as a publicly owned power source at the expense of electricity and oil"; the chance to embarrass President Truman in the run-up to the upcoming election season; and "the fact that Lilienthal is of Jewish descent. That fact, it is reported, has been the subject of discussion among some Senators." See *New York Times,* February 16, 1947.

136 Stason, "Law and Atomic Energy," pp. 95–98.

137 Byron S. Miller, "A Law is Passed: The Atomic Energy Act of 1946," *University of Chicago Law Review* 15 (1948): 799, 780. A careful summary of the similarities and differences among the different bills that were considered within the framework proposed by President Truman was published during the period of lawmaking by the executive secretary of the American Association for the Advancement of Science. See Meyerhoff, "Domestic Control of Atomic Energy," pp. 133–36.

138 Such was the case, for example, when the House adopted an amendment offered by May of Kentucky, which was backed energetically by Robert Lee Sikes of Florida and Harold Cooley of North Carolina, to require the head of the commission's Division of Military Applications to be an active army officer.

139 *Chicago Daily Tribune,* July 13, 1946.

140 *Congressional Record,* 79th Cong., 2d sess., July 19, 1946, p. 9482.

141 With a cohesion score of just 22.

142 *Congressional Record*, 79th Cong., 2d sess., July 16, 1946, p. 9141.

143 Ibid., July 17, 1946, pp. 9261, 9253. It was Short who had moved earlier in the day to kill the bill by recommitting it to the Military Affairs Committee. This was a closer-run vote, failing by 146–195. While the great majority of votes to recommit, 128, were Republican, a few southern Democrats—Harold Cooley of North Carolina, Carl Durham of North Carolina, John Folger of North Carolina, Andrew Jackson May of Kentucky, John Rankin of Mississippi, and Robert Thomason of Texas—voted with them, arguing that the bill did not do enough to fight Communism because it put the commission in civilian hands and gave the federal government too much power with which to constrain the market economy. For a discussion of the passage of the bill in the House following the attempt to kill it, see *New York Times,* July 21, 1946.

144 Johnson, *Congress and the Cold War,* p. 8. For a consideration of how these powers worked in practice in the 1950s, see H. L. Nieburg, "The Eisenhower AEC

and Congress: A Study in Executive-Legislative Relations," *Midwest Journal of Political Science* 6 (1962): 115–48.

145   These representatives served in the Republican 80th Congress. With the Democratic majority restored in both the House and the Senate for the 81st Congress, elected in November 1948, the Democratic membership increased to ten. In the Senate, Millard Tydings of Maryland was added to the party's cohort, while in the House, Paul Kilday of Texas replaced Lyndon Johnson, who had just been elected to the Senate. In turn, Johnson replaced Tydings, and thus returned to the committee, in the 82d Congress. Russell served longest, from 1946 to 1970.

146   Herbert S. Marks, "Congress and the Atom," *Stanford Law Review* 1 (1948): 27–29.

147   Cited ibid., p. 29.

148   *Los Angeles Times,* July 25, 1946. The Soviet Union, like the other permanent members of the Security Council, had pledged at San Francisco to use the veto sparingly, only when its most vital interests were at stake. In the UN's first year, it blocked majority decisions eight times by its veto, essentially on minor matters where its preferences were being outvoted.

149   Feaver, *Guarding the Guardians,* pp. 110–11.

150   *Chicago Tribune,* January 29, 1947. The Smyth Report "was startling" even to the scientists who had worked on the bomb in a compartmentalized way. See H. H. Goldsmith, "The Literature of Atomic Energy of the Past Decade," *Scientific Monthly* 68 (1949): 295. On its security limits, see David Kaiser, "The Atomic Secret in Red Hands? American Suspicions of Theoretical Physicists during the Early Cold War," *Representations* 90 (2005): 33.

151   U.S. Atomic Energy Commission, *In the Matter of J. Robert Oppenheimer: Transcript of Hearing before Personnel Security Board. Washington. D.C., April 12, 1954 through May 6, 1954* (Washington, DC: U.S. Government Printing Office, 1954), p. 69.

152   David M. Hart, *Forged Consensus: Science, Technology, and Economic Policy in the United States, 1921–1953* (Princeton, NJ: Princeton University Press, 1998), pp. 184, 190.

153   Miller, "A Law Is Passed," p. 821. For a discussion along these lines, see Michael S. Sherry, *In the Shadow of War: The United States since the 1930s* (New Haven: Yale University Press, 1995), p. 137.

154   Millis, *Arms and the State,* pp. 159–60.

155   Harry S. Truman, "Our Armed Forces Must Be Unified," *Collier's,* August 26, 1944, p. 63.

156   Cited in Millis, *Arms and the State,* p. 146.

157   See http://trumanlibrary.org/publicpapers/index.php?pid=508&st=&st1=.

158   Key works that focus on the complex process that ultimately culminated in the National Security Act of 1947 as an instance of fierce bureaucratic infighting between the army and navy, and as a struggle to find the right balance between a tightly integrated military and civilian control, include Demetrios Caraley, *The Politics of Military Unification: A Study of Conflict and the Policy Process* (New York: Columbia University Press, 1966); and Hogan, *A Cross of Iron*, pp. 23–68.

159 Robert H. Connery, "American Government and Politics: Unification of the Armed Forces—The First Year," *American Political Science Review* 43 (1949): 40.

160 Cited in Hogan, *A Cross of Iron*, pp. 34, 36.

161 Elias Huzar, "Reorganization for National Security," *Journal of Politics* 12 (1950): 130.

162 Hogan, *A Cross of Iron*, p. 65.

163 A useful summary of these agencies and functions can be found in Gus C. Lee, "The Organization for National Security," *Public Administration Review* 9 (1949): 36–44. For a discussion of the planning activities of the National Security Resources Board, see Robert Cuff, "Ferdinand Eberstadt, the National Security Resources Board, and the Search for Integrated Mobilization Planning, 1947–1948," *Public Historian* 7 (1985): 37–52. The NSRB and the Munitions Board, which produced the benchmark *Industrial Mobilization Plan for 1947*, were assessed by Ferdinand Eberstadt as "far more advanced in our planning than even those people who keep in touch with industrial mobilization would have believed possible" (p. 45).

164 Memorandum to Joint Psychological Warfare Committee, October 24, 1942; cited in Tim Weiner, *Legacy of Ashes: The History of the CIA* (New York: Doubleday, 2007), p. 3.

165 Athan G. Theoharis et al., *The FBI: A Comprehensive Reference Guide* (Westport, CT: Greenwood Press, 1998), p. 182. September 19, 1945; cited in Jeffreys-Jones, *The CIA and American Democracy*, p. 25.

166 On August 29, 1945, J. Edgar Hoover wrote to Attorney General Thomas Clark to complain about the potential loss of FBI functions in Latin America:

> There have been certain developments in this situation in the last twenty-four hours, about which I wanted to advise you. I have ascertained that General William Donovan has recently seen President Truman and is writing him a letter with reference to a proposed program for the operation of a World-wide Intelligence Service. It is reasonable to assume, I believe, that the plan which General Donovan will advance to the President will be similar to the one which he has heretofore advocated and about which I have advised you in detail. From outside sources I have learned that Colonel Frank McCarthy, new Assistant Secretary of State, has discussed the FBI's operation of the Western Hemisphere Intelligence Service with Secretary of State

Byrnes. From the statements made by Mr. Byrnes to Colonel McCarthy, it appears obvious that the Secretary of State is not adequately or fully informed as to the nature, scope or effectiveness of the Bureau's operations in this field.

See http://history.state.gov/historicaldocuments/frus1945-50Intel/d5.

167 I am relying here on Jeffreys-Jones, *The CIA and American Democracy;* Weiner, *Legacy of Ashes;* David M. Barrett, *The CIA and Congress: The Untold Story from Truman to Kennedy* (Lawrence: University Press of Kansas, 2005); and the CIA's invaluable official history, written in 1952 and 1953 by its first official historian but not released for over a quarter of a century: Arthur B. Darling, *The Central Intelligence Agency: An Instrument of Government to 1950* (University Park: Pennsylvania State University Press, 1990).

168 For a discussion of these concerns, see Sherman Kent, *Strategic Intelligence for American World Policy* (Hamden, CT: Archon Books, 1965), p. 79. From 1952 to 1967, Kent, a Yale historian, chaired the Board of National Estimates in the CIA's Directorate of Intelligence. See Robin W. Winks, *Cloak and Gown: Scholars in the Secret War, 1939–1961* (New Haven: Yale University Press, 1966).

169 Cited in Jeffreys-Jones, *The CIA and American Democracy,* p. 39; and Weiner, *Legacy of Ashes,* p. 24.

170 The text of NSC 10/2 can be found in Thomas H. Etzold and John L. Gaddis, eds., *Containment: Documents on American Policy and Strategy, 1945–1950* (New York: Columbia University Press, 1978), pp. 126–28.

171 Anna Kasten Nelson, "President Truman and the Evolution of the National Security Council," *Journal of American History* 72 (1985): 360–78.

CHAPTER 12 · ARMED AND LOYAL

1 The structural advantage southern patterns of representation conferred on the Democratic Party was considerable. Democrats secured 52 percent of the popular vote for the House but fully 61 percent of the seats, thanks to the low-turnout, essentially one-party South.

2 This Democratic majority of 235–199, with one Farmer-Labor independent, was achieved despite a dead heat in the popular vote.

3 The only limit it imposed was the condition that the CIA not have any police functions within the United States.

4 Cited in David McCullough, *Truman* (New York: Simon & Schuster, 1992), pp. 367–68.

5 Tim Weiner, *Legacy of Ashes: The History of the CIA* (New York: Doubleday, 2007), p. 41.

6 See Clarence G. Lasby, *Operation Paperclip: German Scientists and the Cold War* (New York: Atheneum, 1971).

7   See http://trumanlibrary.org/publicpapers/index.php?pid=1195&st=&stl=.

8   Robert H. Connery, "American Government and Politics: Unification of the Armed Forces—The First Year," *American Political Science Review* 43 (1949): 45. Liberals worried that high defense spending would crowd out the welfare state and displace domestic development; conservatives wanted tax cuts and a smaller national state.

9   David Alan Rosenberg, "The Origins of Overkill: Nuclear Weapons and American Strategy, 1945 to 1960," *International Security* 7 (1983): 10. For an overview of American strategic doctrine, including its origins in the Truman years, see Scott D. Sagan, *Moving Targets: Nuclear Strategy and National Security* (Princeton, NJ: Princeton University Press, 1989), pp. 10–57.

10   *Congressional Record,* 80th Cong., 1st sess., July 19, 1947, p. 9416.

11   Michael S. Sherry, *In the Shadow of War: The United States since the 1930s* (New Haven: Yale University Press, 1995), p. 134.

12   *Los Angeles Times,* March 22, 1946.

13   Bernard Brodie, "Implications for Military Policy," in *The Absolute Weapon: Atomic Power and World Order,* ed. Brodie (New York: Harcourt, Brace, 1946), p. 91. Brodie, who taught at Yale, was arguably the country's most important atomic strategist in this period, a nascent moment that connected military strategy to statecraft. For an evaluation of his role and work, see Barry H. Steiner, *Bernard Brodie and the Foundations of American Nuclear Strategy* (Lawrence: University Press of Kansas, 1991).

14   David Alan Rosenberg, "U.S. Nuclear Stockpile, 1945–1950," *Bulletin of the Atomic Scientists* 38 (1982): p. 26; see also Thomas B. Cochran, William M. Arkin, and Robert S. Norris, *The Bomb Book: The Nuclear Arms Race in Facts and Figures* (Washington, DC: Natural Resources Defense Council, 1987).

15   Brodie, "The Atom Bomb as Policy Maker," *Foreign Affairs* 27 (1948): 24, 30 (italics in original).

16   David Alan Rosenberg, "American Atomic Strategy and the Hydrogen Bomb Decision," *Journal of American History* 66 (1979): 70.

17   Rosenberg, "The Origins of Overkill," pp. 18, 16.

18   Cited ibid., pp. 13, 14.

19   On the tests, see Lloyd J. Graybar, "The 1946 Atomic Bomb Tests: Diplomacy or Bureaucratic Infighting?," *Journal of American History* 72 (1986): 888–907.

20   Cited in Rosenberg, "American Atomic Strategy and the Hydrogen Bomb Decision," p. 67 (italics in original).

21   Edward A. Kolodziej, *The Uncommon Defense and Congress, 1945–1963* (Columbus: Ohio State University Press, 1966), p. 79.

22   *Congressional Record,* 80th Cong., 2d sess., April 14, 1948, p. 4452.

23   Ibid., April 15, 1948, p. 4536.

24   Ibid., p. 4530.

25   The classic study of the budget process for that year is Warner R. Schilling, "The Politics of National Defense: Fiscal 1950," in Warner R. Schilling, Paul

Y. Hammond, and Glenn H. Snyder, *Strategy, Politics, and Defense Budgets* (New York: Columbia University Press, 1962), pp. 5–266.

26 Ibid., p. 80.

27 *Congressional Record,* 81st Cong., 1st sess., April 12, 1949, p. 4429. During the period, the navy was stoutly resisting the idea that America's defense should depend first and foremost on the strategic atomic bombardment capacity of the air force, arguing the case that navy airpower could do the job.

28 Rosenberg, "The Origins of Overkill," p. 11.

29 Rosenberg, "American Atomic Strategy and the Hydrogen Bomb Decision," pp. 72, 75. The author was Lt. Gen. Hubert R. Harmon. President Truman never received a hard copy, just an oral briefing (pp. 76–77).

30 Rosenberg, "The Origins of Overkill," pp. 19–26.

31 David M. Hart, *Forged Consensus: Science, Technology, and Economic Policy in the United States, 1921–1953* (Princeton, NJ: Princeton University Press, 1998), p. 192.

32 The Allison and Symington memoranda are cited in Marc Trachtenberg, "'A Wasting Asset,' American Strategy and the Shifting Nuclear Balance, 1949–1954," *International Security* 13 (1988/1989): 24, 25; for a discussion of the term *free world,* see John Fousek, *To Lead the Free World: American Nationalism and the Cultural Roots of the Cold War* (Chapel Hill: University of North Carolina Press, 2000).

33 Peter Douglas Feaver, *Guarding the Guardians: Civilian Control of Nuclear Weapons in the United States* (Ithaca, NY: Cornell University Press, 1992), pp. 137–39, 143. For a discussion of the role atomic weapons played during the Korean War, see Roger Dingman, "Atomic Diplomacy during the Korean War," *International Security* 13 (1988/1989): 50–91. Dingman observes that the United States entered the war with three assumptions in place about atomic weapons: that the US had nuclear superiority: "that such superiority ought, somehow, to be useable"; and that the atomic threat had worked during the Soviet blockade of Berlin (pp. 51–52).

34 An excellent comprehensive overview is provided by Paul Y. Hammond, "NSC-68: Prologue to Rearmament," in Schilling, Hammond, and Snyder, *Strategy, Politics, and Defense Budget,* pp. 267–378.

35 See http://us.history.wisc.edu/hist102/pdocs/nsc68.pdf.

36 Curt Cardwell, *NSC 68 and the Political Economy of the Early Cold War* (New York: Cambridge University Press, 2011), p. 13. Cardwell argues that this document was not just a geopolitical assessment but also an effort to protect and advance global capitalism. An excellent comprehensive overview making the more traditional case is provided in Hammond, "NSC-68," pp. 267–378. See also David T. Fautua, "The 'Long Pull' Army: NSC-68, the Korean War, and the Creation of the Cold War U.S. Army," *Journal of Military History* 61 (1997): 93–120.

37 Warner R. Schilling, "The H-Bomb Decision: How to Decide without Actu-

ally Choosing," *Political Science Quarterly* 76 (1961): 46. For a discussion of "The Soviet Union: The Bomb and the Cold War," see Andrew J. Rotter, *Hiroshima: The World's Bomb* (Oxford: Oxford University Press, 2008), pp. 228–69.

38   Kai Bird and Martin J. Sherwin, *American Prometheus: The Triumph and Tragedy of J. Robert Oppenheimer* (New York: Alfred A. Knopf, 2005), p. 422.

39   Schilling, "The H-Bomb Decision," pp. 35–36; for an overview of "The Battle over the H-Bomb, 1949–1950," see James G. Hershberg, *James B. Conant: Harvard to Hiroshima and the Making of the Nuclear Age* (Stanford, CA: Stanford University Press, 1993), pp. 464, 490.

40   Rosenberg, "American Atomic Strategy and the Hydrogen Bomb Decision," pp. 62, 85.

41   For overviews, see Daniel J. Kevles, "The National Science Foundation and the Debate over Postwar Research Policy, 1942–1945," *Isis* 68 (1977): 5–26; Jessica Wang, "Liberals, the Progressive Left, and the Political Economy of Postwar American Science: The National Science Foundation Debate Revisited," *Historical Studies in the Physical and Biological Sciences*, 26, no. 1 (1995): 139–66.

42   An excellent overview can be found in Jessica Wang, *American Science in an Age of Anxiety: Scientists, Anticommunism and the Cold War* (Chapel Hill: University of North Carolina Press, 1999), pp. 10–43.

43   K. A. C. Elliot and Harry Grundfest, "The Science Mobilization Bill," *Science* 97 (1943): 76.

44   See http://www.nsf.gov/od/lpa/nsf50/vbush1945.htm#ch6.3.

45   The legislation described the purposes of the new independent agency as that of promoting "the progress of science; to advance the national health, prosperity, and welfare; to secure the national defense." The foundation did not include a division for the social sciences.

46   *Congressional Record,* 81st Cong., 2d sess., February 27, 1950, p. 2432.

47   G. Pascal Zachary, *Endless Frontier: Vannevar Bush, Engineer of the American Century* (New York: Free Press, 1997), p. 328.

48   Ibid., p. 329.

49   Hart, *Forged Consensus,* p. 185.

50   Ibid., p. 181; Zachary, *Endless Frontier,* pp. 315–16.

51   David Kaiser, "Cold War Requisitions, Scientific Manpower, and the Production of American Physicists after World War II," *Historical Studies in the Physical and Biological Sciences* 33, no. 1 (2002): 132.

52   Wang, "Liberals, the Progressive Left, and the Political Economy of Postwar American Science," p. 147.

53   James Bryant Conant, *Modern Science and Modern Man* (New York: Columbia University Press, 1952), p. 30.

54   Henry L. Stimson, "The Challenge to Americans," *Foreign Affairs* 26 (1947): 8, 10.

55   Ibid., p. 8.

56   This appeared in a 2004 unpublished statement concerning a project on the Cold War as global conflict.

57   Robert E. Cushman, "Civil Liberty after the War," *American Political Science Review* 38 (1944): 1, 11, 13, 15, 16, 10.

58   Robert E. Cushman, "Civil Liberties in an Atomic Age," *Annals of the American Academy of Political and Social Science* 249 (1947), pp. 60, 61, 62, 63, 65.

59   A useful summary written shortly after this executive order can be found in Walter Gellhorn, *Security, Loyalty, and Science* (Ithaca, NY: Cornell University Press, 1950).

60   Arthur M. Schlesinger Jr., "What Is Loyalty? A Difficult Question. For It Touches Both Civil Liberties and the Right of Government to Protect Itself," *New York Times, November 2, 1947.*

61   This executive order is reproduced in the appendix to Seth W. Richardson, "The Federal Employee Loyalty Program," *Columbia Law Review* 51 (1951): 558–63.

62   In addition to Ramspeck, Jennings Randolph of West Virginia, Carter Manasco of Alabama, Graham Barden of North Carolina, and James Morrison of Louisiana. The only nonsoutherner in this longest-serving group was Henry "Scoop" Jackson of Washington.

63   Cited in Richardson, "The Federal Employee Loyalty Program," pp. 559, 562. For a largely sympathetic overview, see Roger S. Abbott, "The Federal Loyalty Program: Background and Problems," *American Political Science Review* 42 (1948): 486–99. The first list issued by the attorney general contained 82 suspect organizations; that number grew to nearly 200 by 1950. See Eleanor Bontecou, *The Federal Loyalty-Security Program* (Ithaca, NY: Cornell University Press, 1953), pp. 157–204.

64   I am indebted to Andrew Grossman for first introducing me to the character of this extrajudicial process. For an overview of its civil liberties deficiencies, see Marver H. Bernstein, "The Loyalty of Federal Employees," *Western Political Quarterly* 2 (1949): 254–64; for a summary synopsis see Ellen Schrecker, *Many Are the Crimes: McCarthyism in America* (Princeton, NJ: Princeton University Press, 1998), pp. 266–305.

65   This 143-page analysis singled out HUAC as having created the model for extrajudicial investigations that had been adopted by the executive branch. See Thomas I. Emerson and David M. Helfeld, "Loyalty among Government Employees," *Yale Law Journal* 58 (1948): 1, 7, 8–12.

66   Emerson and Helfeld, "Loyalty among Government Employees," pp. 77, 141; on the use of confidential information, see pp. 101–9.

67   J. Edgar Hoover, "A Comment on the Article 'Loyalty among Government Employees,'" *Yale Law Journal* 58 (1949): 401.

68   The shift in President Eisenhower's April 27, 1953, executive order was from a standard of dismissal based on "reasonable doubt as to the loyalty of the per-

son involved to the Government of the United States" to the requirement that federal employment of any person be "clearly consistent with the interests of national security." Any doubt could lead to prompt dismissal; the burden of evidence shifted from the national state to the individual who was thought to be a security risk. See Robert N. Johnson, "The Eisenhower Personnel Security Program," *Journal of Politics* 18 (1956): 625–50.

69   Henry L. Shattuck, "The Loyalty Review Board of the U.S. Civil Service Commission," *Proceedings of the Massachusetts Historical Society* 78 (1966): 80.

70   Jessica Wang, "Science, Security, and the Cold War: The Case of E.U. Condon," *Isis* 83 (1992): 258.

71   Senate, *Employment of Homosexuals and Other Sex Perverts in Government* (interim report submitted to the Committee on Expenditures in the Executive Departments by its Subcommittee on Investigations Pursuant S. Res. 280), 81st Cong., 2d sess., 1950, S. Doc. 241; cited in Richard M. Valelly, "LGBT Politics and American Political Development," *Annual Review of Political Science* 16 (2012): 313–32. See also Margot Kennedy, *The Straight State: Sexuality and Citizenship in Twentieth-Century America* (Princeton, NJ: Princeton University Press, 2009). The term *Lavender Scare* was coined by David K. Johnson. See Johnson, *The Lavender Scare: The Cold War Persecution of Gays and Lesbians in the Federal Government* (Chicago: University of Chicago Press, 2004).

72   Peter J. Kuznick, *Beyond the Laboratory: Scientists as Political Activists in the 1930s* (Chicago: University of Chicago Press, 1987); Alice Kimball Smith, *A Peril and a Hope: The Scientists' Movement in America, 1945–1947* (Chicago: University of Chicago Press, 1965).

73   For an overview, see Jessica Wang, "Scientists and the Problem of the Public in Cold War America, 1945–1960," *Osiris* 17 (2002): 323–47.

74   For a discussion written at the time, see Gellhorn, *Security, Loyalty, and Science.*

75   Wang, "Science, Security, and the Cold War," p. 238; see also David Caute, *The Great Fear: The Anti-Communist Purge under Truman and Eisenhower* (New York: Simon & Schuster, 1978).

76   Edward A. Shils, *The Torment of Secrecy: The Background and Consequences of American Security Policies* (Glencoe, IL: Free Press, 1956), p. 185.

77   This scientific system had an elective affinity with democratic currents, the sociologist Robert K. Merton had insisted in 1942, because of its ethos of universalism, open collaboration, and organized skepticism. His 1942 "Note on Science and Democracy" is reprinted as "Science and Democratic Social Structure" in Robert K. Merton, *Social Theory and Social Structure* (Glencoe, IL: Free Press, 1957), pp. 550–61.

78   Committee on Security and Clearance, "Loyalty Clearance Procedures in Research Laboratories," *Science* 107 (1948): 333–37; Scientists Committee on Loyalty Problems, "Loyalty and Security Problems of Scientists: A Summary of Current Clearance Procedure," ibid., 109 (1949): 21–24.

79   Allen Weinstein and Alexander Vassiliev, *The Haunted Wood: Soviet Espionage in America—The Stalin Era* (New York: Random House, 1999).

80   *New York Times,* November 10, 1999.

81   For a review of the key studies of the Rosenberg case, which after a long period of controversy have developed a consensus about guilt, based in part on evidence that has come to light since the fall of the Soviet Union, raising questions about the definitiveness of our knowledge, see Bernice Schrank, "Reading the Rosenbergs after Venona," *Labuor/Le Travail* 49 (2002): 189–210. The authors of the leading work that argued they had been framed, Walter and Miriam Schneir, have concluded otherwise decades later. See Walter and Miriam Schneir, *Invitation to an Inquest* (New York: Doubleday, 1965); Walter Schneir (with a preface and afterword by Miriam Schneir), *Final Verdict: What Really Happened in the Rosenberg Case* (Brooklyn, NY: Melville House, 2010).

82   Wang, "Scientists and the Problem of the Public in Cold War America," pp. 335–336.

83   Morton Grodzins, *The Loyal and the Disloyal: Social Boundaries of Patriotism and Freedom* (Chicago: University of Chicago Press, 1956). "The danger," he warned, "is that democracy will fail because it fails to be democratic" (p. 258). For a different perspective, one that argued in 1952 that "perhaps it is a calamitous error to believe that because a vulgar demagogue [referring to Wisconsin senator Joseph McCarthy] lashes out at both Communism and liberalism as identical, it is necessary to protect Communism in order to defend liberalism," see Irving Kristol, "'Civil Liberties,' 1952: A Study in Confusion," in Irving Kristol, *The Neoconservative Persuasion: Selected Essays, 1952–2009* (New York: Basic Books, 2011), p. 49. This position, he predicted, "will surely shock liberals."

84   Andrew D. Grossman and Guy Oakes, "The Fifth Column Tactic: Predatory Investigations and the Politics of Internal Security in the 80th Congress," unpublished paper presented at the September 2004 Annual Meeting of the American Political Science Association, p. 6.

85   See Robert C. Carr, *The House Committee on Un-American Activities, 1945–1950* (Ithaca, NY: Cornell University Press, 1952); Telford Taylor, *Grand Inquest: The Story of Congressional Investigations* (New York: Simon & Schuster, 1955).

86   Wang's "Science, Security, and the Cold War" is devoted to an examination of "the case of E. U. Condon." See also Wang, *American Science in an Age of Anxiety,* pp. 130–47.

87   On McCarran, see Michael J. Ybarra, *Washington Gone Crazy: Senator Pat McCarran and the Great American Communist Hunt* (Hanover, NH: Steerforth Press, 2004).

88   For a discussion, see Cornelius P. Cotter and J. Malcolm Smith, "An American Paradox: The Emergency Detention Act of 1950," *Journal of Politics* 19 (1957): 27.

89   A memorandum of September 18, 1950, outlining "Pros and Cons on Signature or Veto of the McCarran Bill," was prepared for President Truman by Richard Neustadt, who, after his service in the White House, went on to a distinguished career in political science at Columbia and Harvard. See William Randolph Tanner, "The Passage of the Internal Security Act of 1950" (Ph.D. dissertation, University of Kansas, 1971), pp. 463–64.

90   See http://trumanlibrary.org/publicpapers/viewpapers.php?pid=883.

91   Schlesinger Jr., "What Is Loyalty?," pp. SM7, 50, 48. A similar search for a balanced policy was written for the Committee on Economic Development by Harold D. Lasswell. See Lasswell, *National Security and Individual Freedom* (New York: McGraw-Hill, 1950).

92   Clinton L. Rossiter, "Constitutional Dictatorship in an Atomic Age," *Review of Politics* 11 (1949): 418, 395. For an exception to Rossiter's lament about the absence of relevant considerations, see Arthur Bromage, "Public Administration in the Atomic Age," *American Political Science Review* 41 (1947): 974–55. Bromage drew on the experience of desolation after the mass bombing of German cities during World War II to project the political and administrative aftermath of an atomic attack on the United States.

93   Rossiter, "Constitutional Dictatorship in an Atomic Age," p. 398.

94   Ibid., pp. 408, 412.

95   Ibid., p. 418.

96   For a discussion of this recursive possibility, see John Fabian Witt, "Anglo-American Empire and the Crisis of the Legal Frame," *Harvard Law Review* 120 (2007): 786.

EPILOGUE · JANUARY 1953

1   *Christian Science Monitor,* December 6, 1952.

2   *New York Times,* November 17, 1952.

3   Ibid.

4   *Los Angeles Times,* December 6, 1952.

5   Ibid.; *New York Times,* December 6, 1952.

6   Robert Patrick McCray, "Project Vista, Caltech, and the Dilemmas of Lee DuBridge," *Historical Studies in the Physical and Biological Sciences* 34 (2004): 339; *New York Times,* December 5, 1951; *Washington Post,* December 8, 1951.

7   *Manchester Guardian,* December 21, 1953; Kai Bird and Martin J. Sherwin, *American Prometheus: The Triumph and Tragedy of J. Robert Oppenheimer* (New York: Alfred A. Knopf, 2005), pp. 474–76; http://downloads.bbc.co.uk/rmhttp/radio4/transcripts/1953_reith6.pdf.

8   Roger Dingman, "Atomic Diplomacy during the Korean War," *International Security* 13 (1988/1989): 50–91; the discussion of the January 25 NSC meeting appears on p. 69.

9   See http://www.bartleby.com/124/pres13.html.

10   Alan Brinkley, *Voices of Protest: Huey Long, Father Coughlin, and the Great Depression* (New York: Alfred A. Knopf, 1982). See also Sander Diamond, *The Nazi Movement in the United States, 1924–1941* (New York: Disc-Us Books, 1974); Francis Macdonnel, *Insidious Foes: The Axis Fifth Column and the American Home Front* (New York: Oxford University Press, 1995), Philip Jenkins, *Hoods and Shirts: The Extreme Right in Pennsylvania, 1925–1950* (Chapel Hill: University of North Carolina Press, 1997).

11   *New York Times,* November 2, 1952; *Washington Post,* November 22, 1952; *New York Times,* November 28, 1952, December 4, 1952; *Chicago Daily Tribune,* December 14, 1952; *New York Times,* January 13, 1953, January 18, 1953, January 19, 1953.

12   *New York Times,* January 21, 1953.

13   See http://www.bartleby.com/124/pres54.html.

14   Guy Oakes, *The Imaginary War: Civil Defense and American Cold War Culture* (New York: Oxford University Press, 1944); Andrew D. Grossman, *Neither Dead nor Red: Civil Defense and American Political Development during the Early Cold War* (New York: Routledge, 2001).

15   *Wall Street Journal,* January 21, 1953.

16   Both editorials are cited in the review by the *Los Angeles Times* of "How Nation's Press Viewed Ike Address," January 21, 1953.

17   http://avalon.law.yale.edu/20th_century/eisenhower001.asp.

18   Martin Conway, "Democracy in Postwar Western Europe: The Triumph of a Political Model," *European History Quarterly* 32 (2002): 59–84.

19   Arthur Schlesinger Jr., *The Vital Center: The Politics of Freedom* (Boston: Houghton Mifflin, 1949), p. 1.

20   *Washington Post,* January 21, 1953. When Johnson first was elected to the Senate, his maiden speech of March 9, 1949, was repeatedly punctuated by the phrase "We of the South." Lasting well over an hour, this was a contribution to a southern filibuster that opposed President Truman's civil rights program. Fifteen years later, it was President Johnson who had become a rhetorical and practical leader of racial change. Southern Democrats no longer could prevent such laws as the Civil Rights Act of 1964 or the Voting Rights Act of 1965 in the face of defections from their ranks by some border-state colleagues. Over the course of the decades that followed, the South shifted partisan allegiances. By the mid-1990s, the once-unthinkable had happened. Most white southerners voted Republican. Most southern House and Senate seats were held by Republicans. And the core constituency of the Democratic Party in the South had become African-American. While southern congressional influence eroded within the Democratic Party, it was propelled into a leading role for the Republican Party.

21   Alexis de Tocqueville, *The Old Regime and the French Revolution* (1856; reprint, Chicago: University of Chicago Press, 1998), p. 95.

22 David B. Truman, *The Governmental Process: Political Interest and Public Opinion*, 2d ed. (New York: Alfred A. Knopf, 1971), p.xlvii.

23 "By a 'boundary condition,' I mean a set of relatively permanent features of a particular context that affect causal relationships within it." See J. David Greenstone, *The Lincoln Persuasion: Remaking American Liberalism* (Princeton, NJ: Princeton University Press, 1993), p. 42.

24 Karl Polanyi, *The Great Transformation: The Political and Economic Origins of Our Time* (Boston: Rinehart, 1944), pp. 257, 244 (italics in original).

25 Gilbert Murray, *Liberality and Civilization: Lectures Given at the Invitation of the Hibbert Trustees in the Universities of Bristol, Glasgow, and Birmingham in October and November 1937* (London: George Allen and Unwin, 1938), p. 57.

26 Bruce Ackerman, *We the People, vol. 1, Foundations* (Cambridge: Harvard University Press, 1991); Bruce Ackerman, *We the People, vol. 2, Transformations* (Cambridge: Harvard University Press, 1998). For a contrary view, minimizing the importance of the New Deal in shaping a constitutional revolution, see G. Edward White, *The Constitution and the New Deal* (Cambridge: Harvard University Press, 2000), p. 311. For an earlier statement by Ackerman, focusing on the radical challenge to legal doctrine by both the quality and quantity of New Deal interventions in the market economy, see Ackerman, *Reconstructing American Law* (Cambridge: Harvard University Press, 1984), especially pp. 6–11. Accounts of the centrality of shifts in governing authority are central to Karen Orren and Stephen Skowronek, *The Search for American Political Development* (Cambridge: Cambridge University Press, 2004).

27 This is the position inscribed in the subtitle to the second edition of Theodore J. Lowi, *The End of Liberalism: The Second Republic of the United States* (New York: W. W. Norton and Company. 1979). The first edition (1969) was subtitled *Ideology, Policy, and the Crisis of Public Authority*. Lowi has often portrayed the New Deal as revolutionary. See, for an example, Theodore J. Lowi, "The Roosevelt Administration and the American State," in *Comparative Theory and Political Experience: Mario Einaudi and the Liberal Tradition*, ed. Peter Katzenstein, Theodore J. Lowi, and Sidney Tarrow (Ithaca, NY: Cornell University Press, 1990).

28 Daniel T. Rodgers, *Contested Truths: Keywords in American Politics Since Independence* (New York: Basic Books, 1987), p. 201. For a discussion along these lines that similarly identifies what was new about the New Deal's orientation to interests groups, see David E. Hamilton, *From New Day to New Deal: American Farm Policy from Hoover to Roosevelt* (Chapel Hill: University of North Carolina Press, 1991).

29 Ibid., p. 207.

30 Robert A. Dahl, *A Preface to Democratic Theory* (Chicago: University of Chicago Press, 1956), pp. 124–51; Truman, *The Governmental Process,* pp. 50–51.

31 E. E. Schattschneider, *The Semi-Sovereign People: A Realist's View of Democracy in America* (New York: Holt, Rinehart and Winston, 1960), p. 30.

32   This theme is developed in the rich review by Donald Brand, "Three Generations of Pluralism: Continuity and Change," *Political Science Reviewer* 15 (1985): 109–41.

33   J. David Greenstone, *Labor in American Politics* (New York: Alfred A. Knopf, 1969); Fred Block, "The Ruling Class Does Not Rule: Notes on the Marxist Theory of the State," *Socialist Revolution*, 7, no. 33 (1977): 6–28. For an empirical portrait of pre–New Deal patterns of interest representation in Washington, see E. Pendleton Herring, *Group Representation before Congress* (Baltimore: Johns Hopkins University Press, 1929).

34   For a comparative overview, see Alfred Stepan and Juan J. Linz, "Comparative Perspectives on Inequality and the Quality of Democracy in the United States," *Perspective on Politics* 9 (2011): 841–56.

35   Theodore J. Lowi, *The End of Liberalism: Ideology, Policy, and the Crisis of Public Authority* (New York: W. W. Norton, 1969), p. 76. See also J. David Greenstone, ed., *Public Values and Private Power in American Democracy* (Chicago: University of Chicago Press, 1982); and the book on which its essays comment, Grant McConnell, *Private Power and American Democracy* (New York: Alfred A. Knopf, 1966).

36   Hans J. Morgenthau, "Another 'Great Debate': The National Interest of the United States," *American Political Science Review* 46 (1952): 970–71, 978, 987; see also Hans J. Morgenthau, *In Defense of the National Interest: A Critical Examination of American Foreign Policy* (New York: Alfred A. Knopf, 1951).

37   *New York Times,* November 12, 1952.

38   C. Wright Mills, *The Power Elite* (New York: Oxford University Press, 1956). Daniel Bell, a sharp critic, made this observation about the place of decisions regarding violence in Mills's book. See Daniel Bell, *The End of Ideology: On the Exhaustion of Political Ideas in the Fifties* (New York: Collier Books, 1961), p. 54.

39   Robert A. Dahl, "Atomic Energy and the Democratic Process," *Annals of the American Academy of Political and Social Science* 290 (1953): 1–2, 6 (italics in original).

40   The only dissenter was Justice Harlan Stone. This decision was reversed in 1944 in *West Virginia State Board of Education v. Barnette;* Justice Frankfurter dissented.

41   Harold D. Lasswell, "The Garrison State," *American Journal of Sociology* 20 (1941).

42   Tony Smith, *America's Mission: The United States and the Worldwide Struggle for Democracy in the Twentieth Century* (Princeton, NJ: Princeton University Press, 1994); Michael S. Sherry, *In the Shadow of War: The United States since the 1930s* (New Haven: Yale University Press, 1995); Michael J. Hogan, *A Cross of Iron: Harry S. Truman and the Origins of the National Security State, 1945–1954* (New York: Cambridge University Press, 1998); Aaron L. Freedberg, *In the Shadow of the Garrison State: America's Anti-Statism and Its Cold War Grand Strategy* (Princeton, NJ: Princeton University Press, 2000); Elizabeth Borgwardt, *A*

New Deal for the World: America's Vision for Human Rights (Cambridge: Harvard University Press, 2005); Robert David Johnson, *Congress and the Cold War* (New York: Cambridge University Press, 2006).

43　For an assessment of the "single, glaring fact" about the modern United States "as a 'security state,'" see Bartholomew H. Sparrow, "American Political Development, State-Building, and the 'Security State': Revisiting a Research Agenda," *Polity* 40 (2008): 358.

44　Harold D. Lasswell, *National Security and Individual Freedom* (New York: McGraw-Hill, 1950), p. 1.

45　For outstanding empirical overviews, see Michael Paul Rogin, *The Intellectuals and McCarthy: The Radical Specter* (Cambridge: MIT Press, 1967); David Oshinsky, *A Conspiracy So Immense: The World of Joe McCarthy* (New York: Free Press, 1983); Ellen Schrecker, *Many Are the Crimes: McCarthyism in America* (Princeton, NJ: Princeton University Press, 1998). For incisive theoretical considerations, see Morton Grodzins, *The Loyal and the Disloyal* (Chicago: University of Chicago Press, 1956); Edward A. Shils, *Torment of Secrecy: The Background and Consequences of American Security Policies* (Glencoe, IL: Free Press, 1956). Especially interesting is Daniel Patrick Moynihan, *Secrecy: The American Experience* (New Haven: Yale University Press, 1998).

46　For a spirited treatment, see Garry Wills, *Bomb Power: The Modern Presidency and the National Security State* (New York: Penguin, 2010).

47　Theodore J. Lowi, *Poliscide: Big Government, Big Science, Lilliputian Politics* (Lanham, MD: University Press of America, 1990); David M. Hart, *Forged Consensus: Science, Technology, and Economic Policy in the United States, 1921–1953* (Princeton, NJ: Princeton University Press, 1998).

48　*Los Angeles Times,* May 11, 1950.

49　The most thorough overview is Barton T. Bernstein, "The Oppenheimer Loyalty-Security Case Reconsidered," *Stanford Law Review* 42 (1990): 1383–1484.

50　"The Eternal Apprentice," *Time,* November 8, 1948, p. 76.

51　See http://en.wikisource.org/wiki/Letter_from_William_L._Borden_to_J._Edgar_Hoover,November_7,_1953.

52　Bernstein, "The Oppenheimer Loyalty-Security Case Reconsidered," p. 1440.

53　In addition to Bernstein, "The Oppenheimer Loyalty-Security Case Reconsidered," see Robert Erwin, "Oppenheimer Investigated," *Wilson Quarterly* 18 (1994): 34–45; Charles Thorpe and Steven Shapin, "Who Was J. Robert Oppenheimer? Charisma and Complex Organization," *Social Studies of Science* 30 (2000): 545–90.

54　Cited in Erwin, "Oppenheimer Investigated," p. 43.

55　See Michael J. Neufield, *Von Braun: Dreamer of Space, Engineer of War* (New York: Alfred A. Knopf, 2007); Wayne Biddle, *Dark Side of the Moon: Wernher Von Braun, the Third Reich, and the Space Race* (New York: W. W. Norton, 2009).

56 Rodgers, *Contested Truths,* p. 209.

57 For a discussion of the lesser evils that are permitted as societies confront greater evils, see Michael Ignatieff, *The Lesser Evil: Political Ethics in an Age of Terror* (Princeton, NJ: Princeton University Press, 2004).

58 Avishai Margalit, *On Compromise and Rotten Compromises* (Princeton, NJ: Princeton University Press, 2010), p. 13.

59 Ibid., p. 2.

ACKNOWLEDGMENTS ▶

I F NOT FOR TWO PERSONS, it is unlikely that I would have written this book. First is Frima Rosenbaum, my maternal grandmother. She is the source of my first political memory. It dates to a Sunday family visit to her Washington Heights apartment in northern Manhattan shortly before the presidential election of 1952. I was eight years old, too young to quite understand why my father and mother, who worshipped Adlai Stevenson, were so visibly stunned to learn that she did not plan to vote. Striking her dining room table with a copy of the Yiddish-language *Daily Forward*, Bubbeh Frima explained, "Since Roosevelt, they are all pygmies."

Sometimes it feels as if I have been considering her historical claim ever since. In truth, it was not until the late 1980s when I was teaching at the Graduate Faculty of the New School for Social Research that I began to think about the New Deal in a scholarly way. Well before that, however, during my decade at the University of Chicago, J. David Greenstone persistently challenged me to think harder and more broadly about the American experience. When I took up a post there in 1974, he quickly became my fast friend and mentor. Since I had earned a Ph.D. in history, David served as a surrogate for the graduate school political science teachers in American politics I never had. More than anyone before or since, he prodded me to integrate questions drawn from the stock of political theory with systematic empirical methods. David died in 1990, just fifty-two. I fervently wish he had been able to critique earlier drafts of this book, and assess its concerns with race and labor, both being subjects about which he wrote with great acuity.

At the New School, with support from the Ford Foundation, I constituted a research group that first sought to compare the ambitious conservative program of the Reagan administration with the liberal initiatives of Franklin Roosevelt's presidency. As it turned out, the articles I wrote with Kim Geiger, Daniel Kryder, and Bruce Pietrykowski, the primary graduate student participants in that project, focused almost exclusively on the 1930s and 1940s. With their help, I had begun to find my subject. Concurrently, my commitment to write analytical history deepened. I spent countless hours talking about historical analysis in the social sciences with the consummate practitioners who constituted the Committee on Historical Studies, including Richard Bensel, Eric Hobsbawm, Elizabeth Sanders, Charles Tilly, and Louise Tilly. My closest colleague in this group was Aristide Zolberg, with whom I taught a proseminar on politics, theory, and policy, and convened a MacArthur Foundation workshop on national security, democracy, and postwar American liberalism, the very themes that later came to animate this book.

Since I moved to Columbia University in 1994, it proceeded in fits and starts. For a long span, I pursued mostly other projects but continued to wrestle with the New Deal. At Columbia, my work has been nourished by colleagues and students in an outstanding political science department in the tradition of Franz Neumann and David Truman that places the study of institutions front and center, and an exceptional history department in the tradition of Richard Hofstadter and Fritz Stern that seeks to deepen the long-term study of political affairs. I have profited especially from interactions in the cross-disciplinary workshop on American politics and society that Alan Brinkley and I have been convening for more than a decade and a half. Working relationship, joint teaching, hearty discussions, and shared endeavors at Columbia—with Karen Barkey, Volker Berghahn, Akeel Bilgrami, Charles Cameron, Partha Chatterjee, Eric Foner, Alice Kessler-Harris, Sudipta Kaviraj, Robert Lieberman, Mark Mazower, Nolan McCarty, Justin Phillips (with whom I enjoyed a period as a visiting scholar at the Russell Sage Foundation), Alfred Stepan, Nadia Urbinati, Gregory Wawro, and well over a dozen others—fashioned a particularly productive environment in which this book has been crafted.

Along the way, I have profited from the intellectual stimulation and superb substantive and technical assistance offered by Columbia's graduate students. Counted among them especially are John Lapinski, Rose Razaghian, Sean Farhang, and Quinn Mulroy, who compensated for my deficiencies in statistical skill and legislative research experience. Each became a coauthor. Each served as a research assistant at the American Institutions Project, housed at Columbia's Institute for Social and Economic Research and Policy, before moving on to assistant professorships, respectively at Yale, Yale, Berkeley, and Syracuse. Other key participants in AIP have been Melanie Springer, Chrissy Greer, Thomas Ogorzalek, David Park, Amy Semet, and Alissa Stollwerk. The project also gained much from its Columbia College and Barnard College research assistants, including Rachel Barza, Donna Desilus, David Goldin, Olivia Gorvey, Elysse Ross, Dennis Schmelzer, Ellen Yan, and, most notably, Seth Weiner, whose detailed legislative histories instructed me in the nooks and crannies of southern congressional preferences and strategies. Thanks also are owed to the institute within which AIP has been housed, for first making it possible for Greg Wawro and me to launch an annual conference on the theme "Congress and History," from which I have learned much that informs this book.

Over the years, I have spoken about parts of *Fear Itself* at too many venues to properly name and thank. They may not remember, but I cannot forget the prodding comments offered at these events by Anthony Badger, Brian Balogh, the late Brian Barry, Walter Dean Burnham, James Cobb, Joshua Cohen, Lizabeth Cohen, Daniel Carpenter, Michael Delli-Carpini, Ariela Dubler, Jonathan Fanton, Janice Fine, Morris Fiorina, Jess Gilbert, Michael Goldfield, Andrew Grossman, David Hart, Matthew Holden, Robert Horowitz, Meg Jacobs, Jeffrey Jenkins, Michael Katz, Anne Kornhauser, Margaret Levi, Nelson Lichtenstein, Michael Lipsky, the late Harry Magdoff, Jane Mansbridge, Cathie Jo Martin, Anthony Marx, David Mayhew, Uday Mehta, the late Robert K. Merton, Sidney Milkis, Gary Mucciaroni, Carol Nackenoff, Norman Nie, Anne Norton, Alice O'Connor, Ann Orloff, Benjamin Page, Sunita Parikh, Kim Phillips-Fein, Paul Pierson, Frances Fox Piven, Gretchen Ritter, Eric Schickler, the late Arthur Schlesinger Jr., Ellen Schrecker, Theda Skocpol, Stephen Skowronek, Rogers Smith, Bat Sparrow, Thomas Sugrue, Mary Summers, Kathleen Thelen, Richard Valelly, Eric Wanner, Dorian Warren, Margaret Weir, Heather Williams, William Julius Wilson, John Witt, Erik Olin Wright, Julian Zelizer, and Olivier Zunz.

I owe a distinct obligation to Martin Shefter, who, by enticing me into a project concerning international influences on American political development, persuaded me that I had to devote more time and words than I had intended to the global dimensions of the New Deal. I also am indebted to the librarians and collections at the remarkable research libraries of Columbia University and Cambridge University; and to Fred Coccozzelli, Benjamin Fishman, Maura Fogarty, Jessica Olsen, and Cheryl Steele, who hauled books, photocopied articles, checked data, and otherwise lent support to this project.

When much of the penultimate draft was complete, Brian Balogh convened an extraordinary helpful session at the Miller Center of the University of Virginia, at which three brilliant scholars—David Kennedy of Stanford University, Daryl Scott of Howard University, and Richard Valelly of Swarthmore College—offered detailed and uncommonly helpful comments and criticisms. Further, once I had a full draft, Alan Brinkley, Eric Foner, Michael Janeway, William Janeway, Alice Kessler-Harris, James Patterson, and Richard Valelly read and commented in detail either on all or on large chunks of what I had written. So you can see how beholden I am to many persons, none of whom is responsible for what I have written, but each of whom has improved the book at hand.

My recitation of appreciation is not done. Gloria Loomis, whose literary agency has represented my interests, guided me to understand how the architecture of this book could build on my prior *When Affirmative Action Was White* and prodded me to take chances as I moved ahead. My penultimate draft was made much clearer, better organized, and more direct by the application, in London, of Tessa Harvey's uncommonly fine editorial intelligence. At Liveright in New York, a revived imprint at W. W. Norton, *Fear Itself* has benefited from extraordinary editorial care. Bob Weil is an editor without equal. Guided by historical learning and distaste for infelicitous prose, he read every line more than once and, to the profit of my readers, heavily marked the script. Bob identified Carol Edwards as the best possible, tough-minded copyeditor. Her professional skill further honed its prose and worked to ensure exactness in its references. Bob has been ably assisted by Philip Marino in the book's early stages and Will Menaker as it moved through production toward publication. Further, Roby Harrington nudged the manuscript along, both as a friend and as a Norton editor who loves books.

My sweetest supporters are my wonderful family. I dedicate this book to

Deborah Socolow Katznelson and her ever-expanding bounty. Ever since we met as undergraduate Young Democrats at the House of Representatives in January 1964, her loving and critical intelligence has deeply shaped all that I do. We share enormous pride in our children, Jessica, Zachary, Emma, and Leah, their spouses Brad, Isabel, Yosi, and Josh, and our growing brood of grandchildren, so far including Rachel, Nathan, Cleo, Azai, and Ezra. Nothing matches these satisfactions. Our growing family continues to offer gifts of affection, energy, and circumstance that support my authorial ambitions. I wish I knew how to say a proper thank you.

CAMBRIDGE, ENGLAND

July 2012

PHOTOGRAPH CREDITS

INDEX

Page numbers in *italics* refer to illustrations.
Page numbers beginning with 487 refer to notes.

Truman administration, 12, 18,
426–27
Truman Doctrine, 417–18, 424, 637
tuberculosis, 171
Tugwell, Rexford, 229, 232, 235, 236,
242, 246
Tunnell, James, 220
Turkey, 104, 277, 362, 417, 424
Turner, Roscoe, 61
Tydings, Millard, 161, 215, 254, 259,
378, 423, 426, 431, 443, 451, 466,
645

Ukraine, 41, 55, 82
Ulysses (Joyce), 55
UN Atomic Energy Commission, 420
uncertainty, 33–34, 48, 51, 232, 298
Underwood, Oscar, 145, 147, 148, 541
unemployment insurance, 252, 386–
87, 625
Unemployment Relief Act (1933), 123
Unemployment Service, U.S., 344
unions, 23, 25, 30, 43, 49, 144–45, 162,
172–85, 207, 257–59, 326, 386–
400, 402
African Americans and, 174–75,
392–93, 395–96, 550, 553
House investigation of, 330
in South, 183, 371, 389–90, 549
in Soviet Union, 51
Taft-Hartley's constraint on, 372
United Cafeteria and Restaurant
Workers, 89
United Fruit, 273, 398
United Garment workers, 174
United Mine Workers, 174, 230, 627
United Nations, 42, 81, 358, 359, 407–
9, 415, 417, 419, 434, 617
United Nations Atomic Energy Com-
mission, 636–37

United Nations Conference on International Organization, 595
United Nations Convention, 102
United Rubber Workers (URW), 173
United States:
calls for dictatorship in, 118–20
émigré intellectuals in, 48–51
Fascist Italy as model for, 93–94, 95
freedom in, 353–54
Germany and Italy's declaration of
war against, 281, 320
as global leader, 362
in NATO, 418
popular opinion on World War II
in, 277–78
postwar defense spending in, 406
science and technology mobilized
in, 346–50
size of military of, 13–14, 19–20,
52, 103, 416–17, 452–53, 493
as threatened by Japan, 315
wartime economy of, 342–46
World War II as unifier of, 317–18,
323–24
World War II casualties of, 41–42
World War II spending by, 345–46
see also South, U.S.
United States Steel Corporation, 273,
307
United Textile Workers of America,
174
uranium, 431
urban poverty, 127
Urey, Harold, 414, 430
USO, 220
Uzbekistan, 357

V-2s, 484
Vandenberg, Hoyt, 447
Vanderberg, Arthur, 422, 431

Water Power Act (1920), 147

Watson, Henry, 236

Webb, Beatrice and Sidney, 55

Weber, Max, 100, 114

Webster Progress, 285

Wechsler, Herbert, 200, 205, 559–60

Wehrmacht, 361

Weill, Kurt, 62

Weimar Constitution, 98, 110, 113

Weimar Republic, 39, 46, 104, 110, 113

welfare state, 36, 162

Welles, Summer, 361

Wells, H. G., 488

Western Union, 273, 398

Westinghouse Electric, 348

Westinghouse Research Laboratory, 415

West Virginia, 136, 165, 211

What Maisie Knew (James), 22

What the Negro Wants?, 138

Whelchel, Benjamin, 292

When Affirmative Action Was White (Katznelson), 24

Whitaker, John, 511

White, E. B., ix

White, Edward Douglass, 335

White, Walter, 160, 167, 210, 429, 545

White Sea Canal, 39, 80

Whither Solid South? (Collins), 139

Whitten, Jamie, 85

Whittington, William, 85, 143, 269, 380

Wierton, 398

Wiesbaden, Germany, 111

Wiley, Alexander, 315

Williams, Aubrey, 176

Williams, John Bell, 428

Willkie, Wendell, 311, 559, 604

Wilson, Edmund, 56

Wilson, George Howard, 456

Wilson, James Mark, 267

Wilson, Joseph, 422

Wilson, Woodrow, 44, 67, 104, 105, 145–46, 149, 158, 165, 288, 289, 290, 325, 337, 471

Winner, Henry, 638

Winthrop, John, 17

Wolfers, Arnold, 600

Woman's Auxiliary Corps, 601

Women's Airforce Service Pilots, 220

Women's Auxiliary Ferrying Squadron, 220

Wood, John, 395, 443, 464

Wood, Robert E., 595

Woodrum, Clifton, 437

Woodward, C. Vann, 127

Woolworth, 88

working class, 22, 23

Works Progress Administration, 217

Works Project Administration, 330

World, 531

World Court, 290

World Disarmament Conference, 102

World Economic Conference, 38

World War I, 31–32, 41, 42, 43, 45, 100–101, 102, 110, 122, 147, 289, 297, 298, 305, 310, 311, 323, 325, 335, 347, 382, 539

World War II, 7, 8, 31, 92, 416, 421, 423, 461

  bombing campaigns in, 350–51

  as "crusade," 367

  and dangers to racial order of South, 16

  effects of, 42–43

  end of, 403–6

  FDR on meaning of, 320–21